# The Emotions and the Will

# THE EMOTIONS

### AND

# THE WILL.

BY

## ALEXANDER BAIN, M.A.,

PROFESSOR OF LOGIC IN THE UNIVERSITY OF ABERDEEN.

**SECOND EDITION.**

LONDON:
LONGMANS, GREEN, AND CO.
1865.

23 1/2 4

Phil 5241.2.10

1873. Mar. 15
By exch. of dupl.
bought with Hollis Fund

# PREFACE.

THE present publication is a sequel to my former one, on the Senses and the Intellect, and completes a Systematic Exposition of the Human Mind.

The generally admitted but vaguely conceived doctrine of the connexion between mind and body has been throughout discussed definitely. In treating of the Emotions, I include whatever is known of the physical embodiment of each.

The Natural History Method, adopted in delineating the Sensations, is continued in the Treatise on the Emotions. The first chapter is devoted to Emotion in general; after which the individual kinds are classified and discussed; separate chapters being assigned to the Æsthetic Emotions—arising on the contemplation of Beauty in Nature and Art—and to the Ethical, or the Moral Sentiment. Under this last head, I have gone fully into the Theory of Moral Obligation.

It has been too much the practice to make the discussion of the Will comprise only the single metaphysical problem of Liberty and Necessity.

iv PREFACE.

Departing from this narrow usage, I have sought to ascertain the nature of the faculty itself, its early germs, or foundations in the human constitution, and the course of its development, from its feeblest indications in infancy to the maturity of its power. Five chapters are occupied with this investigation; and five more with subjects falling under the domain of the Will, including the Conflict of Motives, Deliberation, Resolution, Effort, Desire, Moral Habits, Duty, and Moral Inability. A closing chapter embraces the Free-will controversy.

As in my view, Belief is essentially related to the *active* part of our being, I have reserved the consideration of it to the conclusion of the Treatise on the Will.

The final dissertation of the work is on Consciousness. Although it was necessary at the outset to assume a provisional definition, I considered it unadvisable to discuss the subtle problems involved in Consciousness in the abstract, until the detailed survey of the facts of mind had been completed. Whatever opinion may be formed as to the conclusions, I think the expediency of the method will be admitted.

LONDON, *March*, 1859.

# PREFACE TO THE SECOND EDITION.

IN the present edition, I have introduced extensive emendations into both divisions of the work.

The chapter on Emotion in general has been wholly re-cast; and the deriving of emotion from sensation, according to general laws of the mind, has rendered it possible to define and classify the emotions more precisely. The analysis of the special emotions has been carried out in conformity with the general views. I have added, in the Appendix, an account of the various classifications of the Feelings, both English and German.

Under the Will, the chapters on the first commencement of voluntary power have been considerably modified; and numerous amendments will be found throughout.

The discussion of the meanings of Consciousness has received additions and corrections. And, finally, all that regards the connexions of mind with physical processes has undergone careful revision.

ABERDEEN, *November,* 1865.

# TABLE OF CONTENTS.

## THE EMOTIONS.

### CHAPTER I.

#### OF FEELING IN GENERAL.

|  | PAGE |
|---|---|
| 1. Divisions of Mind. Subdivisions of Feeling . . | 3 |
| 2. General principle of the concomitance of mind and body—Law of DIFFUSION . . . . . | ib. |
| 3. Examples of the law . . . . . | 4 |
| 4. Bearing on the Unity of Consciousness . . . | ib. |
| 5. Counter-doctrines to the theory of Diffusion . . | 5 |
| (1.) Independence of mind and body . . | ib. |
| (2.) Sensation dependent on the lesser ganglia . | ib. |
| (3.) Restriction of the wave to the encephalic mass . . . . . . . | 6 |
| 6. The theory of the Reflex Actions in accordance with the law . . . . . . . . | ib. |
| 7. Also the Habitual or routine actions . . . | ib. |
| 8. Circumstances that limit the diffused manifestations of feeling . . . . . . . . | 7 |
| (1.) A certain energy of stimulation necessary | ib. |
| (2.) Physical condition of the active organs . | ib. |
| (3.) Different emotions have different manifestations . . . . . . . | 8 |
| (4.) Primitive outbursts modified by education | ib. |
| (5.) There may be voluntary suppression . | ib. |
| 9. Stimulus of an Active Impulse . . . . | ib. |

## TABLE OF CONTENTS.

10. Concurrence of *organic* effects with mental states—the capillary circulation; Blushing . . . . 9

#### CHARACTERS OF FEELINGS.

11. Feelings may have other characters besides Pleasure and Pain . . . . . . . . 11

*Emotional Characters of Feeling.*

12. Every feeling has a PHYSICAL SIDE and a MENTAL SIDE 13
13. *Feeling as Happiness or Misery.* Pleasure a state of transition. Pain a Disturbance of the system; modes of restoration . . . . . . *ib.*
14. *Feeling as Indifference or neutral excitement.* Tested by engrossing the mind . . . . . . 14

*Volitional Characters of Feeling.*

15. Feelings may be estimated and described by their influence on voluntary action or conduct . . 16

*Intellectual Characters of Feeling.*

16. The persistence, and recurrence in idea, of feelings, their intellectual property . . . . . 17
17. The revival of a feeling in idea depends on the intellectual forces . . . . . . . 18

*Mixed Characters of Feeling.*

18. The power of sustaining volition in the absence of the object, a compound of Volition and Intellect . . 19
19. *Control of the Intellectual Trains and Acquirements.* Attention stimulated by pleasure, by pain, and by neutral excitement . . . . . . 21
20. Retentiveness stimulated by feeling, distinct from the natural retentiveness,—Taste and Faculty do not necessarily go together . . . . . 23
21. *Influence of Feeling on Belief.* The feelings act partly through the Will, and partly through the trains of Thought . . . . . . . 24

## TABLE OF CONTENTS.

ix

PAGE

22. Examples of operation of the feelings on Belief. Intellectual perversion thereby engendered in common affairs, in History, and in Science . . . 25

### CRITERIA FOR INTERPRETING FEELING.

23. Means of ascertaining and estimating the feelings of others . . . . . . 28
24. The fixing on some standard feeling, or common measure . . . . . . 31
25. Interrogating other men as to their experience . . *ib.*

### REMARKS ON THE DEVELOPMENT OF EMOTIONS.

26. An emotional wave has a certain continuance . . 32
27. The Periodicity of the feelings . . . 33

## CHAPTER II.

### THE EMOTIONS AND THEIR CLASSIFICATION.

1. The Emotions are secondary, derived, or compound feelings . . . . . 35
2. Rules for their classification . . . .
3. Enumeration of Classes, Families, or Natural Orders . 36
4. Pleasure and Pain not a distinction to found classes upon 39

## CHAPTER III.

### EMOTIONS OF HARMONY AND CONFLICT.

1. Consequences of our being liable to plurality of impressions . . . . . 41
2. Physical basis of mental Harmony and Conflict . *ib.*
3. Harmony promotes mental elation, on the law of Self-conservation . . . . . *ib.*
4. Conflict painful. Situations of harmony and conflict 42

# TABLE OF CONTENTS.

## CHAPTER IV.

### EMOTIONS OF RELATIVITY.

|   | PAGE |
|---|---|
| 1. Certain Emotional states are specially dependent on Universal Relativity | 43 |
| 2. NOVELTY.—Objects | ib. |
| 3. Physical circumstances of Novelty | ib. |
| 4. The Emotion one of pleasure. Counter pain of Monotony | ib. |
| 5. Species of Novelty | 44 |
| 6. *Variety* | 45 |
| 7. WONDER.—Examples of the Wonderful | ib. |
| 8. In some respects an emotion of conflict | ib. |
| 9. Wonder as an æsthetic pleasure requires surpassing excellence, and is allied to the Sublime | 46 |
| 10. Elation of tone caused by the emotion | ib. |
| 11. Every-day wonders | 47 |
| 12. Wonder a corrupting emotion in matters of truth and falsehood. Alleged decay of Wonder. Effect of advancing science on the emotion | ib. |
| 13. FREEDOM and RESTRAINT.—Restraint a case of conflict; the system may become adjusted to a continued restraint | 49 |
| 14. Freedom the deliverance from restraint.—Circumstances necessary to the feeling of rebound. Pleasures associated with Liberty | 50 |
| 15. POWER and IMPOTENCE.—Their importance requires a distinct chapter | 51 |

## CHAPTER V.

### EMOTION OF TERROR.

|   | |
|---|---|
| 1. Terror defined. Its object the apprehension of coming evil | 53 |
| 2. PHYSICAL SIDE of Terror.—A sudden transfer of nervous energy | 54 |
| 3. Likely mental consequences of a diversion of vital energy | 55 |

## TABLE OF CONTENTS.

xi

PAGE

4. MENTAL SIDE.—Characters as Feeling . . . 55
5. Volitional aspect . . . . . . . 56
6. Relations to Intellect.—Undue impressiveness of ob-
    jects of terror. Influence on Belief . . . ib.
7. *Species of Terror.*—Timidity of the Lower Animals . 57
8. Fear in Children . . . . . . . ib.
9. Influence of Strangeness on Animals and on Children
    —admits of two interpretations . . . . 58
10. Slavish Terror . . . . . . . . ib.
11. Forebodings of Disaster and Misfortune . . . 59
12. Anxiety . . . . . . . . . 60
13. Suspicion . . . . . . . . . ib.
14. Panic . . . . . . . . . 61
15. Superstition . . . . . . . . ib.
16. Fear of Death . . . . . . . . 62
17. Distrust of our Faculties in unfamiliar operations . 63
18. The being Abashed by the human presence . . 64
19. Counteractives of Terror. Courage . . . . 65
20. Instrumentality of Terror in Government and Education 66
21. Use of the passion in Art . . . . . 67
    The Eleusinian Mysteries, *Note* . . . . . 68

## CHAPTER VI.

### TENDER EMOTIONS.

1. Objects of Tenderness.—The stimulants of the feeling
    are massive pleasures, great pleasures, pains, touch
    in certain localities, the wail of grief, lustrous ob-
    jects, associations with weakness . . . 70
2. PHYSICAL SIDE.—The organs involved are the Lachrymal
    Gland and Sac, the Larynx, and probably the
    Digestive organs generally; the Lacteal secretion
    in women . . . . . . . 73
3. Link of sequence, physical and mental, between the
    stimulants and the manifestations . . . 74
4. MENTAL SIDE.—As Feeling, a voluminous pleasure
    suited to inaction and weakness . . . . ib.
5. Volitional attributes.—The soothing of undue excite-
    ment . . . . . . . . 75

xii                TABLE OF CONTENTS.

PAGE

6. Relating to the Intellect.—A feeling easy to sustain
   and to recall, and ready to form associations, called
   Affections . . . . . . . .    *ib.*
7. *Mixed* characters.—Operating on the will in absence .    76
8. Tenderness in the state of Desire . . . .    *ib.*
9. Influence on Attention . . . . . .    77
10. Influence on Belief . . . . . .    *ib.*

### SPECIES OF TENDER EMOTION.

11. The feeling vents itself on human beings and on the
    companionable animals . . . . .    *ib.*
12. Its outgoings or demonstrations suppose another per-
    sonality . . . . . . . .    72

#### *Family Group.*

13. Mother and Offspring . . . . . .    78
14. Explanation of the vicarious operations of Tenderness,
    or the pleasure of working for the beloved object .    79
15. Relationship of the Sexes . . . . .    80

#### *The Benevolent Affections.*

16. Sympathy the essential constituent of Benevolence.
    Pleasures of Benevolence . . . . .    82
17. Compassion or Pity . . . . . .    83
18. Gratitude. Spectacle of Generosity . . .    84
19. Benevolence between equals . . . . .    85
20. The Lower Animals inspire tender feeling and warm
    attachments . . . . . . .    *ib.*
21. Form of Tenderness towards Inanimate things . .    *ib.*

#### *Sorrow.*

22. Pains that we are liable to in connection with beloved
    objects.—Consoling influence of tender feelings .    86

23. Social and Ethical bearings of Tenderness . .    87
24. Tender affection a moral lever for the elevation of
    mankind . . , . . . .    *ib.*

# TABLE OF CONTENTS. xiii

### *Admiration and Esteem.*

PAGE

25. Admiration the response to superior excellence . . 88
26. Esteem has reference to useful qualities not necessarily
    pre-eminent . . . . . . . *ib.*

### *Veneration—the Religious Sentiment.*

27. Components of the Religious Sentiment, 'wonder, love,
    and awe.' Religion of the early Greeks, *Note.*
    Supernatural government the essential of Religion.
    Veneration towards human beings and the past . 90

## CHAPTER VII.

### EMOTIONS OF SELF.

1. Meanings of the term 'Self' . . . . . 94
2. Meaning intended in the present chapter . . . 95

#### SELF-GRATULATION AND SELF-ESTEEM.

3. Object of the emotion, some excellence beheld in self . 97
4. PHYSICAL SIDE . . . . . . . 98
5. MENTAL SIDE.—Tender emotion directed upon self as a
   personality . . . . . . . *ib.*
6. Characteristics of self-complacent sentiment generally 102
7. *Specific forms :*—Self-esteem, Self-conceit, Self-confidence, Self-respect, Pride . . . . 103
8. Self-pity . . . . . . . . 104
9. Emulation, Superiority, Envy . . . . . *ib.*
10. Modesty and Humility . . . . . . 105
11. Humiliation and Self-abasement, Remorse . . *ib.*

#### LOVE OF ADMIRATION.

12. Ways in which Approbation, Admiration, and Praise,
    operate on the sentiment of self . . . . 106
13. Approbation . . . . . . . . 108

xiv                    TABLE OF CONTENTS.

                                                              PAGE

14. Praise and Admiration ; Flattery and Adulation ;
    Glory, Reputation, and Fame ; Applause, Compli-
    ment ; Vanity and Vainglory    .    .    .    .    108
15. Arts of *Politesse*    .    .    .    .    .    .    110
16. Censure, Disapprobation, Dispraise, Abuse, Libel,
    Scorn, Infamy    .    .    .    .    .    .    .    111
17. Shame    .    .    .    .    .    .    .    .    *ib.*
18. Bearing of education or culture on the emotions of self    112
19. Employment in Art .    .    .    .    .    .    .    *ib.*
20. Self-love and Selfishness.   Prudent calculation    .    113
21. The most disinterested actions still a part of Self    .    114


## CHAPTER VIII.

### EMOTION OF POWER.

1. Pleasure of mere exercise.   Further pleasure of the
   ends of pursuit    .    .    .    .    .    .    115
2. Proper pleasure a rebound from weakness or difficulty    117
3. Different modes of transition or comparison    .    .    118
4. PHYSICAL SIDE.—Increase of energy ; erect attitude ;
   Laughter    .    .    .    .    .    .    .    119
5. MENTAL SIDE.—Characters of the pleasure    .    .    120
6. *Specific forms.*—Position of headship in industrial
   operations    .    .    .    .    .    .    .    121
7. Working for objects of affection    .    .    .    .    *ib.*
8. Bending the Wills of other men    .    .    .    .    122
9. State office ; wealth ; leadership of a party ; adviser
   in affairs    .    .    .    .    .    .    .    *ib.*
10. Command given by Science    .    .    .    .    123
11. Superiority in the effects of Fine Art ; Eloquence    .    *ib.*
12. Love of influence working in society generally    .    124
13. Summary view of the pleasure of Power    .    .    *ib.*
14. Pains of Impotence.—Failure ; sense of Littleness    .    125
15. Jealousy    .    .    .    .    .    .    .    126
    Relation of sentiment of power to emotions of self, *Note*

# CHAPTER IX.

### THE IRASCIBLE EMOTION.

|  | PAGE |
|---|---|
| 1. Objects of the emotion persons, the authors of pain or injury | 127 |
| 2. PHYSICAL SIDE.—An outburst of excitement and activity; manifestations due to the pain of the offence, and the pleasure of retaliation. Acute shocks most exciting | 128 |
| 3. MENTAL SIDE.—The pleasures of Malevolence | 129 |
| 4. Analysis of the pleasure.—(1.) Fascination for suffering; (2.) the pleasure of power; (3.) prevention of farther pain by inducing fear | 132 |
| 5. Volitional, intellectual, and mixed qualities of the emotion | 133 |
| 6. Anger in the Lower Animals | ib. |
| 7. Demonstrations in Children | 134 |
| 8. Sudden resentment | 135 |
| 9. Deliberate resentment.—Revenge | 136 |
| Revenge of Hannibal on the inhabitants of Himera, *Note* | 137 |
| 10. Antipathy | 138 |
| 11 Hatred | 139 |
| 12. Hostility | 140 |
| 13. Question as to the genuineness of the pleasure of Malevolence | 141 |
| 14. Righteous Indignation: Noble Rage | 144 |
| 15. Relation of the passion of anger to Morality | 145 |
| 16. Education needed as a check on the passion | ib. |
| 17. Artistic handling | 146 |

# CHAPTER X.

### EMOTIONS OF ACTION.—PURSUIT.

|  | PAGE |
|---|---|
| 1. Attitude under a gradually approaching end.—Pursuit and Plot-interest | 148 |

xvi TABLE OF CONTENTS.

PAGE

2. PHYSICAL SIDE of the situation.—Intent occupation of
    one of the senses, with or without active exertion . 148
3. MENTAL SIDE.—Abeyance of Self-consciousness in the
    intensity of the objective regards. Other anæsthetic
    influences . . . . . . .
4. Uncertainty or Chance heightens the interest . . 152
5. Animals chasing their prey . . . . . 152
6. Field Sports . . . . . . . . *ib.*
7. Contests . . . . . . . : . 153
8. Games of Chance . . . . . . . 154
9. Operations of industry as involving the emotion of
    pursuit . . . . . . . . 155
10. Positions occurring in the sympathetic relationship . 156
11. Pursuit of knowledge . . . . . . *ib.*
12. Position of the spectator of a chase . . . . 158
13. Literature of Plot-interest . . . . . . 160
14. Pain connected with pursuit.—The end unduly pro-
    tracted . . . . . . . . 161

## CHAPTER XI.

### EMOTIONS OF INTELLECT.

1. The operations of the Intellect give rise to feelings . 163
2. Emotion of similarity in diversity a species of surprise *ib.*
3. Emotions arising out of Science . . . 164
4. Illustrative comparisons. Pleasures of knowledge . 166
5. Comparisons in Poetry. Harmony in the Fine Arts
    generally . . . . . . . 167
6. Feeling of Inconsistency; regard to Truth . . 168

### SUMMARY OF THE SIMPLER EMOTIONS.

Recapitulation of the simpler emotions with reference
to the general laws of Association, Relativity, and
Harmony . . . . . . . .

## CHAPTER XII.

### SYMPATHY AND IMITATION.

1. Groundwork of the aptitudes of sympathy and imita-
    tion . . . . . . . . 172

TABLE OF CONTENTS. xvii

PAGE

Tendency to assume attitudes or movements observed in others, or in any way suggested to the mind . 174
Assumption of a mental state through its physical accompaniments . . . . . . . 177
Character for infectiousness proper to the various simple emotions . . . . . . . 178
Fellow-feeling in great part the echoing of pain or pleasure . . . . . . . . 179
Alliance and Contrast between sympathy and tender emotion . . . . . . . . *ib.*
Sympathy a source of pleasure and mental support to the receiver. Not necessarily pleasurable to the giver . . . . . . . . 180
Consequences in human life. Tendency to uniformity of character and opinions . . . . . 182
Obstructives of Sympathy . . . . . 183
IMITATION. Relates to voluntary actions . . . 184
Circumstances that promote imitation . . . *ib.*
Contrast between the imitative and the self-originating temperaments . . . . . . . 185
Examples of imitation . . . . . . 186
Mimicry . . . . . . . . 187
Intellectual imitation . . . . . . *ib.*
Imitative Arts. Some of the Fine Arts imitative, others not . . . . . . . . *ib.*
Interest arising out of faithful imitation by an Artist 188


## CHAPTER XIII.

### OF IDEAL EMOTION.

Persistence of an emotional wave after the cessation of the cause . . . . . . . . 190
Purely ideal subsistence of states of feeling . . 191
First condition, the state of the physical organs . *ib.*
Specific temperament as regards emotion . . . 193
Individuals are constituted so as to entertain some omotions in preference to others . . . . 194
Repetition and habit may give an emotional bent . 196

xviii TABLE OF CONTENTS.

PAGE

7. Influence of physical stimulants, narcotics, &c. . 197
8. Other physical circumstances . . . . . 198
9. Mental agencies concerned in supporting a wave of
   ideal emotion . . . . . . . 200
10. Operation of the intellectual forces of Contiguity and
    Similarity . . . . . . . 201
11. Application of the foregoing considerations, to explain
    the predominance of the Ideal, over the Actual, in
    human life . . . . . . . . 202
12. Day-dreams and illusions of the fancy, based upon the
    strong emotions . . . . . . . 204
13. Pleasures of the Imagination . . . . . 205
14. The Emotional life . . . . . . . ib.
15. Influence of the ideal in the Ethical appreciation of
    conduct . . . . . . . . 206
16. The Religious sentiment an outgoing of the ideal . 207
17. Fine Art must adapt itself to ideal longings. Imagina-
    tive sensibility . . . . . . . 208

## CHAPTER XIV.

### THE ÆSTHETIC EMOTIONS.

1. Peculiarities that circumscribe the æsthetic pleasures 210
2. The eye and the ear the avenues of Artistic impressions . . . . . . . . 211
3. The muscular and sensual feelings may be brought in
   when contemplated *in idea* . . . . 212
4. Problem of the Beautiful . . . . . . 213
5. Circle of æsthetic qualities . . . . . 214
6. No one comprehensive generalization attainable . 216
7. Element of Sensation in Art :—Senses of Hearing and
   Sight . . . . . . . . ib.
8. Co-operation of the Intellect . . . . . 218
9. Simple Emotions touched by the Artist . . . 220
10. Reasons why the Emotions of Science do not enter into
    Art equally with the others . . . . . 221

### SPECIFIC EMOTIONS OF ART.

11. *Melody and Harmony in Sound.*—Pleasing and con-
    cordant sounds . . . . . . . 222

## TABLE OF CONTENTS. xix

| | PAGE |
|---|---|
| 12. Time in music | 224 |
| 13. Varying Emphasis | 225 |
| 14. Cadence | ib. |
| 15. Composition | 226 |
| 16. Melody of Speech | ib. |
| 17. *Harmonies of Sight.*—Harmony of Colours. Light and Shade. Lustre. | 227 |
| 18. Muscular susceptibility of the Eye. Harmony of Movements, Intervals, and Proportions. Laws of Proportion; the German critics; D. R. Hay | ib. |
| 19. Straight Outlines | 229 |
| 20. Curved Outlines | 230 |
| 21. Pressure and Support | 231 |
| 22. Appearance of Ease in objects employed in giving support | 232 |
| 23. Symmetry | 233 |
| 24. Beauty of Movement | 234 |
| *Note* on Complex Harmonies. Unity; Variety | ib. |
| 25. *Fitness, the Æsthetic of Utility* | 235 |
| 26. Order; Cleanliness; Polish | 236 |
| 27. *The Sublime.* Objects and emotion | 237 |
| 28. Sublime of Support. The mountain, precipice, and abyss | 238 |
| 29. Sublimity of Space. Commanding prospects in scenery | 239 |
| 30. Greatness of Time. Relations of Terror to the Sublime | 240 |
| 31. Sublime of the Human Character. Human Power the literal Sublime | ib. |
| 32. *Natural Objects in general.* Mineral and Vegetable Kingdoms. Surface of the globe | 242 |
| 33. The Animal Kingdom; its beauties and deformities | 243 |
| 34. The Human form | 244 |
| 35. Beauties of Movement and Expression | 245 |
| 36. Beauty and grace in Human Character | 246 |
| 37. *The Ludicrous.*—Causes of Laughter | 247 |
| 38. All Incongruity is not Ludicrous. Degradation essential to the Ludicrous. Degradation viewed as reflecting Superior Power | ib. |
| 39. Ludicrous Degradation as a mode of Release from constraint.—The Comic a rebound from the Serious | 250 |

XX                    TABLE OF CONTENTS.

## CHAPTER XV.

### THE ETHICAL EMOTIONS; OR THE MORAL SENSE.

| | PAGE |
|---|---|
| 1. *Punishment* the test of Moral Obligation . . . | 253 |
| 2. Variety of Moral Theories . . . . . | 255 |
| 3 Right Reason ; the Fitness of Things; the Will of the Deity . . . . . . . . | ib. |
| 4. Self-interest . . . . . . . . | 258 |
| 5 The Doctrine of a Moral Sense . . . . | 259 |
| 6. Qualified form of the doctrine of an innate sense of rectitude, as set forth by Dr. Whewell . . . | ib. |
| 7 There is no abstract standard, either of Truth, or Rectitude . . . . . . . . | 260 |
| 8. All propositions are propositions affirmed or believed by some individual minds . . . . . | 263 |
| 9. Truth in the Abstract is correlative with Belief in the Abstract . . . . . . . . | 265 |
| 10. There is no such thing as a Universal Conscience . | 266 |
| 11. Alleged Uniformity of men's moral judgments. The uniformity consists, first, in the common necessities of society . . . . . . . . | 268 |
| 12. Secondly, mankind have been unanimous in imposing restraints of *sentimental* origin . . . . | 269 |
| 13. Theory of Adam Smith . . . . . . | 271 |
| 14. Principle of Utility . . . . . . | 272 |
| 15. Utility must be qualified by Liberty . . . | 275 |
| Objections to Utility principally resolve themselves into sentimental preferences . . . . | ib. |
| 16. Existing moral rules founded partly on Utility, and partly on Sentiment . . . . . . | 277 |
| 17. Examples of Sentiment converted into law and morality | 278 |
| 18. Process of *enactment* of moral rules . . . | 280 |
| 19. Example from the anti-slavery opinion . . . | 281 |
| 20. The *abrogation* of moral rules . . . . | 282 |
| 21. CONSCIENCE follows and imitates external authority, instead of preceding it . . . . . | 283 |
| 22. Development of Conscience in the individual . . | 284 |

TABLE OF CONTENTS.                    xxi

|  |  | PAGE |
|---|---|---|
| 23. Varieties of the sentiment of obligation : the narrower and the wider regards | . . . . . | 286 |
| 24. Other varieties of conscience | . . . . | 287 |
| 25. The self-formed, or Independent conscience | . . | 288 |
| 26. Sense of duty in the abstract | . . . . . | 290 |
| 27. Moral judgments on the conduct of others | . . | 291 |
| 28. Virtue and merit | . . . . . . | 292 |

# THE WILL.

## CHAPTER I.

### THE PRIMITIVE ELEMENTS OF VOLITION.

#### THE SPONTANEITY OF MOVEMENT.

1. Recapitulation of the arguments in favour of the spontaneous beginning of movements . . . 297
2. Review of the groups of moving organs in the animal body . . . . . 299
3. Necessity of an isolated spontaneity, as a prelude to separate voluntary control . . . 301
4. Supposed cerebral conditions of isolated discharges . 303
5. Instance of the external ear . . . . 304

*Circumstances governing the spontaneous discharge.*

6. Natural vigour of the constitution . . . *ib.*
7. Excitement . . . . . . 305
8. Mental stimulants.—Pain ; Pleasure ; Opposition . 306
9. Explanation of the occurrence of the larger outbursts 307

#### LINK OF FEELING AND ACTION.

10. Necessity of something more than spontaneity to account for volition . . . . . 308
11. Self-conservation furnishes the rudiment of the Link connecting Action and Feeling . . . *ib.*
12. Question whether emotional movements may offer the beginning requisite for voluntary control . . 309
13. Volitional branch of the Law of Self-conservation. Summary of the foundations of the Will . . 310

xxii TABLE OF CONTENTS.

PAGE

14. Prompting of the will by Pleasure. Apparent exception of soothing Pleasures. Exhaustion of the strength. Prompting of Pain directly arrests action ; the relief from pain, like pleasure, promotes action . . . . . . 311

## CHAPTER II.

### GROWTH OF VOLUNTARY POWER.

1. Growth of volitional associations with the Muscular Feelings . . . . . . . 315
2. Organic Sensations.—Pains of Muscle.—Cramp . 316
3. Appeasing of Thirst . . . . . 318
4. Feelings of Respiration.—Warmth and Chillness . 319
5. Sucking . . . . . . 320
6. Mastication . . . . . . 323
7. Snuffing sweet Odours, and recoiling from the opposite 326
8. Cherishing agreeable sensations of Touch . . 327
9. Avoiding painful Touches . . . . 329
10. Training of the whip . . . . . *il.*
11. Avoiding painful, and courting pleasurable, sounds . 331
12. Movements to attain the pleasures, or avoid the pains of Sight.—Beginnings of Attention . . *ib.*
13. Appetites and their gratification.— Sex . . 333
14. Movements to the lead of the special emotions . 334
15. *Intermediate Actions and Associated Ends.*—Associates of warmth, food, &c. . . . . 335
16. Chase for food by the lower animals . . . 337

## CHAPTER III.

### GROWTH OF VOLUNTARY POWER—*continued.*

1. Transference of acquired connexions between movements and sensations to new uses . . . 339
2. Acquirement of a more general control of the voluntary organs.—The word of command . . 341
3. Faculty of Imitation . . . . 343
4. Imitation of movements at sight . . . 347

## TABLE OF CONTENTS. xxiii

PAGE

5. Graduated command of the muscles for the execution of nice operations . . . . 348
6. Imitation of movements of the features.—Teaching the deaf to speak . . . . . 350
7. Power of acting on a *wish* to move a member . 351
8. The idea of a movement must be the antecedent for bringing it into play . . . . 352
9. Association of movements with the effects produced on outward things . . . . 354
10. Working to pleasure or from pain in *idea* . . 356
11. Examples from the Voice.—Associations entering into the voluntary power of speech . . . 357

## CHAPTER IV.

### CONTROL OF FEELINGS AND THOUGHTS.

1. Volition crowned with powers of general command . 360

#### CONTROL OF THE FEELINGS.

2. The direct power of the will confined to the muscular organs . . . . . . 361
3. How to control the portions of the emotional wave that are not muscular . . . . 362
4. Growth of this department of voluntary power . 365
5. Control of the feelings a good test of the volitional energy of the individual character . . 369

#### THE MIXED EXPRESSION OF THE FEELINGS.

Examples of Expression of Feeling determined by voluntary action . . . . . 371

#### COMMAND OF THE THOUGHTS.

6. Instrumentality of the will in directing the current of the thoughts or ideas . . . . 372
7. Command of the thoughts a test of volitional energy 375
8. Constructive association a voluntary process . 376
9. Aid afforded by the command of the thoughts, in controlling the feelings . . . . 378

xxiv TABLE OF CONTENTS.

PAGE

10. Suppressing or rousing emotional displays, by the assistance of ideas . . . . . 379
11. Converse fact, of the feelings governing the thoughts 380

## CHAPTER V.

### OF MOTIVES, OR ENDS.

1. Various forms taken on by the things operating as motives . . . . . . 384
2. The ultimate ends of pursuit ought all to be found in the enumeration of feelings of movement, sensations, and special emotions . . . 385
3. Ideal persistence of the various feelings that operate on the will . . . . . 387
4. *Of aggregated, derivative, and intermediate ends* . 392
5. Adoption as a final end of what was originally a means.—Money ; Formalities in Business and in Science 394
6. Association of feelings with things more persisting in the mind than themselves . . . 396
7. *Excited, impassioned, exaggerated, irrational ends : Fixed Ideas.*—Passion may mean only intense pleasure or intense pain . . . . . 397
8. Cases where action is out of proportion to pleasure or pain. Disturbing force the tendency of a vivid idea to force itself into action.—Fear . . . *ib.*
9. State of antipathy or disgust . . . 399
10. Undue excitement on the side of pleasure.—A ruling passion . . . . . . *ib.*
11. Statement of the point attained in the exposition . 402

## CHAPTER VI.

### THE CONFLICT OF MOTIVES.

1. What happens when two states of feeling come together, viewed simply as emotions . . 404
2. Conflict of a voluntary stimulus with the spontaneous impulses of the system . . . . 405
3. Struggle between a voluntary stimulus and physical exhaustion . . . . . 406

## TABLE OF CONTENTS.

XXV

PAGE

4. Opposition of two states of present pleasure or pain.—
The result shows a fact of character . . . 407
5. The same pleasure or pain acting on different occasions, and in different persons . . . 410
6. Conflict of the actual with the ideal . . . 411
7. Ideal emotions supported by associations . . 414
8. Conflict between ideal ends . . . . 416
9. Aggregated ends in conflict . . . . 417
10. Impassioned ends . : . . . *ib.*

## CHAPTER VII.

### DELIBERATION.—RESOLUTION.—EFFORT.

1. Deliberation a voluntary act, prompted by the known
evils of hasty action . . . . 419
2. Example . . . . . . 421
3. The deliberative position gives opportunity for all the
elements of decision to come up . . . 423
4. Franklin's *Moral Algebra* . . . . 424
5. Method of recording impressions from day to day
during a period of deliberation . . . 425
6. Deliberative process different as it deals with things
experienced or unexperienced . . . 427
7. Deliberation in full accordance with the theory of the
Will . . . . . . *ib.*
8. RESOLUTION.—Action suspended till a certain time has
elapsed . . . . . . 428
9. Resolutions often extend over wide periods, and are
therefore liable to fall through . . . 430
10. The order of human life a train of resolutions . 431
11. EFFORT.—Feelings connected with voluntary acts· . 432
12. Supposition that all mechanical power must originate
in mind . . . . . . *ib.*
13. There is usually a certain consciousness accompanying
volition . . . . . . 434
14. The real antecedent of power put forth is the expenditure of the material organism . . . *ib.*

xxvi  TABLE OF CONTENTS.

PAGE

15. There can be neither consciousness nor voluntary power without the processes of physical renovation and decay . . . . . 435
16. When we say Mind is a source of power, we must mean mind together with body . . . 436
17. The habitual actions tend to become unconscious . 437

## CHAPTER VIII.

### DESIRE.

1. Desire supposes a motive to the will without the ability to act . . . . . 438
2. Form of Desire in protracted operations for ends . 439
3. Question as to the courses open when no volition is possible . . . . . . ib.
4. Endurance . . . . . . ib.
5. The stimulus to endurance is the pain of conflict . 440
6. Ideal or imaginary action . . . . 441
7. Persistence of a feeling in absence, a condition of imaginary gratification . . . . 443
8. Examples of ideal activity . . . . 444
9. Emotions suited to imaginary gratification . . 446
10. The memory of pleasure has a sting of pain from the sense of its being below the reality . . 447
11. Provocatives of desire . . . . 449
12. Susceptibility to ideal inflammation . . . 451
13. Desire most effectually stimulated by growing pleasure 453

## CHAPTER IX.

### THE MORAL HABITS.

1. The force of plastic adhesiveness operates to increase or diminish the strength of motives . . . 455
2. Control of Sense and Appetite . . . 456
3. Examples.—The habit of early rising . . 457
4. The proper initiatives of habits . . . 459
5. Habits of Temperance . . . . 460
6. Control of Attention . . . . . ib.
7. Suppression of Instinctive movements . . 462

# TABLE OF CONTENTS. xxvii

|    |    | PAGE |
|----|----|----|
| 8. | Changing the emotional nature as a whole | 462 |
| 9. | Lowering or raising of special emotions | 464 |
| 10. | Habit of Courage | ib. |
| 11. | Tender Emotion | 465 |
| 12. | Sentiment of Power.—Command of the Temper | 467 |
| 13. | Pleasures of Sport and Plot-interest.—Emotions of Intellect | 468 |
| 14. | Taste and Æsthetic culture | ib. |
| 15. | Sudden conversions, as opposed to the slow course of habit | 469 |
| 16. | Habits modifying the original spontaneity | 470 |
| 17. | Repression of Desire.—Contentment | ib. |
| 18. | Domestication of the animal tribes | 471 |
| 19. | Habits in opposition to intellectual trains.—Concentration of thought | 472 |
| 20. | The more important conditions of the growth of habit | ib. |

## CHAPTER X.

### PRUDENCE.—DUTY.—MORAL INABILITY.

|    |    | PAGE |
|----|----|----|
| 1. | *Prudence.*—The bearing of the constitution of the will on this —Self-promptings | 474 |
| 2. | Promptings supplied from without | 475 |
| 3. | Leisurely meditation an element of prudence | 476 |
| 4. | Characters moulded on the prudential cast | ib. |
| 5. | Forces hostile to prudence | 477 |
| 6. | It is possible to predict the future conduct of an individual from the past | 479 |
| 7. | *Duty.*—Self-promptings | 480 |
| 8. | Prohibition by penalties the first source of the Moral Sentiment.—The Slavish Conscience | 481 |
| 9. | Elements that concur to form the Citizen Conscience | 483 |
| 10. | The Independent Conscience | 486 |
| 11. | Aids to conscience | 487 |
| 12. | Counter-impulses to duty | 488 |
| 13. | *Moral Inability* | 489 |
| 14. | Plea of moral inability put forward by an offender | 491 |

xxviii TABLE OF CONTENTS.

## CHAPTER XI.

### LIBERTY AND NECESSITY.

| | PAGE |
|---|---|
| 1. The practice of mankind involves the assumption of the uniformity of human actions . . . | 493 |
| 2. Examples of problems surrounded by factitious difficulties.—The question of the Will affected in this way | 495 |
| 3. The phrases *Liberty, Freedom, Free-will.*—Their inappropriateness as applied to volition . . | 498 |
| 4. There is a real contrariety of opinion as respects the Will.—The doctrine of invariable sequence in human actions may be denied, as it was in substance by Socrates . . . . . | 500 |
| 5. *Necessity* . . . . . | 503 |
| 6. *Choice, Deliberation,* as bearing on the question of Liberty . . . . . | 504 |
| 7. Meanings of *Spontaneity and Self-determination* . · 507 |
| 8. Self can only mean the sum total of motives . . | 509 |
| 9. *Consciousness of Free-will.*—Is consciousness an infallible testimony ? . . . . . | 511 |
| 10. Where consciousness is infallible knowledge is not, where knowledge begins consciousness is fallible . | 513 |
| 11. Assertions that have been put forward under the infallible attestation of consciousness . . . | 517 |
| 12. The doctrine of Free-will not of the kind that consciousness can testify . . . . | 518 |
| 13. *Moral Agency* . . . . . | 519 |
| 14. *Responsibility.*—Limits to the imposition of punishment | 520 |
| 15. Punishment may be efficient for its end, but objectionable on the score of humanity . . . | 521 |
| Responsibility for Belief, *Note* . . | 522 |

## BELIEF.

| | |
|---|---|
| 1. In the primitive aspect of Volition, belief has no place | 524 |

## TABLE OF CONTENTS. xxix

| | PAGE |
|---|---|
| 2. It appears in the performance of actions that are but *means* | 525 |
| 3. Belief implies some cognisance of the order of nature | 526 |
| 4. Affirmations may be detached from actions or immediate ends | 527 |
| 5. Belief is a source of happiness or misery | 529 |
| 6. Relationship of Belief to Terror.—Doubt | *ib.* |
| 7. Belief in coming evil | 532 |
| 8. Joy and Depression as caused by belief | 533 |
| 9. Sources of belief | 534 |
| 10. The different sources are apt to be mixed together | 535 |
| 11. I. Intuitive tendencies | 537 |
| 12. Belief accompanies action and precedes experience | 539 |
| 13. Fallacies grounded in instinctive beliefs | 540 |
| 14. II. Experience as a source of belief | 541 |
| 15. III. Influence of Emotion | 544 |
| 16. Opposition of Confidence and Fear | 546 |
| 17. Emotions considered as operating to elevate or depress the mental tone | 547 |
| 18. Belief in Testimony | 548 |
| 19. Agency of Desire in producing conviction | 549 |
| 20. Hope, Fear, Despondency | *ib* |
| 21. Religious Faith | 550 |
| 22. Line of demarcation between belief and notions without belief | 551 |
| 23. How can we be said to believe in things beyond the scope of possible action? | 553 |
| 24. Belief in our own sensations, present and past | 554 |

## CONSCIOUSNESS.

| | |
|---|---|
| 1. Prevalent meanings of the term Consciousness | 555 |
| 2. General tendency of the several meanings. First, mental life, and its degrees. Second, the occupation of the mind with itself. Third, Belief | 561 |

### CONSCIOUSNESS AS FEELING.

#### 1. *The Passive States.*

| | |
|---|---|
| 3. Pleasure and Pain. Characteristics of Neutral Excitement | 563 |

XXX                    TABLE OF CONTENTS.

                                                                    PAGE
4. Neutral excitement can stamp impressions on the
   intellect . . . . . . . 564

                2. *The Active States.*

5. Consciousness of energy. Cognition of the Extended
   Universe· The Volitional Consciousness, *Note* . 565

            THE INTELLECTUAL CONSCIOUSNESS.

6. The great problem lies in defining the common ground
   of Emotion and Intellect . . . . 565

                *Sense of Difference.*

7. Discrimination the fundamental fact of Intelligence . 566
8. Change of impression essential to consciousness in every
   form . . . . . . 567
9. The transition that wakens up discrimination may be
   described as a shock of *surprise* . . . 569
10. We are conscious in proportion to the greatness or
    abruptness of the transition . . . 571
11. Points of contrast of the emotional and intellectual
    consciousness.—Occupation of the mind with plea-
    sure or pain excludes discrimination. Neutral
    excitement may not always be intellectual. *Note* . 572
12. The most intellectual minds are the most discriminative
    with the least emotional shock . . . 574
13. Discrimination is the intellectual property of all our
    sensibilities . . . . . 575
14. It is a part of our intellectual culture to form new sus-
    ceptibilies to difference . . . . 576
15. The feeling of difference precedes the operation of the
    laws of association . . . . 577

                *Sense of Agreement.*

16. Agreement causes a mental shock, if accompanied with
    diversity . . . . . . 578
17. The feeling of Agreement underlies those elements of
    knowledge termed generalities, &c. . . *ib.*

                *Sensation and Perception.*

18. Sensation differs greatly as it inclines to the Emotional
    or the Intellectual side . . . . 580

# TABLE OF CONTENTS.

xxxi

PAGE

19. A sensation is, in every view, a conscious element of the mind . . . . . . 581
20. Perception means sensation and something more . 583
21. Illustration from the acquired perceptions of sight . 584
22. Supposed perception of an external and independent material world . . . . . 585

### *The Nature of Cognition.*

23. How are we affected when we are said to know a thing ? *ib.*
24. Dispute as to the origin of our knowledge in sense . 586
25. Sensation and perception pre-supposed . . *ib.*
26. Knowledge is not co-extensive with sensation.—It is select or specialized sensation . . . 587
27. Specializing forces . . . . . 588
28. Relation, or comparison, essential to knowledge . 589
    Relations of Co-existence and Succession. *Note* . *ib.*
29. Illustrations derivable from literature, art, and science 591
30. The use of language fixes attention on select impressions 592
31. Summary of the essentials of Cognition . . *ib.*
    Subject and Object.—The External World. *Note* . 593

---

# APPENDIX.

A. *On the most general physical conditions of Consciousness.* —Laws of Relativity and Diffusion. Combined statement. Mr G. H. Lewes on Reflex Acts . 599
B. *Classification of the Emotions.*—Mr. Herbert Spencer's criticism and classification; Reid's classification; Dugald Stewart: Thomas Brown; Sir W. Hamilton; Kant; Herbart; Waitz; Nahlowsky; Wundt 601
C. *Distinction of Reflex and Voluntary Acts.*—Mr. Spencer's criticism. The doctrine of hereditary transmission applied to the Will and to other supposed Instincts . . . . . . 613
D. *Meanings of Consciousness.*—Hamilton on the priority of Knowledge or Cognition in the divisions of the mind. Ulrici on Consciousness . . . 614

# THE EMOTIONS.

'But, although such a being (a purely intellectual being) might perhaps be conceived to exist, and although, in studying our internal frame, it be convenient to treat of our intellectual powers apart from our active propensities, yet, in fact, the two are very intimately, and indeed inseparably, connected in all our mental operations. I already hinted, that, even in our speculative inquiries, the principle of curiosity is necessary to account for the exertion we make; and it is still more obvious that a combination of means to accomplish particular ends presupposes some determination of our nature, which makes the attainment of these ends desirable. Our active propensities, therefore, are the motives which induce us to exort our intellectual powers; and our intellectual powers are the instruments by which we attain the ends recommended to us by our active propensities:

" Reason the card, but passion is the gale." '

DUGALD STEWART, *Philosophy of the Active Powers*, p. 2.

# CHAPTER I.

## OF FEELING IN GENERAL.

1. MIND is comprised under the three heads—FEELING, VOLITION, and INTELLECT.

FEELING includes all our pleasures and pains, and certain modes of excitement, to be afterwards defined, that are neutral as regards pleasure and pain.

Under the Muscular Feelings and the Sensations of the Senses, I reviewed in detail those feelings of a primary character, due, on the one hand, to the putting forth of muscular energy, and, on the other, to the action of the outer world on the organs of sense. There remains a department of secondary, derived, or complicated feelings, termed the Emotions.

2. In my former volume, I adduced facts to prove the dependence of all the mental workings on bodily organs ; and, in treating of the sensations, gave in each instance the physical side as well as the mental ; all which is applicable to the Emotions.

The most general principle that we are able to lay down respecting the concomitance of mind and body may be called the LAW of DIFFUSION. It is expressed thus : 'When an impression is accompanied with Feeling, or any kind of consciousness, the aroused currents *diffuse* themselves freely over the brain, leading to a general agitation of the moving organs, as well as affecting the viscera.'

I may quote, as an illustrative contrast, the so-called Reflex actions (breathing, &c.), which have no feeling, and are operated through a narrow and confined nervous circle.

It is not meant that every fibre of the brain is affected in

4                    OF FEELING IN GENERAL.

the course of the diffusion, but that a spreading wave is produced enough to agitate the collective bodily organs.

The organs first and prominently affected, in the diffused wave of nervous influence, are the moving members, and of these, by preference, the features of the face, whose movements constitute the *expression* of the countenance. But the influence extends to all the parts of the moving system, voluntary and involuntary ; while an important series of effects are produced on the glands and viscera—the stomach, lungs, heart, kidneys, skin, together with the sexual and mammary organs.

3. The facts that establish the companionship of feeling and diffusive action have been abundantly quoted in the description of the sensations. Each of us knows in our own experience that a sudden shock of feeling is accompanied with movements of the body generally, and with other effects. So well are we convinced of this, that we judge of the intensity of feeling in others by the extent and energy of their manifestations. Sleep is accompanied with stillness of the bodily movements ; the waking to consciousness has for its physical side the renewal of the active energies of the system, with a series of changes in the organic functions.

It is well known that impressions fail to produce consciousness, when the mind is strongly pre-engaged. In the heat of a battle, wounds may be for a time unfelt. A person very much engrossed with a subject gives no heed at the moment to words addressed to him, but should his attention be relaxed before the impression fades from the ear, he will probably return an answer.

One of the remedies for pain or uneasiness is to divert the attention and activity, or even the current of the thoughts.

We are able in some degree to restrain the feelings by the power of the will. Now as the will can act only on muscles, it follows that the moving organs must participate in the embodiment of the feelings.

4. This doctrine has an important bearing on the Unity of the Consciousness. A plurality of stimulations of the nerves may co-exist, but they can affect the consciousness

## DOCTRINES OPPOSED TO DIFFUSION.

only by turns, or one at a time. The reason is that the bodily organs are collectively engaged with each distinct conscious state, and they cannot be doing two things at the same instant. The eyes cannot minister to one feeling, the ears to another, and the hands to a third; for, although the feeling may not be strong enough to involve the activity of all the organs, yet those unemployed must either be at rest or engaged in mere routine functions, such as walking, that are not necessarily accompanied by consciousness.

5. The counter-doctrines to the theory of Diffusion are the following :—

First. It may be maintained that the mind is not dependent on bodily processes throughout. Admitting that there is an occasional accompaniment of outward agitation with inward feelings, one may hold that this is merely casual and incidental, and not at all essential to the existence of the feelings. It may be said that, although certain energetic emotions have bodily manifestations, a great many feelings rise up without affecting any bodily organ. Some of our emotions, it may be contended, are of so tranquil a nature as to have only a pure mental existence, and produce no disturbance in any part of the physical system.

It is here maintained, on the contrary, that no feeling, however tranquil, is possible without a full participation of the physical system; the apparent tranquillity merely signifying that the diffused wave is too feeble to produce observable effects.

Secondly. The uniform connexion of mental states with bodily conditions may be admitted, but with the supposition that one or other of the ganglia, or lesser grey centres of the brain, is all that is necessary to sensation. The corpora quadrigemina have been called the ganglion of the sense of sight, as the olfactory bulb is the ganglion of smell; and it has been supposed that these are enough for mere sensation. I, on the contrary, am disposed to maintain that the hemispheres are requisite to consciousness in every shape; and that these hemispheres are the medium of the accom-

**6**            OF FEELING IN GENERAL.

panying diffusion of stimulus to the collective system of muscles and glands.

Thirdly. It is not uncommon with those that fully believe in the participation of the brain in every mental experience, to restrict it to the brain. To this view, I oppose the doctrine of the farther participation of the outcarrying nerves, the muscles, and the viscera. If we suppose, for example, that a shock of Fear could be prevented from actuating the moving organs, the stomach, the skin, the heart, or any other organ usually affected, our mental experience would not be what is characteristic of the emotion.

6. The theory of Reflex, or Automatic, actions is in strict accordance with the view now taken of the physical accompaniments of feeling or consciousness. These automatic actions, such as the movements of the heart and lungs, the movements of the intestines, &c., are proved to depend upon the spinal cord and medulla oblongata, to the exclusion of the cerebral hemispheres. A reflex action is an isolated response from some one single centre, or some limited portion of grey matter, and not a diffused influence over the system at large. With such local restrictions is associated the property of unconsciousness, or want of feeling, attaching to this class of actions.

7. The Habitual, or routine, actions, which make up the acquired ability and skill of men and animals, have sometimes been termed ‘secondarily automatic.’ The reason is that they resemble in a great degree the actions just alluded to, the reflex, or primary automatic. They are performed almost unconsciously; that is to say, the more thoroughly they attain the character of routine, or habit, the less is the feeling that attends their exercise. Such actions as walking, turning a wheel, stitching, may be sustained without giving rise to any but a feeble conscious impression, so as to leave the mind free for other exercises or emotions. Now, the only view that we can take of the physical machinery of those actions, is to suppose that the originally diffused wave that accompanied them has become contracted within some narrow circles of the brain,

## LIMITS TO DIFFUSED MANIFESTATIONS. 7

which just suffice for the bare performance of the operations implied in them. The first time that the hand clenches a wooden or iron handle, a sensation is produced having all the characters of a feeling fully manifested. There is, perhaps, a pleasurable or neutral consciousness, an occupation of the mind, a responsive expression and attitude of the whole body. All sensations have originally these characters ; they are *conscious states*, and for the time being constitute the exclusive mental experience, and impart movements of expression to the members that are in alliance with the cerebral system. But at a later stage, such an action as the grasping of a handle agitates the brain almost through one solitary channel of influence—that, namely, which suffices for stimulating certain muscles of the arm concerned in rotatory motion. This remarkable narrowing of the sphere of influence of a sensational or active stimulus is one of the effects of education ; and the comparison between the routine and the reflex operations seems most just and accurate. The character of unconsciousness would appear to arise exactly as the cerebral wave gets contracted.

8. Let us now attend to the circumstances that limit and control the diffused manifestations of feeling.

In the first place, a certain energy of stimulation is necessary to produce those gestures, changes of feature, vocal outbursts, and alterations in the state of the viscera, that are apparent to an observer. One may experience a certain thrill of pleasure, without even a smile ; it is nevertheless a fair inference that a nervous wave is diffused to the muscles of the face, and to all the other muscles ; the failure in expression being due to the mechanical inadequacy of the central stimulus. A certain degree of emotional excitement is possible without the full and proper display, but not without the tendency in that direction.

In the second place, something depends on the character of the active organs themselves. Irrespective of the intensity of the feelings, the energy of the demonstrations may vary in different individuals, and in the same person at dif-

## OF FEELING IN GENERAL.

ferent times. There is a certain vigour and freshness of limb, featuie, and voice, disposing those parts to activity, and seeking only an occasion to burst forth. Age, feebleness, and exhaustion, paralyse the display, without destroying the susceptibility of feeling. There are individuals and races characterised by the vivacious temperament; we may instance the ancient Greeks and the modern Italians. It does not follow that the strength of the feeling corresponds in all such cases to the degree of demonstration. We need other criteria besides this to determine the intensity of the mental excitement.

Thirdly. The different emotions differ in their manifestations. The distinct modes characterising pleasure and pain have been formerly described and accounted for. (See *Instinctive play of feeling*, § 20.) There are other distinctions besides. Wonder is different from self-complacency; the pain of fear and the pain of a bodily hurt do not manifest themselves alike. Acute emotions, as wonder, stimulate the movements; massive, as tender feeling, are more connected with glandular effects.

Fourthly. The primitive outbursts of emotion may be greatly modified by education. Articulate speech and song are new and refined outlets for the emotional wave. In the exaltation of triumph, instead of savage laughter and frantic gestures, the hero of cultivated society vents his emotions in magniloquent diction or splendid music. The natural language of the feelings is cast into a mould in a great degree conventional; so that the same emotions would be differently manifested by a Frenchman and by an Englishman, by a man of society and by a boor.

Fifthly. It is possible, by force of will, to suppress the more prominent manifestations of feeling—namely, the movements depending on voluntary muscles. The organic effects, such as blushing, are beyond our power. The suppression of display may become habitual, but the feelings will still occur, although not unmodified by the refusal to allow them the natural vent.

9. *Stimulus of an Active Impulse.*—The law of diffused

## DIFFUSION FROM AN ACTIVE IMPULSE.

manifestation accompanying consciousness is seen in starting from movement, as well as when the impulse is a sensation. So strong is the tendency for other parts to join with the one immediately called upon to act, that we often find it difficult to confine the energy to the proper locality. Thus an infant attempting any operation with its hands always displays a great many movements that are not necessary to the thing aimed at. So in speech, any outburst of utterance is sure to carry with it a number of involuntary movements and gestures, as if it were impossible to isolate the course of the nervous current, or restrict it to the proper instruments of the volition put forth. The awkward gestures of a child learning to write are one of the cares of the schoolmaster. Beginners in every art are in the same way encumbered with the uncalled-for sympathies of irrelevant members. The suppression of these accompaniments is the work of education, and the distinction of mature life. But this extinction is never complete at any age. All that is deemed ungraceful in the extraneous accompaniments of speech is repressed among the cultivated classes of society, but gestures that have not this character are preserved, and even superadded, for the sake of the increased animation that they impart to the human presence. Thus it happens that the diffused cerebral wave, whereby some one action rouses the outlying members into co-operation, is made available in the Fine Art of theatrical and oratorical display, and in the graceful accompaniments of every-day converse. In the uncultivated ranks of society, and more especially in races of low artistic sensibility, the instinctive diffusion of an active impulse produces very harsh effects. We may at all times note individual instances where the secondary actions are of the oddest kind. We shall find persons who cannot answer a question without scratching the head, rubbing the eyes, or shrugging up the whole body. In the excitement of energetic speech, no one is able to keep the other members tranquil.

10. In the volume on *The Senses*, I reviewed the parts of the body concerned in the expression of emotion, and endea-

# 10 OF FEELING IN GENERAL.

voured to generalize the physical adjuncts of pleasure and pain.

The concurrence of *organic* effects, or of alterations in the action of the viscera, with mental states, has not been observed with the care that it deserves. One important fact, however, has been determined experimentally, namely, the influence of mental causes on the capillary circulation.

The small blood-vessels by which the blood is brought into proximity with the various tissues of the body are kept in a state of balanced distension between two forces,—the one the propulsive power of the heart's action which tends to enlarge them; the other an influence derived from the nervous centres, and acting upon the muscular fibres so as to contract the vessels. The first of the two agencies, the heart's action, is so evident as to need no farther demonstration. The other reposes upon the following experimental proofs :—When the sympathetic nerve proceeding to the vessels of the head and face of an animal is cut, there follows congestion of the blood-vessels, with augmented heat over the whole surface supplied by the nerve. The ear is seen to become redder; a thermometer inserted in the nostril shows an increase of temperature, the sign of a greater quantity of blood flowing into the capillaries. The inference from the experiment is that, the counterpoise being withdrawn, the force that distends the small blood-vessels has an unusual predominance. It is farther proved that this nervous influence acting upon the minute muscular fibres of the small vessels is of central origin, for by cutting the connexion between the brain and the ganglion on the neck, from which the above-mentioned nerve proceeds, the restraining influence ceases, and congestion takes place. By stimulating the divided nerve galvanically, the suffusion disappears, the vessels shrinking by the contraction of their muscular coats.

The agency now described is of a piece with the action of the cerebrum upon involuntary muscles, such as the heart and the intestinal canal, and through it many organic functions, namely, digestion, nutrition, absorption, &c., may be affected

## INFLUENCE ON THE CAPILLARY CIRCULATION.    11

by those cerebral waves that are the concomitants of mental states. It is well known that mental excitement has an immediate influence upon all those functions; one set of passions, such as fear, have a deranging effect, while exhilaration and joy within moderate bounds would appear to operate favourably upon them.

The specific expression of *blushing* is no doubt due to this mode of action. The region affected by blushing is the face and neck; and the effect arises from the suspension of the cerebral influence that keeps up the habitual contraction of the smaller blood-vessels over that region.

It is a point not yet finally determined, whether the nervous centres can act upon the organic processes of secretion, absorption, &c,, by an immediate agency, or a power apart from the control of the circulation as now described. Various physiologists have affirmed that there is such an immediate influence, and Ludwig has recently endeavoured to establish it by experiment; but as this implies an altogether new and distinct function of the nerves in the animal economy, other physiologists suspend their judgment on the matter for the present. It is almost certain that the cerebral agency put forth in the exercise of the will can tell only upon muscles; and by analogy it is probable that the emotional wave is confined to muscles also. Nevertheless, the existence of a more direct kind of influence upon the organic processes is open to experimental proof.

### CHARACTERS OF FEELING.

11. In my previous volume (p. 88, 2d edit.) I have given the scheme of a full description of the Feelings. A few remarks may be added here, as preparatory to the department now to be entered on.

The most palpable distinction among our feelings is the contrast of Pleasure and Pain. Next to that is the difference of degree in both kinds. Thus far the matter is plain. Paley, in taking what he considers the practical view of

12                    OF FEELING IN GENERAL.

human happiness, holds that pleasures differ only in continuance and intensity.

His words are :—' In which inquiry (into the nature of
happiness) I will omit much usual declamation on the dignity
and capacity of our nature ; the superiority of the soul to the
body, of the rational to the animal part of our constitution ;
upon the worthiness, refinement, and delicacy of some satisfactions, or the meanness, grossness, and sensuality of others ;
because I hold that pleasures differ in nothing but in continuance and intensity ; from a just computation of which,
confirmed by what we observe of the apparent cheerfulness,
tranquillity, and contentment of men of different tastes,
tempers, stations, and pursuits, every question concerning
human happiness must receive its decision.'—*Moral Philo-*
*sophy,* Book I., Chap. 6.

For my own part, I doubt the completness of a theory of
happiness restricted to the consideration of those two attributes.  The distinction in pleasures (and in pains) between
the acute and voluminous or massive (Intensity and Quantity)
is pregnant with vital results.  Then, again, the attribute of
Endurability, or continuance without fatigue, and the farther,
and related attribute of ideal persistence, are grounds of
superiority in pleasures, being the main circumstances implied in refinement.  Even with all these points taken into
account, the problem is still burdened with serious complications that a man like Paley would rather not grapple with ;
I mean more particularly the nature of disinterested action,
and the sway of mixed ideas.

The characters of Feeling are, 1st, those of Feeling proper,
as Pleasure and Pain, which we call Emotional ; * 2dly,
Volitional characters, or the influence on the Will; 3dly, Intellectual characters, or the bearings upon Thought; we may add,
4thly, certain mixed characters, such as the relations to
Forecasting or Sustained Volition, Desire and Belief.

---

* See, on the use of this adjective, *The Senses and the Intellect*, second
edition, p. 625.

## FEELING AS HAPPINESS.

### *Emotional characters of Feeling.*

12. Every Feeling has its PHYSICAL SIDE, to which a certain share of attention is, in my judgment, always due. In the Sensations of the Senses, we can point to a distinct physical *origin)* or agency, as well as to a *diffused* wave of effects. In the Emotions, the physical origin is less definable, being a supposed coalition of sensational effects with one another and with ideas; and our knowledge is clearest as regards the diffusion, or outward manifestations. The notable contrast, on the physical side, lies between the Pleasurable and the Painful, and between their various gradations; but our power of discrimination does not stop here. Wonder, Love, and Power are all pleasurable, and yet differently embodied, or expressed: Fear, Anger, and Grief are painful, but with outward characters special to each.

On the MENTAL SIDE, we recognise *Quality*, that is, Pleasure, Pain, or Indifference; *Degree*, in its two modes of Intensity and Quantity; and *Speciality*, or points that may distinguish states substantially equivalent in quality and in degree. These distinctions have been largely illustrated under the Muscular Feelings and the Sensations; and a very few additional observations will here suffice.

13. *Feeling as Happiness or Misery.* Our conscious life is made up of Pleasures, Pains, and states of Indifference. Our Happiness may be considered either as the sum of our pleasures, leaving the pains out of account, or as the surplus of pleasure over pain, representing, as it were, the value of existence to us.

The aptitude for Pleasure is the aggregate of all the sensibilities of the constitution in the degree special to each person; and the pleasure realized is according to the extent of stimulus accorded to these, with the observance of due limit and alternation.

The state of Pleasure, strange as the assertion may seem, is a state of transition and unrest; it is always coming or going; there is no complete repose except under Indifference.

14 OF FEELING IN GENERAL.

The proofs are found in the nature of the state, which originates in sudden change, begins to fade as soon as manifested, and urges the will for continuance or increase.

That Pain is a state of unrest will be more willingly conceded. Here, too, there is a shock of change in some organ, the brain being necessarily included, with collateral disturbances, and a series of promptings to voluntary action for relief. The course run through is a complicated one; and it is interesting to survey the various outgoings of the system for restoring the equilibrium. In severe pain, the violence of the gesticulations has a derivative and sedative, although exhausting, effect; the stimulus of the glandular organs brings into play some of the sources of pleasurable emotion, as in grief; the voluntary powers are engaged in alleviation; all available pleasures are sought for their neutralizing efficacy; and, finally, the nervous system, disturbed by the shock, commences a process of adjustment and adaptation to the new state of things, proceeding, it may be, to insensibility, or to death. These rectifying measures put a limit to possible agony. In attaining the maximum of pain, as of pleasure, the infliction must be remitted, the healthy condition restored, and the irritation applied to some different sensibility. It is to be hoped that the ministers of the Inquisition never understood the full bearings of the principle of Relativity as applied to human suffering.

The shock of a great irreparable loss rectifies itself in a similar manner. At first, the agony is extreme and wasting; in time, the system, adjusting itself to the altered condition, assumes a tranquil but reduced tone; there may be comparatively little pain, but the moments of pleasure, few in number and feeble in intensity, are scattered over sterile tracts of indifference; while a great expansion is given to the workings of the tender sentiment.

14. *Feeling as Indifference or neutral excitement.* We may be mentally alive without either pleasure or pain. A state of feeling may have considerable intensity, and yet be neutral. Surprise is a familiar instance. Some surprises give us

## NEUTRAL EXCITEMENT. 15

delight, others cause suffering, but many do neither : yet in all cases we are emotionally moved. The diffusive wave is present ; the mind is awake, alive, stirred ; we are not made either happy or miserable, but we are occupied and engrossed for the time being. So Fear, essentially a painful emotion, may chance to be deprived of the sting, without ceasing to exist. The Tender feeling, which is a principal source of our happiness, may be strongly roused in circumstances devoid of that accompaniment. The mother, in her love for her child, may have much more excitement and occupation of mind than she has pleasure or pain. A man's aspirations towards a high position are not necessarily proportioned to the enjoyment he either feels or anticipates in that connexion ; all that can be certainly affirmed is, that the sentiment of honour or love of power has got a footing in the mind. There is such a thing as being laid hold of, through a sort of infatuation, by a feeling that in no way contributes to our happiness. We may be unable to discard from our thoughts the image of a person that we hate ; or we may be goaded on to a pursuit merely because we cannot shake ourselves free of a certain train of ideas. The fascination of a precipice, or of a serpent, belongs to this species of emotional influence. When an emotion reaches the pitch termed ' passion,' it sometimes happens that the pleasurable element, supposing that to be the character of it, rises to the same high degree, but it may also happen that the excitement is far beyond the pleasure. Insanity illustrates this position. The victim of a delusion is not happy to the degree that his mind is possessed with a fixed idea of grandeur or power, nor unhappy according as he supposes himself enchained to some horrible destiny. An emotion may seize any one as a fixed idea, and exert by that means a disproportionate influence on the conduct ; be it love, self-complacency, power, malevolence, wealth, or knowledge. We shall afterwards see how the action of the Will is indirectly influenced by these pre-occupations.

The excitement now supposed having neither a pleasurable

**16** OF FEELING IN GENERAL.

nor a painful quality, cannot be estimated or described otherwise than by a reference to its detaining or engrossing the mind. A shock of surprise, which may neither please nor pain me, lays hold of my mental framework, my attention and regards, preventing other influences from developing themselves, and leaving a certain impression behind, which becomes one of my recollections afterwards. A great *intellectual* efficiency belongs to these emotions, albeit they are neither pleasurable nor painful. Awakened attention is a consequence of every state of excitement, whether neutral or otherwise.

### Volitional Characters of Feeling.

15. Although the operations of the Will are conceived by us as something distinct from, or superadded to, the operation of Feeling proper, yet in every volition, rightly so named, the stimulus, or antecedent, is some feeling. The genuine antecedents are pleasure and pain. The neutral emotions just discussed, have no immediate power of stimulating activity—their efficacy is indirect. A pleasure, present or prospective —a feast, a concert, or an acquisition of property—makes me go forth in a course of active pursuit; an impending evil makes me alike active in a career of avoidance. A neutral feeling spurs me in neither way by the proper stimulus of the will; nevertheless, by keeping a certain object fixed in the view, it is liable to set me to work, according to a law of the constitution different from the laws of volition, namely, the tendency to convert into actuality whatever strongly possesses us in idea. I am possessed with the notion of becoming acquainted with a secret, which, when revealed, would add nothing to my pleasure; yet, by virtue of a sort of morbid occupation of my mind on the subject, the idea shuts out my more relevant concerns, and so works itself into action.

Thus our conduct is ruled by our pleasures and pains, through the proper and legitimate operation of the Will, and by our other emotions, through the stand they take as persisting ideas. Hence, by marking the line of action dictated by an emotion, we have a further means of characterizing it. If it be a pleasure intensely felt, the fact is shown by the efforts made to secure the continuance of the delight; if a pain, a corresponding energy, with a view to deliverance, attests the circumstance. The volitional character of a feeling, therefore, is an indication of its pleasurable or painful nature, liable only to the disturbing influence of a fixed idea. All our pleasures stimulate us more or less to active pursuit; all our pains to precautionary efforts. When we see a man's avocations, we infer what things give him satisfaction, or cause him suffering. We read the pangs of hunger, cold, and disease, and the pleasures of exercise and repose, repletion, warmth, music, spectacle, affection, honour, and power, in the everyday industry of mankind. The freely-chosen conduct of any living creature is the ultimate, though not infallible, criterion of its pleasures and pains. Accordingly, I shall still abide by the method observed in discussing the sensations, of specifying under each emotion the conduct flowing from it, or the manner and degree of its stimulation of the Will.

*Intellectual Characters of Feeling.*

16. In describing the successive classes of sensations, I adverted to the power that they possess of continuing as ideas after the actual object of sense is withdrawn. This property of Persistence, and also of recurrence in Idea, belonging more or less to sensational states, is their intellectual property; for intellect is made up of ideas, and these are first stimulated in the mind by realities. The same distinction applies, although in a less marked degree, to the emotions generally; some are more disposed than others to leave traces and be recovered without the original exciting cause. The Tender emotion, as a general rule, has an easy persistence, while Anger more speedily exhausts itself. The emotions of Fine Art are said to be 'refined,' owing partly to the circumstance of their existing as remembered, or anticipated, emotions more readily, and at less expense to the system, than some of

B

18                    OF FEELING IN GENERAL.

the other pleasures. Moreover, each separate emotion has modes of manifestation both gross and refined—as in the contrast of vulgar marvels with the novelties of scientific discovery.

17. The revival of an emotion in idea depends upon various conditions, such as have been discussed under the law of association by contiguity. Besides the circumstance just alluded to, namely, that some kinds of feeling are, by nature, more persisting, it is a peculiarity of Individual Characters to retain certain emotions in preference to others. One man, for example, has a facility in keeping up the emotion arising from the love of gain, another lives more easily in family pride, and a third in fine art. Then, there is to be taken into account the fact of Repetition, so largely concerned in acquisition in general. An emotion often felt, is apt, in consequence, to be more readily remembered, imagined, or acted upon, than one that has been but rarely experienced. And in addition to all these permanent causes, there are Temporary Circumstances that affect the restoration of an emotional state. The prevailing tone and temper of the moment favours the assumption of one class of feelings, and repudiates other sorts. The state of fear is necessarily hostile to the feeling of confidence ; love, in the ascendant, renders it difficult to revive even the idea of hatred or indignation. We may note, lastly, the state of the Bodily Organs, and the nervous system generally ; for a certain freshness or vigour in those parts is requisite both for emotions in their full reality, and for their easy recurrence in idea.

The recovery of an emotional state after a lapse of time, independent of the original stimulus, implies some link of Association between it and other things, through whose instrumentality the revival takes place. When we remember the feelings experienced during the recital of some stirring tale, we do so in consequence of the presence of an associated object or circumstance—such as the place, a person present at the same time, or otherwise. There must, therefore, be a process of Contagious adhesion between emotions and the imagery of the world at large. This is one of the intellectual properties of emotion, and has been exemplified in the exposition of the law of contiguity (§ 46). The more intellectual classes of feelings are the most disposed to this alliance with things in general. The same peculiarity that fits an emotional state for existing as an idea, fits it also for being linked with places, persons, names, and all sorts of objects, so as to put it in the way of being resuscitated.

The re-instating force of Similarity in difference applies to the Emotions no less than to the Emotional Sensations (*Similarity*, § 15). The same emotional state may arise sometimes in one connection, and sometimes in another; a certain shade of Fear, Anger, or Self-complacency, may be developed in a variety of circumstances; it will then happen that, by the attraction of similars, the one occasion will suggest the others. This is a strictly intellectual process, although relative to the workings of emotion.*

### *Mixed Characters of Emotion.*

18. There are certain important aspects and characteristics of our feelings that do not belong exclusively to any one of the three foregoing heads, but which are of a mixed or compound nature. When a feeling prompts the will strongly, as, for example, hunger, it is farther to be ascertained whether the same power belongs to it as an idea, a recollection, or an anticipation. This last circumstance obviously involves the property of intellectual continuance; if the feeling is one that does not persist, the action on the will ceases when the pressure of the reality ceases. If, on the contrary, the feeling is retained as an idea, the influence on the will is a more enduring nature; we have then a perpetual resolution and not a mere impulse of a moment. *The power of causing a sustained volition, or perpetual will*, is therefore a compound attribute, involving both a volitional and an intellectual property.

---

* The whole subject of Ideal Emotion is so important, that at a later stage I shall devote a chapter to the elucidation of it in detail.

## 20 OF FEELING IN GENERAL.

All the systematic provisions and precautions of human life grow out of feelings thet spur us to action, both when they are present in reality, and while existing only as ideas. The constant labour for food implies that the sensation of hunger has an intellectual persistence as well as an active stimulus. There are not a few examples of states of sensation, very powerful in prompting action while they last, but having scarcely any force when the reality becomes a mere idea. Our organic pains are often of this nature; a fit of neuralgia or dyspepsia, for whose removal no sacrifice would be thought too great, if happening but seldom, is apt to be unheeded after having passed away. It is the frequent recurrence of such attacks that at last produces the perpetual will of precautionary prudence; repetition makes up for the natural deficiency in the intellectual property of existing as an idea. There are other pains that from the very first take a deeper hold on the mind, and maintain their volitional influence in the absence of the reality. The feeling of disgrace is an instance. Most people retain a lively sense of this danger, so as to be always ready to avoid whatever is likely to incur it. The pain of disgrace may not be greater for the moment than the pain of toothache; but, to whatever circumstance owing, the ideal persistence of the one is so much beyond the persistence of the other, as to make the enormous difference between the preventive measures maintained against the two evils.

Individual constitutions differ considerably in respect to the classes of pains that take the greatest hold of the intellect, and thereby influence *the course* of action. In some minds, the physical sensations of organic pain are forgotten as soon as passed, and consequently the least possible care is taken to obviate them; with others, a lively sense of their misery presides over all the actions of life.

In the conflict of opposite motives, it is common to have one feeling in the actual opposed to another in the idea. This is the case when present gratification is restrained by the consideration of remote consequences. In order that the

CONTROL OF THE THOUGHTS. 21

dread of the future may prevail over the present, it is necessary that the intellectual hold of the absent evil should be sufficient to keep alive the volitional spur belonging to the reality. Thus it is that what is termed self-control, prudential restraint, moral strength, consists in the intellectual permanency of the volitional element of our feelings.

A parallel illustration holds with reference to pleasures. Weakly remembered, they do not, in absence, stimulate the voluntary efforts for securing them; more strongly remembered, they become standing objects of pursuit. It may be said, in this case, that if we had the memory of them in full, more is needless; just as a man that has a book by heart cares not to take up the volume; but memory in matters of enjoyment is seldom, if ever, full actually. The usual case is to have the remembrance of the pleasure, with the consciousness that it falls short of the reality; and this is a spur to obtain the full fruition. Such is *Desire*.

19. *Control of the Intellectual Trains and Acquirements.*— Among the effects produced by states of feeling are to be reckoned those that enable us to store up impressions of the outer world, constituting the materials of our knowledge or intelligence. The exercise of the senses upon things around us is a mode of voluntary action, and is governed more or less by the accompanying feelings. Objects that please the eye receive in turn a protracted gaze; and in consequence they are more deeply stamped upon the recollection. Things utterly indifferent to us pass unheeded, and are forgotten. A painful spectacle repels the vision; but in this case the state of revulsion so excites the nervous susceptibility that a very strong impression may be left, although the glance has been never so transient. Thus it is that both pleasure and pain are, although in different ways, stimulants of the attention and aids to intellectual retentiveness. We hence become conversant with all things that have the power of kindling agreeable or disagreeable emotion; our minds are stored with recollections of what we love or hate.

There is something at first sight anomalous in the pro-

## OF FEELING IN GENERAL.

duction of a common effect, such as that now described, by two agencies oppo3ed to one another in their general influence on the conduct. It is only the natural and proper operation of the will, when we are arrested and detained by objects that give us delight. I keep my eyes directed upon a pleasing picture, exactly as I drink an agreeable beverage ; but the carrying out of the same law of volition would lead me to turn away from a painful spectacle, and, if it had already impressed me before I was aware, make me attempt to dismiss it for ever from my thoughts ; so that the greater the pain, the deeper the forgetfulness. Here, however, the action of the will is liable to be crossed and rendered impotent ; not from any exception to the general principle of courting the agreeable and repelling the disagreeable, but because of the property belonging even to neutral emotions—namely, the power of possessing the mind and remaining in the recollection. Whether a feeling be pleasing, painful, or neither, it holds the attention for the time being, and leaves a trace behind it, the effect being greater according to the intensity of the *excitement*. In the case of pleasure, there is the additional force of the voluntary detention, whereby all things having any charm receive an additional stamp. In pain, on the other hand, the will operates to withdraw the active regards and diminish the time allowed for taking in an impression, but does not annihilate the one already received. I go away as fast as I am able from what revolts my view, but I cannot divest myself of all thought and recollection of what I have seen. If the disgust I experienced was intense, I have a more abiding remembrance of it than of most things that give me pleasure, although the will would be stimulated, in the one case, to resist the impression, and, in the other, to nurse and deepen it. Given equal degrees of delight and suffering, the occasion of delight would acquire the deepest hold, the volition making the difference ; but volition does not give to the first all its impressiveness, and endeavours, but in vain, to deprive the last of any.

The same thing applies to neutral emotions, which the will

neither favours nor discourages. They all have the power of stamping the memory as well as occupying the present attention, in proportion as they are intense, or exciting. An effect of the marvellous may neither please or displease, but it will impress. Unaided by a volitional spur, these emotions will detain us less than pleasing emotions equally exciting, and more than painful emotions discountenanced by the will.

20. We see, therefore, that it is a property of feeling to attract and detain the observation upon certain objects by preference, the effect of which is to possess the mind with those objects, or to give them a prominent place among our acquisitions. The abundance of the associations thereby formed leads to their recurrence in the trains of thought; and the same fascination causes them to be dwelt upon in recollection, and largely employed in the mind's own creations. The poet, and the man of science, if they are so by natural disposition, dwell each respectively in their own region of objects and conceptions; and a stinted place is left in the mind for all other things. Whence it is that the direction taken by the spontaneous gaze, and the easily recurring trains of the intellect, afford a clue to the predominant emotions.

The interested, charmed, or *stimulated attention* to things, is frequently seen in contrast with what may be called the *natural retentiveness* of the brain, which often inclines towards a different region from the other. It is a true and common remark that Taste and Faculty, or power, do not always go together. The objects that please and fascinate us may not be those that take the deepest hold of our minds, so as to constitute our highest intellectual grasp. One may feel a deep charm for the conceptions of science, without possessing that tenacity of mind in scientific matters which is indispensable to high attainments in them; and the same person may have a really powerful intellect in some other department without experiencing a corresponding charm. We may exert real power in one field, and derive pleasure in another. A great statesman like Richelieu finds a superior fascination in composing bad tragedies; an artist of incontestible genius is

24 OF FEELING IN GENERAL.

supremely happy in abortive mechanical inventions. Granted that a certain pleasure must always flow from the exercise of our strongest faculties, it still may happen that we take a far higher delight in a class of things where we could hardly attain even to mediocrity. There is no law of mind to connect talent and taste, or yet to make them uniformly exclude each other; all varieties of relationship may exist, from the closest concurrence to wide separation. When the two happen to coincide very nearly, or when the thing that fascinates the attention most, also coheres in the intellect best independently of this fascination, we have then the most effective combination that can exist for producing a great genius. Throughout the exposition of the law of contiguity, there was assumed, in the first instance, a natural adhesiveness for each different species of objects; and, in the second place, the efficacy of the emotions to inspire the attention.

21. *Influence of Feeling on Belief.*—In a subsequent chapter we shall have to enter fully into the nature of the state of mind denominated Belief. The full investigation of the subject would be premature in this place; still it would be a great omission not to allude here in explicit terms to the property of swaying our convictions common to all kinds of strong emotion.

The influence is of a mixed character. In the first place, it would arise in the ordinary action of the Will. A thing strongly desired, in other words, an object of intense pleasure, is pursued with corresponding urgency; obstacles are made light of, they are disbelieved. We cannot easily be induced to credit the ill effects of a favourite dish. If I am right in my view of belief, it is strictly a phase of *action;* to act strongly cannot be separated from believing strongly for the time.

In the second place, the influence is farther connected with the power of the Feelings over the Trains of Thought. When we are under a strong emotion, all things discordant with it are kept out of sight. A strong *volitional* urgency will subdue an opposing consideration actually before the

INFLUENCE ON BELIEF. 25

mind; but intense feeling so lords it over the *intellectual* trains that the opposing considerations are not even allowed to be present. One would think it were enough that the remote considerations should give way to the near and pressing ones, so that the 'video meliora' might still remain with the 'deteriora sequor;' but in truth the flood of emotion sometimes sweeps away for the moment every vestige of the opposing absent, as if that had at no time been a present reality. Our feelings not merely play the part of rebels or innovators against the canons of the past, they are like destroying Vandals, who efface and consume the records of what has been. In a state of strong excitement, no thoughts are allowed to present themselves except such as concur in the present mood; the links of association are paralyzed as regards everything that conflicts with the ascendant influence; and it is through this stoppage of the intellectual trains that we come into the predicament of renouncing, or, as it is called, disbelieving, for the moment, what we have formerly felt and acted on. Our feelings pervert our convictions by smiting us with intellectual blindness, which we need not have even when committing great imprudence in action. It depends upon many circumstances what intensity of emotion shall be required to produce this higher effect of keeping utterly back the faintest recollection of whatever discords with the reigning fury. The natural energy of the emotional temper on the one hand, and, on the other, the feebleness of the forces of effective resuscitation, conspire to falsify the views entertained at the moment.

22. Intense Pleasure or Pain, while inspiring the actions and influencing the intellectual acquisitions, also tells upon the judgment of truth and falsehood. The emotion of Terror proves the greatness of its power, by inducing the most irrational beliefs. In the extreme manifestations of Anger, a man will be suddenly struck blind to his most familiar experiences of fact, and will for the moment deny what at other times he would most resolutely maintain. Take also Self-complacency. The habitual dreamer is not instructed by a

26                    OF FEELING IN GENERAL.

thousand failures of pet projects; he enters upon each new
attempt as full of confidence as if all the rest had succeeded.
We note with surprise, in everyday life, that an individual goes on promising to himself and to others, with sincere
conviction, what he has never once been known to execute;
the feeling of self-confidence lords it over the experience
of a life. He has not stated to himself in a proposition the
conflicting experience. He does not know that he never fulfils his purposes. So with the Affections that have others
for their objects; love's blindness is the world's oldest pro-
verb.

The falsehood, mistakes, confusion, and fatality growing out of this property of the feelings, ramify in every
province of affairs and every relation of human life. I
speak not at present of the conscious lie—to that our illustration does not now extend. The perverted views of
matters of common business, the superstructure of fable
that envelopes the narration of the past, the incubus of
superstition and blind faith, have their foundation and
source in the power of emotion to bar out the impressions of
reality.

The deep-seated intellectual corruption due to the ascendancy of the Feelings has been a theme for reflecting minds
to dilate upon, and yet we cannot say that it has been sufficiently set forth. The cloud of legend and fable, unhesita-
tingly accepted for ages as the genuine history of foregone
times, has only just begun to be dispersed. The pages of
early Greek and Roman story had been filled with narratives relying solely on faith and feeling; and the introduction
of the canons of evidence appealed to in all matters of recent
date, is felt as a cruel and remorseless operation, by which
the keenest susceptibilities, and most favourite fancies, are
cut to the quick. Warm emotion had bred and nursed those
ancient stories; and in an early uninquiring age, the realities
of nature were set at naught by the very minds that had to
face them as the experience of every hour; such experience
being unable to restrain the creations of an unbridled fancy,

or to check the reception given to the wildest tales and most extravagant inventions.*

In the sciences, the perverting influence of the feelings has been no less conspicuous. It is the nature of scientific truth to express with punctilious accuracy the order and sequences of the world, so that its statements shall hold good at all times and to all observers. The mind that is engaged in collecting the facts of nature for this purpose ought, so far as they are concerned, to be utterly devoid of emotional bias. Neither liking nor disliking, favouritism nor repulsion, should show any traces in the result; the eye, cold and indifferent, should see nothing that cannot always be seen the same, and the mind should keep record in like manner. But this attitude of observing and generalizing the phenomena of the

---

* See Grote's *History of Greece*, Vol. I., Chapters 16 and 17, where the author, in entering at large into the mental tendencies determining the creation and reception of the early Grecian legends, illustrates the principle set forth in the text. In an article in the *Westminster Review*, No. 77, for May, 1843, the subject is taken up by the same hand. From that article I extract the following paragraph.

' Father Malebranche, in discussing the theory of morals, has observed, that our passions all justify themselves—that is, they suggest to us reasons for justifying them. He might, with equal justice, have remarked, and it is the point which we have sought to illustrate by the preceding remarks on the Byronian legends, that all our strong emotions, when shared in common by a circle of individuals, or a community, will not only sanctify fallacious reasonings, but also call into being, and stamp with credulity, abundance of narratives purely fictitious. Whether the feeling be religious, or political, or æsthetic—love, hatred, terror, gratitude, or admiration—it will find or break a way to expand and particularise itself in appropriate anecdotes; it serves at once both as demand and supply; it both emboldens the speaker to invent, and disposes the hearers to believe him without any further warrant. Such anecdotes are fiction from beginning to end, but they are specious and impressive fictions; they boast no acknowledged parentage, but they are the adopted children of the whole community; they are embraced with an intensity of conviction quite equivalent to the best authenticated facts. And let it be always recollected—we once more repeat —that they are radically distinct from half-truths or misreported matters of fact; for upon this distinction will depend the different mode which we shall presently propose of dealing with them in reference to Grecian history.'

## 28 OF FEELING IN GENERAL.

world is not natural to the human intellect, as the generations of actual men have been constituted. In primitive times, the scientific spirit had no existence ; the strong emotions always interfered with the observation of nature in everything but the matters of routine industry for supplying the wants of life. The representation of surrounding nature was left to the poet, or the religious seer, whose professed purpose it was to gratify, instead of suppressing, the prevailing tone of feeling. Even when cool accuracy was brought to bear on the examination of the order of the world, the progress was slow, as of a cause labouring under a heavy load of obstruction. Mechanical science has not been long constituted with philosophical rigour; the subjects of chemistry and physiology belong to the last and the present century. The first book of the 'Novum Organum' of Lord Bacon stands out distinguished among his remarkable writings as an almost singular exposure of the mental corruption wrought by the intrusion of the feelings in scientific speculation. The 'fallacies' recognised by the logician are inadequate to characterise scientific errors, implying, as they do, little else than the feebleness, want of training, or other involuntary deficiency of the intellect.

### CRITERIA FOR INTERPRETING FEELING.

23. It belongs to the present subject to consider the indications whereby the emotional states of individuals can be ascertained with some degree of definiteness and precision. To observe and estimate the different modes of human feeling, as they display themselves in actual life, is an indispensable portion of the task of an expositor of mind.

Each man has the full and perfect knowledge of his own consciousness; but no living being can penetrate the consciousness of another. Hence there may be modes of feeling belonging to individual minds which can never be made known to mankind in general. Only such aspects of the consciousness as have some external characters to distinguish them, can be recognised by fellow-beings. Even with those states that do distinctly manifest themselves by outward act or gesture, it must always be a doubtful point whether the same expression means precisely the same mental condition in different individuals. But for our purposes, and for all purposes, two states of feeling must be held as identical when an identity exists between all the appearances, actions, and consequences that flow from, or accompany them. If there be any peculiar shade, tone, or colouring of emotion that has no outward sign or efficacy, such peculiarity is inscrutable to the inquirer. It is enough for us to lay hold of the outward manifestations, and to recognise all the distinctions that they bring to light.

The various properties of feeling that we have been engaged in discussing are, each and all of them, criteria for discriminating individual feelings. The expressive gestures growing out of the diffusive stimulus, the volitional energies stimulated, the influences upon the intellectual trains, and the appearances that result from various combinations of these, are our means of judging of what is passing in the interior of the mind. When to these we apply our own consciousness as a medium of interpretation, we have done what the case admits of. Having lain on the watch for all the significant acts of another man's mind, we refer to our own feelings, and endeavour to arrive at some one mode of consciousness in ourselves that would have exactly the same accompaniments. This is to us what the other man feels.

In using any one class of external manifestations as our principal medium of interpretation, we require to check the reading by some of the other classes, and the more checks we employ, the surer is our result. Thus, if we refer to the emotional expression, properly so called, or to the various gesticulations prompted ·by the diffusive tendency, we are liable to err, owing to the circumstance that the same feeling (as evidenced by the signs) does not prompt a similar or equal display in different persons. We cannot, for example, estimate physical pain by expression alone; neither do the same pleasures manifest themselves alike in the variety of human

## OF FEELING IN GENERAL.

characters. We must not, therefore, trust to outward demonstration solely; we must include also the resulting conduct. Looking to the power that a feeling has to stimulate the will either for conservation or for abatement, we can thereby correct mistakes that we might be led into by trusting to the demonstrative aspect.' When we see a man strongly impelled to action by his feelings, we conclude that he feels strongly. If expression and volition concur, we are much more safe in any inference that we may draw. Still the experience of the human constitution shows us that both the demonstrative apparatus and the volitional apparatus may work unequally under an identical stimulus of emotion, and other checks have still to be invoked. We might then refer to the modes of operation upon the intellect—the persistence, the effect upon belief, and so forth—by which we should approximate still more to the reality of the case. Another course of proceeding is open to us.

The ambiguity of the demonstrative manifestation taken by itself, or of the volitional and intellectual effects viewed separately, is owing, as already said, to the fact that in some minds these effects are more strongly manifested than in others, when there is reason to believe that the consciousness is not much different. Now this must arise from a peculiarity of constitution, pervading the whole manifestations of the individual; and means may be taken, once for all, to ascertain the degree and manner of it so as to make a proper allowance for it on every occasion. We have in fact to gather, by an inductive process, the demonstrative, volitional, or intellectual temperament of the person in question, and having arrived at this, we are in a position to give the true reading of any class of indications. We find some minds excessive in demonstration; and, accordingly, we are not carried away by any violence of outburst on their part into the belief that they are necessarily suffering under violent emotion. In like manner there is such a thing as a temperament active, or volitional, in the extreme, and a slight amount of emotion may give the rein to very energetic proceedings.

## STANDARD OF COMPARISON OF FEELINGS. 31

And although strong feelings impress themselves more on the intellect than weak ones, there are yet differences of quality in the intellectual constitutions of individuals, whereby a weak emotion in one will persist as tenaciously as a stronger in another. Likewise in that fatal power of obliteration of the past, through which the feelings pervert the view of the present, more resistance is offered, according as the intellectual training has been good; and emotion in this case does not produce the full effects that would otherwise arise from it.

24. The thing to be desired in reality is to fix if possible upon some case wherein every one, as far as can be ascertained, feels almost alike; and, using this as a standard, we can determine the peculiarities of individuals as regards these various points of character. It is difficult to say whether any good standard exists; for, even with regard to the most common physical sensations, there may be great differences both in the degree and in the kind of susceptibility. The sweetness of sugar, the exhilaration of wine, the gratification of hunger, do not affect all persons alike. We are therefore at last reduced to the method of taking the *average* of a great number of cases. It is in this way that we form our judgment of demonstrative, volitional, or intellectual temperaments. By such a system of averages, we have the only means of discriminating between the general temperament and the energy of particular emotions. It is the difference between one expression and another, or between one volition and another, in the *same* individual, that is the surest criterion of intensity of feeling.

25. We obtain much of our knowledge of other men's feelings by interrogating themselves as to their own experience. There is in this case also a necessity for some standard, or common measure, between their consciousness and ours. The thing that a person can really do when interrogated as to his modes of feeling is to compare one of them with another; he can tell us which of a number of tastes is to him the sweetest; he cannot compare his con-

32 ON FEELING IN GENERAL.

sciousness with ours until something like a common measure has been set up between us. But for the purpose of declaring agreement or difference among the feelings of the same person, the plan of interrogation goes farther than any other method, inasmuch as there are many states of feeling that never attain to visible manifestation. Our not being able to question the inferior animals is one great disadvantage that we labour under with them; another is the wide difference that separates them from us. Separation is our difficulty with our fellow-men; it is owing to constitutional differences that we are debarred from interpreting at once their consciousness by our own—the short and easy method of untutored minds.

Supposing that we are able to obtain a common standard between ourselves and those whose feelings we are endeavouring to estimate, the leading precaution to be observed in dealing with the generality of mankind is, not to put too much reliance upon the accounts that may be given us of past, or *remembered*, states of feeling. Any veracious person may be trusted to represent an emotion actually present, but there are few that have the power of representing faithfully on all occasions an emotion that exists only in the memory.

### REMARKS ON THE DEVELOPMENT OF EMOTIONS.

26. An emotional wave once roused tends to continue for a certain length of time. Both the physical tremor, and the mental consciousness, pass through the successive stages of rise, culmination, and subsidence. There is no one rule for regulating the course that is thus passed through, there being the greatest variety observable regarding it. In some temperaments the fury of excitement is intense for the moment, but quickly subsides. In others a feebler wave, lasting longer, is what we observe. Each constitution has a certain total of feeling which it can afford to keep up, and this may be expended either in violent gusts or in more tranquil persistence.

The moral, usually drawn from the cycle, or successive

## PERIODICITY OF EMOTION. 33

phases of an emotional outburst, is to avoid the moment of culmination of a feeling that we have to oppose, and take it rather on the subsiding phase.

27. Another observation to be made, regarding the development of emotions, is their disposition to assume a certain periodicity, so that their return comes to be a matter of rule and prediction. This does not apply to all possible modes and varieties of human feeling ; still with reference to the more fundamental aspects of our emotional nature, there is good evidence for the remark. The recurrent craving of the bodily appetites—hunger, exercise, rest, &c.—extends to the affections, likings, or tastes, that seem to have no regard to mere bodily preservation.

The feelings of tender affection have in all probability a tendency to recur in the same manner as the sexual, or other appetites, and from a similar cause in the bodily organization. There being a well-marked glandular secretion associated with this emotion, we are subject to the alternations of fulness and discharge, and to corresponding moments of susceptibility to the associated mental states. If this be the fact, the emotions in question will have a real, or natural, periodicity as distinguished from the still larger number of cases where the recurrence is determined by habit. Our regular gratifications are known to engender a periodical craving or susceptibility, almost of the nature of a physical want; but most of all such as are based upon the real or organic cycles, like those above mentioned.

The alternation of exercise and repose, which gives a periodic character to the outward bodily life, extends to the inward depths of the mental life. Every emotion whatsoever both exercises and exhausts some one portion of the physical framework of mind. Certain circles of the brain, certain muscles and organic processes are involved in each case, and these are liable to weariness after a time, while by repose they become charged with new vigour. Hence every department that has been severely drawn upon, ceases to support its associated mental condition, and every department that

## OF FEELING IN GENERAL.

has been long dormant is ready to burst forth on the application of the proper stimulus. We all know the delight of a feeling long restrained ; the dullest emotions can yield a moment of ecstasy when their strength has been allowed to accumulate, instead of being incessantly dribbled off. A very ordinary amount of affection for one's native land rises to a fervid burst of delight on returning after years of absence. The feelings that are discharged from day to day are hardly appreciated from the smallness of the amount, but the slender current dammed up for weeks or months rises at last to a mighty overflowing. Some of the intensest moments of pleasure ever enjoyed by man are preceded and prepared by long privation ; they are exceeded only by the sudden relief from some lasting pain. (Some additional observations on the laws of Feeling in general are given in the Appendix, A.)

# CHAPTER II.

### THE EMOTIONS AND THEIR CLASSIFICATION.

1. THE Emotions, as compared with the Sensations, are secondary, derived, or compound feelings. The emotion of wonder, for example, inspired by a human being of gigantic size, is the result of a comparison of the present impression on the sight with our recollected impressions of ordinary men and women.

The coalescence of sensations and ideas, involved in an emotion, may assume various aspects. The simplest case is a *plurality* of sensations in the same sense, or in different senses, in mutual harmony or in mutual conflict; such are the pleasures of concord or harmony in the one case, and the pains of discord or distraction in the other. In many instances, the harmony or discord is between something present and some past recalled by it; as in Wonder, the feeling of Contradiction, and in discoveries of Identification. A second mode is the *transfer* of feelings to things that do not of themselves excite them; as in the instances of the Sublime and the Beautiful by association. A third mode, very extensive in its operation, is the *coalition* of a number of separate feelings into one aggregate or whole; as in the Tender Emotion, Sexual Love, the Irascible Emotion, and the Moral Sentiment; the fusion of elements in these cases being such as to make them appear simple feelings, until analysis shows them to be compound. The sentiment of Property is a remarkable case of aggregate feelings; in its form of the pleasure of Money there is also a transference or derivation.

If the foregoing statement be correct, the theory of

## 36 THE EMOTIONS AND THEIR CLASSIFICATION.

Emotion will consist in the statement of the general laws that regulate the concurrence, coalition, transfer, or aggregation of the primary feelings—the Muscular states and the Sensations; and the analysis of the several Emotions will be the account of the component feelings in each, and the mode of their composition under some of these general laws. Now in addition to the adhesive property of Contiguous Association, two great principles operate in the concurrence of different feelings:—the Law of Harmony and Conflict, and the Law of Relativity. I will, therefore, begin by stating and illustrating these two laws, in which illustration several species of emotion will rise at once to the view, and receive their appropriate handling. I will then enumerate the remaining species in the order that seems most natural; and, in the detailed explanation, it will be seen how far the origin of each can be accounted for in the manner now supposed.

2. In the endeavour to classify the Emotions, a knowledge of the origin and composition of each variety, so far as attainable, is an important clue to their distinctive characteristics, but does not supersede a reference to our own direct consciousness of them, and our observation of their workings in other beings. We must proceed on the golden rule of classification, which is to bring together under one head such as agree in the greatest number of important characteristics, and to keep apart such as most widely differ on points of importance. There are a few well marked genera that have always been recognised, for example, Love, Anger, Fear; and there are some, as Beauty and the Moral Sentiment, that have been erroneously considered as ultimate and irresolvable sensibilities or feelings.

3. I. We will begin with the LAW OF HARMONY AND CONFLICT. The principle that Harmony is connected with Pleasure, and Conflict with Pain, is probably an offshoot of the Law of Self-Conservation.

II. There are certain emotions essentially depending on THE LAW OF RELATIVITY. Such are NOVELTY, WONDER, and the feeling of LIBERTY. These are all purely relative to certain

TENDERNESS.—SELF-COMPLACENCY. 37

other states that go before ; Novelty and Wonder presuppose the ordinary, or the common; Liberty implies foregone restraint. The emotion of Power also subsists upon comparison with some allied state of impotence.

III. The emotion of TERROR is a wide-spreading influence in human life. The revulsion from suffering implied in our volitional nature, instead of producing always the simple effect of inspiring actions for relieving the pain, not unfrequently excites a convulsive trepidation of the whole system, accompanied with a new state of suffering, and with other important consequences. This special outgoing belongs to certain modes of pain rather than to others ; and all sentient beings are subject to the condition although in very unequal degrees. As a general rule, the susceptibility to terror is a weakness and an evil, and the consideration of the means of avoiding or subduing it is of great practical moment.

IV. The extensive group of feelings implied under the title of the TENDER AFFECTIONS constitute a well-marked order or genus of emotion. Being principally manifested towards living beings, their first development in the child comes with the recognition of personality. When they are once made to flow freely, human attachments begin to be formed ; and a considerable portion of the pleasure of life springs from this fountain-head.

If it were permitted to writers on the human mind to advert specifically to the feelings of the sexual relations, these would find an appropriate place anterior to the present division.

V. When a human being recognises or imagines in himself the qualities that draw forth admiration, love, reverence, esteem, when seen in others, he is affected by a peculiar kind of emotion, which passes current under such names as SELF-COMPLACENCY, Self-gratulation, Self-esteem. I am disposed to think that there is here only a special offshoot or diversion of the tender sensibility.

A still further emotional effect is produced by being the subject of the admiration or esteem of our fellows, which is

## THE EMOTIONS AND THEIR CLASSIFICATION.

commonly denominated by the phrases APPROBATION, Praise, Glory, Reputation, and the like.

VI. The elation of superior POWER is a very marked and widely ramifying sentiment of our constitution : implying as its correlative, the depression of Impotence, inferiority, and insignificance.

VII. The IRASCIBLE EMOTION is a notable attribute of our humanity, the peculiar characteristic of which is the pleasure arising from *malevolent* action and sentiment.

VIII. Under Action there are certain distinct modes of feeling to be mentioned, as contributing largely to the interest of life. Besides the pleasures and pains of Exercise, and the gratification of succeeding in an End, with the opposite mortification of missing what is laboured for, there is in the attitude of PURSUIT a peculiar state of mind, so far agreeable in itself, that factitious occupations are instituted to bring it into play. When I use the term PLOT-INTEREST, the character of the situation alluded to will be suggested with tolerable distinctness.

IX. The Exercise of the INTELLECT gives birth to certain species of emotions which it is interesting to study. The routine operations sustained by mere contiguity evolve no feeling ; the more perfect the intellectual habits, the less consciousness is associated with them. A practised accountant approaches to a calculating machine. But in the operation of the Law of *Similarity*, where new identifications are struck out, there is an emotion of agreeable surprise accompanying the flash. Hence, although routine is unconscious, originality is intensely stimulating. Part of the pleasure of works of genius proceeds from this effect, and we shall see in it one of the rewards of intellectual pursuit.

Under the same head is to be reckoned the very characteristic pain produced by *Inconsistency*, on the susceptibility to which temperaments differ greatly. The genuine love of Truth is greatly fostered by the desire of escaping from contradictions.

X. The foregoing classes have in them each a certain

THE MORAL SENSE 39

unity and distinctness as respects their origin in the human constitution. The next class is one that has been very commonly regarded as a unity in the investigations of philosophers. I mean the emotions of FINE ART, expressed by the single term Beauty, or the Beautiful. There is doubtless a strong individuality in the feeling that mankind have agreed to designate by the common phrase, 'the feeling of beauty,' but this community of character implies little more than a pleasurable sentiment. If we take the productions of Fine Art, and examine the sources of the delight that they give us, we shall find a very great variety of species, notwithstanding the generic likeness implied in classifying them together. Many of our simple sensations, and many of the feelings belonging to the different heads just enumerated, are brought into play by artistic compositions.

XI. The MORAL SENSE in man, like the sense of beauty, has been very generally looked upon as one and indivisible. But whether we search into the roots of this sentiment in human nature, or survey the field of outward objects embraced by it, I feel satisfied that we shall discern various kinds of influence at work. The generic peculiarity that circumscribes the moral sentiment is the fact termed *moral obligation*, or *duty*, the precise nature of which we are called upon to define. The feelings concerned in right or wrong are not only capable of acting on the will like many other feelings, but they are required to have a paramount force in the case of a conflict; and when this superiority of volitional stimulus does not exist in the individual mind, we supply the defect by stimulants from without, namely, the sanctions, or *punishment*, of society.

4. A very natural remark may occur on the perusal of the above scheme, which is, that the vital distinction of Pleasure and Pain is nowhere apparent as constituting a line of demarcation. The answer is, that this distinction pervades all the feelings of the mind—Sensations and Emotions; it enters into the species and individuals of every class. Both pleasures and pains are contained in each one of

## 40 THE EMOTIONS AND THEIR CLASSIFICATION.

the eleven families now enumerated, just as the natural orders of plants may each contain food and poison, sweet aromas and nauseating stinks.* In constituting our natural families, we endeavour to bring together species that have the greatest number of points of resemblance, instead of sinking nearness of kindred in some one distinction that happens to have a great practical interest. Accordingly, I shall treat our pleasures and pains as species arising in the different orders or families as we have set them forth. Inasmuch as suffering treads always on the heels of delight, and each kind of sweet has its cognate bitter, it would be divorcing the closest relationship to partition the human feelings into pleasures and pains as the primary division of the whole. (For remarks on the principles and modes of classifying the Emotions, see Appendix, B.)

---

* To take an instance or two. The natural order *solaneæ* includes both the wholesome potato, and the deadly nightshade; celery and hemlock are members of the order of *umbelliferæ;* and the genus *orchis* contains, with species distinguished for fragrance, one of the most fetid plants in nature (*orchis fœtida*).

# CHAPTER III.

### LAW OF HARMONY AND CONFLICT.

1. WE are constantly liable to a plurality of impressions —whether sensations or ideas ; sometimes these are harmonising or mutually supporting; at other times they pull, as it were, in opposite ways. The one position is attended with pleasure, the other with pain. Artistic harmonies and discords, success and failure in pursuit, sympathy and hostility, consistency and inconsistency in matters of truth and falsehood—come under this general head.

2. We may, with great probability, suppose that the physical basis of the situation is made up of conspiring nerve currents on the one hand, and of conflicting currents on the other. The nervous energy is economised in the first case, and, in the second, wasted. According to the Law of Self-Conservation, there would be a corresponding opposition in the mental effects. Two concurring stimulants, in themselves agreeable, must become more so, when pointing to a common attitude, and thereby rendering mutual support.

3. Whether or not this be the true account of the physical situation, harmonising impressions are a source of pleasurable elation, great or little, acute or massive, according to the circumstances. Devoid of any marked or characteristic peculiarity of consciousness, such as belongs to the muscular feelings and the sensations of the five senses, we may describe it as a general exhilaration of mental tone, like the effect of a stimulant. There is, for the time, a real increase of vital energy, as is proved by the increased capabilities of the individual, bodily and mental.

## 42 LAW OF HARMONY AND CONFLICT.

4. Equally well marked are the pains of Conflict. Discordant impulses, while enfeebling the vitality, depress the mental tone in the same manner as exhaustion of the nervous system. In some instances, the pain is highly acute, as in the jarring of discords to a musical ear; in others there is a general depression, as in the failure of an enterprise. The physical influence of the shock may be so great as to occasion nervous derangement, and accompanying neuralgic aches.

The situations of harmony and conflict will often appear in the detail of the various emotions. The Æsthetic Harmonies are treated of in the Fine Art Emotions. The pleasures of successful, and the pains of unsuccessful Pursuit come under the Emotions of Action. A separate chapter is devoted to the workings of Sympathy. Consistency and Inconsistency in truth and falsehood give rise to emotions that are related to the exercise of the Intellect.

In the following chapter, the general situations will be farther illustrated in conjunction with another comprehensive law of our constitution—the law of Relativity.

# CHAPTER IV.

## EMOTIONS OF RELATIVITY.

1. THE fact or property expressed under the Law of Universal Relativity, besides being the basis of all consciousness whatever, developes itself in certain specific emotional states, which are also more or less connected with the situations of harmony and conflict just described. The emotion called the pleasure of NOVELTY, and the closely-connected emotion of WONDER, are pure instances of Relativity. Also, the feelings of Power and Impotence, of Liberty and Restraint, are correlated pairs.

2. The Objects of the Emotion of NOVELTY are as well understood as any definiticn could make them. No one needs to be told the difference between the stale and the fresh in sensation, between what has tired us by repetition, and what has come upon us for the first time.

3. The *Physical* circumstance accompanying the mental fact of agreeable novelty, is doubtless the change in the locality of the nervous action—one set of fibres and cells relapsing after excitement, into comparative quiescence, and another set, formerly quiescent, commencing to operate. The alternation may extend to the organs of the senses, and to the muscles. That pleasure should arise from varying the parts and organs stimulated, is a necessary consequence of the fact that stimulation is pleasurable.

4. As to the Emotion itself, we may pronounce it a pleasure, considerable in degree, often rising to charm and fascination. Change of impression being the condition alike of feeling, and of knowledge or intellect, the pleasure of No-

44                    EMOTIONS OF RELATIVITY.

velty is mixed up with the acquisition of knowledge, and is
hence called an intellectual pleasure. It is a leading inducement to intellectual labour, as well as to many other kinds of
exertion and adventure.

This pleasure is, in fact, the primitive charm of all sensation, before it has been dulled by continuance and satiety.
The first thrill of the virgin fibres of the brain, gives the
utmost pitch of attainable delight. It is only by long
intervals of remission, that we approach to the same state
afterwards.

The counter pain of Monotony is a species of weariness,
arising from certain parts being fatigued, while others are
never called into play. The uneasiness is aggravated by the
desire of enjoyments formerly known and now withheld.

5. In illustrating the species of the Emotion of Novelty,
we may allude first to the simple Sensations, as tastes, odours,
sounds, &c. Such of these as are in their nature pleasing, are,
in the first experience, pre-eminently so. The youthful initiation into the various pleasures of sense—as, for example,
stomachic relishes, and alcoholic stimulants—is a time of high
enjoyment. The new emotions of puberty are at their maximum on newly bursting forth. The first thrill of a success is
never reproduced in the same degree.

The primary sensations are speedily gone through, and fall
into the ordinary routine of pleasures, which by being remitted or alternated, continue to afford a certain measure of
delight. The charm of novelty then belongs only to new and
varied combinations, and in that form it may be sustained,
although with decreasing force, to the end of life. New
scenes, new objects, new persons, and new aspects of life, constitute the attractions of travel. Novelty in incidents and
events, is furnished by the ongoings of life, and by the pages
of story. Inventions in the Arts, and discoveries in Science,
have the initial charm of novelty, as well as the interest of
permanent utility. In Fine Art, whose end is pleasure, the
powerful effects of novelty are earnestly invoked ; pleasurable
surprises are expected of the artist in every department

## NOVELTY.

beauty must be enhanced by originality : and the passion for change, uncontrolled, leads in the end to decadence. Last of all, in Fashion, Novelty is supreme. Throughout the whole, but one rule prevails ; other things the same, the greater the novelty, the greater the pleasure.

6. Next to Novelty is *Variety,* alternation or change. Besides catering for the new, we can find gratification in varying the old. Stimulants tend to recover their efficacy after being for a time in abeyance ; and by a long interval of suspension, we may even come near the pristine charm. Our happiness must rely mainly on the rotation of familiar pleasures ; some of us enjoying but a small round, others a large. It is the proof of our aptitude for a particular form of delight that it can be long sustained, and easily refreshed ; but the demand for remission is absolute.

It is needless to enter into the details illustrative of this phase of the Law of Relativity. The summary above given for pure Novelty, applies also to Variety. After due intervals, we can go back upon the same work of Art, time after time, with little diminution of zest.

7. The emotion of WONDER likewise derives its essential character from Relativity. It is, however, something more than mere novelty, or change. The Wonderful is whatever startles us by deviating from its kind, something that rises above, or falls beneath, what we have been accustomed to. The dweller in provincial towns finds the metropolis wonderful. St. Peter's and the Falls of Niagara are wonderful. These are on the side of greatness. An unusually stupid man, a superior force allowing itself to be defeated, are wonderful on the side of littleness. The correlative state to Wonder is the Common, customary, ordinary, or average standard of the class ; the opposition or conflict of the two leads to a shock of Surprise.

8. Thus, while Wonder is an emotion of Contrast or Relativity, it is besides an emotion of Conflict, the suddenness of which makes the stimulation more lively. As a general rule, Conflict brings pain ; and, in many instances, wonder,

## EMOTIONS OF RELATIVITY.

astonishment, and surprise are names for painful disappointment. When baulked in any fond expectation, we are apt to
signify our astonishment, but the direct mode of describing
the state is some expression of pain or acute distress. On
the other hand, an unexpected piece of good fortune, giving
at first the painful shock of a momentary collision, is followed
by a more acute pleasure through the excitement of the
conflict. Yet it is known that persons have died from being
suddenly made rich, the violence of the transition being more
than could be redeemed by the genial effects of joy.

9. It is not, however, in these examples that the distinctive features of the Wonderful are to be seen. * We must
inquire into the circumstances rendering it, like novelty, one
of the æsthetic pleasures. We then discover it to consist of
things occurring in nature, in life, or in history, such as to
*surpass* the ordinary routine of our experience. The Admirable is the æsthetic wonderful. In our habitual immersion
in things stale, insipid, and commonplace, we seek in the first
instance for novelty, and next for the additional seasoning of
the Marvellous.*

With all this variety in the forms of Wonder, there can be no
common Physical Embodiment. Painful astonishment is accompanied with loss of nervous power and outward collapse;
pleasurable surprise is an acute stimulant like all sudden pleasures;
the elated tone of Admiration supposes the accession of a favourable stimulus, perhaps best studied in the emotion of the
Sublime. When a thing falls below its kind, the spectacle is
depressing in the first instance, but we often console ourselves by
contempt, or by ridicule.

10. The characteristic feature of Wonder is thus an elation
of tone connected with the spectacle or contemplation of
superior qualities, whether natural grandeur or human ex-

---

* Among the various meanings of Wonder, we find some illustrating the
transitive application of words. Thus it sometimes expresses mere ignorance
and uncertainty with the desire of being informed: we wonder who was the
author of Junius. Again, it indicates the interest of a plot: we wonder how
a story is to end.

WONDER. 47

cellence. It supposes us already to appreciate those qualities and to know their indications ; in regarding them, we feel, as it were, raised towards their high level, and rejoice in the conscious elevation. The pleasure is one of considerable value in human life.

11. The every-day wonders are chiefly manifestations of power. The acrobat and the rider in the circus astonish by their feats of muscular strength. The singer and the actor inspire us with admiration of their rare gifts while imparting the peculiar charm of their art. Every man that can impress us in a more than ordinary degree is looked at with a feeling of wonder. Small causes producing great effects are tokens of power and occasions of wonder,—a spark exploding a mine, a few strokes of a pen convulsing the world.

The emotion of Wonder as thus defined does not essentially differ from what is termed the sentiment of the Sublime.

12. In matters of truth and falsehood, wonder is one of the corrupting emotions. The narrations of matter of fact are constantly perverted by it ; while in science Bacon might have enrolled it among his ' idola.' *

---

* 'The love of the marvellous is remarkable for its influence in corrupting our faculties in the search after natural truth. From the fascination and stimulus of this class of objects they are purposely brought together in romantic and other compositions intended for agreeable excitement. What is familiar, ordinary, common, being apt to lose its interest and become stale, we take delight in encountering what is extraordinary, startling, and opposite to our usual experience. The stars cease to arrest our gaze, but a meteor flashing across the sky draws every eye upon its course. The sun and moon become objects of intense interest when in the rare and striking situation of an eclipse. Events either strongly contrasting with the usual run of things, or rising far above ordinary in magnitude, grandeur, or imposing effect, are the seasoning of life's dulness. To see, and afterwards to relate, uncommon occurrences and objects at variance with all experience, is delightful to wise and ignorant alike; but to rude ages and uncultivated minds, novelties, rarities, and marvels are especially agreeable.

' Now this itch for marvels is very apt to interfere with the cool observation of facts, and still more with the record and narration of them to others. Of course in phenomena of a rare and striking kind the difficulty of avoiding exaggeration is increased. In such things as earthquakes, meteors, eclipses, and rare and extraordinary productions, none but a highly-disciplined mind

## EMOTIONS OF RELATIVITY.

Carlyle has uttered a lament over the decay of wonder following on the scientific explanation of the world.* But it

---

is capable of giving unvarnished statements to others, or forming an accurate conception to itself.

'There are two subjects where the love of the marvellous has especially retarded the progress of correct knowledge—the manners of foreign countries, and the instincts of the brute creation. To exaggerate and make known signs and wonders is the standing vice of travellers, even when they do not absolutely manufacture fictions. The early travellers, going abroad with the notions of superstitious ages, and with little discipline in the arts of observation and correct writing, could in general be so little trusted that the cautious part of the public looked with suspicion upon marvellous statements in general, and in some instances discredited what was actually true. The greatest traveller of antiquity, and the earliest accurate historian (Herodotus) repeatedly and expressly refrains from mentioning what he saw from anticipating the incredulity of his readers, who, while delighting in certain kinds of the marvellous, might bring into play another instinct of uncultivated human nature—namely, the tendency to measure the whole world by the narrow standard of their own limited experience.

'It is extremely difficult to obtain true observations of the instincts of animals from the disposition to make them subjects of marvel and astonishment. Many people take delight in storing up tales of the extraordinary sagacity of dogs, cats, horses, birds, &c. in doing things quite incomprehensible and inexplicable on any law of nature whatsoever. It is nearly as impossible to acquire a knowledge of animals from popular stories and anecdotes, as it would be to obtain a knowledge of human nature from the narratives of parental fondness and friendly partiality.'—*What is Philosophy? Chambers's Papers for the People*, No. 92.

* 'You remember that fancy of Aristotle's, of a man who had grown to maturity in some dark distance, and was brought on a sudden into the upper air to see the sun rise. What would his wonder be, says the Philosopher, his rapt astonishment at the sight we daily witness with indifference! With the free open sense of a child, yet with the ripe faculty of a man, his whole heart would be kindled by that sight, he would discern it well to be Godlike, his soul would fall down in worship before it. Now, just such a childlike greatness was in the primitive nations. The first Pagan Thinker among rude men, the first man that began to think, was precisely the child-man of Aristotle. Simple, open as a child, yet with the depth and strength of a man. Nature had as yet no name to him; he had not yet united under a name the infinite variety of sights, sounds, shapes, and motions, which we now collectively name Universe, Nature, or the like—and so with a name dismiss it from us. To the wild deep-hearted man all was yet new, unveiled under names or formulas; it stood naked, flashing in on him there, beautiful, awful, unspeakable. Nature was to this man what to the Thinker and Prophet it for ever is, *pre*ternatural. This green, flowery, rock-built earth, the trees,

## FREEDOM AND RESTRAINT.

is the nature of all changes of view to abolish some emotions and substitute others in their stead, which to minds partial to the old is always felt as depravation. The discovery of uniform laws makes wonder to cease in one way by showing that nothing in nature is singular or exceptional; but even out of this very circumstance the scientific expositor will often find out new matter of surprise. How the same force can produce effects very unlike and far removed from one another is an impressive theme in the mouth of Faraday. Indeed, the 'wonders of science' have in our day come into rivalry with the marvels of fiction.

It is, nevertheless, the case that science and extended study naturally bring a man more or less to the position of 'nil admirari,' depriving him of the stimulating emotion bred of inexperience. Even the unexplained phenomena can be looked at with composure by the philosophic mind.

13. Let us next advert to the Emotions of FREEDOM and RESTRAINT, which involve both Conflict and Relativity.

To commence with RESTRAINT. This appears at the first glance a pure case of conflict. When we are checked in any of our impulses, we suffer all the distress and depression of opposing forces within. The active spontaneity repressed,

---

the mountains, rivers, many-sounding seas; that great deep sea of azure that swims overhead; the winds sweeping through it; the black cloud fashioning itself together, now pouring out fire, now hail and rain: what *is* it? Ay, what? At bottom we do not yet know; we can never know at all. It is not by our superior insight that we escape the difficulty; it is by our superior levity, our inattention, our *want* of insight. It is *not* by thinking that we cease to wonder at it. Hardened round us, encasing wholly every notion we form, is a wrappage of traditions, hearsays, mere *words*. We call that fire of the black thunder-cloud 'electricity,' and lecture learnedly about it, and grind the like of it out of glass and silk; but *what* is it? Whence comes it? Whither goes it? Science has done much for us; but it is a poor science that would hide from us the great, deep, sacred infinitude of Nescience, whither we can never penetrate, on which all science swims as a mere superficial film. This world, after all our science and sciences, is still a miracle; wonderful, inscrutable, *magical* and more, to whosoever will *think* of it.— *Lectures on Heroes*, p. 10.

50

EMOTIONS OF RELATIVITY.

the free vent of emotional diffusion arrested, the voluntary movements opposed, the aims and wishes thwarted—are cases of intestine conflict, and are painful according to the energy neutralized, which measures the waste of nervous power.

It is an aggravation of the pain of Restraint that sudden opposition is a stimulant, and evokes new power; thus rendering the conflict still more exhausting, if the obstacle is not thrown down.

The operation of the principle of Relativity on the position of restraint is interesting to study.

In the first place, a prompting steadily thwarted, may at last cease to be generated. The system is perpetually adjusting itself to new impulses (another way of stating the law of Relativity), and in long-continued conflicts the weaker, as it were, gives up the struggle. The process of suppression may be a work of time; and there may be impulses that, however opposed, are never quashed ; but the general law still holds good ; and to it we refer the great fact of our becoming reconciled to inevitable destiny.

14. The second application of the law of Relativity to the condition of Restraint is to give origin and meaning to the counter state of FREEDOM. Freedom is the deliverance from a foregone bondage, the loosening of a restraint, the cessation of a conflict.

The joyous outburst of feeling on the release from some great bondage is not simply the restoring of the position antecedent to the bondage. It is a state determined by the emergence from a painful restraint. The system was in the process of becoming reconciled to a lessened standard, without altogether forgetting the previous condition ; and now there is a sudden giving way of opposition currents, and enlargement of the vital energy, which (on the law of Relativity) is the condition of a lively and pleasurable consciousness. If the subject of the restraint continues to kick at his bonds, and to oppose nature's efforts at adjustment, deliverance is merely the remission of the conflict and the restoration of the previous state. And if, in the other extreme, a restraint has been so long kept up, and so thoroughly acquiesced in, that the antecedent state is effaced from the mind, freedom brings no joyous rebound to the slave. This fact was singularly exemplified in the overthrow of the Bastille; many of the poor wretches, moulded by long confinement, failed to realize the enlargement of liberty. It is a circumstance of great moral and political import, that men can become accustomed to servitude beyond even the wish for change.

The pleasure of Liberty is thus not merely relative to foregone restraint, but is also dependent on the way that the restraint has operated. The intensity of the pleasure will be according to the amount of vital energy released, and suddenly bursting forth; by the law of conservation, every such rise is accompanied with an elated mental consciousness.

With the stirring name of Liberty, we associate effects far beyond the thrilling moment of actual emancipation. It is in the power to work out our own pleasures in our own way, that we obtain, or think we obtain, our greatest happiness: and those that are fortunate to enjoy much of this privilege, are perpetually made conscious of it, by knowing what it is to be restrained, and by seeing the restraints of others.

15. The emotions of POWER and IMPOTENCE, like the foregoing, depend on transition or contrast, in other words, Relativity. A rise in the consciousness of our own might or energy, is attended with elation of mind, a fall brings depression; an even continuance of the same state is indifferent. Any circumstance occurring to reflect or illustrate our superiority, as success in a competition, gives a thrill of satisfaction; the unsuccessful are correspondingly mortified and depressed.

The physical circumstance of these emotions must still be considered as an increase or diminution of vital or nervous energy, in accordance with the Law of Conservation.

The situation of Power has much in common with Liberty; restraint or opposition so far as it extends, and is successful, is tantamount to impotence. But power has a wider range;

bodily and mental energy, high command, leadership, wealth, are not fully expressed by mere liberty.

This emotion is of sufficient importance to receive a detailed illustration, which will be given in a succeeding chapter.

In the two preceding chapters, I have adverted to the two great laws that pervade the composition of the Emotions generally; these, together with the law of Contiguous Association, will frequently appear in our analysis of the remaining species.

# CHAPTER V.

## EMOTION OF TERROR.

1. THE emotion of Terror originates in the apprehension of coming evil. Its characters are—a peculiar form of pain or misery; the prostration of the active energies; and the excessive hold of certain ideas on the mind.

Adverting first to the *object*, or cause, of the emotion—the apprehension of coming evil—we may remark that it is doubtful how far present or actual pain, uncoupled with anticipation, can give rise to the state of fear. Nothing surpasses in efficacy a present smart viewed as the *foretaste* of a greater infliction to follow; but this is apprehension in its most impressive form.

The apprehension may arise under a variety of circumstances. In the first place, there may be the prospect of known and *certain* evil, as when a penalty has been incurred, a painful operation decided on, or some loss or privation announced. The mere idea of suffering brings depression, but when accompanied with belief in an approaching reality, the idea acquires both intensity and persistence. Unavailing volitions and desires make it all the more distracting and engrossing.

A second case is when the giving way of a support leaves us to *uncertain* dangers, or evil possibilities, as in the partial reverses of a campaign, or in the desertion of allies. Here it is not certain mischief on the wing, but an abatement of the state of security, which is accompanied with a painful and haunting impression. The condition of security or confidence may be represented as a balance of good against evil, the first

## EMOTION OF TERROR.

preponderating; a sudden withdrawal on the side of good gives an unhinging shock, which must depress the mental tone, and fasten attention on the cause. Any new form of danger, as an epidemic, operates in this way.

Whenever we are plunged into uncertainty, darkness, or strangeness, we come under the liability now described. A *habitual* state of ignorance has not the same effect; the power of adjustment, implied under the Law of Relativity, accomodates us to the permanent. Fear has to do with 'new monsters,'

—grave ne rediret<br>
Seculum Pyrrhæ nova monstra questæ—

2. We will now consider expressly the *physical* side of Terror. No passion is more marked in outward display.

The great fact pervading all the manifestations is *a sudden transfer of nervous energy*. Power is withdrawn from the general system to be unduly concentrated in the organs of perception, on a particular class of ideas, and in the movements corresponding to these. Accordingly, the appearances may be distributed between effects of *relaxation* and effects of *tension*.

The *relaxation* is seen, as regards the Muscles, in the dropping of the jaw, in the collapse overtaking all organs not specially excited, in tremblings of the lips and other parts, and in the loosening of the sphincters.

Next as regards the Organic Processes and Viscera. The Digestion is everywhere weakened; the flow of saliva is checked,* the gastric secretion arrested (appetite failing), the bowels deranged. The Expiration is enfeebled. The heart and Circulation are disturbed; there is either a flushing of

---

* This circumstance is the foundation of the custom in India of subjecting suspected criminals to the ordeal of the morsel of rice. The accused is made to take a mouthful of rice, and after a little to throw it out. If the morsel is quite dry, the party is believed to be guilty—his own evil conscience operating to paralyse the salivating organs. It is needless to observe that this would be an effect of fear which, like blushing, might overtake an innocent as well as a guilty person under such an ordeal.

PHYSICAL ACCOMPANIMENTS.

the face, or a deadly pallor. The skin shows symptoms of derangement—the cold sweat, the altered odour of the perspiration, the creeping action that lifts the hair. The kidneys are directly or indirectly affected. The sexual organs feel the depressing influence. The secretion of milk in the mother's breasts is vitiated.

The increased *tension* is shown in the stare of the eye and the raising of the scalp (by the occipito-frontalis muscle), in the inflation of the nostril, the shrill cry, the violent movements of protection or flight. The stare of the eye is to be taken as an exaggerated fixing of the attention on the dreaded object; and there concurs with it an equally intense occupation of the thoughts in the same exclusive direction. Whatever movements of expression, or of volition, are suggested by these thoughts, have a similar intensity.

3. If we wish to account physically for this diversion of the vital energies under a stroke of terror, we must look to the circumstance of sudden deprivation of nervous power at one point, which may not unnaturally, from our experience of the human system, lead to undue excitement there, at the expense of other parts. But in the obscurity of the subject, we can do little beyond offering a plausible conjecture.

That such a physical condition of combined relaxation and tension, proceeding upon loss of nervous energy, should be accompanied with intense mental depression, is in accordance with the great law of Self-conservation. We saw (*Instincts*, § 20) what are the organs that, in their altered vitality, most powerfully affect the mental tone; namely, the digestion, the skin, and other glandular organs; while in mere muscular excitement there may be little or no pleasure. Now in the case of Terror, the sensitive viscera are all suddenly deprived of nervous stimulus and blood; and, on the other hand, the augmentation of energy is intellectual and muscular, which is no atonement for organic depression.

4. Let us next advert in detail to the *mental* side of the emotion. Considered as *Feeling*, we can only repeat that it is painful in quality, and in degree a mass of misery, which we

## EMOTION OF TERROR.

can in some degree estimate by the amount of pleasure or happiness that a shock of fright can destroy or submerge.

5. As regards *Volition*, the important circumstance is the great defalcation of energy for active exertion, except in the one direction where it is morbidly concentrated. It is matter of notoriety that fear cows the spirit of men, paralyzing their power of action. Panic in the field is defeat. Fear, as something apart from the mere infliction of pain, is of old the engine of domination, temporal and spiritual.

6. The relations of fear to the *Intellect* are of special moment. The power diverted from the organic functions flows towards the perceptive powers and the intellectual trains. Hence the extraordinary impressiveness of objects of alarm. One of the effects of acute pain in general is to quicken the memory. The whipping of boys at boundary lines was intended to ingrain the remembrance of the landmarks. But the perturbation of fright, in its excitement of the perceptive powers, makes a more indelible stamp than even an acute bodily infliction. An instance came within my knowledge of a person whose house had taken fire, and who was ever afterwards preternaturally sensitive to the odour of burning wood.

It is in Fear, that we see the extreme case of the 'fixed idea,' or the influence of the feelings upon the conduct, through the medium of the intellectual trains. It is not the regular action of the will, leading us from pain and to pleasure, on the whole, but the action following from the engrossing persistence of an idea, that blinds the view to consequences generally, and overturns all rational calculation. When a man is thoroughly terrified, his intellect is no longer at his command. The minor forms of fear, expressed by anxiety, watchfulness, care, use up the powers of thought, and exclude all impressions of a foreign nature. The poor man whose daily bread is in constant uncertainty, the mother of numerous children, the trader deep in speculations, are unapt subjects for liberal culture or enlarged mental acquisitions.

The influence of Fear on Belief follows from its character-

THE LOWER ANIMALS.—CHILDREN. 57

istics, as a depressing passion, and as engrossing the intellectual view. Mental depression, however arising, is exaggerated distrust of good and anticipation of evil; and an idea that cannot be shaken off, is believed for the time to be the true representation of the facts.

7. We pass now to the consideration of the forms, or Species, of the emotion of Terror.

The lower Animals furnish some salient illustrations of the working of this feeling. Numerous tribes are characterized by timidity as a part of their nature, while others present a contrast equally illustrative. The panic and the flight induced, by a very small demonstration, upon the feathered multitude, the awe impressed upon the most powerful of the quadrupeds by the touch of a whip or a commanding tone of voice, show how completely the exaggerations of fear can take possession of the animal mind. The mental system of such creatures is discomposed, and the diversion and discharge of the nervous currents brought about, by the slightest influences. To their weak and limited understanding every strange or sudden appearance rouses the state of apprehension; and it is only in select instances that this can be overcome by artificial means. The taming of birds and quadrupeds consists in part in conquering the dread of the human presence. The susceptibility to panic is perhaps the greatest disadvantage attaching to the condition of the lower animals.

8. The operation of fear in Children corresponds with the peculiarities of their position. The first manifestations of the state are seen in the general perturbation caused by over-excitement, or mere intensity of sensation. A sudden glare of light, a loud sound, a rough contact, or any other pungent effect, without being necessarily painful, is discomposing to the nervous system, much in the manner of a fright. When the infant is so far advanced as to recognise familiar objects, anything strange that arrests the attention gives rise to the perturbation of fear. The child revolts from the grasp of an unknown person, and manifests all the quakings of genuine terror. At the still later stage, when pain is connected with

58 EMOTION OF TERROR.

specific causes, as when the child knows what it is to be plunged into cold water, to take a bitter draught, to be scolded, or to be punished, the emotion appears in its proper form, as the apprehension of coming evil; the only speciality in the case being what is due to the weakness of the subject. Darkness is not necessarily a source of terror to children, or to any one, although very easily becoming so. The reasons must be sought, (1) in its being a cause of mental depression, or the withdrawal of a source of exhilaration, (2) in the increase of the subjective consciousness, by abolishing the objective regards, and (3) in its giving unbounded scope to any cause of apprehension.

9. The influence of mere Strangeness, as a cause of terror in Animals and in Children, admits of two different interpretations. On the one hand, we may suppose that there is, in the animal, and in the human constitution, a primitive nervous susceptibility, whereby the functions are at first easily disturbed by any cause; while experience and habit enable the weakness to be conquered. Many of the facts undoubtedly favour this view. In children especially, there are many liabilities to derangement that disappear in the adult. The overcoming of fear would seem to be a hardening process of like nature with habituation to cold, fatigue, flurry, or the acquirement of self-command generally.

On the other hand, it has been suggested by Mr. Herbert Spencer, as in accordance with the hypothesis of development, and also as consonant to facts, that the animal and infantile fear of strange appearances, and particularly of the human presence, is the transmitted experience of evil encountered from human and other agency. It would thus conform to the generic character of the passion—apprehension of evil. The commonly alleged fact that, in uninhabited islands, animals show no fear at the approach of man, is a striking testimony in favour of Mr. Spencer's view; for in such a case the strangeness is at its maximum.

10. We may enumerate Slavish terror as a notable species of the emotion. Any one placed in subordination to the will of another, has constantly before his eyes the risk of incurring displeasure and punishment. When the power of the superior has a distinct limit, the subordinate can clearly comprehend

the worst evil that can happen to him, and, in the cool exercise of his active faculties, can take an amount of precaution exactly corresponding to this amount of evil. This is the position of the citizen of a country governed by written laws, and of a servant in a free community. The subject of a government by law has before him a more or less definite penalty for each offence, and is moved to avoid that penalty exactly in proportion to the degree of pain implied in it. This is not fear, but a motive to the will, like hunger, or curiosity. So the servant in a free community, has before his mind the loss of his connexion with his present master as the limit of the master's power; and, notwithstanding his subordination, may rise superior to the incubus of terror.

Slavish terror takes its rise under a superior unlimited in power, capricious in conduct, or extreme in severity. The possibility of some great infliction is itself necessarily a cause of terror. That uncertainty which one knows not how to meet, or provide against, is still more unhinging. It is not possible to preserve composure under a capricious rule, except by being in a state of preparation for the very worst. The Stoical prescriptions of Epictetus, himself a slave, are in harmony with such a situation. Another circumstance tending to beget slavish fear is the conscious neglect of duty on the part of the inferior, he at the same time being unprepared calmly to face the consequences. The state of slavery is a state of terror from the power and arbitrary dispositions of the master; the free-born servant has mainly to fear the effects of his own remissness.

11. The Forebodings of disaster and misfortune, in our future prospects generally, deserve to be mentioned as one of the prevalent forms of the passion. Every one's mind is occupied more or less with his future. A clear prospect of the attainment of what we most desire, yields that confidence already dwelt upon as the opposite of terror. On the other hand, Misfortune, announced as at hand, unhinges the system in the manner described under the present emotion, until such time as we find means of neutralizing the blow. But Un-

## EMOTION OF TERROR.

certainty, with a tinge of probable evil, is to the generality of men the most disquieting situation. It takes much natural courage, or else a light-hearted temperament, to anticipate with calmness some likely but undeclared calamity; to know the worst is generally esteemed a relief.

12. The condition of mind termed Anxiety relates itself to our various interests in the distance. There is here the same ambiguity and confounding of different facts, as belongs to other names connected with the present subject. The rational and measured exertions to meet our known emergencies may be said to indicate anxiety of mind. But the phrase is not properly applicable unless something of the perturbation of fear be present.* The anxious condition of mind is a sort of diffused terror, a readiness to take fright on all occasions of apprehension or uncertainty. As no one's future can be clear throughout, there is never wanting the matter of anxiety to a mind susceptible of the state. The lives of some are spent in a constant flutter of agitation, varied by moments of inexpressible relief, when the dark shadows disappear, or the mind rises into a vigorous or buoyant mood.

13. Suspicion is a mode of our present passion, representing the influence of our fears upon Belief. The state of alarm

---

* There is a well-known anecdote related, if I remember aright, of some great general who read on a tombstone the inscription—'Here lies one who never knew fear;' and upon this, remarked, 'Then such a one could never have snuffed a candle with his fingers.' Here the revulsion from pain, operating in every sane mind, at every moment of life, is confounded with the perturbation of terror, which is only occasional, and may be almost entirely absent from the character. The same ambiguity is seen in Dr. Thomas Brown's exposition of what he calls the prospective emotions. (Lecture 65.) With him fear is simply the contrary of desire. These are some of his expression.:—'Our *fears*, which arise equally from the prospect of what is disagreeable in itself, and from the prospect of the loss of what is in itself *agreeable.*' 'We *fear* to *lose* any source of pleasure possessed by us, which had long been an object of our hope.' The want of a good term for the opposite of desire is probably the reason of this abused application of 'fear' to denote simply what stimulates efforts of avoidance. The true antithesis lies between fear and coolness, composure, or measured expenditure.

## PANIC.—SUPERSTITION. 61

being by its very nature the breaking up of confidence, things in general become the objects of distrust. Slight incidents that the mind in its ordinary coolness would pass by, as unmeaning or irrelevant, are interpreted as ill omens; and the persons whom we never doubted stand forth as compassing our ruin. These effects are ascribable solely to the disturbance wrought by fear. As affecting the conduct towards others, the outgoings of suspicion are most disastrous. We witness them constantly in private life, and they are exhibited on a great scale in the proceedings of nations. Times of political disorder like the civil wars of Rome, or the first French Revolution, are rendered more calamitous by the exaggerations of suspicion, and the credit given to the suggestions of fear.*

14. Panic is an outburst of terror affecting a multitude in common, and rendered more furious by sympathy or infection. When an army is seized with panic, all is lost. The habits of discipline are paralysed by the draining off of nervous power. The strength of a human being is turned into weakness at such a moment; what vigour remains is expended in a disordered flight. Courage, which gives to man a pointed superiority over the lower animals, is notoriously of more worth than numbers in the emergencies of war, or the trials of public disaster. The nerve that can surmount a popular panic is of genuine stuff.

15. I shall include under one comprehensive species, the terrors of Superstition. Man's situation in the world contains all the elements of fear. The vast powers of nature dispose of our lives and happiness with irresistible might and awful aspect. Ages had elapsed ere the knowledge of law and uniformity, prevailing among those powers, had been arrived at by the human intellect. The profound ignorance of primitive man was the soil wherein his early conceptions and theories

---

\* It is well known that in new epidemic disorders, the physicians in ignorant countries are usually suspected of poisoning the wells. Alexander the Great crucified the physician that attended his friend Hephæstion. This was a despot's wrath inflamed by suspicion.

62　　　　　　EMOTION OF TERROR.

sprang up; and the fear inseparable from ignorance gave them their character. The essence of superstition is expressed by the definition of fear. An altogether exaggerated estimate of things, the ascription of evil agency to the most harmless objects, and false apprehensions everywhere, are among the attributes of superstition. The fictious embodying men's terrors in the presence of nature, have assumed an endless variety. The personification of natural powers uncertain and often destructive—the winds and the thunder, the rivers and ocean,—makes part of the ancient worship of our race, a worship largely prompted by men's fears. The ritual of sacrifice and expiation asserts the prevailing sentiment. The creation of malign deities, evil spirits, and the inferior class of tenants of darkness, described under the names of ghosts, hobgoblins, evil genii, imps, and fairies, all bear the impress of terror; and under that influence do they make their way into the general mind. While even the regular and ordinary march of things —the alternations of day and night, summer and winter, seed-time and harvest, birth and death—keep up a certain mystic dread, the exceptions to use and wont, reanimate the sense of terror to the intensity of panic. A solar eclipse fills every bosom with awe; a comet is a portent of horrible calamity; an irregularity of season begets a crushing sentiment of the anger of the gods. The life of infant humanity is overshadowed with terrors; the wild gleams of rejoicing shoot out of a diffused blackness.*

16. The Fear of Death is naturally the crowning manifestation of the feeling under discussion. Still the aspect of the last enemy is so exceedingly different in different circumstances, that the sentiment produced has little of a common character. The one fact of the situation is the unknown future that the being is ushered into.† The loss of 'life's

---

\* ' Where you know nothing place terrors,' says Helps, speaking of the popular notions respecting remote countries, previous to the voyages of Columbus. In the quarters of vast and unknown possibility, the soil is already prepared.

† Ay, but to die, and go we know not where;

　　To lie in cold obstruction, and to rot;

## FEAR OF DEATH.

pleasures, interests, and relationships, is felt according to the value set upon these ; the darkness of the shadow of death is essentially calculated to strike terror. This is the deepest midnight gloom that the human imagination can figure to itself; and from that quarter emanate the direct forms of apprehension and dread. It is the fact respecting death common to the whole human family. If we were to specify individual varieties, we should find every degree between the extremes of placid courage or pious exultation on the one hand, and the depth of horror aud despair on the other.

17. I shall conclude the detail of specific forms of the emotion with two other examples of frequent occurrence, the one the dread on entering on a new operation, the other the discomfiture felt on appearing in a new presence.

The Distrust of our Faculties in unfamiliar operations is a true case of fear. The element of uncertainty, with the apprehension of failure in consequence, has the tendency to unhinge the mind, and induce the quakings and the disturbance that we have been describing. The amount of the evil involved in the failure, and the degree of conscious imperfection on our part, are the two circumstances operating to produce the effect. The attempt to leap a chasm, or a stream of such width that the utmost effort can barely suffice to gain the bank, induces the agitation of fear. In all untried situations, in the exercise of imperfect powers and acquisitions,

---

This sensible warm motion to become
A kneaded clod ; and the delighted spirit
To bathe in fiery floods, or to reside
In thrilling regions of thick-ribbed ice ;
To be imprison'd in the viewless winds,
And blown with restless violence round about
The pendent world ; or to be worse than worst
Of those, that lawless and uncertain thoughts
Imagine howling !—'tis too horrible !
The weariest and most loathed worldly life,
That age, ache, penury, and imprisonment
Can lay on nature, is a paradise
To what we fear of death.

64                    EMOTION OF TERROR.

and in the commencement of enterprises where we can only
partly see our way, we are liable to a certain degree of terror,
manifesting itself in proportion to the stake and the uncertainty combined. The word 'danger' expresses both circumstances. The state of apprenticeship, in general, has this
situation frequently repeated. New trades, new tools, new
exercises in every art, employment, or occupation of life, dis-
compose the mind often with severe terrors and mental
anguish. This is one of the disadvantages of early years, and
a source of both weakness and misery, to be set off against
the superior vigour and spirits of youth. The pain of a young
surgeon at his first capital operation may amount to agony.
Great responsibility maintains the excitement of apprehension
in minds alive to the sense of it, even although well-experi-
enced in the operations required. Anxiety is apt to attend
all great posts.

18. The being Abashed before a strange face, or a new
company, is remarkable as one of the manifold influences of
the human presence upon the human kind. The principal
circumstance is unquestionably the feeling caused by the aspect
of power, with the uncertainty belonging to the exercise of it.
In every human being there is a vast possibility of action
beneficial or hurtful; and it takes much familiarity to be
assured of each person's dispositions and tendencies. The
infant, in its helplessness, is the subject of many misgivings.
Being dependent on other persons for everything, the child
associates safety with the care of the nurse ; but with a strange
hand, and a new face, there is an apprehension not yet overcome. It is the same with later years. We get to know more
and more the power for evil that lies wrapt up in a living
being; while we require a distinct experience of each one to
give us confidence. It is the nature of apprehension not to
wait till hurtful dispositions are actually manifested, but to
demand decisive assurances that such do not exist.

The dread inspired by the aspect of man, or beast, naturally grows with the estimate we are led to form of their
power. A child going to school for the first time is awed by

## COUNTERACTIVES OF TERROR.

the presence of the master, from having heard so much of his high-handed proceedings towards its elders. Persons in power are approached with dread by the mass beneath them. But more discomposing than almost any single human being is the presence of an assembled company. The power of the concentrated gaze of many faces is something appalling to any one making a public appearance for the first time. The state commonly known as 'stage fright' is agonizing and unsettling in the last degree.*

The dread that we all live in from the censure of other persons, or the loss of good opinion, keeps up a certain tremulous circumspection of manner in general society, until extensive usage has set us at our ease. The uncertainty of our position with the persons that we come in contact with, the not knowing what dispositions to ourselves we inspire them with, is a great source of disquiet and pain in our intercourse with others. Hence the comfort of the long familiarity that has set all doubts of this nature at rest.

The shyness of manner induced between the sexes is of the same nature, and proves the influence of mutual regard, by the apprehension on either side of not standing well with the other.

19. The characteristics of Terror are farther illustrated by its opposites and counteractives.

In the first place, Robustness of Constitution is a means of overcoming fear, in common with the other depressing passions. Everything that supports the natural health and vigour of the system, is in favour of composure of mind; while exhaustion, disease, and pain, have the opposite tendency. In the next place, the Active or Energetic Temperament is naturally related to courage; a large stock of energy holds out longer than a small. Again, the Sanguine Temperament rises superior to the disturbing passion, by casting off serious cares and burdensome obligations, and

---

* In my own case, the first attempt to address a large audience produced a momentary loss of vision and a feeling as of sinking through the ground.

E.

66                    EMOTION OF TERROR.

by making too light of real calamity, actual or prospective. Once more, the quality of Resoluteness of Mind, the moral strength that carries men through labours and difficulties to their ends, includes a superiority to fear as part of its nature.

Courage is one of the results of education, or habit. The soldier has the cannon fever in his first engagement, but, at length, meets danger with coolness. The public speaker disporting himself at ease before a large assembly, is a striking instance of acquired composure.

When terror springs from ignorance, the remedy is knowledge. Supernatural fears are dispelled by the discoveries that reveal the laws of the world. Eclipses, comets, and meteors have no terrors in the present day. Our experience of life enables us to rise superior to shocks and surprises ; and when baffled ourselves, we are reassured by the knowledge of others. The bodily ills we are accustomed to, cease to unsettle the mind ; but a new symptom fires up our alarms, until the experienced practitioner has sounded its depths. The arduous labours of the intellect in storing up knowledge, find one source of reward in composing the fears ; and the share that we take in the turmoil of life has a similar good consequence.

Courage is one of the most essential, the most comforting, the most striking characteristics of the human mind. The physical courage of the soldier, the nerve that can submit calmly to a surgical operation, or remain cool on the rack, uncomplaining in the agony of disease ; the moral courage that can appreciate danger unmoved, and retain composure under vast responsibility, that can cling to convictions in spite of opposition, that can remain immovable in adversity, and retain faith in the midst of apprehensions, that can go to the stake for conscience, or live a life of trial,—are appearances among the sublimest that humanity presents ; being among the most impressive of all exhibitions of the might and greatness of the spirit of man.

20. In Government and Education, it is an object to overcome individual impulses, and this is done both by definite

## TERROR IN GOVERNMENT.

punishments, and by indefinite terrors. Nations must be governed, and the young disciplined somehow; still the employment of unbounded fears is a reckless waste of men's energies and happiness. Those in government have a natural partiality for an instrument that wakens up the careless and tames the proud. Terror has a specific effect upon the self-will, the haughtiness, and the independent spirit of human beings—not merely supplying a motive for submission, but sapping and debilitating that part of our nature where these qualities have their root. The quakings of fear are incompatible with the self-erectness and personal dignity of man. In fact, this is surrendered when fear has crept in. Hence, to engender the virtue of humility, recourse is had to terror.

The definite penalties of a regular government, or a considerate teacher, are simple motives to guide the conduct; but irregularity of procedure, uncertainty and caprice, inspire the feelings of apprehension. Likewise the suggestion of vague and intangible evils, such as the wrath of the supernatural powers and the punishments of a future life, is calculated to terrify and take hold of the mind.

The Religious Sentiment might be introduced here, as being a compound, of which fear is a principal ingredient. I prefer, however, to notice it in the following chapter, when we shall have all the elements before us.

21. Our concluding observations relate to the use of the passion in Art. The expression of fear makes a subject for the artist, whether painter or poet.* The actor brings it on the stage both in tragic and in comic exhibitions. Pictures and tales of thrilling interest are sometimes created out of the deepest horrors that reality or imagination can furnish.

A genuine fright is undoubtedly an experience of pure

---

* ' I could a tale unfold, whose lightest word
    Would harrow up thy soul; freeze thy young blood;
    Make thy two eyes, like stars, start from their spheres;
    Thy knotted and combined locks to part,
    And each particular hair to stand on end,
    Like quills upon the fretful porcupine.'

68    EMOTION OF TERROR.

misery; but a slight fear, with speedy relief, occurring in times of dullness and stolid composure, acts like a stimulant on the nervous system. In the flush of high bodily vigour, danger only heightens the interest of action and pursuit. The hunting of tigers is the most exciting of sports. The steeple-chase is the highest achievement of this kind at home.

But it is in the *fictitious* terrors that the sting of pain is most effectually extracted, and only the pleasurable stimulus left behind. In proportion as the reality of evil is removed far from ourselves, we are at liberty to join in the excitement produced by the expression of fear. The skilful dramatist is able to adjust the dose—although the greatest of all has not always done so. The genius of Shakspeare has not been able to submerge the painful horrors of Lear. Some minds can endure a large amount of this element, having that robustness of nerve that can throw off the pain, and not be too much excited by the depicted horrors. Murder, calamity, and mis-rule, are no more than interest to such minds. For others, the misery-causing element would predominate. The spectacle of gladiators, bull-fights, contests in the ring, &c., contains both pain and exciting interest; and the taste for them is determined according as the one or other prevails. The ancient 'mysteries'* are generally supposed to have had terror

---

* 'The *Eleusinian mysteries* were celebrated every year, in September, and the festival occupied ten days. Both sexes and all ages were admitted; but foreigners and bad characters at home were excluded. It was con-sidered a duty of every Athenian citizen to go to Eleusis at least once, for the sake of being initiated. The intending communicants on each occasion formed themselves into a procession, and marched on foot from Athens to Eleusis, a distance of ten or twelve miles. Various ceremonies of purifi-cation were gone through, and sacrifices ordered, with solemn processions, and the carrying about of lighted torches. Sports and contests, as was usual at all festivals, were regularly exhibited. The ceremony of initiation was nocturnal, and took place in a large building called the Temple of the Mysteries. The candidates entered with myrtle crowns and clean garments, dipping their hands in the holy water at the door as they passed. The hierophant, or chief actor of the mysteries, received them with a solemn admonition to preserve their minds pure and undefiled on so august an occasion; and then read out of a book the import of the mysteries. He next

## FICTITIOUS TERRORS.

for their basis, and their influence was considered favourable, as well as stimulating to the mind.

---

put certain questions to them, as to whether they had duly prepared themselves by fasting, &c.; to all which they returned answers in a set form. A vast exhibition of strange objects and scenes then opened up before them; thunders and lightnings alternating with pitch darkness, noises and bellowings, apparitions of horror, and dramatic spectacles of the most terrible excitement. The sad mythical history of the goddess was represented, it would appear, with an exaggeration of details that struck dread into the spectators. Obscene rites and symbols seem also to have been mixed up with the revelations. The shock given to the spectators must have been terrible. The whole scene was an extreme instance of tragedy, according to Aristotle's account of its intention—namely, to purify the heart by pity and terror. It was an accumulation of all the objects and stimulants of the most tumultuous passions of pathos and terror. The motive of the display would appear to have been to operate as a counteractive to these passions in ordinary life, by the abiding remembrance of one volcanic outburst of emotion. There was a saying, that persons that had once visited the cave of Trophonius, where a similar dish of horrors was served up, were never known to smile afterwards; and perhaps some permanent solemnizing effect was anticipated from the exhibition of the mysteries.'

# CHAPTER VI.

## TENDER EMOTION.

1. TENDERNESS is an outgoing of pleasurable emotion, comprehending the warm affections, and benevolent sentiments, and drawing human beings into mutual embrace.

The *objects*, causes, or stimulants of this emotion, are, properly speaking, human beings, and other sentient creatures. A species of it seems to be developed towards inanimate things; but that must be pronounced a figurative, or analogical form of the sentiment.

To speak more particularly. Among the stimulants of tender feeling, we are to include, first, all the pleasures that are massive or voluminous, rather than acute. We have recognised, under this head, slow movements, dying movements, repose after exercise, repletion, agreeable warmth, pleasing odours not acutely sweet, soft contacts, gentle and voluminous sounds, mild sunshine. All such pleasures have the double effect of soothing or calming down the activity, and of inclining to tenderness; and the relationship thus brought out, between the passive or reposing condition of the animal system and the tender emotion, is a notable fact of our constitution.

In the next place, very great pleasures incline to tenderness. Under the agitation of extreme joy, the affections burst out into warm displays, and demand a response from others. Occasions of rejoicing are celebrated by social gatherings and profuse hospitality.

Further, we have to enumerate pains among the causes of the tender effusion. This is the singular paradox connected

## OBJECTS OF TENDER EMOTION.

with the present subject. All discrimination of exciting causes would seem to be at an end when pleasures and pains are declared to operate exactly alike. But when we look a little deeper, the seeming contradiction is a real agreement. In times of pleasure, tender emotion flows as a tributary to the stream of enjoyment. In the agony of pain, the same influence rises in mitigation of the suffering. Any pleasure coming within the range of the human susceptibility may be used in the very same way to drown the sense of pain; and the tapping of the fountains of tenderness is one of the most universally accessible of the assuaging influences that can be employed for this end. In children, in weak natures, in cases where fortitude is undermined by disease, and in persons with largely-developed affectionateness—the resort is a very frequent one. Moreover, it is but natural that pains involving the affections, such as domestic calamity, should be more ready than others to stir up this source of consolation.

Besides those three classes of general causes—massive sensation, great pleasures, and great pains—we have to recognise certain things that have a more specific influence in raising the feeling now before us. Thus, with regard to Movement and Touch, there is a peculiar local region of the body that is immediately related to tenderness. The breast, neck, mouth, and the hand are more especially devoted to this emotion, in conjunction with the movements of the upper members; whereas sexual excitability is localized in the surfaces and movements of the inferior members. These local associations are no doubt owing to the general arrangement whereby any organ is more liable to be acted on by a stimulus applied to its immediate vicinity; the form of the affectionate embrace is determined by the special susceptibilities now mentioned, if it be true that the organs of tender emotion are those stated afterwards. There are also some notable specialities among the sensations of Hearing and Sight. The high and mellow note, occurring sometimes in the wail of grief, and adopted in order to give pathos to the address of the preacher, has especial efficacy in touching the tender

72 TENDER EMOTION.

chords. In virtue of this coincidence, by which one of the notes in the instinctive utterance of grief is also an instinctive cause of tender feeling, there is a primitive power in the outburst of grief to rouse the tender feeling in others. The same effect does not belong to all the utterances prompted by suffering; the sharp and shrill tones of a more violent outburst close up the issues of compassion in the bystander. There are cadences in music that belong to the pathetic class. The 'dying fall' may be noted as a peculiar instance. Compositions in the minor key are supposed to have this character throughout. I think these effects are to some extent primitive, although extended by subsequent associations. Finally, among sensations of Sight, we cannot omit the remarkable power of objects seen through a transparent covering to operate in the same way. I have already alluded (*Sight*, § 11,) to the superior fascination of this class of objects, and I cannot doubt that it is connected with the influence we are now considering. The clear rivulet not only charms, but seems almost to melt and subdue the sensitive mind, very much in the manner of objects of tender affection. The fascination of the human eye is owing to the same cause; and the superadded tear-drop is merely a repetition of the influence. In situations quite unconcerned with humanity, the sight of the clear water-drop often stimulates the watery secretion of the eye. This, too, is another of those pre-established coincidences by whose means the state of tender emotion in one human being is instantly awakened in another. It is only by experience that we can interpret the expression put on by the features, remarkable as that may be; but the pathetic wail, and the watery eyeball, have an original tendency to affect other minds with the same feeling.

Association imparts to a variety of other things the power of exciting this emotion. The alliance of tenderness with inaction renders it suitable to the condition of weakness. A strong man laid prostrate is apt to feel this emotion as being the one most kindred to his state. The dying Nelson craved to be kissed. The feeling of anger implies a certain vigour

PHYSICAL SIDE. 73

without which it cannot be sustained as an emotion; when the last remains of active power have flowed out, and a condition entirely passive has supervened, tenderness is the only mood compatible with the situation. Hence, whatever readily suggests to the mind a predicament of extreme weakness is liable to induce this emotion. The helplessness of infancy, of age, and of the sick bed, stimulates it. Even among inanimate objects, slender and fragile forms take hold of our minds on the same side. The interest thus kindled towards the delicate in natural objects has been reckoned a point of beauty; and the beautiful was identified by Burke with the slender, the feeble, and the diminutive.

2. The *physical* side of Tender emotion is characteristic, and in no small degree complicated. The full and outspoken manifestation of the feeling, the goal that it always tends to, is the loving embrace. Keeping this before us, we will review the bodily organs and processes concerned. Foremost of all is the Lachrymal Gland and Sac, which is specifically acted on during an outburst of tender feeling. It is to be presumed that during the genial exercise of the emotion, all that happens is a slight increase of the healthy secretion; the profuse flooding of the eyes in pain and grief is a morbid stimulation of the gland. Next are the movements of the Pharynx, or muscular cavity where the food is swallowed. In violent grief these muscles are so convulsed as to be unable to swallow the food; in ordinary tenderness they are the seat of an indescribable sensibility, characteristic of the emotion. Considering that these muscles are but the commencement of the series of muscular fibres embracing the alimentary canal throughout its whole length, and harmoniously co-operating in the same function; considering also the popular testimony implied in the phrase ' bowels of compassion,' we may surmise that the digestive organs at large participate advantageously in the wave of tender feeling. Lastly, as regards the Muscular manifestations. The features, voice, and carriage take on a pleased and tranquil expression; the conspicuous movements end in the embrace.

74                    TENDER EMOTION.

The Lacteal secretion in women no doubt co-operates with the lachrymal, as a physical basis of tender feeling. Even without the stimulus of maternity, the mammary glands may be supposed to be in a state of fluctuating activity; and any rise in the degree is likely to be accompanied with a genial feeling, entering into the aggregate of tenderness, and consummated by finally squeezing some living object to the breast. If this be so in the ordinary state, we can imagine the increased development given to it in the mother giving suck to the child.

3. The link of sequence, both physical and mental, between the objects or stimulants of tender feeling and the allied manifestations, must be sought in the common character of the two sets of phenomena, and in the tendency of any pleasurable stimulus to feed itself from all available sources. If we happen to be under any of the influences of massive and serene enjoyment, we are urged, through the law of Conservation, to retain and enhance the state by tapping the allied fountains. Balmy odours, sunshine, and soft music suggest living companionship as a congenial extension and harmonious accompaniment of the same condition.

4. Let us, then, consider more fully the *mental* side of Tenderness. Pleasurable in quality, and massive in degree, it is not merely a tranquillizing emotion, but is fitted to maintain itself in periods of repose and exhaustion. Great as the intensity of it may sometimes be, the capability of being sustained over long tracts of time, and under a condition of the lowest vitality, is more remarkable than the degree attainable at any one moment. This renders it the refuge after toil, and the solace of the sick bed. It may be doubted whether the human constitution can yield the same amount of pleasure at so little cost by any other means. The extent of pleasurable influence diffused over life, from the employment of the tender affections, may be vaguely estimated by the extent of toil and privation cheerfully incurred to keep up the flow, as in the mutual devotion exhibited in families happily constituted. Not only can the emotion be frequently

## RELATIONS TO WILL AND INTELLECT. 75

stimulated without painful satiety, but the vibration from each stimulus is able to persevere long after the stroke. Were this source of sentiment withdrawn from human life the manner of our existence on the earth would be wholly revolutionized.

It is the character of a voluminous excitement to affect lightly a large surface, as opposed to an acute pleasure, which stimulates intensely a small; the tender feeling in all its forms is pre-eminently of the voluminous character, and we need look no farther for the foundation of the property now described.

5. As regards *Volition*, or action, the tender feeling, while operating like other pleasures as a motive for its own continuance, has the efficacy belonging to all voluminous feelings, of soothing or tranquillizing undue active excitement. The effect is doubtless due to the substitution of a new stimulant for one that we willingly forego as soon as we have the requisite aid to conquer it.

6. The relations of Tenderness to the *Intellect* are worthy of attention. The expenditure of nervous force in maintaining it being small, it can be easily kept up, and also, by means of association, recovered in idea. Hence, when any of the objects are strongly recalled to mind, the feeling will revive with them. But there is something farther.

It is to be carefully noted that this feeling is an effect co-operating with, and enhancing, the proper pleasures of the senses; as Terror is something superadded to the mere anticipation of pain, and poetic description an addition to the delight of scenery. A beautiful person, a generous action, or a work of Art, might give sensuous pleasure without inspiring Tender emotion; but, in minds so disposed, they cause the farther effects whose culminating point is the living embrace of some fellow being.

Now, when any one person has repeatedly drawn forth the stream of tenderness, there occurs a process of adhesion, or association, whereby the feeling arises on the mere presence or mention of the person, without the circumstances that originally caused it; which habitual or associated Tenderness is what we mean by Affection. It is easy to understand, how, under the principle of Contiguity, the Affection may pass to collateral persons and accompaniments such as of themselves have no power to stimulate tender feeling; by which means these indifferent objects then become pleasing and consoling influences on the mind.

7. Of the more *mixed* and various characters attaching to our tender feelings, the first to be noted is that combination of volition and intellect which gives them a power to operate on the will when not present in reality. It is necessary for this end that they should persist as ideas or recollections, and carry along with them into this ideal state something of the volitional prompting that characterizes their actual presence. When we affirm that the ideal continuance of the tender emotion is naturally great, we imply a corresponding power of ruling the conduct, or of dictating a sustained course of action. That is to say, according as we consider this feeling to contribute to the pleasures of our being, do we maintain an active career with the view to its fruition. It is found, in fact, that persons susceptible in a high degree to the tender influence, are prone to expend a very large share of their energy in that direction. Any illustration that this position may seem to want, will occur in the subsequent detail.

8. The same combination of the volitional and the intellectual yields the state of Desire, or longing, without active pursuit. In circumstances when no exertion on our part can bring us within reach of the objects of our affection, there is nothing left but that ideal form of action termed desire. Such a state of craving comes to stimulate the imagination, or to substitute action in idea for action in reality. There is a mixture of the pleasurable and the painful in this condition; pleasurable, in so far that the emotion is still maintained in its proper character by intellectual retention; painful, from the labour of feeding upon ideas, and from the poverty of mere imagined bliss. But in an easily sustainable feeling like the present, a sensible amount of happiness may be derived

INFLUENCE ON ATTENTION AND BELIEF. 77

from the mere contemplation of the objects, while in other feelings the painful craving may predominate over the pleasure. Love is often satisfied with objects purely ideal; implying a wonderful power of keeping up the flow of the feeling upon a very slight suggestion. But human nature is not fairly dealt with when so great a strain is placed upon the intellectual forces; a mixture of the real with the imagined is the happiest arrangement for our constitution.

9. The influence of the feeling upon the Attention, or the tendency of it to control the observation and the thoughts is one of its important aspects, and an apt criterion of its power in general. The storing of the intellect with a certain class of images and recollections, and the occupation of the mental trains with the same class of thoughts, are the results of any predominant emotion. These consequences are remarkably shown in the stronger relations of tender feeling.

10. Lastly: We must notice the influence on Belief, which also manifests the power of the feeling. The strong partialities induced by affection and friendship, the blindness to obvious facts, the incapability of entertaining injurious interpretations, are among the most notorious and irresistible characteristics of human nature. The stronger kinds of affection are able to sustain the wildest hopes, and to convert dreams into convictions. The mind dwells in other worlds with as much certainty as on anything seen or realised around it.

### SPECIES OF TENDER EMOTION.

11. Leaving the description of generic characters, we now proceed to the various forms or species of the feeling. As its nature is to vent itself on persons, we trace it principally in the relationships of human beings, while the companionable animals are not excluded from its range. A human being combines, within a small compass, a plurality of the influences above described as stimulants of tenderness. The soft touch, the rich and glossy tints appearing on the surface, the lustre of the eye, and certain strains of vocal utterance,—unite with

78                    TENDER EMOTION.

the rounding of the form, and the more graceful of the movements, in making up a complex whole, capable of awakening the sentiment with great force. These causes, common to the generality of human beings, are very much heightened in particular instances, by a more than usually felicitous conformation, or by a relationship that adds other influences besides. We have seen with what power the element of weakness operates as an exciting cause; a circumstance which tells more especially in the case of infancy.

12. The special outgoings or demonstrations that constitute Tenderness, as something added to sensuous pleasure, suppose another person. The shake of the hand, the embrace, under which the special organs of the sensibility are stimulated— the lachrymal gland, the pharyngeal muscles, &c.—occur between two living personalities. The more intellectual manifestations of soft and unctuous speech involve the mental development of human beings ; while the additional operation of sympathy, in whose absence we should consider the feeling incomplete, requires the attribute of sentient life.

## *Family Group.*

13. Beyond all question the relation of Mother and Offspring is the most replete with tender feeling. Nor is it difficult to indicate the elements and distinguishing features of the relationship. The infant, as a sensuous object, is conspicuously endowed with the properties that excite the feeling. The skin soft and pure, the eye fresh and clear, the outline rounded ; the diminutive size and helplessness ; the interest of the comparison showing so much likeness to the full-grown individual ; the action so different and yet so similar ;—render the child an impressive object of tenderness to every one. And in the case of the mother, there is superadded a powerful element of regard, arising out of the original relation to herself, and the special engagement of her energies in supporting the infant's existence. Such a combination of self-interest and the associations of a strong solicitude would, under any circumstances, stamp an object on the mind ; a

MATERNAL FEELING. 79

house, or a garden, so situated grows upon the feelings of the possessor. When, however, the object is a human being of the age most fitted to act on the tender susceptibilities, we can easily understand how this relationship becomes the crowning instance of intense personal regard. If we cite in detail the various properties of emotion, we shall find our experience attesting that every one of them is strongly manifested by the maternal mind. The expression is copious and persistent; and there being no disguise observed, this alone is a sufficient criterion in the case. Other indications concur in showing that the feeling is large in quantity, sustainable in an eminent degree, and capable of imparting a valuable stock of satisfying pleasure. Being trained, or attuned, to this special stimulant, the mind thrills with a sort of fascination under its influence. The action on the Will is an equal proof of the intense development of the feeling. The ordinary observation sets the child-regarding motives as above all others in the maternal breast; so strong, indeed, that a struggle is scarcely felt when conflict ensues. In the Intellectual aspect we note a degree of retentiveness corresponding to the present power of the excitement, and sustaining both the feeling and the conduct through the intervals when the object is not actually present. The Desire, or longings of the state, contain more of the pleasurable than of the painful, from the same cause. The influence on the Attention—the observation, the trains of recurring thought, the constructions and imaginations of the mind—is all-powerful; things and ideas find a sure access to the intellect, if they can claim connexion with filial interests. There is occasionally an engrossment of mind, probably much beyond the pleasure that is imparted, exaggerating the relationship to the pitch of irrationality, a property of emotion noticed already, and to be still farther dwelt upon afterwards. And in the last place, the power to control Belief is no less signal; the mother's faith in the child passes every other form of credulity.

14. It is requisite, before going farther, to consider specially the prompting to labour for the good of the beloved one,

80 TENDER EMOTION.

which usually characterizes Tender emotion, and constitutes its high social value. The superficial observer has to be told that the feeling in itself is as purely self-regarding as the pleasure of wine or of music. Under it we are induced to seek the presence of beloved objects and to make the requisite sacrifices to gain the end; looking all the while to our own pleasure and to nothing beyond. As incidental to the pursuit, we must perform good offices; we cannot obtain the desired fruition otherwise. But to enter into the feelings of another person, and to seek the gratification of these, in preference to our own, to live the vicarious life of affection, so well shown in the mother, is a result, not of Tenderness, but of Sympathy. Closely as the two facts are allied, they are not inseparable; there may be great Tenderness with little Sympathy (as in children), and great Sympathy with little Tenderness. What we can affirm is that where the power of sympathy exists, beloved objects, by gaining a hold on the attention, receive the largest share; affection is one cause determining the direction that sympathy takes. A strong attachment may be the means of arousing disinterested impulses generally; any one emancipated from exclusive self-regard, by this means, is in some degree disposed to enter into the feelings of indifferent persons. This, too, is shown in the maternal disposition.

The Paternal relationship involves essentially the same modes of feeling and acting, with some few variations. If there be less of personal contact, there is the damming up of the excitement for stronger outbursts; and if the maternal temperament is more alive to tenderness, the father is more struck with the effect of contrast.*

15. The relationship of the Sexes is grounded in the first instance on the sexual constitution, out of which grows an

---

* 'Children,' says Hobbes, 'are a man's power and his honour.'
See in Mill's *Analysis of the Human Mind*, Chapter XXI § 2, a delineation of the Family feelings, in which full justice is done to them without sentimental inflation.

RELATIONSHIP OF THE SEXES. 81

intense appetite, and a special form of physical enjoyment. The element of mere sensual pleasure has always had great potency in human life, as is shown by the institutions and manners of every people. There is, besides, that difference of personal conformation, which makes the one sex a variety as it were to the other, possessing a distinct order of attractions. There can be no doubt of the extensive working of this principle, which puts a limit to the influence of the most perfect forms, and the highest excellence. The merits that we carry about with us are apt to pall upon our taste, and the objects that interest us must be something different, even although inferior.* The greatest affinities grow out of the strongest contrasts ; with this important explanation that the contrast must not be of hostile qualities, but of *supplemental* ones. The one person must not love what the other hates, but the two must mutually supply each other's deficiencies. Affections grounded on disparity so qualified exist between individuals of the same sex. The Platonic friendship was manifested chiefly between men of different ages, and in the relation of master and pupil. But in the two sexes there is a standing contrast, the foundation of a more universal interest. The ideal beauty arising from conformation is on the side of the woman : the interest of the masculine presence lies more in the associations of power.

The feelings stirred by this relationship have been more dwelt upon than any other human sentiment; showing the hold that they take of the human breast both present and in idea, as well as the aptness that there is in them for artistic handling. The real power is not, however, to be measured by poetic language. We can set aside the habitually exaggerated modes of expression, and appeal to the criterion of conduct, to the labours and sacrifices that they give birth to, and the evident satisfaction that they furnish. The excite-

---

* It will be seen, when we come to examine the nature of Self-complacency in the following chapter, that this principle is not unlimited in its operation.

F

## 82 TENDER EMOTION.

ment at its highest pitch, in the torrent of youthful sensations and ungratified desire, is probably the most furious and elated experience of human nature. By every test applied to estimate the force of a state of feeling, this condition ranks supreme. Even at a later stage, under the influence of familiarity, matter of fact, and occasional discords, an amount of interest is maintainable between the opposite sexes that, more than any other circumstance, attests the force that draws them together. Of the attracting bonds, the most constant and enduring is the element of tender emotion. Whatever other feelings are excited, they never fail to evoke this accompaniment, which always remains as the staple of the relationship. Ceasing to be fed by the charms of sense, and quenched by the growth of dislike, affection may come to an end ; but so long as there is anything to attract, the relation is one of tenderness, and all its fruits and manifestations are such as have been described.

### *The Benevolent Affections.*

16. In Benevolence, the main constituent is Sympathy ; which, however, as we have seen, is peculiarly liable to be excited by the tender emotion. The displays familiarly designated Love, Compassion, Kindness, the Heart, are in fact compounded of Sympathy and Tenderness.

Love is tender feeling awakened by an object possessed of charms. Under it the attention is gained, and the sympathies evoked in their fullest measure. Our best energies are at the service of those we love, whatever be the form of the relationship.

It is common to speak of the pleasures of Benevolence, the delight of doing good, but there is a complication here, which the following considerations may help to resolve.

In the first place, love or tender feeling, is by its nature pleasurable, but does not necessarily cause us to seek the good of the object farther than is needful to gratify ourselves in the indulgence of the feeling. It is as purely self-seeking

PLEASURES OF BENEVOLENCE. 83

as any other pleasure, and makes no enquiry as to the feelings of the beloved personality.

In the second place, from a region of the mind quite apart from the tender emotion, arises the principle of Sympathy, or the prompting to take on the pleasures and pains of other beings, and act on them as if they were our own. Instead of being a source of pleasure to us, the primary operation of sympathy is to make us surrender pleasures and to incur pains. This is that paradox of our constitution, already dwelt on *(Senses and the Intellect,* p. 350) and to be again more fully considered.

Thirdly. The engagement of the mind by objects of affection gives them, in preference to others, the benefit of our sympathy; and hence we are specially impelled to work for advancing their pleasures and alleviating their pains. It does not follow that we are made happier by the circumstance; on the contrary, we may be involved in painful and heavy labours.

Fourthly. The *reciprocation* of sympathy and good offices is a great increase of pleasure on both sides; being indeed, under favourable circumstances, one of the greatest sources of human delight. This is not difficult to understand, as will appear when we come to the full explanation of sympathy.

Fifthly. It is the express aim of a well-constituted society, if possible, never to let good offices pass unreciprocated. If the immediate object of them cannot or will not reciprocate in full, as when we relieve the destitute or the worthless, others bestow upon us approbation and praise. Of course, if benevolent actions, instead of being a tax, were self-rewarding, such acknowledgment would have no relevance.

Sixthly. There is a pleasure in the sight of happy beings, and we naturally feel a certain elation in being instrumental to this agreeable effect.

17. Compassion or Pity means sympathy at the instance of weakness or distress. The first step here, too, is an outburst of tenderness. There may be an absence of fascination from sensuous or other charms, and therefore of love in the

# 84 TENDER EMOTION.

full meaning of the word, but it is the peculiarity of the tender feeling, as already explained, to connect itself with states of weakness in ourselves, and to be stimulated in consequence by weakness or distress in others. It is in this situation that the two separate facts of tender feeling and sympathy are so fused as to be indistinguishable; the same name signifying both. An act of discernment is required, such as makes the first step in sympathy, to be aware that a fellow-being is in distress; and becoming aware of it, we are affected by the emotion suitable to distress in ourselves, namely, tenderness, which towards others is compassion, or ' heart,' and puts on the usual display of tender feeling, and also prompts to the completed act of sympathy in rendering assistance or good offices. In tender-hearted constitutions, the melting mood is abundant; in constitutions where sympathy proper is highly developed, the good offices are the chief fact; the one extreme is pointed at by the reproachful term 'sentimentality;' the other, hard and business-like, seems to carve too little interest from the occasion. The tender-hearted will always bestow a tear; the man of un-tender sympathy would provide a remedy if he could, but failing that he does nothing, and appears wanting in heart. The difference is the same as between the person that in his own distresses sits down to bewail his fate, and him that begins a course of exertion for his recovery, deriving no consolation from the other source.

18. The receipt of favours inspires Gratitude, which, simple and natural as it appears, has all the complication that runs through the emotions we are now considering. In one of its aspects it is pure tender feeling, but its real foundations are in sympathy, while it touches on the highly complex sentiment of Justice. The situation of receiving benefits is one of pleasure, and calls forth warm emotion towards the giver, in proportion to the greatness of the pleasure; the unsympathizing mind of childhood stops at this point, the point of thorough selfishness. But with sympathy developed, we enter into the pleasures and pains of the person that has thus engaged our regards, in all respects as with any object of affec-

GRATITUDE. 85

tion. With reference to the highest form of gratitude, which induces us to reciprocate benefits and make acknowledgment in some proportion to the benefits conferred, this must be pronounced an application of the principle of Justice, and, so far from being innate, is an elaborate product, formed for us by society, and varying with social growth and improvement.

The tender feeling is illustrated in a salient manner by the operation of a stroke of signal and unexpected gen erosity. When an enemy, or an injured party, renders good offices, even the indifferent spectator is touched and melted. The mind being totally unprepared, the stimulation would appear to operate as a shock, apart from which circumstance, I see nothing beyond the usual tendency of benevolent actions to inspire a loving outburst.

19. In the equal relationships of life, as in brotherhood, friendship, co-membership of the same society, the occurrence of positions of inequality makes room for the mutual play of benevolence and gratitude ; and the effect is to soften the severe business intercourse of mankind.

20. The Lower Animals are fit subjects of tender feeling, and inspire warm attachments. Their total dependence forbids the rivalries that introduce the taint of anxious watchfulness into the relationships between human beings. By their sensuous charms, their vivacity, their contrast to ourselves, their services, and their devotion, the domestic species are able to touch the chord of tenderness, and enlarge the sphere of our affectionate interests.

21. There is not wanting towards Inanimate things a form of tender sentiment. . A man comes to look upon his house, his fields, his wealth, the implements of his trade, his collections of art and curiosity, his local environment, with something of the associated emotion shown to his family or friends. His regard for these things assumes the character of affection ; when he is deprived of them, the pain is a kind of sorrow.

It is, doubtless, from their original power to give pleasure that such things instigate the tender passion, but as they are unsuited to its proper consummation, the indulgence is ima-

## 86 TENDER EMOTION.

ginary or fictitious, like the love felt towards a person beyond
our reach. We derive a certain satisfaction from personifying
the impersonal objects that give us delight, since by complying with the forms, we can in some measure experience the
reality, of tender regard.

### Sorrow.

22. The pains inflicted upon human beings through their
tender sentiments are of various grades, from the gentle longings of brief absence, to the overwhelming sorrow of the
new-made grave. They are as manifold as the ills that can
happen to any beloved object. They may be mainly summed
up in two classes. On the one hand, our own loss by the
withdrawal of those we love, and, on the other, our share in
the evil that befals them, are the two sides wherein we are
vulnerable through our affections.

With respect to the first case—the deprivation of what we
have become attached to—the pain is deep and intense, according to the power of the attachment, and the pleasure it affords.
When we have cultivated an object of tenderness as a principal
ingredient of our life's comfort, the cutting off of that object
has a reaction of misery and distress, and charges a cup of
bitterness to be drained to the dregs. There is in this effect
much that is common to the pain of severe loss or disappointment in any region of things. The baulking of a dear revenge,
an insult to personal dignity, the wreck of some cherished
hopes, pecuniary losses, a sudden check in anything that the
heart is bent upon, the failure of a prop—all lead to an intensity of mental conflict, constituting one of the severest
forms of human suffering, A large range of associations that
used to yield pleasure and support have suddenly stopped
payment; the cheerful future is all at once darkened. To the
first shock succeeds a physical depression of the brain,
rendering it unfit to be the medium of any ray of comfort;
the spirits are weighed down as with an atmosphere of lead.

Although the first effect of the situation we are supposing
is of a kind common to most forms of heavy loss, the after

SORROW. 87

stages assume a character peculiar to the present class of emotions. When time has healed the rupture, and adapted the mental currents to the new state of things, the tender affection still survives as one of the pleasures of life. The property of ideal persistence that belongs to it, renders it a possession even when the objects have ceased to be. Doubtless the regret continues to have a mixture of the sting with the tenderness, which is what we mean by Sorrow; but the one may abate while the other remains. Grief and lamentation give way to cherished memory.

23. The Social and Ethical bearings of Tender feeling are of high importance, although the best part of the effects is due to the co-operation of sympathy proper. The mere circumstance that we take pleasure in the contact with other beings, makes us court society, and labour to attract, instead of repelling our human kindred. The brutes are moved to this extent, and for the most part prefer companionship to solitude. The effect would be more uniform through all grades of sentient beings, were it not for the presence of other strong passions tending to disunion, which only the higher forms of civilization have been able to subdue in a partial degree.

24. So marked is the influence of tender affection in creating a counter affection in the object of it, that this is naturally considered a great moral lever for the elevation of mankind. Unfortunately it fails with the lowest natures ; owing to the nearly total absence in them of the aptitude for sympathy. An infant, a savage, or even a wild beast, in the act of receiving benefits, embraces the giver, and after repeated kindnesses, may contract a species of affection ; but it is all mere selfishness ; the power of sympathy does not exist, and is not to be evoked ; moral virtue in the proper sense makes no progress. It cannot be too much reflected on that sympathy is an intellectual endowment, and flourishes only under a certain development of intelligence ; the amount requisite being scarcely attained in many individuals and tribes of the human family.

## 88 TENDER EMOTION.

### *Admiration and Esteem.*

25. We may treat as supplementary to the present chapter certain feelings that are not exclusively based upon tender emotion, but either contain it as a principal element, or come into easy alliance with it.

When the feeling of the Sublime suggests a responsive expression to the object of it, we call that response *Admiration.* I mean by the sublime the elation of mind from the spectacle of superior might or excellence, or anything that raises us above our ordinary standard; although the word usually implies only the higher degrees of the feeling. This pleasurable elation easily inspires love as well as wonder, unless the object is marred by ingredients inimical to affection, as when great powers are ill employed. The physical strength of a Hercules, manual skill and dexterity of a high order, artistic power, intellectual force, eminent moral qualities, beauty and refinement, and even the adventitious circumstances of wealth and rank—all tend to raise us above ourselves; and the resulting expression is wonder mixed with love, that is, Admiration. The recognition of superior excellence, in some quality or characteristic that we are strongly alive to, is a frequent beginning of love.

26. *Esteem* is a sentiment applicable to many things that can hardly be said to rouse our admiration. Referring to useful qualities principally, we do not demand for it the attributes of rarity or surpassing excellence. The feeling excited in us towards those that perform their part suitably and well in the relations of life, however numerous they may be, is esteem. We do not compare one man with another; we rather compare a work to be done with the manner of executing it.

The objects of our esteem, therefore, may be said to be all those about us that fulfil the tasks imposed upon them by their situation, or display the virtues that make men useful in society. Industry, independence, fidelity to trust, integrity, truthfulness, practical good sense, are qualities that command our esteem, although they may have no charm to excite admiration. The utilities of life, in the narrow sense of the phrase, imply those precautionary offices valuable only for the prevention of evil, and having in themselves no immediate power of fascination. An artist touches the sources of pleasure by an immediate impulse, a magistrate, lawyer, or physician is valued because of the evil that he can ward off or remove.

The emotion of esteem is a reflected or associated feeling, growing out of our sense of the mischief prevented, and the good achieved, by the performance of the social virtues. Knowing well the miseries that accrue from neglect and carelessness of every description, we feel a lively and cheering sensation of relief from an opposite kind of conduct, which easily passes into a certain tender regard towards the persons. The feeling of being saved from impending or possible miseries is a very prevalent one, varying chiefly in degree according to the nature of the danger. There is always a distinct trace of pleasure, and a cheering tone connected with it, and in extreme cases the effect may rise to a burst of delight. The removal of actual pain yields the condition in the most effective form ; next to that is the prevention of anticipated pain. This ideal form of the pleasure is what connects itself with the labours and precautions of human industry, and makes us feel an interest in the character of our fellow-workers. The cheering sentiment of misery prevented rises up when we see a man skilled in his vocation, and faithful to all his engagements. The prompting of tenderness that the pleasure involves with it, helps to constitute our esteem or regard for the individual.

The sentiment of esteem, although not of itself a first-class emotion in respect of contributing to our happiness, is nevertheless a calculable element ; and the more so that we are keenly alive to the evils of careless living. When at all strongly developed, as in the case of persons coming much under our observation, a current of considerable strength flows habitually in the presence or recollection of those persons. Not only do they give us that amount of pleasure signified by the phrase 'causing an interest,' but they become

## 90 TENDER EMOTION.

a power over our actions, opinions, and sentiments. All this is implied in the meaning of the words 'regard,' 'respect,' which indicate an interested gaze with a deferential disposition. In the bustle of life, where every one is struggling to maintain a position, we make room for those we esteem, showing them preference, and finding a pleasure in serving them.

Our illustration of the state of fear, or terror, may have served to lay open still more fully the roots of this emotion of regard, by showing the condition of mind that we are delivered from on the occasion when it is felt. The blessings of the state of confidence ought there to have appeared in a strong light.

Admiration and Esteem are emotions well suited to promote our happiness as members of society. Not only do they bind us in warm relationship to a number of our fellow-beings, but their expression in language is an easy and agreeable effort, and a bond of sympathy between us and third parties. Our conversation is frequently made up of allusions to those that we esteem and admire ; and when we address persons sharing in the same feelings. the effect is animating and agreeable.

### Veneration—the Religious Sentiment.

27. The sentiment of Veneration is a compound of tender feeling with other emotions.

I postponed the discussion of the Religious Sentiment to the present chapter, that we might have all the ingredients of it clearly before us. The composition of this feeling is well expressed by the familiar collocation, 'wonder, love, and awe.' The vastness of the power presiding over the world stretches the feeling of wonder, or the Sublime, to the utmost limit. The paternal and benign aspect of Deity prompts a Tender sentiment. The sense of Dependence, the irresistible might and the governing hand, working under the shroud of darkness, inspire Fear and submission. The elevation and purification of the religious sentiment consist in making the

## ELEMENTS OF THE RELIGIOUS SENTIMENT.

two first elements predominate over the third. The grossest and most grovelling superstitions are those where terror prints its deepest mark.*

---

\* The following remarks relate to some of the influences that seem to have operated in drawing forth the religious regards of the early Greeks.

1. The grand and imposing powers of nature, including all the objects that act on the human mind through the sense of might, terror, fascination, or other subduing emotions. The aspect of immense power, force, or energy, always tends to put the bet.olders into a submissive mood, and to impress upon them the main feature of religious regard. The will and power of the individual man is utterly abashed and confounded in presence of the stormy winds or the ocean billow; and the contemplative mind cannot but feel that a superior and overruling might dwells in the sun, the moon, and the firmament of stars. The germ of religious feeling is found in the first outgoings of the subdued spirit towards these mighty objects. Not only is there an irresistible inducement to bow the head and bend the proud will before the vastness of nature, but there is also a strong feeling of comfort and delight in the exercise. Moreover, the submissive mind readily passes to the conception of the benignity and kindness of the supernatural powers, while the stubborn spirit can count upon nothing but fiery hostility and indignation. Man, feeling himself weak, naked, ignorant, in the midst of a vast and terrible creation, is in general but too glad to acknowledge and feel his weakness and dependence, and to express this feeling in whatever way he is able.

The aspect of *might* and power is thus the foremost of all religious influences. The effect of this is enhanced by every species of danger, or by the additional influence of *terror*, which in the early stages of the world is almost inseparable from the contemplation of nature. Terror is the fruit of uncertainty. If we see a large agency at work, we feel ourselves subdued into deferential feeling by the sight; but if we understand clearly its whole character and the course of its proceeding—if we can tell whence it cometh, and whither it goeth—we feel no terror at the movement. But this clear knowledge of the course of the world, was impossible in the early ages; no man could tell all the consequences bound up in an eclipse, or assign the causes of an epidemic, and the painful uncertainty as to the larger operations of the world, kept up a perpetual susceptibility to fear or terror. But terror is preeminently a subduing influence; it can drive the mind of man to the most debilitating prostration; it produces an amount of submission approaching to abjectness, and the loss of all self-reliance and independence of spirit. Hence this, in addition to the natural influence of mere might and majesty, readily explains the submissiveness of tone so early assumed towards the great powers and aspects of the world. The sun, the moon, the stars, the winds, the seas, the mountains, the rivers, have all a naturally subduing influence upon minds susceptible to grandeur and power, and would inevitably

## 92 TENDER EMOTION.

Veneration is the name given to the state of mind comprehending both religious regard, and a sentiment drawn out by the more commanding and august of our fellow-beings. The emotion is directed towards objects of majesty and greatness, that have also the power of touching the mind with awe. An element of love is essential also, seeing that we are drawn with a certain fondness to whatever we venerate. That attitude, and those actions implied in worship, are the embodiment and outgoings of the emotion, and all have their spring

induce feelings that could readily take the shape of religious reverence and awe.

There is, over and above the subduing effects of might and terror, an influence of irresistible *fascination* exerted by some objects over the human mind. Probably every one has had experience of some object or other whether a person or an inanimate thing, which attracted the attention, and regards with a power of complete entrancement and fascination; and this effect, although most commonly occurring towards persons, is not unfrequent towards natural objects. Dr. Kitto, in his work on Deafness—a calamity which had befallen himself—informs us that there were two objects that always acted on his mind with a power of fascination so intense that it took an effort to prevent him from regarding them as divinities (this, but for his rational convictions, he would have done with the greatest zest and delight): these were the moon and a tree. With reference to these two things, not only could he conceive the facility of their becoming objects of divine worship, but he had a difficulty in conceiving the possibility of resisting their fascination. The worship of the heavenly bodies, and the consecration of groves and plantations in minds constituted like his, would have been unavoidable.

Much of the fascination that now expends itself in poetic feeling and mere sensuous enjoyment, would, in the early ages, form an inducement to that submission of heart and soul which led to the deification of nature. Wordsworth states, that to his mind everything in nature seemed *clothed with being*, or induced in him a train of thoughts and feelings corresponding to life, activity, and animation, which effects he endeavoured by his poetry to induce on other minds, that thereby the face of the world might become more rich, suggestive, and stirring. Prohibited from attributing actual vitality and personal functions alike to the grandest and the meanest of material things, the poet now-a-days must do so by conscious fiction; but in times when the actual properties of objects were little known, when a bewildering haze of mystery and terror overspread everything, and when the minds of men cherished rather than discouraged this mode of looking at nature, a far bolder flight was admissible, and the agreeable fiction might be set forth with all the air of truth and reality.

## RELIGION IMPLIES GOVERNMENT.

in one or other of the component elements now assigned. The language of admiration is coupled with expressions of fond regard and profound homage; and the symbolical acts and detailed ritual are of the same character. The feeling itself is deep, powerful, and engrossing in minds once attuned to it, constituting much of the happiness or misery of life— ruling the conduct, directing the thoughts, and influencing the belief to an extent corresponding to the magnitude of the emotions that enter into it. The task of reducing the proud mind to the requisite tone of submissive reverence, makes the great struggle of the religious life; and it is only after this is accomplished, that the warm and comforting character of devotion is a matter of experience.

An absolute power over the human destiny is the essential feature of any religion. There may be combined with this an ethical code for the guidance of men's conduct in their earthly relations; there may also be added a highly artistic ritual, and a poetic strain of conceptions; but religion is different from morals, and is not to be confounded with fine art. It is the rule of a supernatural governor that makes the wide distinction between devotion and theatrical excitement.

Human beings are occasionally objects of veneration, as when power is mixed with benignity, and wisdom sits upon age. To parents and benefactors we pay this homage. Those that are long dead affect our imagination with a mystic awe, which swells the sentiment of reverence by the dread power connected with death. To nations, such as a large portion of the Chinese, who refrain from the conception of supernatural government, and therefore are devoid of religion, the Past has still a power to awe and fascinate; departed ancestry receives the attentions of worship.

# CHAPTER VII.

## EMOTIONS OF SELF.

1. THERE are various important meanings attached to the term 'self,' besides the one specially intended in the present chapter.

I. It being impossible to recognise existence in any shape, except as related to the individual mind, each one's universe may be looked upon as coinciding with self. This is the doctrine usually termed Idealism.

II. It is common to recognise a distinction between the Subject mind, and a something supposed to be distinct from, external to, acting upon that mind, called matter, the external or extended world, the object, the non-ego, or not-self. There is undoubtedly a distinction between the mind as sentient and the thing felt, between the percipient and the perception, the concipient and the conception, and so forth; but not as I imagine amounting to self in the one case and the negation of self in the other. The real difference between the subject and the object self, I have already endeavoured to indicate (*Contiguity*, § 38).

III. There is an act of Introspection whereby we regard the feelings and operations of the mind as something to be controlled or to be studied; presenting a contrast to the employment of the organs upon outward things. When we restrain our fears, or our anger, with a view to mental discipline, or when we study the laws of thought and feeling as a matter of information, we are sometimes said to be *self-conscious* as opposed to ploughing, spinning, building, or the acts and operations performed upon the outer world.

IV. The Impulsiveness, spontaneity, or original tendencies of our nature, viewed in contrast with the check, guidance, or influence of impressions from without, is an aspect of self. The difference is great between the outburst of natural vigour, reckless and uncontrolled, and Circumspection, or restraint imposed by a lively sense of consequences. There is here a fundamental difference in the characters of individuals; some abounding in spontaneity, and little sensible to good or bad results, while others are sensitive in the extreme, and perhaps deficient in natural impulse. The vice of the one is rashness, and of the other, inaction.

V. The total pleasures and pains, wants, desires, aims, and actions of an individual, constitute self in contradistinction to all indifferent things. What touches our own welfare, and still more, what we feel and act upon as such, is our end of life, the collective engrossment of our being. This Life-interest is a well-characterized meaning of the term in question.

VI. There is a certain class of our collective interests that does not include the welfare of any other beings, either simply passing them by, or positively detracting from them; the sentiments of friendship, love, devotion, our sympathies and duties being left out. Self-love (or, when intended to be blamed, Selfishness) is the specific designation of this region of our regards.

Even when we adopt one or more living beings into the circle of our regards, we may in our devotion to them oppose a selfish aspect to all who are beyond. As members of a family we may renounce self, one to another, but assume it in a high degree towards strangers. Self-love, therefore, starts, not simply from the individual, but from the smaller societies in whose separate interiors devotion may reign.

2. We are at present to consider a class of emotions still more narrow and select, having reference to our own possession of the qualities that, when seen in other men, inspire the sentiments of love, admiration, reverence, esteem, or the opposites of these. Whatever attributes impress our minds

96    EMOTIONS OF SELF.

as displayed by our fellow-men, produce also a peculiar effect as belonging to ourselves. There is a strong pleasure in observing and contemplating our own excellence, power, grandeur, or other imposing characteristics. This is a very special mode of self-regarding emotion ; the name ' self-gratulation ' is not inappropriate to express it. ' Pride' and ' conceit ' are other names. ' Self-esteem ' implies the habitual or formed estimate that each person has of self. ' Self-complacency ' brings into view the pleasure or delight experienced in contemplating one's own good qualities.

The emotion takes a somewhat different turn, and is usually much more satisfying and intense, when the characteristic excellencies of the individual call forth open manifestations of admiration, love, or esteem from those around. For this gratification, and for the desire that it begets, we have such names as 'vanity,' ' love of approbation,' ' desire of fame or glory,' and so forth. The situation of being admired by others would seem at first sight to be more simple and elementary than being admired by self; but I think it will turn out that this last is the more elementary of the two.

There is a third sentiment differing from either of the above, although liable to be mixed up with them, namely, the feeling of the possession and exercise of Power of any sort. The passion for influence, domination, and the production of large effects on the face of the world, is a marked form of egotism not to be confounded with either self-gratulation or the love of glory, both which may follow in the train of the sentiment of power, although they may also be absent from it. The pleasure of disposing of vast interests, and moving a wide machinery, may be so absorbing as to induce a complete disregard alike to self-approbation and to the voice of the multitude. The exposition of that sentiment will be taken apart. The present chapter will comprise the two other groups of feelings, with a slight reference to the more extended self-interest and egotistical promptings indicated in the fifth meaning above referred to.

## SELF-GRATULATION AND SELF-ESTEEM.

3. Here, as already said, the *object* of the emotion is some quality, excellence, or distinction, beheld in one's self, of such a nature as to draw forth demonstrations of lively admiration, reverence, love, or esteem, when displayed by a fellow-being. We have seen, in discussing these last-named forms of manifested emotion, what are the things that call them into exercise. Beginning with Bodily Strength, we find it both admired when seen, and also exciting in the possessor a feeling of satisfaction. So Mechanical Skill, ingenuity, dexterity, strike a beholder with wonder, and to a similar extent please the individual's self. The various modes of Intellectual Power have the same twofold efficiency. According as we are moved to astonishment and ecstacy by a great display of intellectual power, whether in thought or in speech, in originality, or in acquired knowledge, we are apt to receive delight from the notion of ourselves as exerting those powers. In like manner, the Artist feels elated by the production of a work such as he would account great if another man were the author. In short, any kind of productive talent or ability, in whatever region manifested, is a source of pleasure to the possessor, provided he is of a nature to be impressed and pleased with the particular effects. The youth, whose soul is charmed by military achievements, is already formed for taking pleasure in the profession of arms.

There is another class of objects of the emotion, different from the putting forth of imposing active energies, namely, those accompaniments of the person that impress the beholder, without any expenditure of bodily or mental force, such as personal attractions, the decorations of dress and equipage, material splendour, property, rank, high connections, and dignified associations. By these artificial adjuncts, a human being destitute of active ability, and abstaining from every mode of useful exertion, may still be an imposing object of regard. The <u>Great Lama</u> of Thibet, and the monarch that

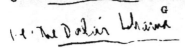

98                 EMOTIONS OF SELF.

reigns, but does not govern, have this kind of impressiveness over and above any derived from their own qualities. By these attributes, too, the owner is affected with the pleasurable feeling of complacency when naturally susceptible to their influence.

4. The *physical* side of self-complacency is a mere variety of the expression of pleasure. If the emotion is not an ultimate phase of the mind, neither is its embodiment. The elements that we resolve it into, will determine it physically as well as mentally. What appears to the spectator, is a certain pleasing, cheerful expression, a look of serene satisfaction and passive enjoyment, with close relations to the aspect of tender feeling, but wanting the element of outward regards. Perhaps the strongest feature in the expression is the smile.

5. To come now to the *mental* side, or the emotion itself. I cannot reckon it one of the primitive emotions of the human mind. It seems impossible that it should be so, considering that the circumstances do not arise until a certain development of the individual powers has been reached. We must first have that appreciation of bodily or mental superiority which inspires us with admiration, fascination, or awe; we are then prepared for the further effect begotten when we discern, or think we discern, such high qualities in ourselves. The question therefore arises, whether the pleasure accruing from the situation is a distinct mode of consciousness arising for the first time, or whether some emotion already operating is made to vibrate in a new manner. If we can resolve the feeling into one more general, we make the desirable step of shortening the description by a reference to known, or previously ascertained properties.

I am of opinion that the self-complacent feeling results from a burst of the *tender emotion*, directed upon self as a personality or as an object of habitual regard, solicitude, and affection. As the mother contracts a constant bent of care and fond attentions to her infant, so any one may build up a framework of associations with their own collective personality. A man may not only be the subject of successive emotions,

## EMOTION OF SELF-COMPLACENCY.

pleasurable or painful, and the author of a series of acts and operations, but may also form in his mind an idea of the totality of those feelings and energies, and make that total the root, origin, or centre, of a strong sentiment, such as that of the mother, just alluded to. For example, each of us bestows certain attentions upon our outward person, being moved thereto by the pains incurred through neglect, and the pleasures resulting from acts of cleansing, &c. Now it is possible, in consequence of these recurrent attentions, to fall into a train of special sentiment or regard towards this portion of self, to allow our tender emotion to flow, and the mind to be engrossed, during those operations, until at last an exceedingly strong bond of affection is knit between our mental regards and that element of our corporeal concerns. Or the individual may be so constituted as that this peculiar growth may never be formed. The impulses to perform the daily routine of bodily purification may exist and prompt the needful observances; but the bent of the mind, and the flow of tender feeling, may never take a direction towards this particular object. In such a case, the motives that one commences with remain without being added to; no new or associated pleasure is generated, and no tendency to enlarge the spot occupied by this department is found to exist. To take another example: one may be stimulated by a natural curiosity to go forward in the acquisition of knowledge, so as to sustain the pursuit, day after day, throughout a whole life. The same motive of curiosity may continue unchanged and unmodified from the first to the last. The mental situation is here a very simple one. There is a renewed pleasure from every additional piece of information, a craving growing out of absence from the sources of knowledge, and an exercise of voluntary energy to read, observe, or study, as the opportunity presents itself. But now, as in the former case, the repeated exercises of the body and mind in this field of pursuit may themselves occupy the attention and regard. Along with the original emotion of the love of knowledge, there may spring up an associated or acquired emotion towards the machinery

## EMOTIONS OF SELF.

and operations of the individual mind whereby the search is maintained. This is not more wonderful than the factitious feeling towards books in general that grows up in the mind of the student, or towards money in the miser. Besides the interest taken in the primary end, there is an interest also taken in that part of the personality that has so often realized for us our desired pleasure.

There are, then, a number of original stimulants planted in our constitution, each working its own proper course towards a distinct object—appetite for food, for warmth, for knowledge, &c. There is a superadded effect when these various operations are themselves made a subject of attentive interest and regard, as we might regard a fascinating natural object, or as the mother is attracted to the child. The bent of the constitution may be such as to abstain from this secondary reference, being entirely engrossed and satisfied by the primary pursuit. Cases approaching to this exclusive externality of regard may be met with. There are persons so completely engaged in following out their first impulses, as scarcely ever to attend to themselves in the act of doing so. Such persons are destitute of self-consciousness; they neither constitute self into an object of affectionate regard, nor would they be qualified to render any account of their thoughts and feelings as a department of knowledge. On the other hand, there is a tendency in men more or less to form out of themselves a certain portion of the self-conscious interest—to look with a warm eye upon some portion of their activity, and acquire a tenderness for that as for a second person. This favoured region may be some select part of the individual— as the manual vigour, or the personal display; or the tendency may become general, and embrace all the principal phases of the emotional and active life. A new interest is thus formed, a centre of gratification and of disappointment, with appropriate stimulants and applications. The original impulses remain in their strength, while an addition is made to their number by the habit of taking cognizance of them at their work. There is thus a broad and solid distinction between

## TENDER EMOTION TURNED TOWARDS SELF. 101

the conscious and the self-conscious, between the human being that simply feels and acts accordingly, and the human being that has made that train of feeling and acting itself an object of affection and consideration, as if it were another personality. This is a step to be gone through, a process that is often, though not always, fallen into ; but when once entered upon, we are then not only conscious, but are, over and above, self-conscious. When the acquisition is made, the individual is a fit subject for the peculiar sensibilities discussed in this chapter. The collective amount of all the regions of our being that have drawn forth these regards, constitutes that self wherein we can feel complacency and enjoy admiration. If, as is quite possible, we do not contract any fond interest in some portion of self, the susceptibility is not generated. We may instead have concentrated all our attentions and all our warm feeling upon another being—a child, or beloved person; that, with the primary interests of our own being, may absorb our mental resources. We should then derive our pleasures partly from our original susceptibilities, and partly from the exercise of fondness towards this other being. We should enjoy the spectacle of its excellences, and the approbation conferred upon it from without; while in consequence of not having cultivated a similar strain of fondness towards our own personality, we should have little delight in the excellences displayed, or the approbation earned in that quarter.

In the explanation of the feeling before us, therefore, we start from the case of tender emotion developed and made habitual towards an outward object, whether a person or a thing. The affection thus formed and cultivated is a source of delight ; we receive a throb of satisfaction every time the beloved object appears to the view, or rises to the thoughts ; the constant presence of it is a cheering and supporting influence diffused over the life. All the good that comes to it is so much additional pleasure conferred upon us. If we can discover in our friend any qualities that would excite our admiration towards a stranger, a twofold delight is experienced ;

## EMOTIONS OF SELF.

and the greater the affection, the greater the delight. The same remarks equally apply to the case of the tender regard contracted to self. This object of our attention, consideration, and fond love, supposing we have made it such, has all those properties now described as belonging to a child, a friend, a pet, a piece of property, &c. The tenderness of our being is thereby stimulated ; the discovery of good qualities in self causes a glow of mingled admiration and fond love ; an occasion of special good towards this object is a moment for the outburst of elation and tender feeling. The two cases are parallel, not to say identical. The real source of the emotion is the copious fountain denominated tenderness, which overspreads the whole environment of our being, attaching us to a wide circle of living persons, inanimate instruments, memories of the past, ideas of the distant, and imaginations of the future. Allowed to run often, and long, in one favoured direction, that emotion knits a threefold cord, and fascinates and sways our daily career. This is true whether the exaggerated current tends outwards, or overflows one's own personality. Wherever the sentiment exists, one or more of those intense links is sure to be forged ; and circumstances will determine whether an egotism or an altruism is reared. Most commonly both the one and the other are found, although with varying proportions.

6. If such be the proper account of self-complacency as a sentiment of our nature, it is not necessary to dwell at great length upon the systematic description of its character. Referring to the characteristics of the generic sensibility as set forth in the foregoing chapter, and to the familiar experience of ourselves and our fellows, we need not hesitate to pronounce it as eminently pleasurable in quality and large in quantity ; as remarkably enduring in continuance, and enjoyable at little cost. When we are unfit for everything besides, in the depths of exhausted nature, and in the last throbs of sinking existence, complacency, as well as love, may glow and burn. Both as a stream of positive gratification, and as neutralizing pain, disappointment, and sorrow, the well-developed passion at-

SELF-ESTEEM. 103

tests its power. In counting up the catalogue of his own excellences, the self-complacent man may beguile a weary hour; from the multitude and splendour of his outward appendages, he may find solace in the midst of pain. As regards Volition, everything advanced respecting the tender sentiment in general is applicable here; while the mode of Intellectual persistence is the same in both. The feeling is one mighty to direct the attention, and influence the current of the recollections and thoughts; thus storing the mind, and quickening the memory with incidents bearing upon self. Notable, too, is the power of this, as of every strong emotion, upon Belief; in putting forward the favourable aspect of self, and so utterly excluding other aspects, that we can only take account of the good side.

7. Let us now attend shortly to the specific forms of the feeling before us.

What is expressed more particularly by Self-complacency, is the act of taking pleasure in the contemplation of one's own merits, excellences, productions, and various connexions; the carving out of morsels of delight from the indulged affection towards all that relates to self. There is an open display of the feeling, accompanied at the same time by the desire of sympathy, when one endeavours to engage the interest of others by narrations and details relative to one's individual history and concerns.

Self-esteem and Self-conceit imply a settled opinion and habitual estimate of the value of our own capabilities, to which follows a train of consequences exactly similar to what we have noted on the subject of esteem generally. The preference of self to those less esteemed, the respect for our own good qualities, is shown in various ways, and perhaps most conspicuously in the feature of Self-confidence. The trust in our own powers, and the conviction in our own opinions, because they are ours, if not a sign of mere sanguine temperament, are criteria of our self-esteem. A still further test is supplied by the contentment derived from the estimate of self, and the independence of any concurring estimate from

104 EMOTIONS OF SELF.

other persons. This Self-sufficing affection is respectable, as evincing moral strength, although somewhat repulsive from its isolation.

Self-respect and Pride indicate the force of the feeling as a volitional spur, or a motive in the conduct. Having embraced a high valuation of our own character, we are induced to save that intact, by avoiding every course incompatible therewith. It becomes an aim to honour the esteem that we feel for ourselves by acting up, on all occasions, to the standard thus fixed; and our actions, in addition to their primary intention, have a charm through their keeping with this self-estimation. The workman has a proper pride in not dismissing from his hands a performance unworthy of his character for skill in his own eyes. The man that values his own integrity, takes proportional pains not to impair it.

8. A marked variety of the emotion here treated of is Self-pity, which strongly illustrates and confirms the above view of the emotion generally, since it is an unequivocal effusion of genuine tender feeling towards self—a most real feeling, not well understood by superficial observers and often very strong in the sentimentally selfish, but quite real in all who have any tender susceptibilities, and sometimes their only outlet.

9. Emulation and the sense of Superiority are related to the present head. Rigorously speaking, there is no such thing as positive or absolute excellence. Comparison is the means of determining merit, and the occasion of awakening the susceptibility to worth. A tool may be well adapted to its end, and for that reason may cause us to value and esteem it; but we become alive to the circumstance by seeing the great superiority it has by the side of a number of others. This feeling of superior merit is, therefore, the ladder whereby we ascend to the highest elevation of self-esteem—as the highest mountains are elevated in appearance by those beneath them. No doubt there are other sentiments mixed up with the comparison, besides the one occupying us at present, but they are not such as to impair the force of the above observation.

The feeling of Envy is much more general in its application. Referring to everything that is desirable in the condition of some more fortunate personage, there is combined a strong wish for the like good to self, with an element of malevolence or hatred towards the favoured party.

10. There is now another side of the emotion which needs to be glanced at. And first of Modesty and Humility; which imply the absence or suppression of those various forms of self-gratulatory feeling. The modest or humble man draws but moderately on the pleasure arising from complacency, and keeps within the mark, in the estimate formed of his own virtues. The beauty of this character, in the view of the spectator or critic, lies in the sort of *generosity* in renouncing a considerable portion of one of the prized luxuries of human life. To pretend to take no pleasure in self, and to set no value on one's good qualities, is completely to overstretch possibility; but exactly as a generous man surrenders to others a share of his worldly means, a modest man remits a portion of his self-esteem to allow a freer scope to his esteem for others.

11. Humiliation and Self-abasement result from a lively sense of the weakness, worthlessness, and demerits of the individual. This is a state of positive pain—the pain of wounded self-tenderness—which may be compared to what we feel when a beloved object has turned out worthless. The flow of affection usually carries with it a sentiment and belief of good qualities inhering in those we love, and the discovery of the opposite, is a shock of revulsion of a most distressing kind. The situation is not confined to the present case, but arises whenever any strong feeling is violently checked. The anguish of a sense of demerit is severe, because of its being liable to recur indefinitely. Just as the death of a friend is more easily surmounted than his disgrace, so a fall in our own eyes leaves a rankling sting behind; perhaps the very worst quality that can belong to suffering. The term Self-abasement implies the consequence, and, in some measure, the remedy, of a sense of demerit; inasmuch as it supposes that

106 EMOTIONS OF SELF.

the individual has surrendered the previous estimate of self, and adopted one suitable to the altered circumstances. By Remorse, we understand the strongest form of self-reproach, arising from the deep downfall of self-respect and esteem. The awakened criminal drinks a cup of bitterness from this source, before experiencing the other fruits of his misdeeds. The intensity of the infliction is great, in proportion to the pitch of self-respect, and to the degree that the act in question runs counter to it. The Hindoo betrayed into tasting animal food is visited with the pangs of remorse, while iterated perjury leaves his mind at peace. Sometimes for real crimes against society, and at other times (like Œdipus) for involuntary offences, or ceremonial infringements, human beings have given themselves up to a life of incurable remorse, presenting some of the sternest and most tragic exhibitions of human history. The Greek drama has immortalized more than one development of this melancholy situation.

### LOVE OF ADMIRATION.

12. It is next to be seen in what way Approbation, Admiration, and Praise operate upon the sentiment of self. It is a fact that one of the most intense human delights grows out of the commendation of our fellows ; the pleasure being akin to the foregoing, but greatly heightened in amount. As on a former occasion, we must here revert to the working of the great principle of sympathy, by which every feeling of our nature may be increased in degree and protracted in duration. There are many cases where pleasure is limited by the inability of the system to support more than a given amount. The emotions all tend to consume the vital energies ; and apart from the introduction of various and far-fetched stimulants, the capability of happiness (or of unhappiness), might be indefinitely augmented by adding to the strength, or in some way economizing the expenditure of the physical powers. Now, the sympathy and support of others have an effect in lightening the pressure of any excitement, thus enabling it to burn

## SUPPORT GIVEN BY APPROBATION.

brighter and last longer.* Just as the faltering courage is reanimated by the confident and emphatic assurances of a friend, and as a sentiment of hope may be kindled in despair by the elation of a multitude, so the feebly-felt satisfaction of self-complacency may become a power of joy when a second party joins in sympathetic accord. The susceptibility to other men's expressed emotions is a thing acquired during early experience, and there are very various degrees of its development, as I shall afterwards illustrate; but so far as the property has been evolved, there is attaching to it this power of extending the support and diminishing the waste of emotional excitement. Such is the main operation of an influence from without.

Not only is the power of enjoying our self-gratulatory sentiment extended by sympathy, but we are also confirmed in that estimate of self, and in that fond affection which is the foundation of the whole. Indeed, it is possible that the impulse to self-consciousness may have its start in foreign' influence; our own good qualities, bodily or mental, may become for the first time the object of attention and regard by the notice taken of them by those about us. The self-regarding tendency may be checked in the bud by the chilling discouragement of parents and teachers, or exaggerated and fostered by a system of lavish approbation. In the very same way would our attachment to a second person be promoted by the influence of a third.

We may remark farther that an offering of praise makes an occasion for the self-complacent emotion to flow out, being one of the appropriate stimulants of the emotion. As a sweet odour to the sense of smell, and a melodious sound to the ear, so is a compliment to self-complacency. The opportunities for this feeling partly arise within one's own circle of avoca-

---

* Sympathy may, however, operate as a new or exciting cause, and make a sum total still more exhausting. I mean that it is easier to keep up a certain amount of self-gratulatory feeling with the aid of other people's expressed approbation and support, than by contemplating our merits in lonely isolation.

108    EMOTIONS OF SELF.

tions, as in the various displays that we make of our powers and appendages. The notice of our fellows contributes an additional round of stimulants.

Nor must we overlook a circumstance that renders one's need of the good opinion and favourable sentiments of others more near and direct than the need of one's own good opinion; which is the association of numerous substantial benefits with that favourable expression, and of equally, if not more, numerous evils from the opposite. Although this is a secondary, or derived, effect, we cannot easily over-estimate the influence of it on the human mind, so habituated to the dread of possible, probable, and actual suffering from other beings, as to feel a cheering glow whenever anything is conveyed that gives assurance of the contrary.

The pleasure of Approbation, and the counter pain of Disapprobation, belong manifestly to the general group of emotions of Harmony and Conflict; and accordingly their respective characteristics are fitly described as elation and depression of mental tone. Likewise, as emotions of Relativity, their degree is essentially governed by comparison or contrast; there must be novelty in the circumstances to give the full effect to a tribute of praise.

13. Having premised these general observations upon the altered character of the sentiment of self under foreign stimulation, we must now glance rapidly at the new aspects thus evolved, as we find them signified in the current phraseology.

Mere Approbation implies the lowest, or most moderate form of intimating a favourable opinion. There is supposed by it a certain doubt that has to be set at rest; and frequently, as in the case of superiors with their servants, nothing more is intended than that a piece of work has come up to the mark. Approbation may, therefore, mean only that we have passed an ordeal without incurring censure or rebuke.

14. Praise and Admiration are always something positive, and usually give rise to a throb of self-complacent feeling in the person addressed. Compliment is a name for the more

## APPLAUSE.—FAME. 109

familiar forms of praise, such as any one may be supposed capable of earning. Flattery and Adulation imply excess, if not untruth, in the matter of compliment. The bestowal of these (within certain assignable limits) is cultivated in polite society as a pleasure-giving art. Glory expresses the most open and ostentatious form of human admiration. The triumphal procession, the crowning in the Capitol, the trumpet notes, 'the tumult of acclaim,' thrill and intoxicate the susceptible bosom beyond every known influence. For such rewards pain is despised, fatigue endured, danger braved, life perilled. Reputation, Fame, may be bestowed in public ovation, or in the multiplied echoes of a wide society. To extend one's name over the world, and to distant ages, fires the human breast as the sublimest destiny that any mortal can succeed to. Posthumous fame, indeed, has been treated as an absurdity and a paradox, since it does not begin till the subject of it is dead. But this is only one of a thousand forms of ideal satisfaction, or the pleasure derived from anticipation, and the imagined. The heir of fame is fired, while yet alive, by the honours that will attend his name; and the acts of homage paid to those already departed operate in reality upon him. Honour includes all those tokens of respect, consideration, and deference instituted in society for those in elevated place, whether through office, rank, or reputation achieved. Applause may come from the many, as in the theatre, or from the few, as in the more recondite walks of the human intellect. In either case, the effect on the recipient is materially determined by his reciprocal feeling towards his admirers. The hurras of the mob have in all civilized nations been distinguished from the esteem of qualified judges. There are a number of less demonstrative forms of giving honour. The mere gaze of the eye is a symbol of esteem, accepted as such by the praise-thirsty soul. Compliment can be conveyed by implication or innuendo, and in this form is free from the objection to open flattery, which often shocks a sensitive mind. The *invidia* that accompanies high honours is strongly felt by some constitutions, and is probably one of the circum-

110                    EMOTIONS OF SELF.

stances that make one revolt from the grosser forms of praise.
Modern society has thrown a certain discredit on the enjoyment of the self-gratulatory pleasures, and hence a feeling of
shame is apt to be engendered when a person is marked out
as the subject of formal applause. For all these reasons, the
transformation of the open into the more covert modes of pay-
ing honour has been thought a refinement. Vanity and Vain-
glory signify that the individual is active in the cultivation
of self-importance, canvassing as it were for distinction. The
open boaster, not satisfied with his own feeling of esteem,
insists on the concurrence of others, and, if people do not
choose of their own accord to pay him regard, he detains them
on every opportunity with the circumstantials of his own
glorification.

15. The arts of *Politesse* lie mainly within the circle of
our present subject. The courtesies of life to a certain extent
manifest kindliness and sympathy, but the larger portion
refers to the *amour propre* of the person addressed. The
compliment direct, the demonstration of respect, the tendering of honour, and the expression of deference, are the positive forms of politeness ; while an equal attention is enforced
to all the methods of avoiding whatever might wound the
self-importance of our fellows. The self-complacent sentiment
is the basis of one of the great ' interests ' of society, like life
or property, and laws are made for protecting it. It is not
allowable even to declare one's honest convictions when the
dignity of others would suffer mortification. People are not
always at liberty to speak the truth to ' ears polite.' *

We are thus led to recognise the present emotion as giving
birth to a pretty. large fraction of the gratifications and
delights of human life. Founded, as we have seen, in the
great region of tender feeling, the outgoings of the sentiment
are a pleasure superadded upon the affectionate relationships.

---

\* It is worth remarking here that this restraint on sincerity is carried
too far ; and in more barbarous times and places, still farther, as in Oriental
politeness.

## DISAPPROBATION. 111

A man's happiness, says Paley, is very much dependent upon the reception he everywhere meets with. To have so impressed those about us with feelings of love and esteem, as to be continually encountering the tokens of their regard, is a grand object to aspire to, and a rich harvest of fruition. There is a reciprocal effect of admiration in drawing forth the kindly sentiments, and as it were the gratitude, of the admired object. Hence a mode of conciliating the favour of others, and also of corruption for the gaining of ends.

16. As applause is but the agreeable heightening of self-gratulation by sympathy, and reflected heat, so Censure, Disapprobation, Dispraise, Abuse, Libel, Scorn, Infamy, increase the feeling of self-humiliation, or at least increase the pain of it. According as the opposites of these make the warmth and sunshine of existence, do they themselves affect the mind with misery and terror, and the sense of outer darkness. If any one is conscious of wrong, of some crime against society, of a gross failure in undertakings, of remissness in duty, or of assuming undeserved privileges, the public indignation crushes him to the dust; seized with penitence and remorse he resigns all claim to consideration, and is ready to compound with the offended powers by a criminal's doom. It is to be noted, however, that disapprobation has usually more in it than merely taking down the self-complacency of the individual. In many cases the tender feelings are outraged as well, while often, as above remarked, it is but a prelude to more substantial evils. As we are accustomed to follow up admiration with other advantages, so when a man has strongly roused our disfavour, we are not content with slighting his personal qualities, but are ready to damage his happiness in many ways besides.

17. The feeling of Shame is resolved by a reference to the dread of being condemned, or ill-thought of, by others. Declared censure and public infliction, by inviting the concurrent hostile regards of a wide circle of spectators, constitute an open shame. One is also put to shame by falling into any act that people are accustomed to disapprove, and will cer-

## 112 EMOTIONS OF SELF.

tainly censure in their own minds, although they may refrain from actually pronouncing condemnation. This is the most frequent case in common society. Knowing the hard judgments passed upon all breaches of conventional decorum, we are mortified when conscious of a slip; we can too easily imagine the sentence that we do not actually hear. The character of the pain of all such situations exactly accords with the pains of expressed disapprobation.

18. We may remark before concluding, on the bearing that education and culture should have on the emotion now passed in review.

Having personal excellence for its principal object, and being a large source of human gratification, this feeling prompts powerfully to self-cultivation and active usefulness. Whatever good qualities strike our own minds, or impress the community that we live in, are sure to be sought after with especial ardour, while those that are in bad odour are kept in subjection. On the other hand, the sentiment of self-esteem is one exceedingly liable to over-indulgence; that is to say, there is a tendency to engross an unfair amount of the general stock of praise, honour, or admiration. We might probably furnish an explanation of the indulgence of self-regard and complacency, by remarking how much easier it is in general to fall into the contemplation of our own character and actions, than to be arrested by the good qualities of others. It is the susceptibility to be fascinated, and -to sympathize, with our fellows, and with things away from self, that constitutes the check or counterpoise to excessive *amour propre*. Admiration, love, and sympathy in general, are powers that take us out of ourselves, and enable us to find pleasure in seeing, if not adding to, the good that others possess.

19. There is a language and expression of the self-complacent feeling that finds its way into Art, and more especially into comedy. Boasting and self-praise are the outright manifestations of self-complacency. The usurping of men's attention on all occasions in season or out of season, the constant desire to show off, the gloating over praise, the recollection

### SELF-LOVE AND SELFISHNESS. 113

and retail of compliments, the turning of every incident in the direction of one's own glory,—all enter into the embodiment of an obtrusive self-gratulation. Inflation, as a substitute for real dignity, is peculiarly adapted for ludicrous effects, and hence the abundant use of this characteristic in comic literature. Vainglorious fools, bragging cowards, are good stage subjects; witness Sir John Falstaff and the Bombastes Furiosos of the comic drama. Indeed, a spice of bombastic self-importance is a principal ingredient in most of the dramatic personages formed to be laughed at. The same remark applies to romance, as we may see in Don Quixote and his squire, and in Addison's finest creation.

20. I observed at the outset of this chapter that Self-love and Selfishness embrace a much larger circle of feelings than those now discussed. A few remarks upon these designations are not out of place in the present connexion. Self-love is a species of self-consciousness or self-regard, that makes the collective wants and pleasures of existence an aim and a solicitude. A sentient being not only feels hungry, but retains the recollection of the hungry state, and of its steady recurrence from day to day. This memory of conscious states, with a view to acting upon them, is a mode of self-consciousness. Present hunger prompts to present action; that constitutes a single or isolated fact of animal consciousness or feeling. When, however, the sensation of hunger is remembered and noted as a recurring appetite, and when means are taken on the large scale to meet the sum total of its demands for many months, the regards take a higher sweep, and some term is needed to express this totalized object that is operating upon the will. The word 'self' is used for this purpose, and self-love becomes identical with forethought and prudence. A man treats self, in this acceptation, as he does his child, or his horse, foreseeing their wants, and providing for them in the gross. We are here, therefore, brought face to face with that exceedingly important phase of human conduct implied under such terms as 'forethought,' 'prudence,' 'calculation,' which, although admitted to be in the main an essential virtue of humanity, is

H

## EMOTIONS OF SELF.

sometimes stigmatized as if it were a vice. The worship paid on particular occasions to blind self-abnegation, or even to the blindness of the self-abnegation, shows that there is something interesting in costly sacrifice that more than makes up for the bad calculation often attending it. The fond mother wastes herself profusely in attention to her sick infant, and no one ever reproaches her for the permanent loss to herself, and to the rest of her family, which a little considerate calculation might have saved, without, perhaps, leaving the other duty undone.

21. Of the narrow love of self called Selfishness, I think it worth while to remark again that nothing implied in it can ever favour the notion of any one being actuated by motives entirely apart from themselves. If a man has been so moved by his tender sentiments, his philanthropic leanings, his love of justice, to include among the objects of his pursuits a large mass of good to others, or if, like Howard, he makes the relief of foreign misery the one aim of his life—he is still evidently following out the impulses of his own personality, while deserving to be ranked with the noblest and best of men. The selfishness that we reproach not only does not comprehend others, but actually robs them of what is their own—as in the reckless pursuit of gain, the suppression of freedom by unbounded authority, or the insatiable grasping of attention, honour, or applause. This is the self of a conquering Alexander.

# CHAPTER VIII.

## EMOTION OF POWER.

1.* IN my preceding volume, I have dwelt upon the various feelings begotten in the Exercise of the muscular organs. These are highly pleasurable when the body is healthy, strong, and fresh, and are one ingredient in the

---

* Dugald Stewart has stated, with great perspicuity and accuracy, the general workings of this sentiment, and I therefore transcribe his account, by way of introduction to the view I have here taken of the foundation, or origin, of the feeling in our constitution :—

'In general, it may be observed, that, whenever we are led to consider ourselves as the author of any effect, we feel a sensible pride or exultation in the consciousness of *power*, and the pleasure is in general proportioned to the greatness of the effect, compared with the smallness of our exertion.

'What is commonly called the pleasure of activity is in truth the pleasure of *power*. Mere exercise, which produces no sensible effect, is attended with no enjoyment, or a very slight one. The enjoyment, such as it is, is only corporeal.

'The infant, while still on the breast, delights in exerting its little strength on every object it meets with, and is mortified when any accident convinces it of its own imbecility. The pastimes of the boy are almost, without exception, such as suggest to him the idea of his *power*. When he throws a stone or shoots an arrow, he is pleased with being able to produce an effect at a distance from himself; and, while he measures with his eye the amplitude or range of his missile weapon, contemplates with satisfaction the extent to which his power has reached. It is on a similar principle that he loves to bring his strength into comparison with that of his fellows, and to enjoy the consciousness of his superior prowess. Nor need we search in the *malevolent* dispositions of our nature for any other motive to the apparent acts of cruelty whichhe sometimes exercises over the inferior animals—the sufferings of the animal, in such cases, either entirely escaping his notice, or being overlooked in that state of pleasurable triumph which the wanton abuse of *power* communicates to a weak and unreflecting judgment. The active sports of the youth captivate his fancy by suggesting similar ideas—of strength of body, of

116 EMOTION OF POWER.

agreeable consciousness growing out of active pursuit. There
is, too, a corresponding pleasure in mental effort, considered
merely as the exercise of an activity of the system. This
may not only be observed as a fact, but is also a natural consequence of the view we have taken of the mechanism of ideal
action. Repeating words in idea is to perform the same
round of nervous movements as repeating them aloud, and
ought to yield the same feeling slightly modified. When the
nervous system is in good condition, both the one and the
other exercise are exhilarating and delightful. The difference
between them is perhaps this, namely, that in the purely
mental exertion the circles of the brain are most excited, and
the resulting consciousness is more intense and more exhausting ; tending to a species of painful fatigue peculiar to mental
exercise. On the other hand, the muscles, when brought
powerfully into action, draw the circulation off from the brain,

---

force of mind, of contempt of hardship and of danger. And accordingly such
are the occupations in which Virgil, with a characteristic propriety, employs
his young Ascanius :—

> ' " At puer Ascanius mediis in vallibus acri
> Gaudet equo ; jamque hos cursu, jam præterit illos ;
> Spumantemque dari pecora inter inertia votis
> Optat aprum, aut fulvum descendere monte leonem."

' As we advance in years, and as our animal powers lose their activity
and vigour, we gradually aim at extending our influence over others by the
superiority of fortune and station, or by the still more flattering superiority
of intellectual endowments, by the force of our understanding, by the extent
cf our information, by the arts of persuasion, or the accomplishments of
address. What but the idea of power pleases the orator in managing the
reins of an assembled multitude, when he silences the reason of others by
superior ingenuity, bends to his purposes their desires and passions, and,
without the aid of force, or the splendour of rank, becomes the arbiter of the
fate of nations !

' To the same principles we may trace, in part, the pleasure arising from
the discovery of general theorems in the sciences. Every such discovery
puts us in possession of innumerable particular truths or particular facts, and
gives us a ready command of a great stock of knowledge of which we could
not, with equal ease, avail ourselves before. It increases, in a word, our
*intellectual power* in a way very analogous to that in which a machine or
engine increases the mechanical power of the human body.'

## PROPER PLEASURE OF POWER.

and their fatigue induces a soothing repose. The exercise of the senses is midway between purely mental activity and bodily exercise. In long-continued acts of attention with the eye, or the ear, the preponderance of pressure is upon the circles of the brain, the muscles engaged being too small in bulk to operate a diversion. The same observation applies to much speaking. All these various modes of exerting the human powers are agreeable within the limits proper to each, and disagreeable when carried beyond those limits.

There is, besides, a satisfaction in attaining the Ends of our active pursuit; the fact of their being ends implies as much. In all *voluntary* effort, therefore, there is a double influence upon the mind—the influence of the state of activity or exercise, and that of the end, or thing aimed at. The animal roaming for its food, the peasant tilling his ground, experience this two-fold effect. Thus, labour, which is exercise for attaining a gratification, or for the avoidance of an evil, is a complicated or compound situation, and the consequent emotion is likewise compound. The great variety of modes of active exercise on the one hand, and of agreeable effects on the other, lead to a numerous class of composite emotions referable to the region of our activity. When some very congenial exertion on our part produces an effect also very gratifying, the confluence of the two pleasures must needs beget an intense delight. Such happy combinations are not the usual case; either the kind of exercise that delights us most brings little other fruit; or, to attain our favourite ends, we must take up with uninviting labours.

2. The proper pleasure of Power is something beyond mere exertion for ends. It arises on comparing the easy with the difficult performance of operations. When the laboriousness of an operation is of a uniform character, the feelings connected with it are the two above-mentioned—the pleasure (or pain) of the exercise, and the pleasure of the end. But let us suppose a work at first performed with great pain or difficulty, and afterwards with ease; in that case, the transition from the one state to the other, gives rise to a new feeling, of the

## EMOTION OF POWER.

class founded on Relativity or Comparison,—a joyous and hilarious rebound; intense according to the greatness and the suddenness of the change; there being a corresponding depression of mental tone when the course is in the opposite direction, or from ease to difficulty. So, when after a protracted and doubtful struggle, we are victorious, there is an outburst of joyful excitement peculiar to the situation of contrast.

3. I formerly described this emotion as the consciousness of superior POWER, energy, or might; there being present to the mind some inferior grade to give the comparison. This is the most general way of expressing the numerous and varied aspects of the emotion.

One mode of transition has been quoted—the passing from difficulty to ease in performing the same work, as happens in the growth of the powers, and in the progress of the learner. Every advance in physical strength, skill, or mental accomplishment, is accompanied with a thrill of elation, which is one of the pleasures attending our progress from infancy onwards. The consciousness of self-improvement is grateful and cheering; the decline of our powers is one of the gloomy adjuncts of age.

A second mode of transition is the increased productiveness of the same efforts, as when we obtain better tools, or when we transfer our labours to a more genial soil, or a more bending material. Any circumstance that enables us to obtain a greater return for exertions, besides conferring the enjoyments of greater material abundance, gives the agreeable stimulation of enlarged power. The teacher of a promising pupil enjoys the effect of contrast in the better yield of his labours. To this form of the sentiment belongs also a rise in the position of command.

The third mode of obtaining the requisite transition, is the comparison with others. When we try our strength against an equal, and come off superior, we are elated with the joy of power. The man of superior endowments, as he passes his fellows in the race of life, is the subject of this grateful senti-

PHYSICAL ACCOMPANIMENTS. 119

ment. The situation of permanent superiority to other men, gives a certain degree of elation, although much less than appears to the looker-on, who rarely allows, in the case of others, for the inexorable subsidence of the emotion in a state of sameness. By every advance in ability or in position, we raise at the same time the standard of comparison, and are no longer elated by the same class of effects. The slave compares himself with his fellow-bondsmen, and rejoices in his points of superiority ; becoming a free citizen, he quits the former comparison, and is now affected, only as he can excel his new associates.

4. The *physical* accompaniments of the emotion of power are well marked, and in full accordance with the general law that connects pleasure with increased vitality. A certain erect and lofty carriage, denoting surplus vigour, is looked upon as the natural consequence, and the fitting demeanour, of superiority to others ; while inferiority, dependence, and defeat, are betokened by an attitude of bending or collapse, the too obvious renderings of impaired vital energy. But we must advert to the appearances on a fresh outburst, to judge what the accession of power does to raise the vital forces. At the moment of overcoming a difficulty, of rising a step in the consciousness of might or skill, of defeating a rival, of promotion to command,—the flush of pleasurable elation is represented by a burst of physical energy, as if some tonic or stimulant had been administered. Compare the successful with the unsuccessful man, in a contest, and the difference is not to be mistaken. The physical and the mental tone will be found to rise and fall together. The successful man is invigorated for his next undertaking ; the unsuccessful man, in being mentally dispirited, is physically disabled.

There is a specific tendency in the elation of a stroke of power to stimulate the outburst of Laughter. Some forms of the expression rebut the hilarious manifestation as unsuitable or unbecoming ; but, throughout the multifarious instances of the wide-spread emotion before us, laughter is found as a ready concomitant. The elation of the spirits accompanying

120          EMOTION OF POWER.

a stroke of superior energy would seem to ally itself with this special manifestation. When we come to enquire into the feeling of the ludicrous, we shall find the sentiment before us at work under many disguises; and although Hobbes's explanation may not be literally correct, yet he has touched upon the chief point of this much disputed phenomenon. There are a plurality of causes of the hilarious outburst, some purely physical, and the rest mental; among these last the production of a telling effect is one that cannot be disputed. We see it in the glee of children, in the sport of youth, and in the demeanour even of grave old age. Not in physical effects alone, but in everything where a man can achieve a stroke of superiority, in surpassing or discomfiting a rival, is the disposition to laughter apparent. The chuckle of a rogue at a successful piece of knavery is prompted not simply by the acquisition that it brings, but also by the success of the enterprise, as illustrating his superior powers.

The effect of the sudden attainment of power in liberating nervous energy may be brought under the general law of Harmony and Conflict. Difficulty or Impotence is obviously a conflict of the forces; the sudden cessation of which, that is, the attainment of harmony, cannot be otherwise than a redeeming of nervous power.

5. As regards the mode of *consciousness* of the emotion we are discussing, little need be said except to resume what has already come out in the course of the foregoing paragraphs. We are to regard it as a feeling intensely pleasurable, great both in amount and in degree. It is a pleasure of the elating or intoxicating class, inasmuch as it produces a general rise of tone, a superior mental energy for the time being, and an atmosphere of excitement wherein other pleasures burn brighter. The thrill is apt to persist as a grateful tremor for a considerable time after the actual occasion, and to be readily revived as an ideal satisfaction. The intensity of the hold that it takes of the mind is shown in inspiring the will to pursue objects corresponding to it; such as station, office, or other instrumentality of superior command. Ambition in-

## CHARACTERS OF THE EMOTION. 121

volves the attainment of power as a principal signification; even honour is not a satisfying good unless there attach to it a certain amount of real influence. Thus it is that power may be described as a sentiment born of our active energies, and qualifying them for still higher efforts; as a copious spring of human pleasure, operating on the will, and persisting in the intellect in no ordinary degree; giving a place in the thoughts to everything appertaining to one's own superiority; and largely swaying the convictions. It is an emotion of the first magnitude; the favourable side is shown in laudable efforts to attain bodily and mental efficiency, and to promote the general good; the unfavourable aspects, if fully enumerated, would bring to view many of our most odious vices. Arrogance, insolence, cruelty, tyranny, oppression, persecution, derision, scorn, abuse, contempt, opprobrium, antipathy, excessive interference, and the passion of anger—fall under that black catalogue.

6. Let us now pursue the exemplification of specific forms of the sentiment. When, by the command of animal power, of natural agencies, or of other human beings, a single person can accomplish Large Operations for his own sole behoof, not only has he a greater yield to his activity, but he has also that exalted sense of power and efficiency now described. Having constantly before his eyes the much lower efficiency of the endeavours of the generality of men, he takes his own measure by the comparison, and feels elated by the wider response to all his movements. The proprietor of land and capital, the owner of manufactories, and ships, and warehouses, receives in return for his toil, or perhaps without any toil, a large share of the good things of life; but besides this, he feels himself elevated when he sees the extent of his command, and the multitude of effects resulting from his will. The chief in a business establishment is no less jealous of his position of mastery than of his actual property.

7. Even in the matter of working for those we love, there is room for the supplementary element of superiority. The mother exerting her powers for her children has all the happi-

## 122 EMOTION OF POWER.

ness of exercise to a favourite end; but she may also aim at the distinction of surpassing the generality in what she does for them. In working to secure the affection, admiration, esteem, or following of others, there is already the twofold satisfaction of putting forth our active energies, and compassing a highly gratifying return; yet at no point of our nature does the extra ingredient insinuate itself more forcibly. It is not simply the pleasure of being loved, admired, esteemed, followed, but the being one or all of these in *superior* measure that the human breast often craves for. The enjoyment of love and esteem is not enough without distinction and monopoly. At least such is the tendency of the unchecked pursuit of the luxury of power. This is one form of Jealousy.

8. There is a great pleasure in Bending the Wills of other men by force, authority, terror, or persuasion. This comes home at once to the feeling of superiority. We measure ourselves by another person whom we utterly subdue and prostrate, and feel elated by the degree that our agency passes his. The terrified aspect, and the submissive gestures, of the weaker party feed the sentiment of power in the stronger, and that quite apart from the comparison with third parties incapable of such effects. The conventional bearing of inferiors to their superiors is meant to echo and acknowledge power by submission. The headship of a family gives scope for the sentiment of power in various ways; and in some minds this is the principal enjoyment of the position. The schoolmaster can both command and form his pupils. Every grade of wealth and rank, above the lowest, brings in the pleasure of influence. The action of man upon the lower animals extends the position of power in humanity generally. To command the service of some animals, and to trample upon and destroy others, are modes of exercising the pride of ascendancy. The sports of the field would be neutralized by men's tender sympathies, but for the gush of exultation felt in bringing a living creature to the dust.

9. The possession of State Office gives in a high degree the sentiment of power, and this is the return for the labours

of government to the inheritors of wealth and fortune. The sovereign, the minister, the official, the military officer, the judge, the magistrate, the ecclesiastic, have each their quota of the sweets of authority. When a man wielding the power of a nation goes forth to conquer other nations, he but panders still farther to this boundless craving. The acquisition of enormous wealth has no other fruit than the luxury of power. The millionaire feels the ascendancy that he exercises, and has often a still more intense delight in imagining the many possible ways that he could make his influence tell. In a free community, the price of power is perhaps by no one more enjoyed than by the chosen leaders of large parties. Men that have attained an influence from their eloquence, or their wisdom, naturally plume themselves by a comparison with inherited power. It is grateful to be consulted in matters of high importance, and to be permitted to suggest or originate large schemes and operations. Without being called in, men are exceedingly prone to offer counsel to the state, or to interfere in cases of imposing interest.

10. The position that Science gives is occasionally of a very commanding kind. The application of scientific laws sometimes imparts great power in practical operations ; and at other times gives a solution to perplexing enigmas. Hence a feeling of elation may be generated by the discovery of new facts or principles, by the possession of extensive knowledge, or by the opportunity of promulgating ascertained truth. The pleasure thus derived is shown by the desire to get at new truths, for the sake of the effect experienced through having the lead in so great an agency. Pretenders to discoveries generally go in advance of the real discoverer, and the anxiety for success relaxes the attention to evidence.

11. The masterstrokes of Fine Art peculiarly affect the artistic mind with the feeling of superior and commanding ability. Before the public are admitted to judge, the artist has judged for himself, and has been elated with the sentiments of power and complacency. In proportion as the effects in fine art are more telling than many other effects, the plea-

124    EMOTION OF POWER.

sures of the operating mind are more intense. Take, as a familiar example, the gifts of speech, as in oratory or colloquial brilliancy. The charm of such effects is so great, and, because the reward is immediate, reacts so powerfully on the mind that can produce them, as to give a more than ordinary elation, and to lead to the employment of unscrupulous means. It is only necessary to indicate the practice of sacrificing truth to point and effect both in oratory and in conversation.

12. The operation of the love of influence may be traced deep in the familiar habits of society. The expansion of one's sphere is sought by interference with the liberty of our fellows; by censoriousness and judicial assumption over the conduct of others; and by the tendency to meddle and push one's self forward in everything that happens. Intolerance has its firmest root in the passion for the exercise of power. It is not enough that people form opinions and contract likings or aversions to act upon for themselves, they must also impose the same line of conduct upon all around them. The love of power shows itself as paramount over the love of sensual indulgence; in the exercise of ascetic self-control, men have found a compensation for the loss of other enjoyments. This choice would be shown in its purity, if such persons were always content with imposing privation on themselves, but when they require also the concurrence of every one else, it is at best but the relinquishing of individual indulgence in return for a wide command.

13. We have thus rapidly indicated a few of the prominent examples of the sentiment in question, and in so doing have signalized the features of the emotion. The quality of it is remarkable, not merely for intensity of pleasure, but for endurability and continuance, both in reality and in idea. Being connected with the exercise of our active power, as decidedly as tender emotion allies itself with repose, we naturally expect to find it developed in the active temperaments. Indeed, we may pronounce it the essential sweetness of activity. Ranking as a first-class emotion, there is in it something remarkably cheering, supporting, and hilarious, giving an erect carriage,

PAINS OF IMPOTENCE. 125

and an easy bearing as of one well-sustained by inward vitality unabated by obstruction. According to the intensity of the feeling in any one case, do we find it operating to inspire voluntary efforts, possessing the mind, directing the trains of thought, and influencing the convictions. There is, however, a peculiarity attending it of great practical importance ; namely, the circumstance dwelt upon from the outset—that being essentially a feeling of reaction and relief, it subsists upon comparison, and dies away as the contrasting condition ceases to be felt. Hence it inflames the imagination of minds labouring under obstruction, difficulty, and inferiority, these having the most lively estimate of that which power gives a deliverance from. Such minds utterly exaggerate the . pleasure of a position of actual sway and unchecked abundance. This consideration has not been overlooked by moralists and preachers, in attempting to supply correctives to ambitious fancies and dreams of bliss attainable through the removal of some actual pressure. The moment of success gives a thrill that is not exaggerated ; but this can be renewed only through the renewal of the foregone struggle, or the lively presence of the contrast. A still more grave consideration attaches to the sentiment of power as a habitual gratification, which is, that no high measure of it can be enjoyed except by a small number of persons at the cost of the great mass of living beings.*

14. The pains of Impotence are shown under resistance, frustration, difficulty *not* overcome. The misery of Failure, besides the loss of some wished-for advantage, is liable to contain the farther mortification of a disclosed weakness. In the case of a menial or inferior position, there is the sense of littleness in the result of one's labours ; the whole existence

---

\* There is room for much additional remark upon the simple concurrence of agreeable exertion with agreeable results (apart from the sentiment of elation at superior might), wherein lies a good part of the substantial happiness of life. To be successful in a congenial profession, or pursuit, expresses a large volume of felicity. A succeeding chapter will incidentally contribute to the examples of this position. See Chap x.

126                    EMOTION OF POWER.

of one person being spent in contributing to, perhaps, the hundredth part of the existence of another person.* Still worse is the posiʰion of absolute dependence, which aggravates powerlessness by terrors. But perhaps the situation of greatest chagrin is to be defeated in a fairly matched contest.

15. I shall notice farther only one other aspect of the painful side of the exercise of power; namely, the form of Jealousy experienced when one's importance is interfered with, or detracted from, by other persons. It applies to every species of superiority, command, influence, ascendancy, direction, and to the love, admiration, or esteem falling to one's share. In proportion as these are cherished by the mind, does one feel hurt, shocked, grieved, or enraged by the attempt to derogate from them in any way. This sentiment of jealousy is the most odious aspect of exaggerated self-importance. Great superiority of position is at best an invidious thing, from implying so much inequality among mortal men, and rather needs to be softened by bearing one's honours meekly, than made more stern by jealous exaction.†

---

* A great expended force with a trifling result has a contemptible effect in the eyes of a spectator, unless pity, anger, or some other passion is roused as an antidote. This is one of the occasions of many-caused laughter. 'Parturiunt montes, nascetur *ridiculus* mus.'

† Something, perhaps, is needed to define more clearly the relations of the feeling now discussed with the egotistic sentiments forming the subject of the foregoing chapter. I am of opinion that Self-complacency and the exultation of the consciousness of Power have totally distinct roots in our system—the one springing from tender emotion turned self-wards, the other occurring in the exercise of our activity—and yet the two mingle their branches together in actual experience. A man, not much given to self-consciousness and self-regard, may still have, in a high degree, the pleasurable sentiment of his own superior efficiency; if he has, besides, indulged a fond affection towards his own personality, as he would to a son or a friend, there is a feeling of complacency and self-admiration superadded. The tender and passive emotion is in this case evoked to supplement the emotion of activity. It depends upon the tone of the individual constitution whether the sentiment of power shall be enjoyed in its singleness, or whether a tributary from the fountain of tenderness shall mingle largely in the current. Hard natures, little prone to warm affection in any shape, dwell in the active emotion. These are the men, like the elder Dionysius, the despot of Syracuse, who enjoy power to such a degree as to despise public approbation, and possibly also self-approbation.

# CHAPTER IX.

## THE IRASCIBLE EMOTION.

WE now proceed to the consideration of an emotion in nearly all respects the contrast of one already handled. Instead of pleasure begetting pleasure, as in the case of the Tender affections, we have here suffering terminating in suffering, while a certain stage of the feeling is still capable of affording delight. The analysis of this phase of our constitution is both interesting and important; and the varieties of the state include some of the most formidable manifestations of the human mind.

1. The *objects* of Irascible feeling are persons, the authors of pain or injury. Pain arising from an impersonal cause, as in the rise of the wintry blast, leads to the usual manifestations of feeling, and to alleviating efforts of volition; but proceeding from a person, or in any way assignable to personal agency, it kindles anger. The general rule is, the greater the pain, the greater the anger; but there are various exceptions and qualifications; and the study of these casts light on the workings of the passion.

It may happen that pain causes terror, or grief, and not anger; the result depending more upon the constitution of the individual than upon any specific distinction between different sorts of injury. Naturally enough, suffering inflicted on the tender side of human nature vents itself by preference in grief. So when the agent is some being of irresistible might, fear is more likely to be inspired than anger. Or, we may note, as a possible case, that the injured person may

## 128 THE IRASCIBLE EMOTION.

coolly set to work to find a remedy without any ebullition of angry feeling.

2. As regards the *physical* mechanism, there is considerable obscurity as well as complication. We cannot trace in the human subject any specific glandular secretion, such as the lachrymal flow in the case of tenderness, or the still more decided example in connection with the sexes ; nevertheless, there is evidence to prove that the state of anger is associated with extensive derangement of the general secretions of organic life. The nature and amount of this derangement cannot be defined, and are possibly not constant ; but both in the alimentary group of organs—the stomach, intestines, liver—and in the exhalations of the skin, most palpable changes are manifested under this excitement. The popular notion as to ' bile ' being in excess during angry passion, is not much to be trusted. Nor are we to take in the analogy of the discharge of poison by some of the lower animals, although apparently very close to our purpose ; that discharge I am obliged to look upon as a proper exercise of volition, and not as the mere diffusion arising from feeling.

In fact, the muscular expression, and the influence on the breathing, the circulation, and the secretions, are a compound of emotional diffusion and the voluntary activity that is so apt to be mixed up with this passion. If we set aside, on the one hand, the manifestation due to mere pain, and on the other hand, the acts having retaliation for their object,—the feeling of pure resentment, being in the main a pleasure, really gives birth to a pleasurable expression, well understood as the grin of a satisfaction that is devoid of tenderness. The various demonstrations of scorn, sneering, loathing, correspond to different turns of the sentiment.

The excitement of the Activity, often to a frenzied pitch, is a characteristic deserving of special attention. There are many ways of bringing on an active outburst;—Spontaneity, after rest and nourishment; more irritation of the nerves anyhow ; a pleasurable stimulus; an acute smart; opposition not insurmountable ; a shock of fear (causing excita-

## CHARACTER OF THE EMOTION. 129

tion in some parts, with depression in others). In pure Anger, the two prominent causes are the disturbing shock of pain, and the thirst for retaliation and revenge.

An acute shock is efficacious as being more exciting ; and anger is essentially a mode of excitement. Again, a sudden and unexpected attack is eminently disturbing to equanimity of mind, and on that ground favours the rise of the angry state. On the other hand, a crushing blow kills the sentiment of anger ; the destruction of vital power is the loss of the all-important requisite of active energy. Proverbially, small grinding inflictions are the most irritating.

3. Next as to the character of the *emotion* itself. The first and natural effect of a painful stimulus, after showing itself in the ordinary wave of diffusion, is to excite the will, or to inspire some actions for escaping from the infliction. It is the nature of any sharp and sudden stroke to prompt some very violent exertion by way of relief. There is nothing more in this than that primordial link between feeling and action, which is the foundation of all voluntary power. We are not to confound either the contortions expressive of pain, or the violent endeavours to escape from it, with angry passion, although all the three are very apt to be mixed together. In children we see the two first from an early period ; the last does not appear until the notion of per-sonality, and the sense of the effects of action on others, have been developed. The distinctive feeling of anger implies *the impulse knowingly to inflict suffering upon another sentient being, and to derive a positive gratification from the fact of suffering inflicted.* We must first be able to read, and to enter into, the pleasures and pains of our fellow-creatures ; and then as the pleasure enjoyed by another gratifies our tender sensibility, so may suffering manifested by another gratify our irascible sensibility. The satisfaction thus derivable from malevolent sympathy is a means of soothing the original wound.

What we have really to explain, therefore, is, not the fury and vehemence of angry excitement, but the root or origin of the *pleasure of malevolence,* which, however we may disguise

I

## 130 THE IRASCIBLE EMOTION.

it, is a fact of the human constitution. We had to perform a nice and circuitous analysis to find out by what steps the tender feeling leads us to take delight in the enjoyment felt by others, and we found that the intervention of sympathy was a part of the process ; and now we have to apply a similar analysis to the contrasting phenomenon of pleasure growing out of other men's pains.

Starting from the circumstance that we ourselves are put to pain, through the agency of another person, the mere volitional impulse would lead us to react upon that person, so as at least to deprive him of the power of injuring us. This is the course we take with offensive animals ; we put them *hors de combat* for our own protection, and having once felt pain and peril, we experience in our deliverance a corresponding satisfaction. Still this does not reach the essence of the irascible sentiment.

To get at the true character of anger we must look at the feeling that remains after our enemy has been deprived of the means of committing farther injury. The fact that we have suffered harm at the hands of another person leaves a sting behind in the violation of the sanctity of our feelings. This presupposes doubtless the sentiment of self-regarding pride, the presence of which gives birth to the best developed forms of anger, although we may have genuine specimens without such co-operation. In any case, the pain actually inflicted upon us by a personal agent, with the contemplation of deliberate purpose in the act, gives us, in addition to the actual pain, a degree of mental discomposure that survives the mere mischief. We forget the suffering caused by inanimate things, or by the mere inadvertence of our fellow-beings. But injury done us with design, or from neglect, is not so easily wiped away. Some positive application is needed to heal a wound that is of the nature of a fretting sore. Two kinds of application are found to answer the end ; the one the voluntary self-humiliation of the wrongdoer, the other a compulsory humiliation inflicted upon him. True anger thus supposes a discomposure of mind through harm received from another person, and the cure of that discomposure by the submission or suffering of the agent.

4. In endeavouring to explain the phenomenon of the pleasures of Anger, we may remark, in the first place, that a *fascination for the sight of bodily infliction and suffering* is one part of the complex interest in personality. Singular and horrible as the fact may appear, the evidence is incontestible. It is enough to quote the delight of children in torturing animals, and the zest of multitudes in witnessing public executions. In the absence of an adequate counteracting sympathy, the writhings of pain seem to furnish a new variety of the aggregate of sensual and sensuous stimulation due to living beings. The indications of a state of suffering that we are happily exempt from, and do not choose to conceive in its dread reality, instead of revulsion, impart a species of excitement pleasurable to many.

In the next place, I conceive that *the pleasure of power*, enters as a very large ingredient of malevolent feeling. The putting of other beings to pain is a startling illustration of power and superiority. The childish delight in making a sensation is at the extreme point, when some one gives evidence of being put to pain. The rampant fury of boyhood exults in victimizing an animal or a beggar in the streets. The orator does not feel his own power, till he see, in the wincing of his opponents, that his thunders have told. But for our compassionate sympathies, our fears of retaliation, punishment, or censure, and the other elements of conscience, the delight in such manifestations would be unrestricted and universal.

Now, what happens when another person puts us to pain? How does this affect our ordinary state of mind considered as under the opposing solicitations of the pleasures of causing suffering on the one hand, and the sentiments that confer a sanctity upon the persons of our fellow-beings on the other? I answer, the effect of an injury received is to suspend for the time the feelings of compassion, sympathy, and dutiful respect, and to leave the field free to the other passions. It

## 132 THE IRASCIBLE EMOTION.

is declaring the individual an outlaw, withdrawing the barriers of a flood always ready to overflow, opening a battery constantly charged, whence only one result can ensue. The protection that habitually surrounds a man, but for which he might be at any time a victim of the sport of every other man, is for the moment removed when he is the cause of pain to some one, and he is liable to the uncounteracted swing of the excitement of inflicting suffering, and the sentiment of power in the person aggrieved. I am prevented by the humane side of my nature, and by my sense of duty, from kicking a dog that passes by; an effect which would, doubtless, gratify other feelings in me. But if the animal bites, or barks at me, the pain and apprehension tend to destroy my tender feeling towards it, and suspend my sense of its rights as a sentient being, and I am thereupon prompted to repay myself for the suffering by a glut of the pleasure of inflicting pain. I might even go farther, and use the occasion as a pretext for deriving far more pleasure than was equivalent to the pain; but this would be to exceed the measure of ordinary human exigency, which is to seek an amount of gratified superiority corresponding to the suffering received.

A third circumstance is the association of *preventing farther pain to ourselves by inducing fear* of us, or of consequences, in the person causing the pain. There is always a great satisfaction in being relieved from the incubus of terror, one of the most depressing agencies that human life is subject to. Many minds that neither boil up in savage excitement, nor take especial delight in manifested superiority, are yet very much alive to this sort of satisfaction, it being only the rebound consequent on deliverance from oppressing apprehensions.

These three considerations are all that I can find at the bottom of the irascible sentiment considered as a source of pleasurable indulgence. One of them will be the prominent circumstance in one person, and another in a second; but taken altogether they seem to me to amount to an explanation, so far complete as to dispense with assuming an independent foundation in our constitution for this peculiar vein of emotion.*

5. The volitional, intellectual, and mixed qualities of the irascible emotion merely illustrate farther the degree of hold that it takes of the mind as a source of pleasure. The intellectual persistence is probably of that medium kind that distinguishes the stronger emotions from the organic feelings on the one hand, and from the sensations of the higher senses on the other. Only in natures specially prone to the state, or under special cultivation, can pure resentment become a standing pursuit for the mere sake of the pleasure. So in the attributes of occupying the attentions and thoughts, and of influencing the belief, we may consider that there is a tolerably close proportion to the general intensity of the feeling. In the detail of species that we are next to enter upon, the generalities now advanced will receive their exemplification.

6. The recognised modes of the operation of Anger are very various, and some of them are not pure instances of the passion. I shall commence with the Lower Animals, many of whom exhibit in a marked form what passes for violent irascibility. The beasts of prey destroy and devour their victims with all the outward symptoms of a furious wrath. Even herbivorous animals, as the bull and the stag, fight to the death the members of their own tribe. The poisonous reptiles and insects discharge their venom on whatever creature encounters them. But in none of all those cases am I able to recognise anything beyond the putting forth of the

---

* The advocate of the hypothesis of evolution might suggest that the irascible outburst in civilized man is a counterpart of the destructive propensities essential, in an earlier stage, to the struggle for existence. To the phrenologists also, *Destructiveness* still appears the appropriate heading of the sentiment, which shows that there is something to be said for that mode of viewing it. Still, I see nothing either in the evolution hypothesis, or in the phrenological examples, to make me depart from the view, prevailing alike in ancient and in modern times, that puts forward, as the *central fact* of anger, the pleasure of malevolent infliction. For a criticism of the phrenological handling of the passion, see *The Study of Character*, p. 79.

## 134 THE IRASCIBLE EMOTION.

volitional energies of the animal under the stimulus of some sensation or feeling. There being, in the system, destructive weapons and an active temperament, the weapons are put in action at first spontaneously, and afterwards at the instance of the animal's various sensibilities, such as hunger and the like.

These powers are the active machinery proper to the constitution of the creature, and in the use of them no emotion is implied beyond the ordinary physical sensations and wants of the individual. In the more highly endowed quadrupeds such as the dog, some notion of personality is gained; and when we see the attacks that sexual jealousy will sometimes inspire, we may there suppose that the victorious animal has a certain pleasure beyond the mere getting rid of a rival by the exercise of a superior might. The animation of two fighting cocks has in it some of the genuine elements of rage,—the stimulated energies, and, on the part of the victorious animal, probably the sensual excitement, and the glut of power.

7. In the wrath of Infancy and Childhood, we may trace a gradual unfolding of the different features of the passion. In the first months of infant existence, pain gives birth to purely emotional displays, more or less energetic according to the intensity of the pains and the physical vigour of the constitution; after the commencement of volitional power, the voluntary action has a corresponding energy; but neither of the two modes can be termed anger. Another appearance that may be noted, is the effect of opposition or thwarting in adding to the violence of the demonstrations—a stimulating influence whose workings are especially apparent in childhood, being probably a mixture of reflex stimulus with volition proper. A somewhat different aspect is presented, when the irritated infant energetically refuses every proposal of the nature of a substitute for what it is bent upon. The proper feeling of Anger passes beyond all these; beginning only when the notion of another person's suffering is attained, and the signs of it understood; a state fully manifested at the

## SUDDEN RESENTMENT.

age of from two to three years, at which period genuine sympathy may also commence.

8. The varieties of the emotion in mature life turn in part upon the various character of the pain, hurt, or injury constituting the original stimulus. There are wrongs inflicted on the person, on the property, on the reputation, on the sympathetic relationships, and in other ways. Sometimes the injury is confined to a single act, at other times a door is opened to an indefinite series of wrongs. Moreover the view taken of the *intention* of the offending party has very much to do with the feeling engendered. An unintended harm is easily satisfied as far as moral reparation is concerned ; whereas the indications of a set purpose of doing us evil, stir up our resentment to the depths. The forms of angry feeling differ greatly among individuals and races, and are modified by civilization and historic changes. Out of all these possible differences we shall select for illustration some of the well-recognised species, such as have received characteristic designations.

And first, of the distinction between Sudden and Deliberate resentment.

The Sudden outburst is what arises from an unexpected blow or shock, and depends on the excitability of the constitution. Some temperaments are described as *quick*, meaning that the operation of all the passions and movements is rapid. Not only anger, but fear, wonder, and all other passions, as well as the voluntary impulses, are propagated with energy and speed in such temperaments. The term *nervous* is applied to characterize the same mode of mental discharge, from the supposition that the nerves by their superior susceptibility are somehow involved in the effect. The aspect of the angry feeling, when suddenly aroused, corresponds to the more natural, that is, the more deeply ingrained, impulses of the individual. When we are abruptly forced into action of any kind, both the original instincts and the confirmed habits show themselves without disguise. In such a case, too, the prompting arises solely from the actual blow, and excludes all

136                 THE IRASCIBLE EMOTION.

reference to circumstances or collaterals. Hence sudden resentment is very apt to be excessive as well as hasty, from which circumstance arises the principal evil attaching to it. In the complicated relations of life, instantaneous decisions must often be bad, and the hurried impulses of a sudden resentment only furnish matter for repentance. Nevertheless the equanimity of the temper is, as already remarked, especially liable to be disturbed by anything either acute or sudden; the preventive volition, the flow of bitterness from violated personality, and the temper of retaliation, are roused into a vehement gush, aggravated in intensity when the temperament is quick or nervous. Thus, while on the one hand, these sudden impulses stand in need of the check of a promptly summoned resolution from within, let all men beware of needlessly provoking them from without.

9. Under Deliberate anger we might include a wide range of illustration. Implying, as this does, a consideration of all the circumstances attending the original injury, as well as all the consequences of retaliation, we may consider it the generic name for the passion as displayed in cultivated minds, and among civilized communities. It gives room for the introduction of some principle of procedure, such as a rule of justice, the dictates of religion, or the received maxims of society. The punishment of offenders, and the maintenance of discipline, belong to this head. We shall speak of these presently.

The term Revenge expresses the angry passion carried to the full length of retaliation. The need of inflicting pain for appeasing the offended person is strongly suggested by this designation. Where the passion exists in great force, the spirit of revenge is sure to display itself, being in fact the course of conduct whereby anger is attested. Where an injury of great magnitude has been committed—or where the magnitude is simply imagined, and when the wounded personality is difficult to be satisfied—we are accustomed to see the workings of a retaliation that knows no bounds. The implacable temper is exemplified on the widest scale in past

REVENGE. **137**

history. The wars of extermination between tribes and peoples, the vengeance of the conquering side, the proscriptions of rivals in power fill the pages of every country's annals. Sometimes revenge has the aspect of mere satisfaction applied to a rankling wound, a relief from real misery; at other times, it would seem as if the wound were purposely kept open in order to enjoy the sweets of vengeance. Numerous instances may be brought to attest the reality of this species of luxury. The case of the Carthaginian general Hannibal may be quoted in point.*

---

* Hamilkar, the grandfather of Hannibal, had been slain at Himera, in Sicily, and his grandson, in the year 409 B.C., in a successful invasion of the island, captured this town by storm. He checked the slaughter of the citizens by his soldiery in order to a signal demonstration of his wrath, described and commented on as follows by the historian of Greece :—

' It was a proud day for the Carthaginian general when he stood as master on the ground of Himera; enabled to fulfil the duty, and satisfy the exigencies, of revenge for his slain grandfather. Tragical, indeed, was the consummation of this long-cherished purpose. Not merely the walls and temples (as at Selinus), but all the houses in Himera, were razed to the ground. Its temples, having been first stripped of their ornaments and valuables, were burnt. The women and children taken captive were distributed as prizes among the soldiers. But all the male captives, 3000 in number, were conveyed to the spot where Hamilkar had been slain, and there put to death with indignity, as an expiatory satisfaction to his lost honour. Lastly, in order that even the hated name of Himera might pass into oblivion, a new town called Therma (so designated because of some warm springs) was shortly afterwards founded by the Carthaginians in the neighbourhood.

' No man can now read the account of this wholesale massacre without horror and repugnance. Yet we cannot doubt, that among all the acts of Hannibal's life, this was the one in which he most gloried; that it realized in the most complete and emphatic manner his concurrent inspirations of filial sentiment, religious obligation, and honour as a patriot; that to show mercy would have been regarded as a mean dereliction of these esteemed influences; and that if the prisoners had been even more numerous, all of them would have been equally slain, rendering the expiatory fulfilment only so much the more honourable and efficacious. In the Carthaginian religion, human sacrifices were not merely admitted, but passed for the strongest manifestation of devotional fervour, and were especially resorted to in times of distress when the necessity for propitiating the gods was accounted most pressing. Doubtless the feelings of Hannibal were cordially shared, and

138          THE IRASCIBLE EMOTION.

10. The formidable state of mind named Antipathy ought not to be omitted in this connexion; being one of the many shades or varieties of malevolent passion. Implying, as it does in the first instance, some exceedingly painful exciting cause, although the pain may be of a fanciful or factitious nature, it is followed up by demonstrations of the most furious hostility, and the most destructive wrath. When we would designate hatred in its strongest forms, we make use of this word. Our antipathies are various, according to the points of greatest sensibility; but it is not mere pain that determines the degree of them; there is the farther circumstance that for some things more than others we are in the habit of pronouncing that sentence of outlawry preparatory to the hunting down of a victim. It is not always the author of an offence against person, property, or good name, that rouses this extreme manifestation; something that affronts our mere æsthetic sensibility, as certain animals and human beings that create disgust, will provoke the requisite suspension of protective sympathy. The usages, customs, and opinions of foreigners often rouse the sentiment. The exercise of free thought in dissenting from the doctrines that we hold in especial reverence, is a common source of our antipathy. Here, however, there creeps out the wounded pride of power, which, by prompting to signal revenge, repays itself, as it were, in kind. Dissenters, heretics, schismatics, have always had their full measure of hatred from the mother Church, whose communion and government they have renounced.

An infusion of fear is a potent element in antipathy. This is partly owing to the greater susceptibility of the mind under fear, and partly owing to the need of preventive efforts against harm. The animals that rouse the greatest force of aversion, are those that sting or poison, as well as present a repulsive aspect. Antipathy once excited against any one, can

---

the plenitude of his revenge envied by the army around him. So different, sometimes so totally contrary, is the tone and direction of the moral sentiments, among different ages and nations.'

HATRED. 139

be very much inflamed, by suggesting a certain amount of dread; this, however, must not be carried too far, else another effect will arise, namely, the subjugation of the active energies, under which the irascible feeling can no longer be sustained.

11. Hatred is another name for malevolent emotion. We recognise under this title a permanent *affection* grounded on the irascible, as love is on tenderness. The sense of some one wrong never satisfied, the recognition of a standing disposition to cause harm, an obstructive position maintained, are among the ordinary causes of hatred. A mere aversion to the character and conduct, or even the appearance of another person, without reference to their being hostile, will often engender an habitual dislike. The repetition of occasions of angry feeling ends in a permanent attitude of resentment, under which the individual is always prepared for acts of retaliation, and for relishing occasions of discomfiture. To be a good hater one needs only to be irascible by nature, and to be placed in some relationship of frequent encounter with the authors of offence. Hence rivalry, the exercise of authority, great inequalities of condition, are among the causes of hatred. Party spirit is one of the most notable species. Under the influence of this sentiment men are affected in all the ways wherein strong emotion can manifest itself. They derive a portion of their happiness from their feelings of animosity, they are powerfully prompted to action for the sake of this pleasure, they retain the feeling by an intellectual hold, and have their minds frequently occupied with the objects of it. Last of all they are led to believe of the opposing party whatever suits, or chimes in with, their hatred. The banding together into sects or factions gives scope for a large body of sentiment; on the one hand engaging the sympathies of fellowship, and on the other provoking the equally natural outbursts of antipathy. Hence people's relations to their party or sect, whether religious, political, or otherwise, usually constitute one of the large interests of their life. The existence of the spirit of sectarian bitterness through all periods of history proves how congenial to man is the passion of hatred, and how much

140                THE IRASCIBLE EMOTION.

satisfaction is mixed up with the painful element of angry feeling.

12. Some further elucidations of our present subject may be derived, if we survey the situation of Hostility, Warfare, or actual Combat between opposing parties. This I shall preface by some remarks on the point of view wherefrom the offending party is regarded. Involuntary offence may cause a sudden or momentary outburst, which usually subsides and is easily satisfied. As soon as we know that no harm is intended, we accept an apology and are appeased. Aware that absolute inviolability is impossible in this world, and that we are all exposed by turns to accidental injuries from our fellows, we have our minds disciplined to let unintended evil go by without the satisfaction of inflicting some counter evil upon the offender. Since the wrathful sentiment is not necessarily unappeasable without a full exercise of vengeance, the same discipline could be extended, if need were, to all other cases. Again, when involuntary offence is of the nature of carelessness, the wounded personality is not so readily appeased. We then look upon the offender as omitting the proper line of precautions to which we are all equally bound, and which, if universally neglected, would produce extensive mischiefs; and feeling that an injury is done to ourselves and to others, we are exempted from the obligation to suppress our anger unappeased. A third case is that presented when another person, not wishing or intending us harm, still pursues his own ends in utter disregard of our feelings and interest. This is an exceedingly common source of injuries. Persons that harbour no ill-will to their fellows are often nevertheless entirely reckless of other people's happiness in the pursuit of their own, feeling no compunction at the misery they cause. We consider ourselves still less called upon to suppress our wrathful sentiments towards this species of offenders; our legitimate indignation seems the right and proper check to such selfish disregard of others. The fourth and highest species of wrong is the case of deliberate and intended offence, limited or unlimited in its character. This opens before us

STATE OF WARFARE. 141

such a state of mind, and such a range of possible damage, that our angry sentiments are deeply moved and call for vengeance. Nothing is wanted to complete the provocation, but the consciousness on our part that we have given no cause for such a demonstration, and are deliberately and gratuitously wronged by a fellow-being.

When, in retaliating upon the object of our anger, we encounter resistance and opposition, the state of warfare ensues. Each party, inflamed with a sense of injury, directs his whole might to bring about the ruin of the other. That prompting to extraordinary efforts of volition, which we have noted as a consequence of pain, and still further of resistance, is seen at the uttermost pitch in actual combat. Even without the bitterness of wounded personality demanding vengeance, the position of the combatant so stimulates the voluntary energy as to exhibit the human powers at their highest point. The superadded spirit of vengeance brings out the fury of a fiend.

The weapons of hostility change greatly according to the circumstances and characters of the contending parties. Passing from the physical encounter of men engaged in mortal conflict, we remark the substitution of other modes of attack for bodily damage. Calumny and abuse is the favourite weapon of factions and rivals living in the same society; and we have all seen the lengths that this will go. Any contested election, a local dispute, or family quarrel, will recall examples to any one's recollection. With intellectual refinement, sarcasm and innuendo take the place of open slander and vulgar scurrility. Sometimes a lawsuit is the arena of the struggle. Still farther removed from the grossness of a bodily combat is the struggle of debate between opposing views or doctrines. The spirit of hostility is here unchanged, but the mode of action has taken an altered shape. A turn for polemics, the love of contradiction and a fondness for paradox, are modifications of irascible feeling.

13. Dr. Chalmers, in a dissertation entitled 'The Inherent Misery of the Vicious Affections,' &c., has adopted a line of

142                    THE IRASCIBLE EMOTION.

illustration that implies doubts as to the genuineness of the
Pleasure of Malevolence.* But although the exercise of
resentment is beset with numerous incidental pains, the one
feeling of gratified vengeance is a pleasure as real and indisputable as any form of human delight. The injury and

---

* 'Kindness, and honesty, and truth, are, of themselves, and irrespective of their rightness, sweet unto the taste of the inner man. Malice, envy,
falsehood, injustice, irrespective of their wrongness, have of themselves, the
bitterness of gall and wormwood.' 'The most ordinary observer of his own
feelings, however incapable of analysis, must be sensible, even at the moment
of wreaking the full indulgence of his resentment, on the man who has pro-
voked or injured him, that all is not perfect within; but that, in this, and
indeed in every other malignant feeling, there is a sore burden of disquietude,
an unhappiness tumultuating in the heart, and visibly pictured in the
countenance. The ferocious tyrant who has only to issue forth his mandate,
and strike dead at pleasure the victim of his wrath, with any circumstance
too of barbaric caprice and cruelty, which his fancy, in the very waywardness
of passion unrestrained and power unbounded, might suggest to him—he may
be said through life to have experienced a thousand gratifications, in the
solaced rage and revenge, which, though ever breaking forth on some new
subject, he can appease again every day of his life by some new execution.
But we mistake it if we think otherwise than that, in spite of these distinct
and very numerous, nay daily gratifications if he so choose, it is not a life of
fierce internal agony notwithstanding.'

Far more just and true to actual experience are the reflections quoted above,
from the most philosophical historian of Greece, on Hannibal's sacrifice of
prisoners at Himera. With a like dispassionate accuracy does the same
author depict the luxury of gratified revenge experienced by the Athenians
on the condemnation of Phokion. After the subversion of the Athenian
democracy by the Macedonian general Antipater (B.C. 322), Phokion lent
himself to the execution of the victor's decrees for humiliating and prostrating
his country, and continued to administer her affairs as the principal agent of
the Antipatrian rule. On the death of Antipater, another Macedonian
general (Polysperchon) acquired the ascendancy in Greece. He restored the
numerous political exiles, and granted free constitutions to the various cities,
Athens included. This event brought Phokion before the Athenian people
as a prisoner accused of the criminality of his past conduct. The Assembly
before which he stood was composed in great part of citizens just returned
from all the hardships of the exile that Antipater had condemned them to.

'When these restored citizens thus saw Phokion brought before them,
for the first time after their return, the common feeling of antipathy against
him burst out in furious manifestations. Agonides, the principal accuser,
supported by Epikurus and Demophilus, found their denunciations wel-
comed and even anticipated, when they had arraigned Phokion as a criminal

## REALITY OF THE PLEASURE OF MALEVOLENCE. 143

violation involved in the original offence, the further damage
incurred in chastising the offender, are only part of the evils
belonging to the case. The presence in the same breast of
tender sympathies and warm affections is often the cause of
an exceedingly painful struggle in addition to those other
sources of pain. But if we were to admit contrariety of
impulses as a proof of the inherent misery of angry emotion,
we must equally consider it a proof of the misery of tender
emotion. There are times when the exercise of our affections
is exceedingly painful, the object of them having excited our

---

who had lent his hand to the subversion of the constitution—to the sufferings
of his deported fellow-citizens—and to the holding of Athens in subjection
under a foreign potentate; in addition to which, the betrayal of Peiræus to
Nikanor, constituted a new crime, fastening on the people the yoke of Kas-
sander, when Autonomy had been promised to them by the recent imperial
edict. After the accusation was concluded, Phokion was called on for his
defence; but he found it impossible for him to obtain a hearing. Attempting
several times to speak, he was as often interrupted by angry shouts; several
of his friends were cried down in like manner; until at length he gave up the
case in despair, and exclaimed, 'For myself, Athenians, I plead guilty; I
pronounce against myself the sentence of death for my political conduct; but
why are you to sentence these men near me, who are not guilty?' 'Because
they are your friends, Phokion,' was the exclamation of those around. Phokion then said no more; while Agonides proposed a decree, to the effect that
the assembled people should decide by a show of hands, whether the persons
now arraigned were guilty or not; and that if declared guilty, they should
be put to death. Some persons present cried out that the penalty of torture
ought to precede death; but this savage proposition, utterly at variance with
Athenian law in respect to citizens, was repudiated not less by Agonides than
by the Macedonian officer, Kleitus. The decree was then passed; after which
the show of hands was called for. Nearly every hand in the assembly was
held up in condemnation; each man even rose from his seat to make the
effect more imposing; and some went so far as to put on wreaths in token
of triumph. To many of them, doubtless, the gratification of this intense
and unanimous vindictive impulse—in their view not merely legitimate, but
patriotic—must have been among the happiest moments of life.'

The above is perhaps the most remarkable instance afforded by the ancient
world. In modern times it is even surpassed by the burst of furious exultation that accompanied the execution of Robespierre. See the description in
Michelet, *Histoire de la Révolution Française*, Liv. xxi. chap 10.

Dr. Young's tragedy, entitled *Zanga; or, The Slave's Revenge*, is a poetic
handling of the same theme.

**144**     THE IRASCIBLE EMOTION.

wrathful sentiment. At those moments, it is a great misery to harbour tender feelings, and it were better for us to have nothing but irascibility in our constitution. Accordingly, in cases where the sympathies and affections are little developed in the character, and where the contrary passions possess an unusual vigour, the enjoyment derivable from pure malevolence is intense and unalloyed. Nothing but the retribution accruing from a course of mischief and wrong inflicted upon others, can occur to interrupt the joys of gratified resentments, whence, with precautions for his own safety, the actor might be truly happy. Instances of this devil-like character are not unfrequently to be met with in real life; and in romance it often occurs as a creation. The Quilp of Dickens is a recent, and highly illustrative specimen. The irascible temper, in a state of surcharge, does not need an actual offender; any person or anything, the most innocent or irrelevant, receives the shock.

14. The resentful feeling sometimes receives the name of 'Righteous Indignation,' from the circumstance that some great criminality or flagrant wrong has been the instigating cause. The open law-breakers that encroach upon the rights of the orderly citizen, and the tyrants and oppressors of mankind on the great scale, are examples of the fair application of the sentiment. A nation rousing itself to shake off the yoke of a despot may well be moved with a righteous anger. This form of the passion has always been considered as not unbecoming in the greatest and most high-minded of men, being justified by the occasion that called it forth. Somewhat different, although akin, is the meaning of 'Noble Rage,' which represents the interesting, engaging, or poetic aspect of anger; being what makes a fine display, an attractive spectacle, or a stirring drama. The wrath of Achilles was a theatrical, rather than a righteous, indignation. The developments of irascible passion, as we shall presently notice, are interesting to behold from the point of view of a mere spectator; and we dignify by the term 'noble' what inspires a lofty æsthetic interest. The very tyrant who has

DISORDERS RISING OUT OF ANGER. 145

kindled a flame of righteous indignation, becomes, by his carriage and demeanour when standing at bay before the excited populace, a subject for the poets and painters of after times ; such is the difference between our artistic and our moral sentiments.

15. In Morality, and in preserving the order of the world, resentment is a powerful instrument. Not merely the hurt that anger prompts to, but the very expression or aspect of the passion inspires dread and makes men exert themselves to avoid rousing it. Our anger is a wall of fire around us. In the government of human beings the display of angry feeling is a check on disobedience.

On the other hand, this passion is one grand spring of the disorders that trouble human life. Injury, real or supposed, excites the thirst for vengeance, the outgoings of which, if unable to crush the offender, only stimulate new acts of aggression. Thus, by a process of action and reaction, the evil goes on multiplying itself, while every step puts the hope of reconciliation at a greater distance. Slight irritation grows to irreparable feud, individuals are injured, the laws are broken, and the evil principle reigns triumphant. Strong remedies are called for to avert consequences such as these. Some powerful third party must lay his hand upon both, and oblige them to retrace. The interference of an acknowledged superior is never more wanted than in allaying quarrels. A different method, applicable where the other is not, consists in the mediatorship of one disposed to bear the brunt of either party's resentment. The spread of the angry flame may be checked when some one appears who is not only indisposed to kindle at offence, but ready to make sacrifices and render good for evil. Such are the peace-makers of society.

16. Education is especially needed to act upon the revengeful passion, with a view to restraining it. The ebullitions of wrath in children have to be held in check, and themselves disciplined to bear up against offences. The purely malevolent aspect of the feeling, the delight in taking vengeance, should be compressed within the narrowest limits.

K

## 146 THE IRASCIBLE EMOTION.

Self-protection and good order may be served by extending to human life generally the cool and calculating spirit of the law in dealing with wrong-doers. The policeman, the judge, the legislator, display nothing of the wrathful in their proceedings. Having a certain end in view, the preservation of the public, they go calmly to work in adapting their means accordingly. So, in private life, it is possible to take whatever steps are necessary for our protection, up to the infliction of salutary pain, without the sting of malevolence. The outburst of resentful vengeance is not wanted so much for others as for ourselves. As with the flow of tears, we derive a great relief from opening the flood-gates of our anger; while, in both cases, it is in general preferable to restrain the current. The immediate effect of soothing the wounded spirit is purchased at the cost of exhaustion to ourselves as well as annoyance to others. Irascible people, ill-tempered men and women, scolds, are justly accounted the pests of life. Theirs . is ignoble wrath.

17. Our concluding observations on the subject of this chapter refer to the Artistic handling of the passion of anger. In addition to the natural expression of the feeling, there is a range of artificial or cultivated expression, whereby civilized men are wont to display their anger. Threats, curses, oaths, and intense language generally, are the spoken manifestations, still farther expanded in denunciation, calumny, or abuse. More ingenious and theatrical devices are also resorted to. The withdrawing of oneself into sullen isolation, the infliction of indirect annoyances, are happily pourtrayed by the masters of comedy in representing the passion on the stage.

The artistic interest growing out of the developments of the irascible sentiment is of various kinds. The mere display of marked human expression arrests and fascinates the gaze; the peculiar intensity of this passion giving a grand prominence to its outward appearance. Hence, when dignified by a fitting occasion, the wrathful demeanour is appropriate to the hand of the painter or the sculptor. The poet, too, finds it a theme for energetic description and imposing

## ARTISTIC INTEREST. 147

phraseology. The wrathful ebullitions and lofty indignation of gods and men have often been depicted in epic and tragic metres ; while less worthy forms have found a place in comic art. The interest that we take in the display of the passions of human beings is complicated, and perhaps difficult to analyse—there is, nevertheless, a real foundation for it in human nature. The personified principle of evil ought, properly speaking, to cause us only dread and loathing. Nevertheless, the artist has often worked up his most interesting creations by the employment of this as a subject. Not in the *Paradise Lost* alone is the malign personage the real hero of the piece.

Another form wherein this passion enters into Art, is in the exhibition of vicious characters and mischief-workers to excite our wrath by their crimes, and gratify it by their punishment. In the plot of an ordinary romance, the sinner after many doublings, is made to feel 'the strong hand of poetical justice' at last. Even in history we have such a thing as 'celebrated crimes,' and the procedure of our courts of justice occupies a notable share of the interest we take in what is passing around us.

# CHAPTER X.

### EMOTIONS OF ACTION.—PURSUIT.

1. IN the situation of voluntary activity, or working for ends, we have already counted three kinds of feeling—the satisfaction of the end, the pleasures (or pain) of the exercise, and the pleasure of superior (or pain of inferior) power. There remains the mental attitude under a gradually approaching end, a peculiar condition of rapt suspense, termed Pursuit and Plot interest.

Some desirable end spurs us into action : we wish, for example, to cross a ferry, to go into the country, or to visit some object of interest. In proceeding along, we keep a look-out upon the goal, and watch it coming nearer and nearer ; our attention is increasingly engrossed, rising to a climax at the final consummation. With the full attainment of the end, the watching attitude dies away and gives place to the state of fruition.

Much use is made of this situation in the recreations of life. As an incident of our industrial pursuits, it furnishes a certain relief to tedium, and at times rises to a positive zest. It contributes to our interest in the affairs of the world at large ; and it is brought into play in the various arts of pleasure and amusement, as in the literature of plot-interest—the drama and the romance.

2. On the *physical* side, the situation of pursuit is marked chiefly by the intent occupation of one or other of the senses, accompanied with a fixed attitude generally, so far as the concurring active exertions will allow. The fixed stare of the eye, the alertness of the ear, the groping touch, are well known

## PHYSICAL ATTITUDE. 149

manifestations. If, as sometimes happens, we have no share in the active proceedings, we are 'all eye, all ear,' all observation; the attitude being one of stillness, and of suitability to the process of seeing, hearing, touching, or other sensibility engaged; as, for example, when we are the spectators of a race, or the listeners to a judicial decision. If, on the other hand, we are agents as well, we are divided between observation and productive exertion, as in hitting a mark. In either case, there is a strong and concentrated activity; the stray currents of energy are recalled for a special effort; recipiency of impressions is reduced to a point; the system is open at a single avenue and closed at the others. The currents of the brain are not available for the diffusion of an emotional wave; and hence the feelings are kept under, if not altogether suppressed.

Bodily exercise, or muscular action generally, is antagonistic to the development of feeling. Were it not for the occasional remission of the active strain, the muscular feelings themselves would remain unmanifested. Acting and feeling tend to exclude one another. Every kind ot bodily labour restricts the play of emotion; it is only in the unavoidable intervals, that we can become fully awake to our feelings. It is not enough that we are stimulated to pleasure or to pain, we must lapse into muscular quiescence to realize either.

3. Our *consciousness* under pursuit is found to accord with what has now been said. The great intensity of the object-regards—into which a muscular strain necessarily enters—excludes the subject-regards, the feelings proper, as pleasure and pain. According as we are engrossed with things beyond ourselves, self-consciousness is in abeyance; and if the engrossment attains an extreme pitch, there is an almost entire suspension of feeling or emotion; pleasure and pain, even though arising out of the situation, cannot be felt, until there is some intermission or relaxation of the attention to the objects. When a new scene bursts on the view, calculated to give astonishment and delight, so long as we are occupied in scanning its dimensions and following its details, we are

## 150 EMOTIONS OF ACTION.—PURSUIT.

restrained from indulging in these emotions; we cannot be, in a high degree, object and subject at once; we must remit the object tension to let feeling arise; the scrutinizing gaze being renewed, there is a renewed suppression of the feeling. Consequently, our most powerful instrument of controlling the development of feeling, of varying the mental attitude, of checking the wear and tear of the emotional consciousness,— is the engagement of the mind objectively, that is, with outward things.

The situation of pursuit, or Plot-interest, has the power of attracting the outward regards in a special degree. Doubtless, the motive, in the first instance, is a feeling, the interest in the end; but when an activity so engrossing is prompted, the mind is, for the time, transported out of feeling. This temporary abeyance of the subject-states is valuable from the circumstance that the object-regards are much less exhausting; being a welcome interruption even to our pleasurable outbursts. Objectivity is of the nature of an anæsthetic.*

---

* The means of allaying and diverting mental excitement, either totally or partially, possess a high practical interest.

The physician has a class of drugs for quelling the fever of the brain, and for bringing on sleep under morbid wakefulness. Opium, in its numerous preparations, and Hyoscyamus, have this special virtue. The stimulants, Alcohol, Chloroform, Chlorodyne, &c., are also narcotics.

Changes of Temperature have a lulling efficacy, within certain limits. Cold, in such measure as makes it a healthy stimulant, reduces the congestion of the brain. Genial warmth, as in the hot bath, diminishes the undue cerebral excitement, by lowering the circulation generally, and by increasing the action of the skin.

Among mental causes, we must give the foremost rank to the massive or voluminous pleasures. I have already remarked on their sedative efficacy, and have endeavoured to assign the link of physical causation (p. 75). If the over-excitement is simply due to pain, the abatement of the pain, or a neutralizing pleasure, is the obvious remedy. Excessive excitement, unaccompanied by pleasure or pain, is best subdued by some *gentle* continued diversion; the difficulty being to find a stimulation such as will not increase the evil. Hence the efficacy of the pleasures characterized by quantity or extent of stimulus, rather than by intensity—slow movements, repose after exercise, warmth, repletion, balmy odours, soft touch, gentle music, agreeable and un exciting spectacle, tender feeling, self-complacency, &c.

## INFLUENCE OF PURSUIT ON THE MIND. 151

That there is, in the background, a feeling of more or less intensity, repressed and asserting itself by turns, must be pronounced a part of the case. Ordinarily the feeling is some good or evil in the distance, an ideal end prompting us to labour for realizing it ; the regards are intent upon the end, and more especially when its approach is rapid and near. Such a moment is favourable to that entranced attention, under which the mind is debarred from feeling, and from all thoughts extraneous to the situation. Nevertheless, we remit, at short intervals, the objective strain, falling back into emotion or self-consciousness; we then experience the full intensity of the primary motive, until such time as we are once more thrown upon the outward stretch.

Through the need that there is of upholding a certain proportion of objective regards, we can see how even pain might increase a man's happiness. We have only to suppose a state of inaction, and the total absence of pursuit, with or without abundance of gratifications ; the consequence would be the drag of an unbalanced subjectivity ; and the introduction of a pain such as to stimulate exertion, and a forward look, might be more than compensated by the abatement of ennui.

---

After an absence from one's home, spent in turmoil and worry, the return to the usual routine, and to the old associations, is highly soothing, and the more so, that these associations are on the side of pleasure.

The power of change of scene and circumstances, as in foreign travel, new society, and unwonted amusements, is explicable entirely on the principle of relativity or change of impression.

The power of self-control, originating in an energetic effort of the will, and confirmed into habit, may serve to suppress on many occasions, the over-excitement of the brain. No better application of voluntary power, and no better subject for self-discipline, could be suggested to those that have the infirmity of too susceptible nerves.

It is impossible not to desire a much greater extension of our catalogue of anæsthetic agents. It is, I think, a matter of regret that the mesmeric sleep is not more cultivated in this application, having nothing of the drawback of the drugging opiates.

I have gladly adopted the term ' anæsthesia' into the phraseology of mental science.

## EMOTIONS OF ACTION.—PURSUIT.

4. It is known that an element of Uncertainty, or Chance, heightens the interest of pursuit. The operation is twofold. In the first place, uncertainty, as an agency of terror, throws the mental energies into the organs of perception; and in the second place, certainty of attainment, being almost as good as possession, relaxes the attention to the approaching goal. A small infusion of uncertainty, and a moderate stake, render the situation perfect as a source of interest. On the other hand, a great risk is attended with too much fear to be agreeable; the spur to objectivity is intense, but the moments of remission give full play to the misery of dread.

5. Whenever an interval occurs between the conceiving of an end and the fruition of it—the interval of action—there is scope for the situation now described. Hence we may study it in the Lower Animals. A beast of prey, actuated by hunger, and seeing in the distance one of its victims, commences the pursuit. The gaze is fixed on the fugitive, the remaining energies are occupied with the run. The emotions in the back ground are furious, but they drop out of consciousness at that moment of engrossment, when the eye is measuring a nearer and nearer approach. Such at least is the interpretation that we should put upon the mental state of the animal, from the analogy of our own experience. If the yelping of a pack of hounds were taken as expressing the emergence of feeling proper, it would be for observation to determine at what points this is manifested, and at what repressed. There might, however, be a certain vocal accompaniment in the general tumult of the energies, such as would not betoken genuine feeling.

6. Field Sports are the imitation by human beings of the exciting circumstances of the life of the wild beast. The end in view, namely, the killing or catching some species of quadruped, bird, or fish, is one extremely grateful to the sporting mind; while the pursuit is one that prominently contains the peculiar elements of interest. The active exertion required is agreeable and healthful, and both this and the condition of suspense are protracted by the flight of the animal, or by its non-appearance giving a necessity for search. With the ob-

## FIELD SPORTS.

ject pleasurable, the exercise congenial, and the end nearing in the view, and yet not too soon attained, the situation is complete. A fair amount of success attending on a day's sport gives a very high exhilaration to the spirits—bright points of victorious achievement separated by intervals of of suspense and emotional stillness, like brilliant stars over the azure spaces.* Danger and difficulty, as in boar or tiger hunting, let loose a more fiery interest upon the mind.

In Shooting, the piquancy of the destructive interest is perhaps at the highest. There is something fascinating to the sense of power in the distant shot; the far-darting Apollo was an eminently imposing personation. Deer-stalking is reckoned one of the best of the sports of the gun, because the animal is of a superior order, difficult to track, and seldom exposing itself to an easy aim. Angling is flat in comparison; but with many minds there is in the handling of the rod a wonderful power of sustaining the pleasurable suspense. In such cases the pleasure of each successful throw needs to exert a lasting influence on the mind, rendering it easy to go on for a long time without a take. All those ends that support a protracted pursuit must have this power of easily occupying the mind in idea, and of spontaneously maintaining the rapt attention and suspense characteristic of the state. Snaring and Trapping have much of the interest of angling. The physical expenditure is small, but the exercise of cunning, skill, and circumvention, is one of the agreeable forms of self-elation, and sustains the 'patient thought' of the operator. In the Chase, the ultimate effect is small and pitiful; the pleasure lying in a long-sustained run, for which the animal furnishes a pretext. The high excitement is mainly caused by the multitude, the race, and the animation of the hounds. There is something of the stir of a battle-field without the danger.

7. Contests present the situation of suspense and pleasur-

---

* All this applies eminently to the chase, guiltless of blood or suffering, sustained by the botanist.

## 154    EMOTIONS OF ACTION.—PURSUIT.

able engrossment in considerable force. The end being a very keen emotion,—the manifesting of one's superiority in the snatching of some advantage away from another party,— it is not surprising that the mind should be deaf to everything while the issue is pending. Two combatants, actually engaged, have their whole disposable force thrown into the two energies of plying their weapons and of rapt attention to the approaching termination of the struggle. Hence combats are introduced for the mere purpose of creating moments of intense interest, as in youthful play, and in the amusements of grown men. Athletic contests put the physical powers to the utmost stretch, and are suitable to muscular constitutions. The games of the field, and the green, combine skill with strength, and are to that extent more mental in their character. In the operations of the Intellect, combats may spring up, as in disputation, controversy, or pleading before an assembly. Here, too, there is that state of stillness of the mind from all foreign emotions, with a fixed gaze in the nearing moment of decision. The intellectual Greeks introduced the contests of wit into the programme of their banquets.

8. The presence of Chance, as already remarked, makes the occasion more exciting. In Games generally, there is a combination of skill and chance; the last, while giving hopes to an inferior player, stimulates the circumspection of the most skilled. Cricket, football, golf, bowls, are contests affected by chance, and leading to sanguine hopes and excited calculations. A corresponding energy of the state of suspense is manifested while the result of a stroke is pending. Billiards is a game of skill with just enough of good or bad luck to keep up the interest between two unequal players, and, as it were, to re-open what would be otherwise a settled question. Chess and draughts are contests of almost pure skill. But when we come to Cards, the element of chance is a large determining agency, and uncertainty keeps up the suspense and the interest. In dice, roulette, and the like, hazard is triumphant, and the bad characteristic of gambling is complete. The kindling of insane hopes out of the wide possibilities

PURSUIT IN INDUSTRY. 155

of such games is their demoralizing feature. On the other extreme, it is to be remembered, in connexion with the emotion of pursuit, that, in proportion as the end is clearly foreseen, the interest of suspense dies away, and what is sure of being realized, although still future, is already enjoyed. The contest of a strong man with a weak has little exciting interest.

9. The extended occupations of life afford scope for the interest of pursuit, even without this being their principal design. The business of war notoriously contains this element; the end is exciting and yet uncertain; a series of actions brings it nearer step by step, sustaining the attention to the very close. The desires of each human being engage him or her in action for attaining their objects, and involve also, to a more or less degree, the attention and suspense towards the approaching end. The commencement of any career generally sees the mind already fixed upon the goal; the starting on an adventure clears the attention of all foreign matters to await the one issue at stake. Moreover, it is to be remarked that the more lengthened undertakings are made up of sequences of minor ends, plots, and adventures, subdividing the large periods into short cycles of near accomplishment. The life of the agriculturist is divided into seasons, having the harvest-time for the principal prospect. Every season has its stages of ploughing, sowing, &c., each containing the interest of a forward look. The artisan has his separate fabrications, and in every one the interest of a beginning, middle, and conclusion. We are so apt to feel languid and discouraged under toil that has no end nor definite term, that we make artificial terms to give the awakened attention and suspense that enable us to pass the time more easily. On a long journey by sea or land, we look out for the minor stages in succession. The labourer in a monotonous and stageless employment is driven for interest to the expectation of his meals, the end of his day, and the receipt of his wages.* In all professions, the cheerful

---

* 'As the servant looketh towards the shadow (on the dial), and the hireling to the reward of his work.'—JOB.

## 156 EMOTIONS OF ACTION.—PURSUIT.

effect of nearing a conclusion is experienced. The physician has his patients, whom he sees through, one after another, to some termination. The attorney's business is made up of his cases, disposed of in succession. Minds, dissatisfied with the degree of excitement arising in an ordinary business profession, have recourse to the more uncertain avocations of war, navigation, and the discovery of new regions. This is to stake high, and leave a large scope to chance, in short, to gamble. The profession of the miner often exemplifies this species of hazard.

10. In the Sympathetic relationships we may experience the interest of pursuit. In addition to the union of occupation and end, as in the mother working for her child, there is a plot-interest attending every stage and crisis of the beloved object. The epochs, the trials, the successes and the triumphs occurring in the development of each human being, are looked forward to by parents and friends with earnest anticipation, and at times with breathless attention. The gratifying of our affections being of itself an end, as keenly pursued as any other felt in the same degree, the turnings and windings, and progressive fulfilment of our longings can keep up the interest of the passing day, and operate in the room of actual enjoyment. As in other cases, the requisites are some object of strong emotion, capable of being sustained as an idea, and in the way of being actually realized—conditions often found together in affairs of the heart. The characteristics of the tender feeling fit it for constituting an easy plot-excitement, as well as a congenial and satisfying emotion. It is, however, too well known, in all these cases, that depressing uncertainties often mar the good of the situation.

11. The love of Knowledge, in minds susceptible thereto, is a good instance of an end adapted to stimulate the forward look, and the growing intentness of the chase. Curiosity once awake, the earnest student is on the alert, until a mystery is unravelled, a truth demonstrated, a discovery achieved. The subject matter of knowledge being something for the intellect to lay hold of, we find it easy to retain in the

## PURSUIT OF KNOWLEDGE. 157

mind, as an abiding desire, the thing that we wish to know. No mother can sustain the interest in her progeny more enduringly, than a mind of intellectual cast can keep up the freshness of the attainment of knowledge. The character of refinement belongs in an eminent degree to such an aim as this. Original research, introducing an element still more capable of arresting the forward regard, is by no means a gentle excitement, but capable of making up a powerful life interest, and yielding moments of almost unnerving suspense. The art of the Teacher is shown in rousing the feeling of curiosity, and thereby securing the attention. When we speak of the influence of pursuit in producing a partial lull, or anæsthesia, of the feelings and thoughts, it is not meant that the mind is made torpid or put to sleep. What happens is the calling in of the stray movements or wanderings of the faculties, the instituting of one engrossing outlet with a shutting up of all the rest. This must often be a real economy of the mental energy. By substituting the tension of the eye for the numerous currents of the brain, involved in the wandering of the thoughts under excitement, we perform an important service to the overworked machine. The fixing of a single organ has a tendency to fix all the rest, and although these effects imply a certain draft upon the central brain, they are less costly than the maintenance of the waves of emotion. It is in this sense that I understand the advantage gained on the whole, by inducing the state of suspense characteristic of the present emotion.* Nothing, therefore, can

---

\* We have here one point of contrast between subjective, and objective or outward regards, showing the more healthy tone accompanying the outward. There is undoubtedly a quieting influence in the steady gaze inspired by an approaching consummation. We feel it often when the mind is suffering from inward distractions and wanderings : anything that, as the phrase goes, takes us out of ourselves, has a medicinal efficacy in stilling the tumult of brain. But the interest attaching to the diverting object ought to be just enough to make a nucleus, or point of subsidence, and no more. One's morbid trains would be all too effectually diverted by being told that the house was on fire.

It is common to prescribe some employment as a cure for sorrow, ennui,

158　　　　EMOTIONS OF ACTION.—PURSUIT.

well be more suited to the imbibing of intellectual impressions, than this attitude when inspired towards the exact object of study. We have seen the power of terror to stimulate the intellectual attention, but awakened curiosity is in every way a preferable instrumentality.

12. We pass now to the position of the Spectator of a chase. Much interest and amusement are derived from standing by, and seeing others moving on to some goal a-head. We are capable of entering into the situation of the actors, of becoming invested for the time with their mode of excitement, and of thereby sharing in the inspiration of the plot. The case follows the usual laws of sympathy, one of which is that we are most ready to assume through outward contagion the states belonging to our own individuality. The ambitions man is easily excited by the spectacle of a fellow-man struggling to rise to power ; the sportsman looks on with suspense, while his companion is aiming a difficult shot. The kind of interest attending this position, is of the same character as the other ; making allowance only for the difference between being actually engaged,

---

or satiety. A chase will often extricate the mind from melancholy broodings, and reanimate the flagging interest of over-indulgence. I doubt not that this is a fact in human nature, as well as a favourite theory of our poets. Tennyson's *Maude*, the comedy of *Used Up*, lately in vogue, and the character of the Duke of Buckingham in *Peveril of the Peak*, show the estimate formed by the authors of the efficiency of a stirring object of pursuit for the purposes now mentioned. As an incitement to active exercise, when other motives are wanting, and as enabling the mind to derive satisfaction from pleasures, merely by seeing them on the way, thus diluting fruition with anticipation—the setting up of some distant goal to be laboriously reached is a device to be tried, when other means fail to stem the downward career towards settled melancholy and despondency.

Physicians warn their patients against too much attention to their maladies ; a practice favoured by the unoccupied condition of the invalid. Sir Henry Holland remarks (Mental Physiology, chap. iii.) that ' the symptoms of the dyspeptic patient are exceedingly aggravated by the constant and earnest direction of his mind to the digestive organs, and the functions going on in them ;' it being in fact the case that such introspection relaxes the nervous influence that aids the digestive process.

## THE SPECTATOR OF A CHASE. 159

and ideal engagement. In the present case, the stress is more upon the mind, and the excitement not being counterbalanced by actual exertion, is apt to be more exhausting. Stirring contests are the most resorted to, for interest as a spectacle. Horse-racing brings out all the features of a begun and completed pursuit, and stands as such to every individual of the assembled throng. With an end in view that strongly engages the feelings, there is a string of preparations intently watched; the start is the commencement of a still higher stretch of attention, which is then kept up, and increased with every new situation of the race, till the grand result has released the breathless suspense. This extreme instance can scarcely be looked upon as lulling the mind, although the power of diversion is complete : the reason being that the diverting influence, is itself a furious excitement, and the intensity of the stiffened gaze is a greater expenditure than any ordinary state of unchecked wandering. Still, the intentness upon the end is made to expand an interest over a length of time, and a great variety of transactions, sustaining a tone and condition of mental engrossment that is esteemed happiness by those concerned. The other contests that have been drawn into the circle of public amusements, as athletic games, gladiatorship, bull-fights, and the like, differ in no essential feature. Sometimes the spectator has a high stake upon the issue; while, perhaps, to the general multitude, the end is only to resolve a doubt, or be confirmed in a belief, of comparative superiority. But to all there comes the excited gaze, the moments of elation, or dread, as the action inclines to one side or another, and the growing concentration of the mind on the eve of the final blow. In the fights where life and limb are concerned, there is the coarse excitement of destructiveness, in seeing some creature laid low in the midst of its vigour ; a feeling that it is to the credit of modern refinement. to have somewhat discouraged. All the conflicts formerly mentioned, as inducing the interest of suspense in the combatants themselves, are coveted as spectacle by some class of lookers-on. A lawsuit, a contested election, a debate, the de-

160 EMOTIONS OF ACTION.—PURSUIT.

cision of a public assembly, a controversy between opposing parties—arouse the attention, both of those concerned in the result, and of the lovers of plot-excitement. People will sometimes work up for themselves a factitious interest in some pending decision, in order to enjoy the animation, and experience the diversion, of the struggle. It is needless to say that all other kinds of pursuit may engage the sympathizing looker-on to the same degree as the instances now dwelt upon. We may follow with excited gaze the operations of another man's industry, and view with breathless anxiety the approaching completion of some great design, the success of an enterprise, or the discovery of a truth.

13. Before quitting the subject, the Literature of Plot-interest claims some notice. The position of the spectator of moving events, is greatly enlarged by language, which can bring before his mind, scenes witnessed by other men; and, in so far as he is able to conceive what is thus related, he catches the fire of the actual witness. This is the interest of story, which is such a widely-spread source of excitement. The narrative of a chase, a battle, an adventure, places the hearer under the dominion of the situation we are considering. The interesting stake, at first remote and uncertain, but gradually brought nearer, as the successive incidents are recounted, keeps up that animated suspense, felt alike by the actor, the spectator, and the hearer or reader, rendering it difficult for the mind to entertain any new subject, till the declaration of the final issue. The recital of what befalls our friends, and the men and societies belonging to our generation, is the commonest and directest mode of stirring up our attention and suspense. We can also be affected by the narratives of past history, some of which are more particularly adapted for this kind of interest. The struggles that have preceded vast changes, contests, revolutions, keep the reader in a state of thrilling expectation; while the inner plots and minor catastrophes serve to discharge at intervals the pent-up currents, and vary the direction of the outlook. Whatever the achievements are that rouse the feelings of a reader—whether wars,

## LITERATURE OF PLOT-INTEREST. 161

conquests, human greatness, or progress and civilization,—
the moments when these were pending in doubtful issue, are
to him moments of earnest engrossment.

While the historian is bound by fact and reality, the
poet or romancer is able to accommodate his narrative so
as to satisfy the exigencies of plot-interest by devices suited
thereto. Calculating how much suspense the mind of a reader
can easily bear, and how this can be artificially sustained and
prolonged; casting about also for the class of events best
able to awaken agreeable emotions in a story; the artist in
narrative weaves together a tissue of incidents aiming at some
one conclusion, which, however, is to be accomplished through
many intermediate issues. Epic and dramatic poetry were
the first forms of plot fiction; the prose romance or novel is
the more modern and perennial variety. Many strings of
interest may be touched by a highly-wrought romance, but
the dissolution of the plot would destroy what is essential in
the structure, and leave the composition lifeless and tedious
to the mass of readers.

14. The chief form of *pain* mixed up with the situation
of pursuit, is that arising from the pursuit being unduly protracted. The failure in the thing aimed at causes the suffering
due to the loss sustained, whatever that may be; by failing
in a contest, we experience the sense of deprivation of the
prize contended for, as well as the humiliation of defeat. But
as far as the pursuit goes, we are made miserable when expectation once aroused is baulked by postponement. I go a long
journey to see a contest, and find that it does not take place;
I am roused by a great issue at stake, and no movement is
making towards the decision; or hear the commencement of
an exciting story, and am left to wait for the conclusion. This
is one of the modes of the pain of disappointment and
thwarted aims, which we have had more than once to bring
into view. The mind put on the stretch for a certain object,
and that object not attained, there is produced a regurgitation
and jar of the system, causing for the moment a shock of
acute distress, which, however, in the present instance, is not

L

162          EMOTIONS OF ACTION.—PURSUIT.

very severe or lasting.   The mental attitude is soon readjusted
to something else, and no permanent wound is made.

The very full discussion to be given of the active and
volitional part of our nature in the second part of this volume
will bring out incidentally other cases of the pleasures and
pains related to Action, and likewise set in a clearer light
those now expounded.   The element of 'Belief' has not been
brought forward as yet; and therefore I have not dwelt, in
the present chapter, on the emotional state of Hope, which is
the forward look in combination with a certain amount of
confidence in the result.

# CHAPTER XI.

### EMOTIONS OF INTELLECT.

1. THE operations of the Intellect give occasion to a certain select class of feelings, which concern both our pleasures and our actions. The expanded illustration of the processes of intelligence in my former volume has brought into view the greater number of those feelings, and all that is needful at present is to resume them in a consecutive order, and to note their characteristic properties.

The trains of Contiguous association, as exemplified in memory and routine, present no special stimulant of the emotions. They constitute a case of mere exercise, and gratify or pain the individual according to the condition of mental vigour and freshness at the time. It is under Similarity that the great fund of emotion-giving situations is placed. Those identifications of likeness in remote objects, and under deep disguises, strike the mind with an effect of surprise, brilliancy, exhilaration, or charm. This may not be precisely the same for all the different subjects which the identifying faculty has to work upon; original discoveries in science do not affect us in the way that we feel under felicitous comparisons in poetry; and the sentiments of proportion and fitness in industry and in design have to be discriminated from both. Again, Inconsistency, want of Unity, or positive Discord, are forms of pain that influence us to a considerable degree, and derive importance from inspiring the virtues of Truth, Integrity, and Justice; being, in fact, a constituent element of the Moral Sense.

2. The emotion of Similarity, or the feeling excited by a

164 EMOTIONS OF INTELLECT.

flash of identification between things never regarded as like before, is generically of the nature of agreeable Surprise ; being, in fact, an outburst of Novelty. When we suddenly discover, or have pointed out to us for the first time, a likeness between two objects lying wide apart, and never considered as of the same class, we are arrested, startled, and excited into a pleasing wonderment. Travelling in new countries where nature is different in nearly all her phases— climate, vegetation, animal life, being all changed—an unexpected coincidence arouses us, as when we recognise the same genera and species under greatly altered modes of development. Similarity in manners affects us when the whole basis of society is distinct, as when we read the history of past ages, or the habits of strange races. A characteristic trait of our common humanity has a striking effect where we are wound up to look for the extraordinary and superhuman ; poetical and mythical antiquity furnishes many such surprises. Accustomed as we are by our earliest impressions to see great diversity among the things around us, every new identification gives a pleasing stimulus. When the young plant rises with all the characters of the old, when we see in children the features and characters of their parents, when likeness is traced in unrelated individuals, an agreeable interest is felt in the circumstance ; our attention is awakened and held fast upon the objects with a sort of temporary fascination. Recurring forms in plants and animals, repetitions in the structure and stratification of the globe, give an analogous excitement.

3. The peculiar mode of the pleasurable surprise varies with the subject, and I shall therefore touch upon the several classes of identifications already delineated in the second chapter of the exposition of the INTELLECT. In the identities struck by Science—the generalizations, abstractions, classifications, inductions, and deductions that constitute scientific discovery—the sudden shock of wonder is accompanied with a marked degree of the pleasure of *rebound*, the lightening of an intellectual burden, or the solving of a difficulty that formerly weighed on the mind. I have dwelt upon this result in

## ADVANCE OF KNOWLEDGE. 165

speaking of these operations.* The labour of intellectual comprehension is reduced by every new discovery of likeness ; and the first feeling of this gives a rush of delight, the delight we feel when we are relieved of some long-standing burden, or discharged from a laborious obligation. If the effect is to solve an apparent contradiction, there is the same gladdening reaction from the depression of embarrassment. Great generalizations, such as the atomic theory of Dalton, give a sense of enlarged power in dealing with the multiplicity of nature, and are more than a momentary surprise.†

When new knowledge has a Practical bearing, the emotion is that produced by the more easy fulfilment of practical ends, and is a deliverance from labour, or an enlargement of effect. The invention of the steam-engine, besides novelty of contrivance, took off incalculable burdens from the shoulders of humanity, and immensely extended the efficiency of labour. In whichever of the two lights we may choose to regard it, the contemplation is pleasurable. Whether we reduce a man's toil or increase the produce of it, we give him a feeling of elation and joy.

Truth is tested by application to practice. The naviga-

---

* To vary the expression to the reader, let me quote a paragraph on the same theme from Mr. James Mill: 'First, the operation of classing ; when the philosopher endeavours to range the objects of his consideration under heads, and as many of them as possible under one head ; so that he may obtain propositions true of as great a number of them as possible. Such propositions are found to be of the greatest utility. And the man who in this way subjects the largest province of human knowledge to the fewest principles, is universally esteemed the most successful philosopher. This is what Plato called " seeing the one in the many," and " the many in the one." And he said he would follow to the end of the world the man whom he should discover to be master in that art.'

† The love of truth, consistency, and simplicity is the proper emotion of pure philosophy. Beside the gratification that may arise from the active exercise of intellect in its peculiar sphere, we may lawfully derive all the enjoyment that accrues from the tracing of similarity in apparent diversity, of unity in variety, of simplicity in complexity, of order in confusion. The clearing up of mysteries, and the successful comprehension of what seemed utterly beyond the ken of our faculties, may likewise delight the spirit even to ecstacy.'—*Chambers's Papers for the People*, ' What is Philosophy ?'

166                    EMOTIONS OF INTELLECT.

tion of the seas by means of lunar distances is the triumphant and telling demonstration of the theory of the moon's motion. The prediction of eclipses is a coincidence between calculation and experience, which both strikes with surprise and exalts the sense of human power. All discoveries that have this prophetic accuracy are a secure foundation for practical operations, and give that confidence in issues, so cheering to the mind beset with many fears.

4. To pass next to Illustrative comparisons, or those strokes of identity whereby an abstruse or obscure notion is rendered lucid by some familiar parallel. When the lungs are compared to a common bellows, we are made in an instant to comprehend their mechanical working. The obscure process of communicating disease by infection is in some degree illustrated by the action of yeast. Nervous action is made more intelligible by comparison with the Electric Telegraph. Now in these cases also, the emotion accompanying the surprise is of the nature of intellectual relief. The mind, labouring and struggling to understand what is difficult, is suddenly illuminated by the help of the well-chosen analogy, and enjoys the buoyant reaction. Such is the pleasure of a felicitous exposition. Whatever the device may be that brings the unintelligible within the reach of comprehension, we experience the lightening sense of a deliverance from toil.

We may sum up the pleasures of Knowledge in the following particulars. First, the feeling of mere intellectual novelty, from being brought face to face with a succession of new objects, new properties, and new operations. The field of nature, as explained by science, is enough to occupy a life with new wonders. Secondly, the flash of agreeable surprise from the great discoveries of identification that exhibit similarity in diversity, and unity in multitude, enlarging the intellectual grasp, and diminishing the toil of comprehending the universe. Lastly, the interest in those applications to practice that extend the conveniences and comforts of life. Nor should we omit the counteraction of the terrors inseparable from ignorance.

## COMPARISONS OF FINE ART.

167

5. The comparisons of ornament and Poetic beauty are next to be considered. The metaphors, similes, and parallels, which every great poet originates to adorn his composition withal, besides the surprise of novelty, have at least two distinct effects; the one is the pleasure of having presented to view some interesting object or image; the other and main effect, is something quite different, and comes under the most characteristic property of the productions of fine art. First, the striking objects of nature, the remarkable events of history, and the touching incidents of human life, excite our feelings not only in the actual encounter, but in any reference made to them; and the literary artist avails himself of this circumstance. ' Like *a star* unhasting, unresting ;' what habitually acts on our feelings in the reality, has an influence in the mere citation.

The second property of poetic comparison goes much farther than the mere recall of what has often stirred us. There is an effect produced in the various fine arts which is, in fact, the very essence and cream of art itself, or the most genuine artistic impression. It is what is called harmony and melody in music; picturesqueness in painting; keeping in poetry; and fitness and suitableness of the parts, exquisite adaptation, and the essence of beauty, in all the regions of art. When we put a number of like things together, as soldiers in a line, there is an agreeable feeling of order and uniformity; but the force of art lies still more in joining two or more things of different composition and make, so as to produce a harmonious feeling. It is in Greek architecture, the harmony of the columns and the entablature; in Gothic, the harmony of the spire with the arch; and in all styles, the harmony of the decorations with one another and with the main body. In sculpture, it is the suiting of expression to mind, and of attitude and drapery to expression. In painting, it is the composing and grouping of things such as will in different ways excite the same emotion. In speech, it is the suiting of the action to the word, the sound to the sense. In poetry, which combines the spirit and effect of music and painting, the scope for fine harmonies is unbounded.

168

EMOTIONS OF INTELLECT.

I have already referred to the general law of Harmony and Conflict (Chap. III.). In accordance with it we are prepared to expect that impressions from different quarters concurring to the same effect should economise power, while conflicting or discordant impressions are attended with waste. In a march or a dance, the accompaniment of the music is an aid or support, as well as a pleasure on its own account. Harmonising circumstances in an artistic group have an efficiency in sustaining the feeling of the main situation. If we are desirous to body forth to ourselves the gloomy feelings of a mind plunged in tragic despair, such illustrations as the following are calculated to aid and sustain the attempt; where, besides the excitement of the subject, we have the feeling of being powerfully ministered unto in our endeavours to grasp it :—

> ' 'Tis now the very witching time of night;
> When churchyards yawn, and hell itself breathes out
> Contagion to this world : Now could I drink hot blood,
> And do such bitter business as the day
> Would quake to look on.'

6. Leaving any further remarks on this head to a succeeding chapter devoted to fine art in general, we shall next consider the feeling produced by Inconsistency, which seems naturally to centre in the intellect. Contrary statements, opinions, or appearances, operate on the mind as a painful jar, and stimulate a corresponding desire for a reconciliation. When we hear the same event described by two persons that contradict each other, we are said to be distracted, or pulled two ways at once. This susceptibility is most felt in minds where the intelligence is highly developed ; indeed, with the great mass of men it counts for very little except with reference to further consequences. Any strong emotion is sufficient to make the untutored mind swallow a contradiction with ease; but they that have been accustomed to sift opinions, and reject the untenable and contradictory, feel an intellectual revulsion when conflicting doctrines are propounded. This intellectual sensitiveness usually leads to the abandonment of one of the contraries, or else to a total

LOVE OF TRUTH.

suspension of judgment, that is to say, a repudiation for the time of both the one and the other.

The above, however, is not the only way that contradiction wounds our sensibilities. A far more operative evil is that bound up with the practical consequences. The traveller bent upon his destination, and directed oppositely by equally good authorities, feels much more than the pain of an intellectual conflict. The obligation to act with the inability to decide, causes a torment of opposing volitions, than which in extreme cases no agony can be more acute or heart-rending. This is what gives such importance and emphasis to the virtue of Truth and accuracy in statement as to make mankind in general urgent in enforcing it. It is not that contradiction lacerates the sensitive intellect, but that without consistency—in the various shapes of punctuality, fulfilment of promises, correspondence of statement with fact—the operations of daily life would be frustrated, and every society pass into disorganization.

The regard to Truth, therefore, besides the positive attractions inspired by the great discoveries that comprehend the vastness, and illuminate the obscurity of nature, is fortified by two deterring beacons ; the one influential according as intellect is prominent in the character, the other acting upon the practical interests of all mankind. When we speak of the love of truth for its own sake, we mean to exclude this last motive, and to put the stress upon the first. No form of the feeling can be more pure or disinterested than the desire to attain knowledge coupled with the revolt at inconsistency as such. The genuine affection for the true, implies a laborious testing of evidence founded on an acquaintance with the canons and criteria of sound decision. A meretricious image of Truth has often been decked out by poets and rhetoricians, and much sentimental homage has been rendered to the goddess ; but by bringing to bear the touchstone of painstaking inquiry, and the mastery of evidence, we can soon expose the hollowness of this kind of worship.

170 EMOTIONS OF INTELLECT.

### SUMMARY OF THE SIMPLER EMOTIONS.

Having defined an Emotion as a plurality or coalition of some of the primary elements of feeling—the muscular states and the Sensations—governed by certain great laws of the mind, as Association by Contiguity, Relativity, and Harmony; we may now recapitulate the simpler Emotions, and consider how far it has been possible to resolve them according to this view.

NOVELTY, WONDER and LIBERTY, were given as direct applications of the principle of Relativity. POWER also, which, on account of its importance, had a chapter devoted to it, is a pure example of the same principle. In the total of the sentiment of Power, as we usually recognise it, there is, besides the gratification of exercise for some agreeable end, and the elation peculiar to felt superiority, the feeling of the attainment of our desires generally. It is therefore intensely associated with the general pervading sense of enjoyment which accompanies or follows the state of gratified desire.

The various emotions arising in the exercise of the INTELLECT have been also shown to spring from the operation of Relativity upon simpler feelings of the mind.

TERROR was defined as a state caused by the idea of evil, known as such from past experience, and believed to be approaching. Here we have (1) a primary feeling of pain, or a pain compounded of primary feelings; (2) the operation of Intellectual Retentiveness, constituting an *idea* of pain, and giving ideas of the collateral circumstances so as to suggest its recurrence; and (3), an element of Belief, which will be afterwards examined, but which is here considered to be a property of our active or volitional nature, modified by intellect and by feeling. Lastly, we found that the physical derangement and mental depression characteristic of fear would, under the circumstances, be a consequence of the general law of Self-conservation.

The TENDER EMOTION was regarded as a harmonious coalition of sensations having the character of massive pleasure.

## ANALYSIS OF THE EMOTIONS.

The sensations of the ordinary senses having this character evoke a kindred group of organic feelings—those connected with the lachrymal secretion, the pharynx, and probably other digestive organs—and the two sets are fused into a complex whole. A similar coalition may be studied in the Sexual Emotion; the organic sensibility that enters into the compound being unmistakeable.

The EMOTIONS OF SELF and the IRASCIBLE EMOTION were considered as not formed directly from primary sensibilities, but as compounded of other emotions.

As regards PURSUIT and PLOT-INTEREST, the only remaining species, we have, not so much the production of a special kind of feeling, as a mode of controlling our emotions, with the view of abating their painful, and enhancing their pleasurable efficacy; all which takes place under recognised laws of the mind.

In Tenderness and in Irascibility, the growth of *affections* or *moods* founded on these emotions had to be traced. It may be remarked, however, that this operation of Contiguity or Retentiveness is general; we may have affections of Fear, of Power, of Wonder or the Sublime, &c. The circumstance limiting the growth of affections is the law of Relativity; the joyful outbursts of Liberty or the Marvellous fade away; but in so far as the feeling can persist, it may be associated with the objects in the form of an affection. This is well seen in Admiration and Reverence.

# CHAPTER XII.

## SYMPATHY AND IMITATION.

THERE remain now two groups of emotions to complete the classification laid down in the second chapter; those, namely, relating to Fine Art, and those that enter into the Moral Sense. But, previous to handling these, I propose to make a digression for the purpose of taking up the important operation termed Sympathy, already referred to several times in the course of the exposition.

1. Sympathy and Imitation both mean the tendency of one individual to fall in with the emotional or active states of others, these states being made known through a certain medium of expression. To rejoice with them that rejoice, and weep with them that weep, to be carried away by the enthusiasm of a throng, to conform to the society that we live among, and to imbibe the beliefs of our generation, are a part of the human constitution capable of being generalized under one commanding principle. The foundation of sympathy and imitation is the same; but the one applies itself more to our feelings, the other to our actions. We *sympathize* with grief, anger, or astonishment; we *imitate* the handicraft, or the behaviour, the elocution, or the language, of one that we consider a model. Imitation, too, is more frequently voluntary on our part, and a very large number of our acquisitions is obtained by this means.

I have already endeavoured to show that both the power of interpreting emotional expression, and the power of moving our organs, as we see others do, are acquired. But it has likewise come under our notice as a fact, that some of the

## MEDIA OF SYMPATHY.                                                173

manifestations of feeling do *instinctively* excite the same kind
of emotion in others.   The principal instances occur under
tender emotion ;  the moistened eye, and the sob, wail, or
whine of grief and pathos, by a pre-established connexion or
coincidence, are at once signs and exciting causes of the same
feeling.   There is, too, something in the *pace* of movement
of one person that induces a corresponding pace in the
movements of the beholder, or listener.   The medium of connexion in this case is not difficult to specify, and I have already
alluded to it in my former volume, (p. 275).   The tendency to
a harmonious pace of action throughout the moving system is
one of the primitive facts or instinctive arrangements of our
constitution.   'Rapid movements of the eye from exciting
spectacles make all the other movements rapid.  Slow speech
is accompanied by languid gestures.   In rapid walking, the
very thoughts are quickened.'  Now, in the infection of the
passions, this fact will often count for a great deal.  The
violent expression of extreme joy, rage, or astonishment, will
induce a disposition to active excitement in the spectator,
which needs only to be guided into the channel specific to the
passion.

Along with these primitive helps to the understanding
and assumption of the manifested emotions of others, we have
the still wider range of acquired, or experimental connexions
between feeling and expression (*Law of Contiguity,* § 50).
By a process of observation and induction, every child comes
to know the meaning of a smile or a frown, of tones soft and
mild, or harsh and hurried.  The young learner observes in
himself these connexions, and extends his knowledge by the
observation of others.  This is the earliest of our acquisitions
respecting our own nature.  The child connects the state
of acute pain or distress with the violent outburst that accompanies it, and presumes the presence of the feeling on witnessing the expression ; while the effect of such observations
is not confined to mere knowledge, or to the cold recognition
of the circumstance that a companion is elated with joy or
plunged in sorrow ; there is a further tendency to put on the

174                 SYMPATHY AND IMITATION.

very expression that we witness, and, in so doing, to assume the mental condition itself. The power of the idea of a state to generate the reality, of which so many illustrations can be given, leads to the assumption of the exact movements, gestures, tones, and combinations, made strongly present to the mind by an actual display ; and when the expression is assumed, it is difficult to resist the corresponding emotion.

2. There are, therefore, two steps in the sympathetic process, involving two different laws, or properties, of our nature. The first is the tendency *to assume a bodily state, attitude, or movement, that we see enacted by another person*, the result of an association between the actual movements in ourselves, and the appearance they give to the eye as seen in operation. The effect of this association is not by any means absolute or unconditional ; that is to say, because a link is established between each sound that we utter, or each vocal exertion, and the sensation of that sound through the ear, rendering the sensation a power to stimulate the act, it does not follow that on every occasion the one must necessarily give birth to the other. All that can be said is that there is a *disposition* to fall in with the manifested emotions and actions of those about us, and when other circumstances are favourable, the assumption actually takes place. (1) The leisurely and unabsorbed frame of the mind at the time is one condition of our being easily acted on in this way ; a strong prepossession operates as a bar to the effect. We may be so much occupied with our own thoughts and affairs as to be incapable of entering into the distresses or joys of any second person, while in a moment of disengaged attention the same exhibition of feeling would at once cause a sympathetic response. (2) In the next place, it is to be taken into account that some modes of feeling are more natural, habitual, or easy to us than others ; consequently these are assumed on the instigation of another person, in preference to what is unfamiliar or remote from our experience. The mother easily feels for a mother. (3) Further, the energy of the expression may be such as to overpower the influence that holds us for the time ; the violence

## CONDITIONS OF SYMPATHY. 175

of extreme agony, or grief, arrests and detains every passer-by. (4) Moreover, the expression of feeling is more influential as the person stands nearly related to us, or ranks high in our affection and esteem ; in those cases a habit has been contracted of giving a place in our minds to such persons, so much so that a slight indication on their part is enough to realize, as far as need be, the corresponding attitude in ourselves. (5) Something also is to be said respecting the *character* of the expression that we witness, there being the widest disparity in the power of manifesting emotion strongly, clearly, and characteristically, so as to render it infectious to all beholders. Some constitutions, by reason of the lively diffusibility accompanying their emotions, are what is called *demonstrative*—that is, have all their organs decisively pronounced in the expression that they give forth ; and the cultivation that art and society bestow contributes still farther to the same expressiveness. This is the talent of the actor and the elocutionist, and the groundwork of an interesting mode of address in society. It is a common remark that if a man himself feels, he can make others feel ; but this takes for granted that he has an adequate power of outward manifestation—a thing wherein human beings are far from being alike. It is true that Kean, Kemble, or Macready, when affected by strong emotion, could so express themselves as to kindle a corresponding flame in those about them ; but it is not true that any Dorsetshire ploughman could stir the fervours of an assemblage of people merely because his own emotion was strong and genuine.* Given both the inward excitement and the gifts of an expressive language and demeanour, and we have undoubtedly the power to move as we are moved ; while a great actor can dispense with the first, and produce the effect by an outward demonstration that has no emotion corresponding. (6) Finally, there is a susceptibility, greater in

---

* It is proper, however, to remark that the Dorsetshire ploughman, if his strong feeling shows itself unmistakeably in any form, will call forth a certain amount of sympathy, unless counteracted by a vein of contrary feeling in his audience.

## 176    SYMPATHY AND IMITATION.

some men than in others, to the outspoken feelings of their fellows. The tendencies and habits of an individual may be, on the one hand, to follow out strongly the impulses personal to himself, or, on the other hand, to give way to the lead and indications of other men ; making the contrast between the egotistic and the sympathetic temperaments.

The principle now stated is exemplified, in an extreme degree, by those cases where, through disease, or artificial means, a patient incontinently acts out to the full any idea that may be impressed upon the mind from without. By an artificial process, the tendency of the mind to act from within may be overpowered or suspended, leaving the system under the sway of impressions suggested externally. This is one of the effects of the mesmeric sleep. It is a peculiarity accompanying great nervous weakness to take on the movements displayed before our eyes, instead of maintaining a resolute tone of our own. Hence, persons in feeble health have to be withheld from exciting spectacles, and the view of violent emotions. The quietness so much recommended to the invalid is not merely an absence of harsh and stunning sensation, such as the noise of bustling streets, the discharge of ordnance, or the clang of machinery ; but also great moderation in the displays of feeling on the part of human beings. The occurrence of an angry brawl in a sick-room might be fatal to the repose of the patient, by exciting in his weakened system a diseased impression of the scene.

The sound of clearing the throat reminds us so forcibly of the action, or brings the idea of it so vividly before the mind, that it is difficult to resist passing to the full reality. When an expression is so strong and merked as in this instance, there is a natural readiness to form the requisite association between the movement and the sound and sight of it, so that the link comes early to maturity ; and in the next place, the actual suggestion is made comparatively easy. This is only what happens in the contiguous association of all very impressive effects. The yawn is in like manner highly infectious. Laughter, too, is one of the catching expressions,

## ASSUMPTION OF A STATE OF CONSCIOUSNESS.

and in part from the same circumstance. A loud explosion occupies the ear, and the broad grin arrests the eye; and the compound indication is very hard to withstand; still more so when a whole company is moved to a hilarious outburst.

We find ourselves disposed to follow the glance of other persons, so as to give our attention to the same things. We also obey readily a direction given by the hand to look, or go somewhere. The child learns very soon to guide its eyes so as to keep up with a moving object. This is one of the earliest associations constituting a voluntary act; and all our life we are liable to be influenced in like manner even involuntarily, especially if the movements are quick, and the object attractive.

3. The second of the two mental properties recognisable in the completed act of sympathy, is *the assumption of a mental state of consciousness*, through the occurrence of the bodily accompaniment. Having said so much already on the connection of the mental with the physical, I here take for granted that if the entire physical condition accompanying any feeling could be aroused anyhow, the feeling itself would co-exist. Could we put on, by suggestion *ab extra*, the outward gesticulation, the play of feature, the vocal tones, the altered secretions, the interior nerve currents—excited in a burst of grief, we should have the very emotion, as if inspired by its proper antecedent. But it is only an approximation that is possible in any case; a sincere and thorough sympathy will penetrate a great way; while the player learns to draw a line between the visible manifestations and the invisible movements in the interior of the brain. We can acquire a habit of assuming the amount of expression that appears outwardly, and no more; thus checking the course of the sympathetic process, and setting up a merely mechanical echo of other men's sentiments. A consummate actor, as remarked above, is not supposed to feel in himself that emotion externally pourtrayed by his stage declamation and demeanour;[*]

---

[*] It may be true that an actor has had, originally, secondary emotions raised up by the *idea* of the situation which the author conceived.

## SYMPATHY AND IMITATION.

The organs of expression prompted under emotion are nearly all under the control of the will, and may therefore be made to simulate the manifestations of the feelings, while the person is really at heart unmoved. Still it is to be reckoned a general tendency of our constitution, that when the outward signs of emotion are in any way prompted, the wave, passing into the interior, inflames all the circles concerned in the embodiment of the feeling, and gives birth more or less powerfully to the accompanying conscious state. The possibility of sympathizing fully with other minds depends upon this fact in addition to the foregoing.

4. I shall next glance rapidly at the infectious character proper to the various simple emotions. Wonder is peculiarly catching from the boldness and energy of the expression belonging to it, and from the easy susceptibility of most natures to the state. The Tender emotion is also highly infectious ; we have already seen that there is here a natural or instinctive power of begetting the feeling in one mind, by the signs of its manifestation in another. Irascibility, anger, indignation, have that pronounced and violent commotion of feature, voice, and frame, calculated to impress the mind of the beholder at one time with fear, at another time with sympathy. An orator is never more successful than in attempting to bring a multitude into unison with himself in that energetic circle of emotions. The state of Terror is too easily spread, while its opposite, Courage, needs to be backed by the most commanding influences, in order to take possession of a mind already discomposed. The emotions of Action and Pursuit, are so natural to our constitution, that they are inspired not solely by actual display, as in the chase, or the battle-field ; the printed page is able to kindle them to a high pitch. In sympathizing with Egotistic feeling generally, there is an obstacle to be overcome, arising from the egotism of the sympathizer. A certain predisposition to love, admire, or venerate another being is necessary to our entering cordially into an outburst of self-gratulation. The more tranquil delights of the Intellectual workings are difficult to impart

## SYMPATHY AND TENDER EMOTION.

except to minds prepared by much actual experience of them; and in proportion as any feeling is quiet in its exterior manifestation, do we need the assistance of language and art to evoke it by the force of sympathy.

5. A large part of our fellow-feeling with our kindred is shown in echoing some form of Pain or Pleasure. When we see a wound inflicted we are reminded of some past wound of our own, with the attendant suffering; and this is the substance of our sympathetic unison with the sufferer. When we hear, by report, of human beings exposed to hunger, cold, and fatigue, we gather together our recollections of those miseries as experienced by ourselves, and thereby enter into the pangs of the situation. So with pleasure; although in this case there is not the same call for our ready response. The steady and general sympathy with the pleasures of children and of the lower animals, even in persons in whom similar sympathy with those of grown persons is destroyed by egotisms and jealousies, is a source of gratification to the sympathizer's self.

6. Having alluded to the instrumentality of the sympathetic process in human nature, we may now advert more at large to the various aspects and developments of it in ordinary life. And in the first place, we may remark again on the close alliance between sympathy and tender emotion, which has led to the application of the same names to both; as may be seen in the use of the words 'compassion,' 'fellow-feeling,' &c. But our sympathetic impulses extend much wider than our tender affections, for whenever we see strong emotion manifested, we feel ourselves carried away by the current, although our tender feelings would point some other way. The disposition to take on the states of others, irrespective of the warm attachments and likings of our nature, is, as we saw, the real source of our vicarious impulses, and of our generous, humane, and social sentiments; it is the disinterested element of the moral sense. A man may not find much in his fellow-men to attract his tender regards, or inspire the charm of a true love; but, coming within the circle of their wants and miseries, he cannot rest

# 180 SYMPATHY AND IMITATION.

without contributing a mite to their common well-being. Philanthropy may thus arise out of strong sympathies with suffering, without much positive love towards the sufferers. Indeed, in the most conspicuous examples this must be so. A Howard could not delight in the company of the thief or the felon, however much he might be moved to exert himself to mitigate their doom. It was a remark of Mr. James Mill, that some of the best men that have ever lived have had their social feelings weak, which might be interpreted to mean that they have laboured for the good of mankind through sympathy with their sufferings and pleasures, and not from any special charm inspired by human relationships. To be a good man, it is not necessary to have a strong taste for the society of other men; it is only requisite to have an open sympathy, and a corresponding disposition to act for others, as well as to feel for them; all which may consist with an absence of the special affections. Whatever merit there may be in working for those we love, there is merit still greater in not being able to shut our eyes and ears to the necessities of our fellow-beings, whether we love them or not. It is an outburst of pure sympathy that leads one to rescue a drowning man; it is a more sustained and deliberate exercise of the same part of our nature that inspired the life-long labours of Howard and Bentham for the amelioration of their time.*

7. Hitherto we have looked upon sympathy as an impelling power simply, or as the surrender of self to others. The direct and immediate tendency of it is to sacrifice or give up a portion of one's own personality or happiness, without a

---

* As on the one hand affection disposes to sympathy, so on the other, the exercise of mutual sympathy leads to tender feeling, and is in fact one of the sources and beginnings of love. When two people are thrown together and commence a mutual interchange of sentiment, alternately responding to each other, there gradually arises a suffusion of tender emotion, to enhance the pleasure of the relationship. Thus it is, that community of opinions, sentiments, situations, or fortunes, by begetting sympathy, may end in the strongest affection. The 'idem sentire de republica,' is recognised as the basis of friendship between public men.

SYMPATHY A SURRENDER OF SELF. 181

thought of reciprocity or reward. To resolve it into selfishness, on the ground of certain indirect results of a pleasurable kind, is to abolish it as a fact of human nature, and to deny the reality of disinterested action. Some moralists have attempted such a resolution ; but I think without success. Still, we are able to show that, under certain circumstances, sympathy is a source of pleasure to the giver, as it certainly is to the receiver. The circumstances are very obvious. The receiver must reciprocate according to his power and opportunity, and then there is a gain on both sides. This is one of the modes of engendering affection, of making one person an object of tender regard to another. Without reciprocation in some form, it is hard to see how sympathy can be other than a pure loss to the giver. Sometimes, its exercise is a diversion to a mind otherwise a prey to ennui ; the taking one out of one's self may be a positive advantage, even at some cost. Still, the first principle of sympathy is abnegation or sacrifice ; and, unless either the individual benefited, or some one else, or society at large, requite the favour, it stands as so much loss to the author. His own approbation will be but a feeble make-weight against any considerable sacrifice, unless it reflect to his mind the approbation of some of the higher powers.

Sympathy may lead to substantial good offices, as in contributing to the wants of the needy, and in furthering the worldly interests of our friends. It finds a still wider sphere in chiming in with, and supporting, men's emotions, likings, and opinions. To find another person giving powerful utterance to some of our favourite sentiments and views, is an especial charm. Many examples of this could be given. The preacher, the poet, the actor, each exercises the power of reviving in men's minds the emotions that they especially delight in ; and the machinery they employ is some form of the instrumentality we are now discussing. Foreign aid comes in to kindle up a flame which the individual standing alone, does not easily sustain at the same pitch, or for the same length of time. Thus it is that devotion is kept up by the preacher, the crowd of worshippers, and the presence of

## 182 SYMPATHY AND IMITATION.

the symbols and ceremonial suggestive of its objects; and when the mind is wearied, and sick of dwelling on a cherished pursuit, the entry of a friend, ardent and fresh, seems to give new oil to the dying lamp. Often it happens that we take delight in a mode of feeling, that we find a difficulty in keeping up by unassisted strength; as when one finds a charm in science, without possessing scientific force or cultivation. In that case we love to come under the influence of one that wields with ease the matter, and the emotions of scientific truth, and we may in fact have the greater enjoyment of the two. In like manner, the responsive feelings of an assembly, a party, or a nation, tell with accumulated force; and whether it be for encouragement in arduous struggles, or for condolence in the depths of distress, we are sensibly alive to the value of a wide circle of friendship.

8. It is difficult to estimate in any precise form the entire influence of mutual sympathy in human life; but the character and tendency of the influence are easily understood. Individuality is softened down into uniformity, and even to slavish acquiescence in the prevailing turn of sentiment and opinion. Each one of us being brought under the constant influence of other minds, first in the close relationship of the domestic circle, and next in the wide echo of general society, we contract habitual modes of feeling, entirely independent of our innate impulses. Hence the conservation of traditional modes of thinking and feeling, and the difficulty there is in attaining a point of view repugnant to the atmosphere we live in. The tenacity of inherited notions and sentiments in a family, or a people, proves the strength of the sympathetic disposition; while innovation may arise either from obtuseness to the expression of other men's feelings, or from the self-originated tendencies being unusually powerful. It is to be observed, however, that the concurrence of each new generation in the received sentiments of the past, is not always or wholly due to spontaneous fellow-feeling, for compulsion is also used to secure the same end.

The constant subjection to foreign influence falsifies the

OBSTRUCTIVES OF SYMPATHY. 183

natural likings and dislikings of the individual to such an extent, that we rarely follow out our own pleasures in their genuine purity. Acquiring a habit of calling objects agreeable or disagreeable, according to the prevailing standard, the language we use is not always to be interpreted as expressing our real feelings. In designating a landscape, or a picture, beautiful, charming, or the like, we may be echoing what we have heard, and feel no disposition to controvert, but it does not follow that we really enjoy the pleasure that the words imply. Some different criterion must be appealed to, in order to judge of the depth of the real feeling in such a case, as, for example, the power of the object to detain the gaze, to occupy the thoughts, to console in misery, or to stimulate efforts in pursuit of the pleasure.

9. Although it is easy enough to chime in with the current of the ordinary emotions, pains, and pleasures of those around us, many cases arise where a laborious effort is requisite to enable us to approach in our own feelings the state of mind of another person. Two notable disqualifications are found in Disparity of nature, and aversion or Antipathy. As to Disparity : the timid man cannot comprehend the composure of the courageous, in the face of peril ; the cold nature cannot understand the pains of the ardent lover ; the impulsive mind will not sympathize with cautious deliberation. Then, again, we cannot be induced to enter into sentiments that we hate ; the very name 'antipathy' implies the deathblow to fellow-feeling. In the one case the difficulty is intellectual, in the other moral. When we are far removed in natural constitu-tion, in habits, and associations from another mind, and still desire to possess ourselves of the emotions belonging to that mind, as when a historian deals with the hero of a past age, or a poet presents a far-fetched ideal to our view, a laborious constructive process has to be gone into, of which mention was made in a former chapter. In many ways this exercise is exceedingly valuable and instructive ; sympathy enabling us to know other men, as self-consciousness enables us to comply with the precept 'know thyself.'

184 SYMPATHY AND IMITATION.

10. I turn now to the consideration of the IMITATIVE process, which relates itself to our voluntary actions, and supposes on our part a desire to repeat or copy another person. The instrumentality of imitation is acquired, as I formerly endeavoured to show (*Law of Contiguity*, § 52). We commence with the performance of actions spontaneously, and see the effect and appearance of those actions in ourselves; whence an association is formed between each movement, and the appearance presented by it. By untaught and random spontaneity, the child closes its hand; the act of closing is impressed upon the observing eye, and, after a sufficient amount of repetition, the appearance is able to suggest the movement. That is to say, the closing hand of another person recalls the mental situation wherein the same act was performed by self, and if there be any desire in the case, certain movements are commenced, and, if need be, varied until the proper one has been hit upon. The process of trial and error is the grand corrective of crude and nascent imitation. In endeavouring to vocalize a sound heard, the first attempts may be very far from the original, but, by persisting, some suitable movement of the larynx occurs, and the coincidence being once felt, the learner maintains the successful effort; and, in consequence, a fusion takes place between the impression on the ear and the action of the voice, so that on a future occasion it is unnecessary to beat about before hitting the effect.

11. Several circumstances contribute to the power of imitation. (1) The Active Spontaneity of the special organs is a prime condition. A disposition to exercise the hand, prepares the way for handicraft associations; a copious flow of cerebral power towards the vocal apparatus, and a consequent profusion of vocal exercises, soon bring forward those specific acquirements now adverted to. It is a fact that languages are most rapidly learned by them that boldly attempt to speak, leaving themselves to be corrected, instead of waiting till they can speak correctly. It is on the same principle, that I should be disposed to account for much of what is deemed instinctive in those of the lower animals that are actively disposed from the

## CONDITIONS OF IMITATION.

moment of birth. In the alertness to move, every movement brings forth an experience, and the accumulation of these soon makes an education.

(2) The Delicacy of the Sense peculiarly involved in the case, is the second principal condition of a good imitative aptitude. ' A fine and retentive musical ear is one of the essentials of musical imitation ; the natural or spontaneous production of musical tones being the other essential.' (3) The third circumstance is the adhesive power of Contiguity, on which depends the growth of the bond between the two elements— the sensible impression on the one hand, and the active impulse on the other. Besides these three conditions, which apply expressly to imitation as distinguished from sympathy, there are to be included the influences that favour both alike (§ 2). The being disengaged at the time, some familiarity with the operations imitated, the pronounced and energetic character of the original, the clearness of the expression or action, our feelings of admiration and respect, and the natural disposition to come under influences from without—all these are inducements to our copying the actions, as well as imbibing the feelings, manifested in our presence. Moreover, the child falls into the tones, movements, and peculiarities of action of the parent, through the circumstance of their being constantly presented to its imitation ; and finds a peculiar satisfaction in guiding the spontaneous activity into some prepared channel. This last is probably the secret of the childish delight in the imitation of the actions of the grown-up person ; these actions are imposing to the young mind, and to realize them himself, or to make his own activity tally with theirs, is a highly gratifying result. The dramatizing of the actions and scenes around is, perhaps, the most charming of youthful sports ; exercise has, then, besides its own pleasure, the charm of realizing an impressive effect.

12. We may now remark generally on the contrast of different minds, as respects sympathy and imitation,—being one of the many phases of the opposition between self and not-self. Some men are moved principally by impulses

## 186 SYMPATHY AND IMITATION.

peculiarly their own. Instead of copying others, they educate themselves mainly by their own experience wherever this is available. They cannot entertain the suggestions of others nor take in new ideas, until these arise in the course of their own observations or reflections. Theirs is the active, self-impulsive, self-originating, egotistic temperament, as opposed to the passive, susceptible, or impressionable. A more marked antithesis of character can hardly be named. In the one case, the fountains of cerebral power are flowing constantly towards the active organs; in the other, the prevailing currents are toward the senses, and seats of recipiency; action waits, instead of preceding, the guidance of sensation. Illustrations of this contrast will occur to every observant person; life affords both kinds, even to morbid extremes. The over-reflecting Hamlet is seen in company with a man that will not 'look before a leap.'

13. Adverting now to some of the chief instances of the imitative tendency, there is no need for saying much on mere mechanical copying, as in handicraft operations, military drill, dancing, posture, and the like. Granting a sufficient flexibility and variety of the spontaneous movements, that is to say, *facility*, the observant and imbibing *eye* is the next grand requisite. Whether this aptitude arise from the susceptibility of the sense itself, or from a deep charm that detains the mind upon the effect to be produced, no rapid strides can be made without it. We find surprising examples of the overwhelming hold that the mind will sometimes take of an action, or a form, a hold so great that the active members concerned can fall into no other channel but that one. We may see a child imbibe forms so rapidly and vigorously, as to copy them in a moment, as if by an instinct; the explanation being no other than that now given. The imitation of handwriting is a gift arising in the same way. The forms of the original take possession of the eye and the brain, and prevent the hand from following any other course but a faithful representation of them. Substituting the ear for the eye, we can apply the same explanation to musical and articulate acquirements.

MIMICRY. 187

Individuals are sometimes so constituted that their articulation is always a pure copy of some one else. The pre-occupa-
tion of the mind is so great as to guide all the vocal efforts
into a set channel.

14. Mimicry supplies interesting illustrations of the principles now in discussion. The mimic needs in himself a
large compass of actions and movements, or a various spontaneity, and adds thereto a well-marked susceptibility to the
actions and demeanour of other men. In truth, if his talent
is of the highest order, it is because his mind and his actions
are not his own; whatever he does, he is haunted by some
other person's example, or some foregone model. It is related
of Mathews that, while he could imitate the manners and
even the language and thoughts of the greatest orators of his
time, he was incapable of giving a simple address, in his own
person, with any tolerable fluency.

15. The case of Intellectual imitations is in no respect
essentially different from the other kinds. In copying a style
of composition, we absorb the original through either involuntary attraction, or express study; and in this mood all efforts
of our own, fall under the control of the guiding model. Sometimes we imitate what has seized hold of our mind by a special
charm, as with our favourite authors; at other times we get
possessed of another man's ideas, from a natural bent and
impressibility, and reproduce them as a consequence. A large
proportion of literature and art must necessarily consist of
copies and echoes from the great originals.

16. A certain number of the Fine Arts derive their subjects from natural things which they copy and adapt; and
these are called the Imitative arts; they are principally Imitative (as opposed to effusive) Poetry, Painting, and Sculpture;
the Stage and Pantomime; and a small portion of the art of
Decoration. The remaining members of the class, namely,
Architecture, Music, Decoration in general, Refined Address,
are but in a very slight degree imitative of originals in nature,
and apply themselves at once to the gratification of our various
sensibilities, without being encumbered with any extraneous

188    SYMPATHY AND IMITATION.

condition, such as fidelity to some prototype. I cannot regard the imitation of nature occurring in the first-named class, in any other light than as an accident; but the fact once occurring, a certain deference has to be paid to it. Where we profess to imitate, we ought undoubtedly to be faithful. Not, I imagine, because a higher artistic charm thereby arises, but because of the revulsive shock that misrepresentation is liable to produce. If the poet draws from reality, he ought not to give a misleading picture, seeing that we receive his compositions, not solely as pleasing melodies, and touching images, but also as narratives and descriptions of human life. There is, doubtless, a limit to what we are to expect from an artist, who must be mainly engrossed with the effects proper to Art, and cannot be, at the same time, a botanist, a zoologist, a geologist, a meteorologist, an anatomist, and a geographer.

17. Although I conceive that fidelity, in the imitative class of arts, is to be looked upon, in the first instance, as avoiding a stumbling-block, rather than imparting a charm, there are still some respects wherein the æsthetic pleasure is enhanced by it. We are drawn by sympathy towards one that has attended to the same objects as ourselves, or that has seized and put into vivid prominence what we have felt without expressing to ourselves. The coincidence of mind with mind is always productive of the lightening charm of mutual support; and, in some circumstances, there is an additional effect of agreeable surprise. Thus, when an artist not merely produces in his picture the ordinary features that strike every one, but includes all the minuter objects that escape common notice, we sympathize with his attention, we admire his powers of observation, and become, as it were, his pupils in extending our study and knowledge of nature and life. We feel a pungent surprise at discovering, for the first time, what has been long before our eyes; and so the realistic and minute artist labours at this species of effect. Moreover, we are brought forward as judges of the execution of a distinct purpose; we have to see whether he that is bent on imitation, does that part of his work well or ill, and admire the power

## IMITATIVE FINE ARTS. 189

displayed in it, if our verdict is favourable. There is, too, a certain exciting effect in the reproduction of an appearance in some foreign material, as when a plane surface yields the impressions of solid effect, and canvas or stone imitates the human appearance. Finally, the sentiment of reality and truth, as opposed to fiction or falsehood, appealing to our practical urgencies, disposes us to assign a value to every work where truth is strongly aimed at, and to derive an additional satisfaction, when fidelity of rendering is allied with artistic charm. Thus Imitation, which, properly speaking, is immaterial to art as such, just as there is little or no place for it in music, architecture, or the decoration of the person, becomes the centre of a class of agreeable or acceptable effects. These effects are the more prized, that we have been surfeited with the purely æsthetic ideals. We turn refreshed from the middle age romance, to the graphic novel of our own time.

The mental peculiarity of being strongly arrested by his subject original, must attach to the imitative artist. The face of nature must seize his eye, engross his mind, and kindle his feelings ; his pencil is then constrained to follow the outer world, rather than an inner, or ideal one. A Michael Angelo invents forms not found in nature, although observing a certain consistency with what nature presents. Such a man is the reverse of an imitative artist, and provides none of the effects specified in the last paragraph, although abounding in an impressiveness and grandeur of his own.

# CHAPTER XIII.

## OF IDEAL EMOTION.

1. THE object of the present chapter is to resume and expand what has been said in the introduction respecting the persistence of emotional states in idea; the continuance of the tremor and excitement for a certain length of time after the object has ceased, or the stimulus is withdrawn. Much of our pleasure and pain is of this persisting kind; being the prolongation of a wave once commenced, and not immediately subsiding. The pleasurable impression of a work of art, a piece of music, a friendly interview, may vibrate for hours, or cast a radiance over an entire day; while the depression of some mortifying occurrence may cast a shadow of like duration.

A distinction is to be made between the emotion persisting of itself, and the persistence of it by virtue of the ideal continuance of the object. If, in the cases above quoted, we retain a vivid intellectual impression of the thing that awakened the pleasure or pain, as the picture, the story, or the mortifying incident, we retain in our mind, although in an ideal form, the exciting cause of the feeling, and therefore the emotional tremor is not properly self-sustaining. As often as we remember the objects of our agreeable associations, we are liable to recover a certain gleam of their peculiar delight; but here the ideality is, strictly speaking, in the objects themselves. The pleasures and pains of the ideal life, are thus a mixture of two modes of persistence—the one the imagery of outward things, or whatever is the antecedent,

PHYSICAL CONDITIONS. 191

or cause, of an emotional wave; the other the wave, or excited consciousness itself.

Throughout our whole exposition of the feelings, we have been careful to note this character of continuance, or recoverability in idea, as belonging to each in a greater or less degree. We have seen that the muscular feelings and organic sensations have little of the quality, that the sensations of hearing and sight have it in a higher degree, and that the special emotions treated of in the present book are in general endowed with a considerable share of endurability.

2. It is now to be considered what are the circumstances and conditions affecting the ideal subsistence of states of feeling; on which subject we find a considerable complication, amounting even to apparent contradiction. At one time a present feeling will suggest and support one of its own kindred, at another time the present condition will urge powerfully the revival or recollection of some *opposite* one. The actual sensation of cold will, in some circumstances, permit only ideas of cold, in other circumstances ideas of warmth. There are modes of misery that allow of recollections only of misery. There are also modes of actual suffering compatible with ideal bliss. We must endeavour, by a minute investigation, to clear up and reconcile these paradoxical results.

3. The continuance of the emotional tremor has obviously for its first condition the state of the physical organs involved in the act of maintaining it. The central brain, and the different muscles and secreting glands concerned in each case, are the medium and instrumentality for sustaining the excitement, after the stimulus, as well as during its presence. There is a power natural to each constitution of persisting, for a certain length of time, in a wave once commenced. The persistence is, as often remarked, unequal for different emotions; and the nervous system is not always prepared to give a uniform support to the same emotion. A certain health, freshness, and vigour are requisite for the proper carrying on of this, or of any other mental function; and as the

192

OF IDEAL EMOTION.

natural tone of the physical members is abated by the fatigues of the day, by the absence of nourishment, by disease, or by general decay, it becomes less easy to sustain either an actual or an ideal excitement. The young mind can sustain hours of buoyant elation ; the brain, the limbs, the voice, the features, the senses, being all charged with active vigour; while the aged are obliged to alternate moments of excitement with hours of lassitude or stillness.

Respecting this primary condition of constitutional vigour, a distinction is to be drawn between the energy of the brain itself and the vigour of the other organs concerned in the emotional wave. The various parts of the bodily system exist in very unequal degrees of strength. The muscular system may be powerful with a feeble brain ; the brain may be vigorous while the muscles and secreting organs are below the average; the chest may be strong, and the action of the skin weak. Now, in the full development of a wave of emotion there is a concurrence of the cerebral centres, and the muscular and other outlying members ; and the prevailing kinds of feeling will be governed by the relative vigour of the two departments. When the muscular frame is powerful, the more violent and demonstrative feelings can be sustained if sufficiently prompted from within ; when the nervous system is powerful and the muscles weak, the emotional life, although equally intense, will. flow less outwardly, leaving the exterior calm and quiet. Whence it is, that constitutions physically weak, as it is called (the meaning being that digestion, muscle, &c., are not highly developed), may yet maintain a vivid and sustained emotional life ; in this case, the endowments of the cerebrum proper must be of a high order. All experience shows that whatever part of the system may languish, there must be no want of nerve-power, when the mental manifes- tations are unusually fervid. Very often what seems a feeble and worn physical frame is really a good average constitution, where every atom of available substance is expended in feeding an energetic brain. This is really at bottom the import of the observation, when we speak of a strong mind in

# THE EMOTIONAL TEMPERAMENT.

a weak body, a conjunction of very frequent and not surprising occurrence.*

4. Next to the general circumstance of cerebral efficiency, we must place the fact of specific temperament as regards emotion. Some constitutions are so framed that the power of the brain runs mainly to the current of feeling. In them, a wave once generated sustains itself for a long period; the same stimulus yielding a more prolonged excitement than in minds of a different cast.

There is a certain adjustment of the three sides of our inward being that might be pointed out as the best for the individual on the whole—a just balance of the powers, which we often speculate upon, as securing all the interests, and conciliating all the exigencies of our complicated existence; this balance being frequently missed, through the preponderance of some one over the other two.

As there are painful as well as pleasing emotions, the question may be asked whether the same organization will favour the continuance of a painful impression, as well as of the other sort. This is answered in part by referring to the elucidation formerly given of the nature and instrumentality of the emotions (Chap. I. § 2). The diffusive wave prompted by every state of feeling, and essential to its manifestation, assuages, by the secondary waves rising out of the action of the various organs brought into play, all kinds of painful consciousness; and the more powerfully the diffusion operates, the more efficient will this assuaging operation be. Hence a vigorous emotional nature is one that has resources at once for prolonging the thrill of pleasure, and overpowering the shock of pain. The cerebral organization, employing its vigour mainly for emotional excitement, gives full tone to all

---

* Dr. Johnson's definition of Genius, ' Large general powers operating in a particular direction,' would not be inapt as a figure for representing the physical fact implied in great mental capacity. A good physical constitution in general, concentrating all its spare vitality in a good cerebrum, is the best notion we are at present able to give of the corporeal foundations of every kind of mental greatness.

194          OF IDEAL EMOTION.

the notes of joy, and by an abundant and various exercise of the parts ministering to the emotional wave, evolves assuaging stimuli from within itself to overpower the pinch of suffering. The furious gestures, the vehement movements, the stern grimace, the piercing wail, are all fountains of a new excitement, which by itself would be exhilarating to a strong and healthy frame, and which is of avail in lulling the irritation that called them forth. When these natural outbursts are guided and attuned by refinement, by poetry, music, or other art, the means at the disposal of the temperament now supposed for overlaying misery with sources of delight, are most extensive and efficient, and do not pertain to characters of a different stamp.*

5. We must also take into account the undisputed fact that individuals are variously constituted in reference to different kinds of emotion ; the same person keeping up one emotion with ease, and another with difficulty. According to the primitive conformation of the brain, and other organs engaged in supporting states of feeling, there is a preference shown towards some of the leading modes of pleasurable excitement, or a tendency to particular modes of painful excitement. One mind falls in easily with the tremor peculiar to Wonder. An object of this class awakens a powerful current, which continues to run for a length of time after the stimulation has ceased. The person so constituted naturally goes after the wonderful, in other words, chooses this as a main gratification and pursuit. Terror I pass by in the illustration, as being more properly a mode of human weakness, and a source of mental waste and pain, than an emotion counting among our phases of pleasure.† The Tender emotion

---

* It would be necessary still farther to discriminate between temperaments joyous by nature and the opposite, both being varieties of the emotional class. It is also true, as remarked before, that there are depths of misery beyond the power of the assuaging influences above described.

† In each individual temperament there are special modes of pain that take a more than ordinary possession of the mind, causing it to succumb to their influence to an excessive degree, and so persisting after the fact as to

## ENDOWMENT OF SPECIAL EMOTIONS. 195

usurps largely a considerable proportion of mankind, being so alimented by the natural conformation of the system as to maintain its characteristic wave with considerable persistence. This gives great capacity for the affections, great power of sustaining the pleasures of love, friendship, and social intercourse, and great aptitude for the kindly and compassionate sentiments. No one can tell what part of the brain, if it be a local division, or what pervading property, determines the vital power to flow in this direction; nor can we say to what extent the structure of the glandular organs, excited by the wave of tender feeling, is concerned in giving it the requisite support. We are, nevertheless, assured that this emotion is the groundwork of one of the best marked distinctions of the human character. So with the charm of exerted Power, to which some minds are keenly susceptible, leading to the worship of might in self and others. The passion for control and influence may be largely developed in the original constitution, whence it will be easy to dwell upon the objects of it in idea, as well as delightful to attain the reality. Irascibility may draw to itself a large share of the vital sap, by which the feeling will receive an undue prominence in the inner life of the individual. The power of hate, of malice, and revenge, is thus extensively developed; and that aptitude for antipathy, which is strong in general human nature, is still farther increased. We have then a positive fondness for the indulgence of dislikes, and a great reluctance to subside from a resentment once kindled. If the general temperament be

---

occupy an extensive and commanding position in the ideal life. In some cases this is merely a phase of the predominating pleasures, whose privation affects us painfully according as their position contributes to our delight; as when the lover of knowledge is for a time banished from books and sources of information. In other cases, it is that particular kinds of pain prey deeply upon the organism, like the tendency of some constitutions to severe inflammatory or febrile attacks; as when one is more than usually unhinged by disappointed expectations. The pain in this instance may be so severe at the time, and so abiding in the impression, as to keep the person in a continual frame of dread and precaution on this one head, disposing him to incur the loss of a great amount of pleasure rather than risk so trying a shock.

## OF IDEAL EMOTION.

emotional, as described in the preceding paragraph, and if the specific channel made for it is the present, we have a type of malignity and hatred that may give birth to the worst excesses of misanthropic ill-will. Instances of the kind come within the catalogue of every generation of living men. And, finally, to close the illustration, the feelings of Intellect may be those specially fed in the distribution of the cerebral nourishment. And, as in the case of the pleasures of action, it is not necessarily a vigorously developed intelligence that thrills with the most protracted note to the objects of intellectual pursuit. The speciality lies in some conformation of our purely emotional nature, although doubtless modified to some extent by the other. The pleasures of knowledge, the pursuit of truth, and the sciences in general, are the occasions for the outburst of this peculiar variety of emotion.*

6. Repetition and habit increase still further the tendency to special kinds of emotion. If this implied only the confirmation of a bent that originally predominated in the constitution, it would scarcely amount to any new fact; for, as a matter of course, whatever we are naturally prone to, we exercise most freely, and thereby develope into still greater ascendancy. But influences from without are brought to play

---

* The same characteristics in the mental system that enable an impression to survive its original, and be recovered by mental suggestion independently of that original, are doubtless those that enable us to endure a large amount of any one sort of emotion, or to take on the frequent stimulation of it, without fatigue. In the case of tender emotion, for example, the cerebral support and other circumstances, causing this to persist as an ideal gratification, are what enables one to bear a great repetition of the actual indulgence as well. A mind so constituted is not exhausted by much society, and the iterated draught upon the affections arising therefrom. The powers of the system being assumed to run largely in this particular channel, the actual stimulation can be borne to great lengths of continuance, and the ideal condition supported to a corresponding degree. On the other hand, a system soon fatigued by any mode of actual pleasure, is not likely to retain the ideal state, unless it be that the actual exhausts the bodily organs too much, as in physical exercise, and the exhausting physical pleasures, in which cases the ideal is the more supportable of the two, especially in a constitution more vigorously constituted in the cerebrum than in the other organs.

STIMULATING DRUGS. 197

upon the mind of every one more or less, and the power of habit reduces the natural prominence of one bent, and brings forward another. It is thus that we come to identify our standing pleasures and most congenial sentiments with those that surround us. ·A constitution little disposed by nature to vehement antipathies, can be made to take on this characteristic in a community very much given to their exercise. In the same manner, a disposition to dwell in the atmosphere of intellectual pleasures may be worked up by assiduous cultivation. There is a certain length that we may always go in changing the primitive arrangements of the system, developing tendencies naturally weak, and abating such as are powerful; it is on this circumstance that we are able to explain the unanimous prevalence of a common vein of sentiment through a wide society.

7. We cannot omit allusion to the wide-spread fact of *artificial stimulation* of the nervous system, by which currents of strong emotion are generated and kept up, out of all proportion to what would otherwise be produced. It stands to reason, that the proper support of the brain is the nutriment conveyed to it for restoring the daily waste of the nerve substance, but every nation has discovered, among the natural productions of the globe, some agent or other, to quicken the cerebral activity, by an action not necessarily connected with the supply of nutriment.* These are the wide class of

---

* ' Siberia has its fungus—Turkey, India, and China their opium—Persia, India, and Turkey, with all Africa, from Morocco to the Cape of Good Hope, and even the Indians of Brazil, have their hemp and haschisch—India, China, and the Eastern Archipelago, their betel-nut and betel pepper—the Polynesian Islands their daily ava—Peru and Bolivia their long used coca—New Grenada and the Himalayas their red and common thorn-apples—Asia and America, and all the world we may say, their tobacco—the Florida Indians their emetic holly—Northern Europe and America their ledums and sweet gale—the Englishman and German their hop—and the Frenchman his lettuce. No nation so ancient, but has had its narcotic soother from the most distant times—none so remote and isolated, but has found within its own borders a pain-allayer, and narcotic care-dispeller of native growth—none so savage, which instinct has not led to seek for, and successfully to employ, this form

**198**                    OF IDEAL EMOTION.

*Stimulants*, intoxicating drugs, narcotics, which have the common effect of exalting for the time the tone of the cerebral and mental life, making all pleasures more intense, and utterly subduing suffering and pain. Alcohol, Tobacco, Tea, Opium, Hemp, Betel, and the other narcotics, are the resort of millions, for the production of mental elation, or soothing irritation and pain. Even in our plainest food, elements occur that are supposed to exercise a stimulating influence on the nervous system. That ingredient of flesh, ' called *Kreatine*, which is rich in nitrogen, has a certain chemical relation to the peculiar principle of Tea and Coffee (Theine), and exercises a special tonic and exhilarating influence upon the system, independent of any directly nutritive quality it may possess.'[*]

The characteristic effects of different stimulants are but imperfectly understood. Their agreement in elevating the mental tone co-exists with great variety in the manner. Physiologists and physicians draw a line between the stimulating, narcotic, and poisonous doses of drugs. Thus, Alcohol, in a small quantity, would appear to heighten the powers generally; causing both mental elation, and increase of all the physical forces. In greater quantities, it paralyzes the nerve centres, diminishing both the mental and the bodily aptitudes, while there may still remain a certain joyousness of feeling. The maudlin of semi-intoxication is a curious feature, whether from stimulating the organic accompaniments of tender emotion, or from the passively pleasurable condition of the mind.

8. In connexion with this subject, there are circumstances different from the action of drugs, capable of exercising an influence on the nervous centres. Cold invigorates the nerves, while warmth relaxes their tone; whence arise the effects of the cold bath on the one hand, and of extreme heat on the other.

---

of physiological indulgence. The craving for such indulgence, and the habit of gratifying it, are little less un'versal than the desire for, and the practice of, consuming the necessary materials of our common food.'—Johnston's *Chemistry of Common Life*, vol. ii. p. 182.

[*] Johnston's *Chemistry of Common Life.*

## PHYSICAL CIRCUMSTANCES.

There is an exact analogy to this in electricity and magnetism High temperature deprives a magnet of its polarity, and destroys the conducting power of an electric wire. The agency of cold, when employed within safe limits, seems to improve the quality of the nerves, without any of the bad consequences of narcotic drugs. Although, in general, an ample supply of nourishment is the main source of cerebral and mental vigour, yet it sometimes happens that light meals, and even fasting for a time, will give a temporary elation. One consideration helping to account for this result is the large amount of nervous power demanded for the digestive process. By relieving the system temporarily from this great draught, there may be an interval of exuberance of high feeling before the coming on of the depression from want of nourishment.* Some such temporary elation, as well as pain and mortification, may have been contemplated in the observance of times of fasting by religious devotees ; the mental brilliancy of the moment being the reward of the self-denial. It is farther to be noted that the nervous system, in all probability, goes through a round of different phases of its own accord, as a mere property of its organic life, and without any reference to the use of stimulants. From no assignable circumstance whatever, it happens that the mental tone is now light and buoyant, while at another time shadows and gloom overspread the prospect. We have no means of accounting for many periods of depression that occur in the best regulated life ; while, on the other hand, moments of intense pleasure and brightness burst out without any seeming cause in lives of protracted suffering.

---

* Thomson, the African traveller, who explored the regions contiguous to the Cape of Good Hope, in describing his experience of protracted hunger, remarks that, when he had been for days almost entirely deprived of food his dreams at night took the form of the most delicious repasts. While the subject most strongly presented to his mind, and therefore likely to be dreamed about, was the obtaining of food, the nervous system had got into such a state as to favour a kind of delirious intoxication during sleep, and to give a corresponding character to the mental revaries. This is a curious and illustrative contrast to the miserably depressing dreams experienced after an actual repast too abundantly partaken of.

## 200 OF IDEAL EMOTION.

As the outward agencies and the course of fortune alternate between good and evil, so the tissues of the body itself, nervous and the rest, have their cycles and changes favourable and unfavourable to mental gaiety and animation.* In certain temperaments the vibration from joy to woe takes a much wider sweep than in others, but it is impossible that the inner life of any human being can have a perfectly equal flow.

9. Leaving the discussion of physical agents and influences, it remains for us now to take account of the agencies properly Mental, that may serve to sustain an emotional wave once commenced. We find often that one feeling can pave the way for a second, or aid in supporting an excitement in actual operation. The manner of rendering this assistance needs to be particularly examined. If, after the action of one exciting cause, such as the meeting of a long absent friend, we come under some second stimulant, as the successful issue of an undertaking, there must needs arise a compound excitement, each of the two promptings working out its natural effect. In such a case we should only say that the mind was doubly excited, there being present two powerful conspiring streams of elation. There would be no propriety in saying that the one emotion fed, or maintained, the other. But there is often presented to our notice, a phenomenon more peculiar than this simple concurrence of two congenial feelings. The second stimulant, instead of producing its own proper hue of emotion, will be found frequently to add to the flame of another and more favourite mode of excitement. The lover, listening to a strain of music, will probably be moved entirely in the direction of the predominating passion. So the votary of ambition is liable to find every source of pleasure acting merely as a stimulant to sustain this one mental attitude, no other enjoying a sufficient cerebral support for its proper mani-

---

* The acute neuralgic pains, as toothache and tic douleureux, come and go without any assignable change of outward circumstances. Many persons subject to nervous disease have attacks at regular periods, which can be counted on.

MENTAL AGENCIES. 201

festation. I imagine that few persons enjoy the pure charm of music, without being led away into some dream of a ruling passion. In this view a certain number of the causes of strong feeling are in reality quickeners of the cerebral activity, whereby the dominant emotion of the individual can come forth into a more potent sway. The minor susceptibilities are so many means of general elation or general depression, giving support to, or withdrawing it from, the great monopolist and master of the mind. Nothing is seemingly more delightful than the burst of relief when a gnawing pain has ceased, or a heavy burden is lifted away ; and yet at that moment we shall often find a man reverting with all the might of the new stimulus to his business gains, ambitious pursuits, or some object of personal affection.*

10. The Intellectual forces, or the associating bonds of Contiguity and Similarity, may be properly reckoned as ministering to the support of an emotional wave. As to contiguous association, the fact is very obvious, and has been noticed already. When 'patriotism is kindled on the plains of Marathon, and piety burns brighter amid the ruins of Iona,' it is the force of a pre-established connexion between objects and emotions that constitutes the energy of the stimulation. We find it much easier to sustain a feeling at its full strength in the presence of its associates ; as tenderness by the graves of departed friends, or through the possession of relics of their friendship

---

\* The influence of the will is also a power operating in the same direction, as the physical and mental agencies now passed in review. The mental tone of the individual is to a certain degree within the limits of voluntary control; by an effort of resolution, we often resist or stave off depression, and keep up a degree of cheerfulness not at all in accordance with surrounding circumstances. Some minds have this power to a surprising degree, and there are few cases where the natural strength of the will is brought to a severer proof. It is an interesting inquiry, which I shall take up at the proper place, to find out through what medium the instruments of the will (these being solely the members moved by muscles) can be brought to operate upon the pervading emotional tone of the individual. The fact itself is one not to be doubted.

202 OF IDEAL EMOTION.

There are other instances of the quickening of emotion that may be referred to the law of similarity. If a passion of our own is fired by the display of the same passion in others, we may call this the suggestion of likeness, or we may term it sympathy ; in either case the force is an intellectual one. When we read the lives of men whose actions and position were exactly what we ourselves delight in, we are fired by our favourite emotions, through the strong presentation of what so closely resembles them in others. This is one of the ways wherein man becomes interesting to man. The spectacle, or account, of those persons that have borne a part in life similar to our own, is capable of moving us with the emotions of our position at times when these would otherwise lie entirely dormant in the mind, or of making them burn with a brighter flame. The enormous actual achievements of Alexander did not dispense with his copy of the *Iliad*, from which he drew an ideal stimulus to his sentiment of military heroism.

11. The foregoing considerations are introduced to explain the enormous predominance of the Ideal over the Actual, in human life. Instead of yielding ourselves up to real and present influences, as they arise in turn, we not only find it easy to resist impressions coming from these present realities, but even set them at nought in favour of something absent and remote, as we would brush off a fly that alighted on the hand. Such is the difference between one feeling and another, that the full actuality in the one case is as nothing compared with a shadowy recollection in the other. In some sudden memory of long past years, we become for a time so completely absorbed, as not to be impressed with the gayest spectacle, or the most stirring drama. Something, in the condition of the cerebral centres at that moment, favours to such a degree the resuscitation of that bygone experience, that the mind is dead to the solicitations of the senses, and the potency of an actual scene. This apparent anomaly of the human constitution, or rather this great inequality in the power of different emotions, shows itself in several well-known

## THE IDEAL AND THE ACTUAL. 203

classes of phenomena. One of these is the often remarked contrariety of mind and fortune, of inward feeling and outward condition, so common in every generation of mankind. The environment of the individual may be blank and cheerless, or may bristle up with positive evils, and yet the mind, fastening upon some choice object, and enabled by some fortifying influence, or natural vigour, to sustain the note thereby struck, may rise superior to the sum total of the depressing influence. To state the opposite case, would only be to condescend upon the rankest commonplace. Not only may ideal delight co-exist with actual pain, and *vice versâ*, but, as just noted, the veritable delights of the mind may run in a tune quite different from what is played in our sphere of reality. Natural temperament, special conformation, nourishment, stimulants, habit, concur to arm the inner being on some one side, and give a persistence to what accords therewith, in spite of very powerful present influences addressed to the less susceptible portions of the mental constitution. There is much truth in the general doctrine that reality is stronger than idea, and present influences more impressive than recollections, but this supposes that the different things compared are pretty nearly equal in the regards of the mind. If we are equally attached to two friends, the one now with us will probably have more weight for the moment in determining our inclinations than the one that is absent; the freshly-uttered living voice has naturally more sway than what exists only in the memory. But this advantage on the side of the actual object now before us, is completely overpowered and nullified, by the disparity that so often exists among our affections and likings. Our absent friend may have such an ascendant place in our esteem, that his words recollected through a lapse of years, are more influential than the most eloquent utterances of our present adviser. This fact is no disparagement to the superior efficacy of present impressions as such, for the superiority of the present is unquestionable, and often mischievous; it only proves the immense hold that some things take of the mind in preference to others.

## OF IDEAL EMOTION.

12. The struggle of the Ideal with the Actual is forcibly illustrated in the day-dreams and illusions that raise the mind into an elevated region, where present evils have no place. Fastening eagerly upon some striking quality in our future prospects, we are so engrossed by the feeling thereby inspired, as to see no accompaniments to mar the looked-for felicity. Another instance is the comparison we make of our lot with some other person's. Admiring in a high degree what we are destitute of, we refuse to entertain the other side of the picture, or to figure to ourselves the never-failing drawbacks of the most fortunate conditions. The mental forces at work, in this very familiar class of facts, relate principally to the great fundamental property of strong emotion, more than once dwelt upon, to exclude incompatible ideas, and rule the convictions of the moment. A battle constantly rages on the field of intellect, between the force of the feelings to retain their own imagery, and the other associating agencies which bring forward the views connected with a cool, intellectual appreciation of the whole case. When feeling is strong, and intelligence weak, there is but one issue possible. The ardent emotions of a young mind, with little experience of life to set against the current, construct the most gorgeous and insane delusions, with a full disposition to risk everything in acting them out. We may enjoy our favourite emotions, in suitable creations of the fancy, without believing in the reality of such creations ; there being a sufficient counterpoise in our rational nature, in our knowledge of the actual, and in the power of making this knowledge always felt, to stem the torrent of excessive emotion, and prevent the total absorption of the mental being by the one strong feeling. A man may dream of becoming prime minister, and may have an hour's genuine delight in ideally occupying that illustrious position ; but he may stop short at the end of the hour, and go to the performance of his humble duties as if his thoughts had never wandered from them. The power of a rampant emotion may, or may not, be held in check by other forces, emotional, volitional, or intellectual ; but whether it gains or loses the day,

the double property of controlling the thoughts, and influencing the belief, is equally put in evidence.

13. Another remark on this hackneyed subject may be introduced for the sake of completing the round of illustrative observations. There are many things that owe their entire mental influence to their ideal efficacy. This is the case with wealth never employed. A man enjoys the imagination of putting forth his property to this and the other application, although in fact he may never go beyond the mere design. We find a great deal of pleasure in scheming plans that do not come to execution, and in forecasting results that are not substantiated. I have formerly remarked, that the paradoxical longing for future fame connects itself with this extensive capability of keeping up ideal emotions. If the enjoyment of human praise be intense in the bosom, and if the cerebral forces go largely to sustain this peculiar thrill, we shall find ourselves able to keep up the charm and the delight long after a time of actual fruition, and to construct occasions and times purely imaginary. We shall see in vision approving smiles never to be seen by the eye, and have our inward ear filled by acclamations that will not pass in by the outward sense. Any strong stimulation applied to a ruling passion, such as this, may intoxicate the mind to the pitch of delirium, with no real occasion or actual cause. These are the 'pleasures of the Imagination,' to which there are counterpart 'pains,' and their groundwork is the existence of emotional waves that have no more than a cerebral, or subjective, support. Remaining after the disturbing stone has sunk to the bottom, they may be equally reproduced by purely inward or mental causes, and may flourish on the imagery that they themselves give birth to.

14. It is difficult to do full justice to the power of self-sustaining emotion in the human mind, adhering at the same .time to something like scientific statements and accurate generalizations. A man or woman with an emotional temperament somewhat above the average, and in the habit of giving way to it, presents, in the course of an ordinary day,

## OF IDEAL EMOTION.

an inward career that persons cast in another mould rarely succeed in conceiving to themselves. With the waking hour a torrent sets in, a fire is kindled, an engine is put in motion, in certain directions, and gives a character to every decision of the day. One or more ruling passions, with certain subsidiary ones, dominate each passing hour, constituting the inner life—the enjoyment and the suffering of the individual, presiding over the conduct, guiding the thoughts and swaying the convictions. Whatever conflicts with the current of the moment is either rudely swept away, or leads to a violent recoil. Duties out of keeping with it are apt to be distasteful, and to get neglected ; actions in accord with the dominant stream make the hours fly like minutes. Everything is measured by emotion. Strong likings are engendered, and equally strong antipathies ; and both are manifested with pronounced energy. He that has to make a stand against the onward roll of the movement needs a stout heart ; for reason is unequal to the combat. In the words of Cowley, applied to times of fervid political excitement, ' the stream of the current is then so violent that the strongest men in the world cannot draw up against it ; and none are so weak but they may sail down with it.'

15. The contrast of Idea and Actuality shows itself in a remarkable manner in the Ethical appreciation of conduct. Practically, human nature revolts at severe restraint and self-denial, while, theoretically, asceticism has with many nations exercised a powerful charm. I cannot doubt that the foundation of the worship of self-denial lies in the pleasure that manifested Power excites, both in the person displaying it, and in the beholder. This is one of the strong emotions growing out of our active constitution, and as such has already come under review. The case now mentioned exemplifies in a signal way the intensity of the feeling. For the sake of this elated consciousness, men will sometimes submit to privation and suffering of the most galling kind. This, however, is not the most usual turn that the sentiment takes in practice. The pleasure of reflected moral energy is not always

## THE IDEAL IN ETHICS.

purchased by actual efforts of repressed appetite and crucified desire. The more common method is, to set up moral theories involving this in a high degree, to be contemplated and admired, with the admission that human nature is not equal to their full realization. So much are we disposed to hug moral strength as an idea, that we are greatly more indignant at any attempt to relax ethical theory than to see the derelictions of practice. It has been remarked that 'any man who should come to preach a relaxed morality would be pelted,' which is only a mode of expressing the adhesion of the mind to the ideal of high moral energy, notwithstanding all the shortcomings of actual conduct. The morality imposed by a community upon individuals partakes of the same admiration of power in the idea. There is, too, the farther satisfaction that each person has, as a member of the society, in imposing rigid rules upon his fellows, which seems more than a compensation for the hardship of being likewise subjected to them. The agreeable sentiment of the exercise of power is thus seen, in more ways than one, surmounting the pleasures of sense, the love of personal liberty, and the sympathy with pleasure generally, which have all very considerable standing in human nature. It would seem a usual tendency of the mental system to run in the channel of the emotions of power; and it is certain that many of the cerebral stimulants, both physical and other, enhance the same general tendency. Under the elation of wine, when the actual exercise of great moral energy, or of anything else, is at the very lowest, the imagination of this quality and the agreeable excitement of it are at the very highest. Under stimulation generally the same effect is liable to occur; in truth, the period of total disqualification for the real is the very acme of the ideal.

16. The outgoings of the Religious sentiment have a reference to the want of accordance between the mind and the world as now constituted; and a portion of the ungratified emotion takes the direction of the supernatural. Nothing could be more accurately expressed than the phrase 'worldly

minded' as opposed to 'religiously minded.' The state of the affections exactly suited by the persons and interests of the present life, gives no footing to the religious nature; the heart completely filled and gratified with the terrestrial, naturally abides in that limited sphere. But the history of humanity shows that this is not the general rule of our constitution. There has always existed a vein of strong emotion,—wonder, love, or awe—that would be satisfied with nothing less than a recognition of some great Power above.

17. In the region of Fine Art the ideal enters as an important ingredient, for reasons that must now be pretty obvious. The creations of art, being intended solely for gratifying the human susceptibilities to pleasure, must needs have respect to those that are not otherwise sufficiently provided for. The imitative artist may, as we have seen in the previous chapter, interest us by effects incidental to able or skilled imitation; but this has never wholly satisfied the human mind. The poet, while working on the subjects of nature and human life, is expected to improve his original by well-managed additions and omissions, thereby furnishing a more adequate vent for our strong sentiments, than the real world affords. This is admitted in all times to be the poetic function.

I may here remark, in conclusion, on imaginative sensibility, and its differences from sensibility to the real. Some of the most sentimental writers, such as Sterne (and Byron), seem to have had their capacities of tenderness excited only by ideal objects, and to have been very hard-hearted towards real persons. Of Wordsworth, again, it has been remarked, that his sensibilities were excited by a thing only after he had 'passed it through his imagination.' The counterpart of Byron's tenderness is Southey's indignation, which, as his friends said (not incredibly to those that have seen him), was wholly imaginative; the man being singularly free from bitterness or antipathy, even such as his opinions made him think were right and becoming.

## LIVING IN TWO WORLDS. 209

Such men live in two distinct worlds, their behaviour in one being no clue to their behaviour in the other. In meditation, and in composition, they enter their ideal sphere, and converse with imagined beings; in real life, they encounter totally different elements, and are affected accordingly.

## CHAPTER XIV.

### THE ÆSTHETIC EMOTIONS.

1. BY the above title I understand the group of feelings involved in the various Fine Arts, and constituting a class of pleasures somewhat vaguely circumscribed, but yet in various respects contradistinguished from our other pleasures. A contrast has always been considered to exist between the Beautiful and the Useful, and between Art and Industry. And we can readily inquire wherein the difference is conceived to lie. The gratifications of eating and drinking, and the other indulgences called sensual, are excluded from the present class, and indeed set in opposition to them, on several assignable grounds. In the first place, as our frame is constituted, these bodily functions, while incidentally ministering to our pleasure, are in the main subservient to the keeping up of our existence, and being in the first instance guided for that special end, they do not necessarily rank among gratifications as such. In the second place, they are connected with the production of what is repulsive and loathsome, which mars their purity as sources of pleasure. And in the third place, they are essentially confined in their influence to the single individual ; for the sociability óf the table is an added element. Two persons cannot enjoy the same morsel of food, or the same draught of exhilarating beverage. Now a mode of pleasure subject to one or more of these three conditions, may belong in an eminent degree to the list of utilities, and the ends of industry, but does not come under the class now propounded for discussion. Again, the machinery of precautions against pain, disease, and death,

## DISTINCTIONS OF FINE ART PLEASURES. 211

—our clothes, our houses, our parapet walls, our embankments, our lightning conductors, physic and surgery,—having in themselves nothing essentially pleasing, are placed in the category of the useful. So bodily or mental cultivation is not pleasurable in itself; very often the contrary. Wealth is disqualified by the third condition, inasmuch as, while in the shape of money, it is confined to some single proprietor. The same may be said of power and dignity, whose enjoyment cannot be divided or diffused,* excepting under one aspect to be presently noticed. Affection is nearly in the same predicament, from the difficulty of extending it over any great number. Anything so restricted in its sphere of action as to cons'itute individual property, and give occasion to jealousy and envy, is not a pleasure aimed at by the producer of fine art. For there do exist objects that can give us delight as their primary end, that have no disagreeable or revolting accompaniments, and whose enjoyment cannot be restricted to a single mind; all which considerations obviously elevate the rank of such objects in the scale of our enjoyments. Though they are not so intense as some of those other agencies of the monopolist class, their diffusion makes them precious like the free air and the light of heaven.

2. The Eye and the Ear are the great avenues to the mind for the æsthetic class of influences; the other senses are more or less in the monopolist interest. The blue sky, the green woods, and all the beauties of the landscape can fill the vision of a countless throng of admirers. So with the pleasing sounds, which certainly may be artificially monopolized, but which in their nature are capable of being enjoyed alike by a numerous multitude. Other things there are that do not perish with the using, but that nevertheless cannot operate upon a plurality of minds at one time, as for example, the whole class of tools and implements employed in our plea-

---

\* National power may be enjoyed as a collective sentiment, thereby approaching to the condition of one of the æsthetical feelings. So may family pride, or the pride of rank.

## 212 THE ÆSTHETIC EMOTIONS.

sures. An easy chair is too confined in its scope to be an æsthetic object.

3. The muscular and sensual elements can be brought into art by being contemplated in the *idea*, in place of being enjoyed in the reality. A painter, or a poet, may depict a feast, and the picture may be viewed with pleasure. Seen at a distance, the objects of sensual delight can take on the æsthetic phase. They are no longer obnoxious to the disqualifying conditions above specified. In such a shape they do not minister to our necessities; their disagreeable accompaniments need not be admitted into the picture; and they are not restricted to the individual consumer.* So with the elements of wealth, power, dignity, and affection, which in their actuality want the liberal character of the true artistic delight; if we can only derive pleasure from the spectacle of them in the hands of the select number of their possessors, they become to us an enjoyment that can be shared by the general multitude. And it is really the fact, that mankind find a charm in contemplating the wealthy, the powerful, the elevated, the illustrious, and take an interest in seeing displays of strong affection wherein they have no part; accordingly such elements are adopted freely into artistic compositions, and attract the admiration of the throng of beholders. The gratification of the spectacle of sovereign dignity, has usually been stronger than the *invidia* of so much grandeur and distinction conferred upon a fellow-mortal; and it is doubtful if history would retain half its interest with the majority, if royal and imperial actors were put aside.

---

* These are the only general assignable conditions that I can seize upon to circumscribe the æsthetic pleasures. I cannot pretend to affirm that they include the circumstances that in every case constitute some pleasures as 'elevating' and refined, as distinguished from others that are sensual and 'degrading;' because, if from no other consideration, a mere arbitrary convention may sometimes make all the difference. The ideal representation of the sensual pleasures comes strictly under the province of Art, but, for prudential and moral reasons, is kept within certain limits, varying in different ages and countries.

PROBLEM OF THE BEAUTIFUL. 213

4. Ever since the dawn of philosophical speculation, the nature of the Beautiful has been a matter of discussion. In the conversations of Socrates, and in the composed dialogues of Plato, this inquiry had a place side by side with others conducted in a kindred spirit, as into the Good, the Just, the Fit. Most of the inquirers laboured under a fallacy of misapprehension, rendering the discussion futile as regarded analytic results ; they proceeded on the supposition, that some single thing could be found, entering as a common ingredient, into the whole class of things named beautiful. Now, excepting the feeling itself, which may be presumed to have a certain uniform character, from the circumstance of the employment of the same name to denote it throughout, there is no one thing common to all the objects of beauty. Had there been such, we should have known it in the course of two thousand years The search for the one common attribute has been an entire failure ; like many other researches, conducted under the same mistaken impulse, for finding a great comprehensive unity in the causes of all natural phenomena. We are now led to recognise the doctrine of the 'plurality of causes' in our explanations of things ; and the instances of this plurality are both numerous and familiar. Motion may be produced by a great variety of agents or prime movers—animal power, wind, water, steam, gunpowder, electricity, &c. The same is true of heat. The agents called useful or good, (hurtful or evil), to living beings are endless, and devoid of any other property in common. .Even such a limited effect as nervous stimulation we have seen, in the preceding chapter, to be operated by an exceedingly wide variety of agents physical and mental ; and yet the effect itself is very much alike under them all. With such examples before us, it is not to be wondered at, that speculative men should have been unable to find any single and exclusive property inhering in all the things that give rise to the common impression, termed the beautiful.*

---

* 'The word Beauty, and, I believe, the corresponding term in all languages whatever, is employed in a great variety of acceptations, which seem,

## 214 THE ÆSTHETIC EMOTIONS.

5. Sublimity, Beauty, Grace, Harmony, Melody, Ideality, Picturesqueness, Proportion, Order, Fitness, Keeping—though they do not all relate to the beautiful, are all involved in the

———————————————

on a superficial view, to have very little connexion with each other; and among which it is not easy to trace the slightest shade of common or coincident meaning. It always, indeed, denotes something which gives not merely *pleasure* to the mind, but a certain refined species of pleasure, remote from those grosser indulgences which are common to us with the brutes; but it is not applicable universally in every case where such refined pleasures are received; being confined to those exclusively which form the proper objects of Intellectual Taste. We speak of beautiful colours, beautiful forms, beautiful pieces of music: we speak also of the beauty of virtue; of the beauty of poetical composition; of the beauty of style in prose; of the beauty of a mathematical theorem; of the beauty of a philosophical discovery. On the other hand, we do *not* speak of beautiful tastes, or beautiful smells; nor do we apply this epithet to the agreeable softness, or smoothness, or warmth of tangible objects, considered solely in their relation to our sense of feeling. Still less would it be consistent with the common use of language, to speak of the beauty of high birth, of the beauty of a large fortune, or of the beauty of extensive renown.

'It has long been a favourite problem with philosophers, to ascertain the common quality or qualities which entitles a thing to the denomination of *beautiful;* but the success of their speculations has been so inconsiderable, that little can be inferred from them but the impossibility of the problem to which they have been directed.

'The speculations which have given occasion to these remarks have evidently originated in a prejudice which has descended to modern times from the scholastic ages; that when a word admits of a variety of significations, these different significations must all be *species* of the same *genus ;* and must consequently include some essential idea common to every individual to which the generic term can be applied.

' Of this principle, which has been an abundant source of obscurity and mystery in the different sciences, it would be easy to expose the unsoundness and futility ; but, on the present occasion, I shall only remind my readers of the absurdities into which it led the Aristotelians on the subject of *causation* —the ambiguity of the word, which in the Greek language corresponds to the English word *cause,* having suggested to them the vain attempt of tracing the common idea which, in the case of any *effect,* belongs to the *efficient,* to the *matter,* to the *form,* and to the *end.* The idle generalities we meet with in other philosophers, about the ideas of the *good,* the *fit,* and the *becoming,* have taken their rise from the same undue influence of popular epithets on the speculations of the learned.

' Socrates, whose plain good sense appears in this, as in various other

## NAMES FOR ÆSTHETIC QUALITIES.

circle of pleasures now before us ; and it is quite obvious that no one fact can run through this variety of designations. There must be a great multitude of agents operating to produce these different impressions, which are related to one another, only by attaching in common to the æsthetic class of compositions. Doubtless, several of these names may be employed to mean the same thing, being, in fact, partially synonymous terms ; as Beauty and Grace,—Proportion, Fitness, and Keeping ; but hardly any two terms are synonymous throughout, and there are distinct conceptions implied in Sublimity, Beauty, Picturesqueness, Fitness, and the Ludicrous.

The objects described in these various phrases may occur spontaneously in nature ; as, for example, wild and impressive scenery ; they may spring up incidental to other effects, as when the contests of nations, carried on for self-protection or supremacy, produce grand and stirring spectacles to the unconcerned beholders, or to after ages ; or when the structures, raised for pure utility, rise to grandeur from their mere

---

instances, to have fortified his understanding to a wonderful degree against the metaphysical subtleties which misled his successors, was evidently apprised fully of the justness of the foregoing remarks—if any reliance can be placed on the account given by Xenophon of his conversation with Aristippus about the Good and the Beautiful. Aristippus, we are told, having asked him " if he knew anything that was good ?" " Do you ask me," said Socrates, " if I know anything *good* for a *fever*, or for an inflammation in the *eyes*, or as a preservative against a *famine* ?"

' " By no means," returned the other.

' " Nay, then," replied Socrates, " if you ask me concerning a *good* which is *good for nothing*, I know of none such ; nor yet do I desire to know it."

' Aristippus still urging him, " But do you know," said he, " anything beautiful ?"

' " A great many," returned Socrates.

' " Are these all like to one another ?"

' " Far from it, Aristippus ; there is a very considerable difference between them."

' " But how," said Aristippus, " can *beauty* differ from *beauty* ? " '—Stewart *On the Beautiful*, Part I. Chap. I.

· The illustration from the Aristotelian notions of Causation is not in point, for these various names designate really different aspects of the relation of cause and effect, or of pre-requisite condition, conceived in a certain manner.

216 THE ÆSTHETIC EMOTIONS.

magnitude, as a ship of war, or a vast building; and lastly, they may be expressly produced for their own sake, in which case we have a class of Fine Arts, a profession of Artists, and an education of people generally in elegance and taste.

6. It will be apparent, therefore, that I contemplate treating of this subject, not with a view to establish any one comprehensive generalization, but to indicate a certain number of distinct and co-ordinate groups, into which the details appear capable of being thrown. With the utmost desire to generalize the common attributes wherever they occur, I see no likelihood of carrying this to the point of including all the objects now referred to, in even a small number of generalities. In a highly-wrought poem or romance—an *Iliad*, a *Macbeth*, a *Don Quixote*, or a novel of Scott, Bulwer, or Balzac—the mind is touched at a great many points, and yet harmoniously; and it would not be good, either for mental science or for criticism, to attempt to fuse the various stimulants, assembled in one of those compositions, under some supposed generality.

Throughout the whole of the preceding exposition in this and my former volume, I have been in the habit of adverting to the employment in Art of the various elements passed in review—the sensations, the intellectual associations, and the special emotions. The first thing to be done here, therefore, is to collect these various allusions, and see how far they will go to exhaust the catalogue of æsthetic effects.

7. As the pure muscular feelings, and the sensations of organic life, taste, smell, and touch, do not belong to Art, unless as conceived in idea, we must start from the sense of Hearing. All the pleasant varieties of sounds may enter into artistic compositions, as in music. Some sounds are characterized as sweet; others are loud and strong, which, within limits, is also an agreeable property. The voluminous sounds are pleasant in a more unqualified manner. The pitch of sound is the basis of musical harmony. The waxing and waning of sounds is an effect particularly impressive. All these qualities are concerned in producing pleasure of the

## BEAUTY UNDER SIGHT. 217

true artistic kind, and the additional circumstance of Harmony is alone wanting.

The sense of Sight supplies a variety of pleasures, all of them worthy to become part of the æsthetic circle of enjoyments. They are not affected by any of the disqualifying conditions laid down at the outset, and they possess in a high degree the attribute of ideal persistence, which recommends them still farther for the same end. Mere light, colour, and lustre, are the three optical sources of pleasure. The combination of the optical with the muscular, gives the pleasures of moving spectacle, of form and outline, including the peculiar effect of the curved line, which, although a simple element, ranks high among the sources of æsthetic charm. There is also the sensation of great magnitude corresponding to the voluminous in sound, and lying at the foundation of what we term sublimity. Objects that are capable of giving any one of those impressions in considerable amount, are important means of exciting human interest. The solar radiance, the rich hues of colour, the lustrous and brilliant surface, are prized even when standing alone, and may be still more effective when joined in Harmony, by the colour Artist.*

---

* 'The first ideas of *beauty* formed by the mind are, in all probability, derived from *colours*. Long before infants receive any pleasures from the beauties of form or of motion (both of which require, for their preception, a certain effort of attention and of thought), their eye may be caught and delighted with brilliant colouring, or with splendid illumination. I am inclined, too, to suspect that, in the judgment of a peasant, this ingredient of beauty predominates over every other, even in his estimate of the perfections of the female form; and, in the inanimate creation, there seems to be little else which he beholds with any rapture. It is accordingly, from the effect produced by the rich painting of clouds, when gilded by a setting sun, that Akenside infers the existence of the seeds of Taste, when it is impossible to trace them to any hand but that of nature.

' " Ask the swain
Who journeys homeward from a summer-day's
Long labour, why forgetful of his toils,
And due repose, he loiters to behold
The sunshine gleaming, as through amber clouds,

218                THE ÆSTHETIC EMOTIONS.

8. Next as to the co-operation of the Intellect, in giving birth to the fitting materials of æsthetic emotion. I have already hinted, that sensations of an inferior rank are capable of being elevated into ideal pleasures. Thus, when muscular exercise, repose, or fatigue, are merely suggested to the mind, as when we look on at gymnastic feats, dancing, skating, &c., they become sources of a more refined interest. Losing altogether their egotistic nature, they may affect any number of persons alike, so that they have the feature of liberality, so essential to art. The sensations of organic life are exalted in the same way. While they are confined to our actual experience, or even our recollected, or anticipated, experience, they are excluded from the present domain, but when viewed in such a manner as to be no one person's property, they are fit subjects for the artist. Thus, the interest that we take in the nutrition and subsistence of animal life, is an unexclusive interest. The circumstances suggestive of the free and fresh air, bringing to the mind the idea of exhilarating respiration, are highly interesting, and are yet sufficiently elevated for the artist's pencil. Indeed, a painter could have no more striking success, than in contriving scenes and touches, so as to make this feeling powerfully present from the sight of his picture. The actual enjoyment of warmth or coolness is, so to speak, sensual, but the suggestion of those effects to the mind of beholders at large by associated circumstances, as by colour, light, and shade, is refined and artistical. The taking of our

---

O'er all the western sky; full soon, I ween,
His rude expression, and untutor'd airs,
Beyond the power of language, will unfold
The form of Beauty smiling at his heart."

" Among the several kinds of beauty," says Mr. Addison, "the eye *takes most delight in colours*. We nowhere meet with a more glorious or pleasing show in nature, than what appears in the heavens, at the rising or setting of the sun, which is wholly made up of those different stains of light that show themselves in clouds of a different situation. For this reason we find the poets, who are always addressing themselves to the imagination, borrowing more of their epithets from colours than from any other topic.'—Stewart *On the Beautiful*, page 275.

## CO-OPERATION OF THE INTELLECT. 219

own food, and our own states of hunger, are an inferior kind of interest, although perhaps to us individually among our most intense experiences; our contemplation of Sancho Panza losing his dinner by the physician's orders, belongs to the elevated sphere of an unexclusive interest. Disinterested sympathy transforms the character of all those purely sensual elements, by giving them an ideal existence, in which shape no one is debarred from the pleasure that they may thereby afford. The appearances that indicate cleanliness, or the absence of whatever causes loathing or disgust, are agreeable associations of deliverance from a serious organic misery. Sweet odours, in picturesque allusion, rise into the region we are now discussing. The fragrant bosom of Andromaché, and of Aphrodité, finds a place in Homer's poetry. Intellectual suggestion is peculiarly operative in giving an æsthetic character to sensations of Touch. A warm, delicately soft contact, may be ideally reproduced by representations made to the eye, as in a picture, and is then a purely æsthetic pleasure.* The objects of hearing and sight, in their own nature, able to constitute liberal and common pleasures, may be still more

---

* 'That the smoothness of many objects is *one* constituent of their beauty, cannot be disputed. In consequence of that intimate association which is formed in the mind between the perceptions of sight and those of touch, it is reasonable to expect that those qualities which give pleasure to the latter sense, should also be agreeable to the former. Hence the agreeable impression which the eye receives from all those smooth objects about which the sense of touch is habitually conversant; and hence, in such instances, the unpleasant appearance of ruggedness or of asperity. The agreeable effect, too, of smoothness, is often heightened by its reflection so copiously in the rays of light; as in the surface of water, in polished mirrors, and in the fine kinds of wood employed in ornamental furniture. In some instances, besides, as in the last now mentioned, smoothness derives an additional recommendation from its being considered as a mark of finished work, and of a skilful artist.

'To all this we may add, that the ideas of beauty formed by our sex are warped, not a little, by the notions we are led to entertain concerning the charms of the other. That in female beauty a smooth skin is an essential ingredient, must be granted in favour of Mr. Burke's theory. Nor is it at all difficult to conceive how this association may influence our taste in various other instances.'—Stewart, p. 296.

220 THE ÆSTHETIC EMOTIONS.

elevated and refined upon by ideal suggestion, as when the word-artist steps in to bring before the mind scenes of natural beauty. Whatever gives a more intellectual character to the objects of delight, provided they are still within the range of easy comprehension by the many, is said to elevate their character by more widely diffusing them. This is the superiority of the literary, over all the other, fine arts.

9. We can easily judge, by means of the criteria already made use of, how far the different simple Emotions of the foregoing chapters can be of avail in the sphere of artistic recreation. We commenced with Harmony and Conflict; and it has been seen already, and will appear more and more as we proceed, that Harmony is the soul of Art. In the next place, Novelty, Variety, and Wonder, are all earnestly sought by the artist. Indeed, those effects have been commonly included in every enumeration of the emotions of taste. The Tender feeling is eminently susceptible of artistic employment, from the large hold that it takes of most minds, and the quantity and quality of the pleasure accruing from it. The only thing demanded of the artist is to give it an ideal presentation, so far as to remove the attribute of monopoly from the picture. The love of a parent for his or her own child is exclusive; while the interest in the Laocoon is unexclusive and æsthetical. All the various objects of tender emotion, inanimate and animate, are freely made use of in the present class of compositions, and are indeed not unfrequently looked upon as synonymous with the beautiful.* The delicate and tender flower, the dependence of infancy, the protectorship of the powerful, and the sentiment of chivalry, are fountains of perennial human interest. The Irascible emotion is also, in some of its phases, a fit subject. When we approve of the occasion of an outburst of wrath, it is pleasing to us to accompany it with our own feelings; and the display of anger may be brought upon the stage, or enter into the epic plot, with

* See Burke *On the Connexion of Delicacy with Beauty; Essay on the* SUBLIME *and* BEAUTIFUL, Part III. Sec. 16.

THE EMOTIONS OF SCIENCE. 221

powerful effects. The passion of Fear may be so handled as to yield æsthetic pleasure, although in itself a painful and debilitating manifestation of human nature. Egotism, as we have seen, is made of universal acceptance by admiration and worship of the object; the self-complacency and cherished importance of our idols give us pleasure; while real power, dignity, and possessions, are a spectacle to inspire fascination and awe. The mere idea or contemplation of superior greatness is a fund of delight. The exercise of actual power is a monopolist pleasure, but Ideal Power is open and free. The judgments and criticism that we pass freely upon our fellow-creatures, and their ways and performances, are a common gratification, partaking of the freedom of thought itself. We have also seen that the emotions of activity give rise to a rich crop of unexclusive pleasures; for, granting actual Pursuit to be purely an individual gratification, spectatorial, or ideal, pursuit, is open and free. The plot-interest of events about us, of history and romance, is the right hand of the narrative artist.

10. A special observation is needed on the last of the simple emotions, as I have enumerated them, those of the Intellect. The feelings of truth and consistency, and the love of knowledge and science, might be conceived as preeminently deserving of being ranked with æsthetic sentiments, if these court an alliance with dignity and refinement. And it is freely admitted that nothing could be more liberalizing, or more open, than such objects. Unfortunately, however, they labour under two special disqualifications of their own, by which they are prevented from sharing in the artistic circle, as men are at present constituted. In the first place, they demand a painful preparatory training, such as only a small number of persons can ever be got to pass through. And, secondly, truth is not the cause of unmingled delight, any more than surgery or discipline; and pleasure is not its immediate end. Any classes of truths that do not fall under the ban of these two conditions are made welcome by the artist, and by the caterer of our amusements. The more

222          THE ÆSTHETIC EMOTIONS.

intelligible and popular discoveries of science are introduced into the evening lecture, the newspaper, the book of the day, or the poet's illustrative simile; and there is a considerable respect generally entertained for the idea of the True, if no disagreeable instances are presented to the mind. But high scientific knowledge manifestly transcends the sphere of Art, just as a highly artistic form transcends the sphere of science. If it could be otherwise, we should be great gainers. If what gives us knowledge and certainty as regards the world, were also of easy comprehension, and the source of a light and fascinating amusement, we should be saved from many pains, and take much higher strides of advancement in the happiness and security of life.

Let us now consider the more usual combinations of these various simple elements.

11. *Melody and Harmony in Sound.*—We have seen what are the simple effects on the ear that are calculated to give pleasure; namely, Sweetness in sound, Loudness or intensity within limits, Volume, and Waxing and Waning sounds. Farther effects arise when different sounds come together, or in quick succession, so as to concur in the ear, or in the mind. The concurrence may be indifferent, or merely increase the mass of sound, as in the din of a market place. It may however, be so arranged as to give a new pleasure, the pleasure of Harmony; which implies also the possibility of a counter pain, the pain of discord.

It has been well ascertained what relation sounds must bear to each other, to form harmony. A certain numerical relationship in the *pitch*, or number of vibrations in a given time, is the foundation of a musical chord. If the rate of vibration of two sounds is as one to two, we have the interval marked as an octave, and the most perfect chord that can exist.* An ear very susceptible to pitch, or the rate of vibration of sound, feels very acutely those several coincidences.

---

\* Other cords are 1 to 3 (an octave and a fifth), 2 to 3 (a fifth), 3 to 4 (a fourth), 4 to 5 (a major third), 3 to 5 (a sixth), 5 to 6 a minor third), 8 to 9 (a major tone), 9 to 10 (a minor tone), 8 to 15 (a seventh), 15 to 16 (a major

## HARMONY IN SOUND. 223

The grateful feelings produced by these harmonized sounds may be supposed to exemplify the general law connecting Harmony with self-conservation and pleasure. But we must consider the circumstances a little more closely. And first, as to the musical note sounded alone. A sound on one continuing pitch is more agreeable than one irregularly varying in pitch, or a mere noise. Now, what is there in such a sound? Mechanically, it consists of a series of vibrations or beats at equal intervals of time, varying from twenty a second to upwards of seventy thousand a second. It appears, then, that even in this very minute scale of duration, equality of times between the shocks on the nerves is more agreeable than inequality. The same fact reappears on the larger scale, in what is properly known as Time in music, meaning the duration of the successive notes of a melody, which to be agreeable must be equal or proportional. It has also its counterpart in the harmonies of Sight, or the pleasures of equality in the succession of visible magnitudes. I cannot with certainty assign the ultimate connection of these regular shocks with a pleasurable consciousness; it is highly probable that the activity of the nerves is in this way promoted with the least expenditure, and without the conflict of disappointed expectation.

The case of concurring or successive notes in musical concord is somewhat more complicated, although the effect, in all likelihood, depends on the same ultimate law. In the concord of an Octave, every second beat of the upper note coincides with every beat of the lower; and between these double beats there is a single beat. The intervals are, therefore, still equal,

---

semitone), 24 to 25 (a minor semitone). When any musical interval can be expressed by the ratio of two numbers not exceeding 5, it is concordant; all others are discordant. This is as regards Harmony, or notes sounded together; but as regards Melody, or a succession of musical notes, all the intervals above enumerated are admissible, being the intervals constituting the common musical scale. In melody, the concord lies between a present note, and the impressions left by preceding ones—between an actuality and an idea, and a greater latitude is allowed in this case. At the same time, the superior chords must be liberally used with the others, in melodious composition.

224          THE ÆSTHETIC EMOTIONS.

but the beats unequal; a double and a single alternating. This is the first departure from uniformity towards variety, and the effect is more acceptable, probably on that ground. In the concord of a Fifth, every third vibration of the higher note coincides with every second of the lower; and between these two coincidences, there are three single beats (two in one note and one in the other) at intervals varying as 1, $\frac{1}{2}$, $\frac{1}{2}$, 1, respectively. In the concord of a Fourth, every fourth vibration of the higher note coincides with every third of the lower; and between the two coincidences, there are five single beats (three in one note and two in the other), at intervals of 1, $\frac{1}{3}$, $\frac{2}{3}$, $\frac{2}{3}$, $\frac{1}{3}$, 1. In these two last mentioned concords, there is a mixture of different sets of equal intervals; the coinciding or double beat, and the single beats recurring in the same order of unequal but proportioned intervals. The pleasure is greater than, or at least different from, the concord of octaves ; and we may still suppose that the introduction of a plurality of various effects, related to each other by similarity, is calculated to yield a heightened stimulation with the minimum of expenditure, and the least falsifying of expectation.*

12. In the foregoing explanations, we have included the effect commonly meant by Time in music, that is, the equal or proportioned duration of the successive notes. The strict observance of Time, not only enables complicated harmonies to be arranged, and large bands to co-operate, but is in itself a part of the agreeable effect of a musical composition. When the ear naturally, or by education, possesses a nice appreciation of intervals of time, any inequality or disproportion acts like a discord, and gives pain to the sense of hearing. The

---

* The views of Helmholtz regarding the composite nature of musical tones, as determining timbre and articulate differences (*Hearing*, § 15), introduce new considerations into Harmony. When two notes are sounded together, effects will arise out of the junctions of ground tones of the one with the upper tones of the other, and out of the junctions of the upper tones of both. In an octave concord, the higher note merely strengthens the first upper tone of the lower note; the concord of a third may therefore be said to be the first departure from unison, and beginning of Harmony.

disappointing of expectation is manifest in this case. The mind is prepared for a certain rapidity of movement, and puts on the corresponding attitude of anticipation ; and when there is an irregularity, or a change of pace, a jar of disappointment is felt, like mistaking the end of a stair.* Whenever a rhythmical arrangement suddenly breaks down, or becomes irregular, the result is the same.

13. The varying Emphasis of music, properly regulated, adds to the pleasure, on the law of Relativity, or alternation and remission, like light and shade. According as sounds are sharp and loud, is it necessary that they be remitted and varied. The gradations of pitch have respect to variety as well as to harmony and melody. As a work of Art aims at giving pleasure to the utmost, it courts variety in every form, only not to produce discords, or to miss harmonies.

14. What is termed Cadence is an effect both in music and in speech, and would seem to refer in the first instance to the fall, or close, of a melody, or period. The mind is revulsed by an abrupt termination, as the body once in motion is jarred and shocked by a sudden halt. To satisfy this feeling, it is a practice to let down gradually all rapid movements and lofty flights, so as to make an easy transition to the state of repose. It is usual to end a musical composition on a low note, or, if otherwise, to let the closing note die gradually away. In speaking, the voice rises towards a middle point of the period, and falls at the end, there being maintained throughout a series of rises and falls subordinate to the principal. This alternation of up and down is the modulation or melody of articulate speech, founded partly on the general craving of the senses for variety, modified by the necessities of cadence as now defined ; and serving as auxiliary to the comprehension of meaning and the impressiveness of the feelings to be conveyed.

---

* Any sound going on while one is attending to something else is much more distressing and distracting if it is exactly rhythmical, and so compels one to listen, and expect, and watch for its successive beats—like a piano in the next house, or somebody beating a tattoo with their hands or feet.

P

226                    THE ÆSTHETIC EMOTIONS.

15. The Composition of a piece of music, taken as a whole, is doubtless nothing more than an adjustment of all those simple effects in such a way as to yield the highest degree of delight. Concord, Time, with the alternation of long and short; Emphasis and Cadence; sounds sweet, voluminous, swelling, dying, and varied,—all duly combined in some one mode and character by the composer's art, are capable of causing the thrill of fascination known to the lovers of music. Nor should we overlook the imitating of emotional expression, whereby the composer can rouse the passions by a direct appeal, as well as gratify the feelings of harmony and variety. Pathos, Awe, Indignation, Triumphant glorification, can be successfully aroused by musical strains. The popular melodies of a nation are some happy simple effects, struck out by original genius, and enhanced by the charms of association and nationality. The elaborate music of modern times is a vast aggregate of effects; a single piece frequently having as many windings as an epic or a drama.

I have already remarked that music may operate merely as an intoxicating stimulant, or excited atmosphere for other passions. When the pleasure derived from it is so great, as to be preferred to any other emotion that might be kindled under its inspiration, the attention is wholly riveted upon the performance, and the recollection of the piece is thereby promoted. The genuine musical mind spurns the intoxicating effect, and abides by the impression proper to the art itself, and so becomes educated for reproducing, as well as for listening.

16. The melody of Speech has an element peculiar to itself, namely, facility of Pronunciation, the principles of which lie on the surface. The ear is sympathetically affected with what is easy or difficult to pronounce, and has besides an independent satisfaction in Variety (articulate and musical), in Rhythm or regularity, and in Cadence or the melodious inflexion of the voice. The details are best given in treatises on Rhetoric and on Elocution. There is no new artistic principle at work.

HARMONIES OF COLOUR.

227

17. *Harmonies of Sight.*—Light and Shade are pleasurable from alternation; they represent in a picture the agreeable cycle of luminous intensity occurring in each day, through which light exercises its cheering influence on the mind. As regards Colour, there are special laws of Harmony. It appears, that whiteness is a balance of all the colours, the effect resulting when all the optic fibres receive their full proportion of stimulus. The eye exposed for some time to one colour desiderates, and is refreshed by, the complement of that, or the colour that with it would produce whiteness.* Next to the complementary colour, the eye can find relief in passing to black, and also, although in a less degree, in passing to white; a strong colour may therefore be agreeably conjoined with black, grey,. and white, in a decreasing scale. We have formerly remarked on the great charm of Lustre. It seems to have a power to redeem bad combinations of colours. Red-yellow is unharmonious as colour, but red-gold is a resplendent effect. The blue lake with its green banks would not be agreeable, but for the lustre of the watery expanse. A lustrous surface reflects the light of the surrounding objects and gives rise to the play of a thin radiance, as of a slight film or gauze, softening without obscuring the colour beneath.

18. Proceeding from the optical to the muscular susceptibility of the eye, we encounter harmonies of Movement, and of Dimensions in space. The movements in a Dance keep Time as in music. As regards objects at rest, a plurality of similar things have to be placed at *equal intervals*, as in rows, tiers, ranks, mosaic work, and other uniform array. To obtain variety, we may introduce larger breaks at uniform distances, as in flower beds ; or objects of larger dimensions, as in ornamental railings. This introduces complex harmony, and the idea of subordination, which is a phase of Unity.

---

* 'Two colours harmonize, if one is a primitive colour, and the other a certain mixture of the two remaining colours : thus red harmonizes with green (formed out of yellow and blue) ; blue harmonizes with orange or gold (a mixture of red and yellow) ; yellow harmonizes with violet (red and blue).

228                THE ÆSTHETIC EMOTIONS.

Wherever any linear object is divided with a view of pleasing the eye, the division must observe some rules of proportion, the determination of which belongs to Fine Art. At first, such proportions were guided solely by the effect; as melodies were composed to please the ear, without reference to musical ratios. At a later period, strict numerical laws were sought.*

* The laws of proportion that reign in admired works of art, such as the remains of Grecian Sculpture and Architecture, are not obvious, and different modes of reaching them have been proposed.

To take the simple case of a vertical elevation, harmoniously divided (as a cross), the German critics have laid down a rule, called the 'golden section,' namely, that the shorter part shall bear the same proportion to the longer, as the longer to the whole; the same rule to hold, in farther subdivisions of the parts, as must happen in a great Architectural front. A second law must regulate the proportions of breadth to height, as the arms of the cross compared with the height of the pillar, and the breadth of a front compared with the divisions of the height. Considerable latitude prevails as to this last relation, but one case may be given as an example of an agreeable and simple proportion ; namely, when the half breadth is a mean proportional between the short and long divisions of the vertical height. (See Wundt's *Menschen- und Thierseele*, Vol. II., p. 82).

Mr. D. R. Hay maintains that the numerical proportionality of the perfect works of art is to be found, not in the lines, but in the angles subtended by the different linear divisions. Thus in a rectangle, the angles made by the diagonal, should have a simple proportion to a right angle, as $\frac{1}{2}$ (in a square), $\frac{1}{3}$, $\frac{1}{4}$, $\frac{1}{2}$, &c. ; which, of course, gives the two parts of the right angle simple ratios to each other,—1 to 1, 1 to 2, 1 to 3, 2 to 3, &c. Mr. Hay named these proportions according to those notes of the musical scale having the same ratios in their number of vibrations ; although it is not apparent what he obtains by the comparison, seeing that both cases fall under the same rule of simplicity of ratios.

The human face and head are, by Mr. Hay's method, resolved thus. An ellipse is formed, whose greater axis is the whole length of the head, from the crown to the chin. The width, or lesser axis, is determined by harmonic considerations, as follows ; the extremities of the major and minor semiaxes are joined, so as to make a right angled triangle, and the acute angles are respectively 30° and 60°, or as 1 to 2; this yields a *dominant* ellipse, based on a dominant triangle, being the same concord as a fifth in music. But now to give the expansion of the cranium. A circle of the same character as the width of the ellipse, overlies it, and touches it at the apex. The combined figure of circle and ellipse, gives the perfect harmonic outline of the face, with a little smoothing away here and there, for greater approximation to nature.

## LAWS OF PROPORTION.

19. The principle we are now discussing applies alike to the two elements of Number and Space, giving to both an artistic capability. In the case of a multitude of objects, we arrange in equal and proportionate intervals; and we subdivide in the same way a blank uninteresting expanse. And there is much of the effect of Outline due to the same feeling, especially as regards right-lined figures,—squares, oblongs, parallelograms, triangles, equilateral polygons, &c., —and the symmetrical curves, the circle and the ellipse. In all these, the eye traces equality, or commensurability, in the

---

As regards the features, the operation is this. From the apex of the head, or the upper extremity of the ellipse, a series of lines are drawn on both sides, making the respective angles, $\frac{1}{3}$ (30°), $\frac{1}{4}$ (22$\frac{1}{2}$°), $\frac{1}{5}$ (18°), $\frac{1}{6}$ (15°), and $\frac{1}{7}$ (12$\frac{6}{7}$°). Through the points where they severally meet the circumference of the ellipse, horizontal lines are drawn across the face, making a series of isosceles triangles. Beginning at the outer lines, with the largest angle, namely $\frac{1}{3}$ or 30°; the line joining these, passes through the centre of the eyes, and consequently is one element in determining their position. The line at the angle of $\frac{1}{4}$ (22$\frac{1}{2}$°), touches the outer circumference of the orbit, and is a second element in determining the eye; the horizontal junction of the two lines, gives the vertical position of the nose. The horizontal junction of the lines of $\frac{1}{5}$ (18°), crosses the top of the upper lip. The lines of $\frac{1}{6}$ (15°), pass through the centres of the eyes, and complete the determination of place and size of the orbits; the horizontal junction gives the lower boundary of the mouth. The horizontal junction of the lines of the angle of $\frac{1}{7}$ give the superior edge of the chin.

By a similar scheme of proportioned angles, Mr. Hay determines the beauty of the Human Figure. He applies the method to the proportions of the Parthenon, and to Architecture generally.

Whether such a device approximately represents the proportions of a beautiful object, or of a work of art, is to be proved or disproved solely by the experimental test of measurement. But if Mr. Hay means to insinuate that the pleasurable feeling of proportion in the mind of the spectator, is a feeling of the proportion of imaginary angles, he advances an incredible hypothesis. It is not to be supposed that the mind, in judging of a face, constructs an ideal diagram, and thereby enjoys a pleasing melody of angles. What the eye fastens upon must be something more within its usual habits of judging than this: the deep angular melody can be accepted only as a mathematical equivalent of some more apparent charm, which Mr. Hay has failed to give any account of. We have still, so far as his views are concerned, to fall back upon the old theory of the sensuous pleasure of curves, as regards curved surfaces; and as regards rectilineal dimensions, we must seek a more palpable order of proportions than his theory provides.

## 230                    THE ÆSTHETIC EMOTIONS.

different sides or dimensions. A triangle or quadrilateral, with all the sides unequal, gives no pleasure to the eye as a form or outline (unless it were, like a discord in music, occasionally introduced); while the square and the parallelogram comply with the desire in question. Parallelism is sustained equality, as much as the equality of intervals in a row of objects. When lines converge, as in a pediment, we look for equality in the two converging sides, and are pleased to discern some further regard to proportion, as in the equality of the three sides of the triangle, or the equality or commensurability of the base, and perpendicular height. When an angle prominently arrests the attention, we prefer 45° or 30° as being aliquot parts of a right angle. The oblique equal-sided parallelogram, with the angles 45° to 135°, is an agreeable subdivision of the small-paned window.

20. On the subject of Form and Outline, we must advert to other principles regulating our appreciation of the effects. We have seen that a curved line is intrinsically pleasing, like a waxing or waning sound, and that a varying curvature is preferable to the rigid uniformity of the circle. The oval is thus a pleasing curve; and still more so is a waving or changing curve, as the outline of a pilaster, or vase. There is an original charm, operated through the muscular sensibility of the eye, in the curved outline, to which are superadded associations of ease, freedom, or the absence of restraint. Accordingly, straight forms are unpleasing in themselves; they refuse the gratification that the eye receives from the other, and they suggest a severe and rigid constraint. The mechanical members of the human body, being chiefly levers fixed at one end, naturally describe curves with their extremities; a laborious cultivation alone enables us to describe a straight line with the hand or foot. Whence, straight forms are apt to suggest this painful discipline.* On the other hand, there are

---

\* A rope or chain running horizontally, and tightened to straightness, reminds us of one of our most difficult mechanical attempts; the catenary curve, or the slack rope, is a form suggestive of ease and *abandon*.

## BEAUTY OF OUTLINE.

circumstances where rectilinear forms are highly acceptable. A straight path is agreeable, because of its contributing to a manifest convenience. In orderly arrangements of every kind, right lines are essential ; or if we depart from these, it is in favour of the regular and symmetrical curves, the circle being the chief. I shall speak presently of the peculiar case of Support ; I am now alluding to the regular and methodical distribution of objects on a horizontal plane, with a view to convenience in all our operations. We should never think of partitioning fields with waving fences, or making the ground plan of buildings of a zigzag curvature. The facility of calculation recommends right-lined surfaces, and they also serve the end of compactness, when things are to be crowded into little space. These various considerations, of utility and every-day convenience, induce us to regard with a certain satisfaction the straight outline, even when the eye, in consulting its own primitive sensibility, would turn away from it.*

21. The dimension of up and down has its outline determined by the paramount condition of sustaining objects against the force of gravity ; thus bringing in the elements of Pressure and Support. We are so unremittingly subjected to that great power, and so much occupied in counteracting it, that the providing of sufficiency of Support on every needful occasion is our foremost solicitude. Experience soon teaches the infant in arms the evil of a failing prop ; the fear of falling manifests itself so early as to be very generally accounted an instinct. But no other explanation of it is necessary than the very decided monitions of falls, and bruises, and stunning pains,—of fractures and scatterings, confusion and loss,—from the giving way of stability. So anxious do we become on this head, that the slightest appearance or suggestion of the unstable, afflicts us with the misery of an

---

* There is something to be explained in the circumstance that all *early* taste in gardening runs to the rectilineal. Possibly the considerations in favour of the straight line, alluded to in the text, recommend it in the first instance.

## THE ÆSTHETIC EMOTIONS.

apprehended fall. Hence we desire all things about us to fulfil the requirements that our experience has shown to be needful for their stable footing. A firm foundation, a broad base, a tenacious and solid framework,—are known to be the only safeguards against a crushing gravitation, and it is distressing to witness any deficiency in those respects. The pyramid is the form that most completely fulfils these conditions. The sloping wall lowers the centre of gravity, and makes an erection exceedingly difficult to turn over. The upright wall is less stable, and demands expedients not necessary in the other ; we must not carry it too high, there must be sufficient thickness, strength, and tenacity of material to make up for narrowness of base. The walls of a house, connected by girders and a roof, are differently situated ; the entire bulk of the building is as one mass, and the stability is then very great. A similar effect is produced, when a row of pillars is joined together by lintels and a pediment.

22. While massive and well-founded edifices satisfy the mind, and give the agreeable feeling of sufficiency, or even superfluity of resistance to gravitating pressure which would otherwise crush and destroy, there is another motive that comes into play to modify the forms of solid erections, namely, the desire to see great effects produced with the smallest expenditure of means, and the appearance of Ease on the part of the agent. This is an aspect of the love of power, which is gratified when small efforts operate large changes, or great effects. The pyramid we are apt to account gross, heavy, awkward, clumsy, when used merely to support its own mass. We feel in that case that a very large amount of material and of space has been used up for a disproportionate end ; (as a sea-wall, or a fortification to resist cannon, the case is otherwise). We are greatly pleased if an object can be raised aloft to a great elevation without such expenditure of material, and such amplitude of base ; we being at the same time assured that the support is adequate. The obelisk is, in this respect, a grand refinement upon the massive pyramid. The column is a still higher effort, inasmuch as its lofty summit is

## BEAUTY OF SUPPORT. 233

capable of being crowned with a mass to be sustained by it. The devices that reconcile us to this bold proceeding are principally—a widening of the foundation, and an expansion of the summit in the lightest way, that is, with the least material that will answer the purpose. Thus the column has the slightly expanded base, and the spreading capital for receiving the superincumbent weight of the architrave and frieze. The pilaster is lightened by being cut away at the lower part, reserving breadth of base as being the primary element of stability. A slender stem, on an expanded base, may thus prove an efficient support, and gratify the mind with a large effect produced at a small outlay. All our graceful forms in objects that give support, such as vases, drinking-cups, and table ware in general, proceed upon these principles, giving at the same time the additional pleasure of curved forms, which is not dependent upon any association. The noble tree with its slender and yet adequate stem, its spreading roots and ample base, supporting a voluminous and expanded foliage—is a telling example of the reconciliation of adequate sustaining power with small outlay of material, and a striking contrast to the grossness of the pyramid.[*]

23. Symmetry is a demand in some cases for mere proportion, and at other times for support. There is a disagreeable effect of violated proportions when the two halves of a human face are not alike; a wasted, or unequal limb maims

---

[*] The light tripos is a good amelioration of the heavy solidity of the pyramidal mass.

The artist judges how far it is safe to go in reducing grossness of dimensions, without detracting from the appearance of adequate support.

Strict adherence to the perpendicular in a wall owes its urgency to the sentiment now discussed. A tall object declining to one side gives the painful impression of an expected fall. The leaning tower of Pisa is said to be quite stable, from having the centre of gravity within the base, but such a declension from the perpendicular is disagreeable to contemplate.

It was formerly remarked (*Contiguity*, § 30), that the Architectural proportions that satisfy the mind must differ according to the *material ;* beauty of design is very different in stone, in wood, and in iron.

234 THE ÆSTHETIC EMOTIONS.

the prop of the figure. A tree with the foliage grown to one side is unsymmetrical in both respects.

24. Beauty of Movement grows out of the cases now considered, in conjunction with the primary susceptibility of the mind to moving objects as seen by the eye. The curved and straight outlines respectively suggest the same emotions in still forms, and in the tracks of moving bodies. A curvilineal movement, as the flight of a projectile, or a bird, or the strides of a graceful dancer, is intrinsically pleasing; straight movements are rendered artistic only by associations of power, regularity, fitness, or some other circumstance that commends them to our regards. An upward flight is the analogy to support in still life—the putting forth of a power to counteract gravity,—and by giving us an idea of great propulsive energy, becomes a striking spectacle. Much illustration might be given of this class of effects, but we have no space for more than the bare enunciation of principles.

The *complex harmonies* brought out in the decorative arts, where colour is suited to form, and both to movement, would be exceedingly difficult to reduce to laws, although attempts are sometimes made with that view.*

---

* I doubt whether any laws of harmony exist between colours and forms in general, such as obtain between colours themselves, and between the different notes of the musical scale. We cannot say that red suits straight forms, or green rounded ones; or that white intrinsically harmonizes with quick movements, and black with slow. In the circumstances of each particular case, we can assign a propriety in the adjusting of particular colours and forms, from there being a common æsthetic character in the two elements for the time being. On an occasion of stately solemnity we can make all the decorations suit the main purpose—bright colours, stately motions, and upright and imposing objects. So in a *ballet divertissement*, the stage master knows how to adjust scenes, dresses, and motions to one pervading character attaching to the piece. Music may be chosen so as to chime in with other effects, without supposing any fundamental concord between certain sounds, colours, forms, and movements. Thus we have the two conspicuous varieties of composition, marking on the one hand the solemn, grave, or melancholy, and on the other the gay or sprightly; to attempt more minute subdivisions leads into the regions where no agreement of individual tastes is to be found. There is in one respect a deep concord among widely different effects, arising in virtue of the common presence of the muscular element with its charac-

## BEAUTY IN MACHINERY. 235

25. *Fitness, the Æsthetic of Utility.*—The ccse of Support just discussed is really a case of the fitting of machinery to a mechanical end, namely, the counteraction of gravity. So much pleasure do we derive from this being effectually, and yet, as it appears to us, lightly done, that we set up structures for the mere sake of seeing them so supported. But all the machinery of human industry is capable of appealing to the same sentiment of power, in the production of effects with a

---

teristic sensibility. To this I attribute the similarity of effect between the dying fall in music and the waving curve in vision; and the harmony between the *pace* of music, movements seen, and one's own movements, as in the dance. Moreover, there are analogous modes of striking the different senses; the distinction between acute or pungent, and the massive or voluminous, reigns throughout. The voluminous sound of the ocean fills the ear in the same way that a wide expanse fills the eye, whence a certain concord may be imagined between the two.

In the arts of decoration and design, the suiting of colour to form must be governed by the taste, fancy, or caprice of the individual. There may be in this, as in many other situations, nothing more than the mere cumulation of pleasing effects, neither lending support to each other, nor introducing discord.

Among the susceptibilities touched by artistic arrangements may be noticed the sense of Unity in multitude, arising when a great number of things are brought under a comprehensive design, as when a row of pillars is crowned by a pediment. This simplification of the mind's grasp is one of the lightening effects, so often alluded to as a prime source of pleasure. The use of simple figures—the triangle, square, circle, &c.—for enclosing and arraying a host of individuals, has this tendency to make an easily apprehended unity out of a numerous host of particulars. In all great works abounding in detail, we crave for some comprehensive plan that enables us to seize the whole, as well as to survey the parts. A poem, a history, a dissertation in science, a lecture, or speech, should have a discernible principle of order throughout

Variety has likewise to be studied as a means of gratification of the æsthetic species. Uniformity is the highest virtue of what we use as means —in the arrangement of tools and apparatus, but in things enjoyed as ends, we get satiated by the continuance of the same sights and sounds.

Some minds (those of high intellectual susceptibility) feel strongly the ennui from repetition, while others lean to Custom, and prefer the appearances they have been habituated to; suffering no tedium from iteration, and enjoying the ease that flows from working in a beaten track. Both principles have their influence in determining men's minds in the estimation of objects and in the ascription of beauty or the opposite.

236　　　　THE ÆSTHETIC EMOTIONS.

small expenditure of toil, A workman, combining great strength with great skill, will execute with ease what another man finds difficult, and the beholder derives a sympathetic pleasure from his power. The possession of superior tools gives the same agreeable distinction. In consequence of the gratification so derived, an actor on the stage feels bound to suppress all the appearances of labour and fatigue, and to put out of sight as much as possible the mechanism of the scenes. In machinery, we desiderate a clean polish and a noiseless action, because rust and noise suggest harsh obstruction and laborious effort. We personify the powers of nature, and sympathize with the apparently easy or difficult attainment of ends. The gentle breeze, giving motion to a huge mass of solid material, affects us with the delightful sentiment of a light finger impelling a heavy body. The noisy thunder, on the other hand, is thought to labour in accomplishing its work. A gunpowder explosion would be grander without the uproar; stillness, or a quiet action, having so much to do with our sentiment of exerted power, unless when the noise is itself a token of the power. The presence of the scaffolding whereby a great work has been reared, takes off from the pleasure of the work itself, by introducing the unacceptable association of painful and protracted labour. Hence the art of concealing art, so long ago announced as a critical maxim. We love to have removed from our sight every aspect of suffering, and none more so than the suffering of toil ; and cherish, on the other hand, every appearance, however illusive, that suggests the easy attainment of the ends of toil.

26. There are certain things, subordinate to the successful prosecution of work, that have an interest to the spectator. We have seen already that regularity and proportion appeal to a primary sensibility of the mind. They come also to be valued, and greatly extended, from considerations of utility. Under the general name Order, we include all the precision, regularity, and suitability, in the array of separate objects, so eminently favourable to the march of industrial operations. The agreeable sentiment that fills the mind of the mere

## BEAUTY OF ORDER.

looker-on is cultivated in many seats of industry, where a degree of orderliness and finish beyond the actual necessities of the case, is given to all the apparatus concerned. We see this in the trimness of a well-kept house, a cotton-mill, or a shop, and in the rigorous discipline and high condition of a man-of-war. Cleanliness is based originally upon the removal of matters intrinsically injurious, and loathsome to the sense. Going one step farther, it aims at giving lustre, brilliancy, or pure whiteness of surface, where those constitute pleasing effects, taking care to wipe off whatever stains a naturally fine surface. The polishing of tools has both an original effect of brilliancy, and the derived pleasure of suggested ease. The neat, tidy, and trim, gratifies us as a part of Order, and, even when non-essential to practical industry, gives evidence of a mind alive to the importance of this great subsidiary. It would be absurd to go the length of some writers in affirming that beauty always implies mind ; but it is a fact of sober observation, that objects are often interesting, from their suggesting to the beholder useful mental qualities. The reverse also holds. Two or three pieces of chopped straw on a carpet, or a small hole in a stocking, would not interfere with any useful operation, or impair the lustre of any other present beauty ; but by suggesting a mind loose and indifferent to orderly qualities, on which so much is dependent on the whole, a great offence may be given to the observer.

27. *Of the Sublime.*—This quality has been generally accounted more simple than Beauty. And justly so, for it is principally a result of the one attribute of superior Power. We have already traced the associations of Power, in Support, and in the Æsthetic of Utility. These become sublime by elevation in degree. The objects of sublimity are, for the most part, such aspects and appearances as betoken great might, energy, or vastness, and are thereby capable of elating the mind with a borrowed sentiment of power. The feeling of our own might is expanded for the moment by sympathy with the might displayed to our view. The towering Alpine summits, the starry concave, the vast ocean, the

238                THE ÆSTHETIC EMOTIONS.

volcanic fires, the hurricane's fury, impress us with an ideal
emotion of transcendent power, which has come to receive the name of sublimity.   So enjoyable is the sense of
power, that we welcome every mode of making it present.
When we have it not in the actual, through manifested energy
of our own, we seek for it in the ideal by witnessing the
energy displayed around us.   The great effects produced in
the world are compared in our minds with effects of ours, and
we transfer to ourselves in some vague fashion, a sense of the
mighty agency that is supposed to be at work.   This gives
birth to a pleasurable elation of the kind arising from power,
in a mind suited to that particular mode of stimulation.  When
fully and fairly manifested, we have in it all the characters of
a highly pleasurable emotion ; being, however, of the ideal
stamp, there is liable to accompany it a sort of boundless
craving for indescribable enlargements of one's scope and condition, sometimes termed the sentiment of the Infinite, which
introduces a certain element of pain from the conflict with
the actual. It is an essential component of the Religious feeling.

28. In touching upon a few of the leading varieties of the
sentiment, the first thing that offers itself to our notice is the
sublime of Support.   We have already seen what opportunity
gravity affords, for the putting forth of either a resisting might
or a propelling power.   Our own unceasing experience tells
us, that every elevation of matter above the ordinary level
demands an expenditure of force; and consequently wherever we
see lofty piles, we imagine the superhuman energy that raised
them.  An upheaved mountain mass, and a projectile shot
high in air, equally suggest a mighty operating cause.  Mere
height is thus an incident of sublimity ; the earth's surface
being our standard, we suppose everything above the common
level carried there, and maintained in its place, by some exertion of power.  Accordingly, the forms of elevated masses
that are most sublime are the lofty and precipitous, as implying the most intense effort of supporting might.  Precipitous
depth below the surface has the same effect, and from the
same causes ; by comparison with the bottom of a deep pit,

THE SUBLIME. · 239

the surface of the ground appears sustained at an elevated height.

29. The Sublimity of Space is vastness, magnitude, or expanse. It has been supposed that this, and not power, is the fundamental fact of the material sublime. There can be no great material agency without a certain amplitude of space; but sublimity may appear within a comparatively small compass, by virtue of the intensity of the forces at work. A lion, a steam engine, a nine-pounder gun, a smelting furnace, a sixty feet cataract, are sublime, although their space dimensions are not great. Still, every natural agent or effect is magnified according as it is extended ; the Amazons river is sublime by its width and volume of water ; Etna is sublime from the amplitude of its base, as well as from its height, both qualities conspiring to determine the force of upheaval represented by it. Extent of space implies corresponding energy to traverse, compass, or occupy it.

But irrespective of active energy, space is sublime from the mere volume or magnitude of its contents. The mind is filled, and as it were distended, with voluminous sensation and feeling ; and the large body of agreeable emotion has an elevating effect. There is an exact parallel in sound ; voluminous sounds, as of a great multitude, a full band, the thunder, the winds, the roar of the sea, exercise a similar power. A mountain prospect is sublime, not from mere extent of vacuity, but, from embracing within a single glance a large area of solid ground with all its activities, interests, and associations ; the volume of feeling is of the highest order. Nor can we entirely separate the notion of power in the strictest sense from a vast prospect ; the epithet ' commanding' implies that we have a superiority of intellectual range, with the resulting elation of conscious might. As regards the Sublimity of Space, therefore, we have to admit both Voluminous Sensation, and the Sentiment of Power, the two also suggesting and supporting each other. The starry expanse is the crowning grandeur of space to a mind that can in some degree enter into the amplitude of its dimensions.

240 · THE ÆSTHETIC EMOTIONS.

30. Greatness of Time has an effect of Sublimity. Not, however, mere duration in the abstract, but time as filled with known transactions and events, which, when suggested in mass, have the elating influence of the voluminous. Here, too, there is the accompaniment of intellectual power from the vast survey of the lapse of centuries. The mere ability to grasp, in one conception, the destinies of many generations elevates us with a species of intellectual might, no less than the wide-reaching prospect of peopled cities. Hence those objects that are able to remind us forcibly of a far by-gone time, or a distant future, affect us with the sublimity of Duration. The relics of ancient empires, the antiquities of the Geological ages,—waken up this sentiment in the reflecting mind, and the more so that the memory is able to recall the intermediate events. A tinge of melancholy and pathos is natural to the retrospect of so many scenes of desolation, and the extinction of so many hopes.

The relations of Terror to the Sublime, have been much discussed. The two were treated by Burke as cause and effect: but if the sublime gives the elation of power, and fear depresses the energy, they must be mutually destructive. Incidental to the sublime, there may be a depressing feeling of our own littleness and dependence, but so far as this operates, it will detract from, and not constitute, the agreeable elation of the sublime. In an object of worship, both sentiments co-exist, but either would be more strongly manifested in the absence of the other.

31. Without dwelling, as I might, on the associations and adjuncts of sublimity—the sound of the hurricane and the thunder, the wreck caused by a storm, the remnants of a battle-field, or a conflagration—we may notice the case of the sublime of Human Character. This is obviously allied with great power or energy.* Any human being that towers

---

\* 'The same considerations appear to me to throw a satisfactory light on that intimate connexion between the ideas of Sublimity and of Energy which Mr. Knight has fixed on as the fundamental principle of his theory. The direction in which the energies of the human mind are conceived to be ex-

## SUBLIME OF HUMAN CHARACTER. 241

above his fellows in force, resolution, courage, or endurance, strikes the spectator with an exalted idea of power. We are for a moment ideally elevated by the contemplation of heroic human beings, and are in some measure worked upon, and permanently influenced, by their great example. Superior intellect also affects us with the sentiment in question. Such minds as Newton and Aristotle, Homer and Shakspeare,—are the standing wonder and admiration of the human race, and it is the custom to illustrate them by comparisons with everything great, lofty, or vast in the external world.

Human power is the true and literal sublime, and the point of departure for the sublimity of power in all other things. Nature, by a bold analogical stretch, is assimilated to humanity, and clothed with mental attributes; and then, far outstripping human limitations, it elevates us beyond the level of our kind.

---

erted will, of course, be in opposition to that of the *powers* to which it is subjected; of the *dangers* which hang over it; of the obstacles which it has to surmount in rising to distinction. Hence the metaphorical expressions of an *unbending* spirit; of *bearing up* against the pressure of misfortune; of an *aspiring* or *towering* ambition; and innumerable others. Hence, too, an additional association, strengthening wonderfully the analogy, already mentioned, between Sublimity and certain Moral qualities; qualities which, on examination, will be found to be chiefly those recommended in the Stoical School; implying a more than ordinary *energy* of mind, or what the French call Force of Character. In truth Energy, as contradistinguished from Power, is but a more particular and modified conception of the same idea; comprehending the cases where its sensible effects do not attract observation; but where its silent operation is measured by the opposition it resists, or by the weight it sustains. The brave man, accordingly, was considered by the Stoics as partaking of the sublimity of that Almighty Being who puts him to the trial; and whom they conceived as witnessing with pleasure the erect and undaunted attitude in which he awaits the impending storm, or contemplates the ravages which it has spread around him. 'Non video quid habeat in terris Jupiter pulchrius, quam ut spectat Catonem, jam partibus non semel fractis, *stantem nihilominus inter ruinas publicas rectum.*'—(Seneca, *de Providentia*, I. 6.)

'It is this image of mental energy, bearing up against the terrors of overwhelming Power, which gives so strong a poetical effect to the description of Epicurus in Lucretius; and also to the character of Satan, as conceived by Milton.'—Stewart, *Essay on the Sublime*, Chap. III.

Q

242          THE ÆSTHETIC EMOTIONS.

32. *Of Natural objects in general.*—A brief survey of the principal forms and objects of nature, notable for æsthetic qualities, will advantageously contribute to the elucidation of the foregoing doctrines. The Mineral kingdom furnishes principally specimens of colour, lustre, and symmetrical forms; our gems and precious stones having no other intrinsic qualities to recommend them. Vegetable nature is much more various in its effects. Colours, pleasing, dazzling, and even gorgeous, are embodied in forms and structures that affect us no less powerfully through other susceptibilities! The curved outline prevails over straight lines. Proportion, symmetry, and harmony, are found in the two halves of the leaf, in the repetition of the same form in each species, and in the structure of the flower; while a certain whole, or unity, is made up out of the multitude of parts. Some plants, by their tall and slender proportions, are tender and graceful, others, by massiveness and size, have a sort of architectural grandeur and beauty. The poet and painter have often dwelt in this region of nature, till a sort of delirious idolatry has overwhelmed their faculty of discrimination; and it is even at this moment hardly allowable to say, that any vegetable species is not instinct with beauty.

The mountains, valleys, rivers, plains, and the general surface of the globe, owe their influence to effects already noticed. The mountain masses are nature's pyramids, and whether we view them from below and contemplate their elevation, or stand on the summits to look down upon the wide expanse beneath, we feel the sentiment of power, or the sublime. The rivers display a vast moving mass, glistening in the light, and bending in graceful curves. The still lake operates differently, its force lying chiefly in composition with the entire landscape. Of landscape beauties at large, we can only remark that a number of the effects above detailed are accumulated into one whole, while there may be superadded a certain harmony or keeping that heightens the general emotion. To find out these harmonies is the vocation of the painter, to which the taste of the spectator responds.

## THE ANIMAL KINGDOM. 243

33. The Animal kingdom contains objects of æsthetic interest in considerable measure, and also the largest part of nature's deformities. Melody of sound, colours, outlines, forms, and movements—graceful or sublime,—may be found among the quarter of a million of estimated animal species ; and associations heighten the effect in numerous instances. All this has been a theme of admiration time out of mind. Perhaps it would now be more instructive, in the way of casting light upon the human mind, to analyse the sources of the repugnance that we entertain towards not a few of the the animal tribes. In some cases, the cause is obvious and intelligible, being simply the presence of mischievous qualities, or the power of inflicting palpable damage to person or property. The beast of prey, the destructive vermin, the sharp tooth, or poisoned fang, are abhorred as our natural enemies ; but to many animals there attaches a sentiment of ugliness or deformity, from their exhibiting qualities in pointed opposition to those we call beautiful. The dingy, sluggish, slimy snail excites a pretty general dislike. The earthworm is less repulsive ; but the crawling centipede excites a wide-spread sentiment of loathing. The frog is the antipathy of some persons. A black beetle appearing suddenly on the floor will make a child scream with terror. The earwig is also very much disliked. It is not always easy to give a reason for these effects. A vague sentiment of fear is manifestly stirred up, from unknown evil conceived as possible to be inflicted by those creatures ; for familiarity reconciles us more and more to their presence. One grand source of terror is their power of *invasion;* it is very much proportioned to the rapidity of their motions ; a black beetle is the nimblest of creatures. It is possible too, that our sense of dignity may be offended, by their crossing our path or lighting on the person uninvited. After all other reasons have been exhausted, we may still have to fall back upon the active principle of disgust and antipathy belonging to our nature, which, directed in the first instance upon objects that really offend the sense and inspire loathing, extends itself to others where the pretext is very

slender, or entirely wanting. It is the nature of a strong emotion to vent itself in some way or other; and the sentiment of disgust is an exceedingly powerful principle, showing its active spontaneity even in children, and remaining in force through the whole of life.

34. The Human form is a fertile theme of æsthetic analysis. A number of the effects are obvious and admitted; the elements of colour and brilliancy—in the skin, the eyes, the hair, the teeth,—of a well-complexioned man or woman, are pleasing both here and elsewhere. The graceful figure is approved on the architectural grounds of adequate, and yet light, support; with the modifications due to forward movement, which determines the shape of the foot and limb. The curvature of the outline passes repeatedly through points of contrary flexure, turning from convex to concave, and again resuming the prevailing convex. This fluctuation is much coveted in the smallest detail, as may be inferred from the value set upon the dimpled cheek, or elbow. The general proportions of the frame are looked at with more or less reference to the ends of movement and action. The masculine type is thus distinguished from the feminine, which last has usually been made use of for the embodiment of the intrinsic charms of support, of curvature, and of numerical harmony, termed the ideal beauties. To great physical strength, a more solid framework is necessary, and for the sake of this we are willing to abandon the flowing outline.

The beauties of the head and face are very complicated. Nature having furnished a certain aggregate of features, symmetrically developed, we are moved by a variety of considerations, in accounting any one individual instance beautiful or otherwise. The ancient model evidently pointed to *proportion* in the first instance, allowing no one feature to be exaggerated beyond a certain prominence, so as to take off attention from the others. The Greek sculptor took upon himself to assign the fair and reasonable dimensions of each part, and the taste of subsequent ages has in the main acquiesced in that measurement. Other races, however, differ-

## THE HUMAN FORM. 245

ently proportioned, and accustomed to their own proportions, would probably dispute the decision. A larger mouth, a smaller chin, a shorter nose, a more retreating forehead, may be deemed just and becoming by the Negro, or the Mongol, and the Greek would not be able to make good his case in opposition to the type thus constituted. It would be absurd, in any people, to set up an ideal form widely at variance with the specimens occurring among themselves, and probably this has never been done. The ancient type is allowed to be a good one, but we can permit considerable departures from it and yet recognise great beauty. Indeed, the allocation of the relative size of forehead, eyes, nose, mouth, chin, is very different to different tastes, and it may be doubted whether the Grecian arrangement has the majority of adherents. There is no fundamental rule to appeal to, for determining the proper proportion of the nose to the rest of the face. It has been surmised (by Sir Charles Bell) that the Greek sculptor took his cue from the points of difference between the human head and the head of the animals next in rank, increasing that difference as far as he safely could without misrepresenting humanity entirely. It is the following out of a similar line of considerations, to account some of the organs more dignified in function than the others, as being more intellectual, or less animal. Thus, the eye is said to surpass the nose and mouth in this respect. But nothing could be more flimsy than such a reason. The mouth, it is true, serves the purpose of eating; but the instrumentality of speech ought to redeem it from any inferiority that may attach to the animal function of receiving and masticating the food. Neither can it be said that there is anything unworthy in the organ of smell. Indeed, I utterly despair of finding any standard, beyond the preference of individuals based on a comparison of the specimens they are accustomed to see.

35. The beauties of Movement and Expression are much more explicable. They belong in part to the primitive effects of movements, in which curves are preferable to straight lines, and in part to associations well understood. The attitudes of

246   THE ÆSTHETIC EMOTIONS.

a person gracefully formed are unintentionally graceful, being merely different ways of exhibiting the original form. In the expression of the face, the formation of agreeable curves and undulations is naturally pleasing. The eye being intrinsically the most dazzling feature, the movements that uncover it widely are apt to impress us. But both the eye and the mouth, being concerned in the indications of pleasure and pain, love and anger, are interpreted so much with reference to these passions, that we have a difficulty in assigning any movements in them that are intrinsically pleasing. A face is often reckoned beautiful, because the features take on, in an especial manner, the expression of kindly feeling ; in other words, the smile in the mouth and the expansion of the eye.

There is nothing difficult to account for, in what constitutes an agreeable manner or carriage in society, or in the still more energetic and pronounced demeanour of the actor on the stage. Reposing in part upon what strikes us originally, and in part upon conventional modes of address, the actor studies every artifice that renders the human presence effective and imposing ; and needs to have a natural framework of body adapted to the purpose. I have already disposed of the superficial notion that mere feeling in an orator, or actor, is enough to inspire such an expression as will make others feel ; the power of a rich elocution and a commanding presence, with some appropriate language and ideas, being an indispensable aid in stirring up other minds.

36. Much is said and felt respecting beauty and grace in Human Character, and here, too, there is a mixture of the primitive with the associated or conventional. Undoubtedly the great foundation of the pleasing in character, is the disposition to surrender self to others. We see this plainly in the virtues of liberality and generosity, of affection and kindness, and, not less than any, in modesty and humility, which mean the surrender or merging of the *amour-propre*. While self-assertion, arrogance, and self-will, are eyed with dislike, almost every form of submission has come to be counted a virtue and a beauty. The cause is apparent. Our

THE LUDICROUS. 247

selfish interest in some cases, our affections and sympathies in others, are touched by benefits conferred or implied; and those sacrifices of importance or free-will, made by one man, enable others to stand forward in dignity and domination, or, at all events, go to the abatement of the multitude of conflicting claims that burden human life.

37. *Of the Ludicrous.*—The causes of Laughter are first *physical*, including cold, some kinds of acute pain, tickling, and hysteria. In the next place, among *mental* causes, hilarity or animal spirits assumes this expression among other modes of joyous manifestation; the laughter of the gods, described in Homer, was the mere exuberance of their celestial joy after their daily banquet. The outburst of liberty in a young fresh nature, after a time of restraint, is an occasion for wild uproarious mirth and glee. The smile accompanies the pleasurable emotion of the tender and kindly sentiment, and is a mode of signifying that state to others. Self-complacent feeling likewise assumes the same outward display. We have seen also that the sentiment of power, awakened by the production of great and striking effects, stimulates the expression of laughter, as observed more especially in the young; the mere sight of such effects caused by others having the same tendency. It would thus appear that whatever imparts a sudden elation to the spirits, by withdrawing restraint, or increasing the conscious energy, raises an emotion of the pleasurable kind, of which laughter is one manifestation. And, farther, it would appear that tender feeling prompts the more subdued form of the outburst, if it be proper to designate the smile as a species of the laugh.

38. It is commonly said that the ludicrous is caused by *incongruity;* 'that it always implies the concurrence of at least *two* things or qualities, that have some sort of oppositeness of nature in them. But the question comes, what kind of incongruity or oppositeness is it that inevitably causes laughter? There are many incongruities that may produce anything but a laugh. A decrepit man under a heavy burden, five loaves and two fishes among a multitude, and all unfit-

## 248 THE ÆSTHETIC EMOTIONS.

ness and gross disproportion; an instrument out of tune, a fly in ointment, snow in May, Archimedes studying geometry in a siege, and all discordant things; a wolf in sheep's clothing, a breach of bargain, and falsehood in general; the multitude taking the law in their own hands, and everything of the nature of disorder; a corpse at a feast, parental cruelty, filial ingratitude, and whatever is unnatural; the entire catalogue of the vanities given by Solomon,—are all incongruous, but they cause feelings of pain, anger, sadness, loathing, rather than mirth

The occasion of the Ludicrous is the Degradation of some person or interest, possessing dignity, in circumstances that excite no other strong emotion. Amid the various themes of Laughter, this pervading fact is more or less recognised. According to Aristotle, Comedy is an illustration of worthless characters, not, indeed, in reference to every vice, but to what is *mean*; the laughable has to do with what is deformed or mean; it must be a deformity or meanness not painful or destructive (so as to produce pity, fear, anger, or other strong feelings). He would have been nearer the mark if he had expressed it as causing something to appear mean that was formerly dignified; for to depict what is already under a settled estimate of meanness, has little power to raise a laugh: it can merely be an occasion of reflecting on our own dignity by comparison. Some of Quintilian's expressions are more happy. 'A saying that causes laughter is generally based on false reasoning (some play upon words); has always something low in it; is often purposely sunk into buffoonery; *is never honourable to the subject of it.*' 'Resemblances give great scope for jests, and, especially, resemblance to something *meaner or of less consideration.*' Campbell (*Philosophy of Rhetoric*) in reply to Hobbes, has maintained that laughter is associated with the perception of oddity, and not necessarily with degradation or contempt. He produces instances of the laughable, and challenges any one to find anything contemptuous in them. 'Many,' he says, 'have laughed at the queerness of the comparison in these lines,—

"For rhyme the rudder is of verses,
With which, like ships, they steer their courses."

LAUGHTER CONNECTED WITH DEGRADATION. 249

who never dream't that there was any person or party, practice or opinion, derided in them.' To my mind, on the contrary, there is an obvious degradation of the poetic art; instead of working under the mysterious and lofty inspiration of the Muse, the poet is made to compose by means of a vulgar mechanical process.

The theory of Hobbes is well-known, and has been greatly attacked. 'Laughter,' he says, 'is a sudden glory arising from sudden conception of some eminency in ourselves, by comparison with the infirmity of others, or with our own formerly.' In other words, it is an expression of the pleasurable feeling of superior power. Now, there are many cases where this will afford a complete explanation, as in the laugh of victory, ridicule, derision, or contempt, against persons that we ourselves have humiliated. But we can also laugh sympathetically, or where the act of degrading redounds to the glory of some one else, as in the enjoyment of comic literature generally, where we have no part in causing the humiliation that we laugh at. Moreover, laughter can be excited against classes, parties, systems, opinions, institutions, and even inanimate things that by personification have contracted associations of dignity; of which last, the couplet of Hudibras upon sunrise, is a sufficient example. And, farther, the definition of Hobbes is still more unsuitable to Humour, which is counted something genial and loving, and as far removed as may be, from self-glorification and proud exultation at other men's discomfiture. Not, however, that there is not even in the most genial humour, an element of degradation, but that the indignity is disguised, and, as it were, oiled, by some kindly infusion, such as would not consist with the unmitigated glee of triumphant superiority.*

Reverting to the statements in the preceding section, (§ 37) that Laughter is connected with an outburst of the sense of

---

* In a Manual of Rhetoric, I have illustrated fully what appear to me the special conditions of Humour, and shall not occupy space by repeating them here.

250    THE ÆSTHETIC EMOTIONS.

Power or superiority, and also with a sudden Release from a state of constraint, we shall find that both facts occur in the multitudinous examples of ludicrous degradation. The foregoing observations apply to the reflection of superior power, actual and ideal, and they might be much extended. One frequent occasion of laughter is the putting any one, or the seeing any one put, into a fright: than which there is no more startling reflection of superiority on the part of some agent. Next to a fright, is the making any one angry, which (if not dangerous) also gratifies the agent's sense of power.

39. Let us next consider ludicrous degradation as a mode of Release from constraint. In this view the Comic is a reaction from the Serious. The dignified, solemn, and stately attributes of things require in us a certain posture of rigid constraint; and if we are suddenly relieved from this posture, the rebound of hilarity ensues, as in the case of children set free from school. If we feel at heart the sentiment either of worship, or of self-importance—that is, if we are thoroughly inspired with either, so as to take to it of our own goodwill— there is no restraint in the case, and no wish to be delivered from the attitude and formalities of respect. On the contrary, we resent any interference with the sacredness of the occasion. The sincere worshipper at church is shocked by the intrusion of a profane incident, while the irreverent and unwilling attender is convulsed with mirth. So it is with the sentiment of self-importance. The mind wherein this is strongly cherished is deeply offended at the contact of anything degrading or vulgarizing, whereas any one that feels the sentiment lightly will join in the laugh at his own expense. It is the *coerced* form of seriousness and solemnity, without the reality, that gives us that stiff position, from which a contact with triviality or vulgarity relieves us to our uproarious delight. We are sometimes obliged to put on a dignity which we perhaps do not feel, as in administering reproof or correction to inferiors; and still oftener have we to assume an attitude of respect and reverence that does not possess our

## LAUGHTER A RELIEF FROM CONSTRAINT. 251

inward feelings. Both the one and the other situation is a fatiguing tension of the system, and we have all the pleasure of a 'blessed relief' when anything happens to give a relaxation. The element of the genuine comic is furnished by those dignities that, from some circumstance or other, do not command serious homage. False or faded deities and dignities; splendour and show without meaning; the unworthy occupants of high office; hollow pretensions, affectation, assumption and self-importance, vanity, airs and coxcombry; all the windings of the hypocrisy that aims at seeming greater than the reality, painful strivings to gain glittering positions,—are among the things that commonly induce laughter, when brought into the embrace of meanness and degrading inferiorities. It is true that, for the sake of the mirthful pleasure, we are occasionally disposed to waive even our serious feelings of respect, and to hail the descent of a true dignity with sparkling countenance; but it is against our better nature to do so, and we are glad when the case is of the other sort.

So intense among the majority of persons is the titillation arising from being suddenly set loose from this peculiar kind of restraint, that they are willing to be screwed up into the serious posture for a moment, in order to luxuriate in the deliverance. The comic temperament is probably determined by a natural inaptitude for the dignified, solemn, or serious, rendering it especially irksome to sustain the attitude of reverence, and very delightful to rebound from it. Be this as it may, the best mode of giving the desired relief is to plunge the venerated object into a degrading conjunction, the sight of which instantaneously liberates the mind and lets the emotions flow in their own congenial channel. The serious and mirthful are in perpetual contrast in human life; in the characters of men, and in the occasions and incidents of our everyday experience. The mirthful is the aspect of ease, freedom, *abandon*, and animal spirits. The serious is constituted by labour, difficulty, hardship, and the necessities of our position, which give birth to the severe and constraining institutions of government, law, morality, education, &c. It is always a gratifying

252        THE ÆSTHETIC EMOTIONS.

deliverance to pass from the severe to the easy side of affairs ;
and the comic conjunction is one form of the transition.*

---

\* 'In a court of justice, or in an assembly of more than ordinary gravity,
a trifling incident causes laughter. We are screwed up into an expression of
gravity and dignity that we do not feel at heart, and the slightest vulgarity,
such as a loud snore, lets us down immediately. All forced dignity of demeanour, as that imposed upon children and giddy people in certain places,
is very apt to explode. In a mirthful mood, every attempt to assume the
decorous and dignified is the cause of new outbreaks, as when a merry party
on the road is interrupted for a moment by a grave and awful passer-by.
Children mimicking the airs, and strut, and weighty actions of grown men are
ludicrous, but in this they are surpassed by the monkey, from its being a
creature so much more filthy, mean, and grovelling, and which therefore in
performing human actions, presents a wider contrast of dignity and debase-
ment. Stage mimicking is made ludicrous by introducing some vulgarizing
accompaniments of manner or dress.

'A common device for causing laughter is to make a person pass at once
from an elevated to a common or degrading action, as in Pope :—

> " Here thou great Anna, whom three realms obey,
>     Dost sometimes counsel take, and sometimes tea."

'Or in the remonstrance to a lady :—

> " Perhaps it was right to dissemble your love,
>     But why did you kick me down stairs ?"

'But the more perfect the fusion of the two hostile ingredients, or the
more impossible it is rendered to think of them separately, the surer is the
ludicrous effect.'—'Wit and Humour,' *Westminster Review*.

In the article now quoted, I have exemplified at length the different kinds
of comic effect ; but what is here given in the text, as being what I now
reckon an important part of the case, is not well brought out there. The
posture of artificial and constrained seriousness demanded by the grave
necessities of life, and occasionally imposed without any great necessity, is,
as it seems to me, one point of departure in the production of the ludicrous.
Our struggles, difficulties, and dangers, screw us up into an attitude of earnest
attention as well as of laborious effort, and the remission of both the one and
the other is a joyful relief. A man is grave in the prospect of misfortune or
death ; in disposing of weighty interests, as legislator, judge, or military commander ; in setting out on a difficult enterprise or taking up a responsible
position. Those that are merely witnesses of such transactions are enjoined
to assume a grave demeanour. If fully possessed of the solemn import of the
occasion, neither actors nor spectators are disposed to shrink from the solemn
attitude, even although severe and exhausting ; but if they are only acting
an imposed part, they welcome any mode of relief. Some constitutions fall in
aptly with the air of solemnity, and to them ' abandon' is nowise entertaining ;

# CHAPTER XV.

## THE ETHICAL EMOTIONS; OR, THE MORAL SENSE.

1. IT is scarcely possible to enter upon an analysis of the peculiar sentiment or feeling termed the Moral Sense, or Moral Approbation and Disapprobation, without first pro-

---

such persons keep up the corresponding forms for their own sake, and render themselves the butt and sport of those of an opposite temperament, who also abound in all societies, and predominate in the light-hearted races. The young are the greatest sufferers by the impositions of gravity, and the most disposed to burst free from them. Hence their habitual irreverence towards superiors, and their indifference to the solemnity of important interests. They entertain a mock solemnity for the intense delight of rebounding from it, just as they toil to the top of an eminence for the sake of the downward run, or dam up a stream to see the barrier suddenly swept away by the current.

In a paper on the Physiology of Laughter, in *Macmillan's Magazine*, March, 1860, Mr. Herbert Spencer has brought forward an explanation based on the physiological distribution of nervous power. When the mind and the body are worked up to a state of high tension, the power must work itself out in some direction or another, and, in one set of circumstances, it takes the direction of laughter. The general principle is undeniable, and Mr. Spencer has made some instructive and original applications of it. I think, however, that he has been incautious in rejecting the fact of Degradation as the governing circumstance of the ludicrous. He says there are 'many instances, in which no one's dignity is implicated, as' when we laugh at a good pun.' I very much wish he had produced such a pun, as I have never yet met with one of the sort. The *Jest-book* published by Mark Lemon is an ample storehouse to choose from, yet I cannot find in it a single instance where a laughable effect is produced without degradation. I quite understand the laugh of pleasure and admiration at a felicitous stroke of mere wit; but no one confounds this with the genuinely ludicrous. Wit, with all its brilliancy and ingenuity, is sadly wanting in unction, if it takes no one down. None of the well-remembered sayings of Sydney Smith and Douglas Jerrold are without the effect of humiliation. Mr. Spencer has quoted (p. 399) certain situations calculated to produce laughter, which he says contain no degrading element; I think most people would say that they do.

254 THE ETHICAL EMOTIONS; OR, THE MORAL SENSE.

pounding some intelligible doctrine in reference to the great Ethical inquiry, viz., what constitutes Morality, Duty, Obligation, or Right.

I consider that the proper meaning, or import, of these terms refers to the class of actions enforced by the sanction of *punishment*. People may dislike a certain mode of conduct, but, unless they go the length of punishing such as pursue it, they do not reckon it obligatory. I am aware that this definition assumes a point in dispute, but my intention is, at the very outset, to lay down what I deem a vital distinction, and afterwards to vindicate the propriety of it. If a man takes the property, or slanders the good name of a neighbour, our dislike goes the length of insisting upon his suffering a penalty ; but if the same person merely refrains from coming forward actively to minister to the distresses of that neighbour, we still dislike his conduct, but not so as to demand his punishment.

The powers that impose the obligatory sanction are Law and Society, or the community acting through the Government by public judicial acts, and apart from the Government by the unofficial expressions of disapprobation and the exclusion from social good offices. The murderer and the thief are punished by the law ; the coward, the adulterer, the heretic, the eccentric person, are punished by the community acting as private individuals, and agreeing by consent to censure and excommunicate the offender. A third power concerned in obligation is Conscience, which is an ideal resemblance of public authority, growing up in the individual mind, and working to the same end. To elucidate this self-constituted variety of moral government is the final intention of the present chapter.

Assuming provisionally, that the imposition of punishment (taken in the large sense above defined) is the distinctive property of acts held to be morally wrong, we are next to enquire on what grounds such acts are forbidden and hindered by all the force that society or individuals possess ? What are the reasons or considerations requiring each one to abstain

## THEORIES OF MORALS. 255

from the performance of certain actions, and to concur in a common prohibition of them, enforced by stringent penalties? The answer to this is the Theory of Morals.

2. A variety of foundations have been assigned for the exercise of this compelling authority; in other words, there are many contending moral theories. The will of the Deity, Propriety, Right Reason, the Fitness of Things, the Decision of the Civil Magistrate, Self-Interest, the unreasoning Dictates of a Special Faculty called the Moral Sense or Conscience, Utility or the Common good of Mankind, have been severally assigned as determining what is to be authoritatively enjoined or forbidden—in other words, right or wrong.

In remarking upon these different views of the origin of moral distinctions, we must not forget that it is one thing to inquire what has been the motive for setting up the rules that we find existing in any community, and another thing to settle the motive that we think ought to govern the imposition of those rules. To explain historically the rise of institutions is different from the endeavour to settle the best principles for modifying the old, or forming new. It may be that some portions of the existing morality have been generated by considerations or motives that we dissent from, although we cannot deny the fact of such motives having operated to produce the result.

3 The arbitrary Will of the Deity, as expressed in Revelation, is seriously maintained by many as the true fountain of right. But many other defenders of the Christian religion have looked upon this view as not only untenable, but full of dangerous consequences to religion itself.*

---

\* 'But whatsoever was the true meaning of these philosophers that affirm justice and injustice to be only by law, and not by nature, certain it is that divers modern theologers do not only seriously but zealously contend in like manner that there is nothing absolutely, intrinsically, and naturally good and evil, just and unjust, antecedently to any positive command or prohibition of God, but that the arbitrary will and pleasure of God (that is an Omnipotent Being, devoid of all essential and natural justice), by its commands and prohibitions, is the first and only rule and measure thereof. Whence it follows

## 256   THE ETHICAL EMOTIONS; OR, THE MORAL SENSE.

Propriety, Right Reason, the Fitness of Things,—are phrases pointing to a Rational or Intellectual theory of Morals.  The determination of Right and Wrong is made an act of intellectual discernment, like perceiving equality or inequality in two compared magnitudes, or deciding on the truth or falsehood of a statement of fact.  If morality is a system of Rules, an act of intelligence is undoubtedly necessary to apply them; when we are told not to injure the person, property, or good

---

unavoidably that nothing can be imagined so grossly wicked, or so foully unjust or dishonest, but if it were supposed to be commanded by this Omnipotent Deity, must needs, upon that hypothesis, become holy, just, and righteous.  For, though the ancient fathers of the Christian Church, were very abhorrent from this doctrine, yet it crept up afterwards in the scholastic age; Ockham being among the first that maintained that there is no act evil, but as it is prohibited by God, and which cannot be made good if it be commanded by him.  And herein Petrus Alliacus, and Andreas de Novo Castro, with others, quickly followed him.

'Now, the necessary and unavoidable consequences of this opinion are such as these, that to love God is *by nature* an indifferent thing, and is morally good only because it is enjoined by his command.  That holiness is not a conformity with the divine nature and attributes.  That God hath no natural inclination to the good of his creatures, and might justly doom an innocent creature to eternal torment, all which propositions, with others of the kind, are word for word asserted by some late authors.'—Cudworth, quoted by Dugald Stewart, *Active Powers*, Vol. I. p. 247.

'In the passage which was formerly quoted from Dr. Cudworth mention is made of various authors, particularly among the theologians of the scholastic ages, who were led to call in question the immutability of moral distinctions by the pious design of magnifying the perfections of the Deity.  I am sorry to observe that these notions are not as yet completely exploded; and that, in our own age, they have misled the speculations of some writers of considerable genius, particularly of Dr. Johnson, Soame Jenyns, and Dr. Paley.  Such authors certainly do not recollect that what they add to the divine power and majesty they take away from his moral attributes; for, if moral distinctions be not immutable and eternal, it is absurd to speak of the *goodness* or of the *justice* of God.  "Whoever thinks," (says Shaftesbury) "that there is a God, and pretends formally to believe that he is *just* and *good*, must suppose that there is independently such a thing as *justice* and *injustice*, *truth* and *falsehood*, *right* and *wrong*, according to which eternal and immutable standard he pronounces that God is *just*, *righteous*, and *true*.  If the mere will, decree or law of God, be said absolutely to constitute *right* and *wrong*, then are these latter words of no signification at all.'"—Stewart, p. 266.

## RATIONAL MORALISTS. 257

name of others, we need the power of distinguishing what is injurious, from what is not. It is another thing, however, to maintain that the rules themselves are founded solely on an operation of judgment; the abstinence from injury to our fellows requires at bottom some motive not intellectual. The intellect can determine the fitness of means to secure an *end ;* but the end itself, must, in the last resort, be some feeling, something desirable or undesirable, some pleasure to be sought, some pain to be avoided, some impulse to be followed out. The Rational Moralists (Cudworth, Wollaston, Clark, Price) give no account of the final end of morality.

The same criticism applies to the dictum of Kant :—' act in such a way that your conduct might be made a law to all beings.' This is an important attribute or condition of right conduct ; no actions can be approved, that might not be generally followed. Still, there is something not expressed, and that something contains the real essence of morality. As fully expanded, the dictum should run thus ; ' Act in a way that might be followed by all, *consistently with the general safety or happiness, or other exigence of society.*' The generalizing of the action puts all men on the same level, and enables the full consequences to be seen, but it does not say what ends should be sought by this uniformity of procedure. It settles no difference between moral usages ; between Monogamy and Polygamy, between castes and equality. Wherever a moral rule prevails, there must attach to it the condition of universal obedience ; what is permitted to one, must be permitted to all the members of the same equal society.

According to Hobbes, the Sovereign, acting under his responsibility to God, is the ultimate judge of right. If he had meant merely that Morality is an Institution of Society, maintained by the authority and Punishments of Society, he would have stated what I believe to be the fact. His theory of government, however, was that when men, to escape the evils of a state of nature, formed themselves into society, they made, or should have made, their last will and testament in favour of some single despotic ruler. This was the practical ques-

R

tion of Hobbes's time, and was decided against him by the events.

4. Several authors have promoted a system of morals based upon exclusively Self-regarding motives. They mean to affirm that men perform the social or moral duties, from a regard to their own individual interests, and consequently that the rules of right are adapted to these interests. But if by 'self' is here understood the gratifications of each person that are not shared by other persons,—such as the sensual pleasures, the love of wealth, power, and dignity, and all other exclusive pleasures,—we may safely deny the alleged constitution of human nature whereon the system is founded. I include here in the term 'constitution of human nature,' the pleasures which have grown up by constant and wide-spread association, as well as the original and primordial pleasures : since both together go to constitute and determine the internal man. There is a class of pleasures whose nature it is to take in other sentient beings, as is implied in all the social affections. We have further a tendency to enter into the pains of those about us, to feel these as if they were our own, and to minister to their relief exactly as we should treat our personal sufferings. This power of sympathy is a fact in human nature of very extensive operation, and is constantly modifying, and running counter to, the selfish impulses properly so called. These two principles of our constitution, Affection and Sympathy, serve as the main foundations of disinterestedness ; and a very large amount of this quality is seen actually reposing upon them. It is not true, therefore, that men have always performed their duties, only so far as the narrow self was implied in them, although, of course, these other impulses belonging to our constitution are likewise our 'self' in another acceptation.

The theory of Self-Interest is still farther falsified by the existence in the human mind of disinterested Antipathies, which prompt us to inflict harm upon others without gaining anything to ourselves. We shall afterwards have to put in evidence those sentimental aversions, of which our fellow-

THEORY OF A MORAL SENSE. 259

beings are the subjects, and on account of which we overlook our own interest as much as in the exercise of our sympathies and affections.

Accordingly, we may say not only that selfishness has never been the sole foundation of men's views of right, but that if we were to propose it for acceptance as such, it would be rejected. Those fountains of the unselfish, now named, so relate us to our fellow-beings, that our ends in life always include more or less of their interests, and we are disposed on some occasions to sacrifice everything we possess, and life itself, to the well-being of others. The comparative force of the two classes of motives varies in different individuals; and the direction taken by the sympathetic motives may also vary; A may be prompted by his affection for B to kill or injure C. But we may be well assured that both will exert their sway in the various arrangements of human life, the social and moral regulations included.

5. The most generally received doctrine concerning the foundations of right is the theory of a Moral Sense. This means that there is a certain faculty in the human mind, enabling us to define what is right to be done in each particular case, and which has given birth to the rules and maxims of morality in common currency. It is affirmed that human nature is universally endowed with this instinctive power of discriminating right and wrong, which is the cause of an alleged uniformity of the moral sentiments, so decided as to constitute an 'eternal and immutable morality.' This theory, undoubtedly the favourite one, is liable to very serious objections, which have been often urged, and never completely met.

6. Although the rigorous mode of viewing the moral sense, which compares it to the sense of hot and cold, or the power of discriminating between white and black, would almost dispense with education, yet this view has never been thoroughly carried out; for the necessity of enlightening conscience, by religious and moral teaching, has been universally insisted on. Accordingly, the following passage from Dr.

260 THE ETHICAL EMOTIONS ; OR, THE MORAL SENSE.

Whewell's *Elements of Morality* may be taken to represent the qualified doctrine of the innate sense of rectitude :—

'It appears from what has just been said, that we cannot properly refer to our conscience as an ultimate and supreme authority. It has only a subordinate and intermediate authority, standing between the supreme law, to which it is bound to conform, and our own actions, which must conform to it, in order to be moral. Conscience is not a standard, personal to each man, as each man has his standard of bodily appetite. Each man's standard of morals is a standard of morals, only because it is supposed to represent the supreme standard, which is expressed by the moral ideas, benevolence, justice, truth, purity, and wisdom. As each man has his reason, in virtue of his participation of the common reason of mankind, so each man has his conscience, in virtue of his participation in the common conscience of mankind, by which benevolence, justice, truth, purity, and wisdom, are recognised as the supreme law of man's being. As the object of reason is to determine what is true, so the object of conscience is to determine what is right. As each man's reason may err, and thus lead him to a false opinion, so each man's conscience may err, and lead him to a false moral standard. As false opinion does not disprove the reality of truth, so the false moral standards of men do not disprove the reality of a supreme rule of human action.'

What then is this standard ? Where is it to be found ? Until it is produced, we have nothing to discuss, affirm, or deny. Is it some one model conscience, like Aristotle's 'serious man ' (ὁ σπουδαῖος), or is it the decision of a public body authorized to decide for the rest of the community ? We have no difficulty in knowing what is the standard of truth in most other matters, but what is the standard conscience? This *must* be got at, or morality is not a subject to be reasoned or written about.

7. Dr. Whewell appears to presume the existence of certain moral ideas without reference to any individual mind whatsoever, correcting every one and yet originating with no one.

## AN UNPRODUCIBLE STANDARD. 261

He sets up for morality a standard having a degree of independent existence, such as can hardly be conceived, and which does not exist with reference to anything else. We have standards of length, of measure, and of weight, which, even although embodied in material objects, can scarcely be said to have the independence here contended for. In constructing the imperial yard, gallon, or pound weight, a certain number of persons concur in adopting a definite unit ; and these persons, being either themselves the governing body of the nation, or being followed by the actual governing body, give the law, or dictate the standard for themselves and all others. It is quite true that individuality is controlled and overruled in this matter, but not by any abstract, unseen, unproducible power. It is one portion of the community agreeing upon a certain choice, and the rest falling in with that. Every dealer must bring his weights and measures to be tried by the authoritative standard, but he is at no loss to say who are the authors and maintainers of that standard. So with Time. When we are all called upon to adapt our watches to Greenwich time, it is not to a standard beyond humanity. The collective body of astronomers have agreed upon a mode of reckoning time, founded upon the still more general recognition of the solar day, as the principal unit. At Greenwich Observatory, observations are made which determine the standard for this country ; and the population in accepting that standard know, or may know, that they are following the Astronomer Royal with his staff, and the body of astronomers generally.

It is a stretch of language to maintain the existence of such a thing as Truth in the abstract—that is to say, abstracted from all perceiving or conceiving minds. Every proposition affirmed or believed must be affirmed or believed by somebody as acceptable to their individual judgments. Many minds instead of judging for themselves, accept, either by choice or compulsion, the judgments of others, and are therefore not the original authors of what passes current. Granting a number of such tamely acquiescent minds, we recognise the

## 262 THE ETHICAL EMOTIONS; OR, THE MORAL SENSE.

rest as the spontaneous originating causes of whatever is maintained as true among mankind.

Much more do these observations apply to morality and the Ethical standard. Those ideas of benevolence, justice, truth, purity, and wisdom, given by Dr. Whewell as the supreme standard, are, and must be, ideas existing in individual minds. There must be a select number of persons, or some one person, holding them in the form that he supposes the typical, the perfect, or the standard form; and what we desire is, that he should name or indicate those persons, as it is possible to name the persons that gave the standard measures. It is no doubt the fact that certain moral ideas are followed by each community, but there ought to be no mystery about either the authorship of those ideas, or the persons through whose influence they are kept up as the standard, in preference to other ideas that might be suggested.

Even in the most unanimous notions of mankind, there can be no such thing as a standard strictly à *priori*, overriding the judgment of every separate intelligence. On such matters as the simple truths of number and extension, the members of the human family, on comparing notes, find that they are affected exactly in the same way, and admit or reject the same things. It is not by virtue of an independent or abstract existence in the Mathematical or Mechanical laws, that they derive their universality as truths, but through the uniformity of men's compared perceptions in that region of phenomena. In matters of Taste, the agreement extends to a limited number of minds, and there stops; the rest not being affected in the same manner. This want of unanimity ought to be a bar to the very notion of a Standard of Taste, except in an extremely qualified form; although it happens in fact, from the imperious dispositions of the human mind, that the feelings of a certain number of persons are apt to be imposed as binding upon all the rest—a proceeding that amounts to the setting up of a standard, like Dr. Whewell's Moral Ideas. It is no uncommon thing to plead in behalf of

## NO MORALITY OR TRUTH IN THE ABSTRACT. 263

certain models of Art, that they have a standard value apart from, and beyond the circumstance of their being accepted by a number of persons in the present and former times ; and those dissenting from them are denounced as erring, and even heretical.* Wherever an agreement is come to by a large or ascendant party, there is a natural tendency to compel the rest to fall in with that, whether it be in Science, in Art, in Religion, or Morality, and this is the real meaning of a standard in the common usage. It is the symbol for compelling minorities to follow the majority, which majority, instead of putting itself forward as the real standard, is accustomed to allege some pure and perfect ideal existing aloft, which it has embraced for itself, and has a right to enforce on every-one else.

8. Every proposition believed or affirmed must be believed or affirmed by some one, as acceptable to his individual judgment. He may agree or differ from others ; but whether he is to enunciate his affirmation in the first person singular, or in the first person plural, he is himself in either case the insepa-rable subject of the affirmation. His own feeling and perso-nality is essentially implicated in the mental fact which his words declare. This fact—his belief, persuasion, conviction—stands out nakedly when he differs from others ; it is overlaid when he speaks as one of the multitude. In a numerous chorus, the voice of each singer may not be separately distin-guishable by an audience ; nevertheless, the voice of each is a distinct effect, produced by his own volition. The result is an aggregate, of which all the authors are distinct and indivi-dual ; there exists no such thing as an abstract universal voice, or an abstract choric agency, apart from the separate choristers, and correlating only with the general effect. In like manner, the universal belief, conviction, or persuasion,

---

* In the case of taste proper (æsthetic taste) an argument might be, and often is, founded on what is naturally agreeable to the *higher quality of mind ;* intellectually, morally, and in point of general development. The reasoning for one taste against another is essentially an appeal from Philip drunk to Philip sober.

## 264 THE ETHICAL EMOTIONS ; OR, THE MORAL SENSE.

is nothing more than an aggregate of individual beliefs ; there exists no abstract universal belief apart from these. And when Dr. Whewell speaks of an universal Reason, he can mean nothing more than the sum total of each individual man's Reason, or the Reason of some persons out of the multitude, chosen by himself as models.

Perhaps Dr. Whewell might ask in reply, 'Is there no such thing as truth in the abstract ? Is nothing true except what is believed to be true ? Are there no real matters of fact which are either unknown or disbelieved ? Was not the rotation of the Earth round the Sun—was not the composition of water from oxygen and hydrogen—as much a truth in the time of Thales, as it is now, though no one then suspected or imagined it ? Will not many truths, now believed, be discovered and proved by future research ? And will not many positions, now accepted as truths, be refuted hereafter as erroneous ? How can it be argued, therefore, that Truth is a matter co-extensive with, or dependent upon, actual belief ?'

I admit the facts as here set forth, but deny the inference built upon them. Propositions may be cited which I, in common with the European scientific world, believe to be truths, and which were believed by no one in the time of Thales. They are believed, upon the warrant of certain facts and reasonings, which are now known, but were not known then. Now, when we say that these propositions were truths then as much as now, what we mean is, to express our full persuasion, that if a scientific man, furnished with all the knowledge of the present day, had been alive then, he would have proved their truth by such evidence as would have changed the belief of intelligent men ; and that if he failed to operate such conversion, the failure would be owing, not to insufficiency of the evidence, but to prejudice, inattention, or misjudgment on the part of the hearers. I say, we express our full persuasion to this effect, when we affirm such and such propositions to be truths ; for this is all that we can by possibility express—we cannot make ourselves sponsors for

## NO BELIEF IN THE ABSTRACT.

the whole human race. The propositions were truths then, though no one believed them, as they are truths now; full evidence might have been produced to prove them : the men of that day, had they been better informed, would have believed them, or at least *ought* to have believed them. Herein we declare our own convictions—full evidence is what we deem full ; *ought* to believe, is measured by our own estimate of logical obligation. It is we who compare ourselves with the believers of the past, affirming that if we, with our present knowledge, had been alive then, we could have shown grounds to them for altering their opinions. So, too, we may compare ourselves with believers of a future day ; we affirm that if we could live again some centuries hence, we should come into possession of extended knowledge, and should adopt many opinions that we are now strangers to. But in all these comparisons we never get away from ourselves and our own convictions, and what we believe are, or ought to be, or would be under certain circumstances, the convictions of others. We do not approach at all nearer to what Dr. Whewell calls Universal Reason, Abstract Truth, a standard of truth impersonal and apart from all believers.

9. Abstract Truth, or Truth in the abstract, apart from the particulars of each individual case, correlates with Abstract Belief, or with Belief in the Abstract. It has no other meaning except in reference to Belief, past, present, or to come. Truth in the abstract, no more exists than Belief in the abstract ; neither of them has any reality except in the concrete. The feeling of belief is one common to all mankind, universally and without exception ; all men agree in feeling this sentiment, though they do not agree in the matters to which it is applied, or in the process whereby it is generated. There neither is, nor can be, any universal standard of truths, or matters which ought to be believed. Every man is in this case a standard to himself. What he believes, he thinks that others ought to believe also. This is inseparable from the fact of sincere belief. If others do not agree with him, he thinks that they are in the wrong ; that the causes, whatever

## 266    THE ETHICAL EMOTIONS ; OR, THE MORAL SENSE.

they be, that have generated belief in him, *ought* to generate the like belief in every one. He can have no other idea of what it is that men ought to believe, except by means of what he believes himself. To a certain extent, the causes that produce belief in one man, also produce it in another ; accordingly, it is often possible for two dissentients, by exchanging facts and reasonings, to arrive at an agreement. But this is often found impossible ; for the harmony as to the producing causes of belief, goes only to a certain point. If they cannot agree, and if there be no third person in whom both place confidence, they must remain dissentient. There is no Universal Reason to settle the question ; for each of them believes that he himself represents Universal Reason.

It is important to remember that the point wherein all men agree is, in having the feeling or sentiment of belief ; and in the farther persuasion, that what they believe, others ought to believe also. In respect to matters believed, the agreement is only partial and fluctuating. All belief is, and must be, individual, belonging to more or fewer assignable persons, and each of these is a standard to himself. This is equally true, whether his belief be founded in reason and argument, or in authority. If one man believes on the authority of Aristotle, and another on that of the Koran, the faith in each case resides in the individual's own mind. The generating cause is in each case a sentiment peculiar and personal ; the Aristotelian will not believe on the authority of the Koran, nor the Mahometan on that of Aristotle. Belief on authority is no less the determination of the individual believer's mind, than belief after rational investigation ; though the process is different in the two cases. The believer is, and must be, a measure to himself—either as to the authority that he follows, or as to the arguments that force his assent.

10. The Universal Conscience is no more to be found than the Universal Reason. Conscience, like Reason, is always individual. It was observed in the preceding paragraph, that all mankind agreed in having the feeling of belief, though they did not all agree as to the matters believed, or as to the

THE SUPPOSED UNIVERSAL CONSCIENCE. 267

producing causes of belief. So, too, about Conscience ; every man may have the feeling of Conscience—that is, the feeling of moral reprobation and moral approbation. All men agree in having these feelings, though all do not agree in the matters they are applied to, or in the producing causes. The agreement among them is emotional.

Dr. Whewell tells us that each man's conscience may err, and each man's reason may err, but that the common conscience of mankind, and the common reason of mankind, are infallible. This is exactly what the Roman Catholics hold in respect to religious belief. They hold that every individual believer is fallible, but that the Church is infallible. Dr. Whewell applies the same principle to all belief ; and if it be true with respect to all belief, it is, of course, true with respect to religious belief, which is one variety of belief. Now Protestants have always argued that an infallible Church could mean nothing else but certain infallible men—a Pope, a General Council or Assembly, as the case may be. They deny infallibility to either. But whether the Pope or the General Council be the persons in whom infallibility resides, this is certain—that if infallibility is to be found, it must reside in some human bosom. It cannot be an attribute floating in the air without a subject. The Universal Conscience and Reason, of which Dr. Whewell speaks as infallible, must reside in some men endued with Conscience and Reason. We ask, who are these infallible men, or this infallible Council ?

The language of Dr. Whewell, that ' each individual man participates in the common conscience and common reason of mankind,' is true in one sense, but not in the sense that will bear out his conclusion. What each man has in common with all others, is, a certain feeling, emotion, or sentiment—conscience, belief, &c. He has a feeling that some actions are right, other actions wrong; he approves the first, he disapproves the last. He has a feeling of belief that some propositions are true, and a feeling of disbelief that others are false. But though two men have each the same feeling of approba-

268 THE ETHICAL EMOTIONS; OR, THE MORAL SENSE.

tion and disapprobation, it does not follow, nor is it the fact, that the same actions that raise the feeling in the one, will also raise it in the other. And if a dispute arise upon this latter point, it cannot be decided by appeal to the feeling common to both. The feeling of each is infallible for him. When an Abolitionist from Massachusetts denounces the institution of slavery, and a clergyman from Carolina defends it, both of them have in common the same sentiment of justice and injustice. But the sentiment is raised by totally different objects. In the Abolitionist, the sentiment leading him to apply the term unjust is raised by the spectacle of a Negro under coercion; in the other disputant, it is not so raised. But the *sentiment* of injustice, in both minds, is the same.

11. I must remark still farther upon the alleged uniformity of men's moral judgments in all ages and countries, as indicating a special faculty in our constitution, analogous to one of the senses.

In order to bring such an assertion to the proof, there ought to be formed for our inspection, a complete collection of all the moral codes that have ever existed. We should then have experimental evidence as to the agreement actually prevailing. In the absence of such a collection or digest, I will take it upon me to affirm that the supposed uniformity of moral decisions resolves itself into the two following particulars.

First, the common end of *Public Security*, which is also individual preservation, demands certain precautions which are everywhere very much alike, and can in no case be dispensed with. Some sort of constituted authority to control the individual impulses, and protect each man's person and property, must exist wherever a number of human beings live together. The duties springing out of this necessary arrangement are essentially the same in all societies. Whether we look at them as the duties of each man towards his fellows, or as summed up in the comprehensive form of obedience to the constituted authority, they have a pretty uniform character all over the globe. If the sense of the common safety were

## UNIFORMITY OF MORAL JUDGMENTS. 269

not sufficiently strong to constitute the social tie of obedience to some common regulations, society could not exist to tell the tale of an exception to the universality of a common standard of right. Man could no more live without social obedience, and some respect for ' mine and thine,' than the race could be continued without sexual love, or maternal care. It is no proof of the universal spread of a special innate faculty of moral distinctions, but of a certain rational appreciation of what is necessary for the very existence of every individual human being living in the company of others. Doubtless if the sad history of our race had been preserved in all its details, we should have many examples of tribes that perished from being unequal to the conception of a social system, or to the restraints imposed by it. We know enough of the records of anarchy to see how difficult it often is for human nature to comply in full with the social conditions of security ; but if this were not complied with at all, the result would be mutual and swift destruction. There must, therefore, be admitted to exist a tolerably uniform sense of the necessity of recognising some rights of individuals living together in society, and of the obligation of civil obedience which is merely another form of respecting those rights. There are to a certain point ' eternal and immutable ' moral judgments on those heads,— in the repudiation of the thief, the manslayer, and the rebel,* but their origin implies no peculiar internal faculty, but only a common outward situation. As well might we contend for a universal intuition as suggesting the uniformity of structure in human dwellings.

12. In the second place, mankind have been singularly unanimous in the practice of imposing upon individual members of societies some observances or restraints of purely

---

\* We must not, however, be too strenuous in urging even this limited position. The rebel, if successful, is admired and honoured. Thieves and manslayers were hardly disapproved of in the Homeric times and in the middle ages. They suffered the full measure of private revenge from the parties concerned, if seized ; but were not, as a matter of course, punished by law and society.

**270** THE ETHICAL EMOTIONS; OR, THE MORAL SENSE.

*Sentimental* origin, having no reference, direct or indirect, to the maintenance of the social tie, with all the safeguards implied in it. Certain things founded in taste, liking, aversion, or fancy, have, in every community known to us, got themselves erected into the dignity of authoritative morality, being so to speak 'terms of communion,' and enforced by punishment. The single instance of the Mussulman women being required to cover their faces in public will suffice for the present to illustrate what is here meant. I shall dwell upon the point in detail a few pages hence. Nobody could pretend to associate the common safety with this practice, which is as authoritative in the mind of the Mussulman as any moral obligation whatsoever; sanctioned alike by the general community and by the educated conscience. In other societies, the same species of obligations may be traced. Here, however, the uniformity lies only in the fact of *imposing something not essential to the maintenance of society;* the observances imposed differ as widely as human actions can be conceived to differ. Not only variety, but often contrariety, marks the detail of the special moral maxims thus originated. The ancient Greek held it as a sacred obligation to drink wine in honour of the god Dionysus; while the Nazarenes among the Jews, and the Mahometans, held the opposite sentiment. The alimentary laws among various nations have been equally authoritative—often ceremonial laws and even sumptuary prescriptions. The modes of regulating the relations of the sexes, which have been usually a subject of very stringent morality, have been various in the extreme; the only agreement has lain in making some one mode a matter of compulsory observance. The feelings respecting caste have generally got the footing of authoritative prescription, but there has been nothing constant in the special enactments on that subject.

It would appear, therefore, that in the rules suggested by public and common necessities, there is a certain uniformity, because of the similarity of situation of all societies; in the rules founded on men's sentiments, likings, aversions, and antipathies, there is nothing common, but the fact that some one or more of these are carried to the length of public requirement, and mixed up in one code with the more imperative duties that hold society together. We can obtain no clear insight into the foundations of morality, until we disentangle this complication, and refer each class of duties to their proper origin, whether in the good order of society, or in some sentiment that has become so predominant, as to be satisfied with nothing less than being imposed upon every member of the community, under the same penalties as those sanctioning the common protection.

13. Adam Smith, in his *Theory of Moral Sentiments*, has given a different turn to the doctrine of the Moral Sense, by laying down as the criterion of right, 'the sympathetic feelings of the impartial and well-informed spectator.' He considers, that when a person imagines to himself, how his actions would appear to a disinterested witness knowing the whole circumstances, he thereby gains a correct estimate of their moral quality. One remark to be made on this modification of the intuitive theory of moral judgments, is that while the bias of the agent is acknowledged, it is assumed that the critic is free from all tendency to error or mistake. But if we look at the matter closely, we shall see that there are dispositions to misjudge on the part of the spectator, as well as on the part of the actor. The love of imposing restraints, or prohibitions, is stronger in the minds of most men than the sympathy with enjoyment, and the impartial umpire is apt to insist on an indefinite amount of self-denial, in the conduct that he is called upon to estimate. It is another weakness of the spectator to look upon an action as a piece of stage effect, or at what is called the *interesting* side, under which aspect the happiness of the agent is made of little account.* To constitute a good moral judge, one ought

---

* 'A good man struggling with adversity is a sight for the gods.' A curious illustration this of the wish to make a striking spectacle out of the conduct of our fellows. Thus it is that the Spartan or the young American Indian undergoes physical torture, to gain the applause bestowed upon the exhibition by the members of his tribe.

272   THE ETHICAL EMOTIONS ; OR, THE MORAL SENSE.

to have the same qualifications as are sought in a good legal judge,—special education, experience, coolness, impartiality, and the observance of all the maxims of evidence, set up to protect the innocent.

But the chief consideration remains. The objection against the Rational theories of Morals applies with all its force to Smith's theory. Where does the impartial spectator get his standard ? Where does he find the rules that he is impartially to interpret ? A judge is provided by competent authority with a legal code ; and the arbitrating spectator is supposed to be provided with a moral code. Now the whole point in dispute is the source or foundation of the moral code itself.

14. Next as to the principle of Utility. This is opposed to the doctrine of a Moral Sense. It sets up an outward standard in the room of an inward, being the substitution of a regard to consequences for a mere unreasoning sentiment, or feeling. Utility is also opposed to the selfish theory, for as propounded it always implies the good of society generally, and the subordination of individual interest to that general good.*

---

\* The statement of the principle by Jeremy Bentham as 'the greatest happiness of the greatest number,' has the merits, and some of the defects, of an epigram. There is something repulsive to the common mind in so broadly announcing the sacrifice of minorities to majorities. In our legislation this happens every day, it being enough for a statesman that one measure does more good to a larger number of people than another. Bentham aimed the principle originally at *class interests*, under which the greatest happiness of the smallest number was the determining motive of public policy.

In Morals, Bentham opposed to Utility, first, Asceticism, and next what he called Sympathy and Antipathy, or the decisions of mere feeling, including the theories of the Moral Sense, the Fitness of Things, Right Reason, &c. He assumed that the production of pleasure, and the avoiding of pain, were the only positive ends, never to be set aside in any instance, except in order to secure them in some greater amount. To aid the requisite calculation, he endeavoured to classify and enumerate our pleasures and pains.

I have elsewhere stated some of the difficulties attending the principle of Utility as thus expressed, but which do not effect its soundness as opposed to a Moral Sense'—(See p. 88 of the *Moral Philosophy of Paley*, with additional Dissertations. W. and R. Chambers, Edinburgh.)

## UTILITY AS THE BASIS OF MORALS. 273

But what is the exact import of Utility as concerns morals? Some limit must be assigned to the principle, for it is obvious that we do not make everything a moral rule that we consider useful. It is useful to make experiments in Chemistry, but this is not a point of morality unless it be a part of a man's professional duty undertaken and paid for. Jeremy Bentham wrote many useful books, but not because of his being obliged to do so under a high moral sanction.

---

Bentham would have contributed still more to the promotion of sound ethical discussion, if he had reversed the plan of his work, and entitled it 'On Legislation and Morals.' He would thus have put forward the more tangible, and more formally and officially constructed department of obligation, to elucidate clearly the less tangible and the unofficial department. There is, as he saw, a precise parallelism between the moral legislation of society in its private action on individuals, and the public legislation through the government, and if this parallelism were closely traced, we should have a much clearer conception of moral obligation properly so called. In both cases, punishment is the instrument and the criterion of the obligatory. Where the law does not prescribe a penalty, it does not make a duty; and so where other authorities and society generally do not think proper to punish, they do not constitute a moral rule.

Then as to the *origin* of moral enactments, and the proper *enacting authority*, we ought to insist on having some positive declaration. Who is it that gives the law in this department to a community, and what is their right to do so founded upon? Is the authority a despotism, a limited monarchy, or a republic? Is public opinion appealed to, and open discussion permitted, before a moral bill becomes a moral law? Or have we received our code from a venerable antiquity, embodied in our religion, and shut up for ever from reconsideration or change? Whatever the case is, let it be stated exactly as we describe the political system under which our other laws are promulgated.

Moreover, we ought to have a written code of public morality, or of the duties imposed by society, over and above what parliament imposes, and this should not be a loosely written moral treatise, but a strict enumeration of what society requires under pain of punishment by excommunication or otherwise—the genuine offences that are not passed over. A system of morals for the guidance of the individual member of society, ought to be composed on the plan of excluding all the virtues that bring rewards, just as the articles of war omit all reference to the virtues of the soldier, and merely enumerate offences and crimes. The very interesting field of human virtue and nobleness should be treated apart, with all the aids that eloquence can bestow, a quality of composition that has no business to be present in a strict moral treatise, any more than in a criminal code, or a digest of justice-of-peace procedure.

## 274 THE ETHICAL EMOTIONS; OR, THE MORAL SENSE.

Many actions pre-eminently useful to society are performed out of the free-will and choice of individuals, and not from any fear, either of punishment, or of inward remorse. A distinction must therefore be drawn between Utility made compulsory, and what is left free.

There are very different degrees of urgency in things known to be useful. The extinction of a blazing house, the arrest of a riot or tumult, the resistance to an invading army, are actions that press before all others. Among social actions, the first degree of urgency belongs to those already alluded to as essential to the very existence of society.

'Social security must be maintained as the highest necessity of men's existence in common fellowship; and whatever militates against it must be considered wrong. On this foundation we establish right, duty, or obligation—as attaching to obedience to law, fulfilment of compacts, justice, and truth; and we employ the sanction of punishment in favour of those classes of actions.

'Moreover, men desire not the lowest security compatible with civil order, but a high and increasing security; and for this end, they put an especial stress on the comprehensive virtue of integrity.

'When something more than social security is maintained as an end carrying rightness and compulsion along with it, that something must be a clear case of the promotion of the general happiness without any material sacrifice of individual happiness. A mere increase of the sum of enjoyment is not to be put on the same footing as the common safety.'*

It is usual to distinguish between the necessary, and the optional functions of government. Defence, security, the administration of justice, &c., are necessary; but whether the government shall undertake the support of churches, schools, theatres, pauperism, or the administration of roads, railways, or the post-office, depends upon a balance of considerations in each case. So it is with morals. Society must keep men

---

* Edition of Paley above quoted, p. 87.

## UTILITY NOT TO BE ENFORCED TO ALL LENGTHS. 275

to their word and punish the promise-breaker; but there is no absolute *necessity* for hereditary distinctions and castes, although it is quite open to any one to adduce arguments in their favour so strong as to justify a compulsory respect towards the favoured class, or to constitute this one of the terms of social communion.

15. It will be seen at a glance that one great objection to the enforcement of utility without exception, or qualification, is the consideration of individual Liberty. (A still greater objection is the fallibility of the social authority.) Every public enactment is a restraint put upon the free will of individuals; and the sum total of the pain and privation thus arising must be set against the positive utility of the measure. There are cases where public authority can do much positive good, at the expense of a small and unimportant amount of individual restraint, as, for example, carrying on postal communication; and in these instances interference is justified. There are other cases of a more debateable kind, such as religious and educational establishments, and the regulation of labour. In a country where questions are settled by the general voice, after free and open discussion, it is difficult to find any other standard than the happiness of the population as calculated by themselves.

The common dislike to utility, as the standard, resolves itself into a sentimental preference, amounting to the abnegation of reason in human life. A man refuses to embrace some lucrative occupation because of family pride, and chooses a life of privation and misery instead; this is the false choice of sentiment as regards the private welfare of an individual. From a feeling of aversion founded on no reason, I refuse the professional assistance of some one specially qualified to extricate me from a situation of misery; so presenting an example of the same antithesis of sentiment and utility. But there are sentiments reckoned so lofty, dignified, and ennobling, and there are utilities reckoned so low and grovelling, that it is conceived no comparison exists between the two. Thus the principles of justice, truth, and purity, con-

276 THE ETHICAL EMOTIONS; OR, THE MORAL SENSE.

sidered in a certain ideal form, are supposed to predominate immeasurably over worldly prosperity. 'Let justice be done though nature should collapse,' is the highest flight of sentimentalism.*

In the case of the individual that would rather starve than abate a jot of his family pride, there is really nothing to be said; as a free man he has made his own choice. If he involves no other persons in his destitution, his friends may remonstrate with him, but no one is entitled to go any farther. And so with any number of men, each carrying out in his own case, without detriment to others, a sentimental preference. Even supposing them to be much less happy than the emancipation from their peculiar liking or dislike would make them, still, as men beyond the state of tutelage, they must decide for themselves. A philanthropic reformer would doubtless wish, by an improved education, or in other ways, to free his fellow-citizens from the incubus of a deleterious sentiment, superstition, antipathy, or the like; but so long as each one confines the operation of the feeling to himself, liberty is in favour of abstaining from anything like interference in the matter. But when one man endeavours to impose his likings or dislikes upon another, or when a mere sentimental preference entertained by the majority is made the law for every one, there is a very serious infringement of individual freedom on the one hand, with nothing legitimate to be set against it in the way of advantage. Herein lies the real opposition of the two principles, as applied to legislation and morality. If a man has a strong antipathy (like what prevails among large sections of mankind) to a pig, this is a good reason to him for not keeping pigs, or eating pork; but if a sufficient number join in the antipathy to make a ruling party in the society that they belong to, and carry the thing so far as to compel everybody whomsoever to put away this animal, they

---

* See an admirable criticism by Mr. James Mill, on the saying of Andrew Fletcher, that 'he would lose his life to serve his country; but would not do a base thing to save it.'—*Fragment on Mackintosh*, p. 267.

## UTILITY AND SENTIMENT CONJOINED. 277

convert a mere physical dislike into a moral rule, and thereby commit a gross outrage on individual liberty. This is very different from such an act as the public prohibition of the sale of arsenic. Nay, if one were to legislate for the American Indians, it might become a grave question whether or not alcoholic liquors should be utterly forbidden, simply because of the want of moral power in the natives to resist the indulgence, to their ruin. Such a measure would have utility for its plea.

16. The foregoing observations on the different Ethical Theories, are intended to pave the way for this conclusion, namely, that *the moral rules found to prevail in most, if not in all communities, are grounded partly on Utility\* and partly on Sentiment.* If we put aside the question as to the legitimate and defensible basis of Morals, and ask simply what has given birth to the codes now, or formerly, existing, we are, I think, compelled to admit that Utility is not the sole explanation, although coming in for a very important share. If, however, we add Sentiment—and Tradition, which is the continuing influence of some former Utility or Sentiment—we can render a comprehensive account of the existing practices. The rules manifestly founded on Utility are all those that protect the persons, property, good name, &c., of the members of each society from violation; that enforce justice and the fulfilment of bargains and engagements; that uphold

---

\* Mr. Mill, in the work above quoted, remarks that 'moral and immoral' were terms applied by men, primarily, to acts, 'the effects of which were observed to be beneficial, and which, therefore, they desired should be performed.' This is to affirm that all moral rules originally had reference to utility, well or ill-considered. This impression is not an uncommon one. We observe a tendency in many writers to seek out some practical intention in the merest ceremonial usages, as in the system of ablution so prevalent as a religious rite. It is sometimes said in defence of the antipathy of the white population of the United States to the persons of the free blacks, that this springs out of a wholesome dread of deteriorating the whole breed by mixture with an inferior race; to which the reply is, that the consideration of bringing forth a vigorous progeny has never been a ruling consideration in any known community, excepting ancient Sparta. It is usual enough to advance utilitarian *pretexts* for sentimental requirements, but the emptiness of such pleas is usually apparent.

278    THE ETHICAL EMOTIONS ; OR, THE MORAL SENSE.

veracity and integrity ; that maintain obedience to constituted authority ;* that extend protection to the helpless, and
so forth.

17. As already remarked, the cases of Sentiment converted
into law and morality differ widely according to place and
time. Some have their origin in sentimental *likings* carried to
the length of public consecration, as the veneration of the
Hindoos for the cow, out of which has arisen a compulsory
homage, with severe penalties for disrespect. The Buddhist
reverence for animal life is of the same nature. The abstinence of the Brahmins from animal food has been prompted
by this sacredness.† Still more numerous are the moral
enactments founded on *dislikes*, disgusts, or antipathies, to
which human nature appears to have a peculiar aptitude and
proneness. The natural causes of disgust are the putrid and
loathsome filth accompanying animal life, the removal of
which constitutes cleanliness. The expression of aversion to
these matters is the most energetic repugnance that we are
in the habit of displaying. Strange to say, however, we are
remarkably ready to be put upon this strong expression, and
even get up cases of factitious uncleanness, having no real connexion with the above-named source. The enunciation of
disgust is a favourite exercise, creating for itself objects to be
vented on ; precisely as the temperament overflowing with
tender emotion finds many things to love. The objects thus

---

* Sentiment often lends itself to aid the duty of social obedience, whose
real foundation is in the highest degree practical or utilitarian. The sanctity
and divine right of monarchs and dynasties are scarcely extinct as feelings
in the present day. Indeed, it is frequently said, that without the help of
the religious sentiment, civil order could not be maintained.

† The conflict of sentiment and utility is painfully exemplified in our
position with the animal tribes. No feeling of our nature is more important
to be cherished than the sympathy with other sentient beings, and yet, for
our own preservation, we are daily compelled to kill vast numbers of these
creatures. But the very same sentiment has to be crucified in our intercourse with humanity,—in the extermination of pirates and other implacable
enemies, in the punishment of wrong-doers generally, and in the discipline of
the young.

sought out, need not offend the senses in any way; if they can only furnish a slight pretext for being called nasty or unclean, it is enough for letting off the charged battery of the powerful organ of disgust. If any class of living beings should happen to provoke this outburst, terrible is their fate. No limits are set to the promptings for evil of this sentiment. The ordinary feeling of irascibility does not come up to it. When we have been so deeply offended as to find the common expressions of anger too feeble, we resort to the language prompted by disgust, and thereby invoke a more furious blast of retributive malice on the victim.

Among strong antipathies made into moral rules, we need only refer to such instances as the dislike to the pig above alluded to. The Hindoo ritual is full of the means of purification from actions deemed unclean. The hatred to classes of men, has often acquired the force of moral enactments. The system of castes implies an outcast population, which the privileged order prohibit their members from dealing with beyond certain limits. Foreigners have often come under this sentiment, as in the feeling of the Jews to idolaters, and white men towards negroes. The sentiment of detestation felt by a good Catholic of the fifteenth century to a heretic was intense to a high degree; no crime against civil society could kindle so furious a flame. As regards unbelievers, the antipathy has persisted to this day. The Jews have come in for a plentiful share of the dislike of Christendom. Not only were these antipathies strong to the hurt of the objects of them, but some of them were enacted as obligatory upon all members of the community, so that any one harbouring the proscribed class, was made liable to the severest penalties. The hatreds of opposite religious sects have been sometimes so intense, that any individual member, showing a coolness on the point, exposed himself to serious danger at the hands of his co-religionists; we have seen this in the case of Catholics and Protestants.

There have usually been certain modes of indulgence, not at all affecting the welfare of society, that have excited feel-

280 THE ETHICAL EMOTIONS ; OR, THE MORAL SENSE.

ings of dislike so strong and so influential, as to place them under the ban of authoritative morality. Wine and animal food have been the subjects of total prohibition. There has been a very prevailing disposition to restrict the indulgences of sex. Some practices are so violently abhorred, that they are not permitted even to be named. Society is apt to look with a severe eye at unshared enjoyments generally, using such odious terms, as 'glutton,' to stigmatize a large eater, and denouncing the pursuit of wealth, and the love of praise, as unworthy springs of action.

18. I shall now advert, in farther illustration of the views here advanced, to *the process of enactment of moral rules.* This will bring into the light what the advocates of a moral sense leave in the dark, the real imposing power, or the supreme standard to which the individual conscience has to adapt itself. History enables us to get at the origin of some parts of our actual morality, and by analogy we can surmise the growth of others.

One well-known source of moral rules is the dictatorship of a religious prophet like Mahomet. Gaining somehow or other a commanding influence over a large community, such a one is enabled to prescribe the practices that shall bind the actions, and shape the consciences, of his own and future generations. The likings and dislikings, personal to himself, are mixed up with his views of public utility in the moral code that he carves out. Ask a Mahometan what is the standard to settle any differences that may arise among individual consciences, and he refers you to the Koran—in other words, to the dictatorship of Mahomet, modified only by the authorized interpreters of his writings. So, in China, Confucius is known to have given the moral tone and specific precepts to a section of the Chinese ; and if we knew the origin of Brahminism and Buddhism, we might find in them too a similar dictatorial authority. But moral enactments have also sprung from *civil* authority embodied in a single person, and erecting his judgments and feelings into public obligation. Whether summoned like Solon, or the traditional Lycurgus, to settle a distracted society, or gaining power by hereditary ascendancy or conquering might, a civil despot may sometimes not only regulate the public laws, but mould afresh the moral sentiments of his time. Thus it was that the religion of Europe, and the accompanying moral code, were changed by imperial potentates, in this case adopting what had been already promulgated from other sources. The assent of the community at large is necessary to complete the legislative process, while every new generation must be disposed to hold fast what has thus been delivered. The proper answer, therefore, to the question, 'What is the moral standard?' would be *the enactments of the existing society, as derived from some one clothed in his day with a moral legislative authority.* The very same remarks apply to reformers, and the founders of new sects generally, who from causes quite assignable by history have obtained influence over a body of followers. The conscience of the Quaker is regulated by the moral code received from George Fox, and continued in the society from his time. In such an instance as this, the popular concurrence was more self-prompted than in the ancient religious dictatorships, and a right to reconsider the original tenets was tacitly reserved by the society. That part of our moral code relating to marriage, and the relations of the sexes, can be historically traced for the most part, and the responsibility of maintaining it in its present shape can be brought home to the proper parties. It is mere trifling to fill our imagination with an unseen, unproducible standard of morality; we need only look about us and read history, to get at the real authority that now maintains, and the one that originally prescribed, almost any moral precept now recognised as binding. Instead of treating morality as a whole, one and indivisible, let us take the enactments in detail, and we shall have no difficulty in ascending to the fountainhead in every case.

19. The change that has come over men's sentiments on the subject of Slavery, would prove an interesting example of the growth of new moral feelings. Until less than two cen-

## 282    THE ETHICAL EMOTIONS; OR, THE MORAL SENSE.

turies ago, the abhorrence of the usage of holding human beings as slaves did not exist; and now, except in the Slave States of America, the repugnance to the practice has almost reached the height of a moral sentiment. The process whereby this new and more liberal theory of the rights of humanity first shaped itself in the minds of scattered individuals, and came by degrees to leaven the mass, might probably be (and has been partially) traced out by the historian; and if so, we should have a sufficient account of the origin of one prevailing moral idea of the present time. This is a case that has just stopped short of the compulsory stage. Many people among us would willingly go the length of making anti-slavery opinions a 'term of communion,' and prohibit all intercourse with persons concerned in the practice; but the class holding such extreme views is not sufficiently numerous or influential to carry their point, and therefore the development of the feeling into a moral sentiment is not complete. The bill has not become law. The example is no less good as an illustration; for any considerable addition made to the intensity of the feeling, would probably suffice to place it in the rank of the obligatory.*

20. The *abrogation of moral rules* may also be quoted as throwing light on the position now advanced. Either something has happened to modify the sentiments of the mass of the community, or a minority becoming stronger has made a successful revolt. Epochs like the Protestant Reformation, and the first French Revolution, are pregnant with such changes. When a restriction is kept up, not by the force of the law, but by the diffused feelings and usages of society, a number of persons banding together may set the general opinion at defiance, and trust to themselves for the mutual sympathy and support that we seek for in society. They will be excommunicated from the mass, they must look for no

---

* I do not give this as an instance of a mere sentiment growing towards an obligation, seeing that the anti-slavery feeling has also the strongest basis of utility. Indeed there is probably no case of moral police more defensible.

## ABROGATION OF MORAL RULES.

favours, but for the reverse, out of their own communion ; but if their cause is a growing one, they may at last vindicate to themselves a full toleration, and so succeed in breaking up one item of social domination. It is thus that Dissent has got a footing in the midst of ecclesiastical establishments,— that the Quakers have stood out against war taxes, and the marriage laws. It was thus that Christianity broke up Judaism.

21. I have purposely deferred the consideration of CONSCIENCE, as a distinct attribute or faculty, from a conviction that this portion of our constitution is moulded upon external authority as its type. I entirely dissent from Dugald Stewart and the great majority of writers on the Theory of Morals, who represent Conscience as a primitive and independent faculty of the mind, which would be developed in us although we never had any experience of external authority. On the contrary, I maintain that Conscience is an imitation within ourselves of the government without us ; and even when differing in what it prescribes from the current morality, the mode of its action is still parallel to the archetype. I freely admit that there are primitive impulses of the mind disposing us to the performance of social duty (just as there are also other primitive impulses which dispose us to perform acts forbidden by social duty), of which the chief are (1) Prudence, or self-interest, and (2) Sympathy which prompts to disinterested conduct; but the peculiar quality or attribute that we term conscience is distinct from all these, and reproduces, in the maturity of the mind, a facsimile of the system of government as practised around us. The proof of this affirmation is to be met with, in observing the growth of conscience from childhood upwards, and also in examining closely its character and working generally.*

---

* I here transcribe from the before-cited work of Mr. Mill, his admirable illustration of the growth of the moral sentiment in the human being from childhood upwards, that the reader may take it along with my own rendering of the same thing, which follows in the text :—

‘ It may be asked, upon what consideration the men of our own age and

284    THE ETHICAL EMOTIONS ; OR, THE MORAL SENSE.

22. The first lesson that a child learns as a moral agent is obedience, or acting according to the will of some other person. There can be nothing innate in the notion thus acquired of command and authority, inasmuch as it implies experience of a situation with other human beings. The child's susceptibility to pleasure and pain is made use of to bring about this obedience, and a mental association is rapidly formed between disobedience and apprehended pain, more or less magnified by fear. The peculiarity attending the kind of evil inflicted, as a deterring instrument, is the indefinite continuance, or it may be, increase of the infliction until the end is secured. The knowledge of this leaves on the mind a certain dread and awful impression, as connected with forbidden actions ; which is the conscience in its earliest germ, or manifestation. The feeling of encountering certain pain, made up of both physical and moral elements,—that is to say, bodily suffering and displeasure—is the first motive power

---

country, for example, at first, and before a habit is formed, perform moral acts ? Or, it may be asked, upon what considerations did men originally perform moral acts.

' To the first of these questions every one can reply from his own memory and observation. We perform moral acts at first from authority. Our parents tell us that we ought to do this, ought not to do that. They are anxious that we should obey their precepts. They have two sets of influences with which to work upon us ; praise and blame ; reward and punishment. All the acts which they say we ought to do, are praised in the highest degree, all those which they say we ought not to do, are blamed in the highest degree. In this manner, the ideas of praise and blame become associated with certain classes of acts, at a very early age, so closely that they cannot easily be disjoined. No sooner does the idea of the act occur, than the idea of praise springs up along with it, and clings to it. And generally these associations exert a predominant influence during the whole of life.

' Our parents not only praise certain kinds of acts, and blame other kinds ; but they praise us when we perform those of the one sort, blame us when we perform those of the other. In this manner other associations are formed. The idea of ourselves performing certain acts is associated with the idea of our being praised, performing certain other acts with the idea of our being blamed, so closely that the ideas become at last indissoluble. In this association consist the very important complex ideas of praiseworthiness, and blameworthiness. An act which is praiseworthy, is an act with the idea of which the idea of praise is indissolubly joined ; an agent who is praiseworthy is an agent

## GROWTH OF CONSCIENCE.

of an Ethical kind that can be traced in the mental system of childhood. There are those other impulses above-named as inducing a regard to others, which make a part of the substance of morality; but as concerns duty strictly so called, the infant conscience is nothing but the linking of terror with forbidden actions. As the child advances in the experience of authority, the habit of acting and the dread of offending acquire increased confirmation, in other words, the sense of duty grows stronger and stronger. New elements come to be introduced to modify this acquired repugnance to whatever is prohibited by parents and teachers, and others in authority. A sentiment of love or respect towards the person of the superior, infuses a different species of dread from what we have just supposed, the dread of giving pain to a beloved object. Sometimes this is a more powerful deterring impulse

---

with whom the idea of praise is indissolubly joined. And in the converse case, that of blameworthiness, the formation of the idea is similar.

'Many powerful circumstances come in aid of these important associations at an early age. We find that not only our parents act in this manner, but all other parents. We find that grown people act in this manner, not only towards children, but towards one another. The associations, therefore, are unbroken, general, and all-comprehending.

'Our parents administer not only praise and blame, to induce us to perform acts of one sort, abstain from acts of another sort, but also rewards and punishments. They do so directly; and further, they forward all our inclinations in the one case, baulk them in the other. So does everybody else. We find our comforts excessively abridged by other people, when we act in one way, enlarged when we act in another way. Hence another most important class of associations; that of an increase of well-being from the good-will of our fellow-creatures, if we perform acts of one sort; of an increase of misery from their ill-will, if we perform those of another sort.

'In this state it is that men, born in the social state, acquire the habits of moral acting, and certain affections connected with it, before they are capable of reflecting upon the grounds which recommend the acts either to praise or blame. Nearly at this point the greater part of them remain, continuing to perform moral acts and to abstain from the contrary, chiefly from the habits they have acquired, and the authority upon which they originally acted; though it is not possible that any man should come to the years and blessing of reason, without perceiving, at least in an indistinct and general way, the advantage which mankind derive from their acting towards one another in one way, rather than another.'—p. 269.

## 286 THE ETHICAL EMOTIONS; OR, THE MORAL SENSE.

than the other. We call it a higher order of conscience to act from love than to act from fear. When the young mind is able to take notice of the use and meaning of the prohibitions imposed upon it, and to approve of the end intended by them, a new motive is added, and the conscience is then a triple compound, and begirds the actions in question with a three-fold fear; the last ingredient being paramount, in the maturity of the sympathies and the reason. All that we understand by the authority of conscience, the sentiment of obligation, the feeling of right, the sting of remorse—can be nothing else than so many modes of expressing the acquired aversion and dread towards certain actions associated in the mind with such consequences as have now been described. Trace out as we may the great variety of forms assumed by the senti-ment, the essential nature of it is still what we have said. The dread of anticipated evil operating to restrain before the fact, and the pain realized after the act has been performed, are perfectly intelligible products of the education of the mind under a system of authority, and of an experience had of the good and evil consequences of actions. If the conscience be moulded principally upon the fear of punishment, the agony of *remorse* means simply the apprehension of the penalty in-curred, as when the soldier has lapsed into a breach of military discipline, or the worshipper under a religion of fear pour-trays to himself inflictions by the offended deity. If love, esteem, and reverence enter largely into the case, the remorse will correspond to the suffering endured from inflicting a wound on those we love, respect, or venerate. If the duty prescribed has been approved of by the mind as protective of the general interests of persons engaging our sympathies, the violation of this on our part affects us with all the pain that we feel from inflicting an injury upon those interests.

23. The Varieties assumed by the sentiment of obligation in individuals are quite endless, but every one of them may be referred to some intelligible origin in the constitution, or the experience and education, of each. The reference to a narrow or a wide circle of interests marks out one important

## VARIETIES OF CONSCIENCE. 287

distinction; the opposition of the family to the community, and of the small society to the general welfare of mankind, brings out the relative strength of the contracted and expansive regards.

The feeling of obligation growing up in the smaller societies is very illustrative of the position I am contending for. Professional honour, or etiquette, in the soldier, or the lawyer,—sometimes even conflicting with the general law, as in regard to duelling,—and the sentiments peculiar to special sects, or fraternities, are among the most obvious instances of the acquired nature of the sentiment of obligation. It is purely by means of the discipline exercised in each society over its members, and by the habitual ascription of praise to some actions, and blame to others, that the code of the society is stamped on the individual mind, and gives birth to a conscience corresponding.

There is no difficulty in assigning the natural temperament, and the modifying circumstances, that determine the adhesion to the narrow circle, or the superior range of sentiment that prefers the larger point of view. Strong personal affection, the habit of engrossing the mind with those in immediate contact with ourselves, and the absence of all that cultivation, study, and knowledge which makes humanity at large an object of consideration and regard, are quite enough to contract the sphere of felt obligation; while, on the other hand, a disposition to sympathize with living beings generally, as distinguished from the special attachments, and wide studies directed to the history and destinies of nations and the human family at large,—cherish the comprehensive sentiment towards mankind.

24. The Religious conscience is characterized by the presence and predominance of the religious sentiment of mingled love and fear towards the Deity; and owes all its power to this circumstance. The feeling of disapprobation would thus resolve itself into the pain of displeasing an object of intense reverence. Again, when the benevolent impulses are the strongest part of one's being, the feeling of obligation is most

288    THE ETHICAL EMOTIONS; OR, THE MORAL SENSE.

severely ruptured by anything tending to inflict harm. Sometimes the mind inclines with special tenacity to the letter of the precepts of morality, so that a breach of form gives a violent shock of remorse; while others accustom themselves to look at the intention and spirit of the requirement, and feel most acutely any departure from this. If there were in the human mind a faculty of conscience by itself, we should not meet with such wide differences in the stress laid upon particular duties; the disposition rather would be, to obey with nearly equal strength of determination whatever was commanded by any recognised authority.

25. We must next take special cognizance of the self-formed or Independent conscience, or that variety of the moral sentiment that is not influenced either by fear of, or reverence to, any superior power whatsoever. On the supposition that external authority is the genuine type and original of moral authority within, the grand difficulty would lie in explaining the cases where the individual is a law to himself. But there is nothing very formidable in this apparent contradiction. The sentiment, at first formed and cultivated by the relations of actual command and obedience, may come at last to stand upon an independent foundation, just as the student educated by the implicit reception of the scientific notions of his teachers, comes by and bye to believe them, or disbelieve them, on evidence of his own finding. When the young mind, accustomed at the outset to implicitly obeying any set of rules, is sufficiently advanced to appreciate the motives—the utilities or the sentiment that led to their imposition—the character of the conscience is entirely transformed; the motive power issues from a different quarter of the mental framework. Regard is now had to the intent and meaning of the law, and not to the mere fact of its being prescribed by some power. An intelligence of superior energy will occasionally detect some inconsistency between the end professed and the precepts imposed and take a position hostile to the existing authority in consequence.

I shall cite a few instances of the growth of independent,

## THE SELF-DERIVED CONSCIENCE. 289

judgments in matters of duty, to show how the mind in emancipating itself from the trammels of the derived sentiment of the obligatory, still adheres to the type of outward authority. A common case is the discovery of some supposed or real inconsistency between a rule imbibed in the course of education, and some practice encountered in the world. The contradiction shocks the mind at first, but in the generality of cases is got over by the same implicit acquiescence that received the rule. There are, however, exceptional minds that cannot swallow contradiction in this easy way, and who accordingly take an independent stand, by choosing either to abide by the rule, and repudiate what is opposed to it, or to fall in with the practice and repudiate the rule. Thus, for example, the literal interpretation of the precept ' swear not,' has led the Society of Friends to refuse an oath in every form. Again, an individual fancies that a moral rule is not so fully applied as it ought to be, and suggests cases where an extension should take place. For instance, some persons consider that the obligation of monogamy, as a Christian institution, implies that neither party should marry a second time. Having made up their minds to such an inference, they feel constrained to comply with it, in opposition to the common usage, with all the strength of sentiment that they have imbibed from that usage in favour of the original doctrine. They are thus the followers of the prevailing opinions, even in the act of dissenting from them in some single instance.*

---

* A man may, in the exercise of independent judgment, embrace views of duty widely at variance with what prevails in the society he lives in, and may impose these upon himself, although he cannot induce anybody else to accept them. This is the only case where conscience is a thing entirely detached from the sanction of the community, or some power external to the individual. Even then the notion, sentiment, or form of duty is derived from what society imposes, although the particular matter is quite different. Social obedience develops in the mind originally the feeling and habit of obligation, and this remains when the individual articles are changed. In such self-imposed obligations the person does not fear public censure, but he has so assimilated in his mind the laws of his own coining to the imperative requirements of society, that he reckons them of equal force as duty, and feels

T

290    THE ETHICAL EMOTIONS; OR, THE MORAL SENSE.

26. I may next remark upon the sense of duty in the Abstract, under which a man performs all his recognised obligations, without referring to any one of the special motives above adverted to. There may not be present to his mind either the fear of retribution, the respect to the authority commanding, affection or sympathy towards the persons or interests for whose sake the duty is imposed, his own advantage indirectly concerned, his religious feeling, his individual sentiments in accord with the spirit of the precept, the infection of example, or any other operating ingredient prompting to the action, or planting the sting for neglect. Just as in the love of money for its own sake, one may come to form a habit of acting in a particular way, although the special impulses that were the original moving causes no longer recur to the mind. This does not prove that there exists a primitive sentiment of duty in the abstract, any more than the conduct of the miser proves that we are born with the love of gold in the abstract. It is the tendency of association to erect new centres of force, detached from the particulars that originally gave them meaning; which new creations will sometimes assemble round themselves a more powerful body of sentiment, than could be inspired by any one of the constituent realities. Nothing that money could puchase affects the mind of the money-getter so strongly as the arithmetical numeration of his gains. So it is with the habitual sentiment of duty in a certain class of minds, and with the great abstractions of truth, justice, purity, and the like. These cannot be proved to be primordial sentiments; nevertheless, we find them in a very high degree of predominance in particular instances; and persons unaccustomed to mental analysis, are apt to suppose that they must be implanted in our constitution from the first. The comparative *rarity* of such high-toned sentiments towards

---

the same sting in falling. The votary of vegetable diet on principle has the same kind of remorse, after being betrayed into a meal of butcher-meat, that would be caused by an outburst of open profanity, or the breach of a solemn engagement.

## MORAL DISAPPROBATION.

abstract morality, if duly reflected on, would satisfy any candid inquirer that they are not provided for in the original scheme of the mind; while the possibility of accounting for their development, wherever they occur, renders it unphilosophical to resort to such an hypothesis.

27. Hitherto, I have supposed the conscience to operate solely on the individual's own self—inciting to act, or punishing for neglect. But the expositition is not complete without referring to our moral judgments respecting the conduct of others, although there is nothing abstruse or difficult to explain in this new case. I must premise, however, in this connexion, that the inquiry should be as to the sentiment, not of moral approbation, but of moral *disapprobation*. I have said already, that a moral rule in the strict sense is not an optional thing, but is enforced by the sanction of some penalty. It is true that the looseness of ethical writers has led to the introduction of precepts of human virtue and nobleness, which undoubtedly deserve to be inculcated, but the compliance with those precepts constitutes merit and earns rewards, while the non-compliance does not entail punishment or censure. The question as to the morality of some line of conduct is, does it inspire a feeling of disapprobation, as violating the maxims recognized to be binding? If so, it is to be supposed that the same sense of duty that operates upon one's own self, and stings with remorse and fear in case of disobedience, should come into play when some other person is the guilty agent. The feeling that rises up towards that person is a strong feeling of displeasure or dislike, proportioned to the strength of our regard to the violated duty. There arises a moral resentment, or a disposition to inflict punishment upon the offender. It is the readiness to punish, that forms the criterion of moral disapprobation, or marks the boundary between a moral sentiment and an allowable difference of opinion. This brings us round again to the first imposition of moral rules. A particular line of conduct is so intensely disliked for some reason, or for none, that we are prepared to resent it and hinder its performance with all our might. A majority of our fellow-

292  THE ETHICAL EMOTIONS ; OR, THE MORAL SENSE.

citizens take the same strong view, and actually employ their power as the majority, to prevent it absolutely; whereby a new article in the moral code of that community is set up. As a matter of course, any one committing the forbidden deed is disapproved of, and handed over to be punished. Every man, whose own conscience tallies with the prevailing moral rules, visits with his indignation the violations of these; whereas the man of independent views of duty, judges according to his own special convictions, whether in his own case, or as regards other persons; only, not having the community with him, he is powerless to enforce his judgments, inasmuch as the sentiment of an individual does not amount to law, although never so well founded.

28. The phrase ' moral approbation' strictly considered, is devoid of meaning. As well might we talk of ' legal approbation,' it being known that the laws never approve, but only condemn. When a man does his duty, he escapes punishment; to assert anything more is to obliterate the radical distinction between duty and merit. It is freely admitted that there may be merit in the performance of duty, when the circumstances are such as to render this so very arduous, that the generality of people would fall short of it. A man may so distinguish himself, and rise into the order of merit ; but the exception here proves the rule, being an example to show that we only praise what we think it would be hard or unreasonable to exact, require, or expect from everybody. Merit attaches itself only to something that is *not* our duty, that something being a valuable service rendered to other human beings. Positive beneficence is a merit. So with good offices and gratuitous labour of every kind for beneficial purposes. These are the objects of esteem, honour, reward, but not of *moral* approbation. Positive good deeds and self-sacrifice are the preserving salt of human life. Too much cannot be said to encourage them, or done to reward them, when under the guidance of a wise judgment; but they transcend the region of morality proper, and occupy a sphere of their own. What society has seen fit to enforce with all the rigour of positive inflictions, has

## MORAL APPROBATION. 293

nothing essentially in common with those voluntary efforts of human disinterestedness and generous feeling, that we characterize as virtuous and noble conduct, and reward with eulogy and monumental remembrance.*

---

\* There is a seeming conflict between the definition of Duty here adopted, and the distinction between duties of perfect and of imperfect obligation, corresponding to perfect and imperfect rights. 'An imperfect law,' says Mr. Austin, 'in the sense of the Roman jurists, is a law which wants a sanction, and which, therefore, is not binding. Consequently it is not so properly a law, as counsel, or exhortation, addressed by a superior to inferiors.

'Many of the writers on *morals*, and on the so-called *law of nature*, have annexed a different meaning to the term *imperfect ;* speaking of imperfect obligations, they commonly mean duties which are not legal; duties imposed by commands of God, or duties imposed by positive morality, as contradistinguished from duties imposed by positive law. An imperfect obligation in the sense of the Roman jurists, is exactly equivalent to no obligation at all ; for the term *imperfect* denotes simply that the law wants the sanction appropriate to laws of that kind. An imperfect obligation, in the other meaning of the expression, is a religious or a moral obligation. The term *imperfect* does not denote that the law imposing the duty wants the appropriate sanction. It denotes that the law imposing the duty is *not* a law established by a political superior ; that it wants that *perfect*, or that surer or more cogent sanction which is imparted by the sovereign or the state.' Austin's *Province of Jurisprudence,* pp. 23—25.

As thus explained, the so-called imperfect duties may still be duties in the fullest sense of the word; they may be enforced by society if not by the law. They may, however, have this peculiarity, which is what Paley and others mean by the term, that they do not create corresponding *rights.* It may be a duty enforced by the social sanction (that is by blame for neglect), to give charity, though no particular needy person can claim it from us. But, in the case of benevolent and philanthropic services, it is more correct to say that they are prompted by the rewards of society, and therefore come under merit, and not under duty.

I must also advert to the doctrine, maintained more especially among Calvinists, that the utmost that even a perfect human being could do is strictly duty, and consequently that there is no such thing as merit.

Upon this I would remark that such a tenet is not Ethical but Theological. It springs not out of the relations between man and man, but out of the relations between man and God.

I am aware that some have endeavoured to make the two fields of Ethics and Theology coincident. Thus Dr. Wardlaw, in his *Lectures on Christian Ethics,* censures the whole series of Ethical writers without exception—including men (such as Butler) no less attached to Christianity than himself—

294 THE ETHICAL EMOTIONS ; OR, THE MORAL SENSE.

for not making the doctrine of the corruption of human nature the corner-stone of their respective systems. But I have already had occasion to adduce the reasonings of Stewart and Cudworth, to show that a vicious circle is formed, the moment that morality is deprived of its independent foundation and made to repose upon religion. The same view has been forcibly urged by Sir James Mackintosh.

The science of Ethics ought, I conceive, to be constructed on broad human grounds, such as are acknowledged by men of every variety of religious opinion, and with reference to what one man can exact from another, as fellow-beings.

Now, man must work by praise and blame, reward and punishment. When he works by punishment or blame, it is duty ; when by praise or reward, it is merit ; such are the very meanings of the words. So, if praise and reward are proper instruments, there must be such a thing as merit in a human point of view.

# THE WILL.

# CHAPTER I.

### THE PRIMITIVE ELEMENTS OF VOLITION.

IN my former volume, I sketched briefly what seems to me the foundation, or germ of volition, in our mental constitution. (INSTINCTS, § 26.) In a subsequent page (CONTIGUITY, § 51), I adverted to the acquired character of the voluntary control of our movements in mature life. The soundness of these views will be put to a severer test in the course of the present Book, in which it is proposed to go into a full detail of the various classes of volitions. In this preliminary chapter, I shall examine at length the two fundamental component elements of the Will, set forth in the passages above referred to. These are, first, the existence of a spontaneous tendency to execute movements independent of the stimulus of sensations or feelings; and, secondly, the link between a present action and a present feeling, whereby the one comes under the control of the other.

### THE SPONTANEITY OF MOVEMENT.

1. Both the character of this Spontaneity, and the proofs of its existence, have been stated in Book I. Chap. I. of the previous volume. It is there laid down, ' that movement precedes sensation, and is at the outset independent of any stimulus from without; and that activity is a more intimate and inseparable property of our constitution than any of our sensations, and, in fact, enters as a component part into every one of the senses, giving them the character of compounds, while itself is a simple and elementary property.' A series of proofs is there offered in favour of this position—such as the physiological fact of a central discharge of nervous energy where no stimulus from without is present as a cause; the

298        THE PRIMITIVE ELEMENTS OF VOLITION.

activity of the involuntary muscles displayed in the maintenance of the respiration, the circulation of the blood, &c. ; the
circumstances of awakening from sleep, wherein movement as
a general rule appears to precede sensation ; the early movements of infancy, and the activity of young animals in general ;
the activity of excitement ; the occurrence of temperaments of
great activity with comparatively low sensibility.  These facts
were dwelt upon, as leading irresistibly to the conclusion, that
there is in the constitution a store of nervous energy, accumulated during the nutrition and repose of the system, and
proceeding into action with, or without, the application of
outward stimulants or feelings anyhow arising.  Spontaneity,
in fact, is the response of the system to nutrition—an effusion
of power of which the food is the condition.  A farther illustration of the doctrine is furnished by what takes place in
parturition.  Here the uterus is prepared for the final act by
the growth of muscular fibres, which are by degrees developed
to a mature state, and at the moment of their ripeness begin
to contract of their own accord for the expulsion of the fœtus.
No circumstance can be assigned of the nature of a stimulus
to commence this act.  Neither the size attained, nor the
pressure of the fluid, nor any other agency that might be
supposed to operate, by mechanical contact or otherwise, upon
the surface of the uterus, can be fairly assigned as the condition that determines the womb to contract.  We have therefore no alternative, but to suppose that when the active apparatus has reached the point of perfect maturity, the inherent
power of the organ spontaneously discharges itself in the act
of parturition.  Nor is there anything intrinsically improbable
or unreasonable, in this mode of considering the manifestation
of active power in the animal frame.  The muscles when fed
with their proper aliment, and the nervous centres when
charged with their peculiar power, are in a condition predis-
posed to give forth any active display ; and, although this
activity is most usually and most abundantly brought into
play by the stimulus of our various feelings, there is no reasonable ground for supposing that a dead stillness would be

PROOFS OF THE SPONTANEITY OF MOVEMENT. 299

maintained, and all this pent-up energy kept in, because every kind of outward prompting was withheld. If a man were fed, and altogether precluded from outward stimulus as well as from movement, he would pass into discomfort and suffering. But besides this, the facts of the case are so strong as not to be easily gainsaid. Perhaps the most striking are those furnished by the initial movements of infancy, and the restless activity of early years generally, and of the young and active members of the brute creation. The bursting and bounding spirit of exercise, in these instances, is out of all proportion to any outward stimulants, and can be accounted for only by a central fire that needs no stirring from without. Next in point of evidence is the state of delirium, under which a rush of power flows from the centres with an almost total insensibility to all around. The natural mode of representing such diseased excitement, is to suppose that the nervous system is in an extraordinary degree disposed to pour out its vital energy ; just as in the state of health there is a proneness to keep up a moderate discharge. I have a difficulty in imagining any strong case against the doctrine in question, nor can I seize upon any fact to show that the animal system waits for something to affect the senses, and rouse up a painful or pleasurable excitement, before it can pass into activity. On the contrary, experience proves that the active tone and tension of the moving members is never entirely at a stand while life remains ; not in rest, nor in sleep, nor in the most profound insensibility that ever overtakes us. We must recognise central energy or activity as a fundamental and permanent property of the system ; and being once established, we are at liberty to suppose that it may show itself in a variety of ways.

2. What I mean to affirm, therefore, with a view to explain the origin of voluntary power, is that, taking the different regions of activity, or the different groups of moving members, these begin to play of their own accord, and continue in action so long as the central stimulus is unexhausted, or until a new direction is given to it. The most notable of the groups of moving members is the Locomotive apparatus,

## 300                THE PRIMITIVE ELEMENTS OF VOLITION.

on whose spontaneity I have already remarked. 'This involves (taking vertebrate animals in general) the limbs or the anterior and posterior extremities, with their numerous muscles, and the trunk of the body, which, in all animals, chimes in more or less, with the movements of the extremities. In the outburst of spontaneous action, locomotive effort (walking, running, flying, swimming, &c.) is one of the foremost tendencies, having the advantage of occupying a large portion of the muscular system, and thus giving vent to a copious stream of accumulated power. No observant person can have missed noticing hundreds of instances where locomotion resulted from purely spontaneous effort. In the human subject, the locomotive members are long in being adapted to their proper use, and, in the meantime, they expend their activity in the dancing gestures and kicking movements manifested by the infant in the arms of the nurse.' The varied muscular endowment of the human arms and hands is prompted into action in the same way, and leads to the execution of many different gestures, and the assumption of complicated positions. The movements of the trunk, neck, and head, which usually chime in with locomotion, may also take place apart from it. The alternation of the jaw is probably an independent prompting of the spontaneity. The mouth and features, where so many muscles participate, may be played upon by a distinct emanation ; and the very important movements of the eyes, to which a large amount of cerebral power is devoted, can doubtless spring up in isolation from the general activity of the frame. 'The vocal organs are a distinct and notable group of the active members. The utterance of the voice is unequivocally owing, on many occasions, to mere profusion of central energy, although more liable than almost any other mode of action to be stimulated from without. In man, the flow of words and song ; in animals, the outbursts of barking, braying, howling—are often manifestly owing to no other cause than the " fresh" condition of the vocal organs.'*

---

\* Other groups are, the muscles of the abdomen, which, besides their connexion with the play of the trunk, have important functions in relation to the

NEED OF AN ISOLATING SPONTANEITY. · 301

3. It is necessary to the commencement of voluntary power, *that the organs which we afterwards command separately or individually, should be capable of isolation from the outset.* For example, I can direct the fore-finger to perform any movement by itself, I cannot do so with the third finger. We have seen that from the original organization of the system, the muscles are grouped and connected in various classes, so that it is much easier at first to perform a plurality of movements together, than to prompt one member while all the rest of the body is still. But if this principle of connexion were absolute, no such thing as an isolated action could ever be started; there behoves to be also a certain degree of separation and independence, such that it is possible for a wave of energy to affect one or a small number of muscles without extending to others. This separateness manifestly exists, although in very different degrees, throughout the system. The isolation of the fore-finger is an instance of the highest degree. We can see in the crude movements of infancy, that this finger receives an independent stimulation from the nerve centres, while the other fingers go generally together. The isolation of the thumb is something intermediate, being less

---

alimentary canal. ' When the pelvis and thorax are fixed, the abdominal muscles can constrict the cavity, and compress its viscera, particularly if the diaphragm be made to descend at the same time, as occurs in vomiting, or in the expulsion of the fœtus, of fæces, or urine.' These actions, though sometimes automatic, are also voluntary in their nature, and have to be acquired from the same original element of spontaneity as the rest.

The perinæal group could be dwelt upon as illustrative of the different points now under consideration. They are so far voluntary in their character as to be brought into play to serve the purposes of the animal, but they are incapable, it would appear, of being separately commanded. It seems not to be in our power to put forth an effort in regulating one of the outlets of this region without affecting the muscles of the other at the same time; a fact implying that the link of primitive connexion is not broken through by an individualizing discharge of the spontaneous influence. Possibly, however, the individualizing impulse may occur at rare intervals, so that if the mind were on the watch at those times, a beginning of separate action might be made; but this is not a region where we are interested to make such special acquirements.

## 302 THE PRIMITIVE ELEMENTS OF VOLITION.

than what distinguishes the fore-finger. The toes go all together, and although it is not impossible to isolate them, as we may see from cases where, in the want of hands, human beings have learnt to write and manipulate with their toes, there is so little original separateness to proceed upon, that the acquisition must be very laborious. The four limbs are grouped so as to be available for locomotion, more especially in quadrupeds, but still the structure is such as to render it possible to isolate the movements of each limb. A central stimulus can proceed to one, without involving the whole. The fore limbs in quadrupeds are more endowed in this particular than the hind limbs; while. in the human subject, the arms are but slightly connected with the lower extremities in the locomotive rhythm, and are extremely impressible by impulses of the individualizing kind. The linking of the two arms is a primitive conjunction, causing them sometimes to alternate, and sometimes to be raised and lowered in conjunction; yet in the depths of the nervous organization, there is an arrangement permitting either to be acted on without the other. The flow of cerebral power can occasionally reach the single channel requisite for raising the right arm, while the other remains unmoved; were this not the case, we should never attain the voluntary command of them singly. The movements of the trunk and head are apt to go in union, but not so as to exclude the possibility of isolating them. Single movements may be performed as well as combined ones; implying distinct primitive currents from the organs of central power. The flexions and extensions of the trunk, and the various motions of the head, are of this independent character in the higher animals, although belonging to an organized system of rhythmical action. The separability of the different *groups* of active members is of a very high order, notwithstanding the tendency of the entire bodily framework to act together whenever any one part takes a lead. Thus the Voice is in a great degree isolated, so as to be the subject of an exclusive stimulation. The same may be said of the Tongue, the Mouth, and the Jaw. The tongue is an organ of great

## CONDITIONS OF AN ISOLATED MOVEMENT.

natural activity, being endowed with many muscles, and having a wide scope of action; the nervous communications between it and the brain are considerable; and the isolation of its movements in the primitive discharges of spontaneous power, corresponds to the remarkable degree of voluntary control subsequently acquired. A like capability of isolation belongs to the movements of the eyeballs, which come very early to the stage of mature volition. If these movements were as closely linked with others as the five toes are linked together, it would be exceedingly difficult to attain a voluntary command of the act of vision. We see the proof of this in the united action of the two balls, which can never be broken up; no provision apparently existing for confining a nerve current to one at a time. The case is different with the eyebrows and eyelids, which, although prone to act together in opening and closing the eyes, are yet so far liable to separate promptings, that we are able ultimately to command each without the other; at least the generality of persons can do so, for there are constitutional differences as regards the extent of the primitive separability of the various individual movements, just as the higher vertebræ excel the lower in this important property. The group of activities contained under the designation of the features of the face, are both conjoined and separate. The mouth, the nasal muscles, and the eyebrows, are disposed to work together, and the two corresponding sides have, as just remarked, a very great tendency to conjoint action; but there is still a sufficient amount of occasional isolation, to furnish a basis for a confirmed voluntary command of any one apart from the rest, as in the education of the actor.

4. It is thus manifest as a fact, but for which the growth of volition seems altogether inexplicable, that the central brain can discharge its power in solitary streams for the stirring up of single movements, and that, while a great number of outlets may appear to be open, one is preferred to the exclusion of the rest. This property of exclusiveness in the currents is compatible with other attitudes of the nervous centres, under

## 304 THE PRIMITIVE ELEMENTS OF VOLITION.

which entire groups of members are moved simultaneously, or in orderly alternation. In some organs, as we have seen, the possibility of isolation is very limited; in others the opposite holds true; in the first, voluntary control comes with difficulty, in the second with ease.

5. To illustrate the necessity of a spontaneous beginning of movement, as a prelude to the command of the will over the particular organ, I may cite the External Ear, which in man is usually immovable, although possessed of muscles. Here we have the absence of a central stimulus from the commencement, and consequently no power of bringing about the effect. Instances sometimes occur of persons able to move their ears, as most quadrupeds can do very readily, and the only account that we can render of this exceptional operation of the will, is to suppose that, from the outset, a proper nerve communication has been established between the brain and the aural muscles, whereby these have shared the spontaneous stimulation of the other voluntary muscles. Even after we have known what it is to command our limbs, trunk, head, jaw, mouth, eyes, voice, &c., if we were attempting to force the ear into motion, we should in all probability fail; in the absence of spontaneity, we have no basis to proceed upon. Should the organ at any time be moved of its own accord, that is the instant for establishing a beginning of voluntary control, and if the attention were directed upon it every time the spontaneous impulse was repeated, we should in the end bring this part of the system into the same subjection as the other voluntary organs.

*Circumstances governing the spontaneous discharge.*

6. It is requisite for the further prosecution of the present inquiry, to advert specifically to the conditions that determine the greater or less vigour of the central discharge. We have to prepare the way for rendering an account of those occasions, when the will operates with a promptness of energy resembling the explosion of gunpowder, while at other times the movements are tardy and feeble.

## DEGREE OF THE SPONTANEOUS DISCHARGE. 305

The first circumstance deserving of mention is the Natural Vigour of the constitution. There are, as we have seen, men and animals so constituted as to give forth a more than usual stream of activity ; and all creatures have their periods of greater or less abundance of discharge. Youth and health, the plentiful nourishment and absence of drain, the damming up of the accumulating charge by temporary restraint—are predisposing causes of a great and sudden outburst, during which the individual's active capability is at the highest pitch. We see this well illustrated in the daily experience of children, whose exuberance is manifested at their first awakening in the morning, after meals, and on release from lessons. On all such occasions, we see evidently nothing else than the discharge of an accumulated store of inward energy. It is not any peculiar incitement from without that is the cause of all this vehemence. The effect is explosive, like a shot, or the bursting open of a floodgate. It would not be difficult at those moments, indeed it would be the natural course of events, to perform some great feat. The boy let out from school, incontinently leaps over ditches, breaks down barriers, and displaces heavy bodies, and should these operations be required at the moment, no special or extraordinary stimulus would be needed to bring the requisite power into play.

7. The next circumstance to be considered is what is termed Excitement. This means an unusual flow of the central nervous energy, brought on by various causes, and followed by exhaustion or premature loss of strength. It is a property apparently co-extensive with mental life, that, by some means or other, the ordinary and enduring currents of activity can be converted into an extraordinary discharge of short duration at the expense of the future. When we speak of an excitable nature, we mean an especial proneness to this fitful or spasmodic exaltation. The exciting causes are sometimes physical, as food, air, intoxicating drugs and stimulants, disease, &c., and sometimes mental, or such as operate through the sensibilities or consciousness, including a large proportion of our pleasures and pains. Whatever may be the cause of

**306**     THE PRIMITIVE ELEMENTS OF VOLITION.

a state of excitement, one effect arising from it is an increase in the vehemence of all the spontaneous impulses occurring at the moment. Any action then performed is done with might. Hence, when an occasion for a vigorous display springs up, one way of preparing the system to meet it, is to induce a general excitement of the system, which being directed into the requisite channel supplies the additional succour that is wanted.

8. The class of proper *mental* stimulants demands a special consideration. First in order, we must place the causes of Pleasure. Whether under the law of Self-Conservation, or under the supplementary law of Stimulation not conservative, whatever gives us pleasure gives at the same time an exalted phase to some portion of our vitality (*Instincts*, § 20.) If the pleasure be great, a general excitement overtakes the system, in which the muscular energies must participate. If it be acute, and still more, if it be sudden, the stimulus is of a very powerful kind. A sudden stroke of success elates both mind and body, and prepares for a discharge of active energy in any direction.

In the second place, stimulation may arise from Pain. By the law of Conservation, pain should be accompanied with depressed energies, and generally it is so; but there is an exception in the case of acute smarts. A crushing blow, or a great depression of spirits, extinguishes exertion ; a sudden smart, not too severe, physically excites the nerves, giving birth to a spasmodic activity. Any quick application to a sensitive surface, whether pleasurable or painful, or merely pungent, is inimical to slumber, tranquillity, or repose. It is not necessary that the shock should be painful, although in point of fact, from its mere intensity, it is liable to amount to pain.

I purposely exclude from consideration the true volitional agency of Pain in causing effects of alleviation ; the present remarks are preparatory to the explanation of the will in its mature state, and refer to the primitive and fundamental processes of the system.

I will next advert to the efficacy of Opposition, obstruction, or resistance, within certain limits, in promoting a flow of heightened energy. While an invincible resistance, as a dead wall, not merely arrests our progress, but suppresses the very attempt to proceed, the check of a smaller obstacle appears to operate physically, like a smart, in exciting the nerve currents. In the full-grown proficiency of the will, we graduate our efforts to suit the work to be done, but there would seem to be a more primitive tendency to put forth energy in encountering a not insurmountable stoppage. It may be partly a kind of reflex action, and partly the stimulus of the sudden shock, operating somewhat like a blow. The actual overcoming of resistance gives the mental elation of the sense of power, and a corresponding physical exaltation of the energies. At the stage when we can be moved with the resentment of wounded pride and thwarted aims, an unexpected opposition awakens us through this sentiment to almost any degree of violence. Whether or not these various considerations exactly square with the phenomenon, the influence of opposition encountered is a fact that goes a great way in explaining how the natural spontaneity may be worked up to energetic discharges.

.9. These various circumstances prepare the way for an explanation of the compass and flexibility, so to speak, of the spontaneous outflow of nervous influence. We see various modes of prompting large effusions to meet those emergencies where an ordinary or average flow would be insufficient. Nor is it difficult to understand how habits may be contracted of emitting the higher discharges upon particular occasions ; for this part of our constitution is as much subject to the great principle of adhesive association as any other. To bring on an active burst in the first instance, the presence of some of the powerful agents now described would be necessary ; but after a time, the effect would come at the instance of some other circumstance having of itself no efficacy to exalt the active tone. The horse at first demands the spur and the whip to prepare him for a leap ; by-and-bye the sight of the

308     THE PRIMITIVE ELEMENTS OF VOLITION.

barrier, or the ditch, is enough of itself to draw out an augmented stream of cerebral energy. To strike a heavy blow with a hammer implies an association between a mere idea— the breaking down of a barrier, or the driving of a bolt—and a rush of nervous energy towards the muscles of the arms and trunk; but even with the firmest association, such as is found in the educated artizan, if it is attempted in cold blood, a little time is required to work up the system to the due strength of discharge. A very sudden blow can be struck, either after being once in heat through a certain continuance, or under a passionate burst, as fright or rage. In a hand-to-hand fight, for example, when the blood is up, the combatants are already under a torrent of excitement. What may be called the volitional *constitution* is identical with a copious central emanation of active power; the volitional *acquisitions* are such as connect firmly the different degrees of central discharge with the signs and signals denoting the amount called for by the various emergencies of life.

### LINK OF FEELING AND ACTION.

10. The mode of operation now supposed, although, as I conceive, absolutely essential as a part, is certainly not the whole fact that we term volition. A second element is wanting for giving direction to those spontaneous workings, in order to invest them with the character of *purpose* or aim, belonging to the proper actions of the will.

11. In my former volume (*Instincts*, § 28,) I endeavoured to find out the rudiment of the LINK BETWEEN FEELING AND ACTION, and traced it to the law that connects pleasure with increased vitality, and pain with diminished vitality—the law of Self-Conservation. From this root there are two branches, which diverge, and yet occasionally come together. One branch is the proper Emotional manifestations, the other enters into Volition.

The Emotional manifestations have been fully described. (THE SENSES AND THE INTELLECT, pp. 277 and 626, 2nd edit.)

They consist in part of movements, of all degrees of energy; and, consequently, in them we have one link at least between Feeling and Action. A painful smart awakens us to activity; an exhilarating draught gives rise to vivacious movements, called the expression of pleasure. But these movements, while distinct from central spontaneity, are not movements of volition. Their selection follows one law, the action of the will follows another law. The most general fact of emotional selection is that stated by Mr. Herbert Spencer, namely, the natural priority of muscles small in calibre and often exercised, as in the expression of the face, the breathing, the voice, &c.; the volitional selection points to those that can heighten pleasure or abolish pain.

12. It may be demanded, whether a movement set a-going under emotional excitement is fitted for eventually coming under voluntary control. Almost all the members of the body are brought into action, in displaying the stronger degrees of emotion; the arms gesticulate in many modes, the limbs are thrown out and retracted, the trunk and head are agitated in many ways, the features are especially acted on, the voice is stimulated, the muscles of respiration are affected; in short, it would seem as if no movement were left dormant in the round of our various manifested feelings. Why, then, it may be asked, have recourse at all to the doctrine of pure spontaneity, in order to obtain a first commencement of action, in the members destined to be subjects of voluntary control? As the chief difficulty seems to be to make the muscles act anyhow at the outset, or previous to that cementing process which gives them a definite and purposed direction, it is but natural to inquire if these promptings of the emotional excitement would not furnish the needful starting-point. Thus there are two views presented of this preparatory stage in the development of volition; the one, the indeterminate spontaneity expounded above, the other the demonstrative portion of our special emotions.

Notwithstanding that this latter hypothesis provides one veritable origin of movements, I still think it necessary to

## 310 THE PRIMITIVE ELEMENTS OF VOLITION.

recognise the other and more primordial source, namely, the spontaneous occurrence of central discharges independent of emotional excitement. In support of this view, I refer in the first place, to the proofs already adduced for the fact of spontaneity, amounting to a force of argument not to be set aside. We have direct and sufficient evidence, that there is such a thing as a tendency to put forth muscular power, in the absence of any emotional wave whatsoever; and this being a genuine and distinct fact of our constitution, we shall find in it a more suitable starting-point for the will than in the other class of movements.

If an additional argument were necessary, I might recur to a circumstance already insisted on, as appertaining to those movements that are developed into volitions; namely, the need of an *isolated* prompting in the first instance, as distinguished from an aggregate prompting. It is the character of an emotional stimulus to impart movement to a number of organs at once; but there seems no possibility of initiating voluntary control, unless we can catch an opportunity of a member moving by itself. We have seen that this is the distinction of the fore-finger, and of several other parts; but the concurrent stimulation of many organs at the same moment, which is the peculiarity of an emotional wave, makes the feelings a bad school for beginning the work of voluntary ascendancy over every separate individual member of the active system.

13. This preliminary question being disposed of, I turn to the second, or volitional branch of the Law of Conservation (see *Instincts*, §§ 28—31). We suppose movements spontaneously begun, and accidentally causing pleasure; we then assume that with the pleasure there will be an increase of vital energy, in which increase the fortunate movements will share, and thereby increase the pleasure. Or, on the other hand, we suppose the spontaneous movements to give pain, and assume that, with the pain, there will be a decrease of energy, extending to the movements that cause the evil, and thereby providing a remedy. A few repetitions of the for-

## STIMULUS OF PLEASURE.

tuitous concurrence of pleasure and a certain movement, will lead to the forging of an acquired connection, under the law of Retentiveness or Contiguity, so that, at an after time, the pleasure or its idea shall evoke the proper movement at once. This is the thesis to be made good by a full detail of examples, in the two following chapters. Except in perhaps a very few instances, (which are our special instincts, more numerous in the brutes), there is no original provision in our mental system for singling out the exact movements requisite to promote pleasure and abate pain. The chief foundations of the super-structure I conceive to be, (1) Spontaneity, (2) Self-Conserva-tion, and (3) Contiguous Adhesion or Retentiveness. The first beginnings of our volitional education are of the nature of stumbling and fumbling, and all but despairing hopelessness. Instead of a clear and distinct curriculum, we have to wait upon the accidents, and improve them when they come.

14. Let us now attend more particularly to the operation of pleasures and pains in stimulating activity for ends, in other words, volition. We find the assumed primordial tendencies at work all through life, and in that circumstance we have the best proof of the doctrine that assumes them.

And first of Pleasure. It is known that a delight tasted urges us to continue and add to it, and that without delibera-tion or delay. Approaching an agreeable warmth, when chilly, we find ourselves giving way to an immediate impulse ; we do not wait for the formalities supposed to attend a de-cision of the will : it takes an effort on our part to resist the movement so long as the pleasure is increasing. An equally convincing example is seen in the act of eating. The taste of food, by an immediate response, adds energy to mastication ; the relish of extreme hunger conjoined with a savoury morsel operates with a species of fury. So in any other sense. The turning of the eyes to a light is a remarkable instance ; the attraction for a flame is at work from the first dawn of volition and never ceases. Humanity seems to share in the fascination of the moth. In the pleasures of children, we see how strongly they are drawn after a tasted delight,

312          THE PRIMITIVE ELEMENTS OF VOLITION.

whether exercise, sport, or the enjoyments of sense. In the transformed character of Desire, the primitive urgency is convincingly apparent. When we can no longer follow in act the lead of pleasure, we are spurred ideally into unbounded longings. There is no limit to the urgency of pleasure begun. Satiety means, not that the system has ceased to be moved by enjoyment, but that we have run up to the bristling point of some pain.

Such I conceive to be the general statement of the facts. The exceptional appearances may be accounted for. Thus, there are pleasures that calm down our active excitement; as warmth, repletion, and the massive pleasures generally. But these cases still conform to the law. There is an arrest put on a painful or morbid activity; a new action or attitude is assumed in accordance with the pleasure, and is kept up and adjusted for increasing it to the utmost. We seem to be passive; but, in point of fact, repose is the essential condition of our enjoyment. Let any one endeavour to drive us out of our quiescent and comfortable state, and the system would prove by the energetic resistance and return, how great is the power of the pleasurable stimulus. The awakening of one asleep is sufficiently illustrative of the point. Still these pleasures have something exceptional in the fact that, under them, we are satisfied and contented, and in a measure exempted even from the longings of desire. One reason may be that we have attained the maximum of delight belonging to them, and can only spoil it by farther exertions, real or ideal. But there is probably another reason. The states of massive enjoyment, not acute, are accompanied with a gradual quiescence of the nerve currents, in other words they are of a soporific character; neither active exertions nor ideal longings are promoted by them. They are our serene, satisfying, unexciting pleasures. They cure the restlessness of activity and desire by sending us to sleep.

Another case where pleasure does not stimulate activity, is when the strength is exhausted. Voluntary pursuit implies a certain freshness of the active organs involved. When

STIMULUS OF PAIN. 313

worn out with fatigue, hunger, or disease, our limbs do not readily answer to the spur, and the relish of felt pleasure is counterworked by the pain that active exertion would induce. Thus it is, that, even under a considerable excitement in the way of agreeable position, our weakness or our indolence may keep us quiescent.

Next, as to Pain. We have seen that the primary and the general influence is to abate energy. The exceptional operation of acute smarts, in stimulating energy, has been sufficiently dwelt upon. In pain, the vitality altogether is lowered, but the state being one of irritation and unrest, movements of some sort are kept up. Still, the typical effect of pain is what is seen when any activity of ours is the cause, and when the abatement of that activity follows as the remedy; as when we are stopped by a prickly hedge, or by knocking against a stone wall. The infliction of pain seldom fails as a cure for over-action.

The opposite case of too great inertness or inactivity, is not so directly met by pain, unless by the rousing efficacy of the smart, inducing a spasmodic and temporary effort. The difficulty here lies in showing how pain can resign its function of abating the active energy, to take up the proper function of pleasure, and stimulate continuous exertion. My opinion is that the operating element in this case is not the pain, but *the relief from pain*, which is, in effect, pleasure. When one is under suffering, any movement bringing a partial remission is kept up and augmented, exactly as when pleasure starts up out of indifference. A diminishing pain and a growing pleasure are all one as regards the elation of vital power, and the continued plying of the happy instrumentality.

In labouring whether for the actual, or for the ideal, abatement of pain, the sustaining influence is the feeling of relief, in fact or in prospect. The exhausted traveller, if he gave way to the direct agency of the sensations of fatigue, would sit down by the way; his flagging powers are kept up by the idea of the better rest at the end of the journey. We

# 314 THE PRIMITIVE ELEMENTS OF VOLITION.

all know what a powerful tonic to the depressed system is the promise of speedy relief, and that, in the absence of hope, pain exercises, in naked display, its real function of damping the active energies.

# CHAPTER II.

## GROWTH OF VOLUNTARY POWER.

1. THE foundations of Voluntary Power being thus assumed to be (1) Spontaneity, (2) Self-Conservation, and (3) Retentiveness, I now proceed to illustrate in detail the rise of the superstructure. What we have to explain is the educational process of connecting definite feelings with definite actions, so that, in the furtherance of our ends, the one shall command the other.

As in the exposition of the Feelings, we commence with Muscular Exercise. Here we have the pleasures of exercise in the fresh condition of the muscles, and the pains of fatigue. The operation of these upon the will is remarkably simple.

Thus, as regards Exercise. Spontaneous movements being commenced, there follows a pleasurable consciousness, with the accompaniment of heightened vitality, or a greater stimulation than mere spontaneity would give birth to. The law of Conservation here operates in its primitive simplicity ; prior to any education, it suggests the course that the educated will would follow. The link between action and feeling, for the end of promoting the pleasure of exercise, is the precise link that must exist from the commencement ; the pleasure results from the movement, and responds, by sustaining and increasing it. The delight thus feeds itself.

The same simple character belongs to the operation of the pains of Fatigue. Without the protracted groping and tedious acquisition necessary in most instances, the pain brings its own remedy under the influence of self-conservation. Muscular expenditure is the cause of the evil, the diminution of this is the remedy, and is what the pain directly involves.

316 GROWTH OF VOLUNTARY POWER.

Every sentient being passes into quietude of its own accord, under the experience of painful fatigue, no counteracting force being present.

We can, however, find instances, in connexion with the muscles, exemplifying the acquired powers of the will. Take the pain of restrained movemeuts, as when spontaneity is checked by confinement. Under self-conservation, this pain would not suggest the true remedy, but would rather work the contrary way; action and not quiescence is the thing needed. We must here suppose the rise of an accidental movement, of such a kind as to extricate the creature from the confined position; as when, by turning itself round, an animal finds an open door; the movement once commenced is kept up under the elation of relief, until perhaps another obstacle re-instates the pain. The round of spontaneity brings new tentatives, and the successful are again singled out and promoted, so long as they yield relief. If, now, we suppose that some one definite movement is a constant remedy for the pent-up irritation, as when an animal has every day to make a way out of the same confined spot, the repeated connexion of the feeling with this one movement (at first accidentally stumbled on) would end in a firm association between the two, and there would then be no more fumbling and uncertainty; the random tentatives, arising through spontaneity and the spasmodic writhings of pain, would give place to the one selected and appropriate movement, and we should have a full-grown volition adapted to the case.

2. Proceeding next to the Sensations proper, we begin with Organic Life. The muscles, besides the feelings belonging to their distinctive function, are liable, in common with the other tissues, to pains from injury and disease. These pains were used to typify the whole class of acute physical pains, and a full description was given of the characters of the class. We shall here notice their alliance with voluntary action. At the outset of life, no special connexion exists between any one kind of physical suffering and the actions calculated to relieve it; there is the general tendency to abate

RELIEF OF ORGANIC PAINS. 317

vitality on the whole, qualified by spasmodic outbursts from nervous irritation. All the special remedies must arise through the usual procedure of the education of the will. For illustration, let us suppose a hurt in any part of the body externally, as by a sharp point or a scald. The spasmodic excitement accompanying the pain (partly reflex and partly emotional), would tend to movements which might withdraw the member, but which possibly might aggravate the mischievous contact. I cannot look upon these movements under a reflex stimulus, or under the excitement of an emotional wave, as at all protective; they might be so on one occasion, and not on another. I conceive that the rise of a protective volition, in the above case, is typically shown by supposing that a limb is in pain through proximity to a hot body, and that in the course of random spontaneity the limb is withdrawn by an *isolated impulse*. The sense of relief would then operate to continue and heighten the impulse. Let a similar conjunction happen a second time. We should still have to wait upon the accidents for the commencement of the proper retractation, and might long wait in vain; but when it did happen, bringing with it the same feeling of relief, there would begin to be formed a link of association, which would go on strengthening with each subsequent conjunction. It is by some such procedure that we at last learn definitely to withdraw each member of the body from a painful contact. A mere reflex stimulus might operate the wrong way; the educated will operates with equal energy, and with the needful precision. This constitutes one class of our voluntary acquirements in connexion with acute pains. (Appendix, C.)

· It is impossible to say what number of chance conjunctions are requisite to generate a contiguous adhesion strong enough to raise us above the uncertainties of the spontaneous commencement. Much depends on the felicitous singling out of the proper movements; any irrelevant accompaniments would stand in the way of the correct union. If the proper movement is never wholly separated from others, the isolating association must depend on its being present more frequently

318 GROWTH OF VOLUNTARY POWER.

than any one else. This obstacle being got over, the progress would be favoured by the mental excitement of the feeling of relief. We know how, in after life, a happy conjunction, following after many ineffectual trials, strikes at once into the mind, and solves the difficulty for ever.

A curious example of an incomplete volition is seen in one of the characteristic muscular pains. An attack of cramp in the limbs does not suggest to people generally the alleviating movements. Owing perhaps to the rarity of the experience, we have not usually a full-formed volition whereby the state of suffering induces at once the best mode of attaining relief, and we are thus thrown upon the primitive course of trial and error. This shows, by contrast with the last-named examples of retractation from a painful contact, the dependence of voluntary power on education. An established link between a cramp in the ball of the leg and the proper actions for mitigating the agency, is as great a desideratum as drawing up the foot when the toe is pinched or scalded; yet no such link exists, until forged by a course of painful experience. The connexion in the other case is so well formed from early years, that it is commonly regarded as instinctive; yet why should there be an instinct for one class of pains and none for another of even greater average severity? The likely explanation is that we are more favourably situated for the process of acquisition in the one case than in the other.

3. Among sensations of Organic Life, I may cite Thirst as remarkable for the urgency of its pressure upon the will. I will not vouch for the truth of an assertion frequently made, that some animals, as the duckling, know water by sight before drinking it. This much is certain, that a thirsty creature having once got water into its mouth feels a very great change of sensation, and this change for the better operates immediately in sustaining the act, whatever it is, that administers the relief. Infants cannot at first perform the act of drinking liquid from a vessel, but in the lower animals the system of nerves and muscles is more highly matured at the moment of birth, and they are able to make

VOLITIONS FOR RELIEVING THIRST. 319

spontaneous movements throughout all their organs during the first hours of life. By this means they stumble upon their most needful operations in the course of a short time. Still it would be a very long period before a creature would, in ordinary circumstances, come upon a pool of water, make experiments upon its properties, and get upon the right movement for imbibing it; if this were requisite for supporting life on the first day, few land animals could live. The satisfying of thirst at the outset is due to the mother's milk, or the moisture of the food; and by-and-bye in the course of its ramblings and pokings, the young animal encounters a stream, and applies its mouth to the surface, putting out the tongue, and executing some of those movements of tongue and jaw already associated with the contact of objects of food. The refreshing sensation that follows maintains, to the point of satiety, the action begun; and an effective lesson is gone through, in uniting by an enduring association the two elements thus brought into conjunction. After a very few such occasions, the contact of the cool liquid with the parched mouth brings at once into play the movements of imbibition, for which we may be assured there was no original provision, independent of successful trials confirmed by the adhesive power of the mind. I shall advert presently to the whole case of taking food.

4. The feelings of the Lungs have been seen to be extremely intense. The most characteristic state in connexion with this organ is suffocation in its various degrees of virulency. The voluntary action required for aiding in such an emergency is to reinforce the movements of the chest. The ability to do this is not likely to be possessed in early infancy. Probably the requisite command of the chest by voluntary agency is first got in some other connexion, and transferred to the present case. We cannot always undertake to state precisely the feeling that brought each voluntary movement first into regular use; because when a movement has got a footing in one connexion, we find it then much easier to bring it into other connexions than to make the start from the original void.

320  GROWTH OF VOLUNTARY POWER.

It may be that the child first learns to make forced inspirations and expirations to relieve the pains of oppressed breathing ; seeing that these pains are very urgent, and that spontaneous impulses are very likely to come towards the muscles of the chest on some of those occasions. There can be no doubt that any alleviating impulse, co-existing with such intense suffering, would be maintained and speedily associated for after times. Possibly, too, the grateful feeling of fresh air, newly encountered after in-door confinement, may be the occasion of learning to heighten the breathing action, by superadding the voluntary impetus to the involuntary movements of the chest ; the opportunity being favourable for the rise of spontaneous impulses. The use of those voluntary efforts of breathing is so exceedingly various, that the order of their acquisition may not be at all uniform.

The feelings of Warmth and Chillness inspire the mature animal to numerous precautions. The commencement of some definite procedure dates from an early period of life. I formerly quoted the case of the infant drawing close to the warm body of the nurse. Animals soon find out that the crouching attitude promotes warmth. By a like experience, accidental in the commencement, adhered to by the spur of felt relief and the operation of the associating bond, other devices are attained. Lying close to one another, creeping into holes and shelters, are portions of the acquired experience of the animal tribes, employed to stave off the miseries of cold, or retain the satisfaction of warmth.

5. I come next to sensations of the Alimentary Canal. These are necessarily the centre of a wide circle of voluntary exertion, and furnish apposite examples of that obscure initial stage of the will which I am now labouring to bring to the light. The earliest actions involved in taking in nourishment are to a great degree reflex, but a certain amount of volition is present at the very beginning, and rapidly extends its sphere. The act of Sucking is generally said to be purely reflex in the new-born infant. The act of swallowing remains reflex to the last. But as I have said before, the giving over sucking,

SUCKING.   ·   321

when there is no longer any relish, is volition in the germ,—
that very typical fact which I have all along insisted upon as
representing the whole. The proceedings of the infant at
this stage are most instructive. The volitional stimulus,
sustaining a movement once begun, so long as pleasurable
gratification is the consequence, must be pronounced to be in
operation from the first hour of life, if it be a fact that the
ceasing to suck is at all dependent on the child's own feelings.
It may be that the purely reflex action which upholds the
first efforts is not amenable to the feelings, and that some
time elapses ere those spontaneous impulses, which arise
from the cerebrum, operate and come under the control of a
concurring wave of sensation. But whatever be the exact
moment when a present feeling first influences a present
action, that is the moment of the birth of volition. We
reach this point by inward growth. Having reached it, the
education of the will is thenceforth a process actually begun,
and ready for improvement. Sucking is the only power
exerted by the infant towards its own nourishment, at
the opening of sentient existence. There is, in the act, a
participation of the movement of the lungs; for it is the
partial vacuum, created in the expansion of the chest during
inspiration, that determines the flow of milk to the mouth.
If all the actions concerned,—viz., the closing of the lips and
nostrils against the ingress of air, the aiding movement of
the tongue, which by an air-tight contact with the opening
of the nipple would cause a flow of liquid on being pulled
away, the inspiration made a little stronger to make up for
the extra resistance to be overcome,—were purely and wholly
reflex, both on the first application of the mouth to the breast
and on succeeding occasions, they never could become voluntary, any more than the action of the heart or the intestines.
As in the breathing action in general, there must be a certain
amount of reflex or automatic movement, with a mixture of
spontaneous impulses from the cerebral centres, ready to be
seized by the concurring painful or pleasurable wave that
they are found to tell upon. The muscles of the mouth,

x

322 GROWTH OF VOLUNTARY POWER.

the tongue, and the chest, are pre-eminently voluntary in their nature,—the tongue especially,—as is seen, both from the great range of their acquired effects, and from the disposition of the youngest infant to impel them copiously and variously. I rely on these considerations as explaining why the act of sucking is so soon adopted from the reflex into the voluntary, and made subject to the feelings of relish and satiety. We see from an early date that the child does not suck merely because it is put to the breast; showing that will has commenced in a decided manner, that in fact the automatic impulse is no longer the prime mover. Probably a regular course has been gone through, whereby the digestive feelings have been completely associated with the active mechanism of sucking; so that hunger brings that mechanism into play, and satiety or distaste suspends its action. We cannot directly verify the stages of the acquisition in this particular instance; at least, I cannot pretend to have done so by any specific observations of my own. The direct proof of the growth of an associating link, converting the random spontaneity into an enduring alliance of definite movements with a definite state of pleasure or pain, must be sought in more favourable cases, such as I trust will be brought to view in the course of the exposition; nevertheless, there are various aspects of the present example that furnish increased presumption on the side of the general doctrines now contended for. The stages subsequent to the very earliest are more open to observation. Thus the child at first, although able to suck when the nipple is placed in its mouth, is utterly powerless to find the breast, just as in the case of the newly-dropped lamb. After some time, we see it directing its head to the place, and applying the mouth exactly to the point of suction. A wide compass of acquisition has been gone through in the meantime. I can describe the process only, as I have already done many times over, by saying, what seems to me consistent with all the appearances, that the child makes spontaneous movements of the body, and finds that these bring it towards the breast and the nipple; that the primordial nexus supports these movements when they are felt to bring

## MASTICATION. 323

gratification in their train ;—and that they at last become so well associated with the sensation as to be brought on at once when that is present. There is an additional element here, which I am anxious not to introduce yet, namely, the acting for a prospective pleasure, and going through a process of several steps, of which only the last yields the result sought. I prefer at present to seek instances exhibiting the volitional connexion in its simplest and most primitive condition. Afterwards the higher complications will come under review.

6. Next to sucking comes the process of Mastication. Here we have, in the first instance, the play of the tongue for rolling the morsel in the mouth. The full maturity of the will is soon arrived at in this case ; the strong feeling of taste and relish on the one hand, and the peculiar readiness of the tongue to come into action, speedily develop a fixed alliance between the two. The tentatives are accompanied with less than usual complication or ambiguity. We must needs suppose that the best of all conditions, for fostering the association of the two elements in question, is when a feeling strong and unmixed co-exists with the one single movement that immediately tells upon it, all other organs being perfectly still. The circumstance that indicates cause and effect in experimental philosophy—the isolation of the sequence—is the thing that enables the primitive volitional instinct to operate fairly, and to begin the permanent alliance which constitutes voluntary power. Now the movements of the tongue seem to be remarkably distinguished for independence or individuality. There is no other organ less disposed, either to be a follower of collateral organs, or to drag those into action with itself. Indeed, the highly endowed muscular and nervous organization of this member implies a distinction over the moving members generally, whatever may be the mode that we may adopt for expressing the superiority. Undoubtedly the supposition just made of a highly independent spontaneity,—of a momentary devotion of the central brain to stimulate some single movement of this one part,—is the very circumstance of all others to promote an alliance between such a movement,

324   GROWTH OF VOLUNTARY POWER.

and the pleasurable state sensibly increased by it.   I can imagine no situation more appropriate than this, and no more elementary mode of stating the ultimate fact at the basis of all volition.   The child has got in its mouth a sugary morsel. If no movement of the tongue arises at that moment, as is quite possible, the morsel will simply melt away at random. No doubt every infant passes through a number of those experiences during its pre-volitional age.   Should, however, an impulse arise at such a moment to elevate the tongue, so as to press the lump to the roof of the mouth, an accession of pleasure is instantly felt, which accession is the antecedent for inducing the continuance of that special movement.   As I have repeatedly said, the more isolated the active impulse has been, the more unmistakeable is the conjunction.   Should the child, for instance, execute at the same time some other movement by a burst of cerebral spontaneity, perhaps even more decided than the one supposed, the augmented pleasure might lead in the first instance to the continuance of that movement. It might be a movement of the fingers, or the arm, or the eyeballs.   The mistaken coincidence would for a moment sustain and perpetuate the wrong impulse.   But then comes in the correcting power of the situation; for the absence of any farther enhancement of the agreeable sensation would permit the false accompaniments to drop, from the want of farther encouragement, and the true cause might then make itself apparent.   However this may be, I cannot hesitate to suppose that the early steps of our volitional education are very much hindered, by the occurrence of a plurality of movements in conjunction with alleviation of pain, or an increase of pleasure.

The use of the jaw in chewing is necessarily late with the human infant.   This circumstance counts in favour of the easy commencement of the voluntary effort; inasmuch as practice improves all the spontaneous tendencies.   When the child begins to chew, the same feeling of enhanced pleasure that promoted the activity of the tongue sustains the co-operation of the jaw, and experience cements the connexion

ACTING UNDER SWEET AND BITTER TASTES. 325

between the sensation, and the movements proper to prolong and increase it. A nauseating or bitter morsel has exactly the opposite tendency, arresting and almost paralysing the concurring action of the jaw and tongue at that moment, and vehemently stimulating any other that may happen to arise of a kind to give relief. The entire process of mastication is thus an example of the spontaneous passing through the usual stages into the voluntary. The members employed have in a high measure the characteristic of individualising spontaneity, and the sensibility developed is of that strong and commanding sort which renders the experiments very telling and decided. The consequence is, that after a brief probation, marked with the usual struggles, the child enters upon the full voluntary control of the masticating organs ; as soon as a morsel is felt in the mouth, it is moved about, and carried backwards, under the increasing relish, until it finally passes into the pharynx. Throughout the alimentary canal the propulsion is involuntary until the termination, when the will again comes into play. In this final act, also, we might elucidate the general principles of voluntary acquisition, all which are fully applicable to the case. The commencing helplessness, the spontaneous movements laid hold of and sustained, when happening at the right moment, the confirming of the link of association after repetition, and the full-grown volition at last, might be all pointed out as belonging in a very manifest way to this part of our mature ability.

In these observations on the influence of the alimentary sensations, I have so far involved the sense of Taste, as to leave little to be said regarding it. Sweet and bitter tastes operate in the same way as relishes and disgusts. In addition to the exertions of the tongue and jaw now described, we acquire at a later period the more difficult act of throwing an ill-tasting substance from the mouth. Prior to the attainment, the child can do nothing but cease to masticate, and with an open wry mouth hold the morsel suspended, perhaps let it flow out of the lips, as we see constantly. It is in vain that we tell an infant to spit the thing out ; we anticipate its voluntary edu-

**326** GROWTH OF VOLUNTARY POWER.

cation, which has not yet reached that point. The act of spitting belongs at soonest to the end of the second year, so far as my observation has gone. Demanding a complex arrangement of the mouth and tongue, coupled with a propulsive expiration, it cannot be expected to arise spontaneously for a very long time. The beginnings of our voluntary power are related to simple acts and easy arrangements, and the conditions are such as to forbid us from arriving at any complex adjustment or combination of movements at the opening of our career.

7. The sensations of Smell contribute their quota to the elucidation of our theme. The sweet and agreeable odours prompt to the exertion for continuing the enjoyment of them, if such an exertion is once hit upon. Hence we contract the habit of snuffing the air when laden with freshness or balmy scent. This is an energy of the lungs, coupled with the closing of the mouth to confine the stream to the channel of the nose. The reinforced action of the lungs is probably one of the spontaneous discharges that come to be linked very early with the feelings that are influenced by it ; we have alluded to it already in the case of relief from suffocation. If this were the only act necessary to inhale a fragrant odour, the young child, or animal, would soon have the necessary connexion established for the performance of it on the right occasion. But, as I have just been remarking, when two acts quite independent of each other must concur to an effect, the probability of their doing so at the right conjuncture is so much less as to delay the commencement of the acquisition. If there were any cause at work, besides random spontaneity, for bringing about the embrace of feelings and actions appropriate to them, these compounded movements might be initiated as quickly as the simple ones. The tardiness in their case coincides perfectly with what we should expect under a system of chance beginnings, but not with any theory that affirms the existence of a more express provision for getting the voluntary powers under way. The snuffing up of a pleasant odour would soon be attained, if the lungs alone

## ATTAINING AGREEABLE CONTACTS. 327

could do it ; the spontaneity of an increased respiratory action is frequent enough to come into the lock of the pleasurable sensation, and to be thereupon sustained until an alliance for the future has made some progress. The inhalation of air, however, with never so much vigour, is of no avail with an open mouth, and the firm closure of the lips is not at all likely to happen at the same moment. Hence the power of smelling actively is a late acquirement, as observation shows. Usually, I think this power is delayed until the child is far enough advanced to be amenable to instruction, or, at all events, until the mouth is subject to voluntary command through other connexions. The dog is also late in arriving at this faculty, and for the same reason, that the concurrence of closed lips with increased inhalation, is not at all likely to be come at in puppyhood. Nearly the same remarks apply to ill smells. To abate the pain caused by them, a strong expiration has to be guided exclusively into the nostrils by closing the aperture of the mouth. This is the proper voluntary accompaniment of the state. The emotional manifestations, so distinctly marked through the untiring play of the muscles that elevate the wing of the nose, have nothing to do with the mitigation of the cause of the evil. No tendency grows out of these to check the course of the deleterious current—if anything, the contrary result would arise.

8. We approach next the fertile theme of the sense of Touch. The sensations of this sense that serve as antecedents in volition, are numerous, and of great practical moment. Some of them were adverted to under the general class of acute pains, but the consideration of these was not exhausted. The characteristic pleasure of touch has been seen to be soft and extended contact, as with the underclothing of the body, or the bed-clothes at night. The movements for bringing on the requisite contact, are the most elementary of any, the earliest to commence by spontaneity, and the most liable to be stirred up in the discharge of the daily store of gathered power. The swing of the limbs, arms, and trunk, is never neglected for a single day in the healthy state ; the central

## 328 GROWTH OF VOLUNTARY POWER.

power collected over night in a robust infant, would not find adequate vent if it had not an opening towards the larger masses of muscle, while the fresh condition of the nourished fibres of the muscles themselves, co-operates in promoting the play of the organs. Thus it is that the spontaneity of these parts is regular in its occurrence; the waking hours are never long without some manifestation of it. Consequently, when a feeling of an agreeable kind—such as a soft warm contact—is induced under some movement, it is not difficult to unite the two into a matured volition. The chances of a tolerably frequent concurrence, and the decided nature of the conscious result, are the two conditions that specially promote a speedy bond of association. The least favourable part of the case, perhaps, is the want of uniformity in the effect of the action, inasmuch as the same movement does not always induce it. The contact being sometimes on one side, and sometimes on another, we cannot associate it with any one motive impulse. We must, in fact, associate it with a great many, until such time as we learn to localize our sensations—that is, to connect each part of the surface of the body with the special movements that protrude or retract that particular part. Before this point is reached, we must resort to the never-failing resource of trial and error; one movement not succeeding is dropped, the one that does succeed is kept up.

Hitherto I have supposed that the warm contact is of something outward, implying definiteness of direction in order to retain, or work up to it; as when the infant closes upon the nurse, or upon its own wrappings—or as when the animal lies down on the soft grass, under a warm shelter, or by the warm bodies of its fellows. There is another mode of securing the same effect—namely, huddling the limbs and body close together. The result in this case being attained always in the same way, an alliance between the sensations and the appropriate motor impulses is probably matured in a short time. The young quadruped soon learns to seek warmth by crouching close upon the ground, taught by a very early experience. Later, the animal finds out the connexion between shelter and

## TRAINING OF THE WHIP.

physical comfort, but this is not obvious enough for the beginner left to itself.

9. The pungent and painful sensations of touch are those involved in the important department of the education of the whip. When we desire to control the movements of an animal, we apply external pain so long as a wrong movement goes on, and withhold the hand when all is correct. But for the fundamental link of the volitional nature, leading the sentient creature to desist from a present active exercise under pain, the whip would be utterly useless as an instrument of training. The animal knows nothing of the hidden purposes of its driver; all that is present to its mind is a series of acute smarts, and its own active energies for the time being. The soreness of the pain disturbs the flow of energy ; other impulses come from the irritated centres, and if under any of these the infliction ceases, that is retained in preference. If the cessation of the pain had no power to induce a continuance in one course rather than in another, the training of a young horse or a dog would be an impractibility. The animal would go on suffering, and perhaps increasing the violence of its spontaneous actions, but would not be deterred from any one course.

10. The training of the whip could not possibly commence at the moment of birth. A certain amount of voluntary development in other ways must be gone through in the first instance. We have reason to suppose that the forming of one volitional link renders it easier to fall into a second, although in a quite different region. The increasing facility may grow out of various circumstances, some of them to be afterwards dwelt upon ; but I apprehend that the mere experience in associating movements with feelings gives a growing distinctness to the act, and that the earliest are in every point of view the most difficult. Hence there is a certain cruelty in forcing on the discipline of a young animal too soon; not that we might not succeed in the attempt, but that the suffering imposed would necessarily be much greater. It is not usual to commence the discipline of children in the first year of

330 GROWTH OF VOLUNTARY POWER.

life, because of the obscurity that still shrouds the connexion of pain with actions, and because of the undeveloped state of the activities rendering it difficult to bring out the one that is sought. The first attempts at infant discipline are suppressive; and the case most commonly presented is intemperate crying and grief. This, however, is a very difficult thing to bring under check, involving as it does a great deal to be overcome. The control of the feelings generally is among the hardest of our voluntary acquisitions; and although in education it ought to be commenced as soon as at all practicable, we must not reckon it among the first or most elementary.

The training of a young animal affords an opportunity of estimating the time required to complete the associating bond between a sensation of pain and the movement that gives a deliverance. The educated horse quickens its pace at once to the touch of the whip or the spur, and checks it to the tightening of the bridle in the mouth. The application of these agents to the colt leads to no definite action. After much suffering, the animal connects in its mind certain movements with the pause of its tormentor; that is the first step. In another lesson, nearly the same course of various struggles is repeated, the desired action emerging at last, and, as in the former case, accompanied with a release from pain. The iteration of this coincidence produces by-and-bye a contiguous adhesion, and every day fewer struggles and errors precede the true impulse. At last, after a length of time and repetition, which might be exactly observed in every case, the two elements are so firmly associated, that the desired pace comes on at once with the sensation of the smart. Thus, one stage of the education of the animal is brought to perfection. Nevertheless, when doubts and ambiguities chance to arise, or when perverse inclination comes in as a disturbing power, it is always easy to fall back upon the primitive force of nature, and apply a persistent smart till the wrong course is desisted from, and a right one assumed. In the greatest maturity of the acquired volitions, the original tendency of a present pain to suppress a present movement, still remains to be

GUIDANCE OF SOUNDS.—SIGHTS. 331

appealed to, and, indeed, up to the last moment of life, is not to be dispensed with.

11. The illustrations from the sense of Hearing may be shortly indicated. As regards sounds painfully loud, harsh, or discordant, there is no obvious movement of protection that the infant creature can readily fall upon; and consequently no volitional alliance of this kind is to be counted among those that grow up in the first epoch. When the power of locomotion is matured, an animal runs away from a disagreeable sound, or is checked by chancing to run up to it. This implies the estimate of direction, which is formed after a certain experience of sounds. But should this not exist, the primordial law of volition will sustain the animal's career under the lessening sound, and restrain it when the pain is increasing. The same thing happens, with allowance for the difference, when a highly pleasurable sound falls on the ear. The listener is detained within reach of the influence, any impulse to move away is suppressed, and the attitude of intent repose, under which the maximum of delight is reaped, maintained by preference. Even the child acquires the power of becoming still to enjoy agreeable sounds, owing to the felt increase of pleasure thus accruing, and the felt diminution arising from restlessness.* I do not enter at present upon the large subject of the connexion between artificial sounds and our voluntary actions, as this implies other associations than those we are now adverting to.

12. The pleasures and pains of Sight fall into an early alliance with specific movements; the reason being that some of our primitive spontaneous impulses tell directly upon those sensations. When a cheerful light is before the eye, a privation is felt on its being moved to one side. The pleasure, however, can be secured by certain very easy movements, which pro-

---

* Apollonius Rhodius describes the Argonautic heroes listening to the harp and song of Orpheus: so strongly did they feel the charm of it that, even after he had finished, they continued immoveable, with heads stretched forward and ears pricked up, expecting more.—*Apollon. Rhod. Argonautica*, i. 516.

332    GROWTH OF VOLUNTARY POWER.

bably every infant performs many times in the course of each day, they being principal outlets of the active spontaneity. The rotation of the head seems to come as naturally as any movement that can be named ; and a chance concurrence of this with the withdrawal of the light would commence an intimacy between the two circumstances, with the usual consequences. Any one may observe that no such power as that of following a moving object exists during the first weeks of infancy ; but the conditions are favourable to the speedy acquisition of it. Both the rotation of the head, and the rolling of the eye-ball, may serve the purpose, and these impulses seem very frequent in the rounds of the cerebral discharge. Occasions of coincidence will therefore arise ; and in proportion as the sensation is intense, will be the influence that clenches the one that is appropriate. Hence a full-formed link grows up to connect different movements of the eyes and head with the directions of moving objects sought as pleasure; while a sensation of pain caused by any spectacle would suspend all such movements, and foster those in an opposite course. Here we have the commencement of voluntary observation, or attention. A further step is made when the adjustment to distance is successfully achieved. According to our general doctrine, the explanation of this would be sought in the spontaneity of the muscles that adjust the eye to distance, namely, the adductors, or external recti, and the internal ciliary muscles. I am not prepared to decide as to the time when this adjustment is finally completed. The adductor muscles have a separate nerve, and, doubtless, some corresponding distinctness of cerebral origin, and are, we may suppose, advantageously situated for an isolating impulse, so that the only thing wanting is an accidental conjunction with the increase of an agreeable, or the doing away with a disagreeable, sensation. Probably the defective part of the case is the rarity of any strongly-marked pleasure or pain, in the mere approach or recess of an object of sight. In the later stages the difference is more sensible, because of the meanings that the child puts upon the appearances ; and it is probably at that time, that the power of voluntary adjustment comes to be matured. The inferior animals have, in this instance, the superiority arising from their precocious locomotion, which gives them an independent measure of distance to compare with the visual changes of the images in the eye. But, as in all cases the great use of adjustment is to give the same distinctness of form through varying distances, there is nothing properly to call it into play, until characteristic form and precise lineaments have become matters of felt importance.

It matters not for the present purpose what is the precise kind of pleasure received, nor what the character of the object. Mere illumination, glaring colour, lustre, form, movement, or æsthetic combination—whatever is appreciated by the eye as delight, keeps up the gaze by virtue of that fundamental link that we are proceeding upon. Even in mature life we find this effect exemplified in the most primitive mode ; that is to say, a strong light, an agreeable spectacle, arrests the gaze by a direct agency, or without those intermediate steps of desire, intention, and conscious putting forth of energy, that we commonly look upon as essential parts of volition. We may often detect our eye drawn towards the light, or towards the interesting objects of the room, when we should say that no effort of will had been exerted ; the fact being, that volition in its most essential and fundamental character is at work. The primitive, and so to speak infantile, mode of the operation may be traced at all stages of life, although a more complex machinery becomes so far the rule, as to be considered the typical case of voluntary exertion. But the attraction of the child towards the light of the candle, or the window, and the still more overwhelming and fatal course of the moth towards the flame, are really and truly volitional impulses, springing from the same original source as the most elaborate determinations of full-grown humanity.

13. So much for the examples that may be culled from the senses, to illustrate the early march of our voluntary education. In these we have anticipated the greater number of what are termed the Appetites, which are, for the most part,

334 GROWTH OF VOLUNTARY POWER.

a small select class of our sensations. I have alluded to Exercise, Repose, Thirst, and Hunger. Sleep is powerful as a motive influence, but considered as a craving, the provision for gratifying it is contained in the system itself. We do not need, properly speaking, to put forth any effort to satisfy this uneasiness, and therefore we have nothing to learn. This remark must of course be qualified for the advanced stages of life, when we require to make certain preparations for going to sleep; but for the period when voluntary acts are first entered upon, no qualification is needed. The remaining appetite, Sex, would constitute an apposite instance, if studied in the animal tribes. The means of gratifying this appetite are not instinctively known, so far as we are able to judge; and therefore a process of groping must precede the mature faculty. The attempt not being entered upon until the animal is in every other respect master of its movements, the difficulty is lessened to a very great degree, but for which one does not see how such an act could ever be hit upon by the generality of creatures. The remarkable intensity of the resulting feeling easily explains the persistence, when once initiation has taken place. (Appendix, C.)

14. As regards the various Emotions treated of in the first half of the present volume, not much need be said in continuation of the theme now in hand; they do not essentially differ in their operation from the sensations of the senses. A pleasurable emotion prompts the continuance of any active impulse that contributes to maintain or increase it, and brings out into full operation such acts as have become associated with it in the accomplishment of those ends. Not many of the special emotions fall to be associated with actions put forth during the initial struggles of the voluntary career. The pain of Restraint and the pleasure of Liberty are felt from an early stage, and are connected with specific muscular discharges; of which one great characteristic is the vehemence that bursts through obstacles. The Tender Emotion is a pleasure of infancy, and is gratified by the loving embrace, which soon, and easily, becomes connected with it. Self-

INTERMEDIATE ACTIONS. 335

complacency, Pride, Power, Anger, are too late in their development to illustrate the initial stages of the will.

15. *Intermediate Actions and Associated Ends.*—In the complete development of voluntary power, the ends in view are often means to farther ends, and the pursuit of the one is sustained by the impulse derived from the other. Even at the early stage now under review, something of this kind begins to appear. When, along with a sensation of pain or pleasure, there is some accompanying object to arrest the attention, that object is linked in the mind with the strong emotion, and acquires the same kind of influence. The connexion between a burn and the sight of a flame may be fixed at a very early date in the mind of the infant, or the young animal; so that the near approach of the flame shall inspire the activity in the same way as the present pain. There is here implied, no doubt, a certain advance beyond the very initial state of the mind. Some progress in intellectuality has occurred to modify the constituents of volition. We suppose a certain persistence of the pleasurable, or painful, feeling, and likewise of other sensible impressions, such as those of sight; and we suppose the ideal fixity and efficacy of these to be so far confirmed as to operate like the reality. Such unquestionably is the case. While those various trials are going on, whereby voluntary power is working its way through difficulties, the impressions of objects of sense are acquiring persistence by iteration, and the life in ideas is entered upon. One notable circumstance in the ideal life is this association of marked pains and pleasures, with their habitual accompaniments, and the adoption of these accompaniments as volitional ends, in avoiding the first and securing the second. We have remarked how speedily an enduring bond may grow up under the excitement of strong pain; and examples of the kind are frequently to be noted in the experience of the young. Very often an irrelevant thing is fixed upon, merely because of its presence at the time, there being no means of establishing the real cause in the midst of the various accompaniments. Repetition, however, or uniform

336 GROWTH OF VOLUNTARY POWER.

agreement, does attest the true cause; and when an object has many times kept company with a strong feeling, there is a presumption in favour of necessary connexion, as well as an adhesive link in the mind between the two. Thus, to take again some of the primitive and perennial sensations, the child associates the agreeable state of warmth with the fire, its clothing, the bath, or other collaterals; and its movements are determined in the direction of these various objects. The sight of the breast becomes a formed image, in firm alliance with the feeling of nourishment, and a volitional tie is constituted, by the usual means, between this and the movements for approaching it. It is a work of time to attain characteristic and abiding images of outward things, even by the most intellectual of our senses; not weeks, but months, must be allowed for such a result. The accomplishment, however, gives an enlarged scope to the schooling of the will; not only are new ends aimed at, but also new means are found for compassing the great primary aims of retaining pleasure, and warding off pain. The all-important sensations of satisfying hunger are seen to connect themselves with many various objects and arrangements. Not merely the sight of the breast to the infant, but the face and figure of the mother, and her various actions in giving suck, are a part of the association. Somewhat later the appearance of the other kinds of food administered, the dishes and different preparations, are firmly associated with the alimentary feelings. The voluntary activity of the child, or the animal, now addresses itself to some of those intermediate effects that hold the principal in train. The opening of the mouth to receive the morsel is an act of the intermediate character, implying a step of association between the main effect and one that has been found subsidiary to it. Still more advanced is the effort of seizing a morsel in the hand to convey it to the mouth. Much must be gone through before so complex a succession can be formed into a chain. The simple arrangement, under which the sensation itself tells immediately upon the one movement that enhances or abates it, has given way to a complication. A secondary

## ASSOCIATED ENDS.

feeling of an indifferent nature has become an end, and an action remote in its influence, is the machinery made use of. What now rules the volition is the sight of a moving thing approaching the mouth; the impulse that determines this approach is sustained by virtue of the fundamental link so often signalized in this discussion, and an impulse in any other direction is arrested or paralyzed. This is an entirely new case, but the operating principle is still the same. The progress of the morsel of food, in the direction of the mouth, is to all intents a pleasure, kindling a bright expression, and sustaining whatever movements favour it. It is, so to speak, a factitious, artificial, derived, associated pleasure; and involves to the full the power of voluntary stimulation. Innumerable pleasures of this sort enter into the life of the full-grown creature, whether man or brute; the pursuit is as fervent, and the energy of the volitional spur as sure, as when an original sensation fires up a movement directly increasing or diminishing it. The movement of the child's hand towards the mouth is sustained by the same inward power that keeps up the process of sucking, or masticating, under the immediate sense of pleasure.

16. The illustration from the associates of food is forcibly presented by the lower animals. As soon as their sensible impressions are so far matured, as to connect the enjoyment of eating with the visible appearance of the food at a distance, or with the smell or touch of it, such a sensation becomes an intermediate end to inspire the pursuit. The power of locomotion possessed by the animal, and at first employed spontaneously, and at random, is found by experience to bring on the encounter with articles of food; and the animal, by understanding the signs that betoken the approach towards the grateful object, is prompted to the corresponding exertion. This implies the attainment of what we term the acquired perceptions of sight, or a class of associations between the locomotive or other movements, and the changing forms and aspects of external things as seen by the eye; which is one part of the education of every animal, and when accom-

Y

338 GROWTH OF VOLUNTARY POWER.

plished opens a new scope for active pursuit. The beast of prey, after a certain time, not merely knows the appearance, to the eye, of the animal that satiates hunger when got in the mouth, but also appreciates the signs of nearing that consummation. The signs are a genuine pleasure, and as such maintain the requisite activity,—the full chase, or the sly concealment while the victim is coming up,—and put an arrest upon whatever is alien to them. This is true volition, somewhat transformed from the initial aspect by the intervention of intellectual processes and acquirements; and everything said of the early stage applies also to the advanced stage. Spontaneous movements are felt to concur in heightening one of these derived pleasures, or abating a derived pain; in the one case the action is kept up, in the other it dies away. Repetition confirms into a plastic bond the union of a feeling with the appropriate action, and the issue is a full-grown volition. The animal, seeing its distant prey, falls at once into the career of forward locomotion, which most certainly it would not do until after a due course of chance coincidences, firmly held by the volitional pincers, and made to adhere through the great plastic force at the bottom of all our education. It happens, moreover, that at the epoch of those acquired perceptions, and permanent imagery of outward things, the voluntary powers have also made great strides in advance; and the struggles and uncertainties characterizing them at the outset are not any longer seen in prominence. But at no time does the primitive force cease its operation. Every random procedure, arrested by failure and sustained by success, shows the principle in its living efficacy.

# CHAPTER III.

## GROWTH OF VOLUNTARY POWER.—*(Continued.)*

1. WE have now to pursue the farther development of the will up to the perfect command of every voluntary organ. The greatest difficulty is the commencement; a very few acquisitions once secured become a basis of operations for succeeding strides, and the progress assumes an accelerated pace.

Allusion has already been made to the transferring of a movement, established in one connexion, to other connexions and uses. Any constituted bond between an act and a feeling, brings that act more frequently into play than if it were left to mere spontaneity, and thus adds to the chances of new alliances. The same movement may happen to answer several emergencies, and introductions being once effected, no matter how, the groundwork of future unions is laid. The motions of the head and trunk, at first purely spontaneous, bring about agreeable effects of warmth, &c., and are very soon associated with those sensations so as to be called out at their instigation. On such occasions, other effects are discovered attending them, as, for example, the exposure to light; and they are now therefore espoused by a new influence, which in time commands them exactly as the first did. The self-conserving tendency is always ready to catch at the coincidence of an active impulse with a heightened pleasure or abated pain; and the probabilities of such coincidences are increased as the various movements are more frequently led out. Take the fertile theme of animal locomotion. This power is at first purely spontaneous, but certain particular modes of it soon form links of attachment with the animal's sensations; these

340 GROWTH OF VOLUNTARY POWER.

modes are then longer sustained and oftener evoked than if there were nothing but spontaneity in the case. The accidents of further connexions are thus greatly extended, just as a more abundant stream of the unprompted cerebral discharge would enlarge the openings for acquisition. I have formerly remarked that great natural activity is singularly favourable to the growth of associated actions, from the number of trials that are made in consequence. Without the primordial instinct that sustains and reproduces what chimes in with a present pleasure or present relief from pain, these trials would end in nothing; but with this, they are in the highest degree fruitful in those special connexions that make up our voluntary power. An action, like the case of locomotion now supposed, from the first highly spontaneous, becomes rapidly associated with a number of sensations, and rendered open to various solicitations which can never be far off. In any difficulty, it will start up to be tried, and whatever use can be served by it, is not likely to be long ungratified. The child soon possesses a number of those actions, the recurrence of which is made more frequent by association with its various feelings. Such parts as the hand, the tongue, the mouth, the jaw—the play of the head, trunk, and limbs—having attained that partial degree of voluntary control constituted by special alliances, are so much the more open to an extension of the same process. Every active organ goes on in this way enlarging its bonds of attachment to states of pain or pleasure, so as to wake up at their instigation, and becomes thus an instrument of free-will to the extent that this detailed acquisition has been carried. Such instances of subjection to separate feelings might be so multiplied as to answer every end of the animal's existence; and the education of the will would then be practically complete. But, in human beings especially, the control of the will becomes, so to speak, generalized by a series of acquirements, different from those hitherto described, to supply the special wants of the living system. This general control has now to be traced to its component elements.

ACTING TO THE WORD OF COMMAND. 341

2. I commence with the Word of Command, since that applies to the guidance of animals as well as men. This is a step removed from the discipline of the whip, which, however, serves as a starting-point in the acquisition. A certain sound falling on the ear of the animal may be in itself so painful, as to spur its movements; whether this be true of the crack of the French postilion's whip, I am unable to say. The harsh, abrupt, and stunning sounds of the human voice are probably painful to the ear of an animal under training, and therefore serve the same end as the smarting of the skin. But the mediation of the whip enables us to associate sounds quite indifferent in themselves, with the actions that we desire to bring about. The animal soon learns to connect each utterance with the movement intended by it, being stimulated to that movement by the accompanying application of an acute smart. Thus the horse is taught to advance, or to halt, to deviate right or left, to quicken or slacken its pace, at the instance of the rider's language of command. Initiated in this vocabulary by the schooling of pain, a process of association gives to the mere sound all the force of the inflicted suffering. Any defect in the goodness of the bond is at all times open to be supplied by reverting to the original instrumentality, which the best education may not wholly supersede. By a careful process of training, a very great number of those connexions between language and movements can be established in the minds of the more docile species. The course of proceeding is the same for all; but the difference of susceptibility to such training between individuals is wide. The explanation is essentially what would be given for human beings, as already dwelt upon under the Law of Contiguity. A good ear for the characteristic tones and articulations made use of, so as unequivocally to discriminate each from all the rest, is one requisite. Without such discrimination, no acquisition of the kind is at all possible; and probably some animals may be wanting in this respect, while many evidently labour under no such deficiency. The other condition is the purely intellectual one of adhesive growth after a certain

342 GROWTH OF VOLUNTARY POWER.

frequency of coincidence, a property belonging in various degrees to the animal organization generally. Granting these two elements, instruction in answering to the word of command may be carried to any length. In the human subject, a very large number of such connexions are formed ; the discrimination of vocal sounds by the ear, being probably superior to what belongs to the most highly endowed of the brutes, while the rapidity of acquisition is also great. The earliest instances of this department of training show all the peculiarities of commencing volition. If we want to associate in the infant mind a movement with a sound, we must wait the opportunity for the spontaneous occurrence of the movement, and then endeavour to provoke its continuance. Thus, if we sought to make the opening of the mouth amenable to command at a very early period, we should have to use a method similar to that for the lower animals, and by a discipline of pain establish a union between the action and the command. With children, the tones and gestures accompanying the first attempts to influence them by language, are like the whip to the young horse ; they paralyse the actions going on at the time, and encourage any movement that makes the torment to cease. Accordingly, the infant, hard pressed in this way, would suppress by turns the various movements under which the urgency was unabated, and abide by the one that brought a sensible relief. The same crudeness of perception and inextricable perplexity that cloud the initial step everywhere, are here observable ; but after a little time things become clearer. When once the child has distinctly connected the action intended with the audible sound and the accompanying tones of painful urgency, a beginning is made, and a permanent alliance will in due time ensue. All that there is to guide it at the outset are the harsh and painful tones that fall on the ear while in the wrong course, and the soft and placid enunciation of the same command when the right course is fallen upon. It is this difference solely that constitutes the determining motive power in the case ; and just as it is felt, so will be the hopes of the experiment. Accordingly, when the child has made some

## MULTIPLICITY OF ASSOCIATIONS IN THE WILL. 343

advance in appreciating the distinction of the two modes of address, and has a decided sensation of pain from the one, and of pleasure from the other—a sensation that is enhanced by various associations—we are able to proceed rapidly with this part of the voluntary education. The infant of a few months can be made to do many simple actions at command, to open and close the mouth, to keep its hands out of the way while fed, to stand erect, and so on. Movements that have as yet formed no other link whereby to instigate them, are made amenable to audible direction, which is therefore to be reckoned as one important species of the antecedents for evoking the energies of the will. Very often it may happen that an infant, or an animal, fails to perform movements in obedience to urgent necessities, while these will spring up at once if the accustomed direction falls upon the ear; the association in the one case by no means implying the other. The voice of one person exercises an influence which the same words uttered by another voice would not possess. The will is a machinery of detail; the learning of a foreign tongue is not more a matter of multiplied and separate acquisitions. The fancied unity of the voluntary power, suggested by the appearance assumed by it in mature life, when we seem able to set a-going any action on the slightest wish, is the culmination of a vast range of detailed associations whose history has been lost sight of, or forgotten. This subjection of the various members of the body to vocal direction has been achieved step by step, through a long series of struggles and laborious iterations, which all disappear from the view when we are practising upon full-grown humanity. Yet there are not wanting instances to show how essentially the whole is an affair of acquisition. We see on the parade ground that the soldier has to learn additional signs of command; that is, to associate his movements with new language, and with the trumpet note, as well as with the human voice.

3. The next great stride in voluntary power is achieved through the acquired faculty of Imitation. I have formerly (*Contiguity*, § 52) adduced arguments in refutation of the

**344** GROWTH OF VOLUNTARY POWER.

supposed instinctive origin of this faculty; and in so doing, have briefly illustrated the gradual formation of it, through a series of struggles such as attend every voluntary commencement. Imitation implies the establishment of a bond of connexion between the appearance presented by a movement as executed by another person, and an impulse to move the same organ in ourselves. This is so far as regards the action of the limbs, trunk, head, mouth, eyes, and features; for the case of vocal imitation, the alliance is between a sound on the ear, and an impulse directed to the mechanism of speech. There is no better example for setting forth the process of voluntary acquirement than is afforded by the beginnings of the imitative faculty. If we make observations upon the first efforts to speak, we shall find that the course so often described above is the one invariably followed. Spontaneous articulation takes the lead; but a sound once uttered impresses the ear as an effect, and if that is a pleasing one, the vocal stimulus is likely to be sustained. A few repetitions cause an adhesive association to grow up between those two elements, so that the order may at last be inverted, and the hearing of the sound provoke the utterance. This would be the course pursued if the child were left to itself; but a forcing process is usually brought to bear in order to quicken the acquisition. The method already described, for teaching subjection to the language of command, is made use of to promote imitation. The child is made to hear certain sounds with those tones of urgency that have the effect of pain in stimulating active exertion. Such attempts are usually begun so prematurely as to be for a long time fruitless. The utter want of a specific connexion, between sounds heard and movements of the larynx, renders the lessons entirely abortive. If, however, the proper sound should chance to come out, the stream of nervous power flowing in that direction may be kept up, and a certain advance made in associating it with the audible effect. Two or three favourable accidents of this kind make the two elements that have to be conjoined less strange to each other. It is not then such a hopeless business,

IMITATION. 345

to force on the right direction of cerebral power, by the urgent presentation of the sound desired. We may still fail in the attempt, but the chances of success are increasing. Every occasion that brings the active utterance and the distinct perception of the sound in company, in the mind disengaged by good fortune for the purpose, is a moment favourable to the work of adhesion; and a limited number of those occasions renders the adhesiveness complete. The first articulations that the child is able to command so as to produce them imitatively, are some of the simpler class, or those that the little range of the organs can readily give birth to. Such sounds as *bah, tah, nah,* arising out of easy situations of the tongue and mouth, are the initial efforts of speech. A great deal of spontaneous play of those very mobile members must precede even this elementary stage; and we find that it is towards the end of the first year that the preliminary spontaneities usually break out. There is no fixed order in the manifestation of those simple articulations; the labials (involving *b* or *p*), and the dentals (involving *d, t,* or *n*), seem about equally accessible to the dawning aptitudes. The gutturals (*r, g*) are, on the whole, perhaps, more difficult and later, but often very little so. The material fact, however, for our present purpose is that the utterance in every case must first come by nature, in order to be coupled with its effect on the mind, and so furnish a handle for being imitatively reproduced. I know no case better adapted for proving, or disproving, the theory herein maintained respecting the will than these vocal acquisitions. They are particularly open to inspection; no part of the process is shrouded in the recesses of the child's own consciousness. The epoch of their occurrence is neither too early nor too late. The primitive germ of volition is still in sufficient purity to manifest its true character. All the circumstances concerned in the establishment of a link of voluntary control are apparent to the view—the spontaneous commencement, the repetitions made each time with less difficulty through a growing attachment, and the link finally become complete. It can be seen whether the

346 GROWTH OF VOLUNTARY POWER.

interval elapsing between the first random utterance, and the imitative facility consummated, is such as would be necessary for the growth of an adhesive association according to the usual rate of such growth. A series of observations carefully conducted, in a variety of individual cases, might settle beyond the possibility of dispute the actual order and genesis of our voluntary energies. The first utterances are necessarily the best for the purpose in view; but every new advance must needs repose upon the same original principle, slightly modified by the antecedent acquisitions. The modifying circumstance consists in this, that after the child has learned to bring forth a variety of vocal utterances on the instigation of the audible sound, there will be a tendency to make some *vocal* exertion when new articulations are urged home, whereas at the outset the connexion between hearing and voice was utterly void. It is something to have gained a few threads of union between the two regions. A road to the stimulation of the voice is thus established, and it becomes so much the easier to rouse it into exercise. We therefore can expect to bring about new sounds to make trial of, with greater readiness, and with less waiting upon fortuitous spontaneities. The circle of wide possibility is narrowed, when we can get the activity to flow to the proper organ instead of running indeterminately over the system. Still, allowing for this advantage, the process described for each additional acquirement is the same. We cannot force on the exact utterance by never so much importunity; we can only clutch the occasion of its spontaneous rise, and drive home the associating nail. We may keep up the stimulation of the voice for this end, but we have no means of ordaining the exact movement to arise in preference to others. Continuing the observations over the whole alphabet of sounds, and into the union of syllables to form names of increasing complexity, and watching the progress of catching accent, or brogue, we shall find a uniform result, with mere variations of circumstance. After a time, the child takes the work of imitation into its own hands, adapting its own movements to chime in with those about it. This is peculiarly the case with accent, which is never taught by express lesson, as the alphabetic utterances are taught. The child in articulating necessarily used some modulation; at the same time the ear is impressed and occupied with the particular mode of those around. There is a certain satisfaction in falling in with this strain to which the ear is so strongly tuned, and a certain pain of discord in the contrary case. The tendency, therefore, is to abide by each intonation that chimes with the model strain; and it is surprising to notice how sure and steady the course of approximation is, through this single instrumentality of holding fast by every accidental coincidence.

The case of learning to sing offers no peculiarities to reward our dwelling upon it. The first imitation of notes musically pitched can be nothing but tentative. A good ear knows when the sound uttered agrees with the sound heard, and the volitional stimulus sustains the exact vocal impulse of that moment; association sets in, and ultimately unites the two mental elements—the sensory and the active, and the imitation can in future be struck at once. Prior to this final stage, trial and error must be resorted to; the sense of discord represses the wrong vocalization, the sense of unison fosters and maintains the right one.

4. The imitation of Movements at sight includes a large part of our early voluntary education. The process is still the same. The child moves its arms, hands, and fingers by natural spontaneity, and sees the appearance of them so moved. Such appearances have a distinct recollection or image on the mind, and are a part of the store of intellectual impressions, persisting and recoverable as ideas. Among a variety of other uses, these ideas become ultimately the handle for rendering the actions themselves amenable to voluntary control. Seeing the movements executed by those around it, the child discerns when they coincide with its own, and if any pleasure happens to attend this coincidence, or any relief from pain, there is a motive for continuing the

348 GROWTH OF VOLUNTARY POWER.

proper act, and refraining from the rest. Thus in the case of bringing the two hands together, as for holding something between them, it is very easy to perceive when the effect is produced; and if a pleasure arises in consequence, or a pain is arrested, the posture once hit upon is adhered to as a matter of course. All the movements of the arms are so broadly apparent to the eye, that after a few months' development of the senses, and their intellectual concepts, there is a good foundation laid for imitational progress in this department. The forcing system may also be resorted to with advantage. The imitative Will cannot work without an appropriate stimulus; either some pleasure must result from bringing about an identity with the model, or some pain be got rid of. If we can bring to bear one or other of those motive causes, we shall soon attain the desired end. Let there be a well-marked gratification attending the lifting of the arm, the closing of the hand, the joining of the two hands, and this, although not at the outset sufficient to bring on the movement, will keep it going if once commenced. Imitation for its own sake is barren to the infant mind; some palpable effect must come of it in order to create a stimulus. When the child sees another person doing something very startling and piquant, the pleasure of doing the same is so strong as to be an active spur to its own exertions; and if imitation is the medium, there will be a motive to resort to it. The early efforts of copying usually have reference to some agreeable effect seen to arise from a particular action. Putting a ball in motion, producing a sound, tampering with a flame, getting something to the mouth, are examples of these promptings. We can never evade the necessity of a spontaneous beginning; and we can always calculate upon the tendency to abide by the true impulse anyhow induced.

5. In those imitations, and in voluntary actions generally, it is not merely a proper direction given to an organ that we want; there must likewise be a certain strength of impetus. Sometimes a gentle discharge of power is needed, at other times a vehement impulse is called for. This does not alter

GRADUATION OF FORCE. 349

the nature of the case, or the steps of the acquirement. We must wait for the moment of a strong impulse happening spontaneously, and keep up that degree of energy by the sustaining nexus of volition, just as we must keep up the stream in the right direction. We attain a command of graduated emphasis exactly as of the right muscles to be moved. The sense of effect is ever at hand, as the corrective of the still imperfect learner ; and when the *degree* is wrongly pitched, the present impulse is made to give place to some other, until the urgency of the moment is finally satisfied.

We have seen in the first chapter what provision there is for vehement or intense discharges of volitional energy. The natural vigour of the constitution generally, the tendency of nervous power to flow strongly towards the active organs, the various causes of temporary increase of the discharge—such as pleasure, the irritation of pain, fright, thwarting, and other stimulants—are sufficient to account for those sudden and explosive bursts needed in great emergencies. In some constitutions there is a too great proneness to excesses of the volitional discharge, while in others of lethargic mould it is not easy to procure an energetic burst. These very intense efforts are, for the most part, less the result of any association than of the stimulation and excitement growing out of the circumstances of the moment. Education does not show itself so much in preparing for vehement exertions, as in giving a proper direction to the active impulses, and in graduating them for delicacy of execution. The fixing of the exact degree of power to be put forth at every stage of a work of skill, is one of the nice points of volitional acquirement. There is a certain primitive quality of the constitution favourable to such an acquirement ; at least such is the supposition that we must make to account for the great individual differences. Just as, in the organization of the senses, delicacy of organ implies susceptibility to minute shades of difference, so, in the putting forth of muscular power, there must be a similar appreciation of minute gradations of force. This constitutes dexterity and nicety of mechanical manipulation.

350 GROWTH OF VOLUNTARY POWER.

Where the original faculty exists, it is easy to comprehend the process of education, that being nothing more than the so often described routine of our volitional acquirements.

6. We might carry on the exposition of imitation into all the postures, gesticulations, and motions of the body at large. As regards the lower limbs and the trunk, there is no essential difference from the case already dwelt upon. The feet seem much less prepared originally for varied voluntary movements than the hands; their accomplishments are both more limited and more laborious, as we see in dancing. The difficulty of imitation is greatest of all in those parts not within the sweep of the eye, as the head and features. Some other medium of discerning the movements must be had recourse to in these parts. A mirror is one way of overcoming the difficulty. Another way is to have some one always at hand to say when the proper movement is hit upon. One of the best examples of the employment of an artificial medium of guidance, is the teaching of the deaf to speak. They being themselves incapable of knowing when their vocal efforts correspond with the alphabetic sounds, as heard and pronounced, it is necessary to indicate by some other plan that they are right or wrong. Suppose a deaf man taught a visible alphabet by the usual methods employed for the deaf; the next thing is to make him articulate something, and should this coincide exactly with any alphabetic sound, he is directed to keep it up, and repeat it, being made aware at the same time which letter he has articulated. An association thus grows up between the various utterances, and the characters as they appear to the eye. With a sufficient amount of pains, the deaf might be initiated into habits of the most accurate pronunciation, and even into a melodious cadence; the only thing wanted is incessant watching, with a view to keep them right when they are so, and check them when otherwise. No doubt this would be a heavy trial of patience both to the subject and to the tutor, but it is nevertheless within the range of possibility.

Enough has probably now been said on the subject of imi-

ACTING TO A WISH TO MOVE A PART. 351

tation, so important as one of the foundations of that *general* command of the organs implied in the full-grown will of the individual. In all those cases where no link is established between our specific pleasures and pains, and the actions bearing upon them, another person steps in and displays the requisite movements to the imitative perception. We are thus saved from laborious experiments of our own, which after all might end in nothing. The inferior animals are at a great disadvantage in being so little imitative; yet they are not wholly devoid of the power. The gregarious nature is a mode of it; and in most tribes the young pick up many of their ways from the old. A well-formed group of imitative associations renders every action possible, that any one individual can exhibit to the observation of others.

7. I must now advert to a still farther advance in the department of general command, namely, the power of acting in answer to a *wish* to have a certain organ moved in a definite way, as when I will to raise my hand, to stand up, to open my mouth, and so on. This case reaches to the summit of voluntary control; it may, however, be pronounced only one degree in advance of the foregoing. Instead of an actual movement seen, we have for the guiding antecedent a movement conceived, or in idea. The association now passes to those ideal notions that we are able to form of our various actions, and connects them with the actions themselves. All that is then necessary is a determining motive, putting the action in request. Some pleasure or pain, near or remote, is essential to every volitional effort, or every change from quiescence to movement, or from one movement to another. We feel, for example, a painful state of the digestive system, with the consequent volitional urgency to allay it; experience direction, and imitation, have connected in our minds all the intermediate steps, and so the train of movements is set on. On the table before me I see a glass of liquid; the infant never so thirsty could not make the movement for bringing it to the mouth. But in the maturity of the will, a link is formed between the appreciated distance and direction of the

## GROWTH OF VOLUNTARY POWER.

glass, and the movement of the arm up to that point; and under the stimulus of pain, or of expected pleasure, the movement is executed. The mind is largely filled with associations of this nature, connecting every conceivable motion or position of all the organs with the precise impulse of realizing them, provided only that the proper instigator of the will is present. It takes a long time to perfect such a multifarious acquisition as this, and there is only one road and one set of means. With every action performed by the hands, arms, or other visible parts, there is an appearance to the eye, and also an appreciation to the muscular sensibility, and these become connected with the central impulse that gives the direction and degree proper for the performance of the act; and the result is, that a mere idea suffices for the guiding antecedent of the voluntary operations, if duly accompanied with the motive or prompting antecedent. What was an entire blank at the opening of the active career is now supplied; channels of communications are established where there existed only blind impulse.

8. From the fact that such is the character of the will in maturity, we are so familiar with it as to reckon it the typical form of the faculty. A somewhat fuller exposition will, therefore, not be superfluous. There is in it an element of conception, ideation, or intellectual retentiveness, whereby we store up impressions of the external positions of things, and of the movements of all the organs in every direction, extent, and degree. We have distinct recollections of the open hand, the closed hand, the spread fingers, the close fingers, the arms straight, the bendings at every angle; we can conceive movements slow, rapid, varying; we can further entertain the idea of much or little force expended. All these particulars, originally experienced only as present and actual, are in the end self-sustaining ideas or conceptions of the mind. I have no difficulty in recalling and retaining the entire image of a firm grasp of the hand, or of the swing of the foot in giving a kick. These are a part of our mental possessions, growing out of our unavoidable experience in life. We may not give much heed to them, but silently they play an indispensable part in our

## THE IDEA OF AN ACTION THE ANTECEDENT. 353

various operations. They enter into associations with the movements that they picture to the mind; and so firm and secure are these ties, that the ideal exertion can determine the occurrence of the real. The hand closed in vision can guide the nervous power into the channels necessary for closing it in reality. I have said that this is a *guiding* or determining association, because, in fact, we find that the proper stimulus of the will, namely, some variety of pleasure or pain, is needed to give the impetus. That primary constitution, so much insisted on, under which our activity is put in motion by our feelings, is still the same to the last. However well a connexion may be formed between the conceiving and the doing of an action, the intellectual link is not sufficient for causing the deed to arise at the beck of the idea (except in case of an ' idée fixe'); just as, in imitation, we do not necessarily fall in with everything that is done in our presence by others. Should any pleasure spring up, or be continued, by performing an action that we clearly conceive, the causation is then complete; both the directing and the moving powers are present. The idea of giving a kick, concurring with an obstacle at the foot, is enough to bring on the act, no counteracting motive existing.

I have formerly remarked, that among the earliest acquirements of the young quadruped, are the alliances between its locomotive movements and the appearances of things approaching to, or receding from, the eye. The enlarging picture is connected in the mind with approach, the diminishing with withdrawal. The human subject has to pass through the experience that leaves the same trace in the mind. This is one important accessory to the operation of the will, in the opposite circumstances of pursuit and flight. The motive element must be present; some pleasure or pain must have possession of the animal, urging a movement in correspondence. If the feeling be to get at some distant object of food, the guiding association is a forward pace; if to escape pain, there is a different course given to the impelling influence through the same experience, and the animal retreats. The

z

## 354 GROWTH OF VOLUNTARY POWER.

rapidity and sureness of the proper action look as if it were an instinct, but, after all, there is nothing but a secure association, the growth being very quick, although still traceable as a growth in the lower animals. Being one of their most interested acquisitions, concerned in their very strongest feelings, there is a great concentration of mind attending the lessons in it. Another case coming under locomotion is the leap over chasms or obstacles, which is also an acquired power, demanding an adhesion to be formed in the mind between the apparent width of the obstacle, and the energy thrown into the muscles that propel the body to a leap. The animal must grope its way to this power by many experiments, abiding by the successful, and shunning the other modes. The lamb, the puppy, the kitten, are at first incapable of such an effort. Their spontaneous impulses of locomotion lead them to make attempts at it, and any attempt causing a hurt is desisted from; after a number of trials and failures the proper adjustment is come to, and finally cemented.

9. The acquired actions of human beings are more various and complicated; for which reason, among others, man is a late learner. The moveable parts of our framework are greatly more numerous, and in the end more variously brought into play, so that the mere ideas that we have to form as the handmaids of the will range over a great compass. Moreover, it is to be noted that these intellectual accessories to volition are not confined to ideas of the appearances of the moving organs; the will to raise the arm is not necessarily led by the notion, or mental picture of a raised arm, although this is one way of inducing the act. We come to look at the effects produced on external things, and associate the appearance of those with the action that brings them on. Thus, to pluck a flower we have, as the intellectual antecedent, the idea of the flower held in the hand and moved away; there being at the same time a notion of power exerted in some definite muscles. We have now departed from the picture of the movements of the hand and arm, and fastened the mental tie between

the changes made on the thing to be operated on, and the operating action. So in driving a nail; although one may put forth this energy under the lead of the ideal motion of the arm and the hand, it is done in fact under the lead of the nail conceived as sinking in the wood at every stroke. In walking from one end of a street to the other, under some stimulus of feeling, the guiding antecedent is the picture of the street through the various phases encountered as we pass along it. This is the intellectual element of the volitional association, which, along with the prompting or motive, gives the power of effectively willing to go from one place to some other. Such is the general case in all our mechanical proceedings, being, in fact, the last stage of volitional acquirement. I have a motive for drawing a circle; after an educational career of many different steps, I find that the mental conception of the desired circle is associated in me with a series of movements and configurations of the hand and arm, and this makes up my ability to draw the figure, when instigated to do so by the motive of pleasure or pain I am under at the time. The sense of chillness urges me to some action for abating it; the instrumentality at the moment is to stir the fire; the intellectual antecedent, initiating the requisite movements, is the appearance of the fire now, coupled with the vision of a brighter blaze, and of the application of the poker. The substitution of these antecedents, for the picture of the play of the arm, is owing to the circumstance that the attention is fixed upon that point where we can judge of the effect produced. In lifting a window to admit the air, we have in the mind the size of opening to be made, which is sufficient to give the lead to the proper muscles, and impart the proper amount of impulse to each, subject to the correcting power inherent in the original organization of the will; which correcting power is always at hand to supply every deficiency in the volitional associations. The highly-trained workman, looking at the thing before him, has in his mind an association between the fracture he is to make and the precise impetus to be thrown into the muscles of the arm, and

356 GROWTH OF VOLUNTARY POWER.

at one blow he produces the exact effect. Another person, less developed in this particular department, does too little or too much; but, having in view the end, continues to operate until he sees it accomplished, falling back upon the primary and natural prompting of volition.

10. We might pursue the examples through the gratification of every sense, and the providing against every pain incident to human nature, but the principles involved would still be the same. We have to deal with pleasure and pain in the state of *idea* as well as actual. But it is a property of our intellectual nature, that for all purposes of action the remembrance, notion, or anticipation of a feeling, can operate in essentially the same way as the real presence. The bitter taste in the mouth inspires the efforts of riddance; the same thing foreseen in idea checks the movement that would bring it near. The child, enjoying the sugary savour, keeps it up by every means within the range of its volitional attainments; after the actual stimulation of the sense has completely subsided, the lively recollection may urge a fury of endeavour to revive the full enjoyment. As we make progress in years we have more and more the ideal presence of things that give us delight, or suffering: consequently our voluntary impulses come into a new service, without in any way altering their genuine character. Without some antecedent of pleasurable, or painful, feeling—actual or ideal, primary or derivative—the will cannot be stimulated. Through all the disguises that wrap up what we call motives, something of one or other of these two grand conditions can be detected. The only appearances of exception to this rule are those furnished by never-dying spontaneity on the one hand, and habits and fixed ideas on the other; but those do not affect the integrity of the principle contended for. I shall afterwards advert to their effect upon the proper course of the will. For the present, I hold it as a rule, beyond all dispute, that there is at the bottom of every genuine voluntary impulse, some one variety of the many forms wherein pain or pleasure takes possession of the conscious mind. Nor is there any intermediate machinery

## PLEASURE AND PAIN OPERATING IN IDEA. 357

between the one fact, the antecedent, and the other fact, the consequent—between a smart and an effort of extrication. Very often in our voluntary operations, we are conscious of an interval of suspense between the moment of painful urgency and the moment of appeasing execution, and in this interval we interpolate a number of impulses having various names— motive, desire, belief, permission, free agency, self-determining impulse, and so on—but these are artificial and accidental complications. Illustrations without number might be adduced to show the instantaneous operation of this causative link, if not interfered with; interference, however, is very frequent, and leads to an aspect of the problem demanding separate consideration. No physical law is more sure and decided in its operation than the checked movement inspired by sudden agony. No consideration, no intervention of the 'me,' no deliberation of free-agency, no passing of resolution through successive stages, is employed in the voluntary suspension that follows a smart. It is the primitive and perennial manifestation of our volitional nature, the unfailing bond between the susceptibilities and the concurring activity, that decides for us at that moment. Only when we have to overbear this native and firmly-rooted prompting, is the other machinery called for; showing that resistance is what introduces complication and suspense into the region of our voluntary determinations.

11. I shall cite a few examples from the Voice, before concluding the present chapter. We have already seen what the power of imitation implies, namely, the linking of a sound falling on the ear with the precise vocal impulse that reproduces it. In our further progress, however, we can dispense with the actual hearing of the note or articulation; we can summon up the vocal exertion at the lead of the mere idea or recollection of the sound. A still higher education connects the movements of the larynx with the sight of the musical stave, and the place of the note thereon. So with articulation. We pass from the state of imitating a present utterance to the reproducing of one remembered; the volitional associa-

358                 GROWTH OF VOLUNTARY POWER.

tions having taken another stride. Then comes the power of
pronouncing words through the sight of their visible characters, which power is merely a further stage of our volitional
acquirements. Usually the voluntary command of speech
may be said to consist in a series of associations, formed
between the words of our language in their ideal state, and the
actual enunciation. This ideal form may be either aural, or
vocal, or both ; that is to say, the notion of the name ' Sun '
may be the idea of the sound of it on the ear, or the idea of
its articulation by the voice, or of the sight of it on a printed
page. When we will to pronounce this word.there is already
present the idea of it in some of these shapes, and there being
a well-knit tie of contiguous adhesion between such notion or
idea and the select stream of cerebral power flowing to the
articulating members, all that is wanted is a motive urgency,
of the nature demanded by the will, in order to consummate
the act. When we have any pleasure to procure, or pain to
ward off by uttering this word, the train of intellectual connexion is so well laid as to bring on the result at once. This
is as regards the maturity of our education in speech ; for it is
easy to go a little way back, and come upon a time in our
individual history when this association was but half-formed,
or did not exist at all. The voluntary powers of speech go
out likewise in the direction above intimated regarding the
mechanical acts. Language being instrumental in guiding
our operations, we form connexions in our mind between
the various phases of an operation and the language of direction, approbation, or disapprobation. Without having before
us any notion of a word to be used. we give utterance to it
merely on the lead of some object that it refers to. We call
a work well or ill done, we give orders, ask questions, impart
information, through a direct link of connexion between the
subject matter and the vocal current. In this sense the work
of voluntary acquisition is advancing during the whole of
life ; every new active faculty that we take on is a branch of
the education of the will, which is homogeneous in its character throughout. We must have, in every case, the two

## VOLUNTARY ASSOCIATIONS IN SPEECH. 359

elements—a proper motive, and a channel of communication formed between the present notion and the desired action. The motive can never be anything but a modification of our pleasurable or painful sensibility ; the other element is the fruit of education. Every object that pleases, engages, charms, or fascinates the mind, whether present, prospective, or imagined, whether primitive or generated by association, is a power to urge us to act, an end of pursuit ; everything that gives pain, suffering, or by whatever name we choose to designate the bad side of our experience, is a motive agent in like manner. In a certain number of cases, experience has prepared within us the very sequence through which to secure our end ; in many other cases this is wanting. To the beginner the intellectual link is absent in every case ; education is constantly cementing the proper associations, which, however, by the very nature of things, are never all complete. The position of entire inability to attain our ends in securing pleasure and evading pain, leads us into a new region of mental deportment, which it also belongs to our subject to notice.

## CHAPTER IV.

### CONTROL OF FEELINGS AND THOUGHTS.

1. IN the development of the foregoing chapter we have seen volition crowned with powers of general command. The gradual subjection of the organs to intermediate ends, to language, to imitation, and to the preconceived notions of movements, and of the changes to be operated on outward things, completes the education of the will, and we seem then competent to anything ; or at all events there is nothing (within certain limits) that we may not be rendered capable of doing by instruction and direction from others. I may not be able to play on the German flute, but my mouth, my chest, and my fingers have become so far amenable to imitation and the word of command, that I can be put on a course of acquiring the power, without going through the full initial process of working my own way by trials and failures. Not that we can ever wholly dispense with the necessity for such corrections inherent in our constitution ; but by being able to follow the lead of another person, we approximate at once to the right action, and limit the range of tentatives or gropings. The associations that have enabled us to go so far, do not supersede the native stimulus of the will ; they are directive and not impulsive. They are ' reason the card,' not ' passion the gale.'

Much yet remains to be considered. We have never yet adverted to the obstructions that may be encountered by the volitional prompting; having all along assumed that if only the way has been prepared to the proper action, that action is certain to ensue. But various circumstances may occur to disappoint this expectation. The physical framework may be too much exhausted to make the effort. The organs may be

VOLUNTARY CONTROL LIMITED TO MUSCLES. 361

vehemently engaged in some other direction ; as when, under
a rapid walk, we are indisposed to stop and examine a wayside
object. Lastly, there may be some counter motive, whereby
a rival power is set up in the mind itself. All these cases
must be fully done justice to. I shall, however, in the present chapter, consider two applications of voluntary power
that present some peculiarities : I mean first the control of
, our emotions, and secondly, the command that we are able to
exercise over our intellectual trains.

### CONTROL OF THE FEELINGS.

2. It is a fact too common to be questioned, that we can
restrain and regulate the course of our feelings in many ways.
We can, under ordinary circumstances, arrest the diffusive
stimulation of the muscles, so as to put on a calm exterior
while a fire is raging within. This is the most simple and
direct mode of bringing the will to bear upon a state of mental
excitement. The muscular part of an emotional wave can be
met by a counter current proceeding to the same muscles.
The tossing up of the arms, and the stare of the eyes under a
surprise, can be prevented, if there be a sufficient motive to
remain still. The two forces being homogeneous, that is to
say, being both of them in the nature of stimulants to voluntary muscles, the one may overbear the other by the power
of the stronger. But when we pass to the other influences of
the emotional wave, namely, the effects upon involuntary
muscles, such as the heart and the fibres of the alimentary
canal, and those further effects upon the secretions and excre-
tions, the operation of the will is not so clear. In fact, the
question has to be fairly met, whether or not the will has any
power out of the circle of the recognised voluntary muscles.

The presumption from facts is all in favour of the one
view, namely, that our direct control is limited to those
muscles. Indirectly, other influences can be exerted, but it
seems quite possible to show that, in all such cases, the
muscles are the medium of operation. I shall have to advert

CONTROL OF FEELINGS AND THOUGHTS.

more particularly in the latter half of the chapter, in speaking of the voluntary control of the thoughts. At present it may suffice to remark, that various organic functions are so connected with muscular movements, that we can often stimulate or check them by means of those. Thus the evacuation of the lacrymal sac, of the bladder, &c., is under the influence of muscles. The involuntary action of sobbing, which the actor on the stage can command without any emotion corresponding, might be forced on by voluntary movements of the parts concerned ; although some of the movements are of muscles not voluntary. Where the connexion between an organic process and the voluntary organs is wanting, or very remote, as in the heart's action, the gastric secretion, &c., no voluntary power is possessed. Blushing cannot be induced or restrained by the will. From such natural connexions as those above noticed, and from others that grow up artificially, the range of voluntary control is extended a considerable way beyond its original sphere, and yet without disparagement to the view now insisted on as to the original limits of its sway. We hear of such extraordinary things as people simulating a swoon or an epileptic seizure, and of the still more singular power of some of the Hindoo Fakeers, who can induce the state of trance, and allow themselves to be buried in the earth for several weeks ; but still, in all probability, the medium of inducing so great changes in the organic conditions, is some mode of directing the voluntary organs.

3. As regards, then, the command of the emotional states, the one thing clearly practicable is to check or further all that part of the diffusive manifestation made up of the movements of voluntary organs. The play of the features, the vocal exclamations, the gesticulation of the arms, &c., come under the domain of our volition. By motives sufficiently powerful, a hilarious demonstration can be arrested, or, on the other hand, all the movements entering into it can be put on without the inward feeling. It is a point of considerable interest, both theoretical and practical, to determine how far the other constituents of a state of emotional excitement are allied with

## SUPPRESSION OF EMOTIONS. 363

the muscular diffusion, so as to take on a check when that is checked, or the contrary. The movements inspired are not the whole of the physical embodiment; there are organic effects in addition, and moreover there is the agitation of the whole nervous system leading to the outward display. This last circumstance is probably the most important. By an impulse of voluntary origin, the action of the various muscles may be suspended, but it does not follow that the nerve-currents of the emotional wave shall at once cease because the free course of them is obstructed. Experience alone can tell us what happens under those circumstances. We find that a feeble wave, the produce of a moderate or faint excitement, is suspended inwardly by being arrested outwardly; the currents of the brain, and the agitation of the centres, die away if the external vent is resisted at every point. I think this position will not be denied for the cases of comparatively feeble excitement. It is by such restraint that we are in the habit of suppressing pity, anger, fear, pride — on many trifling occasions. If so, it is a fact that the suppression of the actual movements has a tendency to suppress the nervous currents that incite them, so that the internal quiescence follows the external. The effect would not happen in any case, if there were not some dependence of the cerebral wave upon the free outward vent or manifestation. An opinion, however, prevails that for very intense excitement it is better, even with a view to the most rapid mode of suppression, to give free course for a time to the full external display. Under a shock of joy or grief, a burst of anger or fear, we are recommended to give way for a little to the torrent, as the safest way of making it subside. In so far as this view is correct, there is nothing more implied than the fact that an emotion may be too strong to be resisted, and we only waste our strength in the endeavour. If we are really able to check the stream, there is no more reason for refraining from the attempt than in the case of weaker feelings. And undoubtedly the *habitual* control of the emotions is not to be attained without a systematic restraint extended to weak and strong. It is a law of

**364**     CONTROL OF FEELINGS AND THOUGHTS.

our constitution that the inward wave tends to die away by being refused the outward vent; and with this the feeling itself disappears from the mind, if it be true, as I believe and have endeavoured to prove, that the diffused nerve-currents are indispensable to the mental or conscious element of the phenomenon. The exceptional cases do not invalidate the rule, they merely indicate some speciality of circumstance that needs to be allowed for. In the case of a great loss, or calamity of any kind, a certain free vent to the feelings is necessary, from the consideration that indulgence blunts our sensibility to the sting, so that we are able after a time to recur to the painful incident without a renewal of the distress in all its pristine severity. I will not undertake to say how far a system of restraint and suppression would be of use in such a state of things, because I cannot measure the exact range of the principle now alluded to. After great indulgence, pleasure loses its charm and pain its sting; excitement of every sort produces at last a dulness of the sensibility, from which consequences, favourable and unfavourable, ensue; and this would seem in some measure to justify a very free expression of sorrow under an irreparable calamity. Accordingly, we spread our lamentation for lost friends over a wide surface, by superadding the parapharnalia of mourning to the natural language suggested by the privation, and so at last the deadening process takes effect, and the loss can be thought of in greater calmness.

It would thus appear that the will, operating through its own proper instruments, the voluntary muscles, reaches the deep recesses of emotion, and by stilling the diffused wave, can silence the conscious state maintained by it. A resolute determination, that is to say, a powerful motive impulse, may trample out entirely a burst of pity, of anger, or of remorse; there being a proper allowance of time and perseverance. It will sometimes happen that the volition will break down before the work is accomplished, but I doubt whether anything is lost by the power actually expended.

By the very same interposition, we may summon up a

## SUMMONING UP DORMANT FEELINGS.

dormant feeling through a volitional determination. By acting out the external manifestations, we gradually infect the nerves leading to them, and finally waken up the diffusive current by a sort of induction *ab extra*. This is the result partly of an original tendency to draw out the nerve centres by commencing the movements, precisely analogous to the above-mentioned principle of restraining them, and partly, without doubt, of association, which brings into relation the external and internal still more closely. Thus it is that we are sometimes able to assume a cheerful tone of mind by forcing a hilarious expression. A few pages later, I shall have to advert to an equally, if not more, efficacious mode of evoking any given passion.

It is not, however, to be supposed that the personation of a feeling, as by a player on the stage, necessarily calls up the reality. Without doubt there is a certain tendency to do so, but various things may come between the outward manifestation and the mental state in accordance with it. The appearances put on for the sake of display, in the presence of other persons, are not precisely coincident with the genuine diffusive manifestation; they are rather adaptations to suit the eye of the spectator. In short, they are a sort of voluntary construction on the model of the natural display, with additions and suppressions in order to make a work of art. The mind of the actor is properly occupied with this end, and not with the assumption of the inward feeling in his own person. He may catch the infection, and come under the reality pourtrayed by him outwardly, and derive from this source suggestions as to the outward embodiment; but it is not absolutely requisite to do so.

4. Having made those preliminary observations as to the extent of the interference of the will, in submerging or evoking our various emotions, we must now attend to the usual mode of growth of this department of voluntary power. Were we to imagine a person attaining all the species of voluntary command indicated in the preceding chapter, merely by such experience as was therein implied, we could easily comprehend the appli-

## 366 CONTROL OF FEELINGS AND THOUGHTS.

cation of all those acquirements to the present case. The submission of the various muscular members to motives operating on the mind, might be easily extended to displays of feeling. The control arrived at over the features, the voice, the upper and lower extremities, and the rest, is available for any purpose of restraining or inducing action that can ever arise. The stare of astonishment might be quelled by a sufficiently strong impulse of pain or pleasure. Even the convulsive outburst of laughter could be held in check, by the command attained over the diaphragm and other voluntary muscles engaged. Usually, however, the control of the feelings is not postponed till the volition is fully educated in all other respects. We commence it when still labouring under the struggles of a yet unformed connexion between the promptings of pain and pleasure, and the executive machinery of the system. The infant has to be indoctrinated betimes into the suppression at least of violent emotion, and is fit to be disciplined to this when very few volitional links are as yet established. By a strong motive, brought to bear in the shape of pain or pleasure, impulses tending to neutralize the movements of a fit of crying may be encouraged and sustained till the end is accomplished. No doubt the case is one of a more serious difficulty than that assumed in the other commencing movements. Not merely are there wanted spontaneous impulses of the right sort, which have here also to be waited for in the round of chances, but an extraordinary degree of energy must be thrown into them to overcome the violence of the emotional wave. Severe practice must be had recourse to at this critical stage. Strong motives of pleasure on the one hand, and of pain on the other, must be plied to make the nascent powers of volition a match for the play of a strong emotion. Nevertheless it is quite possible to initiate the babe of ten or twelve months into the suppression of its noisy outbursts. In the second year, a very considerable process is attainable. The manner of proceeding is precisely that so oft described ; the difficulties are the same as regards the getting of the right impulse under

GROWTH OF COMMAND OF THE FEELINGS. 367

weigh; the method of keeping that impulse at work when once found is likewise the same, with the difference now specified. The treatment adapted for the young restive horse would apply to the beginnings of self-control in the infant. In proportion to the fury of the manifestations to be suppressed must be the spur applied to the germs of counteraction. The difficulties of the case are not to be concealed. That spontaneity, which we count upon for first bringing together in fitting conjunction a feeling and a movement, is favoured by the stillness of the system as regards strong emotion. Being the discharge of surplus power into the various active members, if the system is otherwise drawn upon, it is liable to subside; and without some extraordinary stimulation we cannot hope to call it adequately forth. Still the elements of success in this important endeavour, are within the compass of the organization even at a very early age, and, · as in the other departments of volition, the facility grows with time. If we disregard the suffering occasioned by forcing on the development of the link between a suppressive effort and a certain indication backed by pain, we may begin the discipline when we please. After a few abortive trials, the child will fall upon the connexion desired to be established, and will hold by it when driven by suffering and fear. What we want principally to act upon is the fury of the vocal outburst in a child, as being both an evil in itself, and the key of the entire manifestation. Accordingly we apply ourselves to the task of quelling the excitement at this point, and by concentrating the endeavours so, we can very soon establish a definite link of power with this special region. A certain number of repetitions will enable the child to connect the impulse of vocal suppression with the cessation of the painful urgency brought to bear upon it; and although it is a hard thing to convert a crude volition into a power able to compete with a violent wave of emotion, yet by the grand instrumentality of acute suffering, the will may be goaded into equality in the contest. The discipline may be commenced on an entirely independent footing, that is, without waiting for any other volitional acquisitions to found it upon.

**368**     CONTROL OF FEELINGS AND THOUGHTS.

Or we may delay it until a few links have been established, such as those beginnings in the subjection of the voice to external command made for other purposes. If we suppose the child already familiar with the direction to hush to silence, or if the channel has been formed between certain impressions made on the ear, and a stimulus to the voice, this medium can be had recourse to in reducing a fit of inordinate crying. The intellectual bond being prepared, we need only to supply the proper impulse of the will in sufficient intensity to meet the occasion. There is a certain pitch of pain that will do the work, if pleasure fails. When the child distinctly comprehends the meaning of the term ' silence,' or ' hush,' or ' hold your tongue,' this implies that the way has been laid open to the exact organs to be moved, that the random spontaneity has been reclaimed into a regular road. Then a sufficient degree of volitional prompting will give the needful power. The determination excited to escape from the smartings inflicted will raise a conflict with the fury of the emotion, and may at last gain the day. We cannot but feel a certain relenting pity, in urging the suppressive effort at the early stage of unformed alliance between our indications and the movement intended; when the child, so to speak, has no knowledge of what we require ; in other words, when no association has been formed for guiding the course of power into the true channel. We inspire struggles indeed, and energetic movements, but it may be long ere the fitting one is lighted on, and hence an interval of suffering to no purpose. Still, pain is a surprising quickener of the intellectual progress. The coincidence between the cessation of suffering, and the movement at that instant, will be an impressive one, and not many such coincidences will be wanted to complete the adhesion for the future. The first lessons in the control of the passionate outbursts are unavoidably severe. Every considerate person naturally tries to probe the reason of a child's giving way to a fit of grief ; but when the fury of the outburst is a greater evil than the pain that it helps to soothe, a determined suppression should be attempted. It is no doubt a part of the skill in the management of the young, corresponding to the arts of persuasion devised for grown-up men and women, to find the way to operate a diversion of mind from a ruinous course by the easiest possible means. We try first the whole round of motives on the pleasurable side; and among the pains we single out the smallest in the first instance, reserving the others as a last resource.

5. The overcoming of grief, anger, incontinent animal spirits, &c., continues to be a part of the discipline of self-control, and is carried on through the medium of the various motives available in each case. The intellectual bond for giving a right direction to the course of power is very soon completed, and there remains only the application of a volitional spur, strong enough for the emergency. One of the most common difficulties with children of a certain temperament is to restrain laughter; the outburst being made up of involuntary, as well as voluntary, movements, the control is but partial, and occasionally breaks down. The same may be said of a fit of sobbing, which is a mixture of convulsive spasms extending to parts that are not under the government of the will. There is a peculiar interest in studying this whole department of self-restraint from the circumstance that, under it, we can put in evidence the volitional power of the individual character. What is termed 'force of will' is very fairly brought to the test, by a regard to the greater or less facility in suppressing the outbursts of emotion. When one determination of a voluntary kind overbears another of the same kind, as when a man avoids luxurious living for the sake of health, we have no measure of the energy of the will as a whole, but merely a comparison of two species of motives. But when we array the volitional energy in general against the diffusive current of emotion, we obtain a relative measure of the two great departments of mind in their totality. If we find a person exceedingly deficient in the command of his feelings, being under all the ordinary motives that would inspire restraint, we must represent the fact by saying either

2 A

370　CONTROL OF FEELINGS AND THOUGHTS.

that the emotional wave is unusually vehement, or that the volitional link is naturally or habitually feeble. Supposing two individuals equally urged towards the manifestation of feeling, and prompted to repression by the same pain or the same pleasure, the one that succeeded in the work of control when the other failed, would be said to have the higher volitional endowment. A larger share of the cerebral power is shown to flow towards the region of will in the case supposed. The feeble will is one that needs to be worked upon by a more powerful motive ; a greater severity of pain, or a greater charm of pleasure, must be had recourse to. This is constantly seen in the government of children, in families and in schools, as well as over mankind at large. There is no fairer criterion to be had in this matter than the control of outward displays of feeling ; the only ambiguity attaching to the test is the unequal degrees of the natural diffusive energy of a wave of emotion. Some constitutions flow abundantly towards the diffusive and demonstrative part of our nature, while others predominate in the region of volition proper, whereby they are enabled to suppress the outbursts of feeling by a twofold advantage. A less ambiguous test of genuine volitional power would be to require both the suppression of a given outburst and the assumption of some other in a lively form. A will that can both put down and raise up lively displays of feeling is, undoubtedly, developed in an ascendant degree. If any one moved to intense sorrow, can put on the display of hilarious animal spirits, or, boiling inwardly with rage, maintain a bland and smiling demeanour, if a parent can show righteous indignation to a favourite child—there being at the same time no extraordinary spur in operation— we are bound to pronounce the power of will of a high order. In everyday life we look upon great self-command as regards temper, or any feeling that we know to be strong in an individual, as a test of volitional energy. We shall speedily remark how far this test may be improved by including the command of the thoughts. Instead of dividing volition against itself, as in the case of conflicting determinations, we bring it into

VOLITIONAL EXPRESSION OF THE FEELINGS. 371

collision with forces not at all voluntary, that is to say, with the energy put forth in the operations coming under the two other great divisions of the mind.

The habitual state of the emotional expression is a sort of balance between the diffusive force of the wave and the check of the will. The degree permitted to our various manifestations of pain, delight, sorrow, anger, fear, self-esteem, is governed by motives acting through the voluntary organs; hence, in grown human beings living under social usages, the actual display of a feeling is not to be taken as a measure of the genuine promptings of the occasion.

### THE MIXED EXPRESSION OF THE FEELINGS.

In considering the Expression of the Feelings (*Instincts,* § 13), I enumerated the organs of Expression, and adverted to the attitudes taken on by them under the opposite states of pleasure and pain. I showed that the fundamental law—of pleasure coinciding with heightened, and pain with lowered, vitality—would in a great measure account for the smile, the laugh, the shout, the frown, the sob, the wail. But the expression of the feelings in mature years is more various and complicated; we can then trace a number of attitudes resulting from *volition*, as distinguished from the emotional wave seen in its pristine purity in the infant displays. This is a case where the emotional and the volitional branches of the great first law of Self-Conservation, after growing for some time apart, unite to produce a complex result.

Among the expressive acts and attitudes springing out of volition proper, we may specify, in the first place, those of Self-Protection. An extreme instance is furnished by a combatant in the posture of defence; a posture very expressive, but wholly arising out of the operation of the will, under a particular end. In any apprehended danger, the attitude taken is such as to cover the parts likely to be injured; the hand is raised to protect the head; the body stoops or inclines to one side to be off the line of assault. The act of wincing

372 CONTROL OF FEELINGS AND THOUGHTS.

under an impending blow is of the same class, and it extends even to a remote or ideal danger ; we wince under disagreeable possibilities suddenly suggested, or even under the recollection of past incidents of a distressing kind. The expressive gesture of turning away the head is volitional in its origin ; it is a mode of getting out of the way of something that displeases us. Looking up to the roof is a variety of the same attempt to evade a disagreeable object. The gesture of loathing is chosen with a view to signify the act of repelling ; the head is turned away, and the hands held up in a propulsive attitude. To turn about restlessly from one side to another, to get up and walk to and fro, although to a spectator expressive of mental struggle—are still of the nature of voluntary acts. Drawi g down the eyebrows, to mitigate the glare of the light, is obviously voluntary. A bad odour, besides (emotionally) inducing a pained expression, (volitionally) promotes an attitude of mouth and nose calculated to close the ingress of the nostrils. The movements and attitudes in 'fidgets' are a mixture of the expression of discomfort, and of the actions stimulated by the will for procuring relief. The restlessness of children under constraint shows the expression of pain, and a variety of movements for venting the surplus energy within the narrow limits of the situation. The culprit slinking out of sight exhibits the collapse of a true emotional expression, coupled with an impetus of the will.

On the pleasurable side, we have the attitudes of beckoning, of stretching to, of aspiring after, of embracing—the object of delight ; all which are of the nature of volition.

### COMMAND OF THE THOUGHTS.

6. This is the place to handle more explicitly the topic already introduced under the Law of Compound Association (§ 13), namely, the instrumentality of the will in the current of thoughts or ideas. It is a fact that, by a voluntary endeavour, we can modify or divert the stream of images and recollections coming into the present view of the mind. While I am engaged in one pursuit, I find it possible to keep out irre-

## FIXING THE ATTENTION.

levant thoughts, although arising in the current of associations; my power in this respect is not unlimited, any more than my power of self-control in the suppression of feeling; but I do possess it in a certain measure—more, perhaps, than some men and less than others. I refer to a book on a particular subject —look up the table of contents or index; this starts me off in a great many different trains of intellectual reproduction, all which I refuse and suppress, except the one answering to my purpose or end at the time.

It was said in the place above quoted, that this influence, although genuine and decided, is still only indirect. What the will can do is to fix the Attention. As we can, under an adequate motive, observe one point in the scene before us, and neglect everything else; as we can single out one sound and be deaf to the general hum; as we can apply ourselves to the appreciation of one flavour in the midst of many; or be aware of a pressure on a particular part of the body to the neglect of the rest; so in mental attention, we can fix one idea firmly in the view, while others are coming and going unheeded. On the supposition, that the influence of the will is limited to the region of the voluntary muscles and parts in alliance therewith, something needs to be said in explanation of this apparent exception to the rule. It is not obvious at first sight that the retention of an *idea* in the mind is operated by voluntary muscles. Which movements are operating when I am cogitating on a circle, or recollecting St. Paul's? There can be no answer given to this, unless on the assumption that the mental, or revived, image occupies the same place in the brain and other parts of the system, as the original sensation did: a position supported by a number of reasons adduced in my former volume (*Contiguity*, § 10). Now, there being a muscular element in our sensations, especially of the higher senses, touch, hearing, and sight, this element must somehow or other have a place in the after remembrance or idea; otherwise, the ideal and the actual would be much more different than we find them. The ideal circle is a restoration of those currents that would prompt the sweep of the eye round a

374 CONTROL OF FEELINGS AND THOUGHTS.

real circle; the difference lies in the last stage, or in the stopping short of the actual movement performed by the organ. I know of no other distinction between the remembered and the original, except this stoppage or shortcoming of the current of nervous power, which is no doubt an important one in several respects, but still permitting the power of voluntary control. We can direct the currents necessary for keeping an imagined circle in the view, by the same kind of impetus as is required to look at a diagram in Euclid. Not that we should have had any title to say beforehand, that the volition could operate, as a matter of course, under the restriction now implied; but seeing that it is a fact, we treat it as of the same nature with the power of voluntary attention directed to present realities. This is not by any means an early or an easily-attained aptitude; but when the time arrives for possessing well-formed ideas of things, seen, heard, touched, &c., there is scope for the process of voluntary selection; a spontaneous power in the right direction manifests itself; and is held fast by the urgency of some present feeling. The infant at school can be trained to fix the volatile gaze upon the alphabet before it; a little later the master can compel an arrest of the thoughts upon a sum propounded as an exercise in mental arithmetic. The youthful mind, as yet averse to concentration, may require a pretty sharp goad, and the excitement of fear, but the schoolmaster ultimately triumphs. The power grows rapidly with well-directed exercises, and in the various intellectual professions is so matured as to dispense with artificial spurs. Indeed, none but an idiot (and he not always) is found wholly incapable of mental attention; for this is implied in listening to, and answering the commonest question, or giving the most ordinary information in the proper forms of language. There are very high efforts of the kind belonging to the student, the contriver, the man at the head of complicated affairs; and for such men the qualifying endowment is a mixture of the volitional element with intellect proper. A great profusion of remembered images, ideas or notions, avails little for practical ends with-

## THE PLODDER. 375

out this power of arrest and selection, which is in its origin purely voluntary. We may have the luxuriousness of a reverie or a dream, but not the compliance with a plan of operations, or a method of composition.*

7. We may now see in what way the control of the intellectual trains provides a touchstone for the degree of development of volition as a whole, in the individual character. In the case now supposed, the force of the will is set in array against a power of a different sort, the power of the intellectual associations. Contiguous adhesion, and similarity, call up foregone states with a certain amount of energy. Against this we place the voluntary detention of the inward view upon some one object, and the result shows which is the stronger. I am engaged in watching the demeanour of a person, whom I address with the view of informing or persuading; the appearance of that person tends by association to suggest places and times of former connexion, or other persons having points of resemblance. The earnestness of my purpose, that is to say, the strength of motive growing out of some pain or pleasure, present or apprehended, utterly quells all those resurrections of the associative faculties, and voluntary power is in the ascendant. If it be a usual experience with any one to restrain at all hands the rush of associated ideas, at the

---

\* The common observation as to the plodder taking the start of the man of great natural endowment is in point here. By the phrases 'plodding,' 'industry,' 'application,' 'steadiness,' and the like, is clearly indicated the energy of the will in commanding the intellectual faculties. A mind little retentive by nature of a given subject, as for example, languages, can make up by protracted application or study, under a volitional resolve monopolised by one subject. So as regards the aptitudes growing out of the emotional part of our nature, of which acting, address, and engaging demeanour are the most notable ; the same difference may be remarked between natural gifts adapted to the purpose from the first, and aptitudes that are the reward of study. We have a born actor, like Kean, when the primitive and untutored expression of the feelings, and the general bearing, coincide almost exactly with the maximum of stage effectiveness. When a person of much inferior endowments, seized with the passion for becoming an actor or an orator, 'scorns delights, and lives laborious days,' in training the defective parts of the organisation, the force of the will is the power evoked for the occasion.

## 376 CONTROL OF FEELINGS AND THOUGHTS.

instigation of ends, it is proper to say that such a person possesses volitional energy in a superior degree. It may be that the intellect *per se* is but feeble, and then the comparison would imply little. Could we suppose an instance of great Emotional character as displayed in the sustained vehemence of outward demonstrations, an Intellect unusually strong in the elements of mental reproduction, and a Will, keeping in subjection alike the one and the other,—we should have to pronounce that will something almost superhuman.

8. In the intellectual process, termed, in my former volume, 'constructive association,' I have maintained that there is no new law of association, the additional fact being only an exercise of the will moved by some end to be attained. When I wish to put together a sentence of language, differing from any that I have learnt, I proceed upon some known form, and strike out, or put in, words, also known, till the result answers the effect that I mean to produce. If I am under the hand of the schoolmaster, the spur of his disapprobation on the one hand, and approbation on the other, keeps my faculties at work, trying and erring; and when, in the course of the flow of ideas, brought up by associations, a combination emerges, corresponding with the conditions imposed, I adhere to that, and put a stop to all further currents of associative reproduction. This is the exact tendency of the volitional mechanism so often described, namely, to adhere to what relieves a pain, or yields a pleasure, when that something is once present, and to depart from other objects or movements that have the opposite effect, or no such effect. The higher constructions of the intellectual ingenuity exhibit, in the full-grown individual, nearly the situation of the infant beginner, for in them there is no established channel leading to the movements demanded, and a series of tentatives have to be made, with only the certainty that, if the true thing occur, the primordial instinct of our nature will fasten upon it, and put an end to the search. When Watt invented his 'parallel motion' for the steam-engine, his intellect and observation were kept at work, going out in all

## VOLUNTARY CONSTRUCTIONS OF THE INTELLECT. 377

directions for the chance of some suitable combination rising to view; his sense of the precise thing to be done was the constant touchstone of every contrivance occurring to him, and all the successive suggestions were arrested, or repelled, as they came near to, or disagreed with, this touchstone. The attraction and repulsion were purely volitional effects; they were the continuance of the very same energy that, in his babyhood, made him keep his mouth to his mother's breast while he felt hunger unappeased, and withdraw it when satisfied, or that made him roll a sugary morsel in his mouth, and let drop, or violently eject what was bitter or nauseous. The promptitude that we display in setting aside or ignoring, what is seen not to answer our present wants, is volition, pure, perennial, and unmodified; the power seen in our infant struggles for nourishment, and warmth, or the riddance of acute pain, and presiding over the last endeavours to ease the agonies of suffering. No formal resolution of the mind, adopted after consideration or debate, no special intervention of the 'ego,' or the personality, is essential to this putting forth of the energy of retaining on the one hand, or repudiating on the other, what is felt to be clearly suitable, or clearly unsuitable, to the feelings or aims of the moment. The inventor sees the incongruity of a proposal, and forthwith it vanishes from his view. There may be extraneous considerations happening to keep it up in spite of the volitional stroke of repudiation, but the genuine tendency of the mind is to withdraw all further consideration, on the mere motive of unsuitability; while some other scheme of an opposite nature is, by the same instinct, embraced and held fast. In all these new constructions, be they mechanical, verbal, scientific, practical, or æsthetical, the outgoings of the mind are necessarily at random; the end alone is the thing that is clear to the view, and with that there is a perception of the fitness of every passing suggestion. The volitional energy keeps up the attention, or the active search, and, the moment that anything in point rises before the mind, springs upon that like a wild beast on its prey. I might go

## 378 CONTROL OF FEELINGS AND THOUGHTS.

through all the varieties of creative effort, detailed under the law of constructive association, but I should only have to repeat the same observation at every turn.

9. Reverting now to the first division of the present chapter, we have to consider shortly the additional lever gained in attempting to control the feelings, by the power possessed over the thoughts and ideas. From the fact that our various emotions are wont to spring up on some definite occasion, or on the occurrence of some distinct object, or cause,—as when the re-appearance of an absent friend wakens tenderness, or an injury rouses resentment,—we are to some extent able to bring out the play of those passions by directing the mind upon their objects, or causes. We can work ourselves up into a loving mood, by forcing the attention and the train of ideas upon all the kindness and affection that we may have experienced in the past. By a similar impulse of the will, selecting, out of the current of intellectual reproduction, the catalogue of wrongs that have been inflicted on us, we succeed in warming up the glow of indignation. Dwelling in like manner on the catalogue of our good actions and qualities, the self-complacent condition is nursed into being. So we can do something to turn aside a gush of feeling that has come over us, by diverting the attention from the exciting cause, and still more effectually by forcing the thoughts into the opposite channel, as when we silence a querulous fit by coercing the mind into the act of considering the favourable side of our situation.* We do for ourselves

---

* Dr. Chalmers has expanded this theme with various illustration and eloquent language in different parts of his writings. Many writers have touched upon it, and we see it employed practically in the attempts made to change the prevailing temper and feelings of men's minds under all the emergencies of life. With Dr. Chalmers the grand specific for altering a wrong bias or disposition is what he calls ' the expulsive power of a new affection.' This is a much easier case than the one supposed in the text ; one emotion may be suppressed by the spontaneous rise of the opposite (by which I mean the occurrence of some natural stimulus or occasion) without the intervention of the will ; (so also the counter trains of thought just mentioned in the text might arise independently of volition, as when suggested by some

## COMMAND OF FEELINGS THROUGH IDEAS. 379

what our friends, advisers, comforters, and the public preacher, or moralist, endeavour to do for us, that is, to present forcibly the thoughts, the facts, and the reflections bearing upon the temper that we desire to put in the ascendant. The operation, if successful in any case of real importance, is usually a hard one; in fact, transcending the voluntary power of the generality of mankind. We are not for that reason to omit it from the list of aptitudes falling under our present department, for even the rare instances of manifesting it in a high degree, are to be cherished as precious.

10. The suppressing and exciting of emotional displays, which we have seen to be practicable to a certain length by a direct impulse towards the parts concerned, are very much assisted by means of our control over ideas. It may not be easy to quench a hilarious outburst by a mere volition addressed at once to the muscles; but by carrying the mind away to some quarter of seriousness, the central emotion is damped, and the currents dried up at the fountain-head. When we have to calm down a very troublesome agitation, we commonly bring both methods into play—the direct restraint of the muscular movements, and the transfer of the mental attention to ideas suggestive of the opposite mental condition. The custom of coercing the flow of ideas and the attitude of attention, is an extremely valuable one, both for purposes purely intellectual and for the general government of the temper and feelings. We may consider it as belonging to the highest branch of self-discipline. In restoring some past state of feeling, with all the diffusive manifestation proper to it—a thing not often

---

passing event, or something heard or read at the time). When, under a state of timidity in approaching some strange person of dread presence, we are addressed in the tones and language that inspire confidence and ease, the first emotion is overpowered by the rise of the second. But when we turn aside or suppress a torrent of excitement because of some harm that we are suffering, or are likely to suffer by the continuance of it, or of some pleasure directly or indirectly accruing from arresting it, the effect is a purely voluntary one. The expenditure of power in the case has to be entered in the column of the account that is headed ' Will.'

380 CONTROL OF FEELINGS AND THOUGHTS.

wanted by people generally, but important in special avocations, as the platform or the stage,—the intervention of ideas is more thoroughgoing than the muscular command of the organs of expression, seeing that if we can only resuscitate the feeling itself, all the diffusive accompaniments are sure to follow. True, this is a more costly process than the other, because of the occurrence in this way of organic and other effects not wanted for the purpose in hand, as well as the wear and tear of the emotion itself. But if an actor cannot personify terror or indignation by a simple volition extending to the features, the voice, the gestures, or to the outward display simply, he may, by some recollection of his own, induce the reality of the state with all the collaterals apparent or concealed.

11. While speaking of the ability to summon or expel modes of excitement through the medium of ideas, we are reminded of the contrary tendency, namely, the fact formerly adverted to more than once, that our feelings themselves govern our ideas. It is notorious to observation, that nothing is harder than to introduce with success into a mind roused in some one direction, thoughts or considerations of an opposite kind. This is the way that our feelings lord it over our beliefs or convictions. When, by a stroke of the will, we aim at diverting the current of reflections in profound sorrow or intense anger, we have to fight, by means of this one power, the two remaining forces of our nature leagued against us ; we have to resist the currents of association or intellect proper, and the fury of excited feeling at the same time. But an interesting question is here presented for consideration, whether this power of the emotions to rule the ideas be not properly speaking in part, and on various occasions, a volitional effect. When some intense pleasure keeps the attention fixed exclusively upon one thing, as when listening to music or gazing on objects of deep interest, or when the same process is repeated ideally in the reminiscence, I call this a purely voluntary influence ; it is the proper stimulant of the will impelling to

## ATTENTION NOT ALWAYS VOLUNTARY.

voluntary acts. Some acute pain to be warded off would prove an equally energetic spur upon the bodily or mental attention. Now is not this exactly what happens when a burst of strong emotion, such as tenderness, admiration, self-exaltation, or plot-interest, possesses the mind? Is it not that we cleave to whatever sustains the charm of the moment (which is nothing else than volition) and shrink from whatever would interrupt or do away with it? Clearly, when an emotional state is the bubbling up of pure delight, the will is strongly engaged to maintain that condition.* It is not, how-ever, every mode of excitement that can be described so. We find that an exceedingly painful condition will sometimes operate so as to detain the very causes of the pain. The passion of fear is an instance in point. Happy would it be for the terrified wretch, if the agony of his condition could drive away from his excited vision the imagery and objects that originated his fears. The usual course of volition is manifestly here perverted and paralysed by some foreign influ-ence. So again with anger. I do not doubt that a pleasure is experienced in giving full sway to the outgoings of resent-ment, but certainly the energy of retaliation is out of propor-tion to the pain averted or pleasure sought. I speak not of the calculation of future consequences, which in the great majority of cases would show that the angry ebullition is a mistake in so far as concerns the happiness of the individual; for even as regards the moment, the actions prompted are not according to the measure of a genuine estimate of pain or pleasure. In short, there is in the excitement of the strong feelings a power different from the will, and yet exercising a control over action and thought. It is certainly not from a pleasurable stimulus that all the thoughts entertained by the mind towards the person we are angry with are of the un-

---

* In cases of pleasurable emotion, emotion and volition act in the same direction. In cases of painful emotion, the two act in different and opposite directions, as regards the control of attention, or the retaining or dismissing of ideas and thoughts.—See *Emotions*, Chap. I., Sec. 19.

382    CONTROL OF FEELINGS AND THOUGHTS.

favourable kind. This is a property of the feeling in its strictly emotional character, and not as one of the prompting causes of the will. The way that it occupies the mind, and actuates the framework, is such as to force the intellectual associations into keeping with itself. At the moment nothing can live in the consciousness, so to speak, but what takes on the same fiery aspect. If we would consult our real happiness at that moment, we should find room for considerations that are kept entirely out of view. With regard to those two passions, fear and anger, the case is a very clear one. In both we are compelled to retain and to exclude from the view ideas and facts, without any reference to the suppression of pain or the procuring of delight. They plunge us into misery in spite of the operation of the will, and they overbear both intellectual associations and volitional impulses in the direction they give to the thoughts. Probably, the same observation applies in a less degree to the excessive manifestations of the tender sentiment. Intrinsically, this is one of the most pleasure-giving veins of excitement; but when very much roused, it pursues a course of its own, often at variance with the happiness of the individual. If so, can it be wondered at that emotion proper has all that power over the attention and the trains of thought that is implied in the sway that it exercises over our convictions? We may be under a strong excitement of a perfectly neutral kind, as regards pleasure or pain, and yet this excitement will keep the bodily or mental attention enchained upon one set of objects. This condition, as already remarked, may be realized in the passion of wonder. We may be under a fit of astonishment which we cannot say gives us either delight or the opposite, and which therefore we have no motive to cling to or depart from. In such a predicament, one is able to judge of the nature of mere excitement; and we find that even when of the neutral kind, as regards the proper stimulants of voluntary action, there are manifest effects attaching to it, such as this tendency to fix the intellectual gaze by preference, and thereby to disturb the decisions of the judgment.

## THE FEELINGS COMMAND THE IDEAS. 383

Thus it is that in the voluntary control of the thoughts, we have frequently two powers against one—the tendency of the intellect on the one hand to flow in the direction of the strongest associations, and the tendency of the peculiar excitement of the moment to cherish one class of thoughts and banish the contrary sort. It is not the first of these two influences that renders self-control so difficult as regards the thoughts ; it is the backing that an emotion gives that renders some one kind of considerations omnipotent in the mind. Hence we are constrained to recognise the mediation of the feelings in commanding the ideas, as well as of the ideas in commanding the feelings.

# CHAPTER V.

### OF MOTIVES, OR ENDS.

1. THE discussion raised in the concluding paragraph of the last chapter shows that it is time to consider explicitly, and in detail, the various motives operating in volition. Hitherto we have confined our attention to the general designations, pleasure and pain, as summing up all the causes that have an influence on voluntary action. We see, however, from what has just been said respecting the effect of excitement, that there are important modifying circumstances to be taken into account in estimating the course of action that a human being will pursue. Those passions of fear, anger, tenderness, avail themselves of the instrumentality of the voluntary organs, while urging us on apparently without regard either to pain or pleasure. A fuller explanation on this head is therefore called for. Independently of any anomaly or exception to the general rule on the present subject, there is great room for variety in the operation of motives, according as the pleasure is actual or merely in prospect. The element of intellectual retentiveness is obviously a matter of importance when pain or pleasure operates only in the idea, or anticipation, based on past experience. Moreover, we work largely with the view of compassing ends that of themselves are indifferent, but derive a value from something beyond; which ulterior object, however, in action we often let drop entirely from the sight, being wholly engrossed by those mediate objects. The farmer is as eager about getting his crops gathered in to his farm-yard, as he can be about eating his food or protecting his body from the winter chill. The life of civilized man is full of those intervening or derived ends.

2. If the enumeration that I have given of our various feelings were thoroughly complete, we should now have touched upon every object, circumstance, or agent, that can constitute a simple, ultimate, or underived motive, or end, of Volition. Either among the Muscular feelings and the Sensations brought forward in the first division of the exposition of mind, or under the Emotions, in the present volume, we should find a notice of all the susceptibilities, pleasurable or painful, that can operate as stimulants, in the manner supposed in the foregoing chapters. The proper employment of the active part of our frame may be said to be—the warding off of the large army of possible pains, which threaten us at those numerous points, and the cherishing, retaining, and reproducing the pleasures attainable through the same channels. To refer back for a little to the enumeration as actually given, we encounter first of all a host of troublesome susceptibilities of our Muscular system in the shape of acute pains arising from injuries, and another class consequent on too much exertion. All these are so many points for avoidance, whether actually incurred or only seen approaching. Out of the same region springs a tolerable body of enjoyment to be cherished and cultivated. The Sensations of Organic life involve a certain amount of pleasure, with enormous capabilities of pain, to give occupation to the averting volition. The protection from starvation, hunger, thirst, cold, and suffocation, usurps a large surface of solicitude and endeavour. Here, too, we have the catalogue of ills that flesh is heir to, and here lies the grand stake of life and death. The urgency of the ends thus included is necessarily great and engrossing, commanding a large share of every one's voluntary labour. The cultivation of pleasure is materially trenched upon by the amount of toil to be given to the warding off of organic suffering and disease, with their consequences. The interests of the other senses are important enough, although secondary in their pressure to those comprised in the organic group ; still, according to their several forms of pleasure and pain, do they engage our volitional expenditure. We have to repudiate bitter Tastes, to

386 ON MOTIVES, OR ENDS.

go out of our way to keep at a distance bad Odours, while we are attracted by the opposite species. The pleasures of warm, soft Touches are cherished by us with considerable force of purpose, while we have to repel the pungent and smarting contacts by every means in our power. So with the pleasurable and painful in Sound, to which most natures are sufficiently sensitive to be urged within range of the one class, and deterred from the vicinity of the others. Light has its proper pleasures, no less than its utility as the condition of attaining many other ends; while the varieties of spectacle, movement, scenic effect, and pictured display, enter deeply into the habitual enjoyment of life. We are also liable to many painful and revolting sights, as well as to the gloom of outer darkness, and our volitional energy is kept alive in warding off such predicaments. Passing now to the special Emotions as laid out in the preceding division of mind, we might name under every one of them states of well marked pleasure or of the opposite, at whose instance the will must frequently take proceedings. Novelty and the Marvellous are frequently invested with the highest charm, and are to that degree ends of our voluntary exertions. To pass from restraint to Liberty is an occasional object to every one, and is a greatly prized blessing to many. The Sexual feelings exercise their share of influence. Under the Tender emotion, there are decided pleasures, which one is disposed to use means for reaping in abundance, as when surrounding one's self with family and friends, and entering into the society of one's fellows. Self-complacency, approbation, and praise, and the sentiment of Power and superiority, are objects of intense relish, prompting the will with ardour, and inciting to some of the greatest efforts that human nature is capable of, there being a corresponding energy of revulsion from the opposite feelings. The active part of our nature, as we have seen, furnishes an extensive round of gratification, centering in the attitude of Pursuit; so that there grows up, incidentally to the successful working out of our ends, a pleasure superadded to actual fruition. The delight, growing out of the Intellect, connected with

## IDEAL PERSISTENCE NECESSARY TO ENDS. 387

knowledge and truth, is largely developed in some minds, which are also deeply stung with falsehood or inconsistency, and rendered sad by ignorance ; whereupon the active power is set to work in the direction of intellectual enquiry. The large group of Æsthetic sensibilities divides the energies with our other pleasures, and sometimes engross a considerable share of our means. Finally, under the Moral sentiments, we have much to attain and to avoid. In one or other of those classes, everything that can constitute a motive or end to a voluntary creature ought to be contained ; otherwise the classification of human sensibilities is not complete. Every state denominated pain or pleasure, and tested by operating on the will, is either a muscular feeling, a sensation, or one of the special emotions ; there being also modes of feeling of a neutral or inert character as regards the will.

3. A specific reference must next be made to the *ideal* persistence of those various feelings, whereby they are rendered efficacious while the reality is still remote. I have thought fit to advert to this peculiarity in the several descriptions given in the foregoing Books. The point is most material, as regards the power of any object to engage the will in its behalf. A pain that takes little hold of the memory may inspire our utmost endeavours at the moments of its occurrence ; but between times small attention will be paid to prevent it. On the other hand, when the recollection of some form of misery is good, that recollection will be a spur to our voluntary determinations, whenever there is any opening for a precautionary stroke. Thus it is, that we are constantly keeping up a guard against the causes of disease, against accidents to our property, our good name, our dignity, or against whatever is likely to interrupt our favourite enjoyments, or plunge us into our special aversions. There are many things in everybody's life that maintain a constant efficacy in determining the conduct, whether really present or merely conceived. There are other things that have next to no influence except in the actual contact, while there is a large intermediate class of pleasures and pains that stimulate

388 OF MOTIVES, OR ENDS.

us strongly in the reality, but whose stimulus dies away as that goes farther and farther into the distance. It is a common case to be full of preventive energy against an evil that has just happened, and gradually to lose hold of the bitter experience, so as at last to let it fade from our regards. Shutting the stable door after the steed is stolen, is sufficiently expressive of this weakness. All kinds of suffering tend to persist in the memory, and to keep alive the attitude of precaution for the future; but it is not always the most intense kinds that are best retained. Many circumstances concur to determine the ideal hold that we have of our miseries and delights besides their actual intensity as experienced. All those conditions that modify the growth of contiguous adhesion generally, are applicable to the present instance. (1.) The effect of Repetition, for example, is very notable here. One stroke of suffering is not much remembered, so as to influence the will; but, after a number of recurrences, an impressive reminiscence is constituted, tending to operate powerfully as a stimulant of the actions. The old are more prudent than the young in the avoidance of evil consequences. He that has had twenty attacks of a malady is far more energetically on his guard than after the first or second attack. The experience of pleasure likewise becomes more fixed as an idea, and we come to anticipate beforehand the things that shall really gratify us when they happen. It is repetition that gives that steady appreciation of good, or evil, in the distance, whereby our actions are made to correspond more and more with our happiness on the whole. We should not, however, be stating the full case if we stopped short at this circumstance. (2.) It will be remembered that much stress was laid, in the discussion of the intellect, upon the great variety of individual character, as regards retentiveness of impressions generally, or of some special class in preference to others. Without this we could render no account of the facility of acquisition characterizing some minds, or of those singular aptitudes for particular departments that we constantly witness. In one man we see a strong mechanical turn, in another a

VARIETIES OF CHARACTER AS REGARDS ENDS. 389

facility in acquiring language, in a third pictorial adhésive-
ness, in a fourth the retention of scientific symbols and
reasonings, and so on. Now, I have little doubt that the
variety of primitive endowment extends to the department
of remembered feelings, and that there may be such a thing
as a general tenacity for experienced pains and pleasures at
large, or a specific retentiveness of certain modes. It is not
possible to over-state the value of a good recollection of
those emotional experiences. To have constantly before us
an estimate of the things that affect us, true to the reality, is
one precious condition for having our will always stimulated
with an accurate reference to our happiness. Sometimes individuals may be found having this peculiarity of intellect
well developed. The indication of it would be a precocious
prudence in the aims and pursuits of life ; the natural force of
the mind giving to youth the equivalent of the experience of
age. The opposite character can easily be conceived,
namely, extreme weakness in the hold of what has pained
or delighted us, whence the action of the will inspired by
anticipation is not at all proportioned to the reality. Many
constitutions are keenly alive to organic pains,—nervous
depression, aching disorders, suffocating atmosphere, hunger
and dyspepsia, cold, and the like,—but it does not follow that
each person shall carry away precisely that degree of permanent aversion which represents the real state of the case ;
consequently the will is either too much, or too little, stimulated to avoid the recurrence of the misery. It may happen
that the organic miseries are the things specially retained by
the mind, and, if so, every justice will be done to them in the
framing of the pursuits. Other persons may have a strong
retentiveness for the pains and pleasures of the higher senses,
which will therefore have an abiding influence in determining
the conduct. The pleasures of the ear and the eye will be
worked for, and their pains guarded against, while the miseries
and gratifications of organic sensibility will be less guarded.
So with other feelings ; the vanity of gay attire may strike a
deeper mark than the protection from winter cold. Any one of

## 390 OF MOTIVES, OR ENDS.

the special emotions may have a predominant hold of the intellect, and keep up a persistent motive power; for example, tender affection, self-complacency, or æsthetic sensibility. (3.) Besides repetition and the natural persistence of the intellect, there are other things to be taken into the account in our present calculation, all which are summed up in the Emotional circumstances tending to impress the actual experience on the mind. The intensity of the feeling itself in the original has very much to do with its abiding as an idea; a severe pain being more vividly recollected than one less severe. But a good intellect for pain and pleasure needs neither frequent repetition on the one hand, nor great intensity on the other, to keep alive the details of past experience for the future guidance and stimulation of the conduct. Such are those persons with whom remoteness does not destroy the sense of consequences, who are a law unto themselves without needing the pains and terrors and persuasions of their fellows to secure their good conduct, who early surmount the temptations to injurious excesses, and reduce their scale of life to safe limits. A character of the opposite stamp, retaining a feeble hold of bitter experience, or genuine delight, and unable to revive afterwards the impressions of the time, is in reality the victim of an intellectual weakness under the guise of a moral weakness. There is probably a real difference among minds corresponding to the two great contrasting states of pleasure and pain, such that in some individuals the one is more vividly retained than the other. Certain it is, that to keep up the recollection of painful experiences for the control of our actions makes a well-defined character. By throwing the largest half of the active energies upon the side of preventing evil, an individual stands out prominently as a severely prudent nature, cutting short delights and engrossed with duties. I cannot pretend to say whether the distinction between such a one, and one that looks always to the side of enjoyment, can be ever referred to a purely intellectual peculiarity, like the difference between a verbal and a pictorial mind; but, so far as I am aware, there is nothing to contradict this view. Undoubtedly, in many cases, such varieties are better referred to emotional temperament, than to the department of intelligence proper. There are characters by nature joyous, and disposed to entertain the recollections of that aspect of things, while others seem born to be under the dominion of the painful emotions, in whose minds consequently suffering is magnified. Those alternations that we are all conscious of, from the sanguine to the gloomy, are as it were parted between individuals, some living habitually in the one, and some in the other. Thus the explanation of the great fact regarding the incitement of the will by absent objects, although this be in its very essence an intellectual property, is complicated with considerations of an alien sort. We can see plainly whether it is the repetition of a misery that makes one always ready to exercise caution against it, because we can tell how often experience has been had of it, but when there has been no great frequency of recurrence, and yet one is moved to a perpetual attitude of self-defence, it may not be easy to say whether this enduring impression is owing to the great severity of the shock at the time, or to a special retentiveness of this particular class of pains on the part of the intellect, like the retentiveness for pitch in a musical ear. For example, the feeling of liberty may be an exceedingly operative one, either because we have had such a long course of restraint as to leave a deep impression of misery and aversion, or because the annoyance and distress caused by a single occasion operates like some violent scald in giving a lifelong sentiment of dread, or because the intellect cherishes and sustains with a kind of favouritism of tenacity this mode of misery. (4.) There is a fourth influence that will afterwards be named to give completeness to this list of alternative explanations.

The course of volition under apprehended pain or pleasure is thus as intelligible as under the pressure of the actual state. The mediation of the intellect renders an approaching evil as effective a stimulant as one present. The horse obeys the rider's whip because of the actual smart; the boy at school learns his lessons in the evening to avert the master's cane in

392　　　　　OF MOTIVES, OR ENDS.

the morning. The more completely our intelligence serves us in realizing future good or bad consequences, the more do we approximate to the state of things wherein a real pleasure or a real suffering prompts the will for continuance or cessation. Modes of feeling that are in their nature little remembered in any way, or that the individual happens to have no aptitude for remembering, do not, while at a distance, count among the motives that sway the present conduct, and so we miss the good, or incur the evil, accordingly.*

4. *Of grouped, or aggregated, derivative and intermediate ends.*—The ultimate ends above enumerated, as found in any complete classification of our susceptibilities, and rendered operative in idea as well as in fruition, are, in our daily pursuits, frequently grouped together, and represented by some one comprehensive aim or end. The most familiar of these is the all-purchasing Money, the institution of civilized communities. So there is a general pursuit of what we term Health, implying a certain number of arrangements for keeping off the organic pains and securing the opposite condition. These aggregate ends, for the most part, set up some intermediate goal to be looked to as guiding our exertions. The labourer stepping out into the fields to commence his day's work, is not so much occupied with the ultimate sensations of existence, as with the piece of land that has to be ploughed before evening. This it is that guides his voluntary energies, and it is expedient for him to confine his attention to that

---

* In this act of memory, I do not refer exclusively to the realizing of the actual sensation in its fulness, but include the remembrance of the fact that we were intensely pained, and at the moment prompted to great efforts of avoidance. It is enough if we are distinctly aware of having been strongly urged to action on account of the pain; in short, to realize the *volitional* peculiarity belonging to it; we shall then put forth corresponding energy to prevent its recurrence. I may not remember the exact sensation of a hurt, but I remember all the labour and efforts induced for the amelioration of the suffering, and the recovery from the injury; which is quite enough for putting me on my guard for the future. Another person may forget both the pain, and the exertion and trouble occasioned; in the mind of such a one there will be little or no surviving motive power against a repetition of the accident.

DERIVED ENDS. 393

particular object. The more artificial human life becomes, the more are we called upon to work for ends that are only each a step towards the final ends of all our voluntary labours. Social Security is one of those vast intermediate ends, which we have learned to value for the sake of the ultimate consequences, and strive to compass with all our energy. Each person's enterprises include a small number of comprehensive objects, representative of a much larger number of elementary objects of pain removed, and pleasure gained. Besides those already mentioned, we may specify Education, Knowledge, Professional success, Social connexion and position, Power and Dignity, and an opening for one's special tastes. Every one of those things contains under it a plurality of human susceptibilities gratified, by reference to which the will is inspired to maintain the chase. Without the ultimate elements, directly affecting the human mind, such proximates as gold, a professional *avenir*, the membership of a society, would have no efficacy to move a single muscle of the body ; they are all a species of currency, having their equivalent in a certain amount of the agreeables of the human consciousness. Properly speaking, therefore, their motive value should exactly correspond to an accurate estimate gained from past experience, or from competent information, of the exact amount of ultimate pleasure likely to be realized, or suffering averted, through their means. This is the only measure that a rational being can set up for governing the acquisition of money, of position, of knowledge, of power, of health, or of any of the stepping-stones to these or other ends. Such would undoubtedly be the measure made use of, if one had a perfect mastery of all the preconceptions of the results in substantial enjoyments and protections, accruing in each case. But we have already seen that a very large intervention of the department of intelligence, and a considerable experience already had of good and evil, is necessary to foreshadow the future to the will with a fidelity that shall be justified when that future becomes present.

394 OF MOTIVES, OR ENDS.

5. There is, moreover, connected with those intermediate ends, an additional circumstance that is apt to give a wrong bias to the direction of the energies. It is well known that many things sought, in the first instance, as means, come, at last, to have a force in themselves, without any regard to those ulterior consequences, but for which they would never have been taken up. The acquisition of Money being once commenced, one is apt to get a fascination for the thing itself although, strictly speaking, that has no real value. It would appear that, with the handling of the universal medium of purchase, a new susceptibility is developed, there being something in the form of the object that commends it to the mind. A latent taste is incidentally made manifest, and the gratification of it brings a new end. There is a sort of fascination in the numerical estimate of possessions, and in the consequent certainty conferred upon all our operations of gain and expenditure. The simplification of one's labours is a notable advantage of the use of a money currency. These considerations, at first secondary and incidental, may come, in particular minds, to usurp the primary regards, and throw the actual ends of money into the shade.

The transference now described is, perhaps, still better illustrated by the whole class of Formalities, which, in themselves, are absolutely nothing, but which, as means to genuine ends, are of the highest value. It so happens that many persons, once embarked in this sort of machinery, find themselves drawn to it by a special affection, something in the nature of an æsthetic liking, and carry their devotion far beyond what the original purpose would justify. The keeping of accounts is a common instance. This being an operation of trouble, we should never enter upon it, except as an aid to productive industry. There is a derived or associated importance in our minds attached to book-keeping, and, according as we value the constituent objects subserved by it, we value the process itself. Naturally, however, if we saw occasion for dispensing with such additional labour without sacrificing our chief ends,

## MEANS CONVERTED INTO ENDS. 395

we should be glad to do so. Now, experience shows us that account-keepers are not always ready to abandon their operations, because there is no longer any real occasion for them. It is evident that a special liking for the machinery itself has been gradually contracted, during the time of handling the instrumentality in the furtherance of real pursuits. The avidity for the means is, therefore, no longer an accurate measure of our appreciation of the ends. The Formalities of the Law exemplify the same mental peculiarity. There grows up in the minds of lawyers and judges, and of some persons that are neither, a fascination for the technicalities of procedure, often to the sacrifice of the ends of justice, which originally dictated the whole. The forms that regulate assemblies are often pertinaciously maintained to the injury of the purpose that they serve. We hear of the spirit being made to give way to the letter, as when an ancient machinery is perpetuated that no longer fulfils the original intention, or that even has the very contrary effect. Not merely business, law, and government, but Science also presents the same inversion. An extensive symbolism has been found indispensable to the sciences, and the more so, the further they have been advanced. Mathematics is one continuous fabric of symbolical formalities. Chemistry is largely conversant with them likewise. The Natural History sciences involve a huge machinery of classification. The Logic of the schoolmen is a system of technicalities. Now, in all those sciences, there is frequently good ground for complaining of the conservation of the symbols to the detriment of the primary purpose of the science. So far has this been carried, that we find persons openly declaring a preference of the means to the ends, alleging the importance of an intellectual gymnastic that may or may not lead to the attainment of truth. I shall adduce only one other illustration of this theme, which is the acquired fondness for Experimental Manipulation, beyond all question the greatest source of accurate knowledge of nature. We constantly see the practitioners in this art spending their time in securing a precision irrelevant to the case in hand ; a failing, no doubt,

396                    OF MOTIVES, OR ENDS.

on virtue's side, but still indicative of an undue attachment
to what is only of the nature of means.*

6. I must not pass from this topic without noticing that
the remembrance of our pains and pleasures, which regulates
the voluntary activity in anticipating them as future, is very
apt to cling to some associated object having a more abiding
place in the memory than the feelings themselves. In recalling a violent hurt, we bring up before us the place, time, and
circumstances; and these, by association, aid in reviving the
idea of the pain. States of pleasure and pain by themselves
are not so recoverable as the imagery of the outer world. We
can remember the scenes that have passed before our eyes
during a day's journey, much more easily than we can repossess
ourselves of the various shades of emotion passed through
during the time. It is the same with our aspirations after
pleasure to come. If bent upon rising to a position of honour,
we do not realize to ourselves so much the naked feelings of
that position, as picture forth the pomp and circumstances of
an elevated place, and infer, so to speak, the emotions of the
fortunate occupant. In short, what we look forward to is not
a faithfully conceived idea of the actual enjoyment that a
certain situation will give, but the external appearances that
meet the spectator's eye, and inflame his imagination with
such feelings as he associates with that situation. This is one
fruitful source of deluded and perverted activity. A false
medium is interposed between us and the feelings actually to
be realized in the pursuit of place, distinction, or other glitter-

---

* We have formerly seen (*Emotions*, Chap. XIII. Sec. 26) in discussing
the Æsthetic of Utility, that operations intended purely to ward off evil consequences, sometimes assume an intrinsic interest. This is very much the
case with cleanliness, which, in the first instance, aims at the removal of the
offensive, but, when carried one stage higher, produces a positive effect, by
converting a dull and uninteresting surface into a brilliant one.

It has often been maintained, and is probably the received opinion, that
Justice and Truth are ends in themselves, that is, irrespective of their bearing
on human security and happiness. For my own part, I believe that they are
still of the nature of *means*, and in that character alone assume their momentous importance.

IMPASSIONED ENDS. 397

ing ulterior; and the probabilities are, that in most of our aims pointing towards the untried, we either overstate or understate, or altogether misstate to ourselves the real experience. This is not to be wondered at, if we consider that a difficult effort of construction would be requisite to enable a man to conceive the feelings he is likely to have, when, after years of pursuit, he attains a goal differing materially from anything he has hitherto enjoyed; but we may wonder at the attempt not being made to obtain the proper data for such a construction.

7. *Of Excited, Impassioned, Exaggerated, Irrational Ends: Fixed Ideas.* There are activities wherein we cannot discover any connexion between pleasure enjoyed, or pain averted, and the energy manifested in pursuit. Infatuation, fascination, irresistible impulse, are terms indicating this circumstance. The temptation that seizes many people, when on the brink of a precipice, to throw themselves down, is strongly in point. The infatuation that leads the singed moth back to the flame is something of the same nature. There are sights that give us almost unmitigated pain, and yet we are unable to keep away from them. I doubt not that such is the case with many individuals in every crowd that witnesses a public execution.

8. I have already explained (*Contiguity*, § 11) that we must look for the explanation of this influence, which traverses the proper course of volition, in the undue or morbid persistency of certain ideas in the mind. The obliquity is intellectual in the first instance, and thence extends itself to action. A certain object has, by some means or other, gained possession of us; we are unable to dismiss it; whence by persisting in the view, and excluding other things, it may at last find its way into execution, through that power whereby every conceived act has a certain tendency to realize itself. In looking down the precipice, the idea of a falling body is so powerfully suggested as to give an impulse to exemplify it with one's own person. In the mesmeric experiments of Mr. Braid, and others, the influence is seen in the ascendant, there being

398                OF MOTIVES, OR ENDS.

something in the mesmeric trance that withdraws the counteractive agencies.*

As regards the averting stimulus of Pain, which on certain
occasions causes greater efforts than the pain properly justifies, while there may be various causes to determine the disproportion, the one great and general cause is the emotion of
Fear. Evil felt, or apprehended, in a cool estimate, exercises
a just amount of precautionary motive power ; let the perturbation of terror arise, and the object fixes itself in the mind
with increased force, monopolizes the view so as to exclude
other considerations equally important to the welfare of the
individual, and induces him to act out at all hazards the line
of conduct that has seized the excited vision. Give a child a
fright in connexion with a place, and the idea of avoiding
that place will haunt its mind so vividly that hardly any
voluntary inducement will suffice to overcome the reluctance.
It is the peculiarity of all the modes of the perturbation of
terror, to cause an unusual flow of excitement towards the
senses and the intellectual trains, at the same time confining
the range of their operation to the one subject that caused
the alarm. Hence the strong influence on belief, through
fixing the view upon one class of considerations to the exclusion of all others. Hence, too, the motive influence in action
of these exaggerated conceptions. Seized with panic, we
magnify the danger, and project a scheme of defence on a
corresponding scale. A general may appreciate the force of
his enemy with cool precision, and be heavily pressed with
the difficulty of his position, without any such disturbing excitement. He is moved to do neither more nor less than is
warranted by the fair calculations of the case. This is the
unexcited, unimpassioned, rational, justly calculated operation of
the will.

---

\* Mr. Braid, I believe, was the first to adduce this fact as the explanation of table-turning. He remarked that certain constitutions were especially
prone to fall under the influence of a fixed idea, which worked itself out
quite apart from the will, and therefore with no consciousness of voluntary
exertion.

THE PROPER COURSE OF THE WILL DISTURBED. 399

9. The state of active disgust, abhorrence, or Antipathy is a case of excitement, instigated as an accompaniment to particular modes of painful sensibility, and driving on the energies at an exaggerated pace. There is no limit to the lengths that a man will sometimes go, if once roused to this manifestation in good earnest. Every interest, except one, is cast into the shade, and the individual is urged as if there were nothing besides to divide the forces of the constitution. It is not, however, that the will proper is acted upon directly, as under a genuine pain, it is more that the idea of inflicting suffering on some one has taken such a rooted hold of the mind as to exclude all other ideas, and thereby act itself out to the fullest measure. The murderous prepossessions of the monomaniac are the thorough-going illustration of a force more or less concealed in the generality of cases, by the regular operation of the will. There are not wanting instances of minds that are an easy prey to whatever suggestions are made to them, and feel strongly impelled to put in force any scheme that is once fully entertained.

10. On the side of Pleasure, there are also modes of undue excitement. Any sudden and great delight may give rise to an exaltation of the physical functions of the nature of passion, leading to a disproportionate strain of intellectual and active power in that one direction while the fit lasts. The proper frame of mind under delight, as well as in the former case, is to inspire no endeavours beyond what the genuine charm of the moment justifies, and not to cast into the shade other pleasures, nor to blind us to coming pains. The man that can conform to this rule is in one view passionless, although very far from being devoid of sensibility to enjoyment or suffering. In reality, he it is that has the justest sense and the greatest amount of fruition. It is not true, therefore, it is grossly untrue, that passion * is the best or most valuable stimulant

---

* The name ' passion,' as a synonyme for emotion, must be considered as indicating the intense degrees of emotional excitement, such as destroy the coolness and balance of the system. Under strong emotion of any kind, the object of the feeling will become a ' fixed idea.' Fear, Anger, Love, are the commonest examples of emotions rising to the passionate pitch.

400                    OF MOTIVES, OR ENDS.

of the will. Momentary efforts beyond the justice of the case
are roused, but some other end, also valuable in its turn, goes
to the wall. Nevertheless, it is a fact that almost every
human being has one or more pleasures, that are never enjoyed
or contemplated in perfect coolness. They may not be the
greatest of our possible delights, it may be something in the
quality more than in the amount that makes them tap the
fountains of excitement ; although it may be fairly supposed
that the intensity of them is a principal circumstance.
Whatever this pleasure be that touches the sensibility so as
to agitate the frame, we are to a certain extent victims to it.
Great and valuable may be the contribution arising to our
happiness from such a cause, but the pursuit that is kept
up is out of due proportion. This element of our well-being
is over-rated and the rest under-rated. Among the ends that
commonly induce a heated atmosphere around them, we may
rank as usual and prominent, personal affection, wealth, ambition, fame, knowledge, sport, or some variety of the æsthetic
circle of emotions. Sexuality is a striking instance, perhaps the most striking. Any one of these may be sought after
with an energy proportioned to the gratification reaped from it ;
or there may be a tendency to take on an excited and exaggerated conception, in which case there is a loss of pleasure or
an accession of pain in some other quarter. The susceptibility of special inflammation on some one point, as sexual love,
dignity, reputation, or favourite sport, is a peculiarity of human
nature more or less developed in most individuals. When
very much so, we have what is called the passionate temperament, for which a good deal has been advanced in the way
of commendation. It is, however, a somewhat ominous
circumstance that the extreme development of this character
is one of the phases of insanity. We hear of persons being
hurried on by some demon or infatuation in spite of present
and prospective misery. These are all so many abnormal
positions of human nature, and yet the foundation of them all
is very much alike. It is the temporary exaltation of
the brain and allied functions in favour of some one object,

## EFFECTS OF UNDUE EXCITEMENT. 401

sometimes, but not necessarily an object of intense pleasure ; the effect of which is to magnify all that is related to it, and reduce the estimate of what is not. The poet and the moralist are in the practice of dilating on the importance of this disturbance of the mental equilibrium, provided only the object appears to them a good or noble one. Either despairing of the endeavour to induce a calm and equable current, and a strictly estimated regard in the pursuits of life, or not considering such to be the 'beau ideal' of character, they have been marvellously accordant in praise of a ruling passion well placed. Now, it is impossible to gainsay certain advantages that may be urged in support of this prescription. If we are strongly bent upon securing some one special end, and set at nought every other in comparison, the plan is, not merely to depict the pleasing and valuable results growing out of it, which would be to give it a fair, and only a fair, chance with the will ; but to kindle a blaze of excitement and fury which over-rides all comparisons and annihilates all counter motives. This is the proceeding of a Peter the Hermit, a Daniel O'Connell, or other impassioned advocate of a cause. As regards the work to be done, nothing can be more effectual; as regards the happiness of the agent, the immolation is often remorseless.*

An impassioned pleasurable end is tested not merely by the glow of ecstatic excitement, but also by the display of the painful passions when anything comes to thwart it. The fear, anger, and abhorrence, inspired by opposition, are a just measure of the undue exaltation of the system in favour of the

---

\* In the case of feelings that concern the good of others, or even our own good, when there has been an insufficient cultivation of these from the first, the standard of action is not the pleasure or pain which the agent derives from this source. It is desirable to foster those feelings, so as to make him derive more pleasure or pain from them, and the poet or orator may laudably endeavour for this purpose to inflame the mind to a passionate pitch. The case somewhat resembles the use of terror in education and government, and the employment of Rhetoric generally in the cause of truth. The grand difficulty is, and always will be, to confine the arts of producing exaggerated impressions to these laudable designs.

2 c

402     OF MOTIVES, OR ENDS.

object. Very often these extreme antipathies are directed in the defence of what gives no extraordinary sensation of delight, as when they are let loose upon the violators of some venerated ceremonial, having nothing but usage to commend it intrinsically, and deriving an extrinsic support through the inflammation of these modes of antipathy. The repulsion of the Jewish and Mahometan minds to the pig is a case in point.

So much for the consideration of Ends, or Motives, under the various modifications that they undergo. Present pleasure or pain, future and therefore conceived pleasures or pains, aggregated ends, intermediate and derivative ends, and, finally, impassioned or exaggerated ends,—act on the volition, each according to distinct laws that present no vital exception to the motor efficacy of the two great opposing states of the conscious mind, as assumed throughout the preceding exposition.

11. The point now reached in the development of the general subject is this. In the foregoing chapters, we have traced the rise and progress of the executive part of the will, through the guidance of the great fundamental instinct that causes a present condition of delight or suffering to sustain or arrest a present action. We have seen in what manner experience and association establish channels of communication between the separate feelings and the actions demanded to satisfy them, so as to evoke at once a dormant exertion. Farther, it appears that the intelligence represents, more or less vividly, feelings that are merely impending, whereby the will is roused in almost the same way as by an actual sensation. Our most protracted labours and most incessant solicitudes have reference to what is only looked forward to. The animal pursued maintains its flight through the livelong day, suffering and moved only by an idea. Every step that we take from morn to night is biassed or directed by some foreseen pain or pleasure; or if an intermediate end is the stimulus, the force of that is derived from some ultimate sensibility of our nature, which can live in the remembrance as well as operate in the actual impression.

## POINT ARRIVED AT IN THE EXPOSITION. 403

Having thus traced out the fully-formed executive, and a series of motives capable of impelling it into action, we may be said to have given an account, however imperfect, of the essential phenomena of volition, as they appear in the life of men and animals. There are, however, a number of applications of the general doctrines, interesting in themselves, and serving to elucidate the theory. Indeed, one whole department of the subject still remains untouched, and that perhaps the most fruitful both in vexed problems and in practical considerations. I mean the conflicts of volition. The motives that influence living beings are so numerous, that we should expect beforehand the occurrence of frequent collisions, when of course either no result ensues, or one of the forces gives way. This leads to the denominating of some motor states as stronger than others. A scale of motives is constructed, with reference to individuals, or classes of sentient beings, according to the relative power of stimulating the executive, as tested by the actual encounter. The inner life of every one is a sort of battle ground, or scene of incessant warfare ; and the issues of those recurring contests are often very momentous both to the person's own self and to other beings. The estimate that we form of any creature as an agent, depends upon the motives that predominate in the actions of that creature. The training of the young has a principal reference to the development of certain motives into superiority over the rest. In short, the great departments of Duty, Education, and the Estimate of Character, centre in considerations relative to the rank assigned to certain motives in the outgoings of the voluntary executive. Accordingly, it is necessary for us to set forth these conflicts of the will in some degree of detail.

# CHAPTER VI.

## THE CONFLICT OF MOTIVES.

1. WHEN two states of feeling come together, if they are of the same nature, we have a sum total—as when the occurrence of two pleasures gives a greater pleasure. When a pain concurs with a pleasure, we find, as a matter of fact, that the one can neutralize the other. An agreeable relish, in the shape of some sweet taste, soothes the infant's irritated mind; and all through life we apply the grateful to submerge the disagreeable. In the conflict of the two, one will be lost and the other lowered in its efficacy; the first being pronounced the weaker, and the second the stronger. When the charm of the landscape makes one insensible to hunger and fatigue, the pleasurable part of the consciousness is counted more powerful than the painful; if an interesting romance failed to subdue the same painful solicitations, we should say that the landscape gave more delight than the romance—a fair and usual mode of estimating the comparative influence of objects of delight. I am here assuming the volition as dormant the while, and describing what happens in the meeting of opposite states considered purely as Feeling. Nor is this a mere hypothetical case. Many of our pains are counteracted by enjoyments, and never proceed to the stage of stimulating the will. We use by turns, according to circumstances, either mode of alleviation. A good deal depends here upon the individual constitution; some from having great excess of voluntary energy, deal with suffering by active measures of removal and prevention; others, more lethargic, and developed principally on the side of the emotional manifestations, seek to overcome misery by

## CONFLICT WITH SPONTANEOUS IMPULSES. 405

frequenting the sources of delight, and indulging in a various and soothing expression of woe. The contrast of the two characters is unmistakeable.

2. We will consider first the conflict of a voluntary stimulus with the Spontaneous impulses considered in their primitive character, as growing out of the purely physical conditions of the nervous and muscular systems. In this respect, spontaneity is a separate power to the very last. After every night's repose, and after the nourishment of a meal, the active organs are charged with power ready to explode in any direction. I will not reiterate the proofs already produced on this head. Suffice it to say, that this element of our activity is brought into frequent collision with the genuine impulses of the will, those derived from pleasures and pains. The discharge of exuberant activity is opposed by such motives as urge one to remain in stillness and confinement. The conflict is seen when the healthy boy has a hurt, or a sore, rendering it painful to join the sports of his playmates. It is seen when the horse or the hound is kept in check, in the fulness of the morning's vigour. The more active the animal, or the more highly-conditioned in all that regards health, nourishment, and preparatory repose, the greater is this explosive tendency that carries it into action without any reference to ends, or motives of the true voluntary character ; and the greater is the stimulus, whether of smarting pain or pleasurable charm, necessary to check the outburst. To reconcile the young to a day of indoor confinement, we have to cater largely for their amusement. Whatever any one's peculiar activity consists in, a considerable force of motive has to be supplied in order to restrain the exercise of it when the organs are fully refreshed. It is so with mind as well as with body, with the exercise of the manual and intellectual powers alike. Long restraint prepares the way for a furious demonstration at the moment of liberty. The conflicts thus arising are among the pains of early discipline, for it is impossible to reconcile the process of education with the free discharge of all the centres of power exactly at the moment

406 THE CONFLICT OF MOTIVES.

of their plenitude. Some part of the irksomeness of every professional pursuit, of every continuous undertaking, and the fulfilment of every course of duty, is due to the same cause. In so far as we have the regulation of our daily life in our own hands, we endeavour to suit our times of active exertion to those periods of natural vigour; but this adjustment will often fail; we are obliged to restrain the flow of power when at its height, and force it into play when at the lowest ebb. The irregular operations of the soldier's life continually bring about these crosses, whence, among other reasons, arises the need of that stringency of painful discipline peculiar to the military system. After a lapse of time, a second nature growing up, renders the subjection of the spontaneity less arduous, but the physical fact remains, that at certain stated times each organ attains a fulness of power, and a readiness for action, not possessed at other times, and demanding a certain counteracting motive to withhold it from proceeding to act. The very same thing is true of the spontaneity bred, not of repose and nourishment, but of an exciting cause, as the infection of a multitude, or of some other powerful example. Such, also, is the nature of a passionate stimulus, as fear; and such the morbid persistence growing out of fatigue carried beyond the point of repose. It is of no consequence what is the origin of the current that sets in strongly to rouse the various members into action. If we would neutralize it, we must provide some adequate counteractive in the form of an incitement to the will, and we measure the strength of the spontaneity according to the strength of the pain, or the pleasure, found equal to checking it. Sometimes the stream gets beyond all ordinary bounds, and is better left to exhaust itself. For after all, it is the same nervous system that has to bear the cost of the conquering agency.

3. The struggle that arises when we goad an exhausted system into action, is an interesting study in various respects. We see in this case the extreme importance of physical condition. It is not simply repugnance to the pain arising from working under fatigue, but a positive inaptitude to exertion,

that appears in that case. A time comes when no amount of pain will procure a single muscular contraction. The inability is now physical and not moral. That condition of spontaneous overflow indispensable as a preliminary in the formation of the innumerable links of voluntary control, is still of great moment in the complete establishment of those links ; and although it is possible at the mature stage to whip up action where there is but a very scanty central stimulus, yet, according as the nervous batteries grow feeble, the prompting cause has to be increased, until at a certain pitch of depletion there is a total incapacity of evolving any further quota of power. The associations established in the growth of the will bring forth action where none would well out otherwise ; the horse that has parted with all his surplus power, and would prefer to lie quiet, under the prick of a sharp pain can give forth an additional amount ; this is the stage of conflict, growing more and more painful, until the animal drops down. The rider's spur has to encounter both an opposing volition from the pain of fatigue, and a physical insufficiency owing to the exhaustion of the muscular and nervous power.

4. Let us next proceed to consider in detail the case of Opposing Volitions proper, where two pleasures or two pains, or one of each, solicit the voluntary executive in opposite ways. The instances of this conflict may be as numerous as the various concurrences of the human feelings. It would be both impossible and useless, to attempt to specify every instance of opposing impulses arising within the range of the human susceptibilities to pleasure or pain, present and ideal, aggregated and intermediate ends, and passionate fixed ideas. If we could only make a good selection, suitable for illustrating the general theory of the will, and for elucidating the questions depending on it, we should comply with all the exigencies of the present treatise. In every separate point or region of our susceptibility, an opposition may arise, and the arena of conflict may be indefinitely extended by the concurrence of impressions on different parts of our sensitive framework. The muscular feelings may be divided against them-

## 408 THE CONFLICT OF MOTIVES.

selves; the organic group may quarrel to great lengths; tastes or smells may conflict with one another; so with touches, sounds, or sights. Under the same emotion—tender, irascible, egotistic, æsthetical, &c., there may be encountering objects drawing the system in contrary ways. The emotions that incite us to duty and prudence are notoriously liable to inimical attacks, both from one another and from the rest of the feelings; for we may have opposing duties, as well as opposing affections or tastes.

A brief exemplification will suffice for the case of two *actual* states, pleasurable or painful, concurring at the same moment to suggest incompatible acts. The sensations of Organic Life furnish cases in point. The pleasures and pains of cold and heat are especially liable to run counter to other organic interests. In a warm room we are subject to depression from the close and heated air. Out of doors, in a winter day, the case is reversed. The lungs and nerves are exhilarated, while perhaps the misery of chillness is superinduced. Lying thus, between contradictory impulses, the result shows which is the stronger; for supposing no third sensation, or motive, to step in, one of these two will carry the day, and so will be deemed the more powerful. If I remain out of doors, incurring the winter chillness, it is that the pleasurable exhilaration through the lungs is more than a balance for the pains of cold. Another person in the same circumstances acting differently, must needs be differently constituted; the experiment determines a fact of character as regards relative sensibility to those influences.

In the same way, wherever two present sensations dictate opposite courses, there is an experiment upon the relative strength of the two. The resulting volition decides the stronger, and is the ultimate canon of appeal. A creature left to free will under two influences gives evidence which is the more, and which the less acceptable. By free will, I here mean that the ground is clear of all other moving causes whatsoever, except the two under trial. Place food before a bird in a cage, and at the same time open the cage and the house door, and the choice between a repast and liberty represents the greater pleasure; nor is any higher criterion attainable. The action of a free being having experience of several objects of delight, or of a plurality of evils, settles irrevocably which to him is to be considered the greater, and which the less. Whenever we can have an experiment of this simple kind with two concurring sensations, and no remote consideration in view, we accept it as establishing the comparative estimate of those sensations. The enthusiast for sport, disregarding, for a long day, fatigue, cold, wet, hunger, proves to us as a fact that the one pleasure outweighs the many pains. It is from these conjunctures that we obtain our knowledge of one important region of character, the region of likings and dislikings, in other words, of comparative motive influences upon the will. In circumstances favourable to a good experiment, that is, on an average condition of the individual, and in the absence of extraneous adjuncts and fixed ideas, a result gained is looked upon as conclusive, and rarely needs to be reversed; such is the constancy of this part of the character. Each animal has its favourite amount of exercise, temperature, relishes, tastes, smells, and so on; and whole tribes are found to agree in their choice on these heads. So with pains, when set against pleasures, or other pains; we measure the intensity by the impulses surmounted. Extreme hunger is attested by urging an animal's pursuit under great fatigue, by incurring the pains of a contest with a powerful rival, or overcoming some other great aversion. No principle is involved in those cases; we simply determine a fact, or facts, in the natural history of each man or animal, which we remember for our guidance in future dealings with them. It is only an identical proposition to affirm that the greater of two pleasures, or what appears such, sways the resulting action; for it is this resulting action that alone determines which is the greater. As we can never transfer the actual consciousness of any other being, great or small, to our own consciousness, we must look to action as the ultimate criterion of feeling. No doubt, in human beings, there are

410    THE CONFLICT OF MOTIVES.

other indications, such as the expression of the emotions, and the use of language, but we must come at last to volition as the final court of appeal, subject only to the presence of a fixed idea, which is a real disturbing force, to be allowed for, if we have any evidence of its existence. If we want to know what any one's pains are, we look to their avoidances; if their pleasures, to their attractions. This canon will serve us down to the lowest limits of sentient being; or if we doubt the applicability of it to the inferior tribes, we must pass into total uncertainty respecting them.

5. If we compare the voluntary stimulation taking place on *different* occasions, under pleasure or pain, we are liable to mistake, from the varying condition of the active organs. It does not follow, because one thing wakens up the activity in the morning, while another fails to excite any effort in the evening, that the first is intrinsically a stronger feeling. There are times when the executive of the will is especially prone to stimulation, and times when the opposite happens. We must therefore make the experiment as nearly as possible in the same bodily and mental condition, or repeat it so frequently as to obtain an average under all conditions. This last is the true method adapted to the case, and is what gives us our knowledge of the characters of individual men or animals. Having seen the predominating effect of some one pleasure, such as bodily exercise, food, warmth, music, sociability, self-complacency, power, or knowledge,—under circumstances so various as to eliminate all the differences of general or constitutional activity, we pronounce one or other of those to have a superior rank in the scale of sensibility of the subject. We know that unless there be some special and exceptional considerations present, the taste thus established as standing high in the character, will certainly overbear other tastes, and force the will to surmount obstacles and repugnances. In the same individual, the volitional tendency is a constant fact, subject only to the variations of nourishment, freshness, general health, and excitement; and the thing that puts it in motion by preference is to be considered as touching

## CONFLICT OF ACTUAL AND IDEAL.

a keener sensibility. Excepting that the active ability lies more in some organs than in others,—in limbs, hands, voice, &c.,—the will is one, while the sensibilities are many; the executive is common, and open alike to all, and the one that carries it for the moment is properly estimated as the strongest at the time.

The comparison between one subject and another brings in the element of variety in the constitution of the Will itself, in consequence of which two men unequally moved under the same sensation or emotion, are not thereby shown to differ in emotional susceptibility. In some, as often remarked, the activity is especially developed. We pronounce this to be the case when we see a disposition to be put in action by all motives indifferently; and the opposite character is read in a general inactivity of tone under all varieties of stimulation. One man will bestir himself and go through industrial toil; but his feelings of cold and hunger need not be a whit stronger than, nor even so strong as, another man's originally were, who makes no effort at all. We cannot therefore judge between the one man's pains, or pleasures, and those of the other, until we are able to make allowance for the difference in the degree of the voluntary discharge, or the determination of vital power to the region of activity. This difference we can ascertain by the same system of averages as described above. An industry strongly manifested under motives generally, whether small or great, is the proof of a high development of the will; in a mind of that class, a trifle will overcome the disposition to rest, as effectually as a powerful spur in a constitution of a different stamp.

6. In the foregoing illustration, I have supposed a conflict and comparison of actual impressions; as when, under present sensations of bodily pain or appetite,—a taste, touch, or sound, agreeable or disagreeable,—or any emotion upheld by the pressure of its object. The next step takes us to *ideal* motives, and their conflict with the actual, and with each other. We here open up a much wider field of operations. All the long list of delights and sufferings are things to remain

more or less durable in the memory, and to instigate voluntary acts to bring on, or ward off, the reality, as yet in prospect. A counter stimulus of actual sensation may also be present, and the rivalry takes place between such ideal ends and the real one. I remember the pains of excessive muscular fatigue, and am now enjoying the pleasure of some exciting game, or sport; there is a hostile encounter within; if the pleasure of the sport be very intense, that carries the day; if the pain, as remembered on former occasions, was very acute, and the memory of it now so fresh and lively, as to present it in nearly all its living power to the present view, that will probably prevail, and I shall desist from the present pleasure. The comparison no longer faithfully represents the relative force of the opposing impressions at the moment of their actual occurrence, inasmuch as the ideal retentiveness may be so bad as to do no justice to the force of the actual; what was severely felt at the time when it happened is not severely felt as a mere anticipation. The pains of our various excesses in food, stimulants, and other sensual delights, are often very great, sometimes acute, and sometimes massively depressing; but if the recollection of the suffering vanishes with the reality, there is nothing to counteract the pleasurable impetus to repeat the whole round of indulgence. An important branch of our intellectual acquisitions is constituted by this good and faithful recollection of past pleasures and pains; a certain amount of natural force of adhesive association is the groundwork, and an adequate repetition of the lessons of experience completes the structure. The thoroughly educated man in this respect is he that can carry with him at all times the exact estimate of what he has enjoyed, or suffered, from every object that has ever affected him, and, in case of encounter, can present to the enemy as strong a front as if he were then under the genuine impression. This is one of the points of superiority that age confers; but, as formerly remarked, there may be a special retentiveness for likings and aversions, such as to bring on a precocious maturity·of practical wisdom, just as we may see a precocious mathematician, painter, or poet. When we find persons manifesting

IMPORTANCE OF IDEAL RETENTION OF FEELINGS. 413

energetic volitions in all the points bearing upon the maintenance of Health, we may interpret their conduct on various
grounds. There may be in the constitution a remarkably
acute sensibility to derangements of every kind, so that the
voluntary actions are strongly solicited in the way of preventing such infractions of the sound condition ; the same
circumstance of acute sensibility also leads to an abiding
recollection that serves in absence. If to this be added
a good intellectual adhesiveness for bodily pains, the cause of
protection is still farther strengthened ; while every fresh
experience of the evils of ill-health adds force to the ideal
representation. In such a state of things, the motive of present
pleasure must be strong, indeed, to overthrow a bulwark so
confirmed ; and very acute pain in other departments will be
borne rather than surrender this fortress. Take another case.
Poverty brings with it a round of discomforts and privations
felt in some degree by every human being, although constitutions differ exceedingly in the acuteness of the susceptibility. Scanty, indifferent, food, poor shelter and clothing, few
delights, a position of contumely—are all painful ; but they
do not actually operate at every moment. The stimulus of
the will to ward them off by industry, frugality, temperance,
and all other 'ways to wealth,' is at certain moments supplied
from the pressure of the actual, while, for the remaining time,
the ideal form of the miseries must be the sustaining spur.
If there be a natural dulness of sensibility to all those evils,
conjoined with a repugnance to continuous and regular labour,
only one result can ensue, the slothfulness and degradation of
the lowest races. There may be, however, a considerable
sense of the sufferings of penury under the actual pressure of
hunger, cold, or privation, but an intelligence so deplorably
unretentive as not to represent those miseries to the will in
the intervals of their cessation. The consequence is, that the
preventive efforts are fitful, uncertain, and therefore inadequate. An intelligence of another cast keeps them ever
in the eye of the mind, confronting them with each counter
motive of pleasurable ease and painful toil ; whence emerges

**414**     THE CONFLICT OF MOTIVES.

the man of unfaltering, persevering industry, with the natural consequences.

7. In describing the Special Emotions, I have included a reference to their greater, or less, persistence as ideas with men generally. In the preceding chapter, notice has been taken of the assistance rendered by the *external objects* of the several feelings, in maintaining the recollection of the pleasurable or painful states, as when we revive the gratification of a poem, or narrative, by recalling the main stream of the composition itself. The forms of the intelligence—the sights, sounds, and touches, &c., representing the material world—are the most persistent elements of our mental stock, and we are aided by their mediation in the memory of states of a merely emotional nature. Not only do places, persons, scenes, incidents, operate as the links of association in restoring states of joy, suffering, or excitement, but they contribute to keep alive in the mind, for the purposes of active pursuit or avoidance, those various conditions of our sentient life. The pleasures of music, or painting, should therefore naturally persist in minds that have a strong affinity for the material of either art, and should operate upon the will accordingly. Those occasions of pleasurable or painful excitement, that do not connect themselves with well-remembered objects, are apt to fade from the view, and accordingly lose the day in any conflict with more potent and abiding impressions. In this way, we may really let slip valuable pleasures, and run unheeding upon very malignant pains. Any form of suffering that has a visible, assignable and certain cause, such as a wound, a chill, a harsh discord, a mortifying reproof, a money loss, is peculiarly calculated for being held in the mind as a deterring motive; the cause, being itself a well-remembered fact, or incident, imparts the same property to the effect. On the other hand, those sufferings that spring up we know not how, that have no ascertainable object, or agent, or defined circumstances, give nothing for the intellect to fasten upon, and unless they are formidable enough to excite terror, as mystery is apt to do, they die away and are forgotten. This is the case with the

## ASSOCIATIONS IN AID OF IDEAL MOTIVES. 415

more uncertain and inscrutable ailments that occasionally come over us; they have neither connecting circumstances for the memory to lay hold of, nor assignable antecedents for the will to avoid, and so we are apt not to count them among the miseries that have to be recorded in the list of our voluntary ends. Seeing that emotional states as such are retainable to a much less degree than the appearances that constitute our notions of material things, it is of importance to have a good alliance between them and those more enduring notions. Our recollection of a burst of wonder, of tenderness, of pride, of anger, is always a mixed notion or idea, having the object, circumstances, or occasions, as presented to the senses, in company with the emotional excitement. The remembrance of a pure, detached, or isolated emotion is of rare occurrence. Still, there is a certain ideal persistence in those conditions of pure feeling, which would sustain them without their companion circumstances addressed to the eye or the ear. An acute misery can be remembered in its own proper character; and as such can incite the voluntary efforts to ward off a repetition of it; the remembrance being still farther enhanced by the notion, also present, of the instrumentality or circumstances involved with it. Thus we see how very pertinent the strength of the intelligence is in determining the will, and in representing absent joys, or miseries. A good retentiveness for the material accompaniments is an auxiliary of great force in holding in the view the things to be aimed at, or recoiled from. No doubt, for the purpose in hand, this recollection ought to couple strongly with the outward circumstances the exact feeling bred by them, otherwise we get no good by it. If the recollection of an opponent whom we have to conciliate, or combat, does not carry with it a lively sense of the mischief he is likely to do us, but runs off upon other peculiarities of his character, the proper end, of setting us to work to smooth him down or overwhelm him, is not brought about. So that, after all, the most indispensable part of the reminiscence is the way that we actually felt at the time of the present reality. The very actions stimulated then

**416** THE CONFLICT OF MOTIVES.

ought still to be stimulated under the idea. The perfect balance of the mind consists in this approximation of the present to the absent, whereby the same evil prompts us alike in both conditions, not being too furious in the one, nor too lax in the other.

8. In what has now been said, I have put the case of a conflict of the ideal with the actual, as when a present gratification of the sense is opposed to a future represented by the intellect. We can easily extend the illustration to other conflicts. The opposing motives may be both ideal, as when a prospective day of pleasure is coupled with an array of subsequent pains. Our decision depends first on the comparative intensity of the two as formerly experienced, and next on the faithfulness of the recollection of each. If memory has retained the pleasure in all the colouring of the original, while the painful part is scarcely at all remembered in its deterring power, we shall be sure to give way to the promptings of the side of indulgence, even although in an actual conflict the other were strong enough to prevail. Neither is the case uncommon of a prospective pain debarring us from a course of enjoyment, owing to the circumstance that the enjoyment is feebly represented in comparison of its rival. I may underrate the satisfaction that I shall derive from joining in some amusement, because I have not a vigorous recollection of my previous experience, while I retain strongly the pain of loss of time, or the remission of some other occupation that engages my mind. Having passed through the first much less frequently than the last, the persistence of the two is very unequal, and the will is moved to a wrong choice as regards my happiness. We are thus the victims of unfair comparisons. The well-stamped and familiar pleasure is apt to move us to set aside some still greater delight not adequately conceived, because it is seldom repeated, and lapses into a remote and forgotten past. He that has had few occasions of exciting sport may not do justice to this pleasure as a motive, especially when the very latest experience is now long gone by. It is no doubt possible to make up for the

AGGREGATED OR COMPREHENSIVE ENDS. 417

want of repetition in the actual, by repetition in the ideal, as when one or two days of successful pleasure are able to sustain themselves in the fond recollection of many succeeding years. The mind dwelling in this way upon a very limited enjoyment may give it a power quite unlimited, and as much out of measure in the side of excessive appreciation. This is an exception to the cold operation of the intellect, and implies the intrusion of some degree of passionate warmth. The general rule must be held to be, that, according to the intensity of the original and the goodness of the intellectual representation, is the motor influence of any suffering or delight in the distant approach; and in the comparison of two such ideals, the one that succeeds must needs have a superiority in one or other particular.

9. As regards the Aggregated or Comprehensive ends—Property, Health, Society, Education, Worldly position, &c.—not much needs be said. The force of these ends depends upon the ultimate pleasures that they supply, and the pains that they rebut, and we are urged by them, according to our sense of these; allowance being made for the tendency of some of them to take on an independent charm, from the particular character of the aggregate. We may be too little moved by these great objects of pursuit as well as too much. One may sometimes slight the acquisition of wealth, not because of being naturally insensible to purchasable delights and safeguards, but because the intellect has not been so impressed with those as to keep them before the mind in absence. This is one of the errors of the young, as avarice is said to be a vice of the old. So it is with knowledge and valuable acquirements. The pleasure of their fruition, and the ill consequences of the want of them, may be at times acutely felt; but from too little repetition of the actual, the mind has not that abiding sense that can sustain the will, through a long period of application to the means, against all the countervailing stimulants occurring from day to day.

10. The Impassioned or Exaggerated ends, from their

2 D

418                    THE CONFLICT OF MOTIVES.

very nature, inflame the conceptive faculty on one point to such a degree that the opposing subject is not adequately presented. Strong indeed must be the retention of a very sharp pain that is able to cope with an unduly inflamed prospect of delight. The mind excited at the instance of possessions, pride, fear. or antipathy, is incapacitated to that extent from admitting rival considerations. In fact, the battle contest here may be said to be on the arena of the intellect. No doubt, even an *actual* pain or pleasure of a rival sort is most completely quelled under the storm of an undue excitement; but the influence as against what is merely matter of memory and anticipation is still more overwhelming. Enthusiastic fervour for a cause shuts out the view of difficulties and consequences. Passionate love between persons is of the same blinding tendency. To meet those impulses with success, a motive must be armed with triple powers; the good or the evil of it must be something deeply affecting us in the first instance; the force of intelligence which is to keep it alive in idea, must be of a high order; while the confirming power of a frequent repetition, or the freshness of some recent experience, would be likewise required. When an excitement is *equally* met, not by another (as we may fight enthusiasm by terror, or *vice versa*), but by a cold estimate of pleasure to be trampled out, or pain to be hazarded, our commentary upon the case is, that these consequences are of such a nature as to impress the sensibility to a peculiar degree, and also to be firmly retained throughout the intervals of their actual occurrence.

The present subject will have its illustration prolonged in the two succeeding chapters. I here close the remarks upon the general case, in order to introduce the consideration of the *deliberative* process so much identified in the common view with the operations of free will.

# CHAPTER VII.

### DELIBERATION.—RESOLUTION.—EFFORT.

1. DELIBERATION is a voluntary act, under a concurrence or complication of motive forces. There is implied, in the first instance, at least one opposing couple of feelings, neither being so commanding as to over-ride the other. It is a supposable case, embodied in the immortal illustration of Buridan, that the two hostile motives may be so evenly balanced, that no action ensues. The animal's hunger is baulked because the two bundles of hay are so equal in attraction that he can turn to neither. A pleasure may be opposed to a pain with such a precisely adjusted equivalence, that we remain at rest. This is called being undecided, and is a very usual event. But during the moments of abeyance or suspended action, the current of the thoughts brings forward some new motive to throw its weight into one scale, whence arises a preponderance. A first presentation of the case gives an equality, second thoughts establish a superiority; or, if the first view presents a great inequality that would lead to immediate decision, yet if the action is not at once entered on, subsequent considerations may lead to equality and suspense. I form a resolution on the first hearing of a question, which, if I have space left for continuing the consideration, I abandon afterwards. Knowing all this from our experience, we come to see that it is dangerous to carry into effect the result of the first combat of opposing forces; and this apprehension of evil consequences is a stimulant of the will like any other pain. Accordingly, I term the deliberative process voluntary. The prompting of probable evil, from giving way to hasty decision, arrests action, even although

420    DELIBERATION.

a great preponderance of other impulses is in favour of a particular course. A third element is introduced of sufficient power in many instances to neutralize the ascendancy of the strongest of the two others. Thus, then, either in an equal balance which nullifies all action, or in an unequal contest, where experience suggests the possibility of there being other considerations than those at present before the mind, there is a period of suspense, and an opportunity for the rise of new suggestions through the trains of association or new observations of relevant fact ; but in this operation of delaying the final action, there is nothing extraneous to the nature of the will as hitherto described. It is the memory of past pains, from too rapidly proceeding to act, that constitutes a stimulus to the voluntary organs, by suggesting the renewal of those pains, as a breaker a-head. This is nothing more than the remembrance of a sleepless night restraining one from repeating the excess that caused it. The motive of the deliberating volition is sometimes an excited one ; for the evil of a too quick decision being only a probable and imagined evil, there is room for the perturbation of terror with its exaggerated influence upon the thoughts, and through them upon the will ; and the postponement of action may be carried to an absurd length. It is one of the properties of a well-trained intellect, to make at once a decisive estimate of the amount of time and thought to be allowed for the influx of considerations on both sides of the case, and, at the end of such reasonable time and thought, to give way to the side that then appears the strongest. Among the errors that men in general are liable to, is that of hasty decision on the one hand, and protracted indecision on the other ; and this is according as the evil of giving way to the first show of superior motive is little apprehended by the mind so as to have no influence, or is apprehended under passionate exaggeration of danger so as to have too great an influence. The difficulty of allowing space for deliberation is manifestly increased according as the motive for instant procedure is very great. The impetuosity of youth and of passion brooks no delay ; the feebler sensibilities of age

## DELIBERATION A VOLUNTARY ACT. 421

and languor of temperament make hesitation a matter of little annoyance. We may say, notwithstanding, that the ill fruits of acting, before all the opposing pleasures and pains involved have been fairly arrayed in the view, constitute an end of avoidance of the Intermediate class, which finds a place in the list of stimulants to the will in every well-constituted human being. The door is opened in this way to a very great enlargement of the sphere of voluntary action. This one prompting originates impulses to prevent many painful consequences, of which, indeed, it is but the summary, or the representative. From its operation, springs the opportunity for our various sources of suffering, or delight, to confront one another ideally, before coming to a conflict actually. We are then less and less the slaves of isolated or individual impulses, or to use the common language, we take a higher rank as ' free agents.' By introducing the process of deliberation and suspense of judgment, our decisions approximate more to our interests or happiness on the whole.

2. To take a simple example. A demand suddenly rises for our assistance to a friend, relation, or some one in the circle of our sympathy and esteem. We are here placed between a sacrifice involving pain or privation to self, and the impulse springing out of our tender feeling towards another. An instantaneous decision would show which feeling was strongest at the moment of the first presentation of the case. Experience, however, has taught us that painful consequences are apt to ensue from those instantaneous decisions ; and without perilling the interest that may be at stake, we stop for a little time and permit the influx of other considerations arising out of the case. The deserts and conduct of the person in question are looked at on all sides. Perhaps the assistance demanded will be wastefully employed without rendering substantial good ; which constitutes a motive force against the demand. Perhaps we ourselves have been the recipient of frequent benefits at the hand of the same person, which consideration, rising up to the mind, strengthens the impulse on the other side. Again, what is wanted may amount to a

422    DELIBERATION.

serious reduction of our own means, so as to affect our independence or the discharge of other obligations; considerations necessarily of a very powerful kind, and felt as such when the mind is suffered to dwell upon them. Then comes some fact to neutralize some preceding one, and reduce the magnitude of the opposing array. Every new suggestion tends to add or subtract from one side or the other. At one moment a motive appears in great force, at the next a circumstance comes to view that takes away half its urgency. The well-disciplined deliberative Will meanwhile resists the prompting of the stronger side, until nothing new any longer presents itself; the case is then closed, and the restraining power suggested by the anticipation of evil from rashness of judgment ceases to operate, leaving the will to follow out the side of the case that has mustered the strongest sum total of motives. To allow the proper time for this process, and nothing beyond, is one of the highest accomplishments of the combined intellect and will. In such a consummation, we have to be duly alive, in the first instance, to the evils of hurried conclusions, and so to oppose all promptings of that nature; in the next place, we have to feel adequately the further evil of protracted decisions, so as to overcome the weakness of excessive dread of committing mistakes. Both the one and the other are genuine motives operating on the will; they are pure pains, and deter from the actions that would incur them, as much as any other kind of suffering that we have felt already, and may again be liable to. They are highly ideal in their nature, being, in the majority of cases, represented by the intellect as not certain, but merely probable. Nevertheless, no amount of complication is ever able to disguise the general fact, that our voluntary activity is moved by only two great classes of stimulants; either a pleasure or a pain, present or remote, must lurk in every situation that drives us into action. The deliberative suspense is born of pain; the termination of it at the right time is also stimulated by anticipation of evil; and the development of those two kinds of suffering into motive powers paramount on every occasion, however the

## LATEST THOUGHTS NOT THE BEST.

storm of potent impulses may rage, is a great accession to the practical wisdom and well-guarded happiness of life.

3. The deliberative position is open to another remark in the same general direction. By keeping a conflict suspended, new motives come successively into view; but, in many minds, the last fresh arrival is ever the strongest, from the very fact of its being new, while the others are put into the background. As an actual pain is naturally much more powerful in instigating the will than the same pain in the ideal distance, so the first moment of the rise of a motive into view is the most efficacious; and a training is wanted to prevent us from acting this out to the injury of the others. The sense of bad consequences must, therefore, be our monitor here too. Many a sharp experience has taught us that the latest thought is not necessarily the best; and the feeling so arising is a prompter of the will to resist the too great impressiveness of the newly-sprung up suggestion. The mind, by degrees, undergoes a discipline to keep back the impulse of the strong present, and put it on a level with the fading past, in the decisions that lead to action. Thus, to take an easy example, there is proposed to one the alternative of a life of liberty with small means, and a life of constraint with considerable affluence. Supposing that there is no overpowering strength of feeling on either side, such as an inveterate love of freedom on the one hand, or an all-absorbing love of wealth on the other, the case demands a certain deliberation. Time being allowed for the survey and estimate of all the particulars, favourable and unfavourable, on both sides, there is gradually accumulated a sum of motive power *pro* and *con;* and when everything that can affect the decision has come forward, the account is closed, and the resolution adopted shows which side is the strongest. It may happen that either the pain of restraint, or the miseries of poverty, may stand forth in accidental prominence at the time of the decision, and turn the scale on the side that is weaker on the whole. A knowledge of this possibility would induce an experienced person to postpone the final resolution. We see the danger

## DELIBERATION.

of deciding in such circumstances constantly exemplified both by single individuals and by public bodies. So difficult does it appear to conquer the tendency, that we are often obliged to accept as a sufficient excuse for some wrong judgment, that the minds of men were unduly impressed with some stirring event that just then happened. The condemnation, by the Athenians, of the ten generals after the battle of Arginusæ, because, in a furious storm, they had not rescued from drowning the seamen of their disabled ships, was decided on under the strong burst of family feeling that accompanied the festival of the Apaturia. The historian, speaking of the Athenian people generally, while rebutting the charge of fickleness and inconstancy made against them, accuses them of the weakness, for weakness it is, of being too strongly urged by the impression uppermost at the moment. Any exciting question raised them to the impassioned pitch, and the result was something that they had afterwards probably to repent of.[*]

4. It is, in truth, no easy matter, in a complicated case nicely balanced, to retain in the mind the just values of all the opposing considerations, so as, at the instant of closing the account, to have a true sum total on either side. The great genius of prudential calculation, Benjamin Franklin, has left on record a remarkable letter addressed to Joseph Priestley, entitled *Moral Algebra, or method of deciding doubtful matters with one's-self,* in which he recommends the use, in daily-life questions, of the artificial methods practised in money accounts. I quote the letter entire :—' In the affair of so much importance to you, wherein you ask my advice, I cannot, for want of sufficient premises, counsel you *what* to determine ; but, if you please, I will tell you *how.* When those difficult cases occur, they are difficult, chiefly because, while we have them under consideration, all the reasons *pro* and *con* are not present to the mind at the same time ; but sometimes one set present themselves, and at other

---

[*] Grote's *Greece*, Part II., Chap. LXIV.

FRANKLIN'S MORAL ALGEBRA. 425

times another, the first being out of sight. Hence the various purposes or inclinations that alternately prevail, and the uncertainty that perplexes us.

'To get over this, my way is, to divide half a sheet of paper by a line into two columns; writing over the one *pro* and over the other *con;* then, during three or four days' consideration, I put down, under the different heads, short hints of the different motives, that at different times occur to me, *for* or *against* the measure. When I have thus got them altogether in one view, I endeavour to estimate their respective weights; and when I find two (one on each side) that seem equal, I strike them both out. If I find a reason *pro* equal to some *two* reasons *con*, I strike out the *three*. If I judge some two reasons *con* equal to some *three* reasons *pro*, I strike out the *five;* and, thus proceeding, I find where the balance lies; and if, after a day or two of further consideration, nothing new that is of importance occurs on either side, I come to a determination accordingly. And though the weight of reasons cannot be taken with the precision of algebraic quantities, yet, when each is thus considered separately and comparatively, and the whole lies before me, I think I can judge better, and am less liable to take a false step; and, in fact, I have found great advantage from this kind of equation, in what may be termed *moral* or *prudential algebra.*'

5. Such a method of aiding the understanding by the artifices of formality is not to be despised. In business and in science, auxiliaries of this nature are found indispensable; the human mind could not have taken the strides of improvement that we now benefit by, without a very large amount of formal procedure. Having this conviction, I will venture to suggest another device of a similar nature, which may be resorted to in difficult deliberations. It is more particularly aimed at the weakness last described, of our being too much impressed by the motives present at the moment when the case is closed. I will suppose that we have a certain length of time allowed for deciding between two different courses of action, say a month of thirty-one days, and that the mind is

at work every day entertaining the considerations and feelings on the two opposite sides. We may or may not employ Franklin's method of using a balance sheet; that has its separate advantages without interfering with the plan here intended. What I should suggest is that every evening we record the impression of the day, or put down the side which preponderates according to the balance of motives passing through the mind in the course of that day; and that this record should be continued during the whole period that the deliberation lasts. It would happen that in some days we feel more acutely the pressure of the motives on one side than on others; the preponderance being liable to be reversed from day to day in a question where the total of pleasures or pains is very nearly equal. But by allowing a lapse of time we should reduce the casual or accidental biasses to a general average, and at the end of the period we have only to sum up the records of the days, and see which side has the majority. If we found such a result as twenty to eleven, or nineteen to twelve, our decision would probably be a safe one, while fifteen to sixteen would be of course indecisive, but also of value as showing that no great blunder would be likely to arise in either course. The essence of this procedure lies in its taking account of all the states of mind that we pass through in reference to the opposing questions, and therefore the judgment should be deferred until we have described a complete cycle in this respect. In discussing the choice of a profession, we must look at it through all variety of seasons, circumstances, and states of body and mind, and this cannot be done in a day. Even if the consideration is carried over many weeks or months, the mind may be untrustworthy in recording the successive impressions, and may thus leave us at the mercy of those occurring last; it is to counteract such danger that the method of recording and summing up the separate decisions is here recommended. Another advantage would be that periodical re-hearings of the question, with interlocutory summings up, always advance it nearer to decision, and prevent any of the considerations which have at any time occurred to the mind, from falling again out of sight.

6. The deliberative process is very different in its chances of a good result, according as we deal with things experienced or things unexperienced. Having once gone a long voyage, we can readily decide on going to sea again, but when a youth that has never been on shipboard, is carried away by longings for the seafaring life, we have no criterion as to the likelihood of his being satisfied with the reality. There is a difficult, and often impossible, operation of constructiveness to be gone through, for the prior determination of how we shall actually feel in the situation that we are imagining to ourselves. Not only is time wanted for this, but also a good method of going to work. The recording of the daily impressions is of some use, as showing how the thing appears to the mind in the majority of days, but there may be a false colouring prevalent from first to last. To get at the actual experience, or genuine feelings, of a number of persons that have passed through the same career, is one valuable datum; and if we can find some constituted very nearly like ourselves, so much the better. We can never have too much matter-of-fact information, when committing ourselves to an untried career. The choice of a profession, the change of one's country by emigration, the undertaking of an extensive work which we cannot go back from, the contracting of the irrevocable tie of domestic life, ought all to be looked at with reference to the facts, and the foregone experience of trustworthy narrators; while the deliberation may be fitly aided and protected by formalities such as those now set forth. The feelings of the moment must be resisted by the machinery of the intelligence, at least to this extent that the resolution dictated by three days' consideration shall not have equal weight with the decisions come to in five others.

7. In this whole subject of Deliberation, therefore, there is no exception furnished against the general theory of the Will, or the doctrine, maintained in the previous pages, that, in volition, the executive is uniformly put in motion by some

428 RESOLUTION.

variety of pleasure or pain, present or apprehended, cool or excited. When, instead of acting out the result of the first clash of motives, we resist the impulses to action, and await the incursion of the other motives appertaining to the case, the exertion is a truly voluntary act ; a pain apprehended or conceived, namely, the pain suggested by foregone experience as likely to arise from hurried action in a complicated matter, spurs the activity to resist the prompting of the stronger of two present impulses. There is no essential difference between this operation of a deterring impulse, and the voluntary prompting to keep out of any other mode of impending harm. The distinction lies in the highly intellectual character of the sensibility involved. A careful series of observations on the consequences of our own actions and the actions of other people, or the imbibing of the narrated experience of the past, has impressed us with a feeling of evil or mischief arising from precipitate decisions—by no means a common education—and the conception of bad consequences takes the rank of a pain influencing the will, and casting its weight into every conflict of motives. In the earlier stages of life, this artificial sensibility is but feebly developed ; time, careful training, one's own observations and reflections, bring on the effective maturity of the feeling, and give it that enduring hold of the intellect whereby it takes its stand in arresting a hasty judgment.

8. Let us now make a few observations on the meaning of RESOLUTION as a phase of our voluntary actions. The close of the deliberative process implies that the prompting to delay, begotten of the sense of danger now discussed, ceases, its exigencies being fully satisfied. There would then follow a course of action in accordance with the motives that prevail. Just as, having examined several articles in a shop, we purchase the one that pleases us most, so in every other case of terminated conflict, action follows as a necessary result. There are no intermediate steps to be described, or any power to be consulted, in passing from an awakened sensibility to pleasure or suffering, and the action recognised

## RESOLUTION IMPLIES DEFERRED ACTION. 429

as proper to the emergency. It is the nature of the will to connect at once and decisively a pleasure with the exertion that sustains or increases it, and a pain with the exertion that relieves it. When suspense arises, it is through some new influence that checks the regular and ordinary course of the voluntary faculty. The deliberative veto is one mode of giving a check, but this withdrawn, action ensues. There is, nevertheless, one situation of suspense, which leads us to recognise an intermediate state—of decision without execution —namely, when we have deliberated on a course of proceeding that is still future, so that the execution must wait till a given time has elapsed. In this condition of things we give a name to the unexecuted determination ; we term it a Resolution. The mind having formed such a resolution, that is having deliberated and felt which side is the stronger on the whole, is thereupon urged to a course of action, but cannot at once proceed upon it ; in other words, the train of executive impulses undergoes a certain modification, which may be described as follows. Instead of doing at once what is suggested, a preliminary volition takes place, namely, the act of looking out for, watching or waiting the moment, known as proper to commence the main operations. When a youth is destined for the university, his parents or guardians deliberate beforehand which classes he shall enter. The decision is probably come to some time previous to the opening day. Execution therefore is suspended, but meanwhile a volition is actually working itself out, namely, the act of counting the days and keeping note of the time, and other circumstances appertaining to the act of enrolment. We may say properly that a decision of the will never goes to sleep. If we cannot follow instantaneously the natural prompting of the stronger impulse, left in the ascendant by the cessation of the deliberative veto, we assume the attitude of attention to the time when execution is to begin. Resolution, therefore, means the preliminary volition for ascertaining when to enter upon a series of actions necessarily deferred. The interruption arising in this way is a purely accidental cir-

**430** RESOLUTION.

cumstance, and in no degree changes the proper character of the will, which is to execute at once whatever a motive exists for.

9. In following out a decision of importance, it most frequently happens that the operations are protracted over a length of time. I undertake a piece of work, likely to occupy me six months, and my resolution must sustain my active energies all that time. Nay, we have resolutions enduring with our lives, as in those rules that we propose to ourselves as the means of abating the evils and enhancing the satisfactions of life. Virtue was defined by Cicero as a perpetual will of acting out virtuous precepts. Volitions of this continuous character are in danger of being occasionally overpowered by indolence, the sense of fatigue, passing pleasures, and solicitations of various kinds, whence it comes to be a characteristic of Resolutions, to need occasional aliment or stimulus, as by reminding ourselves, or by being reminded, of the important ends that led to their adoption. Indeed, it may happen that they are utterly overthrown long before they have accomplished the work intended. The middle state of resolution is a state of trial and uncertainty. The strong sense of good to be gained, or evil to be quashed, that originally presided over the determination of the will may fade away, or give place to other feelings leading to an opposite line of conduct. My resolve to rise every morning at a certain hour for a year to come, is prompted at the outset by a certain force of motive which suffices to get me up for a week, but is no longer strong enough to encounter the inducement that keeps me in bed; that is to say, the resolution is broken through.

Every one's life contains a number of sudden or hasty resolutions, conceived under the pressure of an emergency, and wanting that full deliberation above alluded to. It is impossible that a volition requiring protracted labour can be sustained by the prompting of a temporary cause. I feel very much mortified and humbled on some one occasion by meeting a rebuff from being too forward in tendering advice; in the smarting of the moment, I am urged strongly to avoid this danger in future. If on the same day I am brought into a similar predicament, I act out my chosen attitude of neutrality. Time passes, and the painful experience dies away ; an occasion arises where I am prompted again to intrude my opinion into another person's affairs. Perhaps the intrusion is well received in this case, and away go the last vestiges of the former mortification and the resolution bred of it. Perhaps, however, 1 am met with a repetition of the former rebuff ; this would infallibly revive the old resolution with new energy, and the memory would retain for a much longer time the shock of pain, and would keep it alive for the protection of the future. But a temporary resolution, formed without reference to the states of mind that one is likely to pass through, before the execution is accomplished, is sure to fail ; other occasions occur, prompting the contrary course, with quite an equal force, and so neutralize what seemed at the time an all-powerful influence.

10. We exist from day to day under a host of resolutions. The intelligence—itself put in motion by a grand volition, having for its end the harmony of the whole life, which means the avoidance of clashings and failures—arranges the work to be done for each day, and the action to be performed under every situation ; and, as the successive moments arrive, the memory presents the operation with its animating motive, and the organs are inspired accordingly. The result of the whole is multitudinous and complex, but the mental laws are few and simple. We must have a certain development of the intelligence, in the shape of memory, of the succession to be observed, of the behaviour to be adopted under each definite circumstance, and of the pains and pleasures that sustain the requisite labour. We must have an educated executive, or an association between the various sensations of outward things and the acts properly suited to each case, as when the soldier obeys the word of command, or the sound of the trumpet. Each man sent out for a day's work, and actually fulfilling it, is provided with all these requisites. He knows

432 EFFORT.

what to take up first, second, and third; a particular hour is specified for one thing, and his memory retains the connexion, so that when the hour strikes, he proceeds with that; and, should a certain eventuality happen, he is provided with an association suggesting what change or adaptation he must make to meet it, and he is also so far alive to the pleasure of doing, or the pain of not doing, the appointed act, that a volitional spur equal to the occasion is not wanting. Such is a rough description of our industrial life from day to day. An educated activity, motives to the will, and an intelligence to represent those motives when they are not actual pains or pleasures, and to harmonize the succession of our operations,— are the general foundations of all those multifarious doings that constitute the stream of our active life.

11. I have reserved for the close of this chapter the consideration of the feeling of EFFORT, upon which so much stress is laid in the theoretical questions arising on the subject of the will. A voluntary act (as well as some acts not voluntary) is accompanied with consciousness, or feeling, of which there may be several sorts. The original motive is some pleasure or pain, experienced or conceived. The active exertion is accompanied with the muscular consciousness, agreeable in states of vigour, painful under exhaustion or fatigue, and often indifferent as regards pleasure or pain. Now which of these modes of consciousness is properly designated by the term 'Effort'? Probably it includes all the phases of expended energy,— pleasurable exercise, the pain of acting under fatigue, and the tracts of mere indifference; but more particularly the sense of fatigue. There is a common phrase 'costing no effort,' used in contrast to 'labour,' 'pains,' 'taking trouble,' which are modes of effort. So that 'effort' really means the muscular consciousness accompanying voluntary activity, and more especially in the painful stage. It is a case of conflict between a motive urging us to act, and a muscular pain that would keep us from acting.

Great importance has been attached to this peculiar sensibility of the active framework. It has been supposed that

## MIND AS A MECHANICAL PRIME MOVER. 433

here we have mechanical power originating in a purely mental agency. The ancient and prevailing doctrine, representing volition as the source of all moving power, is considered to receive the strongest confirmation from the feeling of effort that accompanies the putting forth of muscular energy. It is, therefore, interesting to examine closely the sequence of cause and effect in the production of mechanical force by the will. I will first extract a passage from Sir John Herschel's *Astronomy*, where the doctrine in question is forcibly expressed.

'Whatever attempts may have been made by metaphysical writers to reason away the connexion of cause and effect, and fritter it down to the unsatisfactory relation of habitual sequence,* it is certain that the conception of some more real and intimate connection is quite as strongly impressed upon the human mind as that of the existence of an external world —the vindication of whose reality has (strange to say) been regarded as an achievement of no common merit in the annals of this branch of philosophy. It is our own immediate consciousness *of effort,* when we exert force to put matter in motion, or to oppose and neutralize force, which gives us this internal conviction of *power* and *causation* so far as it refers to the material world, and compels us to believe that whenever we see material objects put in motion from a state of rest, or deflected from their rectilinear paths, and changed in their velocities if already in motion, it is in consequence of such an EFFORT *somehow* exerted, though not accompanied with *our* consciousness. That such an effort should be exerted with success through an interposed space, is no more difficult to

---

\* 'See Brown *On Cause and Effect*—a work of great acuteness and subtlety of reasoning on some points, but in which the whole train of argument is vitiated by one enormous oversight; the omission, namely, of a *distinct and immediate personal consciousness of causation* in his enumeration of that *sequence of events,* by which the volition of the mind is made to terminate in the motion of material objects. I mean the consciousness of *effort,* as a thing entirely distinct from mere *desire* or *volition* on the one hand, and from mere spasmodic contraction of muscles on the other.—Brown, Third Edition, Edinburgh, 1818, p. 47.'

2 E

## 434　EFFORT.

conceive than that our hand should communicate motion to a stone, with which it is *demonstrably not in contact.*

'All bodies with which we are acquainted, when raised into the air and quietly abandoned, descend to the earth's surface in lines perpendicular to it. They are, therefore, urged thereto by a force or effort, the direct or indirect result of a *consciousness* and a *will* existing *somewhere*, though beyond our power to trace, which force we term *gravity ;* and whose tendency or direction, as universal experiences teaches, is towards the earth's centre.'—*Treatise on Astronomy,* Chap. VII.

Undoubtedly, if we view the whole assemblage of phenomena, occurring in an act of will, there is involved some kind or variety of the feelings of activity. Effort of the painful sort may be entirely absent. On the first start of a chase with the hounds, no living thing concerned feels the sense of effort ; although there is a muscular consciousness of some kind.

But the question arises, is this muscular consciousness, pleasurable or painful, the sole antecedent of the mechanical energy arising from a volition ? Or, putting together all the conscious elements preparatory to the act,—the feelings that constitute the motive, together with the consciousness of the exertion,—can we say that these exhaust the antecedent circumstances rendering sentient beings mechanical prime movers ?

Certainly not. The case is far otherwise. When the field-labourer goes out in the morning to plough a field, he is under a volition, and in this volition there is a certain consciousness—call it ' effort,' ' power,' or anything else, but it is not the consciousness by itself that enables him to stand at his plough. A large expenditure of muscular and nervous energy, derived in the final resort from his well-digested meals and healthy respiration, is the true source, the veritable antecedent of all that muscular power. It is now-a-days a truism to compare a living animal with a steam-engine, as regards the source of the moving power. What the coal by its com-

## ANIMAL ACTIVITY WITHOUT CONSCIOUSNESS.

bustion is to the engine, the food and inspired air are to the living system; the concurring consciousness of expended power is no more the cause of that power, than the illumination cast by the engine furnace is the source of the movements generated.

It seems strange that the consciousness of effort should be deemed the antecedent or cause of the voluntary movements, considering that when the power is at its greatest the effort is null, and when the effort is at its greatest the power is null. The feeling of effort is the symptom of declining energy, the proof that the true antecedent, namely, the organic state of the nerves and muscles, is on the eve of being exhausted.

It is to be observed, farther, that the animal system puts forth active energy without, as well as with, consciousness, but in no case without the expenditure of nutritive material. The consumption of food and transformation of tissue are the essential part of the production of power, the consciousness is the accidental part. In all the reflex, or voluntary operations,—the circulation of the blood, the movements of the chest, the motion of the intestines,—there is mechanical power generated, with the total absence of consciousness. If we are bent on finding the antitype, or explanation, of the powers of nature, in our own constitution, why should we not fasten upon these involuntary actions, as well as upon the voluntary? Then again, it has been, as I believe, demonstrated that movements arise spontaneously in the system, or without any previous sensibility or stimulation of the senses; the antecedent cause being wholly physical. Apart from physical conditions, the most intense consciousness is impotent. So, in the maturity of the will, when the presence of a feeling leads to the rousing of a dormant energy, the consciousness is a determining circumstance in the effect, but if the sytem were not in proper tone and condition at the moment, the action would not result. The energy and persistence of the action do not rise with the intensity of the consciousness, but with the corporeal development, and the material conditions. Voluntary actions are distinguished from reflex actions by the

436　　　　　　　　　EFFORT.

intervention of a feeling in their production ; and the phenomenon is a very remarkable one, introducing us as it were into a new world : but it is simply a mistake to call the one class the pure offshoot of feeling, and the other the working of physical causes. Every portion of moving power coming from the will needs the same transformation of tissue, as an equal portion arising in the involuntary movements of the system.

16. If it so please us, we are at liberty to say that mind is a source of power ; but we must then mean by mind, the consciousness in conjunction with the whole body ;* and we must also be prepared to admit, that the physical energy is the indispensable condition, and the consciousness the casual. Only in one class of animal forces is feeling present; the rest work on in deep unconsciousness. The real lesson derivable from the survey of the living frame, as regards the sources of mechanical momentum, is summed up in the analogy of the steam-engine, where active chemical combinations give birth to moving force, through the medium of a certain mechanism. Physiologists are now pretty well agreed on this point, and the case is brought under the head of the grand doctrine of the interchangeability of the natural powers—Heat, Electricity, Chemical Affinity, Mechanical Force—otherwise termed their ' correlation,' which physical inquirers have of late years been occupied in developing. Instead of mind being the cause of gravity, gravity and the other physical forces are the *sine quâ non* of mind in human beings and animals. Our only experience of mental manifestations is in connexion with a gravitating framework of exceedingly complicated mechanism,

---

* ' Our consciousness in this life is an *embodied* consciousness. Human Understanding and Belief are related, in a variety of ways, to the original and successive states of the corporeal organism, from birth to death. Observation and experiment prove the important practical fact, that the conscious life on earth of every individual is dependent on his organism and its history. This condition of human consciousness affords room for a curious and interesting science, still in its infancy, but to which many eminent minds have applied themselves in ancient and modern times.'—*Rational Philosophy in History and in System,* by Professor Fraser of Edinburgh, p. 122.

PHYSICAL AGENCY RESULTS FROM PHYSICAL FORCES.   437

and concentrating, in a small compass, numerous physical, chemical, physiological forces, balanced and adjusted, in an organization, self-supporting indeed, but requiring perpetual renovation and perpetual means of elimination.   We find that the mental property, in alliance with this corporeal aggregate, is remarkably susceptible to every physical effect and every trifling disturbance.   In a word, mind, as known to us in our own constitution, is the very last thing that we should set up as an independent power, swaying and sustaining the powers of the natural world.

17. Moreover, I have not adverted to the circumstance of familiar occurrence, that the habitual actions, including some of our most difficult displays of power and skill, tend to become unconscious.   A man can walk, turn a wheel, attend on a machine, cast up accounts, play on an instrument, with the mind completely at his disposal for something else.   There are moments in the performance of our routine processes, when the consciousness of them falls under a total eclipse, while at the same time the organs continue to operate. Whatever act is very much repeated, approaches more and more to this predicament ; and although feeling was requisite at the commencement, we come to dispense with it in the end. These are the actions that, from their resemblance to the reflex processes inherent in our constitution, have been termed the secondarily automatic.   The nervous framework is adjusted to perform the one by original conformation, and the other by the plastic property at the basis of all our acquirements. Here, then, is a large mass of various activity, maintained without the co-operation of the mind, or with that in a small and diminishing degree.   Mind, it is true, was concerned in the commencement, but after a time the execution is committed to the purely physical part of the mechanism.   Thus we derive another illustration of the accidental, temporary, and intermitted presence of the mental property, and the indispensable and perennial character of the corporeity, in giving origin to moving power.

# CHAPTER VIII.

### DESIRE.

1. DESIRE is that phase of volition where there is a motive, but no ability to act upon it. The inmate of a small gloomy chamber conceives to himself the pleasure of light and of an expanded prospect ; the unsatisfying ideal urges the appropriate action for gaining the reality ; he gets up and walks out. Suppose, now, that the same ideal delight comes into the mind of a prisoner. Unable to fulfil the prompting, he remains under the solicitation of the motive ; and his state is denominated craving, longing, appetite, Desire. If all motive impulses could be at once followed up, desire would have no place.

The state of craving is thus, in the first place, a want or deficiency, an inferior level of happiness. In the second place, there is the idea or conception of some delight, with the notion that the ideal form is much below the realized condition ; consequent on which is a motive to the will to compass the reality. And, thirdly, there is a bar in the way of acting, which leads to the state of *conflict*, and renders desire a more or less painful frame of mind.

2. We have a form of desire in all our more protracted operations, or when working for distant ends. The suppression of the state of craving is complete, only when the gratification is under the hand ; as, when I become thirsty, having a glass of water on the table before me. If I have to ring a bell, and send some one off to fetch the water, I remain under the urgency, but in a modified shape, seeing that I am bringing about my

ALTERNATIVES WHEN VOLITION IS CHECKED. 439

sure relief. In such cases, Desire is synonymous with pursuit, industry, or voluntary action for distant, intermediate, or comprehensive ends. Many of our pleasures and pains have names that denote them not in their actuality but in the condition of desire and pursuit. Thus, 'avarice' expresses not the fruition but the pursuit of wealth. There is no name for the pure pleasure of knowledge; 'curiosity' signifies the state of active desire. So. with 'ambition;' to indicate the real gratification we are obliged to use complex phrases, as 'the pleasure of power,' 'the sentiment of power possessed and exercised.' It would be mere repetition of what has been already said respecting the regular operation of the will, to exemplify desire in connexion with industrial pursuit. The only form remaining to be considered is the case where the gratification is unattainable.

3. The question then arises, what are the courses open to us, when no volition is possible. It is but too common to experience pains that prompt to action in vain, as regards their alleviation; to feel actual pleasures slipping away before we have had our fill of them; and to conceive ideal pleasures not to be realized. Neither by present exertion, nor by postponed, but sure, opportunities of action, can we obey the mandate to work for pleasure or to remove pain. It is in this state of things that we bring to light the peculiar workings of desire, as contrasted with the routine of proper volition.

4. The first alternative is described by the names *endurance*, resignation, contentment, acquiescence, patience, fortitude. In consequence of the pain of the conflict, and the impossibility of terminating it by fruition, the will is urged to suppress the longing itself, which is possible by dismissing the idea from the thoughts. The craving for unattainable wealth, or for a hopeless affection, may be met by a grand effort not to entertain the ideal as a subject of contemplation. This is to induce the state of contentment. When the longing is for fancied bliss, as when people sigh after honour, splendour, power, or unusable wealth, the coercion of the intellectual trains may be such as to restore the quiet of the mind.

440                    DESIRE.

It is somewhat different when we are under the pressure of some actual pain—as physical agony, destitution, contumely, oppression, the privation of what we are accustomed to ; granting that we suppress the thought of relief, we have still the irritation to bear up against. The counter-volition of endurance now consists in being urged, by the pains of spasmodic gesticulation and fruitless endeavour, to remain still ; not permitting either the diffusive manifestations or the vain attempts at relief. Under this stern regimen, the system sooner adapts itself to the new situation, and the fortitude is rewarded by a mitigation of the pain.

The misery of fruitless endeavour is not the sole motive inspiring this forced composure of the irritated frame. The reflecting and cultivated mind is urged to it by remote considerations also. The waste of valuable strength in these struggles, the feeling of dignity associated in the mind with endurance, the approbation that it brings, and the reprobation so often given to the impatient temper—all concur in moving the counter resolution of forced quietism. The history of the world is full of wonderful feats of endurance, and these not limited to civilized peoples. The fortitude of the old Spartan in physical suffering and privation is rivalled or surpassed by the Indian fakeer, and the American savage. Such displays can often be commanded, when that most overwhelming of all motives, public opinion, determines that they shall be.

5. Endurance is talked of as being either physical or moral. The fact is, that it applies to every one of the long catalogue of our possible pains, whether those that are so in their first origin, or those that arise from the privation of some pleasure. All the disagreeables reaching us through the senses, and all the modes of emotion that belong to the side of suffering, stimulate the will into action, and, if an effectual means of alleviation is known, that will be followed out. If the means are unknown, one attempt after another will be entered upon ; and, if nothing succeeds, the secondary vexation of conflict, disappointment and unrest, will overtake us. Rather than go on with this new evil, we fall back upon the

ENDURANCE. 441

quiet endurance of the first; which, however, cannot be done except by a new act of will, dictated and kept up by the suffering of abortive action, and those other considerations that make up a powerful array of motives in favour of the patient attitude. The same counteractive may be brought into play, when we are torn and exhausted by the extreme outbursts of the emotional manifestation. We have seen that pain may, in one set of circumstances, run out into violent expression, and, in others, to volition. In both cases, we may incur new evil, to a greater extent than we obtain relief, and hence a motive, for total suppression of both outgoings, is brought before the mind. It is within the power of the will to suppress the diffusive movements of a strong emotion, by bringing a force to bear upon the voluntary members in the first instance, and by that control of the thoughts, which is the most direct method accessible to us for affecting the states of consciousness in their inmost recesses. No doubt it is always a question, if the secondary force is strong enough to cope with the first, whether that be a voluntary stimulus or an emotional wave. Anything like the complete endurance of all the incurable pains that come over the human being is not a usual endowment, nor can it be bred without a superior force of voluntary determinations generally, as compared with the other impulses of the system, accompanied by a protracted education on this special head. There is a class of minds specially sensitive to those secondary pains now alluded to, and with whom, therefore, the motive to quietism has more than ordinary efficacy. Goethe may be quoted as a case in point. Being so constituted as to suffer acutely the nervous exhaustion of internal conflict, such minds are strongly induced to throw the whole weight of the voluntary impetus into the scale of prevention, or to concentrate in one conflict the decision of the mind, instead of suffering the distraction of many. It is possible even to form a passionate attachment to a serene mode of life, so as to surrender many positive pleasures rather than not realize the end.

6. So much for one solution of the problem of ungratified

442                    DESIRE.

impulse or desire.* It is not given to every one to succeed in
this method, as bearing on the whole compass of desires, however much we may deem it the preferable course. We have
now to consider what other solution can be resorted to, of a
less severe character as regards the demand for energetic
efforts of the will. There is a mode of an easier kind, which
may be designated by the general title of *ideal or imaginary
action*. We all know what is meant by day-dreaming, castle-
building, and such like terms; as implying that one finds
scope in an imaginary world for the gratification of longings
that are not answered by anything in the realities of one's lot.
This method of proceeding, however, is not of the same universal application as the preceding; it is not every desire that
can be even partially satisfied by imaginary outgoings. If, for
example, we take any of the bodily appetites,—hunger, thirst,
sleep, &c., or any of the other organic sensations,—heat, cold,

---

* I have not introduced into the text any notice of those antidotes common to Desire with all other forms of pain. The uneasiness of ineffectual
craving may be appeased by drawing upon some of our stores of pleasure.
It is in this way that we appease the longings of infancy, and prevent the
mischiefs of a too rampant appetite. It being the prerogative of pleasure to
neutralize the sting of pain, we apply it to silence the restlessness secondary
to suffering as well as the primary irritation. The mind will often accept a
substitute for what is pretty strongly longed for; and we are but too glad to
ply this method of compromise for the blessings of peace and content.

Another device of familiar application is the diversion of the thoughts
from the subject that has caused the state of craving. When this originates
in the conception of some pleasure, and not in a real want or suffering, the
remedy may be found where the evil arose; namely, in the intellect. The
seeing or hearing of some one's good fortune on a point that we ourselves
are susceptible to, quickens our longings if not our envy, and leaves us very
much out of sorts with ourselves and the world. It is at such a moment that
the advent of a friend, the arrival of some stirring news, the necessity for
falling to work at a task, or some other influence suggesting an entire change
of subject, will prove a healing balm. New associating links can always more
or less turn aside the stream of pre-existing ideas, and there are many occasions when this fact exercises a benign power. The consolation afforded by
a spiritual adviser, or a wise friend, has no other basis to proceed upon, and
yet great effects may be operated by the skilful management of this resource.
Nevertheless, there is nothing of special adaptation to the pains of thwarted
desire in the present method any more than in the foregoing.

THE IDEAL GRATIFICATION OF DESIRE. 443

nervous depression, we find that no ideal or imagined relief is
of any practical avail :

> Who can hold a fire in his hand
> By thinking on the frosty Caucasus?

On the other hand, the craving for a return of scenes and
days of bygone pleasure, sometimes contains so much of
the 'pleasures of memory' of the foregone emotions, as to
make it satisfying to a great degree merely to imagine circumstances that shall bring about a return. So, when any
one has deeply offended us, being yet beyond the reach of our
retaliation, we have still some fraction of the full measure of
revenge, by going over in the mind what we should do if the
offender were to cross our path. Any sentiment that is naturally luxuriant in the constitution, being not likely to be met
in all its fulness by the reality, makes up for the defect by a
series of ideal volitions corresponding to its demands. The
sentiment of power is a signal example of this. Each one
whose sphere falls below what this feeling leads him to wish,
finds in imagined domains an outlet for the insatiable craving;
and such may be the peculiarity of the individual, that empire
in conception may go a great way to supply the void.

7. The comparison now instituted between the physical
wants, and certain of the emotions or sentiments, suggests at
once what the circumstance is that enables us to find
gratification or relief in imaginary actions. Referring to a
former chapter (*Emotions*, Chap. XIII.), it will be remembered that a feeling persisting after the fact, or recovered by
mere association, without the presence of the proper stimulus,
can sometimes approach the fulness of the real experience ; so
much so, that we are content in many instances with this bare
conception, or ideal resuscitation. The recollection of a time
of gaiety and excitement, of some interesting conversation or
discourse, or of a book that we have read, may give such an
amount of the feeling of actual experience that we rest satisfied with that, and wish nothing farther. On a matter, therefore, where we have a power of restoring mentally the full-
toned delight of a real experience, it is easy to convert memory

## 444 DESIRE.

into imagination, and to construct future gratifications of the same sort, with or without a basis of reality. We speak occasionally of some one having a strong imagination, when we mean that such a one can body forth an ideal pleasure, so as to derive from it an entire satisfaction of the want of the moment. In the physical cravings, this is an impossibility. Something may be done to stave off for a little the insupportable agony of thirst, hunger, drowsiness, or cold, or to lull the acute pinch of a neuralgic pain, but the actual in these cases is too strong for the most highly stimulated counter-ideal. We have thus two opposite extremes among our multitudinous sensibilities; the one where actuality alone can fill up the aching void, the other where the mere idea amounts to the full demands of the system; and between those extremes lie the whole range of imaginary volition, put in motion at the instance of pains or pleasures, such as we cannot work for in the regular compass of our voluntary exertion.

8. So wide is the operation of these ideal outgoings, that the chief difficulty lies in selecting a good instance, to show how faithfully a course of voluntary action is repeated in the idea. Take the desire of Wealth. The motive growing out of pleasure secured, and pain turned aside, by worldly abundance, stimulates, perhaps, the largest share of the activity of mankind. To work, to husband the fruits of toil, to combine intelligence with handicraft, to exercise self-denial, and surmount the love of ease, are the genuine manifestations of our volitional nature under this cumulative end. The motive, however, may exist, where the means of attainment are from various causes restricted. A man may feel very keenly the sufferings that wealth could alleviate, and may have an appetizing conception of pleasures that it could command, but may be so situated as to be unable to compass the desirable object. It is then that imagination overleaps the barrier, and fills the mind with the ideas of those transactions that in other circumstances would be reproduced in reality. If the young man's obstacle at starting is the want of a certain capital to trade upon, his imaginings take the form of chalking out his

## IMAGINARY ACTIVITY.

line of operations, were he in actual possession of the amount desiderated. If the difficulty is to obtain a certain office exactly adapted to his abilities, he is occasionally led to assume this difficulty overcome, and to sketch in his mind the active proceedings consequent thereon. It is still the stimulus of volition that is the prime mover of the activity; and the activity itself is essentially voluntary, although transferred from the actual operations, to the ideal rehearsal of them. This ideal volition is, in fact, an essential prelude to the lifting of the hand, and the performing of the actual business as it arises. The man that has gained his capital, or his office, has to spend a certain time in the mental work of deliberation under conflicting impulses, before taking the real proceedings ; and the dreamer, moved by the same original motives, goes through these ideal preliminaries, even when they can end in nothing real. And when a man actually has great wealth, his principal enjoyment of it consists in imagining what he *might* buy with it, but does not buy. Take, again, the very estimable end implied under curiosity, or the desire of rational knowledge, which possesses some minds so intensely as to constitute itself an end of pursuit. Suppose the aspirant occupied with routine toil, and removed from libraries and the converse of the learned. What would such a one do, if suddenly released from confining drudgery, and sent off to the metropolis of letters and science, with freedom to drink in knowledge to the utmost ? The urgency of the motive would stimulate a certain deliberation in the first instance, at the close of which he would set out in the full career of execution. Pretty much the same course is described when he allows himself to forget his bonds, and give the rein to his imagination. The train of thought is a train of volitions forecasted as if for being carried into effect, it being possible to become occasionally oblivious to the limits that circumscribe the actual situation. The point to be noted on this subject, is the instrumentality of the voluntary part of our nature, in keeping up the trains of thought that we go through under such circumstances. It is not by mere laws of association

446 DESIRE.

that we expatiate over fields of fancied activity, and reap in idea the fruits of exertion : it is the thought controlled by the will, or by the motives present at the time. The intellect by itself brings up certain trains, some of which are embraced and dwelt upon as suiting the urgency of the moment, while all the rest sink away unheeded. The same process is repeated so often as a choice of objects is before the mind. It is not the magnitude and grandeur of the metropolis, with its shops and shipping, its equipages and crowds, that seize the imagination of a scholar; these would be suggested by the intellectual links of reproduction, but they are not dwelt upon ; they sink away for want of a supporting stimulus in the mind, alive only to the thirst for knowledge. I have said before (*Compound Association*, § 13) that volition is a determining force in the rise of the thoughts, and I think it is pretty clear in what way the influence works. Now, as our actual conduct can be conceived in memory after the fact, and as this memory of the past can be so altered as to construct an anticipation of the future, which anticipation is essential to the deliberative process, so it is possible to go through the same mental operations for some line of conduct that is never realized, and cannot be realized. The general remembers at the end of a campaign all that he has done ; if he is reappointed to a similar post, he makes use of these past experiences, retained in his mind, to construct a future plan ; if, laid aside from service, he still cherishes the love of command and military glory,—this sentiment inspires trains of imaginary campaigns, which not being restrained by reality, are apt to take a grander flight, so as to please to the full measure the emotions that sustain them.

9. The kind of feelings most favourable to these constructions of imagined activity, are those that lie midway between the extremes above mentioned, viz., the class that can give no satisfaction, except in actual fruition of the objects, and the class that are satisfactory in the highest degree as mere ideal emotions. The tender affections, complacency, honour, and the sentiment of power, as existing in the average of persons,

## EMOTIONS FITTED FOR IDEAL GRATIFICATION. 447

make some approach to this middle character. We might say the same of the artistic feelings, and the love of knowledge. But there is, perhaps, hardly any sensibility of human nature that may not prove a basis for day-dreaming in some constitution or other; while in many cases the feelings now mentioned may fail in that respect. It may give one no pleasure at all to imagine the recovery of a lost friend, or to dream of fame, fortune and power. As mere ideas, these may not warm up an agreeable glow, but only reproduce the pain of privation, as when we suffer fatigue, hunger or cold. There is, moreover, a sentiment of our nature that revolts from excessive ideality, namely, the painful sense of conflict between this and our actual condition. In minds alive to the contradiction, the suffering that it gives is so acute, as to be a motive power hostile to the outgoings of the mind in vain imaginings. We call this a healthy check, from the fact that the duties and interests of life are put in peril by the license of roaming desire.

10. It is easy to understand how pain generates avoidance in the ideal as well as in the actual. It is only necessary that the recollection of the painful quality be tolerably vivid—as when we earnestly reflect how to keep at a distance shame or penury. As regards the motives from pleasure, there is something to be explained. If I have in my mind the vivid conception of some favourite delight—as of music, spectacle, or social intercourse—why should I not remain content with what I remember of it? It is quite true that there may be still higher degrees of gratification than mine, but such would be the case, whatever felicity I might attain to. This leads us to consider closly the nature of that state of mind wherein a pleasure in idea craves to become one in reality. There must be something in it different from the mere impulse to add to a present delight up to full satiety. It is a fact that I am much more satisfied with a plain and moderate meal than with the imagination of a feast. There would seem to be a certain pain mixed up with imagined good, resembling the pain of a bodily craving, and I have no doubt that this is

448                          DESIRE.

so. We are said sometimes to set our heart upon a particular
enjoyment, which is a mode of signifying that we have been
worked up to such a condition respecting it, as to feel the
deprivation to be a real want of the system. The desire of
pleasure, in this sense, contains in it the mental sting of an
acute suffering. We are thus brought back to the great distinction made above between pleasures whose memory or
conception is satisfying, and those of an opposite sort. In
cases where we can remember that we were at a certain time
very much elated, but where the remembrance contains in
itself no elation whatsoever, there starts up a painful feeling
urging us to realize that time again, of which to entertain only
the remembrance is an empty notion. We can take hold of
a past emotion by a present effort of the intellect, so as to
recognise intellectually the distinguishing qualities of it—to
compare it with others agreeing or disagreeing with it, while
yet nothing of the genuine thrill is again reproduced. It is
in such a predicament, that volition and desire are roused by
a motive power, which we may concede as in part made up of
pleasure—namely, that very small share that still clings to
the memory, or notion,—but which I believe to spring mostly
out of the pain of so imperfect a realization of what we know
to have been a state of high delight. The ardent Greek, remembering the excitement of an Olympic gathering, has a
certain elated feeling stirred up by the mere remembrance ;
but at the same time he recognises the great difference between
his present tone of enjoyment and that full tide of hilarious
glee that belonged to the days of the great celebration ; and
it is upon this sense of difference that he is moved to be present at another festival, or failing that, to visit it in imagination. The pleasurable part of the state urges the will for an
additional draught ; the sense of shortcoming of the recollection is of the nature of a pain, and operates for its own
removal. If that amount of excitement, stirred up by the
memory of some happy day gone by, could exist in the mind
without any comparative reference, we might probably feel
gladdened, without any spur of desire—it is the idea of still

PROVOCATIVES OF DESIRE. **449**

greater delights that mars the peace of the mind. What happens in our ordinary appetites is illustrative of the two-fold urgency of desire. In the state of hunger there is pain; in the memory of past gratifications there is pleasure; we have therefore the two motives—deliverance from suffering, and the attainment of a positive delight additional to the pleasurable reaction from the pain.

11. A brief consideration of the several provocatives of desire will tend still farther to the elucidation of the point just raised. In the matter of appetite, these can be very readily specified. The wants of the system, implied in the bodily cravings as they come round, waken up the orgasm of the mind. When the watery fluids are dried up, thirst is experienced; when the stomach has long been empty, and the general nutrition is low, hunger takes possession of the animal. Long-continued exercise rouses a state of pain strongly suggesting repose. Such are the main and the proper causes of those various states of bodily craving. If there be any of the deeper emotions, whose periodic venting becomes identified with the serenity and content of the system, they too will make their regular demand as the time comes round. How far nature has implanted in the constitution necessities for giving scope to such emotions as tenderness, the sentiment of power, complacency, admiration, and the sense of beauty, I am not prepared to say. If there were any case of this sort in our original mechanism, I should say, in all probability, that would be the tender feeling. The analogy between this, and the sexual region of sensibility, is considerable; and experience would seem to indicate a very general need of interchanging the sentiments of affection with our fellow-beings. This is probably the most widely-spread of all our susceptibilities to emotion. Fear, anger, complacency, approbation, power, knowledge, fine-art, moral sentiment, are certainly not in the nature of primordial cravings. After being felt they operate in the way of desire or avoidance, but we might go through a long life without recognising the void, if any one of them were left in entire dormancy.

2 F

450                DESIRE

In all cases where a bodily want does not create the uneasiness that prompts the will, or when there is no actual suffering of any kind, we must reckon the *experience of pleasure* as the great provocative of desire. The carnivorous animal, before sucking blood, is not urged to the pursuit of its prey with the fury shown after tasting. The American Indian has no desire for intoxicating liquor until some fatal draught of spirits has once been administered. The simple rustic is too deeply ignorant of town delights to be troubled with any longings for concerts, and operas, and gay spectacle. Those pleasures once tasted give birth to the craving for repetition. They leave behind them a recollection of the fact of their giving an intense enjoyment; while the bare recollection is of itself but the dry bones of the feast.' In some rare minds, a very few actual occasions of high pleasure leave behind them such a vivid track of ideal emotion as to content the mind, and supersede the reality. This is the extreme instance; most commonly the memory of the past is accompanied with a painful sense of the difference between the glow of the dying embers and the full blaze of the original, and it is this contrast that is the sting of desire. Everything, then, that recalls to mind foregone times and occasions of pleasure is apt to engender the state of craving. If ways and means are at hand, and no counter volition exist, we go forth into action for the reality; in circumstances of obstruction, we may find an outlet in imagined pursuit. It is not every moment that we are visited by the recollections of departed joys; some circumstance is necessary as an associating link of revival. To be tempted is to have some consideration or idea brought before the mind, calculated to restore vividly those experiences. The sight of something sweet or savoury fires the craving of the child to partake of it. The display of gold has often stimulated to crime. The pomp and paraphernalia of the rich waken the vain longings of the less wealthy spectator; and mere recitals and narratives of good fortune kindle the same urgency and unrest. Here, however, it is expedient to draw the line between simple remembrance and

## SUSCEPTIBILITY TO IDEAL INFLAMMATION. 451

the constructive imagination of pleasure ; for although the last has its foundation in the first, the workings of the two are in the end widely contrasted. A true and sober recollection of a real pleasure instigates the pursuit of a repetition of it, which pursuit may be either real or ideal, according to circumstances. But we have a great alacrity in using these remembered pleasures, as a stepping-stone to the conception of modes and degrees of delight far beyond anything that we have ever known in the fruition. This is one of our easiest exercises of the constructive faculty. We gather together all our experienced delights into one ideal sum, and picture these to ourselves multiplied many times over, and this vast total is what we proceed upon, in letting loose the fancy in some high ideal chase. The inflammatory agents of desire include all those pictures of unbounded bliss that poetry and romance exhibit to the mind of the absorbed reader. To these we must add the enchanting power of absence, which suggests only what the mind pleases to entertain, and gives full liberty to omit from the account the drawbacks of the reality. Certain objects of sense owe a part of their charm to their inflaming purely imaginary states of pleasure. The clear, pellucid fountain suggests to the mind a delicious coolness under the summer sun. Very different might be the sensation if we were to make the experiment that the fancy indicates. The pleasures of gay colouring, melodious sound, and all the charms that the artist can create,—operate to intoxicate the mind with ideal emotion, and with dreams and fancies of endless enjoyment. Hence it is often said that desire is essentially allied with our greatest pleasures.

12. The susceptibility to ideal inflammation is a peculiarity of our nature, varying with constitutions, and affected by various circumstances which I formerly endeavoured to set forth. I remarked that music had often the intoxicating quality of disposing the mind to entertain elevated day-dreams. Pictorial charms may operate in the same way. A fine landscape, under the hand of an artist, may work up an ecstasy as of fairy land in a passionate beholder. Personal

## DESIRE.

beauty still oftener induces this intoxicating glow; under which the anticipations of possible delight from closer intimacy with the object of so great charm are wild and extravagant to a degree; and it is not to be wondered at, that a condition of intense longing should grow up while those splendid possibilities are in the view. To yield to these frenzied delights is one of our human weaknesses, to which experience applies a partial and painful corrective. I am here, however, concerned principally with the explanation that is to be afforded of what is anomalous and perplexing in the phenomenon. In consequence of the fact, that the pleasures of the unreal are, in the great majority of instances, accompanied with a sense of comparative inferiority to some possible state of happiness, a desire emerges, and with that an ideal chase, which may work up the mind to something of the higher pitch of feeling that was longed for. The poor Bedlamite, imagining himself a king deprived of his throne, sets his wits to work to compass its recovery, and, by a series of brilliant strokes, is at last rewarded with the full consciousness of monarchial possession. Such is the result of a few hours spent in a day-dream. The enjoyment while it lasts may be very intense; the revolutions of the physical system of the dreamer, or the accidental turns given to his thoughts, bring the whole fabric to pieces, and he has to start again from his old position. The elation of wine and narcotics often witnesses the imaginary campaigns and adventures of a mind under inflamed desire. There is, to begin with, a nervous exaltation, physical in its origin, giving a certain tone of pleasurable consciousness, with which one might remain content without passing into dream-land. But it would seem to be the peculiarity of this condition, to encourage the intellect to construct or imagine modes of high delight, by inducing the ruling passion, by suggesting the brightest experiences of the past, and by recalling those gay pictures of happiness that have passed before the eyes, so as, with much present gratification, to bring into view a far larger possibility of bliss. When such is the case, desire and imagination commence their

ILLUSTRATION OF THE LAW OF THE WILL. 453

career, and in the end perhaps succeed in working up a still greater degree of nervous exaltation. The modes of pleasure that have this inflammatory character well deserve to be signalized as a class apart. It might seem as if certain plea-sures could be described as inflammatory in a special degree, while others are soothing and satisfying. I apprehend, how-ever, that all pleasures are inflammatory, by the very law of their being. There are two recognised modes of counter-working the tendency. The one is founded on the circum-stance that voluminous pleasures are soporific. The other is the check of some pain. What is called sobriety in the pur-suit of pleasure is nothing more than the habit of restraint engendered by painful experiences. The shock of recoil, not unfrequently experienced, in passing from those ideal heights to actual things, is a severe lesson, a powerful stimulus to the will, to curb the license of day-dreaming and desire. In short, we come back to the position that we commenced from, namely, that pleasure is a prompter of the will, for continuance and increase, up to the point when it ceases to be such, or until some pain, present or apprehended, plants a barrier. This after all is the principal groundwork of the illimitable in desire. Content is not the natural frame of any human mind, but is the offspring of compromise and collision, and of the intelligent comparison of good and evil, suggesting when to stop, or what is on the whole the best.

13. In the workings of appetite and desire we see the first principle of the will in bold relief—or the self-acting power of increased pleasure and diminished pain. The shock of an alteration of state on the favourable side is a direct and imme-diate stimulus to the active forces of the system. A delight growing with every step is exciting and inflammatory in the highest degree ; a dead level of feeling is accompanied with inaction. A patient that has been long in the same state neither makes exertions nor indulges hopes of improvement ; but let some chance application bring a sensible relief, and he is instantly roused both to action and to hope.

The connexions of Desire with Belief are still to be explained. A succeeding chapter, devoted to this last-named subject, will supply the blank, while endeavouring to elucidate the acknowledged difficulties that beset that whole subject.

# CHAPTER IX.

### THE MORAL HABITS.

1. IN my former volume, I gave a full exposition of the principle of our constitution at the basis of all our acquired powers; reserving, however, the case of moral acquisitions till a later stage. It is well known that the plastic process, expressed under the Law of Contiguity, operates in the conflicts of the will, so as to increase the power of one motive over the other, until what was at first a drawn battle is at last an easy victory. The child is torn asunder with the difficulty of fixing attention for a length of time upon one thing; the full-grown man or woman ceases to have even the semblance of a struggle. The applications of the plastic process to the confirmation both of prudential volitions and of those that respect the interests of others, constitute an important chapter of the human mind.

The principle of cohesiveness is precisely the same in the present class of acquisitions as in those formerly treated of. There must be a certain amount of repetition, which may be aided by other favouring circumstances (*Contiguity*, § § 5 and 81). The most considerable of these accessory conditions, apart from natural differences of character, is the disengagement of the mind from other things, and the absorption of it in the matter in hand. Other aiding circumstances are youth, nutrition, and health. The peculiarity of the moral habits, contra-distinguishing them from the intellectual acquisitions, is the presence of two hostile powers, one to be gradually raised into the ascendant over the other. It is necessary, above all things, in such a situation, if possible, never to lose a battle. Every gain on the wrong side undoes the effect of

456 THE MORAL HABITS.

several conquests on the right. It is, therefore, an essential precaution so to regulate the two opposing powers, that the one may have a series of uninterrupted successes, until repetition has fortified it to such a degree as to cope with the opposition under any circumstances. This is the theoretically best career of moral progress, not often realized in practice.

2. Commencing then from the natural beginning of our subject, I shall first remark upon the control of the volitions f Sense and Appetite. We find, when we come to balance the conflicting interests of life, that the pleasures of sense stimulate us too far in pursuit, and the pains of sense too far in avoidance. The delights of exercise, repose, nourishment, warmth, sweet tastes, fragrant odours, soft contacts, melodious sounds, and the host of various influences operating through the eye, cannot be followed out to all lengths without trenching on other interests present or future ; and we want therefore to have those interests represented with sufficient power to interpose a check at the proper point. For that end, we desire to bring the influence of habit to assist the force of volition, which is best done by means of a tolerably unbroken series of decisions on one side. In like manner, we fly such pains as muscular fatigue, acute smarts, thirst, hunger, and indifferent fare, cold or excessive heat, bitter tastes, repulsive odours, &c. ; there being, however, valuable interests on whose account we occasionally submit to those painful irritations. What is to be done, therefore, is to mark certain objects as paramount to certain others, and to initiate each person into the deliberative preference by gentle stages. We gain nothing by leaving a hungry child within reach of forbidden fruit ; the education not being yet sufficiently advanced to give strength to the motive of restraint. We begin by slight temptations on the one side, while strongly fortifying the motives on the other ; and, if there are no untoward reverses to throw back the pupil, we count upon a certain steady progress in the ascendancy that we aim at establishing. Each case has its special difficulties. Sometimes we have to deal with sensual impulses of inordinate strength, and at other times we

CONTROL OF APPETITE. 457

find individuals precociously disposed to take on prudential volitions, and to be susceptible to those interests of other living beings on whose account so much of this discipline is called for. The one general fact in the case is, that by a series of exercises, where some one consideration is made to over-bear sensual solicitations in an unbroken series of trials, a confirming stream of the nervous power will give new force to the victorious side, enabling it to cope with stronger adversaries, while the sense of struggle and effort gradually dies away. The control over appetite demanded by a regard to health, so difficult in early life, or even in middle age, may become, by the aid of habit, so complete, that the individual scarcely suffers the twinge of temptation.

3. Take the practice of regular early rising. Here we have, on the one hand, the volitional solicitations of a strong massive indulgence, and on the other, the stimulus of prudential volition as regards the collective interests of life. I will avoid all extreme suppositions that would mar the illustration of the point in hand, and will assume that there is neither an unusual indifference to the indulgence of lying late, nor an unusual force of determination in favour of the pursuits and interests of the day. We require, then, in order to consummate a habit of early rising, in the first place, a strong and decided initiative. This is not a case for an easy and gradual training. I should not count much upon the plan of fixing a certain hour not difficult to get up at, and after a time advancing by a quarter of an hour, and so on. The proper means is, either a very strong putting forth of volition on the part of the individual, or an imperative urgency from without ; while the hour that is to be final, should also be initial. Some necessity, that there is no escape from, compels a man from his early youth to be out of bed every morning at six o'clock. For weeks and months, and perhaps years, the struggle and the suffering are acutely felt. Meanwhile, the hand of power is remorseless in the uniformity of its application. And now it is that there creeps on a certain habitude of the system, modifying by imperceptible degrees the bitterness of that oft-

458 THE MORAL HABITS.

repeated conflict. What the individual has had to act so many times in one way, brings on a current of nervous power, confirming the victorious, and sapping the vanquished, impulse. The force of determination that unites the decisive movement of jumping out of bed with the perception of the appointed hour, is invigorated slowly but surely; and there is an equal tendency to withdraw the nutritive power that keeps up the pleasurable sensibility opposed to the act. I cannot doubt that there is such a thing as literally starving a very acute pleasurable or painful sensibility, by crossing it, or systematically discouraging it. So that on both sides, the force of iteration is softening down the harsh experience of the early riser, and bringing about, as time advances, an approach to the final condition of mechanical punctuality and entire indifference. Years may be wanted to arrive at this point, but sooner or later the plastic element of our constitution will succeed. Not, however, I think, without the two main conditions of an adequate initiative, and an unbroken persistence. If the power applied in the first instance is inconstant or merely occasional, and if periods of indulgence are admitted to break the career of the learner, there is very little hope of ever attaining the consummation described. A great change in the direction of the vitality of the system is needed in order that the still small voice of daily duty may overpower, without an effort, one of the strongest of our fleshly indulgences ; and in ordinary circumstances, we can calculate upon nothing less than the persistence of years to establish such a diversion. Here, as in the intellectual acquisitions, there are great individual differences of plastic power. Moreover, the circumstances of life may favour or impede the efficacy of it in such an instance as the present. If a man's existence is regular, free from overwork and harassing trouble, his moral habitudes will prosper accordingly. Eating cares, and excessive toil injure the system at some point or other, and the injury may happen to light upon the property of plastic adhesiveness. Then, too, it is to be considered that the general temper and feelings of the mind may concur with a special discipline, or

## CONDITIONS OF THE GROWTH OF HABIT.

may not. It may be an object congenial to my prevailing emotions and tastes to fall into a mechanical punctuality of life, and to reclaim the morning hours for favourite pursuits. If so, this will enhance the currents that tend to the habit in question. Should I, on the contrary, never feel any liking or interest in the attainment of this habit, the absence of any such supporting stimulation will make the acquirement proportionally tedious.

4. The above example contains all the leading elements of the acquisition of habits running counter to strong appetites. The difficulties to be overcome are very much the same in the other instances; namely, the power of the appetite itself, the inadequacy of the initiative, the occasional backslidings, and the want of any strong inclination in the mind towards the points to be gained by a complete control. With regard to the initiating influences, the most powerful undoubtedly is external compulsion; next to which we may rank example, moral suasion, and those other modes whereby we are acted on by fellow-beings without absolute coercion. Lastly, the mind's own volitions, determined by the pleasures and pains of its own experience, and by motives wherein other men's views have no part, must be the sole agency in a large number of instances. When those that have gone before us, dictate for our guidance the maxims resulting from their experience, we trust our future to their wisdom rather than to our own choice; and this is necessarily the predicament of the young. Rousseau, in his *Emile*, has carried out to extreme lengths the opposite principle of purely self-determining forces. He proposes that no inclination of a child should ever be directly curbed, but that some method should be found of bringing it under a course of trial and error in every instance, so that its own revulsion from pain should be the sole check. He would allow it to feel actually the injurious consequences of misplaced desires, instead of thwarting these by the hand of authority. Unquestionably much may be said in favour of the superior force of dear-bought experience, as compared with mere advice, persuasion, or example, but the scheme of

460 THE MORAL HABITS.

Rousseau is utterly impracticable, if from no other reason than the impossibility of realizing in sufficient time all the evil consequences of imprudences. Besides, some of these are so severe that it is an object to save the child from them. We cannot by any amount of ingenuity place infancy in the position of free self-determination occupied in mature life. Moreover, although authority may be carried too far in human life generally, yet as no human being is ever emancipated from its sway, an education in submission is as essential a preparation for going out into the world as an education in a sound bodily regimen.

5. Habits of Temperance generally belong to the present head, and their illustration might be given in detail if space admitted. A strong commencing volition founded on the pains of excesses, and the pleasures of a healthy frame, would of itself induce acts of self-restraint, and the individual might then be said to be temperate simply by the force of will. If the practice of a rigid self-denial were merely rare and occasional, there would be nothing else in the case; no growth would take place so as to render the volition more easy as life advanced. When, however, the volition is so strong on the point as to operate on all occasions for a lengthened period, the plastic force adds a concurring power that supersedes the necessity of high resolve. This alone is a *habit* of temperance.

6. I shall advert now to a different class of habits based on resistance to the solicitations of sense, namely, the habitual control of the Attention, as against the diversions caused by outward objects. The senses being incessantly open to impressions from without, whenever anything pleasurable occurs, the power of volition cherishes and retains the effect, and takes away the active energies and dispositions from any other thing not so pleasing; and on the other hand, a painful impression stimulates the voluntary operation of getting out of its reach. Now, although the occurrence of intense pleasures, or intense pains, among the sensations occurring at random through the various senses, is not very

## CONTROL OF ATTENTION.

461

frequent, we are liable to a large number of petty pleasures and pains from the objects that strike our sight, hearing, touch, or smell. Every one of these petty impressions has its volitional stimulus, and without the presence of some more powerful agency, either of volition, or of habit, the mind and the activity are constantly tossed about in a multitude of directions. In children, this is seen in full operation. We have to be put under training to resist those various solicitations, and to keep the mind as steadily fixed upon the work in hand as if they did not happen. The process here consists in becoming indifferent to what at the outset caused pleasure or pain. We can never be free from impressions of touch, but we contract the habit of inattention to them. The occupation of the mind upon things foreign draws off the currents of power from the tactile susceptibility, which, in consequence, becomes so starved, that even when there is little else to engross the attention, we are scarcely at all alive to the extensive action of our clothing upon the surface of the body. A still more remarkable instance is presented by the ear. Sounds being, in general, more acute in their impression than touches, it is not so easy to contract an insensibility to them. We may, however, acquire this power under favourable circumstances. It is possible to contract the habit of not attending to noises and conversation. To arrive at this point, we must not be over-sensitive to sound from the first, otherwise the initiation would be extremely difficult. There should be some one thing so far capable of engrossing the attention as to overpower, for the time, the buzz of conversation, or the distraction of noise. Some minds are so susceptible to sound, that nothing can ever place them in this situation of insensibility, even for a single half-hour; and, in their case, the acquisition would be impracticable for want of a commencement. If we can but make a beginning, or find any occasion where indifference can be induced for a short time, the habit will follow. The solicitations of Sight have to be met in the same way, and the very same remarks are applicable. We have to assume an attitude of indifference to the great expanse

462 THE MORAL HABITS.

of the visual scene, every feature of which probably stirs the infant mind with strong and engrossing emotion. We learn to withstand the volitional impulse that would divert the eyes to a more pleasant point of the scene around us, and to abide by the unattractive object under our hands. Living in a neighbourhood full of objects of beauty, we walk about in nearly total indifference to the charm, excepting in those special moments when we give ourselves permission to dwell upon them.

7. Many of our habits are directed against the primitive or instinctive movements of the body. I have endeavoured to show that the rhythm of the limbs is an original provision of the organization, and also that there is a primitive tendency to community of action throughout the entire system (*Instincts*, § 5). This last especially demands educational control. We have to suppress those movements of the limbs which instinctively accompany the play of the voice; to resist that inflammatory action whereby a more local excitement kindles a general activity. These acquirements, however, are so much akin to the mere mechanical education already discussed under the Law of Contiguity, that I do not dilate upon them in this place.

8. The subject of the Emotions presents a wide field for the elucidation of the growth of habit. We have had to consider the control and suppression of emotions by voluntary power; an effort rendered more or less easy according as suppression or indulgence is the prevailing fact. The various demands of life are the motives for diverting the emotional currents, and, after a lapse of years, the commencing struggles are modified by the plastic force now under consideration. A few remarks upon the emotions in detail will bring out their distinctive peculiarities, as respects the initiation and formation of habits on their account.

An observation may first be made applicable to emotional culture in general. It is possible, by education, to raise or lower the position of emotion relatively to the two other divisions of the mind. Each person comes into the world with

## CULTURE OR SUPPRESSION OF EMOTION. 463

a certain relative proportion of the three great departments of the mental nature, and this proportion may be either retained or departed from in after-life. The primitive rush of power in some one direction may be checked or encouraged by the circumstances that the individual is placed in. The natural consequence, in the absence of interference from without, is that the prevailing bent strengthens itself, and what was originally feeble becomes feebler still. The originally powerful intellect, by asserting its own exercise, more and more deepens the penury of the emotional nature; while two of the elements once in the ascendant leave little room for the third. A person constitutionally weak in the emotional region, as shown by such tests as,—being little fired by the common pleasures of mankind, little given to the profuse display of demonstration and expression, not consoled under pain by the resources of laughter or tears,—may be taken in hand so as to be educated into a higher development in that region. The most effective mode of commencing operations would be to ply the influence of example, sympathy, and multiplied pleasures, in such a manner as to encourage the weak side, and discourage the others. Mere authority would not be relevant, and the individual's own volition is not likely to be exerted to change the very foundations of his character. In like manner, by a judicious starving regimen, an over-emotional nature may be toned down, and fuller play given to intellect and volition; an operation, perhaps, more trying to the patient. An exceedingly useful part of our moral discipline relating to this head is the restraint of those exciting motives, more than once referred to, whereby the will is prompted to act to a degree disproportioned to the real enjoyment or suffering of the individual. Every initiative within reach should be brought to bear for the establishment of so valuable a habit; and the difficulty of the case renders all of them not too much. The systematic calming down of physical excitement cannot be over-inculcated in education, nor too strongly aimed at by each one's own volition. The human powers attain their maximum of efficiency only when a confirmed superiority is gained

464     THE MORAL HABITS.

over flurry, excitement, needless fears, and extravagant ebullitions; but as this is a triumph over one of the very greatest of human weaknesses, the whole force of favouring circumstances must chime in with the acquisition. Good initiatives, supported by the aids to plastic growth in their full measure, must be invoked in this all-important struggle.

9. Next, as regards the emotions in detail, something of what has now been said, on the general subject, applies, more or less, to each. We can, by the instrumentality of education, alter the degree of prominence of one of them in relation to the rest; while the naturally strong, left to itself, will grow still stronger. In every instance, the course of habit will be either to increase or diminish an original susceptibility. Take the example of Liberty. The indulgence of the natural roaming impulses, confirmed by habit, will prove an unsurmountable bar to a life of regulated industry. By a well-placed discipline, on the contrary, the pleasure of mere freedom, and the irksomeness of encountering cheeks, may be sapped by discouragement, by usage, and by withdrawing the mind from entertaining them, until they are esteemed as of no account. Such is the condition of the contented slave, and the man whose life is made up of artificial impositions.

10. The state of Terror affords the strongest instance, in support of the point insisted on at the opening of the chapter, as to the importance of an unbroken career in the formation of a habit. If we have to deal with a mind naturally susceptible to fear, it is a notorious fact, that we must do our utmost to avoid every incident that will of a certainty bring on fright. The initiation should be gradual, and the trial never beyond the acquired strength. A single fright may put back the subject of our training for an indefinite period. The case resembles the inuring of the body to fatigue, hardship, or exposure, where the stress should always be within the strength attained. In developing the frame to bear up against muscular fatigue, no wise trainer pushes it beyond the limits of safety to the organism; and in accustoming ourselves to endure the severity of cold and wet, we are almost sure to go backward

EDUCATION IN COURAGE. 465

a good many points, every time that we contract an illness. There is every reason to believe that this is a general principle, applicable to the fortifying of the system against disease and dissolving tendencies ; and as respects the passion of fear, there is ample confirmation of it. A decided fright, taking hold of the mind, scathes and weakens the courageous tone for a length of time, if it be ever entirely got over. To exercise and try the system up to the point of acquired endurance, and yet not to pass that point, is the maxim never to be lost sight of. One must be exposed to occasions of fear in order to have the natural bravery strengthened ; but a premature or excessive exposure might leave the subject more susceptible than ever. The initiatives in carrying on this particular discipline need to be very good, if we desire to prosecute the acquisition far. Example, encouragement, gentleness, health, and an undistracted mode of life,—are the great requisites in the present as in every other difficult moral acquisition. Judging from the physiological differences of animals and of the sexes, it would appear that the quality of courage reposes upon a peculiar mode of nervous vigour, and consumes a definite portion of the nourishment of the frame. To instil this quality, where it is but feeble by nature, would probably demand a considerable diversion of the growing and plastic energy of the system, and hence few examples occur of very successful attempts to erect it on an acquired basis.

11. The Tender Emotion supplies a theme (so also would the sexual) for repeating a similar course of remarks, as to the possibility of exalting or depressing the original development, assigned to it by nature. If strong from the commencement, and supplied with objects to cherish it, there would inevitably follow a progressive enlargement of the susceptibility. A person so situated would find a great and increasing enjoyment in affection, sociability, and humane impulses, and would, as a part of the same endowment, be able to keep up the excitement over comparatively lengthened periods. The currents of energy would go largely into this one channel, leaving other regions, such as intellect and volition

2 G

466 THE MORAL HABITS.

so much less supplied with power. On the other hand, a character deficient in tenderness from the first, might be cherished into an average development, provided attractions are given, and the mind not suffered to be too much absorbed in the direction of greatest strength. We may thus raise or lower the sensibility as a whole, and render it a more or less important item in the sources of enjoyment or suffering; which is an effect entirely distinct from the habitual direction of it towards particular persons or things, termed objects of attachment or affection. No doubt the one effect is ready to go along with the other, but they are not therefore the same. As there are certain things that inspire tenderness at the very first presentation, as for example, infancy, so association constitutes many new objects, and increases the influence of all. Any circumstances that determine the emotion to be frequently felt in one connexion, cause a powerful adhesion to grow up, so as to develop in that special quarter a pre-eminent power to stir up the feeling; and we may have a certain number of those strong attachments to persons or to inanimate things, without rising above our original share of the general susceptibility. For example, self-complacency is, in my view, nothing more than a habitual tender regard to self as an object displaying attractive and admirable qualities. The primitive fund of tenderness may not be very great, but in consequence of its flowing incessantly in this particular channel, there may arise a considerable glow of excitement in that relation, not experienced in any other. Few persons undertake to control it, either in themselves, or even in others; nor would it be very easy to resist its insinuating progress when once the bent has set in. The outward expression can be checked, but the inward course is not much affected thereby. Following close upon self-tenderness, we find vanity and all the forms of love of admiration and applause; and here there is more scope for control. By indulgence, the feeling of praise may be pampered beyond all limits, while, by a careful stinted regimen, it is possible to keep it very much under. The individual's own volition, however, is wanted to concur in the suppression; it being so

## SENTIMENT OF POWER ABATED. 467

easy to get out of sight of a second person, acting as monitor, and fall into stealthy indulgences.

12. Ranking with tenderness as a grand generic source of emotion in the human mind is the Sentiment of Power, to which the same round of observations may be adapted. When already large, habit can make it larger, or reduce it to a moderate scale. The free license given to its development ends in a crop of the worst faults of humanity. An imperious and egotistic temper, encroaching on other men's freedom of action, and hating every brother near the throne, a domineering insolent deportment, a rancorous jealousy ever ready to burst out, an overweening fondness for the exercise of government in every shape—are some of the displays of the love of power cherished by indulgence. It is very hard, too, to keep down this feeling, if, besides being originally strong, there is superadded a certain scope for its exercise. The efforts of the parent and tutor are often baffled by the hydra-headed character of the feeling. A man's own conscience and reflections are never more called for, than in endeavouring to curb the excesses of this region of the emotional nature. With a cordial inward co-operation, something may be done in the course of years to tone it down to sobriety. The strongest counter-forces are the sympathies with other men's feelings and freedom of action; and by entertaining these habitually, we may keep a check upon the domineering spirit, and at last attain a habitual control over ourselves.

I have given it as my opinion, that the Irascible emotion and the strong antipathies are to a certain extent outbursts of the sentiment of power, resorted to, like the tender outburst, as a soothing and consoling influence under painful irritation. Be that as it may, habits of command of the temper are universally allowed to be a prime object in moral education and self-discipline. In the management of the young, the violent manifestations may be quelled by remonstrance and fear, and encouragement given to composure and coolness under provocation. Like most of the foregoing instances, however, the individual must take the work in his own hand, and with his

468                THE MORAL HABITS.

own volition check the risings of the storm, as it first breaks upon the consciousness. The strong passions are able to work under cover to such an extent, that foreign influence is un-availing, unless invited in aid of one's own will, bent upon gaining a mastery over them. If we are strongly alive to the mischiefs of unbridled temper, and are moderately endowed with strength of will, while, at the same time, the worry, distraction, and provocations incident to our condition are not overwhelming, it is no more than a fair probability, that we shall eventually succeed in superadding the force of habit to the force of volition in this instance, as well as in the others.

13. Among the pleasures incident to Action, we ranked Pursuit and Plot-interest, whose fascination sometimes be-comes too great, and requires to be restrained. A certain check must be placed upon the excitement of sport and the engrossment of story in youth, as engendering a species of dissipation inconsistent with the sober engagements of life. When allowed to run riot, the interest in mere narrative and plot becomes a source of serious annoyance. It is needless to say what are the means of initiating a habit of restrain-ing this appetency; I have already mentioned more than once all the modes of initiation, and all the circumstances favourable to a successful issue.

The Emotions of Intellect, like Intellect itself, are for the most part more in want of being cherished than of being checked. A congenial atmosphere of society, access to books and means of culture, freedom from cares, and the absence of strong competing tastes, would enable one to cultivate to advantage the original germs of curiosity, and of the love of truth and consistency, implanted by nature.

14. The region of Taste and Æsthetic culture is subject to the same general laws of plasticity and habit. These emotions as a whole may be nourished or stinted, or some one may be selected for especial aggrandizement. Take a man moderately endowed by nature in this department, and place him in the artistic atmosphere of Rome, or Florence, without much to engross him otherwise, and without any

## CULTURE OR SUPPRESSION OF ÆSTHETIC FEELING. 469

peculiar bent in a different direction, and he will by degrees warm up under the influences around him, and end in being a man of decided æsthetic tastes and susceptibilities. On the other hand, place an artistic nature in an age of high Puritanism; withdraw every influence that would foster the love of art; spur the mind into discrepant pursuits;—and in all probability the original proportions of the constitution will be ultimately reversed. It is within possibility to implant, and to root up, the most deep-seated of human pleasures and dispositions. We must not forget, however, that operations so revolutionary are not performed without a considerable cost, and that more than one such rarely takes place in a single life. The power of education is limited, because the up-building force is itself limited. We cannot concentrate the plastic power, and array the outward circumstances, upon two or three diverse objects of great magnitude. It would hardly be possible to impart artificially to the same person the spirit of science and the love of art, both being feebly cast in the mind originally; nor could we hope to make head against two distinct moral weaknesses, so as to make moral powers out of both.

15. It may be expected that I should say a few words on those great and sudden changes, sometimes operated in the human character, in striking contrast to the laborious pace according to which habits are built up. The explanation of sudden conversions is no doubt to be sought in some over-powering impression upon the mind that supplies a new and energetic motive to the will, thereby initiating a new line of conduct. If we can only strike a blow with such power, as to seize possession of a man's entire thoughts and voluntary dispositions for a certain length of time, we may succeed in launching him in a new career, and in keeping him in that course, until there be time for habits to commence, and until a force is arrayed in favour of the present state of things, equal to cope with the tendencies and growth of the former life. Such changes occasionally happen, but not without terrific struggles, which prove how hard it is to set up the volitions of a day against the bent of years.

470                THE MORAL HABITS.

16. We may next illustrate the class of habits related to the more purely volitional impulses of our nature. That Spontaneity, formerly dwelt upon as an essential element of the will, is modified in various ways during the apprenticeship to life. Originally, the spontaneous outbursts must be supposed to follow the course of nutrition and accidental stimulants. We have to learn to suppress movements, at times when the replenished condition of the centres would bring them on, and at other times to protract them beyond the period when they would be disposed to cease. The operations of Industry cannot be sustained without great additions of power to some centres, perhaps at the expense of others. The sustained use of one organ, such as the voice in a singer or a public speaker, or the arm in a blacksmith, implies that after a number of years a determination of vital power, many times greater than the original measure, now takes place towards every part involved in these activities. It is an element in every man's professional acquirement, to be able to continue without fatigue the activity of some special organ, much longer than would be possible without a special education. There is such a thing, too, as changing the natural temperament as regards the *manner* of acting. A spontaneity prone to vehement and exhausting discharges may be toned down to a slower pace, although considering the deep-seatedness of the peculiarity to be changed, it must be a work of no little time and effort.

17. The subject of Desire brings to our notice various important moral acquisitions. A habit of Endurance as against irremovable pains generally, or against special pains of more than usual recurrence, may be established under the usual conditions. It is a hard thing to support acute, or massive suffering, by a mere unaided volition; and accordingly various helps are sought out in those circumstances. Sympathy, diversion, hope, are resorted to; and, if only we are able to maintain the struggle a number of times with tolerable success, we may count upon a certain contribution from the principle now under consideration. The attitude of mind, designated

DOMESTICATION OF ANIMALS. 471

Contentment, points to a very large field of operations, where habit is thrown into the scale of good resolutions. The quieting of the mind, under the endless solicitations of desires that cannot be satisfied, must needs occupy a considerable share of every man's moral force; and in no quarter does the plastic process interpose to greater effect for individual happiness. Good monitions must be well backed by an individual sense of the evil of frettings and longings, and the mind must have a certain freedom for devoting itself to the work of combating them. Every one is liable to possess some special susceptibility in more than ordinary degree, which, perhaps, the outward circumstances are the farthest from gratifying; whence arises the necessity of a strong discipline directed upon that single point. The love of splendour bursting out in a contracted lot, or ambition in the mind of a serf, opens scenes of contradiction that sometimes interest the poet and writer of romance, but are in reality harrowing to a sympathizing looker-on. We do not often reflect what pains it has taken to arrive at virtues that make a very little show, being but mere negations of conduct. The decisions of frugality as against expenditure, if made with ease, are frequently the crowning display of years filled with mental struggles.

18. Our present theme might be illustrated by the domestication of the animal tribes. It is both curious and instructive to find out what those peculiarities are that render some animals docile, in contradistinction to so many others. The great property of mental adhesiveness is equally owned by all the higher vertebrata, if not in equal degree; and could we but initiate the animal with sufficient energy into any artificial course, a habit would emerge sooner or later. The horse, the dog, and the cat, are not singular in taking on acquisitions. The distinction among animals in this respect must be sought for in some other circumstances. The impossibility of taming the lion or the tiger may be ascribed, perhaps, to the extraordinary intensity of their natural impulses, while they are probably less endowed with the plastic quality of the brain than the members of the canine family. The imparting of a habit of domestication to these ferocious creatures would simply re-

472         THE MORAL HABITS.

quire a very long-sustained and severe discipline, such as we do not choose to enforce. A creature must be subject to the passion of fear, in order to be effectually tamed by the hand of man. The horse and the dog have a certain amount of timidity in their disposition, which we largely avail ourselves of; whereas we seldom take in hand the taming of animals endowed with great natural courage.

19. The opposition to Intellectual trains, or to the stream of ideas ushered in by Contiguity and Similarity, is within the range of volition, and may be confirmed into habit. Two interesting cases may be specified. The concentration of the thoughts upon one subject as against wanderings, digressions, and chance solicitations, is a thing difficult to compel in early life and in untutored minds. Where there is frequent occasion for the exercise of the faculty, and strong motives in addition, the lapse of time will find the effort gradually diminishing, and, at last, the power will become completely dominant. This is a part of the apprenticeship of every highly intellectual profession, and merely follows up into the world of ideas the ability to command the attention against the diverting influence of objects of sense.

The second instance is the power of dismissing a subject from the mind at pleasure. To be absorbed with a matter of business, after it has ceased to be of any practical import, or to keep the thoughts going upon it, is a weakness to be overcome if possible. The force of the will can be interposed to clear out subjects loitering unnecessarily in the field of vision, and, although the first attempts of this kind will be met with considerable resistance, a fair amount of perseverance will not be without its reward. In the active business of life, men are frequently called upon to turn rapidly from one subject to another, forgetting what has just been settled, and applying the whole mind to the thing next in turn. The mere act of the will, in absolutely suspending all consideration of what has been engrossing the ideas for several consecutive hours, is a high and imperious dictation, not by any means obeyed in the early stages of one's apprenticeship.

20. I will here bring to a close the subject of this chapter;

CONDITIONS FAVOURING THE GROWTH OF HABIT. 473

concluding, at the same time, the exposition of the force of Contiguity, Retentiveness, or acquisition. It has not been the object of the present discussion, to bring forward every power of the nature of a moral habitude belonging to our constitution. I might have introduced the mention of a variety of others of equal value to any of those selected. For example, habits of Obedience are created in opposition to self-will, and to the instinctive tendency to follow out one's prevailing temper. Habits of Authority have to be acquired, in spite of the disposition to sympathize with our fellow-beings under all circumstances. Habits of Promptitude, Activity, and Alertness are frequently the result of a long-continued contradiction of the natural character. Habits of Grace and Polite demeanour are, in many persons, a growth forced entirely from without, and not coinciding with a single tendency of the natural man. My purpose was to bring out into prominence the conditions that the growth of habit mainly depends upon; for, although some of those are sufficiently well understood, there are others that we do not always lay sufficient stress upon. It is admitted that repetition sustained for a length of time is a *sine qua non ;* there is not the same adequate recognition of the need of an initiative, so strong and so well managed as to carry the day in every separate conflict, until such time as a considerable growth has taken place. Nor do we always advert in practice to the clearing of the mind from strong pre-occupations, the avoiding of feverish distractions, and over-tasking of every sort. I am not sure whether we do full justice to the fact that ' to him that hath shall be given,' and that, obversely, where there is a weak disposition naturally, the training must be very slow, gentle, and persevering. Some natures are distinguished by plasticity or the power of acquisition, and therefore realize more closely the saying that man is a bundle of habits. The vital energies of the constitution would seem, in their case, to avoid imparting strong natural bents, and to flow towards the consolidation of every artificial or communicated bias. The opposite extreme may likewise be seen in the circle of any careful observer.

# CHAPTER X.

### PRUDENCE.—DUTY.—MORAL INABILITY.

1: BEFORE approaching the closing question of our present subject, the question of the freedom of the will, I propose to set apart a chapter to the illustration of the various motives that play a part in duty and prudence. The principal arena of the conflict of ends is indicated under those designations ; and there is, moreover, the attendant practice of forging motives as make-weights to throw into one side of the scale, with a view to determine the result in that exclusive direction.

*Prudence, Happiness, The Ideal of Pursuit.*—It has been now abundantly seen, that the constitution of the will, from the very commencement, provides for warding off pains and retaining pleasures. The following out of those instigations, the comparing of pleasures and pains with one another when a plurality concur, the having respect at each moment to the future as well as to the present, are the foundation elements of prudence and the pursuit of happiness. Recognising evil and good in the distance, we work for remote ends no less than for present sensations and emotions. We have before us the catalogue of possible evils, on the one hand, and of possible pleasures, on the other, knowing, at the same time, the greater or less probability of finding them on our path. We are aware, too, of certain objects that will afflict and pain us in an extraordinary degree, and of certain other objects that will give us an intense flow of pleasure. All these different sources and varieties of the two great opposing inspirations play alternately upon our voluntary mechanism, and give the direction to our labours and pursuits. We are constantly avoiding physical injuries, organic disease, cold,

## PRUDENCE STIMULATED FROM WITHOUT.      475

hunger, exhaustion, fatigue, and the list of painful sensations and feelings ; we are seeking after the opposites of all these generally, while devoted with express assiduity to something that has a distinguishing charm to our minds. These are the motives personal to each individual, suggested by the contact of each one's susceptibilities with surrounding things. The upshot of the whole, the balance struck in the midst of conflict, is the course of prudence and the search for happiness that we should severally steer by, if left entirely to ourselves. The stronger impulses of our nature would have their ascendancy increased by repetition, and our character would be made up from those two great sources—the original promptings and the habits.

2. We are not suffered, however, to pursue a course so entirely self-prompted as that now described. Foreign influence is brought to bear in determining the will on points whereon one's own feelings have not yet given the cue. We are put under instruction and discipline as to the attainment of pleasurable ends, and the avoidance of painful. We are taught at first to eat and to drink, to clothe, to exercise and to rest, independently of our own promptings. Besides compulsory direction, we are in the presence of persons whose example we imbibe ; and thus the traditions of the past, facing us in the customs of the present, take the initiative of life out of our own hands, and mould it according to a pre-established model. When this system has done its work, we are altered beings. The natural impulses of the individual are not wholly rooted out, but they are modified and overborne by new powers, and the calculation of our character must apply itself to the resultant of the two classes of impelling forces. The influence begun in tender years, by the authority and example of elders, masters, and associates, is continued in after-life by preaching, admonition, advice, persuasive address from tongue and pen, information to warn and to guide, the exhibition of bright examples and great successes, with their contrasts. The friend in private, the authorized monitor in public, are besetting us with motive power to sway our decisions. An-

476 PRUDENCE.—DUTY.—MORAL INABILITY.

other class of persons seek merely to supply us with information to assist our judgment, without dictating the use we are to make of it. One man teaches us the means of preserving health, another the rules of economy and acquisition of wealth, a third points out the ways in which a good name is won and lost, a fourth guides us to the sources of general knowledge. Having applied ourselves to some special end, we adopt all trustworthy suggestions as to the means, and we act accordingly. There is nothing in all this of the lawless, the capricious, the uncertain, the unpredictable. There may be a combination of influences at work, but each one has its characteristic and settled consequence, the same yesterday as to-day. It is difficult to say absolutely that the repetition of the same motive will lead to the same act, but that is only because we are not quite sure but that some other motive has arisen to intrude its efficacy upon the first.

3. The case is not complete until we add the devotion of a certain amount of mind, thought, leisure, to dwelling upon the motives on the side of prudence, and on the calculations and resolutions founded upon them. This is one of the ways whereby an accession of power passes to the side so favoured. When it is known that any one has this reflecting bent, there is confidently expected a greater degree of adherence to prudential resolves on that account.

Distant and future interests are impressed, on a mind given to entertaining them, during periods of deliberate meditation, and are, in consequence, all the more strongly represented in times of conflicting motives. No law of the physical world is more sure than the consolidation of the prudential incitements by such a procedure. He that is devoted to the pursuit of wealth and fortune, by thinking often of such ends as principal, as well as subordinate, is strengthened in his adhesion to them when attacked by the solicitations of ease or indulgence.

4. There is, as before remarked, such a thing as a character moulded at the first for a prudential career. A concurrence of strongly acting Will with an intellect retentive of good

THE GENIUS OF PRUDENCE. 477

and evil, as actually experienced, are the main features of this cast of mind. If the principal end be health and physical sensation, it is necessary that all the pains of disease and low vitality should be strongly remembered by the intellect, and represented powerfully in idea, when there is any danger of incurring them. So with any other end, or with the sum total of objects of pursuit. The intellect must lend itself to the purpose of vividly retaining those ends in their full magnitude, to give them the power of resisting present impulses that conflict with them. There may be, as I have already said, a prudential genius, as well as a mathematical or a musical genius; the fact of intense persistence in idea of the characteristic impressions of the department being common to all. Now, whenever we have the evidence of such an endowment, we take for granted that the person will certainly act in a way corresponding, and in striking opposition to all that class of minds, in whom there is no effective remembrance of the sweet and bitter experiences of life, for the future control of the actions. Our genius of prudence has imbibed a thorough sense of the good and evil consequences of actions; has submitted to instruction and example in favour of a course of careful living; has given good heed to advice, warning, and persuasive address in the same direction; has laid up store of information availing for the furtherance of collective interests against partial and temporary good; is disposed to the practice of meditation above mentioned; and in all ways is employed in building up an immense fortress, a mental stronghold of prudential forethought. The operations of such a mind are singularly amenable to calculation. We know that it is in vain to seduce it into the commonplace dissipation of the unthinking, light-hearted throng.

5. Such being the moving forces on the side of prudence, the counter forces are not difficult to assign. They are chiefly our actual and pressing sensations and emotions, which are by nature stronger than what is merely remembered or anticipated, and gain the day until such time as these others have been artificially invigorated. Intemperance, indolence, pro-

478      PRUDENCE.—DUTY.—MORAL INABILITY.

digality, neglect of opportunities, giving offence to those that
would assist us, and all sorts of reckless behaviour,—are sins
against prudence, incurred simply because the sense of our
lasting interests does not move the will with the same energy
as the relish for stimulants, for ease, for indulgence of
emotions, and such like. There is a volitional or moral weakness in the case, which, if once fairly manifested and put in
evidence, can be assumed as the law of our being, just as it is
the law of smoke to ascend, and of water to descend. It is true
enough, that we are under no compulsion in the common sense
of the word, like the compulsion whereby a child is made to
take physic, or a vagrant sleeps in the open field, because
there is no shelter accessible. But the law of action is just as
sure in the one case as in the other, allowance being made for
the various susceptibility of the mind to various motive
agencies. The person that cannot withstand temptations to
self-injury may be properly said to be under a moral weakness or inability, because the defect is possible to be supplied
by moral means, or by raising new feelings, having in them
strong volitional promptings. The weakness of intemperate
indulgence is not such as can be met only by shutting a man
up, and limiting his meals by the strong hand. This would
. be to pass beyond mere moral inability into the domain of infatuation or insanity. You may make up for any ordinary
weakness by adding new motives on the side of restraint, and
when this is possible, the weakness consists simply in the
character of the impulses that act upon the will. You may
represent to the person's mind the evil consequences more
vividly than they occur to himself; you may interpose autho-
. rity, which means the laying on of new evils of a deterring
kind; you may announce the promise of some pleasure as an
incitement to the same effect; you may preach, warn, exhort,
and fill the mind with examples of the horrors of indulgence,
and the felicity of moderation. By some or all of these means
you rescue your victim, or you do not. If you do, you have
simply been able to add motives enough to supply the
deficient side; very much as you fortify a building against

## HUMAN CONDUCT PREDICTABLE. 479

a storm, or increase the power of artillery to demolish a citadel.

6. As regards any object that a person takes up, as the great or crowning end of life, he will be disposed, more or less, to subordinate all other motives to it. His character is complete as regards the carrying out of the chief end, when nature, the force of will, habits, and concurring circumstances, have succeeded in securing a total subordination. The observations now made with reference to prudential ends apply equally to the ambition of Alexander, the philanthropy of Howard, or the career of any devotee to literature, science, or political amelioration. As a general rule, no one is equal to the full maintenance of the crowning object, against every conflicting solicitation. Nevertheless, we know full well that agencies could be brought to bear that would make up for the insufficient power of a principal end. A man is betrayed by his feeling of fatigue, by his love of some sensual pleasure, by his fear, his affections, his anger, his sensibility to the charms of fine art, to throw away an opportunity of furthering his cause. We note the circumstance, and expect that if all things are the same, he will show the same inability at another time. We know further, however, that if any friend, monitor, or person having authority with him, take to heart the failure thus exhibited, they may ply him with extra motives, which may possibly secure the right determination. We know besides, that if the person himself feels remorse and self-crimination at his own moral weakness, the recollection will be a new motive in favour of his high purpose on the next occasion. After a few experiments, we can tell pretty closely what is the value of repentance as a motive upon the individual supposed. In some we find that remorse is a powerful spur to the will for a long time after, and in others we have to set it down as nothing at all. As our opportunites of watching a person are increased, we are to that degree enabled certainly to foretell how he will behave, and to take our course accordingly. If the event ever disappoints us, we ascribe it to no uncertainty in the sequences of motive and action ; but

to our not being able to foresee accurately the motives that were present. In speculating beforehand on the decisions of a deliberative body, we may know the opinions and inclinations of each member with absolute certainty; but we may not be able to say who are to be present on a given day. Very much the same thing holds in our attempting to predict the decisions of a single mind. We can know from a tolerable experience what will be the result of any one motive when we know it to be present, but it is not always within our power to ascertain beforehand what number of susceptibilities shall be acted upon on each occasion. An untoward event may render a man of open sympathies for a moment obdurate. The irascible temperament may accidentally pass by an affront; or the penurious man surprise us by his liberality. No one ever supposes that these exceptions imply that the connexion between motive and act is for the time suspended by a caprice of nature, or the relaxation of the usual link of antecedent and consequent. The only explanation that we ever think of entertaining, is the presence of some second motive that for the time holds the prevailing bias in check. We should not think of countenancing the supposition, that a man intensely avaricious in the main current of his life, does nevertheless, on certain days, become paralyzed to the love of money, behaving in all things as if the character could never be attributed to him. We know the uniformity of human actions too well to maintain the possibility of an absolute suspension of motive, while we are no less prepared for the interposition of new motives, and the occasional defeat of some of the strongest of men's usual impulses.

7. To pass next to the consideration of *Duty*. The illustration here is of an exactly parallel nature. The various branches of what is termed duty, or obligation, all point to the interests of our fellow-beings, which we have to respect while in the pursuit of our own. Justice, truth, fulfilment of contracts, the abstaining from violence to the person or character of our neighbour, the respect to other men's property and rights, obedience to legal authority,—are so many

modes of conduct enforced upon us as members of a community bound together for common protection. There are in human nature certain primary impulses that would dictate actions falling under the heads now indicated. The operation of Sympathy identifies us with the pleasures and pains of sentient beings at large, and supplies a motive to work for these to some extent as if they were our own. In the small group of Intellectual emotions, there is a feeling hostile to inconsistency, inequality, and unfairness, ministering therefore to the support of the duties of Truth and Justice. These are the slender contributions of our nature to the cause of social duty. Much more formidable is the array of the unsocial feelings that have influence upon the will. Fortunately however, the purely self-regarding impulses can be wrought upon in this cause, otherwise it is very doubtful if the multifarious exigencies of duty or morality could be at all complied with.

8. I have given it as my deliberate opinion (*Ethical Emotions*, § 1) that authority, or punishment, is the commencement of the state of mind recognised under the various names—Conscience, the Moral Sense, the Sentiment of Obligation. The major part of every community adopt certain rules of conduct necessary for the common preservation, or ministering to the common well-being. They find it not merely their interest, but the very condition of their existence, to observe a number of maxims of individual restraint, and of respect to one another's feelings in regard to person, property, and good name. Obedience must be spontaneous on the part of the larger number, or on those whose influence preponderates in the society ; as regards the rest, compulsion may be brought to bear. Every one, not of himself disposed to follow the rules prescribed by the community, is subjected to some infliction of pain to supply the absence of other motives ; the infliction increasing in severity until obedience is attained. It is the familiarity with this *régime* of compulsion, and of suffering constantly increasing, until resistance is overborne, that plants in the infant and youthful mind the

2 H

## 482    PRUDENCE.—DUTY.— MORAL INABILITY.

first germ of the sense of obligation. I know of no fact that would prove the existence of any such sentiment in the primitive cast of our mental constitution. An artificial system of controlling the actions is contrived, adapted to our volitional nature—the system of using pain to deter from particular sorts of conduct. A strong line of distinction is drawn in every human mind between actions that bring no pain except what may arise out of themselves, as when we encounter a bitter taste or a scalding touch, and those actions that are accompanied with pains imposed by persons about us. These actions, and the circumstances attending them, make a deep and characteristic impression; we have a peculiar notion attaching to them, and to the individual persons, the authors of the attendant pains. A strong ideal avoidance, not unmixed perhaps with the perturbation of fear, is generated towards what is thus forbidden by penalties rising with transgression. The feeling inspired towards those that administer the pain is also of the nature of dread; we term it usually the feeling of authority. From first to last, this is the essential form and defining quality of the conscience, although mixed up with other ingredients. As duty is circumscribed by punishment, so the sense of obligation has no other universal property, except the ideal and actual avoidance of conduct prohibited by penalties. This discipline indoctrinates the newly-introduced member of society with the sentiment of the *forbidden*, which by-and-bye takes root and expands into the sentiment of *moral disapprobation*; he then joins with the other members of the community in imposing and enforcing the prohibitions that have been stamped and branded in the course of his own education. Duty, then, may be said to have two prime supports in the more self-regarding parts of our nature—the sense of the common preservation and well-being operating upon a preponderating majority, and the sense of punishment brought to bear upon individuals (who must be the smaller number) not sufficiently prompted by the other sentiment. Order being once established in a society, that is to say, the practice of obedience being habitual to the mass of

## NATURAL FEELINGS TENDING TO SOCIAL DUTY. 483

the community, it is only necessary to apply a disciplining process to the young to prepare them for the same acquiescence in the public morality. The imposition of penalties begets at once the sense and avoidance of the forbidden and the awe of authority, and this is retained through life as the basis of the individual conscience, the ever foremost motive to abstain from actions designated as wrong.

9. It is not implied that conscience is never anything else than the actual and ideal avoidance and dread of punishment. Other elements concur, sometimes so largely as to obliterate in the view the primary germ and characteristic type of the faculty. There are motives that supersede the operation of punishment in a variety of instances; as when we contract a positive sentiment of good-will towards those that the law forbids us to injure. Even then we do not lose the strong feeling implanted in us respecting the forbidden and the authoritative; we simply are no longer in the position of being moved by that alone. Our tender feelings, our sympathies, our sentiments of the fair, the equal, and the consistent, if liberally developed and well directed, impel us, as it were of our own accord, to respect those interests of our fellow-beings that are protected by the enactments of society. Moreover, as already said, there is a certain maturity of the well-disposed mind at which we enter the company of that majority, spontaneous in its own obedience from a recognition of the common safety, and compelling dissentient minorities by force or punishment. The conscience, which was at first derived and implanted, is now independent, or self-sustaining. The judgment of the individual approves of the common prohibitions against falsehood, injustice, breach of bargain, and other injuries, as a prohibition essential to his own security in company with the rest of the society; and conscience therefore passes into a higher grade of the prudential motive.

At this stage, however, it is hardly possible to exclude entirely the generous or disinterested impulses as elements in the case. The most consummate prudence would do no more than make each man look to himself in the totality of his own interests. So long as his public duties coincided with his private welfare, he would perform them to the full, but, if the contrary, he would not necessarily do so. If he saw that by some act of violence to a neighbour, or some act of defiance to the supreme authority, he would, besides the risk of punishment, incur the chance of a state of things wherein his own security would perish, his prudential sense would be a restraint upon him. Not so when a crime would bring him large gain without either punishment to himself, or endangering the common security that he shares in. There are many cases where a man's social obedience—the fulfilment of his bargains, his justice, veracity, respect to other men's rights—costs him a sacrifice with no return, while the omission leads to no penalty. Simple prudence would at such a moment suggest the criminal course. We see men constantly evading obligations, because the law is not able to enforce them, not to mention the crimes committed in the belief of a shroud of secrecy. If each one were disposed to act on a strict calculation of what was for his own individual gratification, all social duties that brought no more good than repaid the outlay, would be surrendered, while no self-sacrifice for public objects would ever happen. Some virtues might be better attended to in a society of intelligent self-seekers than we actually find as men are constituted. It is often remarked, how a certain kind of truthfulness enables a man to prosper in his business, from the sense of confidence created thereby ; not that any one need be a worshipper of truth in the abstract, or go all lengths with the maxim, that 'honesty is the best policy ;' but that he should see clearly how far truth and honesty really served him, and there limit his devotion. On the whole, however, it may be fairly questioned, whether society could be maintained on the principle of a rigorous and far-seeing selfishness, if it were only for this circumstance, that each generation must pay some respect to the interests of those that are to follow. We must include in that sentiment of the mature mind, which adopts the social duties as its own approved conduct, a

THE CITIZEN CONSCIENCE. 485

mixture of prudence as regards self, and of generosity as regards others. The element of generosity—which, as I have often said, is in the final analysis, Sympathy—may be almost entirely wanting, and then we should have a member of the ideal society of intelligent self-seekers conceived above. Or the generous impulses may have a high and ascendant development, giving birth to acts of self-sacrifice and devotion. In actual experience, neither extreme is the usual case. The mass of civilized men as we find them—Englishmen, Frenchmen, Turks, Chinese, &c.—are constituted by a certain balanced mixture of the self-regarding and the *vivre pour autrui*, with that peculiar element of disinterested antipathy formerly alluded to, which rarely permits either a total self-annihilation, or a total disregard to every interest beyond self. The conscience of the average individual of the commanding majority of each society, contains in it, therefore, a certain concurrence in the social duties, partly for his or her own sake, and partly for the sake of relatives, friends, fellow-citizens, humanity generally, and future generations. We adopt, as it were, into self the interests, more or less, of a greater or smaller number of other beings that awaken our tender regards, or our sympathies. The decisions we come to are influenced by these adopted interests, which sometimes entirely submerge the interests of the isolated self. It is enough for us, under these circumstances, to know that a breach of social duty will injure some individual, or class, that we are generously disposed to. We refrain from the act in ourselves, and join in disapproving and punishing it in others. Such, I conceive, is the nature of the *citizen* conscience, as distinguished from the conscience of the child, or the criminal and rebel, who know nothing but the avoidance of punishment. We must all pass through our novitiate in this last-named form, and we may never be able to rise above it. Yet there must be in society a preponderating number, who at last adopt the social duties as agreeable to their own judgment and sentiment, who need not the fear of punishment themselves, and who are sufficiently strong to punish where

486 PRUDENCE.—DUTY.—MORAL INABILITY.

punishment is needed. In a free and equal society, a clear majority of the full-grown members must be of this mind. In many societies, a government once in the ascendant, and residing in a very limited number of persons, has been able to keep up a sentiment of authority and a dread of punishment, without the concurrence of the rest of the community. Temporal and spiritual despotisms have established themselves, and maintained a sense of law and dispositions to obedience, which the general community, freely consulted and not over-awed, would never have responded to. The conscience of a Russian serf, as of a subject of Xerxes or Tiberius, is a sentiment of pure dread; the conscience of an Englishman, or an Anglo-American, must contain a certain approval of the laws he is called on to obey.

10. Having thus distinguished two leading modes of the sentiment of moral obligation—the Slavish Conscience and the Citizen Conscience—it is proper further to recognise a third mode of rarer occurrence, namely, the Independent, Self-originating, or Idiosyncratic Conscience. When an individual dissents from the notions of duty entertained in the community that he belongs to, either renouncing what they impose, or constituting for himself new obligations, he may be said to have a conscience purely his own. That such consciences are very uncommon, proves in the strongest manner how little this part of our nature is innate. It is generally a superabundance of study and reflection—that is, a more than ordinary exercise of the mature observation and intelligence—that developes the dissenting conscience, when not simply a spirit of rebellion against social restraints. The man that obeys all the laws in force in his society, while adopting obligations of his own in addition, certainly does not exemplify the ordinary type of the moral sense. Still he takes the sentiment of authority engendered by his education as the model of those self-originating obligations. If a European came to the conclusion that the destruction of animal life in any shape is sinful or wrong, it would be by finding in this a case of exactly the same nature as the destruction of human life;

## SUPPORTS TO CONSCIENCE.

whereupon he transfers the sentiment of prohibition from the recognised case to the one not recognised, and makes, not so much a new law, as a new application of what is law already. The abstinence from destroying sentient life becomes a point of conscience by *extension* or deduction, and is carried into practice by the individual's own promptings, there being a revulsion of remorse every time he sins against it. The remorse is fed from the same fountain as a breach of the citizen conscience, where the mind has adopted or acquiesced in the rules imposed by the society; and there is the same mental satisfaction in complying with the dictates of each.

11. So much, then, for the power of motive belonging to the faculty of conscience. The same supporting adjuncts, detailed with reference to prudence, operate in the sphere of duty, in forming the conscience itself and in strengthening it to overbear opposition. The instruction and example brought to bear upon early years; the usages of society in punishing and stigmatizing the forbidden acts and extolling those that are enjoined; the pressure of admonition, warning, and advice; the systematic preaching and reminders embodied in religious worship; the literature of moral inculcation; the setting forth of illustrious virtue and of the infamy of crime; the poetic beauty associated with the conduct that is approved— are among the influences from without that constitute a strong prepossession and motive in favour of social duty. Religious fears and hopes, and the ascendancy of revered individual men, classes, castes, or dynasties, fall in with the other contributing impressions. Nor must we omit here, any more than in the search for individual happiness, the effect of the mind's own leisurely reflections upon all these various motive forces, through which every one of them takes an increased hold of the system, and adds to the moral strength in the moment of conflict. When the bent for revolving all the considerations of duty is spontaneous or natural to the mind, and when the intellect is strongly retentive of all the pains and pleasures arrayed in behalf of social duty, there emerges a moral genius, as we have already spoken of the genius of prudence.

12. The counter-impulses to duty include, as in the former head, a number of strong temporary and passionate risings, the excitement of some strong sensations, appetites or emotions, which have to be conquered both for our interest and for our duty. But the calculations of prudence itself, and the deliberate pursuit of our own happiness, or chief ends, are in many instances opposed to our duties, no less than the more temporary cravings or passions. A power has to be built up to deter us from seeking our own good in another man's loss or harm. Every one knows well how serious is the task of rearing any human being to that maturity of self-restraint, wherein the egotistic and passionate influences are in easy subordination to the social obligations. We all know the multitude of hard struggles with bare success ; of occasional slips amid general conformity, and of downright failures with open defiance. In such instances, however, we are not without a clear and intelligible theory of what has occurred, and a distinct notion of what is proper to be done in practice ; neither the theory nor the practice conceding for one moment a want of uniform causation in the sequences that make up the human will. When any one that we are concerned with has failed in a point of duty, we accept it as a fact of character that will certainly re-appear, if in the meantime no change takes place in the mind or the circumstances, and we address ourselves to the task of making some changes sufficient to break the uniformity. We throw new motives into one side, and withdraw them from the other; in other words, by presenting pains and pleasures that were not presented on the former occasion, we hope to avert the repetition of the error or fault. There is no metaphysical perplexity in the mind of the parent, the tutor, the master, the military commander, the civil authority, when punishing for an offence committed, with a view to prevent its renewal, and increasing the severity, if the first application is not powerful enough to deter. As little perplexity hampers the moral teacher, who knows that by judicious and well-sustained lessons he can create a power that shall anticipate punishment by timely obedience. It is

MORAL INABILITY. 489

possible to calculate the general effect of all the various aids
to the performance of duty in opposition to the ordinary
counter-motives; but without uniformity of sequence, calculation is impossible. A fit of remorse tells for a certain length
of time in one person, a rebuke or admonition has a definite
extent of influence upon another; and these causes are of the
same efficacy in the same circumstances. Every one can tell
what to expect from a child neglected and starved; the action
of the moral agencies at work is sure in its issue when we
know enough to make allowance for original differences of
character. The right-minded parent has no doubt as to the
contrast between such a case and the result of a careful application of all the modes of building up a character of moral
self-restraint.

13. In duty, therefore, as in prudence, *Moral Inability* is
simply weakness of motive, and can be remedied by the aid of
new motives. If the avoidance of a fine of five shillings does
not deter from an act of insult or violence to a fellow-citizen,
a higher penalty is imposed. In the family, duty is supported
by rewards as well as punishments, by instruction and admonition, and the evoking of the generous, in opposition to the
egotistic, sentiments. Moreover, the unformed mind is carefully withheld from strong temptations. It is considered unfair
to place a child under very strong motives to disobey, while
the opposing sentiment has as yet gained little strength, and
when nothing short of the dread of some very severe penalty
would be equal to the occasion. Moral inability is a matter
of degree, admitting every variety up to the point where no
amount of available motive is enough. Still the inability may
not pass out of the character of mental or moral. The incontinent and incorrigible thief may not be restrained by all the
terrors of the law, by imprisonment, servitude, or infamy,
nor by the persuasive address of kind monitors, nor by remorse and reflection of his own; yet, after all, the weakness
that everything fails to make up for, is only moral. True,
nothing that can be done at the stage arrived at is of
sufficient force to reform the character so degraded; never-

## 490    PRUDENCE.—DUTY.—MORAL INABILITY.

theless, had influences been brought to bear sufficiently early, the incorrigible state would have been averted, and there are conceivable promptings that would even now effect a reformation. There is necessarily a limit to the power of the law in surrounding the individual with motives, seeing that its power lies in punishment, and it must work by general rules. After a certain trial made of moral influences, the magistrate proceeds to inflict a physical disability by taking away the life or liberty of the delinquent. In the condition of insanity, we have examples of inability going beyond the bounds of the moral, by passing out of the reach of motives. We may imagine such a weakness of intellect as to make a man forget the consequences of his actions; in such a case it would be useless to hold out either punishment or reward as a motive. So under delusions, the intellect is so perverted as to give a false direction to everything suggested to it. What is most difficult to deal with in the way of legal responsibility, is the state termed *moral insanity*, where the subject is not beyond being influenced by motives of prospective pain or pleasure, but has contracted such a furious impulse towards some one crime, that the greatest array of motives that can be brought to bear is not sufficient. If the orgasm were somewhat less, the motives might be sufficient; they have their due weight, but are overpowered by a mightier force. A nice legal question arises when a monomaniac, not being put under timely restraint, has committed an outrage against the law. An attempt is always made by his counsel to represent him as irresponsible, and not a subject for punishment. The case is a somewhat complicated one, from the circumstance that the magistrate must always bear in mind, as a principal consideration, the effect of a present punishment in preventing future crime generally. On this ground, he is not justified in allowing the escape of any man who is not clearly in that state wherein motives have lost all their influence. Moral insanity is merely the extreme form of passionate fury which, for the time being, obliterates in the mind all sense of consequences and all deterring motives; yet, inasmuch as the person can be

THE OFFENDER'S PLEA OF MORAL INABILITY.    491

influenced by future consequences in ordinary moods, the law will not take as an excuse the frantic condition that caused the crime. Any one who has not to deal with a whole community, but with separate individuals apart, and out of sight, does make allowance for moral inability and for inequality of moral attainment. We are bound to prevent every sort of disobedience, but in private life we do not treat every person in the same way. The public administration is hampered by general rules, and is therefore unable to make the same degree of allowance.

14. There is one form of stating the fact of ability that brings us face to face with the great metaphysical puzzle. It not uncommonly happens that a delinquent pleads his moral weakness in justification of his offence. The schoolboy, whose animal spirits carry him to a breach of decorum, or whose anger has made him do violence upon a schoolfellow, will sometimes defend himself by saying he was carried away and could not restrain himself. In other words, he makes out a case closely allied to physical compulsion. He is sometimes answered by saying that he could have restrained himself if he had chosen, willed, or sufficiently wished to do so. Such an answer is really a puzzle or paradox, and must mean something very different from what is apparently expressed. The fact is, that the offender was in a state of mind such that his conduct followed according to the uniformity of his being, and if the same antecedents were exactly repeated, the same consequent would certainly be reproduced. In that view, therefore, the foregoing answer is irrelevant, not to say nonsensical. The proper form, and the practical meaning to be conveyed is this, ' It is true that as your feelings then stood, your conduct resulted as it did; but I am now to deal with you in such a way, that when the situation recurs, new feelings and motives will be present, sufficient, I hope, to issue differently. I now punish you, or threaten you, or admonish you, in order that an antecedent motive may enter into your mind, as a counteractive to your animal spirits or temper on another occasion, seeing that acting as you did, you were plainly in want of

## 492   PRUDENCE.—DUTY.—MORAL INABILITY.

such a motive.   I am determined that your conduct shall be reformed, and therefore every time that you make such a lapse, I will supply more and more incentives in favour of what is your duty.'   Such is the plain unvarnished account of what the master intends in the address to his erring pupil. Though he may not state it so, he acts precisely in the spirit of the language I have now supplied.   Finding a delinquency to arise, he assumes at once that a repetition will occur if the same feelings and ideas arise under the same outward circumstances; and accordingly there is nothing left for him but to vary the antecedents, and make sure that a new and potent spur shall be mixed up with the previous combination, so as to turn the conduct in the direction sought.

I have now brought the discussion of the will to the verge of the last problem connected with it, the problem of Liberty, for which this chapter has been intended to prepare the way.

# CHAPTER XI.

### LIBERTY AND NECESSITY.

1. THE assumption involved in all that has been advanced respecting the voluntary actions of living beings, is the prevalence of Uniformity, or Law, in that class of phenomena, making allowance for the complication of numerous antecedents, not always perfectly known. The practice of life is in general accordance with the theory, so much so, that if any other theory had been broadly propounded, the experience and procedure of mankind would, in all probability, have offered a negative. Ever since men lived in society, they have been in the habit of predicting the future conduct of each other from the past. The characters affixed to individual men, covering the whole of their mature life, could not be sustained except on such a principle of uniformity. When we speak of Aristides as just, of Socrates as a moral hero, of Nero as a monster of cruelty, and of the Czar Nicholas as grasping of territory, we take for granted a certain persistence and regularity as to the operation of certain motives, much the same as when we affirm the attributes of material bodies, —that bread is a nourishing article of food, or that smoke ascends. How comes it then, to what fatality owing, that an enormous theoretical difficulty, a metaphysical dead-lock, a puzzle and a paradox of the first degree, an inextricable knot, should have been constituted where in practice the worst to be said is, that the number and complication of motive forces may elude our knowledge, and render prediction uncertain and precarious? There are problems connected with the world that have severely tried the human intelligence; but then the difficulties have been felt alike in theory and in

# 494 LIBERTY AND NECESSITY.

practice. The explanation of the conditions of health and disease in the animal body, was from the first, and is now, very hard to arrive at ; and the consequence is, that the healing art has come forward slowly, and is still in its infancy. The prediction of the places of the sun, moon, and planets for practical ends, has gone along with theoretical astronomy. In like manner the problems of human society, the philosophy of history, and the theory of statesmanship, are very uncertain ; the deficiency being as great in practical insight as in theoretical comprehension.*

---

\* ' It is surprising that this connexion between motives and actions should have ever been theoretically questioned, when every human being every day of his existence is practically depending upon its truth; when men are perpetually staking pleasure and fortune, and reputation, and even life itself, on the very principle that they speculatively reject. It is, in truth, intermingled in all our schemes, projects, and achievements. In the address of the orator, in the treatise of the author, in the enactments of the legislator, in the manœuvres of the warrior, in the edicts of the monarch, it is equally implied. Examine any one of these. Take, for example, the operations of a campaign. A general, in the exercise of his authority over the army which he commands, cannot move a step without taking for granted that the minds of his soldiers will be determined by the motives presented to them. When he directs his aide-de-camp to bear a message to an officer in another part of the field, he calculates upon his obedience with as little mistrust as he reckons upon the stability of the ground on which he stands, or upon the magnifying power of the telescope in his hand. When he orders his soldiers to wheel, to deploy, to form a square, to fire a battery, is he less confident in the result than he is when he performs some physical operation—when he draws a sword, pulls a trigger, or seals a despatch? It is obvious that throughout all his operations, in marches and encampments, and sieges and battles, he calculates as fully on the volitions of his men, as on the strength of his fortifications, or the reach of his guns.

' In commercial transactions of all sorts there is the same reliance. In the simple circumstance of a merchant's draft on his banker, payable on a specified day, we have it strikingly exemplified. We can scarcely conceive an instance of more perfect reliance on the production of voluntary acts by the motives presented to human beings, than this common occurrence. The merchant dismisses his draft into the commercial world without the least doubt that, however circuitous the course, it will at last find some individual to present it for payment on the appointed day, and that his banker will finally pay it. Here we have, in fact, a series of volitions, the result of which is looked for with unhesitating confidence, with a confidence quite equal to that with which the material of the draft is expected to retain the handwriting upon it.

## PREVALENCE OF LAW IN HUMAN CONDUCT. 495

2. There are not wanting examples of another class of difficulties, so far parallel to the question before us, as to make

---

'It is a received conclusion in Political Economy, that where competition is left open, there is a tendency to equality in the profits of the various branches of commerce. If any one branch becomes more lucrative than the rest, a flow of capital to that department soon restores the equilibrium. This general law is explained with perspicuity by Adam Smith in the case of the builder, whose trade, as he shows, must yield sufficient profit to pay him the ordinary interest of money on the capital expended, and also to replace that capital within a certain term of years. If the trade of a builder affords at any time a much greater profit than this, it will soon draw so much capital from other trades as will reduce the profit to its proper level. If it affords at any time much less than this, other trades will soon draw so much capital from it as will again raise that profit.

'Now, when Dr. Smith asserts that the trade of a builder under the circumstances supposed, will draw capital from other trades, he is not stating a physical fact which will take place in consequence of some material attraction, but he is laying down a result which will ensue from the known principles of the human mind; or, in other words, from motives acting on society with certainty and precision. The secession of capital from other trades is not a mechanical effect, like the motion of water to its level, but the consequence of a number of voluntary actions. It is an event which is produced through the medium of human volitions, although we reason upon it with as much certainty as on the tendency of water to an equilibrium.

'In employing such figurative expressions as these, in exalting trade and capital into spontaneous agents, and investing them with certain qualities and tendencies, we are apt to be deceived by our own language; to imagine that we have stated the whole of the truth, and to lose sight of all those mental operations concerned in the result which we so concisely express. Let us reflect for a moment on all the intellectual and moral processes, which lie hid under the metaphorical description of the trade of a builder drawing capital from other trades. To produce this result, the fact must transpire that the trade is more than ordinarily lucrative; this circumstance must excite the cupidity or emulation of a number of individuals; these individuals must deliberate on the prudence or propriety of embarking in it; they must resolve upon their measures; they must take steps for borrowing money, or withdraw capital before appropriated to other purposes, and apply it to this; in doing which they will probably have to enter into bargains, make sales, draw bills, and perform a hundred other voluntary actions; the result of all which operations will be the employment of a greater portion of the labour of the community in building than formerly, and a smaller portion in other pursuits; and all these, with a number of other occurrences, are marked under the phrase of one trade drawing capital from another.

'It is the same throughout the whole science of Political Economy. The rise and fall of prices, the fluctuations in exchange, the vicissitudes of supply

496                    LIBERTY AND NECESSITY.

it worth while to refer to them by way of elucidation. On
certain subjects, there have grown up theoretical and factitious
puzzles, that have not interfered with practical applications,
while tasking speculative ingenuity to the utmost. The
sophisms of Zeno, the Eleate, respecting motion, are exactly
in point. This philosopher originated a demonstration, as he
conceived, of the impossibility of motion, although the fact
itself is felt by every one as among the most certain of all
human experiences. He said that a body must move either
in the place where it is, or in the place where it is not, but in
neither case is motion possible; for on the first supposition
the body leaves its place; and the second is manifestly absurd,
for how can a thing move in the place where it does not lie.*
Here is, on the one hand, an obvious fact; and on the other,
a theoretical demonstration that belies it.

Again, the same philosopher gave birth to the famous
argument that if Achilles and a Tortoise were to begin a race,
Achilles would never beat the tortoise. Our sense shows us

---

and demand, the return of excessive issues of paper on the bankers, the dis-
appearance of specie, the depreciation of the currency, and various other
events, are to be traced to certain determinate causes acting with regularity
on the minds of individuals and bodies of men; all these phrases are, in fact,
expressions of the result of voluntary actions. Such circumstances furnish as
striking instances of perfect vaticination in regard to the acts of human beings,
as any that can be adduced in regard to material occurrences. Political
Economy is, in a great measure, an inquiry into the operation of motives, and
proceeds on the principle that the volitions of mankind are under the influence
of precise and ascertainable causes.'—*Letters on the Philosophy of the Human
Mind*, by Samuel Bailey. Second Series, p. 166.

   * The extrication of the fact of motion from this puzzle of language is by
no means hard of accomplishment. It will be seen that Zeno, in expressing
the condition of a moving body, employs terms that utterly preclude motion,
and apply only to the state of rest. He puts the supposition that the body
must be *in* a place, but this is the definition of rest, and extinguishes movement as much as if we were to use the phrase ' at rest.' A moving body is
not *in* a place: the essence of the phenomenon is change of place, and we
cannot resort to the language of Zeno without denying motion itself. His
demonstration is tantamount to saying, it is impossible for a body to move,
provided it is at rest or not moving, which is evident enough, being only repeating the same fact in other language.

## FACTITIOUS PROBLEMS. 497

the contrary, and yet it has not been an easy thing to refute the argument.*

It has been attempted to be proved by reasoning that matter must be infinitely divisible, while there is nothing in our actual knowledge or experience to justify such a conclusion, which, being on a matter of fact, ought to have the countenance of a certain amount of inductive proof.

*Ever since the time of Archimedes there has been introduced into mathematics a system of quantities called 'Infinitesimal,' or infinitely small, which have given rise to no small amount of discussion and dispute. The Fluxional or Differential calculus, invented by Newton and Leibnitz, assumes that questionable order of quantities, and yet no practical error has ever been committed by the use of them, while they have lent new power to the solution of the most difficult problems in Mechanics, Astronomy, and other branches of Physical science. Very severe and acrimonious criticism has been brought to bear on the irrationality of a method, that passes out of the region of finite and intelligible magnitudes. Bishop Berkeley denounced the looseness and credulity of Mathematicians in using the fluxional calculus, which was burdened with this sort of auxiliary, and even now there are scruples as to the legitimacy of devices that lead to no practical errors. I believe the fact to be, that Mathematicians are more under the control of verification from practice than almost any other class of reasoners; their results, being numerical, can generally be brought to a rigorous experimental test, and they square their machinery accordingly. Even what is called 'impossible quantities' can be so used as to minister to sound conclusions, in the sphere of the possible and the real.

In the question of Liberty and Necessity, much of the apparent mystery lies in the employment of unsuitable language, and much of it in the subtlety of the phenomenon to be expressed. I admit that it is no easy matter to render an

---

* Mill's *Logic*, Book V., Chap. VII., Sec. 1.

2 I

498                LIBERTY AND NECESSITY.

exact account of the operations of the human Will, but no
more is it easy to seize the abstruser phases of the understanding. There may be a little more or a little less pains requisite
to solve the one problem or the other, but I deny that there is
any such peculiarity in the will as to render it insoluble,
supposing (what it is true has not always been admitted)
other parts of the mind to be susceptible of scientific explanation. The whole of the present Book is my justification
for so saying; and granting any amount of imperfection in
the exposition here attempted, I apprehend that there is no
radical inferiority in it as compared with the explanation
given by me, or by other persons, of the remaining departments of the human mind. I shall now go over in detail the
different phrases in use on the subject of free will and necessity, with the view of showing, that they are, for the most
part, inapt expressions of a phenomenon that is neither inconsistent nor unintelligible.

3. *Liberty, Freedom, Free-Will.*—The notion of a man
being free in his actions appears first among the Stoics, and
afterwards in the writing of Philo Judæus. The virtuous
man was said to be free, and the vicious man a slave; the
intention being obviously, by a strong metaphor, to pay a
lofty compliment to virtue, and to fix a degrading stigma on
vice. In so far as explaining the human will is concerned,
nothing could be worse chosen than these names—an application, however, never meant by those that originated them.
It would be quite as correct, and in some instances more
correct, to say that the virtuous man is the slave, and the
vicious man free, seeing that the man that acknowledges
fewest restraints has the greatest liberty. The doctrine of
Freedom was first elaborated into a metaphysical scheme,
implying its opposite Necessity, by St. Augustin against
Pelagius; and in a later age was disputed between Arminians
and Calvinists; being for centuries a capital controversy both
in Theology and in Metaphysics. One answer to be made to
the advocates of Free-will is, I conceive, the utter inappro-
priateness of the name, or notion, to express the phenomenon

## THE TERM LIBERTY INAPPROPRIATE. 499

in question. We may produce any amount of mystery, incomprehensibility, insolubility, transcendentalism, by insisting on keeping up a phraseology, or a theoretical representation, that is unadapted to the facts. I can imagine some votary of the notion—that polar force (as in the magnet) is the type and essence of all the powers of nature—finding the difficulty of bringing gravity under it, and thereupon declaring that the case of gravity was an insoluble problem. Now it so happens, that the theory of gravitation exemplifies the perfect form of attainable knowledge; it is impossible that any natural phenomenon can ever be more thoroughly comprehended by the human mind, than this has been since the time of Newton. We might render this intelligibility obscure by twisting the phenomenon into some unnatural shape such as polarity; as it now stands nothing is more simple. In like manner, I believe that to demand that our volitions shall be stated as either free or not free, is to mystify and embroil the real case, and to superadd factitious difficulties to a problem not in its own nature insoluble. Under a certain motive, as hunger, I act in a certain way, taking the food that is before me, going where I shall be fed, or performing some other preliminary condition. The sequence is simple and clear when so expressed; bring in the idea of Freedom, and there is instantly a chaos, imbroglio, or jumble. What is to be said, therefore, is that this idea ought never to have come into the theoretical explanation of the will, and ought now to be summarily expelled. The term 'Ability' is innocent and has intelligible meanings, but the term 'Liberty' is brought in by main force, into a phenomenon wherewith it is altogether incommensurable. By the adoption of a course similar to what has taken place in the history of this word, namely; the conversion of metaphor into scientific language, we might have had controversies as to whether the will is rich or poor, noble or ignoble, sovereign or subject; seeing that virtue has been said to make men, not only free, but rich, noble and royal; all which would have ended in transcendental mysteries from the same impossibility of reconciling

500                    LIBERTY AND NECESSITY.

them with the facts, or assigning a decisive reason in favour
of one or other of the contrasting epithets. We understand
the difference between slavery and free-citizenship, between a
censorship and a free press, and between despotism in any
shape and the liberty of the subject, but if any one asks
whether the course of volition, in a man or an animal is a case
of despotism, or a case of freedom, I answer that the terms
have no application whatsoever to the subject. The question
put into some one's mouth by Carlyle, 'Is virtue then a gas?'
is not too ridiculous a parody upon the foregoing. 'Let each
phenomenon be expressed in the language exactly suited to
its nature,' is surely a maxim of sound philosophy. 'Let a
phenomenon be twisted into a scheme of expression at variance
with its very essence,' can be the policy of none but an author
of chaos and confusion.*

4. I do not affirm that the question of Liberty is wholly
verbal, or that, if the present terms were set aside and the
subject discussed in other language, all the disputants would
come to a speedy agreement. There have prevailed, and

---

* As another example of problems created out of inappropriate phraseology
I may quote the application, in the Philebus of Plato, of the terms 'true' and
'false' to pleasures and pains. Mr. Grote well remarks on this point:—'This
is one main defect pervading the Platonic Philebus—the *violent pressure* employed to force Pleasures and Pains into the same classifying framework as
cognitive Beliefs—the true and the false.'

In the Appendix to my former volume (2d edit., p. 632), I expressed
great misgivings as to the propriety of applying the terms External and Internal, derived from the Extended or Object world, to express the fundamental
contrast of Object and Subject. I cannot help accounting this also as a case of
the 'violent pressure' of an unsuitable metaphor. All that we can strictly
say of the relationship of the two great opposing constituents of the universe,
is that mind is *allied* with matter—with a nervous mechanism, &c.,—but not
that it is enclosed in that mechanism, in the manner of the enclosure of the
brain in the skull.

Those theories respecting the nature of mind itself—as in much of the early
materialism—implying an *extended* substance, were guilty of the blunder of
inappropriate predication. The contrast of matter and mind turns upon the
attribute of Extension; this is the fundamental quality of the *object*. Accordingly, it was an advance in correct thinking (by St. Augustin and others
in the 5th century), to declare in favour of the *Unextended* mind.

DOCTRINES OPPOSED TO LAW IN HUMAN ACTION.   501

still prevail, views opposed to the doctrine of uniform causation as applied to human actions.   I may instance, as an example in point, the Socratic doctrine that, as regards human knowledge, some portions were attainable by human study, while others the gods reserved for their own department.*

---

* Xenophon, *Memorabil.* I. 1. 6—9.—' In conversation with his friends, Socrates advised them to perform necessary matters, in the way in which they thought that each matter would be performed best : but respecting enterprises of uncertain result, he recommended consultation of the oracle, to ask whether such enterprises should be undertaken.   He maintained that all who intended to administer either houses or cities well, stood in need of prophetic counsel as a supplementary resource.   For though a man might qualify himself by study, and by the exercise of his own intelligence, to become a competent carpenter, or smith, or husbandman, or inspector of such works, or ruler of men, or calculator, or house-manager, or general—yet in all these departments, the gods reserved the most important results for themselves, so that nothing of them was visible to men.   For the man who has built a house well, cannot tell who will live in it: nor the competent general, whether it will answer to him to undertake command: nor the competent statesman, whether he will gain by becoming leader of the state : nor the man who has for his pleasure married a beautiful wife, whether he shall come to sorrow through her means : nor he who has acquired by marriage powerful relatives in the state, whether he shall through them come to be banished.   Socrates believes those persons to be out of their senses, who affirmed that nothing in these matters was reserved by the gods, and that everything in them was within the reach of human intelligence; those also (he thought) were out of their senses, who resorted to prophecy on points which the gods had assigned to human study to determine : for example, if any one were to ask the oracle, whether it was better to entrust his chariot to a practised or to an unpractised coachman— whether he should take aboard his vessel a practised or an unpractised steersman.   Socrates accounted it impiety to inquire from the gods respecting any matters which might be known by computation, or measurement, or weighing. We ought to learn all that the gods had assigned to be performed by practised hands; and to consult them, through the medium of prophecy, only on matters not cognizable to man: for the gods then give information to persons whom they favour.'

More is said, in the sequel of the chapter, respecting the Socratic distribution of the subject matters of knowledge into *human* and *divine*.   Under the latter head, *the divine*, Socrates ranked physical philosophy, or the philosophy of nature.   He thought that we could not by any study find out how the gods managed the phenomena of nature, and that we offended them by even making the attempt (IV. 7, 6).   He himself confined his study exclusively to the *human* department—discussing ' What are piety and impiety ?   What are the honourable and the base—the just and unjust—sobriety and insanity—

502 LIBERTY AND NECESSITY.

In the one class of subjects, a man, by informing himself of the usual sequence of events, might predict with certainty what would happen, and act accordingly; as regarded the other class, human study was of no avail, and the only resource was to consult the gods. Here then is a distinct and intelligible negation of an intelligible doctrine; the universal prevalence of law and uniform causation, is met by the counter-affirmation, of that prevalence being only partial. In the theology of modern times, instances might be adduced where a position almost similar is taken up. It is obvious, however, that the dispute here is not the handling of a puzzle, but a matter of fact, experience, or induction. Can it be made out, that there are in human actions any class unpredictable from their very nature, apart from the complication that they involve, or the obscurity that surrounds them? One field expressly excepted by Socrates from the domain of human study, is now the crowning instance of human prediction, namely, the motions of the heavenly bodies. There is a greater certainty, at the present day, in anticipating celestial events than in those very matters quoted by Socrates as so thoroughly within man's own study, that it would have been mere impiety to refer to the gods respecting them.

The doctrine of invariable sequence in human actions might be opposed by various negatives, still shutting out the obnoxious terms 'liberty' and 'necessity.' Considering the law of causation, in the view taken of it by Mr. John Stuart Mill in his *Logic*, as nothing more than an induction of observed instances of uniformity, with no unequivocal ex-

---

courage, cowardice—a city and a man qualified for citizenship—the government of men, and the character fit to exercise such government—and other similar matters. Persons cognizant of these he accounted good and honourable: persons ignorant of them he affirmed to deserve the appellation of slavish-minded.—(I. 1. 16).

Even in the department which Socrates recogned as *human*, we see that he pronounced an important fraction of each series of events to be reserved by the gods for themselves, concealed from human research, and discoverable only through supernatural indications.

## NECESSITY AN OBJECTIONABLE TERM. 503

ception, it might be said, that we never can be sure that an exception shall not arise. Until we have experimentally proved the law throughout all departments of nature, and throughout every corner of each department, we cannot tell whether there may not lurk some nest of irregularity, and therefore we cannot affirm the law of causation as absolutely certain. Granting this, however, it is enough that we have examined a very wide portion of natural phenomena, both in matter and in mind, and that no case of anarchy has ever yet been lighted on. Until an exception has been decidedly made manifest, we are entitled to presume the universality of the rule, according to the maxim of philosophizing laid down by Newton, and accepted in the schools of science.

Still, it is competent for any one to constitute the human will a region of anarchy, provided he thinks there are facts that bear out the conclusion. What I most strongly contend for at present, is the discarding of the old '*drapeau*' under which the contest has been so long carried on, being persuaded that the controversy will then assume a very different aspect, and, if not speedily adjusted, will at least be divested of all its paradox, transcendentalism, and incomprehensibility.

5. *Necessity.*—A similar line of criticism may be pursued with reference to this word. In so far as it expresses the negation of Freedom, it is exposed to the very same objections. Moreover, I very much doubt whether the word ought to be retained in any of the sciences, physical or moral ; nothing is ever gained by it. We speak of 'mathematical necessity,' but we might convey the same idea by language equally good, if not better. In common life, the word has a tolerably fixed meaning, suited to ordinary emergencies, and to that sphere we should do well to keep it. I cannot but think that every scientific discussion where people have intruded it, has been perplexed by it. I see nothing but confusion in such questions as 'whether the axioms of Mathematics are necessary,' and 'the necessary connexion of cause and effect ;' the disputes on such points would probably be shortened by agreeing to depart from the present form of predication.

504 LIBERTY AND NECESSITY.

Because a term has once got footing in science, it surely does not follow that a vested interest has been created, compelling us to retain that word after we have discovered the unsuitability of it to the purpose in hand ; and leading to laborious contortions, with a view to abate in a slight degree the excess of the *malapropos !* The tenderness that we show to the feelings of living men cannot be requisite towards inanimate instruments. I consider the word ' necessity ' as nothing short of an incumbrance in the sciences of the present day.*

6. *Choice,—Deliberation.*—The word ' choice' is one of the modes of designating the supposed liberty of voluntary actions. The real meaning, that is to say, the only real fact that can be pointed at in correspondence with it, is the acting out one of several different promptings. When a person purchases an article out of several submitted to view, the recommendations of that one are said to be greater than of the rest, and nothing more needs really be said in describing the transaction. It may happen that for a moment the opposing attractions are exactly balanced, and decision suspended thereby. The equipoise may even continue for a length of time, but when the decision is actually come to, the fact and the meaning are that some consideration has risen to the mind, giving a superior energy of motive to the side that has preponderated. This is the whole substance of the act of choosing. The designation ' liberty of choice ' has no real meaning, except as denying extraneous interference. If

---

* It is not meant that the term should be wholly excluded from speech and composition. What I contend for is, that as a principal term in scientific affirmations, it ought to be dropped as being incurably inappropriate. There are names whose meaning is adapted to the phenomena of the world, as explained scientifically at the present day ; I may quote as examples, ' uniform,' ' conditional,' ' unconditional,' ' sequence,' ' antecedent,' ' consequent,' all which have a precision of meaning, and an absence of confusing associations. If terms of this class are employed in the leading propositions, it matters less that vaguer words are occasionally introduced in connexions that show the exact sense intended. The rhetorical conditions imposed, even upon scientific exposition, do not allow that the one appropriate word shall be repeated on every occasion.

DELIBERATION AN INTELLIGIBLE FACT. 505

I am interfered with by another person compelling me to act in one way, then it may be said, intelligibly enough, that I have not liberty of choice ; the child may be taken to the shop where a dress is to be purchased, but some one else makes the selection. But, as between the different motives of my own mind, there is no meaning in the 'liberty of choice.' Various motives—present or prospective pleasures and pains —concur in urging me to act ; the result of the conflict shows that one group is stronger than another, and that is the whole case. Any person watching me at that moment, and knowing exactly the different prompting considerations, would take a lesson as to my character from the trial, and would have some guidance as to what might be expected from me on similar occasions. He would never think of either liberty or necessity, unless in the exceptional case of my being so overpowered by compulsion from without, that my own likings or dislikings had nothing to do with the conclusion. Even then 'necessity' would be a bad title to employ ; it would be more correct to say that my will was completely suspended in the matter, that I was no party in the decision. The question really is, in such circumstances, not whether my will is free, but whether the action is mine at all, or whether it belongs to some other person, using me as an executive instrument. The expression, in common speech, that 'such a one has no will in the matter' is correct and intelligible, on the supposition of an irresistible power from without. When a strong motive is brought to bear, in the shape of command or dictation under penalties, and when that command is resisted, we can only pronounce that the counter-motives are stronger than the deterring prospect of punishment. So that, in whatever predicament a man or an animal may be placed, there is a simple and strictly apposite mode of expressing the conflict of motives and the issuing decision. In very few circumstances are the terms liberty and necessity in any way suitable, and in none are they the best ; while in the great mass they serve only to breed confusion. Nothing could have been more fatal than to clothe the most general and fundamental fact of

506                LIBERTY AND NECESSITY.

volition, so often set forth in the foregoing chapters, in such a
phraseology. The following up of pleasure, and the recoil
from pain, are the ultimate facts, and most comprehensive
types, or representations of volition; but I am unable to see
how they can be brought under any description involving
those names. I can fancy an equal appropriateness in styling
the mind's proceeding circular or oval, wet or dry, up-stairs
or down-stairs. In truth, the terms in question have weighed
like a nightmare upon the investigation of the active region
of the mind. It is a fact that the progress made in explaining the will bears no proportion to what has been achieved in
the other departments—the senses, the understanding, the
affections, the emotions of taste, &c.—and my only explanation is, that the authors that have contributed to enlighten us
in the human mind have had their strength wasted, and their
pages usurped, by a problem in great part spurious.*

As regards the phrase 'deliberation,' I have already
explained at length what is comprised under it (Chap. VII.).
There is no exception to the general theory, when the mind
deliberates for a certain time before acting. If the opposing
ends are equally balanced, there is a state of indecision, until
such time as new motives gather round one or other of the
two sides. This suspense, under equal and opposing pressures,
is one form of deliberating, the occasion when additional time
for the occurrence of motive considerations is essentially
called for. It generally happens that the course of the
thoughts continuing upon the question, brings up something

---

\* Locke, after stating his view of the nature of Free-will (summed up in
the remark that Voluntary is opposed, not to Necessary, but to Involuntary),
goes on to say :—' I leave it to be considered, whether it may not help to
put an end to that long agitated, and I think, unreasonable, because unintelligible question, viz., *Whether Man's Will be free or no?* For if I mistake not,
it follows from what I have said, that *the Question is altogether improper :* and
it is as insignificant to ask, whether Man's *Will* be free, as to ask whether his
Sleep be swift, or his Virtue square ; Liberty being as little applicable to the
Will, as Swiftness of Motion is to Sleep, or Squareness to Virtue.'—*(Essay on
the Understanding*, Book II., Chap. 21.

## SPONTANEITY AND SELF-DETERMINATION. 507

on one side or the other, converting the equipoise into a preponderance; the fact that a decision is at last come to implies as much. Here, as in the supposed exercise of choice, there is nothing but an accession of motive; no simpler or more exact description can be given. The other mode of deliberation supposes the mind acted on by a decided preponderance of inclination to one of two or more courses; but also subject to the consideration of the evil consequences of deciding too quickly. A new and distinct motive is thus present, to counterwork for a certain period the strong inclination that would otherwise bring about immediate action. There is the same general fact of volition exemplified in postponing an act from the avoidance of prospective evil, known from past experience to be likely to follow, as in any other circumstance where pleasure or pain prompts to secure the one, and escape the other. After a proper interval, the sense of danger from precipitate execution is satisfied, and ceases to operate; whereupon the action is taken according to the strongest urgency; or as the fact might be more correctly rendered, the action shows which is the stronger, decision being the only criterion attainable of strength of motive.

7. *Spontaneity,—Self-determination.*—These names are introduced into the discussion of the will, as aids to the theory of liberty, which they are supposed to elucidate and unfold. That there is such a thing as 'spontaneity,' in the action of voluntary agents, has been seen in the foregoing pages. The spontaneous beginnings of movement are a result of the physical mechanism under the stimulus of nutrition; and they are laid hold of, and linked to the pleasurable and painful feelings, in a manner above indicated at full length. The spontaneous tendency operates all through life, and has a definite influence upon the actions. In studying the conflict of volitions, we found it requisite to allow for this element. After nutrition and rest, every animal tends to break out into some form of active display; if the other motives are indifferent, or equal for movement and for stillness, the central energy decides for movement. To resist it, a certain motive for rest must be

508 LIBERTY AND NECESSITY.

present. There is nothing in all this that either takes human actions out of the sweep of law, or renders liberty and necessity appropriate terms of description. The physical, or nutritive, stimulus is a fact of our constitution, counting at each moment for a certain amount, according to the bodily condition; and if any one knew exactly the condition of a man or animal in this respect, a correct allowance might be made in the computation of present motives. In a general way, we do calculate this element in the instances of pronounced spontaneity, as in youth and activity of temperament. The schoolmaster knows well the times when his pupils are restive, the horseman knows the troubles of managing a steed too long confined to the stable.

'Self-determination' assumes something more than spontaneity, having a lurking reference to some power behind the scenes, that cannot be stated under the form of a specific motive or end. There is one sense of the term that represents a genuine fact, or distinction of characters, to which a brief allusion may be made; that is, the opposition of *permanent* and enduring motives to *temporary* and passing solicitations. When a person remains at one task under a variety of temptations to leave it; or retains a fixed character through many vicissitudes, or a fixed purpose under every variety of outward circumstances,—one way of expressing the character is to represent it as having great self-determination. Not that any new and distinct species of voluntary action is implied; but the motives growing out of the distant, the future, and the collective ends, are so powerfully retained and set forth by the tenacity of the intellectual hold, that they are a match for all counter-motives of present and living sensation. This peculiar case could not have been omitted from an exposition of the will pretending to anything like completeness; and abundant allusion has been already made to it. The opposition of the comprehensive ends of life to the desires generated by things passing around us, is one large region of volitional conflict which ought not to pass unnoticed. One man is said to be the ' creature of circumstances,' another not so. The difference is made by the presence of deep-seated ends, adhered to through all the varying circumstances and moods of the outward life.

8. If Self-determination is held to imply something different from the operation of the motive forces of pleasurable and painful sensibility, coupled with the central spontaneity of the system, there is an imputation on the sufficiency of the common analysis of the mind. Feeling, Volition, and Intellect, as explained with full detail in the present work, must still leave a region unexplored. A fourth or residual department would need to be constituted, the department of 'self' or Me-ation, and we should set about the investigation of the laws, (or the anarchy) prevailing there, as in the three remaining branches. The preliminary question, however, has yet to be disposed of, whether there be any residuum when the phenomena comprised under the common division are taken away. I cannot light upon anything of the sort ; and in the setting up of a determining power under the name of 'self,' as a contrast to the whole region of motives generated in the manner described, I see only an erroneous conception of the facts. The proper meaning of self can be nothing more than my corporeal existence, coupled with my sensations, thoughts, emotions, and volitions, supposing the classification exhaustive, and the sum of these in the past, present, and future. Everything of the nature of a moving power belonging to this totality is a part of self. The action of the lungs, the movements of the heart, are self-determined ; and when I go to the fire to get warm, lie down under fatigue, ascend a height for the sake of a prospect, the actions are as much self-determined as it is possible for actions to be. I am not able to concede the existence of an inscrutable entity in the depths of one's being, to which the name *I* is to be distinctively applied, and not consisting of any bodily organ or function, or any one mental phenomenon that can be specified. We might as well talk of a mineral as different from the sum of all its assignable properties. A piece of quartz is an aggregate of inertia, specific gravity, crystalline form, hardness,

510                LIBERTY AND NECESSITY.

transparency or opacity, colour, infusibility, chemical re-agency,
conjoined in one definite situation; and, if there be any other
known property, we include it in the list. The aggregate is
the quartz's own self, essence, or whatever other designation
marks it off from other minerals. It is impossible that any
object can be more than the assemblage of its known properties; if there were any remainder, the enumeration would
simply be incomplete. A self-determining power, therefore,
in a voluntary agent, is merely another, and not a good,
expression for the ordinary course of the will, as we understand
it. The pains, personal to the agent, incite actions also personal to that agent; the pleasures making a portion of the
collective self operate likewise, according to their nature. It
is quite plain that the great mass of our voluntary actions
have antecedents that can be traced and assigned, and the
presumption is that the whole agree in kind with the majority.
If any acts can be pointed out as unconnected with motives,
or antecedents, of the character that we have recognised
throughout our inquiry into the will, the exception ought to
be made good, and admitted as a new element of voluntary
determination. But, before giving the supposed residual phenomenon an ambiguous title, its existence should first be
established, a work very far from being achieved in the present position of our knowledge of the subject in hand.

The only instance that I can fix upon, as having the semblance of a power contradistinguished from the ordinary
motives, is the perverseness sometimes exhibited by individuals, for the sake of showing that their actions are not to be
predicted by every looker-on. We sometimes take a fancy to
feel humiliation in being the subject of easy calculation by
our neighbours, and go out of our usual course to preplex
their intrusive speculations. There is nothing in this, however, but a new motive, springing out of our sense of humiliation, or pride, one of the most hackneyed of all human impulses. An observer of a still shrewder stamp might predict
the occurrence of this element also. Turn whichever way we
may, there is no escape from the antecedence of motives when

## ARE WE CONSCIOUS OF FREE-WILL? 511

we perform voluntary acts; if we seem to evade one, we find ourselves in the arms of another.

9. *Consciousness of Free-will, Self-determination, &c.*—A bold appeal is made by some writers to our Consciousness, as testifying, in a manner not to be disputed, the liberty of the will. Consciousness, it is said, is our ultimate and infallible criterion of truth. To affirm it erring, or mendacious, would be to destroy the very possibility of certain knowledge, and even to impugn the character of the Deity. Now this infallible witness, we are told, attests that man is free, wherefore the thing must be so. The respectability and number of those that have made use of this argument compel me to examine it. I confess that I find no cogency in it. As usual, there is a double sense in the principal term giving origin to a potent fallacy. I am not inquiring minutely at present into all the meanings of the term consciousness, a task reserved for the dissertation that is to conclude this volume; it is enough to remark, that for the purpose now in view the word implies the knowledge that we have of the successive phases of our own mind. We feel, think, and act, and know that we do so; we can remember a whole train of mental phenomena mixed up of these various elements. The order of succession of our feelings, thoughts and actions, is a part of our information respecting ourselves, and we can possess a larger or a smaller amount of such information, and, as is the case with other matters, we may have it in a very loose, or in a very strict and accurate shape. The mass of people are exceedingly careless about the study of mental co-existences and successions; the laws of mind are not understood by them with anything like accuracy. Consciousness, in this sense, resembles observations as regards the world. By means of the senses we take in, and store up, impressions of natural objects,—stars, mountains, rivers, plants, animals, cities, and the works and ways of human beings,—and, according to our opportunities, ability, and disposition, we have in our memory a greater or less number of those impressions, and in greater or less precision. Clearly, however, there is no infallibility in what we

know by either of these modes, by Consciousness as regards thoughts and feelings, or by Observation as regards external nature. On the contrary, there is a very large amount of fallibility, fallacy, and falsehood, in both the one and the other. Discrepancy between the observations of different men upon the same matter of fact, is a frequent circumstance, the rule rather than the exception. What makes it so difficult to establish even simple matters of experience, in science and in courts of law, if there does not belong to the ordinary mind a great natural deficiency in the power of seizing the exact truth of any phenomenon or incident? There are a few points whereon the senses give a tolerably exact appreciation from the first, and all through; the principal being the comparison of Magnitude or Size. When two rods are placed side by side, there is an entire unanimity among observers in settling the greater or the less, when the difference is not microscopically minute, and perhaps no other quality is so decisively rendered in one way by the multitude of observers. Next in order we may place the appreciation of force, as in the case of Weight, or in the encountering of a moving obstacle. The human system seems to yield on all occasions a distinguishable response to the increase or diminution of force, or pressure, brought to bear upon the moving organs, so as to call forth a greater or less degree of muscular expenditure. I scarcely know of any anomaly, or any mode of derangement, that would make the feeling of a four pound weight seem less than the feeling of a two pound. Next in order may be ranked the discrimination of Colour, which, however, with prevailing agreement, is liable to exceptional discrepancy. I allude to the well-known instances of colour-blindness, and to the differences of power manifested by individuals in marking the gradations of tint. The sensibility to the property of Heat, although in the main uniform, is exceedingly fluctuating. The want of accuracy and unanimity of perception, in these last, and in other properties, such as hardness, softness, roughness, smoothness, taste, odour, musical pitch, has led to the invention of modes of mechanism for

SUPPOSED INFALLIBILITY OF CONSCIOUSNESS. 513

reducing the mensuration of all properties to the first-named property, or criterion, namely extension. Witness the balance, the thermometer, the photometer, &c. If such be the case with the objects of the external senses, what reason is there to suppose that the cognisance of the mental operations should have a special and exceptional accuracy ? Is it true that this cognisance has the definiteness belonging to the property of extension in the outer world? Very far from it ; the discrepancy of different men's renderings of the human mind is so pronounced, that we cannot attribute it to the difference of the thing looked at, we must refer it to the imperfection in the manner of taking cognisance. If there were any infallible introspective faculty of consciousness, we ought as least to have had some one region of mental facts, where all men were perfectly agreed. The region so favoured must of necessity be the part of mind that could not belong to metaphysics ; there being nothing from the beginning to controvert or to look at in two ways, there could be no scope for metaphysical disquisition. The existence of metaphysics, as an embarrassing study, and an arena of dispute, is incompatible with an unerring consciousness.

10. Let us examine for a moment, whether there be at bottom any, the smallest, fact, or pretext, for the assumption that consciousness is the ultimate and infallible criterion of truth. Is there any point of view that can be taken, under which consciousness is to be assumed as evidence above all dispute ? The only case of the sort that I am able to specify is the testimony that each individual gives as to the state of his or her own feelings at any one moment. If I feel pain, and say that I feel it, my consciousness and testimony are final. If the pain disappears, my mind has gone into a new phase, which it may please me to take notice of as a fact or phenomenon, and declare as such ; and there, too, my testimony is final. No appeal can be made from it, no contradiction can be given to it. If, again, I have the consciousness of a blaze of sunshine, followed by another state—darkness, this is to me an ultimate experience—indisputable, undeniable ; and so

2 K

514 . LIBERTY AND NECESSITY.

with all my feelings, whether of pleasure or pain, or of discriminative sensibility without pleasure or pain, if I confine
myself to expressing simply my own momentary changes. Be
it observed, however, that this knowledge which, if not infallible, is at least final and unanswerable, is to the last degree
special and confined. Being applicable in strictness only to
my individual mind, at some one single instant, it contains
the very minimum of information, the smallest portion of fact
that it is possible to express. As regards what we commonly
understand by knowledge, it bears something of the same
proportion that an atom does to a tangible mass. Grant to
it the highest order of certainty, or even the august title of
infallibility, what have you got under it? It enables you to
predict nothing, to affirm nothing beyond the single experience
of a single instant in a single mind; you are not one whit
better or worse for the information. In fact, knowledge, in
the larger and more applicable sense, although reposing upon
this ultimate experience, does not begin to exist until some
step has been taken beyond it. We must make a march of
advance, in order to constitute the smallest item of what is
properly termed information, and although the primitive
experience were never so sure, it is quite another question
how far fallacy may creep in with the new move that constitutes the beginning of knowledge, as commonly conceived.
While infallibility reigns, knowledge is not; where knowledge
commences, fallibility has crept in. Some one informs me
that he at present feels a comfortable soothing sensation. I
grant it; there is no·disputing his consciousness to this
extent. He says, moreover, that along with this feeling he is
conscious of an active state, namely, the act of inhaling
tobacco fumes; which I likewise concede, as on this point
also consciousness is final. (I waive the consideration of the
outward appearances corresponding to action, as being no
part of the illustration.) It is incompetent for me, or for any
one, to deny that the attesting party possesses at the moment
the twofold consciousness spoken of. The testimony is final.
But then what avails it? The affirmation conveyed extends

## MERE CONSCIOUSNESS CANNOT ATTEST OUR KNOWLEDGE. 515

not beyond one period of the life of one person; it neither recalls the past nor points to the future. It has no application to any one else. A statement so limited, therefore, is but the minimum of knowledge. Anything that we term information must be of avail beyond the one moment, or the one locality, where it originally grew. To pursue the foregoing illustration. The same person goes on to affirm, that on former occasions, the same conjunction of mental states has occurred to him. By this step he makes one advance from the barren infallibility of his first declaration to a declaration that involves something like knowledge, although as yet in a sort of inchoate condition. But by the very act of extending the affirmation he trenches upon the region of fallibility. For now he needs a faithful *memory* to support him in the advance that he has made; and we know that memory is anything but infallible. The farther back he goes in the sweep of his assertion, the less sure are we of the certainty of it. Thus, exactly in proportion as knowledge is involved, the testimony of consciousness departs from its primitive certainty. Let the subject of our illustration declare that, on every occasion throughout his past life, the two kinds of consciousness supposed have gone together, or that the consciousness of the activity has been always followed with the other feeling; and although we admit that the sweep of the affirmation is now so considerable as to constitute a genuine fraction of knowledge, we cannot help being aware at the same time, that the testimony of the individual to this point is not to be absolutely relied on. And if he goes on extending his assertion, and raising the value of it as an item of information, by affirming that in after times the same sequence will hold; we thank him very much for putting us on the high altitude of prophetic power, but we plainly see that he has now far transcended in his affirmation what his present, and only infallible, consciousness can reveal to him. In assuming the attitude of the seer, he has come down to an exceedingly humble position as regards infallibility. In order to be trusted now, he must discard entirely the reliance on a present consciousness, and rest his claims upon a

516                LIBERTY AND NECESSITY.

laborious comparison of many past states, and a laborious
method of surmounting the errors and weaknesses that crowd
in at every point of the operation.  So, if progressing still in
the compass of the matter included in the statement under
discussion, the supposed individual tells me that in me also
the same sequence would occur; in other words, if by any
chance I were to induce the consciousness of the action, there
would succeed in me the consciousness of the pleasurable sensation,—this is to me a real and solid donation.  It is knowledge in the completest and best sense of the term, seeing
that it guides my volition for my practical advantage.  But by
what infallible consciousness of his, can my friend assure me
of what is to happen in my consciousness, which never has
been and never will be present to him, and on a point not
even experienced by myself?  I freely grant, that there is an
ample disposition in the human mind, to extend in this way
the application of each one's own narrow point of consciousness
at a single moment to remote places and times ; but in admitting it, I, in common with the generality of men that have
thought on the subject, have to deplore it as a weakness, and
the source of innumerable errors.  The labour to be gone
through, before any fellow-man can carry his own consciousness into mine, is understood only by those that have largely
reflected upon the grounds of certainty in knowledge.  To
whatever extent an affirmation is wide-ranging and fruitful in
consequences, to that extent does it pass out of the sphere of
immediate consciousness into the domain of hard and troublesome verification.  The infallible revelation of consciousness
is an atom (or, if you will, it is *zero*, which is the commencement of a series), while every step made in that series is a
step towards uncertainty, fallibility, and, without numerous
precautions, positive error.*

---

* See the remarks on Observation and Description in Mill's *Logic*,
Book IV., Chap. I., which strongly corroborate the tenor of what is said
above respecting Consciousness, and the ascertaining of true descriptions of
mental phenomena.

## DOCTRINES HELD ON THE AUTHORITY OF CONSCIOUSNESS. 517

11. Now let us consider for a moment the nature of some of those metaphysical assertions that have been put forward under the infallible attestation of consciousness. It is to be seen whether they are contained within the very narrow limit, where consciousness, immediate and direct, is really infallible, or, I should rather say, final. The existence of an External Material world independent of the percipient mind is one of those doctrines ; but does this doctrine confine itself to what my consciousness infallibly assures me of, namely, a certain series of feelings—sensations, ideas, emotions, volitions ? Certainly not. There is a manifest extension of the actual consciousness beyond what it can possibly reveal. There may be good grounds for believing the doctrine, as there are for believing many things that pass beyond immediate and infallible intuition, but it cannot be correct to say that consciousness, pure and simple, is the foundation of the belief. It is not within the sphere of any immediate cognition of mine, that some unknown cause is the necessary antecedent of my sensations, which cause persists when I am no longer affected by it. The persistence of the supposed agency is an assumption beyond the present consciousness, very natural as human beings are constituted, but very fallible, as we know from other things. Innate Moral distinctions are also said to receive the attestation of an unerring consciousness. It cannot require much reflection to show how far such a doctrine steps beyond any single immediate cognition. That I feel at any one moment a sentiment of the kind called ' moral disapprobation,' may be true enough. It is quite another thing to maintain, that there is revealed to me at that moment the mode whereby I became possessed of the sentiment. It is like saying that a New Zealander touring in the British Isles sees that we are an aboriginal population. We do not doubt that a characteristic impression is produced upon the mind of a traveller in Britain, and that he is conscious and convinced of the difference between it and the impression of another country; but it wants much more than observation to shape historical theories.

518                    LIBERTY AND NECESSITY.

12. To return to the case of Freedom. A man may well be conscious of the concurrence, or immediate sequence, of a pleasurable sensation and an action, of a painful sensation and another action, and so on, through the whole sphere of volition. If he confines himself to one instant, or to a short interval of time, and relates exactly the experience of that interval, we give him credit for being upon very sure ground. Yet in this simple operation, there are already two different openings for mistake. His expression, even in that small matter, may not succeed in representing the truth, and he may be unconscientious, and have a motive for deceiving us. How then, when he goes to assemble his past experiences, and generalize them into a theory of the Will? For, say what we may, the doctrines of Freedom and Necessity are generalized theories, affirming a character common to all the volitions of all men. Granting an entire infallibility to the consciousness of a single mental act, it is too much to select one especially difficult generalization, as infallibly conducted by the human mind, which we know to be constantly blundering in the easiest generalizations. The notion of Freedom, for example, is not an intuition, any more than the notion of the double decomposition of salts. There is a collection of remembered volitions, and a comparison drawn between them and one peculiar situation of sentient beings, the situation of being unloosed from an overpowering compulsion from without, as when the dog is loosed from his chain, or the prisoner set at liberty. The theorists that we are supposing compare the whole compass of voluntary acts with this single predicament, and find, as they think, an apposite parallel, under which the will is generalized and summed up for good. But comparison is not an infallible operation of the human intellect. Very far otherwise. Nothing gives us more trouble to obtain and substantiate than a thoroughly suitable comparison, when a great multitude of particular facts of varying hue is concerned. Our existing systems of knowledge have numerous bad comparisons, and these have been probably preceded by still worse. My own judgment, or if you will, my Consciousness, which really means

MORAL AGENCY. 519

all the collective energies of my intellect addressed to the study of the mind, tells me that the comparison of Will in general to the special idea of Freedom is especially bad. I will even venture the opinion, that it is an unlikely and far-fetched comparison, and does not spontaneously occur to any one's mind. We inherit it as a tradition, which we venerate, and strive to reconcile it with the facts from motives of respect. No doubt if the counter-doctrine of Necessity is dressed up in a repulsive garb, and if we are represented as being in all our actions like the dog chained, or the captive physically confined to a given routine of life, we may readily feel the inappro-priateness of that comparison, and repudiate it with some vehemence, declaring that, on the contrary, we are free. In the sense of denying a hypothesis of compulsion, there may be a momentary suitableness in the term liberty; which does not, however, go to prove that the faculty of the will is fairly resumed, or correctly generalized and represented, by the notion of Liberty. It is a great stretch of asseveration to call the construction of an enormous theory a function, or act, of consciousness, so simple and easy that we cannot make a slip in performing it, being practically and theoretically infallible the while.

13. *Moral Agency.—Responsibility.*—It is a common phrase to describe human beings as moral and responsible agents. The word 'moral' has here obviously two meanings, the one narrow, as opposed to immoral, the other wider, as opposed to physical. The same ambiguity occurring in the designation 'Moral Philosophy,' gives to that subject a wide or a contracted scope, according to which of the two meanings is understood; being on one supposition confined to Ethics, or Duty, and on the other comprehending, if not the whole of the human mind, at least the whole of the Emotions and Active Powers. In the large sense, I am a moral agent when I act at the instigation of my own feelings, pleasurable or painful, and the contrary when I am overpowered by force. It is the distinction between mind and the forces of the phy-sical world, such as gravity, heat, magnetism, &c.; and also

520          LIBERTY AND NECESSITY.

between the voluntary and involuntary activities of the animal system. We are not moral agents as regards the action of the heart, the lungs, or the intestines. Every act that follows upon the prompting of a painful or pleasurable state, or the associations of one or other, is a voluntary act, and is all that is meant or can be meant by moral agency. Every animal that pursues an end, following up one object, and avoiding another, comes under the designation. The tiger chasing and devouring his prey, any creature that lives by selecting its food, is a moral agent. It would be well if the same word were not indiscriminately applied to two significations of such different compass; for there can be little doubt that perplexity and confusion of idea have been maintained thereby. Still, nothing can be better established than the recognition of both significations, and we are bound to note the circumstance that the 'moral' which at one time coincides with the 'ethical,' at other times is co-extensive with the 'voluntary.'

14. The term 'Responsibility,' is a figurative expression, of the kind called by writers on Rhetoric 'metonymy,' where a thing is named by some of its causes, effects, or adjuncts, as when the crown is put for royalty, the mitre for the episcopacy, &c. Seeing that in every country, where forms of justice have been established, a criminal is allowed to answer the charge made against him before he is punished; this circumstance has been taken up, and used to designate punishment. We shall find it conduce to clearness to put aside the figure, and employ the literal term. Instead, therefore, of responsibility, I shall substitute punishability; for a man can never be said to be responsible, if you are not prepared to punish him when he cannot satisfactorily answer the charges made against him. The one step denoted by responsibility necessarily supposes a previous step, accusability, and a subsequent step, liability to punishment. Any question, therefore, growing out of the term in discussion is a question of accusing, trying, and punishing some one or more individual beings.

The debateable point arising here is as to the limits and conditions of the imposition of punishment. There are certain

RESPONSIBILITY. 521

instances where punishment is allowed to be just and proper, as in the correction of the young, and the enforcing of the law against the generality of criminals. There are other instances where the propriety of punishing is disputed; as in very young infants, the insane, and the physically incapable. There are, however, two very different grounds of objection that may be taken. The first and principal ground is that the action required under menace of punishment is not one within the capability of the individual, not a voluntary action; in other words, no amount of motive can instigate such an action. It may not be within the range of the individual's powers. One may be asked to do a work that surpasses the physical strength under the strongest spur that can be applied; an unskilled workman may be tasked with an undertaking requiring skill; a mechanic skilled in his art may be deprived of his tools, and yet expected to do his work. All these are obvious cases of the inadmissibility of punishment. So, too, a state of mind which cannot comprehend the meaning of an enactment or a penalty—as infancy, idiotcy, insanity, ignorance of the dialect spoken, excuses the individual from punishment.

15. A second ground of objection is, not the impossibility of bringing about the action by a mere motive urging to it, but the very great severity of motive necessary. You may exact from a man something that is barely compassable by him, when urged to the very utmost limit, by the strongest motives that it is possible to provide. You may threaten to take away the life of your slave if he does not exert himself beyond the point of utter exhaustion, and you will probably succeed in getting a little more out of him. The question now is one of justice, expediency, and humanity, and not of metaphysical possibility. Punishment is a thing competent, a thing not nugatory, whenever the act can be induced by mere urgency of motive; nevertheless, there may be great and grave objections, on the score of just and humane principle, to the application of it. Draconian codes and barbarous inflictions may answer their end, they may confine themselves to what men have it in their power to do or refrain from, when

522                    LIBERTY AND NECESSITY.

overawed by such terrors ; they are not on that account to be defended.

The vexed question of punishability is raised by certain forms of insanity.  Intellectual delusion is the one decisive circumstance that usually exempts from punishment, while placing the patient under adequate restraint ; as when an unfortunate being fancies that every one that he meets is a conspirator against him.  The difficult case is what is called 'moral insanity,' where there are impulses morbidly strong, which can yet be to some degree counterworked by motives, or the apprehension of consequences.  There is a shading off here into the region of mere passionate impulse, such as persons counted perfectly sane may fall victims to.  It is impossible to deal with such cases by a theoretical rule.  They must be treated on their individual merits as they occur.*

---

\* *Responsibility for Belief.*  The dictum of Lord Brougham, that 'man is no longer accountable to man for his belief, over which he has himself no control,' was the occasion of a serious controversy at the time it was uttered (see, among others, Wardlaw's *Treatise on Accountability*).  Reduced to precise terms the meaning is—a man's belief being involuntary, he is not punishable for it.  The point, therefore, is *how far* is belief a voluntary function, for it is known to every one that the will does to some extent influence it.

I. Whatever may be true of the internal conviction, the outward profession of belief is voluntary, and so are the actions consequent upon what we believe.  Now it is these external manifestations alone that society can lay hold of, and they being suppressible, on sufficient motive, the law can supply that motive, and lead to their suppression accordingly.  It is not, therefore, nugatory or absurd, to make laws against belief ; for if every expression of opinion, or consequent proceeding, can be kept down, the purpose is fully served.

II. It has been always open to remark, how completely human beings are the slaves of circumstances in the opinions that they entertain upon all subjects that do not appeal directly to the senses and daily experience.  We see in one country one set of beliefs handed down unchanged for generations, and in another country a totally different set equally persistent.  Seeing, then, that there is so little self-originating, or independent, judgment among mankind, it is evidently possible, by external means, and the power of motives, to make some one opinion prevail rather than another.  I might be a Roman Catholic born, yet with a mind so constituted, as irresistibly to embrace the Protestant faith on examining its creed.  But if I am under a *régime* that

## RESPONSIBILITY FOR BELIEF. 523

appends heavy penalties to my becoming a Protestant, the effect might be to deter me from ever reading a book, or listening to a preacher, or hearing any argument on the Protestant side. It is in the power of my will to open or shut my eyes, although what I am to see when I do open them is not voluntary. The legislator, therefore, in hedging one belief round with heavy penalties may be a tyrant, but he is no fool.

There are many arts of swaying men's convictions. Look at the whole array of weapons in the armoury of the skilful rhetorician. Look at the powers of bribery and corruption in party warfare. Consider also the effect of constantly hearing one point of view to the exclusion of all others. There is the greatest scope for the exercise of arts in swaying men from their own genuine tendencies into some prescribed path. It would be in the last degree incorrect to say that punishment cannot succeed in inducing belief, but whether it be right to employ it for that purpose is merely the old question of political and social liberty.

There is a length that external pressure cannot go in compelling a man's convictions. It is not possible for any power to make me believe that three times four is six. I may for once so far succumb to a tremendous threat, as to affirm this proposition in words, but I feel that if I am to give in to propositions of a like nature generally, I may as well go to the stake at once, for life under such an arithmetic is not worth a week's purchase. If every bargain that I engage in is to be subject to such reasoning, all my security has vanished, and the sooner I quit the better. There are, however, so many affirmations constantly afloat, and never brought to any practical test, that we may swallow a great many inconsistencies without difficulty. So long as action is not entered on we are not obliged to be consistent; and accordingly it is very usual for a man to assent to a number of propositions irreconcileable with one another; while it is still true that in a matter of plain experience, involving one's immediate actions and welfare, it is beyond the power of motive to change one's decided convictions. Sovereign power, whether legal or social, has plenty of room in the outworks of belief, without affecting this inner sanctuary, of pressing and practical experience. The greatest despot stops short of the pence table; he knows that religion, political theories, and many other departments of belief are at his mercy, and to these he applies the screw. After all, therefore, the gist of Lord Brougham's dictum is nothing else than the issue, contested now for centuries, as to freedom of thought and opinion.

# BELIEF.

**1.** IT will be readily admitted that the state of mind called Belief is, in many cases, a concomitant of our activity. But I mean to go farther than this, and to affirm that belief has no meaning, except in reference to our actions; the essence, or import of it is such as to place it under the region of the will. We shall see that an intellectual notion, or conception, is likewise indispensable to the act of believing, but no mere conception that does not directly or indirectly implicate our voluntary exertions, can ever amount to the state in question. The present chapter is devoted to set forth this position in all its consequences.

In the primitive aspect of volition, which also continues to be exemplified through the whole of life, an action once begun by spontaneous accident is maintained, when it sensibly alleviates a pain, or nurses a pleasure. Here there is no place for belief, any more than for plot-interest, deliberation, resolution, or desire. The feeling, that is, the end, prompts at once the suitable exercise of the voluntary organs, and that is all. In this primitive and elementary fact, we have the foundation of the most complicated forms of voluntary procedure, but as yet we have no indication of those subsequent developments. The process in that rudimentary stage might be termed reflex, although differing in a most vital consideration from the reflex actions commonly recognised, namely, the presence of consciousness as an essential link of the sequence. There is an instantaneous response to the state of pleasure or pain, in the shape of some voluntary movement modifying, or sustaining, that state, according as the case may be. Circumstances arise, however, to prevent this immediateness of response, or to interpose delay between the occurrence of the feeling that is the motive and the movements that answer

## INTERMEDIATE ACTIONS INVOLVE BELIEF. 525

to it. We have seen that this condition of suspense is the occasion of those new phases of the will described by the terms desire, deliberation, intention, resolution, choice, and the like ; and the very same condition of suspense is necessary to the manifestation of Belief. If every pain could be met by an appropriate movement for relieving it on the instant, and the same with every pleasure, we might still talk of doing or acting, but there would be no place for believing. When I imbibe the water in contact with my lips, under the pain of thirst, I perform a voluntary act in which belief might by a fiction be said to be implied; but if all my actions were of this nature, the state of belief would never have been signalized as a phenomenon of the human mind, just as no place would be given to deliberation.

2. When the matter is examined closely, we find that it is the class of *intermediate* actions, of themselves indifferent, that give origin to the phenomenon now before us. By the ultimate action of the will, I imbibe the water that sensibly appeases my thirst, but there is nothing in the primordial endowment that would provoke me to lift a cup of liquid to my mouth, or that would inspire the thirsty animal to run to the brook. These movements must be sustained by something else than the feeling of pain relieved, for as yet no such feeling comes of them. That something which keeps the energy of an animal alive, with no immediate fruition, is a new power not involved in the original mechanism of our voluntary nature, but arising more or less as a result of experience. In whatever way it originates, the name that we principally designate it by is Belief. The primordial form of belief is expectation of some contingent future about to follow on our action. Wherever any creature is found performing an action, indifferent in itself, with a view to some end, and adhering to that action with the same energy that would be manifested under the actual fruition of the end, we say that the animal possesses confidence, or belief, in the sequence of two different things, or in a certain arrangement of nature, whereby one phenomenon succeeds to another. The glistening surface of

526 BELIEF.

a pool, or rivulet, presented to the eye, can give no satisfaction to the agonies of thirst; but such is the firm connexion established in the mind of man and beast between the two properties of the same object, that the presentation to the eye fires the energies of pursuit no less strongly than the actual contact with the alimentary surface. An alliance so formed is a genuine example of the condition of belief.

3. While, therefore, Action is the basis, and ultimate criterion, of belief, there enters into it as a necessary element some cognisance of the order of nature, or the course of the world. In using means to any end, we proceed upon the assumption of an alliance between two natural facts or phenomena, and we are said to have a trust, confidence, or faith, in that alliance. ] An animal, in judging of its food by the mere sight, or in going to a place of shelter, recognises certain coincidences of natural properties, and manifests to the full a state of belief regarding them. The humblest insect that has a fixed home, or a known resort for the supply of its wants, is gifted with the faculty of believing. Every new coincidence introduced into the routine of an animal's existence, and proceeded on in the accomplishment of its ends, is a new article of belief. The infant, who has found the way to the mother's breast for food, and to her side for warmth, has made progress in the power of faith; and the same career goes on enlarging through the whole of life. Nothing can be set forth as belief that does not implicate in some way or other the order, arrangements, or sequences of the universe. Not merely the sober and certain realities of every man's experience, but also the superstitions, dreams, vagaries, that have found admittance among the most ignorant and mis-led of human beings, are conversant with the same field. When we people the air with supernatural beings, and fill the void of nature with demons, ghosts, and spirits; when we practise incantations, auguries, charms, and sacrificial rites, we are the victims of a faith as decided and strong as our confidence in the most familiar occurrences of our daily life. In all such cases, the genuineness of the state of belief is tested by the

## BELIEF IMPLICATES THE ORDER OF THE WORLD. 527

control of the actions, while the subject-matter of it is some supposed fact, or occurrence, of nature. The intellect must take hold of a certain co-existence, or succession, of phenomena through the senses, or the constructive faculty, and the mind be, as it were, occupied with this as distinct from being occupied with mere feeling, or mere volition. The state in question, then, having its roots in voluntary action, has its branches spreading far and wide into the realms of intelligence and speculation. As the intellectual functions are developed, and become prominent in the mental system, the materials of belief are more and more abundantly reaped from their proper field; nevertheless, we must not depart from their reference to action, and the attainment of ends, otherwise they lose their fundamental character as things credited, and pass into mere fancies, and the sport of thinking, It is true, however, that that enlarging of the sphere of pure intelligence, which we encounter as we pass to the so-called superior animals and races, leads to the collecting and the storing up of natural coincidences, sequences, and similarities, without any immediate regard to practical ends; as in the vast encyclopædia of ascertained knowledge accumulated to the present time, of which a large amount is possessed by individuals without being turned to any account in the pursuit of pleasure or the banishing of pain; and it has to be shown, that there lurks a tacit appeal to action in the belief entertained respecting all that unapplied knowledge.

4. The beliefs above illustrated, as involved in the pursuits of the inferior creatures, are never separated from the actions and ends where they serve as guides. The stag believes in a connexion between the glistening surface of the brook and the satisfaction of its own thirst, but the intellectual conception has no place except in this one relation. It is only at the moment of thirst that the sequence is produced in the mind; when that has disappeared, the affirmation vanishes, and never recurs until the recurrence of the appetite. The intelligence is awakened solely for the sake of the physical wants and pleasures, and has no detached or independent standing.

528         BELIEF.

Still, in that state of vassalage, there is a genuine display of intellectual power and acquisition. Without those associating forces, and that power of discriminative sensibility, whereby the loftiest flights of reason and imagination are sustained, an animal could not employ the smallest item of mediation in the accomplishment of its ends. But it is possible to restrict the scope of our higher faculty to the exigencies of the physical system. It is also possible to detach those conceptions of sequence, and give them a local habitation out of the routine of practical life. I can suppose a contemplative stag reposing by the brink of a lake, and, without feeling thirst at the moment, recalling to mind past occasions of drinking from the source before him. This would be to entertain a mere reminiscence, or idea, to put forth intelligence without the spur of an end, to view a sequence of nature as pure knowledge. Whether any animal indulges in such disinterested exercises of the intellectual function, it may not be easy to affirm. We should probably be more safe in assigning to such of their conceptions of nature as have no present application, a bearing on the future, as when the same stag chooses his lair with reference to the proximity of a pool to quench his thirst, whereby he manifests an abiding recollection of the connexion of the two things, although the interest that keeps it alive is still practical. It is, however, in the operations of the human intelligence, that the detaching of natural conjunctions and sequences is carried to the greatest lengths. The intervention of language, the coupling of the 'name' with the 'local habitation' gives a distinct existence to those experiences of terrestrial phenomena, and they become a subject of mental manipulation on their own account. We have thus the extensive machinery of propositions, affirmations, abstractions, deductive reasonings; we have, together with names given to all the characteristic objects of nature, a part of speech devoted to the expression of belief, that is to say, the Verb. All the cognisable universe is laid out into departments. each having a body of affirmations, according to the conjunctions and sequences therein relied upon, or accepted as suffi-

THE REALIZING OF FUTURE GOOD. 529

cient for the guidance of such actions as involve them. Sciences, branches of knowledge, theoretical and practical, are the piled-up accumulation of these manifold cognitions of the natural laws; and we attach ourselves to them with no indifferent attitude or empty apprehension, but with a sense of inherent power, a consciousness of the mastery exercised by them over all that we prize in life.

5. As beings, then, that look before and after, the state of belief has in us an extensive footing, and an incessant control over the temper for happiness or misery. In anticipating a want, we forecast at the same time the natural sequence that is to be the medium of supplying it, and in that predicament wherein we are said to have confidence or trust in such a medium, we enjoy a positive satisfaction in the total absence of painful forebodings. So with a pleasure that has taken the form of vehement desire. The fruition is future, but the mind cannot easily assume a present indifference to the subject; we are either disquieted by seeing no prospect of attaining the wished-for good, or elated and comforted by the assurance of its being within reach. In all that regards our future happiness, therefore, and the future of all those interests that engage our sympathy,—belief, when the assurance of *good* in the distance, is the name for a serene, satisfying, and happy tone of mind. Through it, as has been said, we have already the realizing of what we long for. Ideal emotion is consummated in its happiest phase, by this condition being secured. If a man thinks merely of his present, or of the work that is under his hand, the sphere of belief is confined to the narrowest limits, having reference only to the instrumentality of actual operations. In proportion as we dwell in the prospective, we give to the influences that inspire confidence a very large prerogative in relation to our enjoyment.

6. In discussing the emotion of Terror, it was impossible not to be struck with the contrariety, or inverse relationship, between that emotion and the subject of the present chapter; so much so that it was necessary to take both facts together for the elucidation of the one. Speaking *logically*, or with

2 L

530 BELIEF.

regard to the form of the subject-matter, the opposite of belief is disbelief; but as a mental fact these two states are identical. Coming to a place where two roads meet, I believe that the one will conduct me to my home, and disbelieve the same affirmation respecting the other. In either view, my mind is in the condition of certainty, conviction, or faith, and I derive both the means of reaching my dwelling, and the cheering tone that a conviction gives to a person looking forward to a wished-for end. [The real opposite of belief as a state of mind is not disbelief, but doubt, uncertainty; and the close alliance between this and the emotion of fear is stamped on every language. Not that doubt and fear are identical facts, but that the situation called uncertainty, ignorance, hesitation, vacillation, is at all times prone to excite the perturbation of fear. ] Even when stopping short of this effect, owing to the great natural vigour of the mind in retaining its composure, this state is one of discomfort in most cases, and sometimes of the most aggravated human wretchedness. The constituents of it may be to a great extent discriminated by analysis, and we may be able to account for the peculiarity on some of the broad principles already recognised; still, there is in the phenomenon an exceedingly patent and well-marked physiognomy.

In this predicament of Doubt, there is necessarily involved the baulking of some end sought after with more or less earnestness. An uncertainty as to the means is, to say the least of it, tantamount to failing in the end. We may go even farther, and maintain that the failure is accompanied with an aggravation that does not attach to downright impossibility of attainment. When we are assured that some object is altogether out of our reach, we sit down and endeavour to become reconciled to the privation; but when the only obstacle is uncertainty as to the choice of means, we are kept on the tenter-hooks of alternate expedients, encouraged and baffled by turns. Distracted by opposing considerations, keeping up an aim, and yet not making any progress towards it, we suffer all the acute misery so well known to accompany

CONDITION OF DOUBT. 531

such situations of contradicting impulses. The wretchedness can be subdued only by either abandoning the pursuit, or coming to a decision in favour of some one road. Irrespective, therefore, of the additional pains of the state of terror so frequently succeeding to great uncertainty, there is a characteristic form of suffering begotten by the condition of doubt; of which the parallels are the cases, wherever occurring, of being obliged to act while equally poised between opposing solicitations. When fear is excited, the misery is deepened by a new element, and decision still more effectually paralysed. It is hardly necessary to cite particular instances of one of the very commonest of human experiences. Men may be found that can boast of never knowing fear; but who has ever passed through a busy life without knowing what it is to doubt? With all the inequality of characters in respect of constitutional self-confidence and the opportunities of obtaining knowledge, there lives not a human being adequate to the instantaneous solution of every enigma that he encounters in the course of life; and no one can be exempt from moments of painful uncertainty such as now described.

The temper of belief, confidence, or assurance in coming good is, in the first place, the total exclusion of all this misery; in so far the influence is simply preventive or remedial. Assuming the mind to be cheerful and serene, an emergency of doubt would plunge it into acute suffering proportioned to the importance of the crisis. All this is saved, if clear conviction and unhesitating decision as to the course to be pursued are possessed by the mind. The believing and decided temper is ever and anon arresting us on the brink of some abyss of distraction and terror, and thereby conserving in their purity our times of enjoyment, and interfering to save us from new depths of despondency. In this view alone, we derive, from our various sources of confidence as to means, the ends being still supposed desirable, a large addition to the happiness of existence; which would of itself account for the greater buoyancy and serenity of mind belonging to such as are seldom afflicted with uncertainty and doubt. Even

532  BELIEF.

if no positive pleasure were imparted through the possession of certainty and assurance in all occasions of emergency, we should still pronounce the condition of belief to be a source of pleasurable elation; but, besides withdrawing the incubus of the opposite condition, we must give it some credit for stimulating the sentiment of power, which is also one of our cheering influences. As there is a certain humiliation in being placed at bay through ignorance and hesitation, so there is apt to arise a flush of elation at the consciousness of being equal to whatever end we have in view. Beyond these two ingredients, I do not know any other marked way wherein the state of faith operates to sustain and elevate the pleasureable tone of the mental consciousness. Quite enough is herein contained to render the condition a great moral power in the human mind, and to account for all those wonderful effects so often attributed to it in the many forms of its manifestation.

7. I have hitherto confined the illustration to the case of coming good as an object of confidence. Let us now advert to the opposite state of things, the case of coming evil, more or less firmly relied on. The line of observations is here very much the same, allowing for the points of difference. When a future evil is believed as certain, we display as much energy in the corresponding course of action as if it were actually present; and we realize all the misery of the actual, in so far as we are capable of conceiving it. The mere idea of pain is apt to be painful, as when I see another person in distress; the more thoroughly we are possessed with that idea, the more are we afflicted or depressed by it. But the affliction and the depression are much deeper, when the evil is one approaching ourselves, and believed to be certain to overtake us. In so far as this conviction is complete, we have already the evil upon us; we act and feel as if it were really come. The greater the belief now, the greater the misery; doubt is less harrowing than conviction. Any loophole of escape, anything that would invalidate the evidence of the approaching pain, is as welcome as, in the opposite case, an addition

BELIEF CAUSING JOY OR DEPRESSION. 533

to the evidence would be. The comfortable condition of belief, and the suffering of doubt, suppose good in the distance; substitute evil and all is changed. The man mortally wounded in the prime of life, is not at the maximum of his misery so long as the fatal issue is in anywise doubtful. In one sense, doubt is painful even in the matter of future evil, namely, when it paralyses action. There is sometimes a comfort, as commonly remarked, in knowing the worst; the comfort lying in this, that we then address ourselves to the task of meeting it by active operations, or by a resigned spirit. But, as a general fact, doubt is a less evil than conviction, when the subject-matter is ill-fortune; and a weaker conviction is preferable to a stronger.

8. The *idea* of Pleasure, in most shapes, diffuses in the mind that state denominated Joy, which is recognised by every one as characteristic, and distinct from the reality of a sensuous gratification. The idea of good approaching, with confidence in its ultimate realization, is the most powerful stimulus of this condition. A wedding, the birth of an heir, the obtaining of an office, are styled joyful events from their reference to pleasures in prospect. Hence, in familiar language, the conjunction of Joy with Faith and Hope. The state of Joy is, in itself, one of our happy phases of mind, and is, besides, when produced, an exhilarating atmosphere for other pleasures, and an aid to the maintenance of the conviction of coming good against unfavourable appearances; ministering in turn to the cause of its own existence. The condition is one habitual to some constitutions, through organic and other agencies; and is then identical with the sanguine temper.

The idea of a Pain, on the other hand, produces the condition termed Depression, which, and not sorrow, is the true opposite of joy. The more strongly the idea takes hold of the mind, the greater is the influence. But here also, the effect is most decided when it is the idea of pain believed as coming to ourselves. In such circumstances, the mind is apt to be filled with gloom; and is not unlikely to pass one stage farther into the condition of terror. It is possible to stop

534 BELIEF.

short of this final stage; but even courage does not necessarily imply the absence of depression. The strength of the conviction is measured by its power of casting down the mind from the joyful, to the depressed, tone. A less strong belief would be less dispiriting.

When it is said 'the devils believe and tremble,' the subject-matter of the belief is some evil fate, which it would be better to doubt. The belief in our mortality is the reverse of comforting. Ill news operate a shock of depression, if not of alarm; and if the assurance amounts to certainty, so much the worse.

The mind depressed finds it hard to believe in coming good, and easy to be convinced of coming evil. Such is the action and reaction of the two states, of dread and depression, as above remarked of the connexion between the hopeful, or sanguine, and the joyful.

9. I must advert to the SOURCES of this efficacious attribute of our active nature. Looking at the cases introduced at the commencement of this chapter, in which a certain natural conjunction was relied upon in the employment of an instrumentality suitable to certain wants, we should say that the proper, and indeed the only possible foundation of such a belief, is experience of the various conjunctions so trusted to. Unless it could be shown, that there are some instincts of the nature of antecedent revelations of what we are to meet with when we come into the world, there seems no way of rising to the platform of knowledge and belief, except the actual trial; at least until we become the subjects of instruction and guidance by those that have gone before us, in which case it is merely the substitution of one experience for another. It is, however, a matter of fact that other influences are at work in determining our convictions, and it is our business to survey these also. There are instinctive tendencies partly co-operating, and partly conflicting with the principal monitor; and we have had to recognise, in discussing the emotions, a power belonging to every one of them to mould our received opinions in opposition to the interpreta-

## SOURCES OF BELIEF. 535

tions of experience. Delusion, fallacy, and mental perversion could not have obtained so great a sway over mankind, but for the intervention of agencies operating without any regard to what we find in the world as the result of actual experiment and observation.

10. We may divide the sources of belief into three different classes as follows :—First, the *Intuitive* or Instinctive; second, *Experience,* with the reasonings and inferences supplemental thereto; third, the Influence of the *Feelings.* It is not usual to find cases where these different methods act pure and apart; the greater number of the ordinary convictions of men involve a mixture of the different sorts; and hence a strictly methodical exposition of the three classes is scarcely practicable. Experience is very generally modified by instinctive tendencies, while no mere instinct can constitute a belief in the entire absence of the other. In these circumstances, I will first indicate briefly the manner of deriving convictions from actual contact with the world, and then proceed to a minute consideration of the three sources in the order now given. An animal sees the water that it drinks, and thereby couples in its mind the property of quenching thirst with the visible aspect. After this association has acquired a certain degree of tenacity, the sight of water at a distance suggests the other fact, so that, from the prospect, the animal realizes to some degree the satisfying of that craving. Then it is that water seen by thirsty animals inspires the movements preparatory to actual drinking; the voluntary organs of locomotion are urged by the same energetic spur on the mere distant sight, as the organs of lapping and swallowing under the feeling of relief already commenced. This is the state of mature conviction as to the union of the two natural properties of water. I cannot doubt that an animal attains this crowning belief by a gradual process, and that there are stages, when it is proper to say that a less strong assurance is possessed. The criteria of initial inferiority are always these two circumstances, at bottom substantially one, namely, that the pursuit of the means is less energetically

536    BELIEF.

stimulated than the realizing of the end actually in the grasp; and secondly, that the attainment of the means does not give that strong mental satisfaction that is felt at a higher stage of assurance. When we have reached the highest certainty as to the characteristic appearance of water or food, our preliminary operation, for getting the objects themselves, is hardly to be distinguished from the activity manifested in following up the first tasting ; and, moreover, the mental agony is to a great degree done away with by the sight and anticipation. With a glass of water actually in hand, I may be almost said to have terminated the state of suffering due to thirst. All that *depression of mind* caused by the privation has vanished, through the certainty that relief is now come. This is a sure and striking characteristic of the state of belief, marking it out as a thing of degree, and indicating the highest point in the scale. The young animal, little experienced in the great natural conjunction now cited, follows up the lead of the few observations already impressed on the mind, but does not display the same energy of voluntary pursuit on the mere appearance, or feel the same sense of relief in anticipation, as at a later stage. Repetition, and especially unbroken uniformity, are the obvious causes that bring this conviction to maturity. The adhesive influence of Contiguity is in this respect a moral power, giving rise to a certain proneness to pass from the one thing to the other. Still, it would be a great mistake to lay it down as a rule, that indissoluble association of two ideas constitutes by itself an assurance of their connexion, such as to render the one a sure indication of the other. The second circumstance just mentioned, namely, unbroken uniformity, is a most vital ground of our security in a sequence of events. A single breach of expectation will unhinge all that a long series of repetitions has established. Moreover, as regards indissoluble association, there may exist along with this the temper of disbelief. There is an indissoluble association in most minds educated in the New Testament between 'Diana of the Ephesians' and the epithet 'great,' but without attaching any credit to the proposition

## INTUITIVE TENDENCIES. 537

thus affirmed. In fact, to appreciate exactly the power of repetition and association in this matter, we must advert to certain instinctive tendencies operating in alliance with our experience, and I will therefore proceed to discuss that class of influences.

11. I. The foremost rank, among our Intuitive tendencies involved in belief, is to be assigned to *the natural trust that we have in the continuance of the present state of things*, or the disposition to go on acting as we have once begun. This is a sort of Law of Perseverance in the human mind, like the first law of Motion in Mechanics. Our first experiences are to us decisive, and we go on under them to all lengths, being arrested only by some failure or contradiction. Having in our constitution primordial fountains of activity, in the spontaneous and voluntary impulses, we follow the first clue that experience gives us, and accept the indication with the whole force of these natural promptings. In other words, the more strongly we are urged into action by those primitive energies, the more strongly do we cling to that particular line of proceedings that an experience as yet uncontradicted has chalked out. The hungry beast having fallen on a road to some place yielding food, on the faith of a single experiment, goes with the whole impetus of its voluntary nature on that particular tract. Being under the strongest impulses to act somehow, an animal accepts any lead that is presented, and, if successful, abides by that lead with unshaken confidence. It is the very essence of our volition to sustain us under pleasure tasted, or pain mitigated, and this applies to our adherence to means as well as to the fruition of ends ; so that there is contained, in the fundamental properties of the will, a source of the confident temper wherewith we follow up a single successful trial without waiting for repeated confirmations. This is that instinct of credulity so commonly attributed to the infant mind. We are ready to act and follow out every opening, accepting as a sure ground of confidence any one that answers the end on the first experiment. Thus the tendency to act carries with it the state of confidence, if only the smallest

538 BELIEF.

encouragement is present, and there be a total absence of ill-success. It is not the single instance, or the repetition of two or three, that makes up the strong tone of confidence ; it is the mind's own active determination, finding some definite vent in the gratification of its ends, and abiding by the disco-very with the whole energy of the character, until the occur-rence of some check, failure, or contradiction.

All the considerations involved in the primitive constitution of the will, and all the observations of the first start of the intellectual and voluntary powers, are in favour of this view of intense primitive credulity. At the commencing stage, the measure of credulity is the measure of the spontaneous and voluntary energies. The creature that wills strongly believes strongly at the origin of its career. The general ten-dencies of mankind, as exhibited in their mature convictions, show the continued operation of the same force. To be satis-fied that this is so, we have only to look at such facts as these : —Every man, until convinced of the contrary, believes in the permanence of the state of things that he is born into. Not only do we expect that what is will remain, but we con-clude that other places and times must resemble our own. It is constantly noted as a peculiarity of ignorant tribes, to refuse credence to anything different from what they have been accustomed to. The earliest experiences are generalized so as to override the whole unexperienced world, and present a for-midable obstacle to the admission of new facts at a later period. The mind shows an obstinacy in maintaining that the absent must resemble the present, and that other minds are of the same mould with itself. Those first impressions, under which action took place in all the vigour of pristine freshness, have acquired a hold and a confidence that it is difficult to compete with afterwards ; and although contrary appearances happening early would prevent their consolidation into beliefs, they become at last too strong to be unseated by any amount of contradiction. Although repetition cannot but strengthen the confidence in a particular course, it is not true that five repetitions give exactly five times the assurance of one. A

WE BELIEVE FIRST AND PROVE AFTERWARDS. 539

single trial, that nothing has ever happened to impugn, is able of itself to leave a conviction sufficient to induce reliance under ordinary circumstances. It is the active prompting of the mind itself that instigates, and in fact constitutes, the believing temper; unbelief is an after-product, and not the primitive tendency. Indeed, we may say that the inborn energy of the brain gives faith, and experience scepticism. After a number of trials, some of our first impressions are shaken, while those that sustain the ordeal of experiment are all the more confirmed by contrast with the others which have given way. As we become familiar with the breaking down process, we cling the more to whatever impressions have stood every trial.

12. The force of belief then is not one rising from zero to a full development by slow degrees according to the length of experience. We must treat it rather as a strong primitive manifestation, derived from the natural activity of the system, and taking its direction and rectification from experience. 'The anticipation of nature,' so strenuously repudiated by Bacon, is the offspring of this characteristic of the mental system. In the haste to act, while the indications imbibed from contact with the world are still scanty, we are sure to extend the application of actual trials a great deal too far, producing such results as have just been named. With the active tendency at its maximum, and the exercise of intelligence and acquired knowledge at the minimum, there can issue nothing but a quantity of rash enterprises. That these are believed in, we know from the very fact that they are undertaken. In an opposite condition of things, where intellect and knowledge have made very high progress, and constitutional activity is feeble,—a sceptical, hesitating, incredulous temper of mind is the usual characteristic. The respectable name 'generalization,' implying the best products of enlightened scientific research, has also a different meaning, expressing one of the most erroneous impulses and crudest determinations of untutored human nature. To extend some familiar and narrow experience, so as to comprehend cases

540                                    BELIEF.

the most distant, is a piece of mere reckless instinct, demanding the severest discipline for its correction. I have mentioned the case of our supposing all other minds constituted like our own. The veriest infant has got this length in the career of fallacy. As soon as we are able to recognise personalities distinct from ourselves, we presume an identity between them and us; and, by an inverse operation, we are driven out of this over-vaulting position after the severe findings of contrary facts. Sound belief, instead of being a pacific and gentle growth, is, in reality, the battering of a series of strongholds, the conquering of a country in hostile occupation. This is a fact common both to the individual and to the race. Observation is unanimous on the point. The only thing for mental philosophy to do on such a subject, is to represent, as simply and clearly as possible, those original properties of our constitution that are chargeable with such wide-spread phenomena. It will probably be long ere the last of the delusions attributable to this method, of believing first, and proving . afterwards, can be eradicated from humanity. For, although all those primitive impressions that find a speedy contradiction in realities from which we cannot escape, cease to exercise their sway after a time, there are other cases less open to correction, and remaining to the last as portions of our creed.

13. The common notions with reference to Causation are, in the judgment of many persons, with whom I concur, tainted with the primitive corruption of this part of our nature. The method of rational experience would lead us by degrees to recognise with reference to every event, or new appearance, some other assemblage of events or appearances that preceded it, as an established rule; while, in some cases, the same event has a plurality of causes. We should find that this arrangement prevails in a very great number of instances, while there would be a considerable class wherein no prior invariable antecedent was discernible. A just experience would simply confine itself to mentioning the cases of either sort; and if it so happened that, while many appear-

## EXPERIENCE. 541

ances that at first sight could not be connected with any antecedent, came afterwards to show such a connexion, on the other hand, those so connected from the first, continued to be so, there would arise a fair presumption that the existence of antecedents to phenomena or events was the rule, and that the exceptions were likely to disappear as our knowledge was extended. I can conceive no other course to be taken on this matter by the human mind, gathering its conviction solely by the course of experience; but would this lead to the astounding assumption, made even previous to the detailed survey of the world, that everything that exists, not only has, but *must* have a beginning? No amount of experience can either lead to, or justify, this affirmation; and the origin of it is therefore some intuition or instinct. The notion, already commented upon, that *mind* must needs be the primitive cause of natural changes, could not arise from any large experience. The agency of men and animals, beings endowed with mind, is, of course, a fact to be admitted, but there are other natural agencies,—wind, water, heat, gravity, &c.—each good in its own sphere, without any accompaniment of mental facts. Experience unbiassed by foreign impulses would simply put these down as causes side by side with animal power, without resolving them into that agency. But the generalizing impetus of the untutored mind makes use of the near and familiar to explain everything else; and the type of activity closest at hand, is the activity of the animal's own volition. This is to us the most conceivable of all forms of causation, and we presume that it must prevail everywhere, and over all kinds of effects. There is no better authority for the assumption than for the belief that other minds are in all respects like our own, or that water, which is liquid to the dweller in the tropics, is liquid everywhere else.

14. II. So much as regards the intuitive as a source of belief. The second source has been also dwelt upon by way of a contrasting illustration to the first. I must now remark farther, on the subject of the growth of conviction from *Experience*, that the instinctive impulse of Perseverance above explained,

542                BELIEF.

seems requisite to give the *active* element, without which there
is no effectual belief. I can imagine the mind receiving an
impression of co-existence or sequence, such as the coincidence of relish with an apple, or other object of food ; and
this impression repeated until, on the principle of association,
the one shall without fail at any time suggest the other ; and
yet nothing done in consequence, no practical effect given to
the concidence. I do not know any purely intellectual property that would give to an associated couple the character
of an article of belief; but there is that in the volitional
promptings which seizes hold of any indication leading to an
end, and abides by such instrumentality if it is found to
answer. Nay more, there is the tendency to go beyond the
actual experience, and not to desist until the occurrence of a
positive failure or check. So that the mere repetition of an
intellectual impress would not amount to a conviction without this active element, which, although the source of many
errors, is indispensable to the mental conditions of belief. The
legitimate course is to let experience be the corrector of all
the primitive impulses ; to take warning by every failure,
and to recognise no other canon of validity. This does not
exclude the operations termed induction, deduction, analogy,
and probable inference; because these are to be pursued
exactly to the length that experience will justify, and no
farther. We find, after may trials, that there is such a
uniformity in nature as enables us to presume that an event
happening to-day will happen also to-morrow, if we can only
be sure that all the circumstances are exactly the same. I
cut down a tree, and put a portion of it into water, observing
that it floats ; I then infer that another portion would float,
and that the wood of any other tree of the same species
would do so likewise. It is a part of the intuitive tendencies
of the mind to generalize in this way ; but these tendencies,
being as often wrong as right, have no validity in themselves ;
and the real authority is experience. The long series of trials
made since the beginning of observation has shown how far
such inferences can safely be carried ; and we are now in

## CRITERIA OF SOUND BELIEF. 543

possession of a body of rules, in harmony with the actual course of nature, for guiding us in carrying on these operations.*

* It is the province of works different from mine to deal with the entire subject of scientific method and proof. The explanation of the mental state of belief must include alike the cases of assurance well-founded, and assurance ill-founded ; the mere mental fact being precisely the same in all. The state of confidence in the astronomer's mind, as to the occurrence of a calculated eclipse, is not different from the wildest anticipation of a deluded day-dreamer or fanatic. The real distinction between the two is important in the highest degree, but the full account of it belongs more to the theory of evidence, than to the theory of belief. I indicate, in what follows in the text, the sources of misplaced confidence, having indeed already done so to a great extent in the exposition of the emotions in detail, and in the foregoing account of the intuitive tendencies. Still it is not my object to argue fully the position that experience is the ultimate and only valid authority in matters of belief ; the controversies therewith connected are too extensive and weighty to be handled in a corner of a single chapter of a work, whose business it is rather to explain the mental processes, than to adjudicate upon their merits, as regards the practice of life. There are those who contend for an *à priori* origin of scientific first principles, although, to say the least of it, such principles are sufficiently accredited by experience to justify us in relying on them ; I mean such first principles as the axioms of Mathematics. There is also a doctrine current that the law of Causation has an authority derived from intuition, on which the same remark may be made as to the superfluity of any addition to the actual verification. Another class of beliefs relates to matters altogether beyond experience, and therefore purely and exclusively subjective ; such is the metaphysical doctrine of the Infinite—a doctrine believed in even while the substance of it is pronounced to be unthinkable by the human intelligence. With regard to these various convictions, *à priori*, as they are called, or grounded solely in the internal impulses of the human mind, a remark common to them all may be here suggested. It must be conceded that some intuitive beliefs are unsound, seeing that we are obliged to reject a greater or less number, because of the contradiction that experience gives them. But if any are rejected as unsound, why may not all be, and what criterion, apart from experience, can be set up for discriminating those that we are to retain? Man undoubtedly has boundless longings ; and the metaphysical doctrine of the Infinite corresponds in a manner to these. But in actual life, we find very few of our desires fully gratified, not even those most honourable to the human mind, such as curiosity, the passion for self-improvement, and the desire for doing good. How then are we to ascertain which of the longings carries with it its own necessary fulfilment? Moreover, the intuitive tendencies are exceedingly various in men ; and all cannot be equally true. The theory of the instinctive vouching of natural laws and properties seems to me to lie under a load of insuperable difficulties ; although I am unable to give

## 544 BELIEF.

15. III. The influence of Feeling as a source of belief, has been repeatedly touched upon in the previous exposition. In the commencing chapter of this volume, I spoke of the matter generally, and, under each separate emotion, traced specific consequences arising from that influence. Any strong feeling possessing the mind, gives such a determination to the thoughts and the active impulses as to pervert the convictions, and dispose us to trust or distrust at that moment things that we should not trust or distrust at another time. In the elation of a successful enterprise just achieved, we are apt to have a degree of confidence in our own powers that we do not feel in ordinary times, and very much in contrast to what we feel under some miscarriage or failure. The fact as to a man's powers is constant, allowing for the known fluctuations of health and circumstances, not so is his estimate of them. I have sought the explanation of this variability of our convictions, on matters where the reality is unchanged, in the power of the feelings to control the intellectual trains, or to determine what things the mind shall entertain at the time. It happens, in the present class of convictions, that the evidence for them is only probable, there being appearances both for and against the conclusions supposed. In things of experimental, inductive, or deductive certainty—the rise of to-morrow's sun, the flow of the tides, the mortality of living beings—there is no room for the influence of fluctuating states of feeling. Under the highest elation, and the deepest gloom, we count alike on these events. But, in the many cases where exact knowledge of the future cannot be had, we are at the mercy, not merely of conflicting appearances, but of our own changing moods. The prospective tranquillity of Europe, the coming harvest, the issue of a great trading speculation, the behaviour of some

---

an adequate expansion to the subject in this place. Everybody admits that our only practical safety in the operations of life, lies in our close adherence to what we find when we make the experiment; and surely this circumstance ought to give experience an exclusive place in our estimation as the canon of credibility.—See Mill's *Logic*, Book III., and more especially Chap. XXI.

### INFLUENCE OF FEELING ON BELIEF. 545

individual or body in matters affecting us, the recovery of a patient from a critical illness—being unascertainable by any process with certainty, are termed cases of probable evidence, and we decide them differently at different times according to the aspect that turns up. The Stock Exchange measures the daily variation of the public estimate of the probable future of every corporate interest. Now, without any reference to men's feelings, the anticipation of what is likely to happen in this class of events, changes with the new appearances. A political difficulty has passed away, the funds rise in consequence. A distressing symptom has ceased in a patient; the hopes thereupon predominate. But when the speculator in the Stock Exchange, on a day when no new occurrence has influenced the money market, takes of his own accord a more sanguine view of foreign securities than he did yesterday, the cause is some variation in his own temper of mind, or manner of viewing the face of affairs. A change from high spirits to low, or the contrary, a sudden inspiration of esteem or dislike to some Minister or person in power, an accidental stroke of fear having no reference to the subject in hand, and many other causes, are able to modify the estimate that a person shall form of the very same outward facts. I conceive that this happens entirely from the circumstance, that these various emotions, while they do not alter the facts themselves, alter the mode of looking at them ; determining the mind to dwell upon one class of appearances, and to overlook another class as completely as if those did not exist. It is to no purpose that some significant symptom shows itself in the aspect of the future, if there be an agency capable of making us ignore the very existence of it ; which is, I apprehend, the real point where a strong feeling does its work. It is needless to repeat the instances of love blinding us to the defects, or hatred blinding us to the merits of an object ; to the marvellous delusions of self-interest, vanity, and pride ; to the perversions of the strong æsthetic sentiments, or to the effects of passion in every form. The careful examination of these phenomena leads to no other conclusion than this, that, when

2 M

546                    BELIEF.

a feeling strongly occupies the mind, the objects in harmony with it are maintained in the view, and all others repelled and ignored. There is a fight between an emotional excitement and the natural course of the intellectual associations ; facts, considerations, and appearances that would arise by virtue of these associations are kept back, and a decision come to in their absence. It is not that the mind declares that to be a fact, of which the contradiction is actually before it ; it is that, under a one-sided fury, the contradiction that would otherwise come forward, remains in oblivion. Emotion tampers with the intellectual trains, as a culprit would fain do with the witnesses in his case, keeping out of the way all that are adverse to the interest of the moment.

16. These remarks apply to the feelings generally, but we cannot part from this branch of the subject without noticing again the antithesis between belief and the condition of Fear. I have said that the opposite of confidence is Doubt, which is akin to fear, in the sense of being a principal cause of perturbation. Confidence and doubt cannot co-exist any more than hot and cold, fire and water, or acid and alkali. As we establish the one we necessarily quench the other. The confident tone of mind with reference to some event, may be utterly destroyed by a fright from a quite foreign cause, and a restoration of confidence may take place through a mere physical tonic applied to the disturbed nerves. In the case of future good we cannot both fear and believe ; it is only when the subject is coming evil that belief, by first operating depression, may pass on to apprehension, in other words—fear. It is difficult to have a strong assurance of any merely probable good fortune under the condition of alarm, and on the other hand, in a tone of high confidence, we do not give way even to probable evil. There is thus a close alliance between courage, the antithesis of fear, and confidence. In a courageous mood, we are apt to be affected in both the ways characteristic of belief ; that is to say, we go forward into action for a distant fruition as if every step realized the object itself ; and we feel an elation in the prospect as if the reality

STATES OF DEPRESSION. 547

were at hand. The general, believing that a certain force would infallibly enable him to defeat the enemy, makes his attack when he has got the force; and when he is sure of that force reaching him, he feels already the excitement of victory; at least such would be the tests of a perfect confidence.

17. These observations apply not simply to the passion of fear and its opposite, but to the emotions generally, so far as they may be classified under the contrasting heads of elators and depressors of the mental tone. Whatever cause raises the animal spirits, raises at the same time the confident side of the uncertain future. It is the nature of some constitutions to maintain the high buoyant tone as a prevailing quality through all vicissitudes of events. Physical causes may co-operate or may be in antagonism with this happy disposition; and there are also what is termed 'moral' causes, meaning the mental emotions. Success and failure in enterprises may be mentioned as familiar examples of the last-named class. With regard to matters of experimental or demonstrative certainty, these fluctuations of mental tone are at the lowest point of influence; they neither confirm, nor impair our confidence in the refreshing power of food and sleep, or in an arithmetical computation. As we pass from the highest order of certainty, through the stages of probability, down to the depths of total uncertainty, we come more and more under the domination of the physical and moral causes that maintain or destroy the cheerful, buoyant, and happy frame of mind. The man of much knowledge and experience, inured to reflection and the handling of evidence, with habits of submission to proof, carries his tone of rational conviction a considerable way into the region of probability, reclaiming a larger track from the domain where the feeling of the moment gives the cue; but in this, as in other things, there is only an approximation to the absolutely perfect. The soldier in a campaign, cherishing and enjoying life, is unmoved by the probability of being soon cut off. If he still continues to act in every respect as if destined to a good old age, in spite of the perils of the field, his conviction is purely

548                    BELIEF.

a quality of his temperament, and will be much less strong at those moments when hunger and fatigue have depressed his frame, or when the sight of dying and dead men has made him tremble with awe. I formerly quoted a happy expression of Arthur Helps, 'where you know nothing, place terrors;' but, given the sanguine, buoyant, and courageous temperament—given youth, spirits, and intoxication—given a career of prosperity and success—and where you know nothing, you will place high hopes. Under this hypothesis of no positive evidence, elevation of tone and belief of good to come, are the same fact. Where the acquired trust in evidence does not find its way in any degree, belief is no other than happy emotion. Ply the resources that sustain the bright class of feelings, and you sustain a man's trust in the favourable view of the unknown; let the system sink down to nervous and mental depression, and hope passes to despondency. The condition of belief thus has two great opposite poles, Evidence and Feeling. The nature of the subject, and the character of the individual mind, determine which is to predominate; but in this life of ours, neither is the exclusive master.

18. There are various other points of the present subject that must be despatched with a brief notice, although some of them are worthy of a more extended illustration. Belief in Testimony contains all the elements of intuition, experience, and emotion, in varying degrees. We are disposed to accept as true in the first instance whatever we are told to act upon, until we incur the shock of an opposing experience. After many trials, we ascertain the persons whose testimony exposes us to no collision with fact; the intuitive tendency to believe is in their case consolidated by repetition into a strong assurance. So far the case of testimony, therefore, is in no respect different from any other mode of deriving conviction from the actual facts of the world. But there is in testimony an additional source of influence, arising from the peculiar force exerted by one man upon another. All those circum - stances that lend impressiveness to a speaker, and render the orator an artist, dispose the hearers to accept his statements

with more than the deference due to the mere testimony of a single person. Emotion here exercises an interference of its own kind. In like manner, the loud asseveration of a multitude operates beyond its intrinsic worth, by virtue of an emotional ascendancy.

19. There can be now little difficulty in comprehending the agency of Desire in producing conviction. When anything strongly excites our feelings, making us long for the full possession of it, the mind is so much under the sway of the emotion as to suffer the blinding effect peculiar to such a situation. We then refuse to entertain the obstacles in the way of our desire, and eagerly embrace every view and appearance favourable to our wishes. Such is the tendency of any intense longing, and such is the result in a mind not strongly disciplined to hunt out all sides of a question, in spite of the feelings. Desire may, however, be accompanied with even unreasonable doubt as to success; the tone and temper of the individual being unduly depressed, as at other times too much elated.

20. Hope is the well-known name for belief in some contingent future bringing good. Whatever object intensely pleases us, is thought of by us; and if the mere idea is not all-satisfying, the reality is desired. There may be as yet nothing of the nature of a conviction. When an event happens to put this object within reach, so that we have only to put forth some effort of our own to attain it, or to wait a certain time, at the lapse of which we shall possess it, the state of belief is generated. We then make the effort with the same ardour as we perform any voluntary act under immediate realization of the end, and we already enjoy in foretaste the full fruition. The hard-worked official, with no prospect of liberation, has a certain gloomy satisfaction in merely conceiving a holiday. He may allow himself to fall into the state of desire with imaginary gratification, and rehearse in his mind all the delights that he would follow out if he had the reality. But let him be told by authority, that on the execution of a certain task he shall gain a release, he, believing

550                     BELIEF.

this declaration, proceeds to the work with the alacrity of a
person gaining at every moment the very sensations of the
future. Or let him be told simply that on a certain day he
shall be set free, and instantly the ideal picture brightens, and
he feels already as if he began to realize what he has just been
imagining. If, instead of a promise on good authority, he
has merely a surmise with some probability, he makes very
little progress towards the elated tone of full realization. The
strong desire and the sanguine temper may make up to him
for the want of unexceptionable evidence ; but in either way,
the transition from a mere imagined delight to the elation
corresponding to a reality in hand, is the measure of the
power of belief.

The opposite condition is usually named fear ; the proper
title is Despondency, of which the highest degree is Despair.
The belief in approaching evil is an unhinging and depressing
condition of mind, as the belief in approaching good causes a
joyous elation. Likewise, as the joyful mood, already in
existence, disposes to that confidence of good on the way
constituting Hope, so a mind depressed from any cause is disposed to the belief in coming evil. The exhaustion of long
watching by a sick bed is unfavourable to a hopeful view of
the patient ; whence the advent of the physician is a moral
support to an afflicted household. The perturbation of fear is
related to despondency, only as being a depressing agency.
The one state passes into the other through this community
of character.

21. Faith, in the religious sense, is mainly supplied from
the fountains of human feeling, and is, in fact, cherished as
itself a mode of consoling, cheering, and elating emotion.
Direct experience can have but little to do with the subject-
matter of spiritual essences. Testimony, and the accordance
of fellow-beings, may go far to stir up the state of confidence
in a present, presiding, and benignant Deity, and in a state of
future blessedness. Nevertheless, the culture of strong feelings
and affections must ever be the main instrumentality of gaining
the comfort of such assurances. Religious truth cannot, there-

## RELIGIOUS FAITH.

551

fore, be imparted, as has sometimes been supposed, by an intellectual medium of verbal exposition and theological demonstration. Being an affair of the feelings, a method must be sought adapted to heighten the intensity of these.

As in other things, the belief here also may refer to the side of evil, and consist in realizing strongly the threatenings of future misery. The terms ' faith ' and ' believer,' are commonly used to express the comforting aspect of religion, but the fact of belief is as much exemplified in the opposite side. The strongest conviction there is what casts on the mind the deepest gloom.

22. It remains to consider the line of demarcation between belief and mere conceptions involving no belief—there being instances where the one seems to shade into the other. It seems to me impossible to draw this line without referring to action, as the only test, and the essential import of the state of conviction. Even in cases the farthest removed in appearance from any actions of ours, there is no other criterion. We believe a great many truths respecting the world, in the shape of general propositions, scientific statements, affirmations on testimony, &c., which are so much beyond our own little sphere that we can rarely have occasion to involve them in our own procedure, or to feel any hopeful elation on their account. We likewise give credit to innumerable events of past history, although the greater number of them have never any consequences as regards ourselves. Yet, notwithstanding such remoteness of interest, the criterion assigned in this chapter must hold; otherwise there is no real conviction in any one instance.

Every one recognises the old distinction of potentiality and actuality (*posse* and *esse*) as a true account of two states of mind that we practically assume. Besides actually doing a thing, we know what it is to be in an attitude or disposition of preparedness to act, before the emergency has arisen, or while the emergency is still at a distance and uncertain. When I say, if ever I go to America I will visit Niagara, I have put myself into an ideal attitude, perhaps never to be realized,

552                    BELIEF.

but still existing as a fact or phenomenon of my mind. So it is with a proposition that I believe in, although without any actual prospect of founding action, or staking my welfare, upon it. When I believe in the circumference of the earth being twenty-five thousand miles, if I am not repeating an empty sound, or indulging an idle conception, I give it out that if any occasion shall arise for putting this fact in practice, I am ready to do so. If I were appointed to circumnavigate the globe, I should commit myself to this reckoning. If I were to walk due east, from one meridian of longitude to another, I should take all the consequences of the same computation. If there were any hesitation in my mind as to running those risks, my alleged belief would be proved hollow, no matter how often I may have heard the statement, or repeated it, with acquiescence. In truth, the genuineness of a conviction is notoriously open to question, until an opportunity for acting presents itself. Is not this alone sufficient to show the soundness of the criterion that I have insisted on throughout this discussion? Very often we deceive ourselves and others on the point—whether we are in full potentiality or preparedness in some matter of truth or falsehood. There is a very large amount of blind acquiescence, or tacit acceptance, of propositions, which never become the subject of any real or practical stake. These pseudo-convictions, beliefs falsely so called, confuse the line of demarcation now spoken of, and seemingly constitute cases where no element beyond a mere intellectual notion is certainly present. Such is the acceptance that the unthinking multitude give to the statements about things that they are accustomed to hear from the better-informed class. They do not dispute or disbelieve what passes current respecting the facts of science or the transactions of history ; much of it they do not understand ; yet as they would not of their own accord commit any serious interest to such statements, they have no belief in the proper sense of the word. Nearly the same may be said as to the state of belief in the religious creed that has come down by tradition from parent to child. Some are found believing in the full import of the

BELIEF IN MATTERS REMOTE FROM ACTION. 553

term; others, opposing no negative in any way, yet never perform any actions, or entertain either hopes or fears, as a consequence of their supposed acceptance of the religion of their fathers. To all intents and purposes, therefore, the belief of these persons is a nonentity.

23. Within the last few years, astronomers have been able to measure the distances of a number of the fixed stars. The distances so ascertained are believed in by all who are satisfied of the methods pursued for this end, yet it would not be easy to reduce this belief directly to the criterion of action, as in the case of the magnitude of the earth. We shall never make the actual journey to Sirius or any of the others, or stake any interest of ours upon the computations relative to those stars. Nevertheless, the belief may still be shown in the last resort to have the criterion that I have contended for; inasmuch as the same observations and calculations that we ground action upon on this earth are applied to the new case. It is an instance of belief, if I maintain that, supposing Sirius a sphere, his circumference is somewhat more than three times his diameter. I shall never have to proceed upon that affirmation respecting him, but as I am constantly proceeding upon the same affirmation regarding spheres and circles, it is right to say that my belief, in the case removed from any possible action of mine, is still measured by action. My conviction of the events of bygone centuries is nearly in the same predicament. I may show my belief in the history of the Roman empire by using those events as experience to found political maxims upon, which maxims I apply to the conduct of such present affairs as I may have any hand in. Here the criterion of action is unequivocal. But supposing I make no such application of these recorded events, I may still show my belief in them by acting upon precisely the same kind of evidence— namely, that of testimony preserved by written documents— with regard to recent events. I read the history of Napoleon's wars, and travel over Europe, expecting to encounter the fields and the monuments of all the great battles; so, when I consider that a like strength of testimony exists with reference to

554                    BELIEF.

the wars of the Roman republic, I may be fairly said to be in
the state of belief on the subject of those wars, although I do
not take any proceedings thereupon.

24. The last case to be noticed is the belief in our own
sensations, present or past.   It is common to say, that I
cannot have a sensation without believing that I have that
sensation, which belief seems to grow out of the consciousness,
and not to involve any action.   In point of fact, however, we
are constantly acting upon our sensations, as when we avoid
the painful and cherish the pleasurable.   The spectator relies
upon my actions as the surest evidence of my sensations.   If
I am thirsty, I may say that I believe myself to be thirsty,
because I act accordingly.   I cannot assure myself, or any
other person, that I am not under a dream, an imagination, or
a hallucination, in any other way than by a course of voluntary
exertion corresponding to the supposed sensation.   And when
I affirm that I was thirsty yesterday, it is supposed that I am
prepared to act out that supposition also ; as when I make
it the basis of an inference that I shall be thirsty on some
future day, and use means to provide for that emergency.
When no action can be indicated as directly or indirectly
following on the affirmation, the belief in it may be still held
as genuine, if I feel in the same way to it as I do towards
those sensations that I am ready to act upon.   I believe that
I yesterday ran up against a wall to keep out of the way of a
carriage.   I have no disposition to do anything in consequence
of that conviction ; yet I call it a conviction, and not a mere
notion, because I am affected by it in the same way as I am
by another recollection that I do act upon.   I feel that if
there were any likelihood of being jammed up in that spot
again, I should not go that way if I could help it, which is
quite enough to show that, in believing my memory, I have
still a reference to action, more or less remote.

# CONSCIOUSNESS.

1. I HAVE reserved for a closing dissertation the subject of Consciousness as a whole, being of opinion that the subtleties and complications involved in it demand, as a preparation, a survey of the detailed phenomena of the mind. I assumed at the outset a provisional definition, but it would have been inexpedient, at so early a stage, to enter into a discussion of various problems of deep importance that have been suspended upon that term. To clear up the most difficult of all general notions, without first providing an adequate array of particulars, I look upon as hopeless.

As a preface to the systematic exposition of the subject, let us first gather together the various acceptations of the word in current speech. A scientific definition is not to be controlled by unscientific usage; but at the same time we must, for the sake of being intelligible, keep as closely as we can to the meanings that have obtained currency. We want to make those meanings precise, so far as that is possible; where that is not possible, we may then have to adopt a new phraseology.

(1.) Consciousness is a term for the waking, living mind as distinguished from dreamless sleep, fainting, insensibility, stupor, anæsthesia, death. The total cessation of every mental energy is expressed by unconsciousness, among other phrases. In reviving or becoming awake to sensation, emotion, idea, or voluntary action, we are said to become again conscious. The term is thus identified with the whole range of functions included under mind.*

---

* 'The meaning of a word is sometimes best attained by means of the word opposed to it. *Unconsciousness*, that is, the want or absence of *consciousness*, denotes the suspension of all our faculties. Consciousness, then, is

556 CONSCIOUSNESS.

(2.) Our feelings of pain and pleasure are recognised more especially as modes of consciousness. If we are unconscious, there is a complete negative both of the one state and of the other. There are some operations truly mental, that may be performed while we are affirmed to be unconscious of them; but unconsciousness utterly excludes pain and pleasure. Pain is perhaps the most intense and decided manifestation of consciousness. The excitement of the brain is at the maximum under irritation, or suffering. According to the degree of either pain or pleasure, is the degree of feeling, or consciousness.

When we are strongly excited about a thing, without reference to pleasure or pain, we may be described as in a highly conscious condition. The mental function is, for the time being, exalted into unusual energy. I may be very languid, indifferent, or sleepy, over a task, or in presence of a spectacle; another person may be animated, excited, roused; I am declared to be scarcely conscious, half asleep, or the like; the other is more than ordinarily alive, awake, conscious.

The meanings now given—namely, pain, pleasure, and excitement generally—correspond to the mental department of Feeling.

(3.) Attending, observing, noticing, in opposition to passing by unheeded, is often characterized by the name consciousness. The clock strikes, and a person sitting near is not aware of it. I survey the objects in a room, but it afterwards appears that several things, whose picture must have fallen on my retina, have not been recognised by me. It is common to call these facts, being unconscious. They and their opposites, are, however, still better described by the other terms, inattentive and attentive, observant, noticing, and the like. With reference

---

the state in which we are when all or any of our faculties are in exercise. It is the condition or accompaniment of every mental operation.'—Professor Fleming's *Vocabulary of Philosophy*, Art. ' Consciousness.'

The concluding sentence quoted is not in harmony with those preceding. We cannot properly describe as the *condition* of a thing what is the thing itself, conceived and denominated in its highest generality.

MEANINGS OF THE TERM. 557

to the special senses, we might say that we did, or did not, hear, see, &c. ; or that we did not perceive the effect, or object, in question.

(4.) The taking note of difference or agreement among things. People often say they are not conscious of a distinction between two tints, two sounds, two sizes, two persons, &c. So we may be unconscious of agreement, or similarity, in two things that are like. This meaning can he otherwise expressed by saying that the difference is not felt or perceived, that it does not strike us, and so on.

An increase of knowledge respecting some matter is not uncommonly described by the term before us. Some one tells me that he remembers in former days having periods of bodily and mental depression, the cause of which he was then unconscious of, having found out since that the effect was due to the east wind.

(5.) A passive, contemplative, dreaming, indolent existence, as contrasted with the active pursuit of some outward and tangible object, is spoken of as an over-conscious life. I have already had occasion to remark, that the attitude of objectivity suspends or arrests, to a certain degree, the stream of feelings and thoughts, having thereby an anæsthetic tendency. The absence of aim leaves the mind a prey to its own inward activity, or occupation with mere ideas, apart from present sensations or actualities.

(6.) Consciousness is put in opposition to *latent* trains of thought, and to actions that by habit become so mechanical as to be compared with our reflex movements. A rapid intellect, unaccustomed to note the succession of its own thoughts, arrives at remote results, without being able to reproduce the intermediate stages. Something of this is attributed to Newton, who, in the demonstrations of the *Principia*, leaves wide gaps to be supplied by the mind of the reader. It is thought doubtful if he would have been able himself to quote the intermediate reasonings, unless by an express effort of study. In that last consummation of the acquired habits, when a person can carry on an operation

## 558 CONSCIOUSNESS.

while the mind is engrossed with something else, we not unfrequently say that the performance is nearly, if not entirely, unconscious. At all events, ,wide is the distinction between the state of the beginner, whose whole mind is painfully concentrated upon his first lessons, and the experienced workman whose mind is almost entirely at his disposal for other things. The change may be represented as a transition from intense consciousness to something not far off from total unconsciousness. Compare the child's earliest attempts at a sum, with the arithmetical processes of an experienced accountant.

(7.) One man acts out spontaneous and unthinking impulses, careless and heedless of the result, or the manner of acting, while another is anxious both as to the result and the manner. The difference is described as a less or greater degree of consciousness. If I fire a shot at random, not troubling myself where the ball is to strike, I exemplify the quality in its faint degree. If 1 have a mark before my eyes, and gaze steadily upon that with intent to strike it, I may be said to be more conscious. If, in addition, I have in my mind certain rules or directions for the attitude I am to assume, and the manner of holding my piece, so as to be observant of my own motions and postures, I am then most conscious of all. It is a practice of some writers to lavish great praise upon actions unencumbered with the thinking of rules, models, or guidance, in the manner of them; and, in styling this last accompaniment being 'conscious,' they imply a reproach. Nobody denies that it is better if one can work without burdening the attention with the consideration of rules; the only question is what is requisite to have the work well done. The usual course is obviously that mentioned in the foregoing paragraph, to begin in the one predicament, and end in the other; and to stigmatize a recruit at his first day's drill, because he is intensely conscious, is mere childish absurdity.

(8.) It is partly a variety of the same idea when self-examination as to one's motives, merits, guilt, or innocence,

CONSIDERATION OF SELF. 559

is designated consciousness. A man not only acts, but institutes a study of his actions and motives, by comparing them with such and such examples, standards, or rules. We now approach, however, more and more closely to the most special acceptation of the term, namely, the occupation of the intellect with oneself as a subject of consideration or study.

(9.) The indulgence of the emotions that have self for their object is a case for the employment of the same word. The state of self-complacency, or the opposite; the thinking of how we appear in the eyes of others, the hunting for approbation, the mixing up with an operation the view of our own demeanour or merit in it,—are to be conscious in one prevalent meaning of the word. A person little given to any one of these emotions, not entertaining them as ends or intruding them into the common business of life, is occasionally described as little conscious.

(10.) The three last meanings brings me to the definition of consciousness that has been adopted by many of the writers on the human mind. Let me quote from Dugald Stewart, 'This word denotes the immediate knowledge which the mind has of its sensations and thoughts, and, in general, of all its present operations' (see in Fleming's *Vocabulary of Philosophy* a number of quotations to the same effect). The study of the human mind is thus said to be an affair of consciousness; implying that the study of the external world does not involve the same property. I shall have to animadvert upon this presently.

(11.) Certain of our beliefs, termed intuitive, are said to be grounded on our consciousness. This also is a signification peculiar to the science of the human mind, and the metaphysical doctrines mixed up with it. Here, however, there is clearly a step in advance upon the definition last quoted; for the mere cognition of our own mental processes does not contain the knowledge involved in those intuitive judgments. When Stewart says,—'The changes which I perceive in the universe impress me with a conviction that some cause must have operated to produce them. Here is an intuitive

560                     CONSCIOUSNESS.

judgment involving the simple idea of *causation*'—he points
to something beyond the mere study of the mental operations.
It is impossible, by ever so much attention to the phenomena
of my own mind, to gather information as to the order of
events in the so-called external universe. The best that we
can hope for, is to attain a thorough knowledge of our own
mental life. It is, therefore, something new and distinct to
say that consciousness affirms such judgments as that now
quoted. And even as regards certain theories of the mind,
such as the liberty of the will, and an innate moral sense, I
have lately had to show that something more than a simple
act of consciousness at any one moment is requisite.

(12.) It is a natural transition from the foregoing to attach
the meaning of Belief generally to the word consciousness. A
strong affirmation is now and then expressed by the phrase
being conscious of so and so. It is not difficult to show how
the term in question has extended itself to signify belief. It
is the strong instinctive tendency of our nature to believe a
number of things, before we have gone through any large
teachings of experience. The believing function is a prominent attribute of mental activity. We are scarcely able to
feel or act without the operation of belief, or without making
assumptions in anticipation of the reality. We believe first,
and prove or disprove afterwards. Far from denying intuitive
judgments and assertions to be an original and spontaneous
emanation of the mind, I admit that the mind generates them
in great profusion ; I only refuse to them validity, certainty,
or authority, in the absence of good positive evidence.

(13.) Lastly, Memory is occasionally denoted by the same
term consciousness. We say, when we do not remember
something that has happened, we are not conscious of its
having taken place. The connexion of the two meanings is
an explicable one, for in order to an abiding and future
impression of an object, it is necessary that the first impression should be distinctly conscious, or should fully engross
the waking mind for a certain time. If a sound falls unheeded
upon my ear, it is only the natural consequence that I should

PERVADING IDEA ATTACHED TO THE TERM. 561

not afterwards possess an idea of it. What I remember vividly in after times are those things that have, in their original shock, excited and engrossed me for a considerable period to the exclusion of all else.

2. Such is a tolerably complete enumeration of the significant ideas attached to the name in question. There is a general drift or tendency common to them all. Nevertheless we may class them under distinct heads, inasmuch as there are one or two very decided departures from what is evidently the primitive and radical signification.

First, the capital and pervading idea is the one that we commenced with, of which those that follow as far as the seventh, with the exception of the fifth, are mere ramifications. The word consciousness is identical with mental life, and its various energies, as distinguished from the mere vegetable functions, the condition of sleep, torpor, insensibility, &c. Anything that renders the mental activity more intense, that increases the whirl of the brain (such as feelings of pain and pleasure, mental engrossment with a subject, rapid flow of imagery and ideas) is designated by the positive term; the absence, or the lower shades, are expressed by the negative, or unconsciousness. The act of attending as against listlessness is simply a more intense exercise of the mental functions. Even that more peculiar signification—the observation of rules, examples, &c., in contradistinction to mere unthinking impulse, is really a branch of the same meaning, as implicating a larger amount of mental activity in the case. The more considerations I bring to bear upon a particular action, the more conscious may I be said to be. My mind is wakened up in a greater number of directions; the brain is more heavily taxed, and the ideas that remain will be all the more vivid. Consciousness is thus co-extensive with mental life, and is expressed more or less strongly as that life is considered to rise or fall in degree.

Secondly, there are certain of the meanings (5, 8, 9, 10), pointing to the occupation of the mind with itself, in contrast to being occupied with the object world. The relation of this

562 CONSCIOUSNESS.

to the principal signification is not difficult to explain. We have formerly had occasion, more especially with reference to Pursuit and Plot interest, to advert to the anæsthetic character of the object regards. It is in the remission of those regards, that feeling, and other states of the *ego*, attain their full development. Even Pleasure and Pain are in abeyance during a moment of intense objectivity, as in aiming a blow or in watching a race. A nice question is thereupon suggested— Are we conscious in any shape when engaged exclusively upon the object world? It seems to me that we are, and I have called this the object-consciousness, to distinguish it from the elements of the subject-consciousness.

The only other important restriction of the meaning of the word consciousness is the employment of it to signify Belief. Most disastrous have been the effects of this limitation. People have been thereby led to suppose not only that the human mind evolves beliefs of its own accord without reference to, or in anticipation of, actual trial (which is very true); but that these beliefs carry their own evidence with them, and dispense with the confirmation of experience—which is a different proposition, noway admissible. The term consciousness has been the medium for playing off this piece of jugglery. There being one acceptation wherein the name means the final criterion of knowledge, the credit due to that is transferred to a number of cases where the meaning is entirely changed. Let us once dismiss this equivocation, and we shall come face to face with the realities of the questions that concern human knowledge, belief, and certainty. (See also Appendix, D.)

Having thus surveyed the common acceptations of the term in dispute, and commented upon the shifting quicksands introduced by means of it into philosophy, I shall now proceed in a more systematic way to the consideration of the entire subject brought into view by its employment.

## CONSCIOUSNESS AS FEELING.

### 1. *The Passive States.*

3. That we are conscious when under Pleasure or Pain is admitted on all hands. These are our states of feeling by pre-eminence. I have always contended, in addition, for the existence of states of Neutral excitement, where we are mentally alive, and, it may be, to an intense degree. Perhaps the best example of these is the excitement of a surprise. There are pleasurable, and also painful, surprises, but there are many that are neither ; and yet they are genuine emotions. And even our emotions that have pleasure or pain for their usual character, often pass into neutral phases without disappearing, or ceasing to operate as mental excitement. I may be under an attack of fear, and something may occur that takes away the painful part of the state, but I am not thereby restored to the quiescent indifference that preceded the shock. So our moments of pleasurable elation very often lose the element of delight, long before the system subsides into the condition of perfect calm. We feel mentally alive on all those occasions, but neither enjoy nor suffer.

Again, neutral excitement has its emotional wave, or diffusion, as much as the other kinds. The shock of a surprise causes an animated expression and stir of movements and gestures, which are very much the same whether we are pleased or otherwise. When the tremor of a great excitement is thoroughly roused, the system continues to be agitated with it for a length of time, no matter whether we like it or not. The inward or conscious condition is allied with the corresponding outward embodiment, and the two are sustained together. Whence the physical characters or expression, which are the natural accompaniment of an emotional wave, show themselves in connexion with the neutral, as well as with the pleasing, or painful.

Next it is to be noted that as regards the *occupying of the mind*, to the shutting out of other states, the neutral sort of

564 CONSCIOUSNESS.

excitement avails quite as much as pain or pleasure. Under any kind of stimulation we are mentally roused up and engrossed, and so much the less open to subsequent impressions. A stimulation, in itself indifferent as regards enjoyment, may indirectly contribute to our pleasure by displacing a painful mode of occupation, and, on the other hand, it may prevent us from falling under a real pleasure. The mind can thus be taken up with what is neither agreeable nor disagreeable, and it may be a matter of difficulty to find room for any object possessing one or other of these qualities.

4. Further, the wave of neutral excitement has an efficacy as regards the intellect, which should by no means be omitted as a positive characteristic. It is not merely pleasure and pain that keep the mind alive to intellectual impressions, and deepen the stamp of them for after times; the state now before us has the very same power. An object that can strike us with surprise, raises around it a condition of the brain so active as to retain the impression to the exclusion of other objects. We speak of rousing the attention to a particular thing, which does not imply necessarily either suffering or delight, but merely a degree of mental animation. The astronomer, Tycho, walking out one evening, came upon a group of persons gazing on a new star. They were arrested and detained by the emotion of surprise; they could not quit the thing that had so powerfully wakened their attention. We cannot say whether they were pained or pleased; they may have passed through moments of both the one condition and the other. Such moments, however, would be accidental to the occasion; what was essential was the excited detention of the gaze, resulting in a proportionate depth of enduring impression of the object that gave the surprise. All through life the remembrance of that night would probably be fresh. Without either sensibly adding to their happiness, or causing them misery, the new star would occasionally recur to their recollection, and occupy the mental trains and determine the mental attitude for a certain time, as did the original on the night of first breaking on their view. They might rise to the pleasur-

## CONSCIOUSNESS OF ACTIVITY. 565

able pitch of the state of wonder, or they might experience some of the pains of terror, but without either there would be an emotion roused, and an impression engrained.

### 2. *The Active States.*

5. I have frequently spoken of the consciousness of energy put forth as the basis of the objective attitude, the medium of cognising Extension, Force, and the other attributes of the so-called External World. This does not involve pleasure or pain; there may be pleasures and pains of exercise, but the mind, when given up to these, has lapsed into a purely subject condition. It is a kind of neutral excitement, having for its speciality the feeling of degrees of expended energy; to which is added, in the cognition of the Extended Universe, a vast range of associations of potential or possible energy.

### THE INTELLECTUAL CONSCIOUSNESS.*

6. The gravamen of the present subject centres in the intellectual aspect of consciousness. There is a great transition made in passing from the emotional to the intellectual; and no small difficulty is experienced in determining, on the one hand, the common groundwork, and, on the other, the special peculiarities of the two. As suggested by Sir William Hamil-

---

* *The Volitional Consciousness.* It might be expected on some show of plausibility, that a characteristic form of consciousness should attach to Volition, as well as to the two other departments of mind, where a marked antithesis exists. It is not so, however. The modes of consciousness growing up in the course of voluntary action are fully described as either emotional or intellectual. We have, in the first place, all the pleasures and pains connected with the exercise of the active organs, with the pursuit of ends, with desire, and the opposite. There are, further, states of excitement and occupation of mind without either pain or pleasure. Then, again, as to the appreciation of degrees of expended energy, whereon are based the sense of weight, resistance, force, extension, rate of movement, &c.; these are varieties of the intellectual consciousness. The states of Deliberation, Resolution, Desire, Belief, wherein the volitional impetus is under arrest, are states of ideal exertion.

566 CONSCIOUSNESS.

ton, there is often an inverse relationship, or mutual exclusion, one of the other. We are mentally alive while engaged in intellectual operations, and yet, as regards pleasure or pain, we may be in a state of indifference. What is there then that can be a common foundation of two mental modes whose extreme manifestations diverge to opposite poles ? At what point do the two pass into one another, supposing them to shade gradually, or where is the abrupt separation on the contrary supposition ? The bridge is to be found in that property of neutral excitement just explained.

### *Sense of Difference.*

7. As more than once expressly stated in former parts of our exposition (INTELLECT, Introduction) the basis or fundamental peculiarity of the intellect is Discrimination, or the feeling of difference between consecutive, or co-existing, impressions. Nothing more fundamental can possibly be assigned as the defining mark of intelligence, and emotion itself does not necessarily imply any such property. When I am differently affected by two colours, two sounds, two odours, two weights, or by a taste as compared with a touch or a sound, I am intellectually conscious. By such distinctiveness of feeling am I prepared, in the first instance, for imbibing that various experience implied in the term knowledge, and essential even to the lowest forms of voluntary action. There need be nothing of the agreeable or the disagreeable in this discriminative sensibility ; pleasure and pain in this connexion are mere accidents, and not essentials. The fact that I am differently affected by blue and red, by the bark of a dog, and the crowing of a cock, may be accompanied with pleasure, but the mental phenomenon is there in all its fulness, in the absence alike of pleasure and pain. We are awake, alive, mentally alert, under the discriminative exercise, and accordingly may be said to be conscious. The point is to connect, if possible, this new mode of consciousness with what is certainly the broad typical form of it represented by emotion.

## CHANGE OF IMPRESSION ESSENTIAL.

8. It is a general law of the mental constitution, more or less recognised by inquirers into the human mind,[*] that change of impression is essential to consciousness in every form. This is the Law of Relativity so often alluded to in the present work. There are notable examples to show that one unvarying action upon the senses fails to give any perception whatever. Take the motion of the earth about its axis, and through space, whereby we are whirled with immense volocity, but at a uniform pace, being utterly insensible of the circumstance. So in a ship at sea, we may be under the same insensibility, whereas in a carriage we never lose the feeling of being moved. The explanation is obvious. It is the change from rest to motion that wakens our sensibility, and conversely from motion to rest. A uniform condition, as respects either state, is devoid of any quickening influence on the mind. Another illustration is supplied by the pressure of the air on the surface of body. Here we have an exceedingly powerful effect upon one of the special senses. The skin is under an influence exactly of that nature that wakens the feeling of touch, but no feeling comes. Withdraw any portion of the pressure, as in mounting in a balloon, and sensi-

---

[*] 'Sense, therefore, properly so called, must necessarily have in it a perpetual variety of phantasms, that they may be discerned one from another. For if we should suppose a man to be made with clear eyes, and all the rest of his organs of sight well-disposed, but endued with no other sense; and that he should look only upon one thing, which is always of the same colour and figure, without the least appearance of variety, he would seem to me, whatsoever others may say, to see, no more than I seem to myself to feel the bones of my own limbs by my organs of feeling; and yet these bones are always and on all sides touched by a most sensible membrane. I might perhaps say he was astonished (?) and looked upon it; but I should not say he saw it; *it being almost all one for a man to be always sensible of one and the same thing and not to be sensible at all of anything.*'

'For seeing the nature of sense consists in motion; as long as the organs are employed about one object, they cannot be so moved by another at the same time, as to make by both their motions one sincere phantasm of each of them at once. And therefore *two several phantasms will not be made by two objects working together, but only one phantasm compounded from the action of both.*'—Hobbes, *Elements of Philosophy, Body*, Chap. XXV. Secs. 5, 6.

568                    CONSCIOUSNESS.

bility is developed. A constant impression is thus, to the
mind, the same as a blank. Our partial unconsciousness as
to our clothing is connected with the constancy of the object.
The smallest change at any time makes us sensible, or awake,
to the contact. If there were some one sound of unvarying
tone and unremitted continuance. falling on the ear from the
first moment of life to the last, we should be as unconscious
of the existence of that influence as we are of the pressure of
the air. Such a sonorous agency would utterly escape the
knowledge of mankind, until, as in the other case, some
accident, or some discovery in experimental philosophy, had
enabled them to suspend, or change the degree of, the impression made by it. Except under special circumstances, we are
unconscious of our own weight, which fact nevertheless can
never be absent. It is thus that agencies might exist without
being perceived; remission or change being a primary condition of our sensibility. It might seem somewhat difficult to
imagine us altogether insensitive to such an influence as light
and colour; and yet if some one hue had been present on the
retina from the commencement of life, we should incontestably
have been blind as far as that was concerned.*

------

    * To pursue the illustration of this important theme a little farther. The
mountain sheep is entirely destitute of those respiratory pleasures and pains
familiar to human beings, who spend their time partly in the confined air of
houses, and partly out of doors. It is the transition that developes at one time
the oppressive sensation of closeness, and at another time the exhilaration of
fresh air. The animal whose days and nights are spent alike on the mountain
or the plain has no experience of confined air, and therefore no sense of a pure
atmosphere. This does not debar the animal from the good effects following
from uninterrupted purity of respiration, as regards its general health, but it
prevents the possibility of any consciousness growing out of respiratory action
in the manner familiar to us. Again, the fishes in the tropical seas are
without the sensation of warmth. Living in an invariable temperature, the
sensibility of that temperature is dormant for want of varying the experience
by a greater or a less. Never to feel cold is never to feel heat; a transition
from one grade to another is indispensable to consciousness. In like manner,
sightless animals, whom our imagination pictures as living in the gloom of
deepest midnight, in reality have no sense of darkness as we understand it.
It is the loss of light, or of the power of vision, that makes the dark; the

## INTELLECTUAL CONSCIOUSNESS A SURPRISE. 569

9. Considering, then, that change is indispensable to our sensibility, let us see how we are likely to be affected in passing from one impression to another. Suppose a person in darkness, and suddenly exposed to the light. How shall we describe the way that the new influence is likely to affect the cerebral and mental system ? Putting pleasure or pain out of the account, as a mere accident, might we not fairly call the effect a shock, start, or *surprise*, and would not this have very

---

tenants of the Mammoth cave of Kentucky, where no ray of light ever entered, know nothing of darkness.

We have repeatedly seen pleasures depending for their existence on previous pains, and pains on pleasures experienced or conceived. Such are the contrasting states of Liberty and Restraint, Power and Impotence. Many pleasures owe their effect as such to mere cessation. For example, the pleasures of exercise do not need to be preceded by pain ; it is enough that there has been a certain intermission, coupled with the nourishment of the exhausted parts. These are of course our best pleasures. By means of this class, we might have a life of enjoyment without pain ; although, in fact, the other is more or less mixed up in every one's experience. Exercise, Repose, the pleasures of the different Senses and Emotions might be made to alternate, so as to give a constant succession of pleasure, each being sufficiently dormant, during the exercise of the others, to reanimate the consciousness when its turn comes. It also happens that some of those modes of delight are increased, by being preceded by a certain amount of a painful opposite. Thus confinement adds to the pleasure of exercise, and protracted exertion to that of repose ; fasting increases the enjoyment of meals, and being much chilled prepares us for a higher zest in the accession of warmth. It is not necessary, however, in those cases that the privation should amount to positive pain, in order to the existence of the pleasure. The enjoyment of food may be experienced, although the previous hunger may not be in any ways painful ; at all events, with no more pain than the certainty of the coming meal can effectually appease. The pleasures of warmth may count for a share of one's enjoyment, without being alternated with such degrees of cold as to amount to positive suffering ; this is the case, in all probability, with the majority of healthy persons enjoying the means of warmth, although there are instances wherein the pains of chillness preponderate. There is still another class of our delights depending entirely upon previous suffering, as in the sudden cessation of acute pains, or the sudden relief from great depression. Here the rebound from one nervous condition to another, is a stimulant of positive pleasure ; constituting a small, but altogether inadequate, compensation for the prior misery. The pleasurable sensation of good health presupposes the opposite experience in a still larger measure. Uninterrupted health, although an instrumentality for working out many enjoyments, of itself gives no sensation.

570 CONSCIOUSNESS.

much the character of a neutral emotion? We cannot well regard the sudden stroke as a mere agitation of a limited corner of the brain, called the ganglion of vision, or by any other name. I should rather say that there would be a free diffusive influence over the cerebral mass, or a pervading cerebral embodiment, showing itself in the more extreme cases by a lively demonstration. We know, as an experimental fact, that the loss of the cerebral hemispheres leads to blindness, in common with the deprivation of every other form of consciousness. Does not this indicate that a luminous impression must have the cerebrum at large to diffuse itself in, in order that we may be made alive by it? Here, then, is a common ground of the two kinds of consciousness, the emotional and the intellectual. In the shock of an impression of sense, as in the shock of an object of emotion proper, there is at first a cerebral participation, and a diffusive agency, extending to the active extremities of the body. In order to produce any effect on the senses there must be a change, and everything of the nature of change thrills through the brain as a kind of surprise. After a certain exposure to the light, the sudden withdrawal of it is a new change, and a new surprise. The gradations of colour, in passing from one object to another, are so many starts or surprises. Wherever we are sensitive to a difference, we must experience a species of cerebral shock as the accompaniment of the new sensation, and the greater the shock, the more alive do we become. It is in every way improbable that an effect so great as to waken and engross the mental life, and remain stamped as an indelible impression, should be operated in a small locality of the brain. Such a thing would hardly be credible in itself, apart from the contradiction that experiment has given to it. Everything new that strikes us through any one of the senses, must be assumed to prompt the emotional wave, with the consequences accruing therefrom, namely, mental occupation, or detention with that peculiar impression. If I am looking for a length of time on a green surface, and suddenly turn to a red, I am, so to speak, startled, shocked, surprised, and held possessed for the time

## MEASURED BY INTENSITY OF TRANSITION. 571

by that one effect. Such is the intellectual consciousness, and, so viewed, the fundamental identity between it and the emotional consciousness is apparent. When feeling is divested of the accidents of pleasure and pain, and looked at in its most general form of mental excitement and diffused manifestation, there is no essential point or peculiarity to distinguish it from those shocks of surprise that we must receive, in order to be conscious of any impression of sense. At one time I am engaged with objects of vision; my attention, as it is called, is suddenly drawn away by sounds falling on the ear. The change of avenue to the brain gives a character of difference to the sensibility or the consciousness, being one of the ways of stimulating or surprising us. Like the influence characteristic of feeling generally, the change from the eye to the ear takes possession of the brain and the mind by the impetus of novelty, and the attitude now assumed remains for a certain time, so as more or less to preclude other modes of occupying the mental organism, and to take on a certain hardening or confirming process, which enables it to persist in the future without the renewal of the outward shock. The method is precisely the same in listening to a succession of different sounds, or to the alternations of sound and silence. Every change imparts the cerebral thrill that makes us mentally alive with that one mode. Passing from acute to grave, from feeble to intense, from simplicity to complexity, from harmony to indifference, we are startled at every transition, with only a lower degree of what happens under what is admitted on all hands to be a genuine emotion, namely, surprise, wonder, or astonishment.

10. It is a well-known fact that we are conscious, awake, made sensible, or roused to attention, just in proportion to the greatness or the abruptness of the transition that we are subjected to. This is only another mode of saying that the brain is more sharply stimulated, and more forcibly detained in the new attitude, or in the new currents, by reason of the novelty of the impression. There is a common set of phrases for describing the emotion of wonder, or astonishment, and the

572 CONSCIOUSNESS.

distinctness or impressiveness of a sensation of the senses. The clear, distinctive discrimination that we obtain of different things that strike us, which is the very foundation of our intellectual development, is originally bred from those cerebral shocks, not improperly styled surprises. The change from an existing, to a new condition of the mind may not be very great, but if great enough to be felt at all, and to leave a mark behind it, a certain impetus or shock must cause a thrill through the cerebral system.*

11. Having thus recognised a common ground in the two great leading modes of consciousness, let us now consider the points wherein they stand contrasted with each other. There are several such points to be noted. It is incumbent on us to probe to the bottom that inverse relationship, more than once adverted to, of the emotional and the intellectual, and to reconcile it with the common foundation of the two. In the first place, then, there is an important difference of mode between feeling as pleasure or pain, and the surprises above delineated, as (although not exclusively), stamping intellectual difference. If the mind is very thoroughly alive on the point of enjoyment as such, or of pain as such, it is not in a favourable state for being struck with the shades of discrimination of its feelings. Intense delight absorbs the energies of the cerebral and mental system, and the only intellectual consequence arising from it is a certain impressiveness lent to the objects that chime in with, or contribute to, the pleasure. When feeling is strongly roused in either of the two opposites that constitute the happiness or the misery of our being, the neutral forms are

---

* There is a wide distinction between the first shock of a difference, and the degree of excitement of the same transition at later stages of our education. When red and blue are first seen together, they give a start that fills the mind with an acute thrill of surprise, being to all intents and purposes a wave of emotion. At after times, the same contrast is passed over with a comparatively faint excitement, the discrimination still remaining and serving some purpose in our economy, without rousing any shock of surprise. When red is reduced to the function of acting as a signal to perform one operation, and blue another, the emotional excitement attending their original manifestation fades away to very narrow limits. The effect then still occupies the

## INTELLECT AND EXCITEMENT INVERSELY RELATED. 573

thrown into the shade. A mere surprise, that has no effect to impress a difference between two feelings, is but coldly entertained at such a time. We must, to a certain extent, both forego delights, and be free from eating cares, in order to dwell largely among the neutral excitements that stamp difference upon the mind. There is thus, upon a common mental basis, a specific difference of kind, amounting to antithesis, between the pleasurable or painful excitement and the intellectual excitement. This conclusion is not founded on any *à priori* consideration, but on an induction from facts. There is a large experience that can be interpreted in no other way. The devotion of the mind to incessant pleasure, and the incumbency of misery and care, are wholly adverse to the general cultivation of the intellect,—a cultivation which, in the last resort, resposes on the ready sensibility of difference. The best atmosphere for a high culture is a serene condition of mind, with no more pain than is necessary to stimulate pursuit, and no more pleasure than imparts an inducement to go on with life. The energy of the brain is thus reserved for the neutral stimulation that impresses every kind of difference, and in this way stores the intellect with distinct impressions. The maximum of intellectual excellence implies at once a sparing resort to pleasure, and a tolerable exemption from misery. The inverse relationship thus implied is, moreover, a confirmation of the previous doctrine of the common emotional basis. For why should the two states be to a certain

---

mind, or is a conscious effect, but so feebly and for so short a time as to be next thing to unconscious. It is in this way, that what began as emotion and full consciousness, ends as mere discrimination and virtual indifference. We could never commence the act of discriminating, if we were at the outset as little excited with the difference of red and blue, as we become ultimately in using them as mere distinctive marks or signals in some every-day routine operation ; and it is not fair—in fact, not true— to regard this abated and transformed manifestation as the type of primitive sensation. It is one of the effects of habit, easily traceable, to pass from the primordial excitement to the final indifferentism, that indifferentism still retaining the substantiality of discrimination.

574                    CONSCIOUSNESS.

extent incompatible, if they do not, to that extent, avail themselves of a common cerebral diffusion ?*

12.   The illustration of the points of contrast or antithesis
of the emotional and the intellectual, is not complete without
signalizing another circumstance. The true intellectual nature
is what takes on the present sensibility and the abiding impression of difference (and resemblance) with the least emotional shock.  To feel distinctly a faint transition, as of a
slight gradation of tint, or a small alteration of the pitch of
a sound, is the mark of a brain discriminative by nature.  On
the other hand, when the consciousness is not awake, except
under a very broad difference, we consider the mental constitution the opposite of intellectual.  In whatever department
of impressions the nicest sensibility to difference prevails, in
that department will reside, in all probability, the intellectual
aptitude of the individual.  It may be in the delicate appreciation of degrees of muscular force, giving birth to dexterity
of manual or other bodily execution ; it may be in taste or
smell, so as to confer an aptitude for testing substances that
affect those senses ; it may be tactile, and contribute to the

---

* While admitting that both pleasure and pain have a certain intellectual
efficacy in impressing what concerns themselves, as when a man retains a
lively impression of a scene that delighted him, simply because of the delight,
or of a person that injured him because of the injury, we must also admit that
even a neutral excitement may sometimes stand apart from the discriminative
sense of change.   A stirring novelty may set me off in a fit of surprise, and
yet I may very soon pass from the thing itself, and transfer the benefit of the
excitement to something else.   Such a transferable, or mobile excitement, is
not the true intellectual species.   A few hours spent in hurry, bustle, and
noise, put the brain into a fever of unnatural energy, under which everything
felt or done has more than ordinary power.   Such a state is no more favourable, in the long run, for the storing up of differences (and resemblances) than
the extremes of pleasure and pain.   The smart that a change of impression
makes should simply sustain the currents belonging to that impression, stopping short of a general animation of the brain.   It should not prevent the
cessation of the wave, and the taking on of another at a short interval, the
mind all the while being what would be termed perfectly cool.   The stirring-
up of a vague and wasting excitement, which follows on too many stimulants
being applied at once, is as fatal to intellect, as pleasurable dissipation or
wasting misery.

## DISCRIMINATION UNDER A SLIGHT SHOCK. 575

discrimination of solid substances from the texture of their surface; it may lie in some one or other of the properties of sounds, musical or articulate ; or, finally, in the wide domain of the sense of vision. To be markedly sensitive to very minute shades of difference, or to have a distinctive conscious- ness under a very slight shock of change, is the first property of the intellect on any species of subject-matter. We cannot assign any fact more fundamental in the constitution of our intelligence. The laws of association, and the storing-up and engraining of various impressions, imagery, and ideas, pre- suppose the primitive susceptibility to every various mode or degree of primary sensations or feelings.

13. In describing the muscular sensibilities, and the sensa- tions of the senses, I have uniformly adverted to the intellec- tual or discriminative property. We have found, for example, that, besides the pleasure and pains of muscular exercise, there is a discriminative sensibility to degree of expended energy of all the voluntary muscles. There is a distinct shock given to the mental consciousness on passing from quietude to action, and another in relapsing to quietude again. There is also a series of distinctive impressions made through all the varying degrees of force expended, the mind assuming, as it were, a different attitude under each. When I am holding in my hand a weight of four pounds, if some one adds two more, the additional putting forth of muscular energy imparts a certain shock to the cerebrum, and gives a new character to the cur- rents of the brain. The same language describes what happens throughout all the senses, wherever discrimination is to be found. Even in the regions of pleasurable and painful sensi- bility proper, we may be conscious of degree, which is the true intellectual consciousness. When, in tasting something sweet, I find in the course of turning the thing in my mouth, that the sweetness increases or diminishes, that is properly an in- tellectual consciousness ; although the really extensive deve- lopment of the intellectual susceptibility is among sensations and impressions that are quite neutral as regards pain or pleasure. This is evident by looking at the classes of proper-

576 CONSCIOUSNESS.

ties, under the different senses, put down as discriminative—the discrimination of a plurality of points in touch, of articulateness in sounds, and of symbolical or arbitrary forms in sight. Such things are hardly ever reckoned either agreeable or disagreeable, and yet they waken and occupy the mental energy, and monopolize the forces of the cerebrum. We are distinctly affected merely by a change from one sense to another sense, and yet there is nothing in that circumstance to please us or otherwise. Such is the true type of the intellectual consciousness.*

14. An important part of our intellectual culture, consists in forming new susceptibilities to difference by artificial methods. What is called the improvement of the senses, means this, in the first instance; as when the wine-taster acquires a delicate palate, or the chemist a fine nose for the odours that characterize different volatile bodies. By merely practising the organs, they become more discriminative, and differences are felt after a time that would originally have been unfelt. The musician experiences a steady improvement in the quality of his ear, as well as in his execution; the painter is by degrees more and more alive to tints of colour. In the higher intellectual education, much of the acquired

---

* I have adverted in my former volume (*Contiguity*, § 45) to what is perhaps the crowning instance of discriminative sensibility, namely, the bringing out of difference between an impression on the right hand, and one on the left, or between touches on different parts of the body. Originally, on comparing the two impressions right and left, supposing them of the same character, it is impossible to say that there is any difference, yet the fact of their distinct origin and transmission through separate nerves, enables them to suspend separate trains of association, and by this means we localize the different impressions made all over the body. Here is an originally latent difference made patent by subsequent associations. At first, the common saying is applicable to us all, that we do not know our right hand from our left, the distinction in this case being an acquired one; but the acquisition would not be possible without a certain independence and separateness of the nerves, rendering the cerebral attitude, put on by a communication from one, capable of being clearly distinguished from that put on by a communication from the other. Thus, states of consciousness, perfectly identical as regards the intensity of the mental shock, yet maintain an available distinctness according to the quarter whence the impression comes.

ACQUIRED DISCRIMINATION. 577

power lies in tracing differences in matters where the uninitiated feels none. A person untaught in Logic would perhaps see no distinction between two arguments coming under different moods and figures, or between a truth arrived at deductively and one arrived at inductively. The term 'Judgment' expresses those higher forms of discrimination, and also not unfrequently the lower ; and Sir W. Hamilton remarks that Judgment is implied in every act of consciousness, which is quite true on the supposition of its being merely one of the synonymes of discrimination. But, as we shall see presently, there is another mode of the intellectual consciousness, whose mention is requisite preparatory to the full explication of these higher judgments of the mind.

15. The only farther observation to be made under the present head, refers to the impressing of the mind with distinctive forms, notions, and imagery, to be connected by the laws of association, and made use of in guiding present action, and in preparing those higher combinations, designated under the faculties of Reason, Imagination, &c. Were it not for the primitive shock that difference gives, there would be no basis for the intellect. All colours would be alike ; sounds would not be distinct from touches or smells, and there would be no cognition possible in any sense. The feeling of difference, therefore, is the first step ; the impressing of that into an enduring notion, under the plastic property of the mind, is the next. We begin by being alive to the distinctive shocks of red and green, of round and oval, small and large ; by-and-bye, we attain the fixed notion of a rose on its stem ; thence we go on combining this with others, until the mind is full of the most variegated trains of imagery. The law of contiguous association follows up, and does not necessarily imply, or contain in itself, the primordial sense of difference, which is the most rudimentary of all the properties of our intellectual being. Analysis can descend no deeper, explanation can go no farther ; we must take a stand upon this, as the preliminary condition of all intelligence, and merely seek to place its character in a clear and certain light.

2 o

578            CONSCIOUSNESS.

### *Sense of Agreement.*

16. The foregoing remarks proceed on the assumption, that a continuous or unbroken impression supplies no element of the consciousness, and that change, novelty, variety, are what incite the mental being into wakeful manifestation. There are, nevertheless, cases where Agreement imparts the shock requisite for rousing the intellectual wave. It is, however, agreement in a qualified sense, indeed, so qualified as to be really a mode of difference. We have seen at large, in the exposition of the Law of Similarity, that the discovery of identity comes upon the mind with a flash or a shock of the nature of surprise, but the identity in such cases must be surrounded with diversity. It gives no surprise to waken every morning, and see the same objects in the same positions, but it does surprise us to go away into a remote place, where everything is altered and where we are prepared for changes, and find a prospect exactly resembling a familiar scene at home. We are not surprised by seeing friends in their wonted haunts, the surprise is given when we meet them in some region far remote. Agreements of this sort are in reality differences ; they are breaches of expectation, and give us a start exactly in the same way as a difference arising where we looked for agreement. The mind once accustomed to a certain fixed routine of change, is startled by the substitution of uniformity instead. Having often been in a room hung with pictures, and otherwise richly furnished, one feels a rupture of expectation and a violent surprise on encountering naked walls and an empty floor. It is still change, or a discrepancy between a past and a present attitude of mind, that is the exciting cause of the awakened consciousness ; although it sometimes happens that the change consists in producing an old familiar impression in an unlooked-for connexion.

17. Having premised thus much, we have next to study the influence of this new class of surprises on the growth of our intelligence. It so happens that the noticing of agree-

OUR KNOWLEDGE CONTAINS AGREEMENTS. 579

ment in the midst of difference is an exceedingly useful function as regards our knowledge of the world, where amid great variety there is much resemblance. A long chapter having been devoted to the exposition of that fact, and the consequences of it, any laboured demonstration in this place is superfluous. What concerns us at present, is to notice the manner whereby we are made alive to those agreements, so as to stamp them on the mind and make them a part of the permanent intellectual furniture. Take a simple case of classification to illustrate our meaning. The young mind looking again and again at one tree acquires an impression of it merely through the sensibility to difference. We being at last familiarized with the repetition of the very same aggregate of differences, so to speak, there is an end of any special surprise on the presentation of the object, and a gradual tendency to the indifferentism that monotony induces. Let the mind, however, encounter another tree smaller in dimensions but similar in all else ; the similarity recalls the old tree, while the difference gives the stimulus of surprise. We are then awakened as it were to a new circumstance as important as the original fact of difference, and a flow of excitement accompanies the experience, rendering it vivid at the moment, and laying the basis of a permanent recollection. Thus, besides accumulating differences, and enlarging the stock of intellectual imagery grounded upon these, we enter on a new class of impressions, the impressions of agreement in diversity. If these agreements fell upon the mind perfectly flat, like the unbroken continuance of one impression, I doubt whether we should have been able to take any cognisance of the great fact of recurrence in the midst of change, on which depends the operations of classifying, generalizing, induction, and the like. In order to impress upon the mind the existence of a *class* of houses, trees, men, and so on, it seems essential that the recurrence of similarity should give a smart or fillip to the cerebral organism, quite as much as the transition from action to rest, from light to shade, or from rough to smooth. I do not see how those valuable

580                    CONSCIOUSNESS.

elements of knowledge that we term generalities, general
ideas, principles, could have found a standing in the intellectual consciousness but for the shock of surprise that, in common with change in general, they are able to affect us with.
If we were totally indifferent to the occurrence of the feeling
of sweetness in a number of different objects, the faculty of
classifying aud generalizing would never to all appearance be
manifested in our minds.   It is the liveliness of that thrill of
surprise, caused by likeness in the company of unlikeness, that
rouses us to the perception or impression of recurring properties, and uniform law among natural things.   There is a
certain depth of stupidity exhibited by individuals, amounting
almost to total indifference on this peculiarity ; and in such
cases the power both of generalizing and of comprehending
generalities, of forming and applying analogies, will to that
extent be found wanting.   Just as a keen sensibility to difference determines the lively cognition of the variety of natural
properties, which a blunter sense would confound, so the corresponding sensitiveness to the shock of similarity in diversity,
leads to the appreciation and the storing up of nature's generalities, and comprehensive unity of plan.


### Sensation and Perception.

18. It is proper to take notice of the precise meanings of
these names in relation to the present subject. As regards
*Sensation* there is a certain complexity to be unravelled,
owing to the circumstance that sensations extend between
the extremes of emotion and intellect, and have therefore
no uniform character except in their mode of origination.
Some sensations are mere pleasures or pains and little else ;
such are the feelings of organic life, and the sweet and
bitter tastes aud odours.   Others stretch away into the region
of pure intellect, and are nothing as respects enjoyment or
suffering ; as, for example, a great number of those of the
three higher senses.   A sensation in the signification of
one extreme is quite a different matter from one in the

other extreme. The tendency of most writers on Mental Philosophy has been to put an almost exclusive stress on the intellectual, discriminative, or knowledge-giving class ; which meaning, if consistently adhered to, could not be censured. But, occasionally, the other or more emotional class is intended by the term, which is then used in contrast, or contradistinction, to the discriminative element of the mind. Sir William Hamilton's doctrine of the inverse relation of Sensation and Perception involves this meaning ; for he really means to contrast the Emotional with the Intellectual aspect of the senses.

19. A sensation is, under any view of it, a conscious element of the mind. As pleasure or pain, we are conscious in one way, as discrimination, we are conscious in the other way ; namely, in a mode of neutral excitement. A balmy odour wakens up the mind with a certain charm ; the odour of camphor gives no charm and no pain, while causing a certain excitement and a characteristic attitude of the cerebral system. But this is not all. After much contact with the sensible world, a new situation arises, and a new variety of the consciousness, which stands in need of some explanation. When a child experiences for the first time the sensation of scarlet, there is nothing but the sensibility of a new impression, more or less intense, according to the intensity of the object, and the susceptibility of the mind. It is very difficult for us to realize or define this original shock, our position in mature life being totally altered. It is the rarest thing for us then to come under a radically new impression, and we can only, by the help of imperfect analogies, form an approximate conception of what happens at the first shock of a discriminative sensation. The process of engraining these impressions on the mind after repetition, gives to subsequent sensations quite different character as compared with the first.. The second shock of scarlet, if it stood alone, would doubtless resemble the preceding ; but such is the nature of the mind that the new shock will not stand alone, but restores the notion, or idea, or trace that survived the former. The

582                   CONSCIOUSNESS.

sensation is no longer the primitive stroke of surprise, but a coalition of a present shock with all that remains of the previous occasions. Hence it may properly be said, when we see, or hear, or touch, or move, that what comes before us is really contributed more by the mind itself than by the object present. The consciousness is complicated by three concurring elements—the new shock, the flash of agreement with the sum total of the past, and the feeling of that past as revived in the present. In truth, the new sensation is apt to be entirely over-riden by the old; and in place of discriminating by virtue of our susceptibility to what is characteristic in it, our discrimination follows another course. For example, if I have before me two shades of colour, instead of feeling the difference exactly as I am struck at the moment, my judgment resorts to the roundabout process of first identifying each with some reiterated series of past impressions; and, having two sum-totals in my mind, the difference that I feel is between those totals. If I make a mistake, it may be attributed, not so much to a wrong act of discrimination, as to a wrong act of identification. It is as if I could only judge between two substances on the chemist's table, by first finding out, by an effort of identification, which drawer, or which bottle each belonged to; I should then judge not by comparing the specimens, but by comparing the drawers or bottles containing the entire stock of each. If I made a wrong identification to begin with, my conclusion would be sure to be wrong; the similarity being accurate, so would be the difference. All sensations, therefore, after the first of each kind, involve a flash of recovery from the past, which is what really determines their character. The present shock is simply made use of as a means of reviving some one past in preference to all others; the new impression of scarlet is in itself almost insignificant, serving only as the medium of resuscitating the cerebral condition resulting from the united force of all the previous scarlets. If, by some temporary hallucination, a scarlet were to bring up the impression of ultramarine blue, the mind would really be possessed with

## PERCEPTION MORE INTELLECTUAL THAN SENSATION. 583

blue, while the eyes were fixed upon scarlet; just as, in putting an account upon a wrong file, we lose sight of the features of the account itself, and declare its character according to the file it has got to. Sensation thus calls into operation the two great intellectual laws, in addition to the primitive sensibility of difference. The endurance of the impression, after the original is gone, is owing to the plastic power denominated under the law of contiguity. The power of the new shock, to bring back the trace of the first, is a genuine exercise of the power of similarity. When we consider ourselves as performing the most ordinary act of seeing, or hearing, we are bringing into play those very functions of the intellect that make its development and its glory in its highest manifestation.

20. *Perception* has various meanings, and great questions hinge upon some of them. The more that sensation involves cognitive or intellectual processes, the more liable is it to fall under the title of Perception. Thus, in sensation, we are subject and object by turns. We are *object* when attending to the form and magnitude of a conflagration; we are *subject* when we give way to the emotional effect of the luminous blaze. Now, although the name Sensation is used for both states, Perception is the better word for the object attitude.

Again, what has just been said regarding the intervention of intellectual forces in sensation, indicates the same tendency. Supposing the first impress of scarlet is called a sensation, the combined trace of thirty impressions, revived in the presentation of the thirty-first, would be a perception, as being something more than effect strictly due to present stimulus. When 'more is meant than meets the eye,' we are said to perceive rather than to feel. Not that feeling, consciousness, and sensation, are at all restricted to the minimum signification of present effect, unheightened by contributions from the recovered past; but, when the two words are compared, perceiving is generally feeling, and something more. The term sensation might be so narrowed as to exclude the intellectual operations above specified as involved in it; not so perception. On any

584 CONSCIOUSNESS.

view, the intellect participates in every act of perceiving, and when such intellectual participation accompanies a sensation of the senses, it would be allowable to say that a perception took place. The recovery of the past sum-total of sensibilities of redness, orange, blue, of the sound of a bell or a voice, of the touch of marble, or the taste of a peach, being in each case an effect far exceeding the special range of the new encounter by itself, we are at liberty to style the mental state thus produced a 'perception,' or something transcending the mere sensation, as narrowed to the shock of the moment.

21. The tendency to reckon perception a larger mental product than sensation, is still better seen in another of its well-established meanings, of which the best example, perhaps, is furnished under sight. When we talk of perceiving the distances and magnitudes of things about us, more is implied than the sensations can possibly contain. All that I ever can really feel regarding a house before me, is a certain union of optical and muscular sensibility, in which the notion of distance can have no part. That notion is derived through other parts of the system, more especially the locomotive members, and could no more come through the eye, than through the olfactory organs. Experience, however, recognises coincidences between certain optical impressions and certain movements, and after a time the occurrence of the one is able to suggest the other. I may perceive distance by the eye, as I may perceive a mail-coach in the next street by the sound of the horn. Association gives additional meanings to my sensations, and I am thus made to know or perceive what it is impossible for me to feel. The word has now a range of application that usage does not impart to the other; for, although the term sensation may extend to the mind's contribution from the past, at the instance of the present feeling, we should not be disposed to include all those other collateral impressions that may concur, and be associated with, that sum total. It would scarcely be correct to say that I *see* the distance of a hill. On the same principle, we ought not to speak of seeing the size,

COGNITION. 585

meaning the absolute size, for all that we see is the angular expansion measured on the retina. Having made certain comparisons as to the indications for judging of size, we may say, we *perceive* it to be of a certain amount.

22. It is by virtue of exceeding the narrow limits of strict sensation, that perception goes so far as to mean things neither felt nor inferred as experienced adjuncts, but simply assumed or believed to exist. Such is the supposed perception of an external and independent material world.* What is here said to be perceived is a convenient fiction, which by the very nature of the case transcends all possible experience. It is stealing a march upon our credence to use the term perception, which in its first and proper sense, means something decidedly within the domain of past or present experience, to avouch an entity of imagination. The case resembles the elastic use of the chief term consciousness itself; the same name being employed to denote the highest certainties of the human mind, and the wildest longings of illimitable desire.

### *The Nature of Cognition.*

23. It is a problem of no small difficulty, and no light import, to ascertain precisely what is the real nature of the act of knowing, so very familiar to our experience. 'What is it that we do when we are said to know or be cognisant of a thing? I apprehend that the actual subtlety of the question, which is not inconsiderable, is aggravated by the looseness of terminology, which afflicts the whole region that we are now

---

* The step here made may be described thus. I observed above, that the term perception applies to the sum-total of the many past similar sensations, recovered by association with the present sensation. These being all blended in one act of mind, in which the constituent items are not separately discernible, we mistake this sum-total for an unit, and imagine a Something which makes them all one—an object, one and the same, from which all and each emanate. Such transformation of a sum-total of association into a self-existent unit, is a frequent mental illusion. This supposed object is an entity, not of sense, but of imagination and belief, to which we erroneously apply the word perception.

586　　　　CONSCIOUSNESS.

traversing. The power of knowing is subject to the limitations above detailed with reference to consciousness or sensation ; it being clear, whatever else may be doubted, that some mental excitement or consciousness is indispensable to anything that we should call knowledge. Seeing that *change* is a condition of wakefulness of mind, a thing cannot be known unless the action of that thing on the mind is varied or remitted. We had no knowledge of the pressure of the air on our bodies until means were found to alter its degree ; the blank of consciousness is the blank of knowledge.

24. One great dispute, that has agitated the schools of philosophy on the present subject, has been between two opinions, the one affirming that all knowledge is derived through sensation, the other that the mind itself contributes a constituent part. *Nihil est in intellectu, quod non erat in sensu,* expresses the former opinion, to which Leibnitz added, *nisi intellectus ipse.* I do not enter here into this particular controversy, having discussed the origin of most of our simple notions in my previous volume. The reference of many of those elementary notions, such as Extension, Figure, Solidity, to the muscular system, alters entirely the state of the question as originally propounded. If sensation includes all that we derive from the feelings of movement, the first thesis would not be difficult to maintain ; exclude movement, and we render it wholly untenable.

25. At present our concern is, not so much with the first beginnings or sources of knowledge, as with the meaning, or nature of it, at any stage. Now, most that has been above advanced respecting Sensation and Perception applies to explain cognition. It is, I hope, sufficiently evident from the discussion of consciousness, incidentally raised in a preceding chapter (*Liberty and Necessity,* § 10), that the lowest or most restricted form of sensation does not contain an element of knowledge. The mere state of mind, called the sensation of scarlet, is not knowledge, although a necessary preparation for it. We must be discriminatively conscious of different mental states, before either perceiving or knowing in any

## COGNITION IS MORE THAN SENSATION. 587

acceptation. Nay, farther, we may have everything that is implied in the full meaning of sensation, as taking in the past with the present, and yet not rise to knowledge. The sensation of thunder, produced by reviving all the former experiences to enhance the new effect, is a true intellectual element of the mind, and a constituent part of knowledge, without itself amounting to knowledge. So with the lowest meaning of perception, which is identical with this. When, however, we pass to the higher meanings of perception, we enter upon the field of genuine cognition. When two different impressions concur in the mind, and by repetition become associated together, the one recalling the other ; and when we not only have a present experience of their concurrence, but a *belief* of it, we are then said to know something. A single notion by itself does not make knowledge, two notions coupled will not make knowledge in the absence of belief. Knowledge, therefore, is identical with affirmation and belief. In what manner the believing element springs up, and occupies the merely notional groundwork of our experience, as when we not only feel a present concurrence of lightning and thunder, but predict similar occurrences in the unknown future, I have already endeavoured to show. Belief derives its very existence from the active or volitional region, and not from the region of intellect proper. Still there are certain points relating to the merely intellectual constituents of knowledge that afford scope for animadversion, as they have given occasion to wide discrepancy of opinion.

26. In the first place, I should remark that knowledge is far from being co-extensive with sensation, or with distinguishable consciousness. Taking all the varieties of sensible effect, through all the avenues whereby impressions are made upon the mind,—the great range of distinguishable muscular feelings, and the innumerable changes or differing sensibilities of the senses,—hardly any arithmetic could sum up the number of ways wherein we are made discriminatively conscious. It is only a very small selection of these that any ·one person converts into knowledge, or couples into credible affirmations.

588                    CONSCIOUSNESS.

Consider the complicacy of the scene that presents itself to the infant eye, opened upon the outer world. The child may be said to feel, or be conscious of, all that enters the eye or the ear, but it demands a specializing, or selective, consciousness, in order to form any portion of this into knowledge. The act that we term attention, observation, concentration of the view, &c., must supervene upon mere discriminative consciousness, before knowledge commences. The cognitive process is essentially a process of selection, as the mind is moved to special, or monopolized, consciousness of certain portions of its various experience. Of all the sounds that fall upon our ear in the general din of the elements above, and the bustle of human beings beneath and around, only a very few ever attain the position that would constitute them knowledge. The articulate voices, the sounds that betoken human purposes that concern us, the indications noted as preceding the storm on its way,—are a few select impressions that take the rank of knowledge with most minds. Others there are, which are unheeded by some and noticed by others, as the buzz of the insect, or the rush of the rivulet. It would appear, in fact, that different minds have a different motive of selection out of the countless multitude of impressions that we are all alike open to. It is, therefore, a material consideration in the problem of knowledge, to ascertain what are the motives to the specialized consciousness, or the forces governing attention, as something over and above disinterested and equal sensation. In addition to the primitive shock of difference that makes us variously susceptible to different movements, tastes, odours, touches, sounds, sights, and emotions, there are needed some great inequalities in the surprises that come upon us from so many sides, to determine the occupation of the mind with some decided preferences, so that while five hundred stars are painted on the retina, only two or three are in actual possession of the mind, determining its emotions and its trains of thought and imagery.

27. These specializing forces are nothing new in the exposition of the mind. They are mostly reducible to a greater

## COGNITION IS SELECTION.

degree of those general influences already detailed, as essential to consciousness in the faintest manifestation of it. A bolder difference than the rest rouses wakefulness in that individual instance, overpowering the solicitations of the weaker transitions. A cannon fired in the silence of night gives the predominating sensation for the time being. The senses may be open alike for every impression, but some are calculated to obtain the monopoly of the mind, as giving the greater shock of surprise, and these are singled out as the more likely to enter into credible affirmations, or to emerge into knowledge. Not that they have become so yet; there are other stages previous to the final result.

In the same manner, the shock of agreement is a specializing or concentrating consciousness; understanding agreement as of the sort already defined, namely, similarity in diversity. If I cast my eyes over a large crowd of persons assembled before me, the recognition of a face resembling some one familiar to me arrests my attention upon one point of the scene.

28. It is not enough to call these the forces that determine special consciousness; it is further necessary to affirm, that the circumstances implied under them are essential to the very nature of knowledge. We know only relations; an absolute, properly speaking, is not compatible with our knowing faculty. The two great fundamental relations are difference and agreement.* To know a thing is to feel it

---

* The very general attributes that we denominate Co-Existence and Succession are not so fundamental as the feelings of difference and agreement. They are, properly speaking, an opposed, or antithetic, couple; the transition, from an instance of the one to an instance of the other, affects the mind by the change, and so develops the two contrasting cognitions. I am affected in one way, by two birds on the same bush at once, and in another way by one going away, and the other coming. If the two facts made an identical impression, I should not be conscious either of co-existence or of succession. As it is, the sense of difference gives rise to the perception of both attributes, and imparts to each its proper meaning, namely, the negation of the other. If all things in nature preserved an eternal stillness, and if it were possible for the eye to have simultaneous, instead of successive vision,

## 590 CONSCIOUSNESS.

in juxtaposition with some other thing differing from it, or agreeing with it. To be simply impressed with a sight, sound, or touch, is not to know anything in the proper sense of the word ; knowledge begins, when we recognise other things in the way of comparison with the one. My knowledge of redness is my comparison of this one sensation with a number of others differing from, or agreeing with it ; and as I extend those comparisons, I extend that knowledge. An absolute redness *per se*, like an unvarying pressure, would escape cognition ; for supposing it possible that we were conscious of it, we should not be said to have any knowledge. Why is it that the same sensation is so differently felt by different persons—the sensation of red or green to an artist and an optician—if not that knowledge relates not to the single sensation itself, but to the others brought into relation with it in the mind ? When I say I know a certain plant, I indicate nothing until I inform my hearer what things stand related to it in my mind, as contrasting or agreeing. I may know it as a garden weed ; that is, under difference from the flowers, fruits, and vegetables, cultivated in the garden, and under agreement with the other plants that spring up unsought. I may know it botanically ; that is, under difference and agreement with the other members of the order, genus and species. I may know

---

there would be no fact of the nature of succession, and no cognition of, the one prevailing fact, co-existence. We generalize all cases of particular co-existence into the abstract attribute ; and all individual successions into succession in the abstract ; but, without the shock of difference felt when we pass from an instance of the one to an instance of the other, we should have no cognition of either ; and our cognition, as it stands, is explained as a mutual negation of the two properties. Each has a positive existence because of the presence of the other as its negative, like heat and cold, light and dark.

Under Succession, we have the related couple, Antecedent and Consequent—the one giving both meaning and existence to the other, as in the more comprehensive case. An antecedent supposes a consequent, and conversely ; annihilate either, and the entire cognition disappears. Being distinctively conscious of a succession, it is implied that we are conscious of a difference between the member preceding and the member following ; and the two make an item of our knowledge ; neither, standing alone, could constitute a cognition.

it artistically, or as compared with other plants on the point of beauty of form and colour. As an isolated object in my mind, I can have no knowledge regarding it at all. Thus it is that in the multifarious scene and chaos of distinguishable impressions, not only do different minds fasten upon different individual parts, but, fastening on the same parts, arrive at totally different cognitions. 'Like the two electricities, which cannot exist the one without the other, or the two poles of the magnet, which rise and fall together, no mental impression can exist and be called knowledge, unless in company with some other as a foil wherewith to compare it. Left to a single unit of consciousness, the mental excitement vanishes. In the intellect, as in the emotions, we live by setting off contrasted states, and consequently no one impression can be defined or characterized, except with reference to its accompanying foil. We see how difficult it is in language to make meaning explicit by a brief announcement; interpretation, as applied to laws, contracts, testaments, as well as to writing generally, consists in determining what things the writer excluded as opposites to, and looked at as agreements with, the thing named. It is thus everywhere in cognition. A simple impression is tantamount to no impression at all. Quality, in the last resort, implies Relation; although, in Logic, the two are distinguished. Red and blue together in the mind, actuating it differently, keep one another alive as mental excitement, and the one is really knowledge to the other. So with the red of to-day and the red of yesterday, an interval of blank sensation, or of other sensations coming between. These two will sustain one another in the cerebral system, and will mutually be raised to the rank of knowledge. Increase the comparisons of difference and agreement, and you increase the knowledge; the character of it being settled by the direction wherein the foils are sought.

29. The present train of reflections might receive illustation from the course of literature, art, and science, in selecting portions and phases of the countless host of things that people the universe of the mind. There is no limit to the modes of

592 CONSCIOUSNESS.

knowing the world, when we superadd the sphere of art to the more narrowly-defined sphere of science. It is a theme of common remark, how an original genius makes us see what has always been before our eyes. The truth is, that having a thing before the eyes is not seeing, far less knowing. The man of genius, be he Homer or Shakspeare, supplies the foil— the complement that raises the thing to knowledge. The happy comparison—by classification, analogy, or simile,—and the pointed contrast, are the agents that vivify the mind with reference to what formerly lay unheeded before the open eyes.

30. The use of language is a means of fixing the attention upon select impressions, out of the great total that makes our universe. Whatever has received a name is, as it were, pointed at by the finger; and any one hearing the name in connexion with the thing, is made specially alive to that, and in consequence has the chance of knowing it in the proper acceptation of the term—that is to say, through difference and agreement. The stars and constellations, whose names are familiarly disseminated, are better known from that circumstance. Hence to be born under a copious language, or to live in the circles of learned converse, is to be mentally alive to a larger class of our impressions. Space, however, does not permit me to dilate on this topic, or to exemplify in full the other forces that govern the mental attention, so as to coin select impressions into knowledge.

31. The essentials of Cognition, or Knowledge may be summed up thus :—

First. To know any single thing, we must be conscious of it as Differing from some things, and as Agreeing with other things. To this extent, knowledge involves only what belongs to Sensation and Perception.

Secondly. When Knowledge amounts to Affirmation there are usually at least two things taken notice of; and not only so, but the couple must be farther viewed, as coming under a third property, namely, one of the Universal Predicates of Propositions—for example, Co-existence or Succession. 'The

## EXTERNAL PERCEPTION

593

sun is a luminous body;' 'night follows day;'—are higher combinations than the mere knowledge of ' Sun,' 'Night,' ' Day;' they unite simple or elementary cognitions into affirmations or propositions ; and the binding circumstance is one of the comprehensive generalities called Co-existence and Succession.

Thirdly. Into these Affirmations, there must enter the active state or disposition termed Belief (or Disbelief).*

---

* *Subject and Object.—The External World.* The last point to be adverted to, in our rapid summary of the meaning of cognition, is the important distinction of Subject and Object, involving the greatest of all the problems of metaphysical philosophy—the problem of self and an external world. In my former volume (*Contiguity*, § 38) I endeavoured to state the sources of our notions of an external and material world, although a much more extensive handling would doubtless be desirable to place those views beyond the reach of dispute. As happens with all the other vexed questions of mental science, there is a certain amount of real difficulty, and a still greater amount of factitious difficulty, created by unsuitable language, which every one considers himself bound to preserve.

What is true of each item of knowledge within the whole compass of the knowable, namely, that there must be a plurality of impressions under comparison, with difference and agreement, is the thing to be remarked in reference to subject and object. An object has no meaning without a subject, a subject none without an object. The one is the complement or correlate of the other; drop the one to exalt the other into prominence, and you behave like him that would cancel the south pole of a magnet to make it all north. Subject and object are one of the innumerable couples, mutual foils, polar pairs, coined among the universe of our impressions as portions of our knowledge. An everlasting light in the eye would be as good as no light at all. It is the privative darkness that keeps us conscious of, or mentally awake to, positive illumination. Yet as we can think and speak of the light by itself, without express mention of its foil, or indispensable contrast, as we can direct attention to the north end of the magnet leaving the south out of account for the time, so we can think of the object while the subject is tacitly understood, or of the subject, the object being understood. We never could have come to the notion of externality without its contrast, but the notion being once formed, we have the power of abstracting the attention, and looking at one while sinking the other. An absolute object or an absolute subject is a pure absurdity, irrelevance, or impossibility. Not more so, however, than light with no darkness, redness with no other colour, high without low, straight without curved, greater without less.

I have already expressed the opinion, that the contrast of subject and object springs originally from the contrast of movement and passive sensation.

2 P

594 CONSCIOUSNESS.

The impressions that we call feelings of movement, or active energy put forth, are recognised by us as different from the impressions of passive sensation; and through this difference a light, so to speak, is struck up in the mind, an effect of knowing is produced in the transition made, or the comparison instituted. Were our impressions all movement, we should know nothing of movement as a whole, for want of the contrasting alternative. Our knowledge would then be confined to qualities wherein movements differed, or where there was a remission of effect, as quick and slow, action and inaction. So, were our impressions all sensation, there would be no knowledge of sensation altogether, it being impossible to know what cannot be passed from, contrasted, or varied; we should know sensations of sight because we had sensations not of sight, we should know the presence and absence of sensation, the pleasurable and the painful, and so on; but of sensation in general, as now known by the contrasting impression of inborn movement, we should have no notion whatsoever.

Movement and sense are the most marked antithesis among all our present feelings. The change of character experienced, when we pass from the putting forth of energy to passive sensation, is greater, imparts more of the shock of difference, than the passing from smell to taste, or from one sound to another sound. In the presence of the feeling of movement as a foil, we discern something common to all sensation, in spite of the many individual varieties. By being cognisant of movement, therefore, we are cognizant of sensation on the whole, and by being cognisant of sensation on the whole, we are cognisant of movement on the whole. Cut off the one, and the cognition of the other vanishes, being reduced to the cognition of contrasting details. This antithesis is an essential preliminary to the one in question, without entirely amounting to it. In the perception of the Extended, there is involved the world of ideas, or of impressions enduring after the fact; and the contrast, in my judgment, greatly turns upon the difference between the state of things called the present, or actual, and the subsequent state of things called the ideal. There is a marked transition from the state of looking at the sun in the actual to one of the consequences of that, namely, the persistent, or revivable state termed the *idea* of the sun. I have described already what seems to me the characteristic difference of the two states. The actual impression changes with all our movements, and is thus, as it were, embodied in a group or series of moving energies. The closing of the eye, the turning of the head, the raising of the hand, and a great many other movements of ours, would at once extinguish the sensation, or the state called the actual. We must go through a certain amount of bodily exercise to secure and retain it; when it becomes ideal, all that is dispensed with. The transition is thus a very marked one, and impresses the mind with a contrast or mutual foil, in short, a cognition of the first degree. If there were no persisting impressions, that is, no ideas; if actuality were our sole world, we should, to say the least of it, lose one means of attaining to the cognition of subject and object, although we should have still other contrasts, and consequent cognitions; that is, supposing, for the sake of illustration, what is in reality not possible, namely, that knowledge could exist without an impression enduring after the

## OBJECT AND SUBJECT INSEPARABLE. 595

fact. Around this primary antithesis of the actual and the ideal, other contrasts are grouped so as to widen and deepen the resulting cognition. When the same class of movements leads to and controls the sensations of a plurality of senses, as when by the movements of the arm and hand I derive a touch, an odour, a taste, a sight (*e.g.* handling an orange), the cognitive contrast of the situation in the actual, and the subsequent ideal is very much increased. We are compelled to recognise a difference so bold as that between the reality and the imagination of a feast, and our language for the purpose is external and internal, subject and object. It is, however, an extravagance of fancy to project the one into a sphere of independent existence, apart from our whole mental life. The real fact seems to be, that two greatly differing experiences develop between them a cognition, as in every other item of knowledge, and we call this cognition by two names according to the one that is principal for the time. Having emerged from an actual to an ideal, we have the cognition of mind. Having emerged from an ideal to an actual, as above interpreted, we have the cognition of the extended, or not-self. Take away the prior experience, and there being then no transition, there is no cognition.

The great mistake in the ideal theories of the last century, from Berkeley downwards, lay in doing away with the cognitive antithesis, and resolving the state called the actual into the state called the ideal; at all events, the reality of the distinction was not kept up with sufficient care. It is impossible ever to identify the two positions any more than to identify the two magnetic poles. There would be no knowledge of either but for the contrast of the two. In rebutting the assumption of a world totally separated from mind, in the largest signification that we can give to mind, we must not use language to imply that actuality is the same as ideality; the two experiences are experiences of our own, aspects of self, but so widely distinct as to give a shock of consciousness when we pass between them, and thereby to develop a cognition. We shall never be able to sink this cognition, and it is a logical fallacy to convert the two constituents of it into absolute and independent existences.

The comparing of our experiences with other men's, through the signs of communication, enables us to recognise elements of agreement, and elements of difference, in the same predicament of the actual. Take, for example, the attribute of extension or length, made up of sensation under movement; we find that the effect of the same predicament is the same upon all minds. A foot is a foot to everybody's experience. There are other experiences of a very different kind; thus, the sensation of relish is found not to be uniform in different minds, nor even in the same mind, all other things being the same. A new distinction emerges here which we attach to the one already formed of actual and ideal, and the whole is compounded into the object-subject cognition. Metaphysicians have called the elements of universal agreement *primary* qualities of body, and have properly classed them with the object pole. Such are Extension in all its modes, including Figure and Position; also Inertia and Solidity, and Movement. Where the agreement is less general, and more precarious, a number of qualities are designated as *secondary*, and made to cluster round the subject pole; such are Colour,

# 596 CONSCIOUSNESS.

Sound, Taste, Odour, Heat, and some others. These are said to give no indication of externality, and fall in with the subject. The remark to be made respecting them is simply this, that there is a less universal agreement between different minds, and between the same mind at different times respecting them, than respecting the primary qualities. In proportion as we find agreement of feeling in a like situation, we recognise the circumstance by the names externality and independence; in proportion as we find the same movement yielding different sensations in different individuals, we express the fact under internality and dependence. It will be obvious to any one studying the detail of the primary and secondary qualities, that the first are connected with our feelings of movement; extension, figure, solidity, and inertness, are modes of our own active energies; and it is in those that the appreciation of different minds is most nearly identical. The secondary qualities are the impressions due to sensation proper; they are the optical, audible, tactile, odorous, sapid, and organic, impressions; in all which, and more especially in those last named, mankind are very differently affected. Even colour is found to be by no means a uniform sensation. The remarkable instances of colour-blindness show the want of unanimity in optical effect. The contrast therefore between the unanimous or the invariable, and the idiopathic and variable feelings, is one to generate a decided and important cognition, and to receive an adequate designation in language. We place this distinction side by side with the distinction of actuality and ideality, and fuse the two into a kind of whole, described by the contrasting phraseology that has been repeatedly quoted. There are other minor cognitions that go to swell the great aggregate. The contrast between the pleasurable or painful on the one hand, and the indifferentism of intellectual emotion on the other, joins in with the previous mass, the first tending to the subject-pole, and the last to the object.

It has ever been the popular fallacy, sanctioned and propped up by one portion of the philosophic schools, to carry this great cognition far beyond the limits of mere cognition, and to resolve the members of it into absolute and independent existences. A material universe, entirely independent of mind on the one side, and an independent mind on the other, have been postulated and assumed; and, notwithstanding the manifold difficulties in philosophy that have been the result, it is with great reluctance that the hypothesis is surrendered. That universal tendency of the human mind to make belief constantly outstrip experience, and to presume largely upon the distant and the future, has led to the easy reception of the notion of two absolutes, created as it were apart, and brought together in the way of casual encounter. The mind would seem to take a certain comfort in supposing the two independent existences, as if the relativity were something too little to repose upon. No theory of the ultimate nature of cognition can alter the practice of life, the ends that men pursue, and the means that they adopt. It is nevertheless proper to put our knowledge upon its true foundation, and to rebut the fallacious tendencies of the natural mind on this as on all other subjects.

Professor Ferrier, in his *Institutes of Metaphysics*, has contributed very materially towards bringing home the theory of relative cognition, as against

## FERRIER'S INSTITUTES. 597

the Absolutists in philosophy, and the exaggeration of the case by the popular mind. Nothing could exceed the clearness and force of his exposure of the fallacy in question. I allude more particularly to Section I., Propositions third fourth, fifth, and many other passages that I cannot specify in detail. I regret that I cannot coincide with the wording of his first and fundamental proposition, which undoubtedly, in a Geometrical system of exposition like his, ought to be free from the slightest flaw. The proposition is expressed thus: ' Along with whatever any intelligence knows, it must, as the ground or condition of its knowledge, have some cognisance of *itself.*' What I dissent from is the placing of *self* in the relationship of a factor or foil in *all* our cognitions. I grant it to the fullest extent in the great cardinal cognition, subject-object, mind *versus* matter, internal and external. I maintain, however, that this is only one of innumerable cognitions of the human mind, although a very commanding one. Moreover, I grant that everything that we know ultimately takes a part in that great comprehensive antithesis, ranging itself with one or the other pole. Still things might have been known although the subject-object distinction had never emerged at all; it being enough for cognition that any sort of contrast should exist. I can know light simply by the transition from it to darkness; light-darkness is a veritable cognition, a genuine stroke of knowledge, even if carried no farther. The cognition is extended as other contrasts are introduced. Much and little gives the property called degree; white as against coloured is a further enlargement. As yet, the distinction of subject and object has not entered into the case, but that is no hindrance to the possibility or validity of these mental impressions. The further transition, from effects of light to effects of sound, gives a new surprise, a new contrast, foil, or antithesis; and a cognition, good as far as it goes, light-sound, is the product. We now know light as not dark, as much or little, as white or coloured, as not sound,—all which are valid items of our knowledge, being of a piece with knowledge throughout the whole extent of it. We might remain for ever at this point, being distinctly aware of a certain number of qualities without attaining the subject-object cognition. It is true that we do not remain in such a narrow sphere, but carry on our knowledge further and further, until at last every conceivable quality is arrayed round one or other pole of the greatest cognition of all. There is no property that is not finally attached either to the subject or the object divisions of our universe; still every property has many other contrasts whereby it becomes knowledge out of that connexion. I should know extension in very many of its aspects without knowing self, although certainly as object, as something called external, I cannot know it except in synthesis with the other factor of that conception.

I should therefore be disposed to give a different form to the wording of Ferrier's first proposition. There are two ways of expressing it, both which would in my judgment be free from objection. We might either state the general fact of the necessity of a contrast or foil in every cognition whatsoever, or we might confine it to the one cognition which is the main subject of his book, being the main theme of metaphysical dispute. I believe it correct to say, first, 'Along with whatever any intelligence knows, it must, as the ground

598 CONSCIOUSNESS.

or condition of its knowledge, have some cognisance of a quality in contrast to what is known.' It is the contrast that really determines what the knowledge is as well as makes it possible. To know light, we must know something else that affects the mind differently, as darkness. New contrasts give new knowledge. The naming of a quality gives us no information, unless we can find out the contrasts whereby it sprang up.

A second form of the proposition might be ' whenever the intelligence is concerned with anything as an object, it must, as the ground or condition of its knowledge, have some cognisance of a subject.' It is in fact this special point that Mr. Ferrier aims at establishing, and, in my opinion, succeeds in establishing. Wherever he stands upon irresistible ground, as it seems to me, he is engaged in maintaining the position of the mutual implication of object and subject. It is, as regards knowledge generally, what he has well exemplified in the expository method of his book, namely, that to every proposition there must be a counter-proposition either put explicitly or understood implicitly. Negative is not more necessary to positive, than a contrast or foil is to every quality that the human mind can take into its cognisance.

The following extracts from Destutt Tracy are a true statement of our position in reference to the perception of an external world :—

' Nous ne connaissons notre existence que par les impressions que nous éprouvons : et celle des autres êtres que nous, que par les impressions qu'ils nous causent.

'Aussi, de même que toutes nos propositions peuvent être ramenées à la forme de propositions énonciatives, parcequ'au fonds elles expriment toutes un jugement : de même, toutes nos propositions énonciatives peuvent être toujours réduites à n'être qu'une de celles-ci : Je pense, je sens, ou je perçois, que telle chose est de telle manière, ou que tel être produit tel effet—propositions dont nous sommes nous-même le sujet, parcequ'au fond nous sommes toujours le sujet de tous nos jugements, puisqu'ils n'expriment jamais qu'une impression que nous éprouvons.

' Il s'ensuit de là——— Que nos perceptions sont tout pour nous ; que nous ne connaissons jamais rien que nos perceptions, qu'elles sont les seules choses vraiment réelles pour nous, et que la réalité que nous reconnaissons dans les êtres qui nous les causent, n'est que secondaire, et *ne consiste que dans le pouvoir permanent de faire toujours les mêmes impressions dans les mêmes circonstances*, soit à nous, soit à d'autres êtres sensibles qui nous en rendent compte, (encore *par des impressions qu'ils nous causent*) quand nous sommes parvenus à nous mettre en communication avec eux par des signes.'—*Idéologie—Supplement à la première Section*, Vol. IV., p. 164-165, ed. 1825. Duodec.

'On peut même dire que comme nous ne sentons, ne savons, et ne connaissons rien que par rapport à nous, l'idée, sujet de la proposition est toujours en définitif notre moi : car quand je dis, *cet arbre est vert*, je dis réellement, *je sens, je sais, je vois, que cet arbre est vert*. Mais, précisement parceque ce préambule se trouve toujours dans toutes nos propositions, nous le supprimons quand nous voulons : et toute idée peut être le sujet d'une proposition.'—*Principes Logiques*, ch. VIII., p. 231. Vol. IV.

# APPENDIX.

*A.—On the most general physical conditions of Consciousness.—p. 34.*

As regards the most general laws of connexion of the mental and the physical functions, I will add the following observations.

I have repeatedly alluded to the great mental Law of Relativity. Although we cannot with certainty assign the physical counterpart of this law, the following statement is in harmony with our present knowledge both of mental and of physical phenomena.

> The nervous equilibrium disturbed by the application of a stimulus, is perpetually restoring itself.

This is an elementary law of all material forces known to us; comprehending Mechanical momentum, Heat, Chemical force, Electricity, &c. The disturbance of a liquid at rest is an easy example; as in the Tides. The Winds exemplify the same principle in the atmosphere. No reason can be assigned why it should not apply to the nerve force. We may fairly presume that when all the currents of the brain are in a balanced condition, when no one is commencing, increasing, or abating, consciousness or feeling is null, mind is quiescent. A disturbance at any point wakens up consciousness for the time, a second disturbance continues it from another point, and so on; the variety of stimulus in the waking state forbidding the perfect equilibrium of the mind. In full harmony with this view, is the really fitful nature of mind; the stream of consciousness is a series of ebulitions rather than a steady flow. In the calmer moods of the mind, this is not so apparent; but our experience of any intense excitement is in favour of the doctrine.

The second general condition of consciousness is the Law of Diffusion, fully expounded in the text. Coupling this with the physical side of Relativity, we should have to lay down the most general physical condition of Consciousness as follows:—

> An increase or diminution of the nerve-currents circulating in the interior of the brain, sufficiently diffused to affect the combined system of outcarrying nerves.

The concluding clause,—' sufficiently diffused to affect the combined system of outcarrying nerves'—besides embodying the law of Diffusion, is intended to

600                    APPENDIX.

point to the development of a collective and *united* consciousness, as will be illustrated in the following remarks:—

Mr. G. H. Lewes, in his *Physiology of Common Life*, has argued, with great ability, and with seemingly irresistible cogency, in favour of the position that Sensation or Feeling, that is, Consciousness, is a property of all nervous ganglia. He denies the existence of unconscious circuits of stimulation and action, as in the so-called 'Reflex Acts,' sustained by the agency of the spinal cord ; and adduces numerous observations and experiments of the same tenor as the one quoted in THE SENSES (p. 58, 2nd edit.) from Pflüger ; drawing the inference that, in reflex stimulation, there are found the essentials of voluntary action. So far as I am able to see, the weight of evidence is on his side. That every ganglionic excitement whatever (cerebral, spinal, sympathetic) gives birth to sensibility, seems a more likely supposition than that sensibility should attach to certain ganglia (those in the cerebrum) and be absent from others made up of exactly the same combination of the same nervous elements.

Mr. Lewes's theory is in no ways incompatible with the conditions of consciousness here laid down. I presume that when he attributes sensibility to the ganglia in common, he means in conjunction with the nerves ; ganglia without nerves are nothing ; they would be railway stations without rails. It would no more do to localize mind in ganglionic cells than to place it in the pineal gland ; the sensibility co-exists with the completed circles of nervous action, of which the ganglia are an indispensable part.

Again, the theory must be held subject to the Law of Change, or Relativity. Mr. Lewes tacitly assumes this throughout, and occasionally states it in express terms. Speaking of visceral sensibility, he says :—' And, it is to the variety of states which may be determined by *changes* in the circulation, and the conditions of the viscera, that the great variety in the actions of decapitated animals must be attributed.' (Vol. II., p. 240.) We may contend for the sensibility of all the organs of the system that are in any way connected by nerves to nerve-centres, but without a fluctuating condition of these organs, their state would fail to influence the consciousness.

But farther, Mr. Lewes's position is not at variance with the Law of Diffusion. Translated into his language, this law would be that ' sensibility increases according to the extent of the ganglia affected.' The real subtlety here is to lay down the circumstance determining the *Unity* of Consciousness.

It may be quite true, that whenever a ganglion completes a nerve circuit there is sensibility or consciousness in connection therewith ; but if the circuits perform their functions apart, there are so many separate sensibilities like distinct animals. In order to unity, they must somehow run together ; the local feelings must fuse into a collective feeling, or a combined tone, the resultant of all the separate tones. If a reflexion from the spinal cord performs an act substantially amounting to volition, as in the decapitated frog, without in any way relying on cerebral assistance, there may be sensibility or consciousness, as well as volition, in the act, but then it is not, as Mr. Lewis himself admits, the consciousness of the animal, as we understand and interpret that ; it is the consciousness of a separate and inferior animal. And why so ? Because our recognised consciousness is what employs our

## CLASSIFICATION OF THE EMOTIONS. 601

voice to describe it to others, our mouth, eyes, &c. to embody in outward manifestation, our collective members to work for. To whatever extent an outlying nervous centre performs an organic or protective function by its unassisted agency, its consciousness does not properly become our consciousness; it is like the consciousness of a parasite, or of the fœtus in the mother's womb.

I, therefore, assign, as determining the unity of consciousness, and as showing which local currents have found means to actuate the collective currents, the unity of the *executive*; that is to say, the active mechanism and the higher senses. We can employ our organs of expression to express only one feeling at a time; we can employ our senses in only one act of attention, our body generally in only one act of the higher volitions. In so far as these propositions are not rigidly true, to that extent consciousness is not a unity, but in some sort a plurality. Detached operations, as walking, which we may carry on while the attention is available for something else, may have their own consciousness, but they do not affect the central consciousness, whose properties are—to be localised in the cerebrum, to possess unity, and to be alone recognised as constituting our mental history.

### B.—*Classification of the Emotions.* · p. 40.

Mr Herbert Spencer, in an article reviewing 'The Emotions and the Will' (Essays, 2nd Series), has adverted more especially to the Classification of the Emotions, and to the defects in my mode of proceeding. He considers that, while I profess to follow a Natural History method, I have done so but partially and insufficiently. His own view as to the means of arriving at a good classification is stated thus :—

'Thus we may, in the first place, study the evolution of the emotions up through the various grades of the animal kingdom : observing which of them are earliest and exist with the lowest organization and intelligence; in what order the others accompany higher endowments; and how they are severally related to the conditions of life. In the second place, we may note the emotional differences between the lower and the higher human races—may regard as earlier and simpler those feelings which are common to both, and as later and more compound those which are characteristic of the most civilized. In the third place, we may observe the order in which the emotions unfold during the progress from infancy to maturity. And lastly, comparing these three kinds of emotional development, displayed in the ascending grades of the animal kingdom, in the advance of the civilized races, and in individual history, we may see in what respects they harmonize, and what are the implied general truths.

'Having gathered together and generalized these several classes of facts, analysis of the emotions would be made easier. Setting out with the unquestionable assumption, that every new form of emotion making its appearance in the individual or the race, is a modification of some pre-existing emotion, or a compounding of several pre-existing emotions; we should be

## 602 APPENDIX.

greatly aided by knowing what always are the pre-existing emotions. When, for example, we find that very few if any of the lower animals show any love of accumulation, and that this feeling is absent in infancy—when we see that an infant in arms exhibits anger, fear, wonder, while yet it manifests no desire of permanent possession, and that a brute which has no acquisitive emotion can nevertheless feel attachment, jealousy, love of approbation; we may suspect that the feeling which property satisfies, is compounded out of simpler and deeper feelings. We may conclude that as, when a dog hides a bone, there must exist in him a prospective gratification of hunger; so there must similarly at first, in all cases where anything is secured or taken possession of, exist an ideal excitement of the feeling which that thing will gratify. We may further conclude that when the intelligence is such that a variety of objects come to be utilized for different purposes—when, as among savages, divers wants are satisfied through the articles appropriated for weapons, shelter, clothing, ornament; the act of appropriating comes to be one constantly involving agreeable associations, and one which is therefore pleasurable, irrespective of the end subserved. And when, as in civilized life, the property acquired is of a kind not conducing to one order of gratification in particular, but is capable of administering to all gratifications, the pleasure of acquiring property grows more distinct from each of the various pleasures subserved—is more completely differentiated into a separate emotion.'

Mr. Spencer has distinguished himself as the philosophical expositor of the theory of Development, or Evolution, and has carried it out into a great variety of applications; the growth of the emotions being one example. In the composition of the present work, I had in view, as sources of knowledge of the human mind, the inferior animals, the less advanced races, and infancy and childhood among ourselves; and, perhaps, I ought to have gained much more than I did from those sources; but I had not before me in any shape Mr. Spencer's doctrine of Evolution, which I have since studied in his own writings. As an hypothesis for connecting together facts that no other hypothesis can render any account of, I think highly of the doctrine; and I am fully disposed to listen to whatever it suggests as to the analysis of the complex feelings of the mind. Nevertheless, considering that the generic distinctions, in any classification, are determined by our actual experience of the feelings themselves, in preference to every other consideration, I do not see that any attainable amount of insight into their successive stages of development, can radically alter the mode of classifying them. I allude more especially to such well-marked emotions as Wonder, Fear, Love, Anger, which may be better or worse discriminated and described, but can never, as it seems to me, be other than distinct genera under all classifications. Neither can I find anything in the hypothesis of development, as at present expounded, to change the status, or alter the account given, of the Sentiment of Power. We have thus at least five capital emotions of the mind, which will, in my judgment, retain substantially the position they now occupy, in systems of the mind, until humanity itself is radically changed. As they appeared in Aristotle, two thousand years ago, so they are likely to remain for thousands of years to come.

## SPENCER ON THE EMOTIONS. 603

Mr. Spencer, after all, has nothing to offer in the way of amending my views of any of these leading emotions, except a suggestion regarding Fear, which I have adopted in the present edition (p. 58.) His chief illustrations of the backward condition of mental study, are taken from such feelings as Property, Justice, Mercy, Sympathy; all which I look upon as derived states, and endeavour, as far as possible, to analyse. I greatly wish that we had a stock of good observations regarding the lower animals, savages, and children, on all these points; and if I have overlooked any that exist, I shall be glad to have them pointed out. The acquired nature of the feeling of Property, as in the love of Money, is one of the oldest facts of Psychology; it was a common-place to Plato; and I do not see that Mr. Spencer has greatly improved the statement of it with all the help of the comparative and embryological methods. As regards Justice, Mercy, Sympathy,—these are constituent elements of the Moral Sentiment, and the supporters of the acquired character of that sentiment have always endeavoured to analyse these. One of the most elaborate, and I think most successful, attempts of this nature, may be seen in Mr. J. S. Mill's 'Utilitarianism' (Chap. VI., on *Justice*); and I do not think that an appeal to the lower animals, to savages, to the doctrine of development, in the present state of our knowledge, would greatly improve that analysis. The growth of the moral sentiment is seen with tolerable completeness in the history of every human being; little, if any, of it is hidden in the inarticulate depths of infancy; while affirmations either for, or against, its hereditary transmission are, under existing information, extremely precarious.

I have myself laboured to give an account of the ultimate constituents of Sympathy, and have duly noticed the fact of its absence in animals, savages, and children; but there is still room for hypothesis as to the real meaning of that absence. Mr. Spencer appears to treat the faculty as an acquired or developed emotion like property: I am disposed to regard it as a branch of the development of the intellect generally.

If I were called upon to state what I have found the best guide to the analysis and delineation of the emotions, next to the direct experience of their workings, I would say the study of the physical accompaniments. Mr. Spencer is not behind me in this; in fact he thinks me lagging here too. Any improvements that I have been able to introduce, in the present edition, have mainly sprung from increased attention to this much neglected part of the subject of mind. Imperfect as is our knowledge of the brain and the nervous action, it is yet sufficiently advanced to control and guide speculation as to the mental processes; while the appeal to the mental facts themselves can always suffice to check unwarrantable assumptions. On the subject of Fear, I mentioned a suggestion of Mr. Spencer's, derived from the doctrine of evolution; far greater, in my opinion, is the light flowing from the physical workings of that passion. Those great physical generalities stated above (A, p. 601), even in their hypothetical condition, are full of suggestions as to the mental laws.

Having declared my classification of the Emotions as imperfect, and at best provisional, Mr. Spencer sketches one 'in harmony with the results of

604 APPENDIX.

detailed analysis aided by development.' He divides the Feelings into four classes, as follows :—

I. ' *Presentative feelings*, ordinarily called sensations, are those mental states in which, instead of regarding a corporeal impression as of this or that kind, or as located here or there, we contemplate it in itself as pleasure or pain; as when eating.' I presume that this division is fairly represented by the Muscular Feelings and Sensations as given in my former volume, and that, so far, there is no apparent difference between Mr. Spencer and me.

II. ' *Presentative-representative feelings*, embracing a great part of what we call emotions, are those in which a sensation, or group of sensations, or group of sensations and ideas, arouses a vast aggregation of represented sensations; partly of individual experience, but chiefly deeper than individual experience (that is, vague *inherited* experience), and consequently, indefinite.' He gives Terror as an example, and makes the remark already quoted as to the presence of inherited pains in the state of fear. He does not offer any other example; but I see nothing in the language inconsistent with including under this division all the simpler emotions enumerated by me (Chapters III.—XI. inclusive), that is, Novelty, Wonder, Liberty, Terror, Tenderness, Complacency, Power, Anger, Plot-Interest, Intellect. Perhaps he might object to one or two of the members, as he would of course vary the handling of many of them; but so far as appears, if I had chosen to give to that collective group the title *Presentative-representative feelings*, I should have complied with his idea of classification so far as now stated.

To some of these genera (as Terror and Tenderness), I substantially apply the attributes of the above definition, only I do not undertake to specify the supposed hereditary experience, it being so difficult to attain satisfactory evidence on such a matter. Mr. Spencer would say that the undefined pleasures of the love of the sexes, before sensual gratification, is the inherited recollection of that experience, a statement that I can neither affirm nor deny; I treat the feeling as an organic sensibility connected with certain organic functions, but as to the earlier history of it, I say nothing. Again, as regards Novelty, Wonder, Liberty, Power, I consider the language of the above definition cumbrous, if not inapplicable; and prefer to treat them as results of the Law of Relativity; while others are directly allied to the Law of Harmony and Conflict. I admit the propriety of the definition as regards all the products of Contiguous adhesion, or agglomeration—Terror, Tenderness, Sex, Self-Complacency.

III. ' *Representative feelings*, comprehending the ideas of the feelings above classed, when they are called up apart from the appropriate external excitements. As instances of these may be named the feelings with which the descriptive poet writes, and which are aroused in the minds of his hearers.'

In a chapter on Ideal Emotion, following the detail of the genera belonging to the previous division, I have treated this very subject; and, with a very slight adaptation, I could make that chapter precisely tally with the definition. A good deal of what would be said in illustration of these pictorial emotions was anticipated in the exposition of the Intellect, they being obviously the result of the intellectual operations applied to feeling. On the whole, I do

## REID'S CLASSIFICATION OF THE EMOTIONS. 605

not plead guilty to the omission of this class, nor to any fatal dislocation of them, in my general arrangement.

IV. ' *Re-Representative feelings*, under which head are included those more complex sentient states that are less the direct results of external excitements than the indirect or reflex results of them. The love of property is a feeling of this kind. It is awakened not by the presence of any special object, but by ownable objects at large; and it is not from the mere presence of such objects, but from a certain ideal relation to them, that it arises.' ' The higher sentiments, as that of Justice, are still more completely of this nature.'

The love of Property may, I think, be unexceptionably handled in various parts of the exposition of the mind. Being a product of intellectual association, it may be given by way of illustrating the intellect, as I have done. It may also be brought in at a late stage of the discussion of the ordinary Emotions, as being an agglomeration of the collective interests growing out of sense and emotion. Or, a few chapters at the end may be devoted to the greater aggregates of feeling, or composite states, arising out of our common relationships to the world and one another. This is the course preferred by Mr. Spencer, and the course actually adopted by me. In my concluding chapters on the Æsthetic and the Ethical Emotions, I have complied with the spirit, if not with the very letter, of his fourth division. I have analysed Conscience, which, to all intents, includes Justice; if I have not specially noticed Property, it is because I do not consider that I had anything farther to say on that head; and I presume I am right in taking up Beauty and the Æsthetic feelings at the same stage.

It appears, therefore, that I have given a classification as nearly agreeing with Mr. Spencer's, as two independent minds can be expected to agree in so vast a subject; the scheme, whereby he proposes to re-organise, on an advanced idea, the Psychology of the Feelings differing from mine only in form and appearance.

I will next advert to some of the other modes of classifying the Emotions.

In Reid's 'Active Powers,' Emotion is handled in a very defective way. Under what he calls 'ANIMAL PRINCIPLES OF ACTION,' he includes *Appetites, Desires* (Power, Esteem, Knowledge), *Benevolent Affections, Malevolent Affections, Passion, Disposition,* and *Opinion;* and under ' RATIONAL PRINCIPLES OF ACTION,' he brings in *Regard to Good upon the Whole,* and the *Moral Sense.* There is no allusion to Wonder or Fear. There is a total omission of Belief in its bearings upon Action. The *Æsthetic Emotions* are slightly touched on, in the concluding chapter of the Intellectual Powers.

Dugald Stewart, as usual, builds upon Reid's foundation. His ' Active Powers ' are cast into two chief divisions. I. INSTINCTIVE PRINCIPLES OF ACTION (Reid's ' Animal' Principles). These are—1. The *Appetites ;* 2. The *Desires* (Knowledge, Society, Esteem, Power, Superiority); 3. The *Affections* Benevolent and Malevolent. II. RATIONAL AND GOVERNING PRINCIPLES OF ACTION, including Self-Love or *Prudence,* and the *Moral Faculty;* to which he appends certain other principles that influence our conduct, namely, *Decency,* or a regard to *Character, Sympathy,* the *Ridiculous, Taste.*

It is a defect inherent in the two-fold division of the mind (Intellectual

## 606                    APPENDIX.

Powers and Active Powers) that the Feelings cannot be discussed apart from their prompting the Will; the pleasures of Esteem, Society, Power, Knowledge, &c., are considered not purely as pleasures, but under the guise of Desire, which is a compound of Feeling and Will.

Thomas Brown, in entering on the consideration of the Emotions, is in doubts whether to arrange them according to their ultimate elements, or in the complex forms familiarly recognised. He decides on the last course, remarking that, if he were to lay them out in the order of the elementary feelings, these would be Joy, Grief, Desire, Astonishment, Respect, Contempt, and the Moral Sentiment. In arranging the complex emotions, he proceeds upon their relation to Time, and divides them into—IMMEDIATE, including, *Cheerfulness* and *Melancholy*, *Wonder*, *Languor*, *Beauty*, *Sublimity*, the *Ludicrous*, the *Moral Feeling*, *Love* and *Hate*, *Sympathy*, *Pride* and *Humility*; RETROSPECTIVE, *Anger*, *Gratitude*, *Simple Regret*, and *Gladness*, *Remorse* and its Opposite; PROSPECTIVE, the *Desires* (continued Existence, Pleasure, Action, Society, Knowledge, Power, Affection, Glory, the Happiness of Others, Evil to others). By such a scheme the author departs from the simplicity of Reid and Stewart, without remedying any of their defects. He was still less likely, from his point of view, to see the impropriety of bringing forward our chief pleasures in their complication with the action of the Will, or Desire.

Sir W. Hamilton has the material advantage of starting from the three-fold division of the mind: (in which division, however, he places Knowledge or Intellect first, and Feeling second). He classifies the feelings as (1) Sensations, and (2) Mental or Internal Feelings, the Sentiments. His subdivision of the Sentiments, that is the Emotions, is into CONTEMPLATIVE—having reference to the Cognitive Powers or Intellect, and PRACTICAL—having reference to the Powers of Conation, or the Will. It seems somewhat singular that Emotion should have no *locus standi*, except as a mere incident of the two other powers of the mind; a circumstance that may be justified on one ground, namely, that the Emotions are generated from the Sensations, through the operation of intellectual forces; but this Hamilton does not affirm. The CONTEMPLATIVE Feelings are again subdivided into those of the Subsidiary Faculties, and those of the Elaborative Faculty; the first being again subdivisible into those of Self-consciousness, and those of Imagination. Under Self-consciousness he gives *Tedium*, and its opposite. Under Imagination by itself, are placed *Order*, *Symmetry*, and *Unity in Variety*. Connected with Understanding, or the Elaborative Faculty, are *Wit*, the pleasures of *Truth* and *Science*, and the gratification of adapting *Means to Ends*. The joint energy of the Imagination and the Understanding gives birth to *Beauty* and *Sublimity*, in their fullest scope. The PRACTICAL Feelings relate to (1) our *Self-Preservation*; (2) the *Enjoyment of our Existence*; (3) the *Preservation of the Species*; (4) our *Tendency towards Development and Perfection*; and (5) the *Moral Law*. *Self-Preservation* includes Hunger and Thirst, Loathing, Sorrow, Bodily Pain, Repose, Fear, Anxiety, Shuddering, Alarm, Security, and the state aroused by the Representation of Death. The *Enjoyment of Existence* is connected with Joy and its opposites, Fear, Anxiety, Sorrow, &c. The *Preservation of the Species* implies Sexual Love, Family and Social Affections,

## KANT AND HERBART ON THE EMOTIONS. 607

Sympathy, Vanity, Shame, Pride, Indignation, Resentment, Anger, Scorn, &c. The *Tendency towards Perfection* embraces the consciousness of Power and of Impotence, Emulation, and Envy. The regard to the *Moral Law* comprehends Respect to others, Self-Respect, Self-Abasement, the Moral Feeling, Conscience, Remorse.

This must be considered a hasty sketch, a mere beginning, which the author never followed up. The weaknesses of the classification are many and obvious. It is characteristic of Hamilton's inversion of what I think the natural order of (1) Feeling, and (2) Knowledge, that Beauty is made to grow out of Imagination, instead of Imagination catering for Beauty.

The prevalence of the Triple division of the Mind in German philosophy, from the end of last century, might be expected to show itself in the scheme of the Emotions. Kant is regarded as the author of the triple division, but he did little to carry out the subdivisions, by which alone we can see what the main heads are intended to imply. In his 'Anthropology,' he divides Pleasure and Pain (that is, Feeling) into SENSUAL and INTELLECTUAL, which does not exactly coincide with Sensations and Emotions. The SENSUAL pleasures (or pains) come either through *Sense* (Enjoyment) or through *Imagination* (Taste). The pleasures and pains of Sense include Tedium, Contentment, &c. The INTELLECTUAL pleasures and pains arise in connexion with the *Concepts* of the Understanding, and with the *Ideas* of the Reason. This is not unlike Hamilton's method. But it is under the Appetitive Power, CONATION, or we should say the Will, that he includes the ordinary emotions Love, Hatred, &c., thus reproducing, in spite of his more auspicious starting-point, the vice attaching to our own philosophers, who proceeded on the two-fold division of mind. In connexion with the Appetitive or Active Faculty, he distinguishes *Affections* and *Passions*. An Affection is a present feeling of pleasure or pain whereby the power of reflection is for the time overcome. It is a sudden coming-on of sensation destructive of the equanimity of the individual. Passion is inclination too strong for the Reason. The passions are *natural* (Liberty, Sexual passion, &c.), or *acquired* (Ambition, Avarice).

Herbart and his followers are of more importance than Kant in all that regards Psychology, and especially the analysis and classification of the Feelings. Herbart, in adopting the three-fold division of the mind, does so with the express proviso that the three parts, although scientifically divisible, are mutually involved and inseparable in their workings, being all based on one primary element, or primitive mental form, which is the Objective Presentation, viewed as cognition or knowledge—the Sensation in what we should call its intellectual aspect. The other states, intellectual, emotional, and volitional, are of secondary origin. The Feelings arise amid *the mutual re-action of the presentations*, above or under the 'threshold' of clear consciousness; the re-action being either Arrest and Obstruction, or Furtherance and Harmony; in other words, Feeling is *wholly* subjected to the Law of Harmony and Conflict. The definition of Feeling is 'Immediate Perception of Hindrance or Furtherance among the presentations extant at any moment in consciousness'; and, as the presentations express the only active forces of the mind, by which its vital activity can be measured, Feeling may be called

608    APPENDIX.

'the immediate consciousness of the momentary rising or sinking of the mental vital activity.' The distinction between Sensation and Feeling is variously stated by Herbart's followers. Nahlowsky defines Sensation as the state depending on the mere perception of an organic stimulus; and Feeling as the resultant, not of immediate stimulation of the nerves, but of presentations simultaneously concurring in the consciousness; to this the master could have had no objection. Waitz says that Feelings are produced necessarily in the course of the succession of presentations, but are *not mere modified presentations*, or reducible to such; which, in spite of his disclaimer, comes very near the recognition of a distinct element of Feeling; the Emotional is grounded without being altogether merged, in the Intellectual. Wundt, who is not a Herbartian, goes still closer to the mark, when he says that Feeling is every state having a purely subjective reference, thereby including *the subjective aspect of the Sensation*. The great defect of Herbart's views is the common defect of philosophical systems, over-simplicity; while his unity of the mind is a thorough carrying out of the idea (adopted by Hamilton) of basing everything on knowledge or cognition.

The classification of Feelings suggested in part by Herbart, and carried out by Waitz, and others of his disciples, is into FORMAL and QUALITATIVE Feelings. The FORMAL are not bound exclusively to any one mode of subject-matter, but depend solely on the manner of coming together of the presentations (the mutual hindrance or furtherance). The QUALITATIVE depend on the special characters of the presentations. I quote the various subdivisions, and the complementary heads, as given by Nahlowsky *(Das Gefühlsleben* pp. 50-1, 214-5.)

### I. FEELINGS PROPER.

#### A. *Formal.*

*a.* The general, or more elementary Formal Feelings—Oppression and Relief; Exertion and Ease; Seeking and Finding; Success and Defeat; Harmony and Contrast; Power and Weakness. *b.* The special, or more complicated Formal Feelings—Expectation; Hope, Apprehension, Astonishment; Doubt; Tedium; Entertainment (Diversion, Recreation).

#### B. *Qualitative.*

*a.* The lower feelings, or those of Sense—the pleasures and pains of single colours and sounds. *b.* The higher or Intellectual Feelings (Truth and Probability); the Æsthetic; the Moral; the Religious.

### II. COMPLEX EMOTIONAL STATES.

1. Emotional states involving Conation (Desire or Aversion). *a. Sympathetic* Feeling (properly qualitative, but not classified under B, because of involving both the Sensual and the Ideal element). *b. Love*, (both Sensual and Ideal, and also complicated with Desire).

2. States essentially resting on an Organic foundation.

*a.* The *Disposition*, mood or frame of mind—the collective or general tone, admitting neither the prominence of special feelings, nor a reference to any distinct agency—general hilarity in all degrees, &c.

*b. Affections* (not in the sense of love), opposed to the foregoing as the

## AFFECTIONS CLASSIFIED. 609

transitory to the permanent. It was a speciality of Herbart to note under this name the transitory disturbance of the internal equilibrium by some sudden unexpected impression (Fear, Anger, &c.) whereby the organism is sympathetically affected to the loss of calm reflection and free self-determination.

These affections have been variously classified : (1) according as the intellectual activity is heightened or arrested (Drobisch) ; (2) according as the emotional element is varied—or whether the feeling is one of satisfaction or dissatisfaction, agreeable or disagreeable ; (3) according to their influence on action—whether they give rise to desire or aversion (Kant's division into Sthenic and Asthenic) ; (4) according as the bodily tone is heightened or depressed. From a still different point of view (Nahlowsky's, p. 258), they are arranged in two groups.

| A. Affections of the Active, or *Plus*-side. | B. Affections of the Passive, or *Minus*-side. |
|---|---|
| Pleasurable Surprise. | Helpless Amazement. |
| Sudden Mirth. | Embarrassment. |
| Jollity. | Perplexity. |
| Frolicksomeness. | Painful Surprise. |
| Joyful Transport. | Fits of Sorrow and Sadness. |
| Rapture. | Apprehension. |
| Courage. | Depression. |
| Rage. | Faintheartedness. |
| Vexation. | Shame. |
| Admiration. | Fear. |
| Enthusiasm. | Anguish. |
| Ecstacy. | Terror. |
| | Horror. |
| | Repentance. |
| | Despair. |

The *active* nature of the affections in the first column announces itself in the general rise, the massive flow, and quicker rhythm, of the Presentations involved ; along with a feeling of Power, of Muscular Elasticity, Readiness to act, general increase of Vitality.

From the Affection, finally, the Passion has to be distinguished. As the affection arises out of violent sensations, so does the Passion out of unguarded desires. When any higher feeling is hurt, an affection ensues ; when any inclination is thwarted, a passion is excited. Passion is a fixed predominant disposition towards a certain kind of desire that refuses the control of the Reason. This distinction is to me a quibble ; it would not exist but for the arbitrary repetition of the very same states under the heading of Desires. Moreover, any one of the so-called affections rising to intensity, in my opinion does everything that characterises passion.

Wundt, (professor in Heidelberg), in his work, *Vorlesungen über die Menschen- und Thierseele*, Vol. II. (1864), enters elaborately into the nature of Feeling and Emotion. He is at great pains to discriminate the Objective from the

2 Q

## 610 APPENDIX.

Subjective consciousness, which last is the domain of the Feelings. He recognises the pleasures and pains of sense as at the foundation of all feeling, and avoids the Herbartian resolution of feeling into cognition. The Emotions, he remarks, are described in the very terms applied to sensations—Love burns, Care oppresses, Remorse gnaws. Moreover, the emotions are accompanied with sensible or bodily effects—muscular or visceral—so that they are only another form of corporeal excitation.

The Emotions, like the lower feelings of Sense, fall under the grand division of pleasure and pain. They may also be divided into pleasant and painful *Affections* and *Moods ;* the Affection being the more transitory state, the Mood the more lasting. The Affections in their intenser moments rise to *Passion ;* which is the transition to Desire.

The other Affections are, all of them, varieties of the two fundamental and least definite states—*Sorrow* and *Joy.* Sadness, Trouble, Concern, Grief, Affliction, Melancholy, Distress, Mourning, are all different kinds of Sorrow. Some have a more objective reference, or fasten on a specific cause, as Concern, Trouble, and Affliction ; others are more purely subjective, as the Affection of Grief, and the Mood of Melancholy ; while Distress and Mourning incline now to one side and now to the other.

Joy has its different forms, but language does not supply the same range of designations, as for sorrow. As a lasting mood, it is called Joyfulness. It is, the author remarks, a characteristic circumstance that there is no word to express a distinction of objective and subjective joyful affections : joy is, on the whole, he thinks, more purely subjective than sorrow. When either state is a direct result of an impression of some outward thing, it gives birth to the objective reference expressed by Liking or Dislike. We have an affection, as well as a sensation, of Disgust, which last of course implies objectivity.

Wundt, like the others, takes notice that the Affections and Moods differ from the Sensations in requiring a plurality of intellectual presentations ; sorrow for the death of a friend is the complicated result of many thoughts and recollections. An emotion may be excited on a single presentation, but the force and character of it depend on the ideas awakened.

We may pass beyond the simple Affections and Moods to other complications of Sensation and Idea. We have a class depending not on the *matter* of the presentations, as the foregoing are, but on the *mode* of their interconnection, viz., as harmonious or discordant. We are very differently affected, according as the flow of the thoughts is smooth, free, and uninterrupted, or as it is laborious or broken. We have thus the two classes—(1) Feeling of free flow of thought—the feeling of pleasure joined to thought unrestrained and yet not too swift ; (2) the opposite Feeling of the restrained flow, which includes also the too violent or rapid flow. Under these we have a variety of special forms :— Feelings of *Exertion* and *Ease*, as regards both bodily and mental operations, corresponding to the feelings of sense in laborious or easy muscular motion, with which indeed, in a weak form, they are accompanied even when most purely mental. Feelings of *Diversion* and *Tedium*, which specially involve the sense of time ; in Tedium, there is a sort of indeterminate expectation. Feelings of *Success* and *Failure ; Seeking* and *Finding ;*

## WUNDT'S CLASSIFICATION OF THE FEELINGS. 611

*Agreement* and *Contradiction* on the comparison of two sets of ideas; there may be also in the same connexion the middle states of *Doubt* and *Indecision ; Harmony* and *Discord,* in their æsthetic bearings, are applied in the first instance to the sense of sound, but thence extended to other senses and feelings. Harmony (in sound) is expressed by Wundt as a number of sounds falling together into a permanent union ; Discord arises when the simultaneous tones give rise to fluctuating accompaniments, which we endeavour in vain to bring to unity ; both affections in the heightened forms have an affinity with *Dizziness,* which is a regular feeling of sense, being an excessive stimulation of the brain by an object of sense. *Expectation* is the hurrying forward of the thoughts into the future ; another form of it is *Lying-in-wait* (Plot-interest). When the result arrives and is favourable, we have *Satisfaction,* in the opposite case, *Disappointment.* When something ensues differing from Expectation, then we feel *Surprise,* which according to the circumstances is pleasurable, painful, or indifferent ; when there is a difficulty in reconciling the mind to what has happened, the state is called *Astonishment,* and this continued is *Amazement.* Allied to Harmony is *Rhythm,* definable as " the feeling wherein Expectation and Satisfaction always coincide ;" there is a jar of *Disappointment* when the rhythm is destroyed. *Hope* and *Fear* are special forms of Expectation, containing an element of the indeterminate ; Hope is the expectation of a wished-for event, Fear the expectation of one not wished-for. *Anxiety* is the fear of a great evil immediately to follow : to it *Fright* stands related as Surprise to Expectation. *Consternation* and *Terror* are more intense forms ; *Care* is continued Fear.

Wundt, while recognising the existence of affections that arise on occasion of the free or restrained flow of the ideas, controverts Herbart's position that all feelings whatsoever are grounded on this circumstance. He maintains that not only the first-named Affections, and still more the feelings of Sense, depend absolutely on the matter or contents of the presentations whereby they are occasioned, but that the last-mentioned Affections—Hope, Fear, &c., are also more than merely formal, being in reality compounds of both qualitative and formal affections. His exposition of the Feelings is completed by a review of the still more involved emotional states, known as the Æsthetic, the Moral, and the Intellectual feelings.

I refrain from occupying space with a minute criticism of these various arrangements of the Feelings; their points of agreement and of difference with the scheme in the text will be obvious to the attentive reader. In all of them, I should have to remark, more or less, on the redundancy of the designations, the same phenomenon being often expressed under different heads. I have more than once noticed the repetition of an identical state under the form of Desire ; besides which, the mode of introducing the element of Belief (Hope and Fear) is, I conceive, hostile to a correct analysis of the emotions.

C.—*Distinction of Reflex and Voluntary Acts.*—p. 317.

The drawing the line between the Reflex and the Voluntary is one of the most delicate considerations in the theory of the Will. Mr. Herbert Spencer,

612 APPENDIX.

in the review of this work already referred to, finds fault with my saying that Volition includes ' all cases wherein pleasures and pains stimulate the active machinery of the living framework to peform such operations as procure the first and abate the last ;' and he adds that ' then sneezing and coughing must be examples of volition.' He also disapproves of my alleging that ' To withdraw from a scalding heat and cling to a gentle warmth, are exercises of volition.' As he has not himself, in his article, drawn the line in dispute, I am left in uncertainty as to the real point of his criticism. I have maintained everywhere that the voluntary must be distinguished from the reflex by the presence of (cerebral) consciousness, or the spur of pleasure and pain ; and I am unable to assign or imagine any other boundary. I explained in my former volume (p. 263, 2nd edit.) that the acts of sneezing and coughing are of a mixed nature ; they are reflex actions, but combined also with consciousness, which superadds the element of voluntary control. Or, to adapt the statement to Mr. Lewes's view of the reflex process, they are mainly actions of spinal consciousness and volition, although accompanied and influenced by cerebral consciousness and volition—the consciousness written down in our mental history.

I find in Mr. Spencer's Psychology, in regard to the Will, such expressions as the following :—'The difference between an involuntary movement of the leg and a voluntary one, is, that whereas the involuntary one takes place without any previous consciousness of the movements to be made, the voluntary one takes place only *after it has been represented in consciousness.*' This language is suited to the Development hypothesis, under which Mr. Spencer states all his doctrines of the mind. At that stage of growing complexity (in the process of evolution) when detached automatic operations are no longer the sole mechanism of the system, and when the complication of impulses gives rise to mutual conflict, there emerge states of suspense, under which arise Memory, Reason, Feeling, and, with these, the Will. So that Mr. Spencer connects Will with Consciousness or Feeling, after a manner of his own. His expression, however, applies only to what I call the matured volition. When we are sufficiently advanced to be able to select the movement suitable to some emergency, we must have a previous idea of that movement ; if I see a dying fire, and put my hand to the coal box, I must have an idea of the action that I am to perform. But the real difficulty of the Will, as I apprehend it, is at an earlier stage, which Mr. Spencer skips over thus : ' The Will is a simple homogeneous mental state, forming the link between feeling and action, and not admitting of subdivisions.'

My example from the effects of heat and cold has the defects of being ambiguous. Under it, cases may arise (1) of purely reflex action (spinal), (2) of mixed reflex and (cerebral) voluntary action, like sneezing and coughing, and (3) of pure voluntary action, from the centralized, or cerebral, consciousness, as explained in A., p. 600. Any violent scald or pinch would give birth to a purely reflex, or spinal, movement ; and although cerebral consciousness accompanies the state, the reflex tendency will probably have acted before the consciousness has had time to operate. But then the reflex start may be nothing but a start ; it may not be fully and accurately remedial or preventive.

## DISTINCTION OF REFLEX AND VOLUNTARY. 613

In all probability, as Mr Lewes affirms, spinal actions can have purpose in them; the organic functions maintained by the spinal cord, &c., serve a purpose; and in the default of a cerebrum, spinal actions generally might take on the character of purpose. But it is not true of our usual reflex states that they precisely answer the end of removing the evil: too little scope is given to them for that. If a hot cinder has fallen upon the foot, the spasmodic movement will shake it off, merely by the violence of the shock; we cannot say that the movement has been exactly guided so as to have that effect. Even although the spinal consciousness has the fundamental property of self-conservation, like the cerebral or general consciousness, permission is not given to it, in human beings, to pass through the voluntary education that would give it the sense of locality and direction, requisite to a guiding volition. All our voluntary education seems to be expended on the cerebral consciousness. In the case of sudden hurt, the spinal response may be the first to show itself, but the cerebral response follows very rapidly and supplies the guidance that grows out of its higher endowment and education.

If I had said 'To withdraw from an *uncomfortable* heat—is an exercise of volition,' I should have avoided the ambiguity that seems to me the sole basis of Mr. Spencer's criticism, and have given an example of the will in its purity, at least as I have understood it throughout my long discussion of it. By inadvertently quoting a case of violent or sudden shock, I made an opening for the spinal reflex process, where I meant the cerebral voluntary.

I may here remark upon the application of Mr. Spencer's doctrine of 'Heredity,' or hereditary transmission, to explain both Instinct and the growth of Will. I have satisfied myself by observations that the new-born quadruped—the lamb, calf, &c.—has no notions of the things about it; nevertheless, I feel a difficulty in accounting for the extent of acquisition realized within a few hours after birth. The only remark that I could offer, by way of lightening the difficulty, was, that an animal spontaneously active would soon go through a great compass of trial and error, and would, under the Law of Conservation, abide by what gave agreeable sensation; while the plastic power of the system would unite these happy coincidences. I am not altogether confident of the sufficiency of this explanation for the cases now supposed; the rapidity of the proceeding is beyond what we are entitled to assume from the powers of the animal generally. The case is more fully met by supposing a hereditary inclination to certain acts, the result of their incessant performance by many successive generations. In some instances, the acts are fully matured at birth, as in sucking; in others, a certain tentative experience is still necessary, as in the copulation of the sexes among the lower animals, which is barely explicable on the assumption that it has to be discovered anew by every successive couple, or can be learned by imitation; while yet a certain amount of groping appears to be necessary at the outset.

It is also conceivable that, in each animal, there may be, through transmitted experience, a certain vague preparation for its special manner of life; the power being completed after a few attempts, under the connexion of the self-conservative tendency. Mr. Charles Darwin compared the working of instinct to a person sitting down at a piano, and, after a little practice,

614                    APPENDIX.

recovering the memory of a tune long out of mind. Thus, for example, the knowledge of the optical changes that are the signs of approaching to, or receding from, a visible object—which is one of the most frequently repeated mental cognitions—may be to a certain extent a transmitted experience, although quickened into full effect by a brief course of trial and error. In birds that are said at once to peck their food, with perfect precision, the power must be transmitted full and complete.

This last example has an important bearing on the Berkleian Theory of Vision. Believing, as I do, that the interpretation of the visible signs of distance is a matter of experience, and not of instinct in the ordinary meaning of the term, I am not prepared to deny that it may be an instinct in the acceptation of Darwin and Spencer, that is to say, a case of hereditary predisposition. The strongest presumption against referring it wholly to experience in each person *de novo*, is the singular strength and maturity of the association at the earliest period that our recollections can go back to. Now if there be anything intellectual that could work itself into the transmitted nervous organization, it would be an experience so well iterated as this is. The same remark applies to the cognitions of Space, or geometrical truth ; and suggests a third alternative in the dispute as to the origin of our knowledge of the mathematical axioms. (Spencer's Psychology, p. 577.)

### D.—*Meanings of Consciousness.*—p. 562.

The great mystification, as it seems to me, in regard to Consciousness, has reference to the attribute of Knowledge. 'Consciousness,' says Hamilton, ' is the recognition by the mind of its own acts or affections,' which to an ordinary reader suggests Consciousness, not in the large sense of our mental life, but in the narrow sense of the study of our own mind, the definition of Stewart. A pleasure merely enjoyed, and not studied or reflected on, would not be consciousness according to this view. Again, Hamilton says:—' It is evident that every mental phenomenon is either an act of knowledge, or only possible through an act of knowledge; for consciousness is a knowledge—a phenomenon of cognition ; and, on this principle, many philosophers—as Descartes, Leibnitz, Spinoza, Wolf, Platner, and others—have been led to regard the knowing, or representative faculty, as they called it—the faculty of cognition, as the fundamental power of the mind, from which all others are derivative.' This he considered going too far. ' These philosophers did not observe that, although pleasure and pain—although desire and volition, are only as they are known to be ; yet, in these modifications, a quality, a phenomenon of mind, absolutely new, has been superadded, which was never involved in, and could therefore never have been evolved out of, the mere faculty of knowledge. The faculty of knowledge is certainly the first in order, inasmuch as it is the *conditio sine qua non* of the others ; and we are able to conceive a being possessed of the power of recognising existence, and yet wholly void of all feeling of pain and pleasure, and of all powers of desire and volition.' *(Metaphysics*, Lect. XI.) Thus of the three great functions of mind,

# CONSCIOUSNESS. 615

Knowledge is reckoned first and fundamental; it is independent of the two others, while these others are dependent on it.

Hamilton, therefore, is to be held as affirming that every mental state must be at the bottom a state of knowledge; that a pleasure is no pleasure, is not possible as pleasure, unless we are somehow or other taking note of the fact that we are pleased : that it is not the intensity of the feeling that makes the consciousness, but the operation of recognising the feeling as a fact, or a phenomenon of our being. This doctrine is not confined to Hamilton and his followers; it is extensively maintained in Germany. For myself, I cannot concur in it; it seems to me to pervert the facts. I fully admit, that if we have a feeling,—say a pleasure or pain—it is in our power to attend to that feeling, to study it, to recognise it as a fact, to compare it with other feelings; and that no state is a conscious state, unless there be this possibility of cognising it; but I do not admit that the circumstance of knowing it is the fundamental fact, the *conditio sine qua non*, of the feeling. It is the nature of an intense feeling to call attention to itself; but the attention does not make the feeling; if it were so the more attention we give the more we should feel, while, in point of fact, in the case of any strong emotion, the study of it has a sedative efficacy, by employing the forces of the mind in a purely cognitive process.

It seems to me most accordant with the facts, to treat Feeling as a conscious element, whether cognised or not, whether thought of much or little. The three functions of mind are so interwoven that it is scarcely, if at all, possible to find any one in exercise by itself absolutely; we cannot be all Feeling, without any vestige of a cognitive element; it is impossible to be mentally awake without leaving some deposit of an intellectual kind, something that instructs us either of ourselves, or of the extended world. So we cannot be all Will, without either feeling or knowledge. It is, however, maintained by Hamilton that we can be all knowledge, or exist in a cognitive state, without either feeling or will. This I dispute. We may be in a state of knowing consciousness without either pleasure or pain, and consequently, without a motive to the will; but not without something, more or less, of a neutral excitement, which I regard as a shade of Feeling, an accidental moment when the pleasurable or painful elements of feeling happen to be neutralized.

Professor Ulrici, of Halle, in a lengthened criticism of my two volumes in the *Zeitschrift für Philosophie and Philosophische Kritik* (38th Vol., Part II., 1861), takes great objection to my employing the term Consciousness as synonymous with Feeling and Emotion; contending that to feel is one thing, to know that we feel is another thing, and that only this last is proper Consciousness. With respect to the identity in meaning of Feeling, Emotion, and Consciousness, I have altered my views, for reasons already explained (The Senses and the Intellect, 2d edit., p. 625). I have in this volume used ' Feeling' as the name for the genus, of which Sensation (with Muscular Feeling) and Emotion are the two species; and I use Consciousness as comprehending every state of mental life, both the subject life, and the object life. In how far consciousness as Feeling is related to consciousness as Intelligence, I have endeavoured to explain above (p. 565):—I regard the state of neutral excitement as the transition between the two.

# APPENDIX.

Professor Ulrici's contrast between feeling and knowing that we feel, as expounded by him, is tantamount to the difference between so-called reflex stimulation, and sensation with feeling in the ordinary acceptation; and he attributes the first to animals as their sole mental existence, and reserves the second for man. This I take to be, in the first place, a license of speech, and, in the second place, a gratuitous and unprovable assumption in matter of fact. The common use of the word 'feeling' is being mentally awake, or conscious—being pleased, pained, or excited;—and the only real question at issue is that above discussed, with reference to Hamilton's views:—Is Feeling based on Knowing, or are Feeling and Knowing co-ordinate, although inseparable, functions of the mind?

---

PRINTED BY ARTHUR KING & CO., BROAD STREET, ABERDEEN.

CPSIA information can be obtained
at www.ICGtesting.com
Printed in the USA
LVHW080204150720
660741LV00004B/95